Lampedusa
Image Stories from the Edge of Europe

Migrant Image Research Group

Lampedusa

Image Stories from the
Edge of Europe

Spector Books

Migrant Image
Research Group

LISA BERGMANN, artist, Karlsruhe
ESTELLE BLASCHKE, photo historian,
    Berlin and Lausanne
PAULA BULLING, comic artist and author,
    Berlin
ELISA CALORE, visual designer and
    researcher, Venice
MOHAMED & HAITHAM EL-SEHT,
    comic artists / Twins Cartoon,
    illustrators and cultural managers, Cairo
EMILIE JOSSO, illustrator and comic
    artist, Bologna
LEON KAHANE, artist, Berlin and Tel Aviv
ANNE KÖNIG, author, publisher of
    Spector Books, Leipzig
INA KWON, graphic designer, Berlin
ANDREAS LANGFELD, photographer,
    film maker, artist, Düsseldorf
ARMIN LINKE, artist, Berlin
VALERIA MALITO, event coordinator of an
    Italian design magazine, Milan
KAROLINA SOBEL, artist, photographer,
    Karlsruhe
HELMUT VÖLTER, graphic designer, Berlin
JAN WENZEL, author, artist, publisher of
    Spector Books, Leipzig

Contents

ARRIVAL ON LAMPEDUSA

BY EMILIE JOSSO

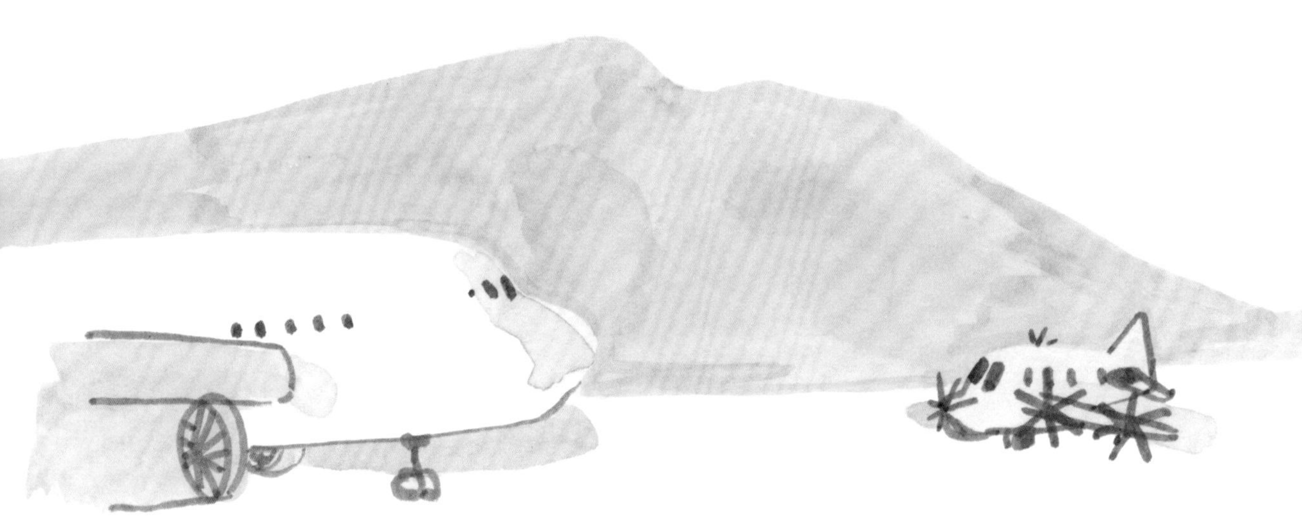

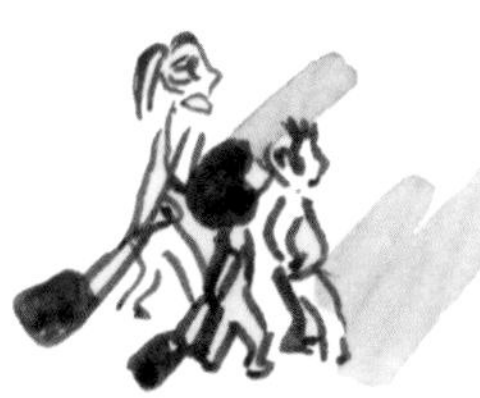

FINALLY GOING THERE, AFTER ALL WE'VE READ ABOUT LAMPEDUSA... THE LAST PART OF THE TRIP IS IN A VERY SMALL AIRPLANE, TAKEN FROM PALERMO'S FALCONE E BORSELLINO AIRPORT, NAMED AFTER TWO LAWYERS WHO WERE KILLED BECAUSE THEY HAD FOUGHT AGAINST THE MAFIA.

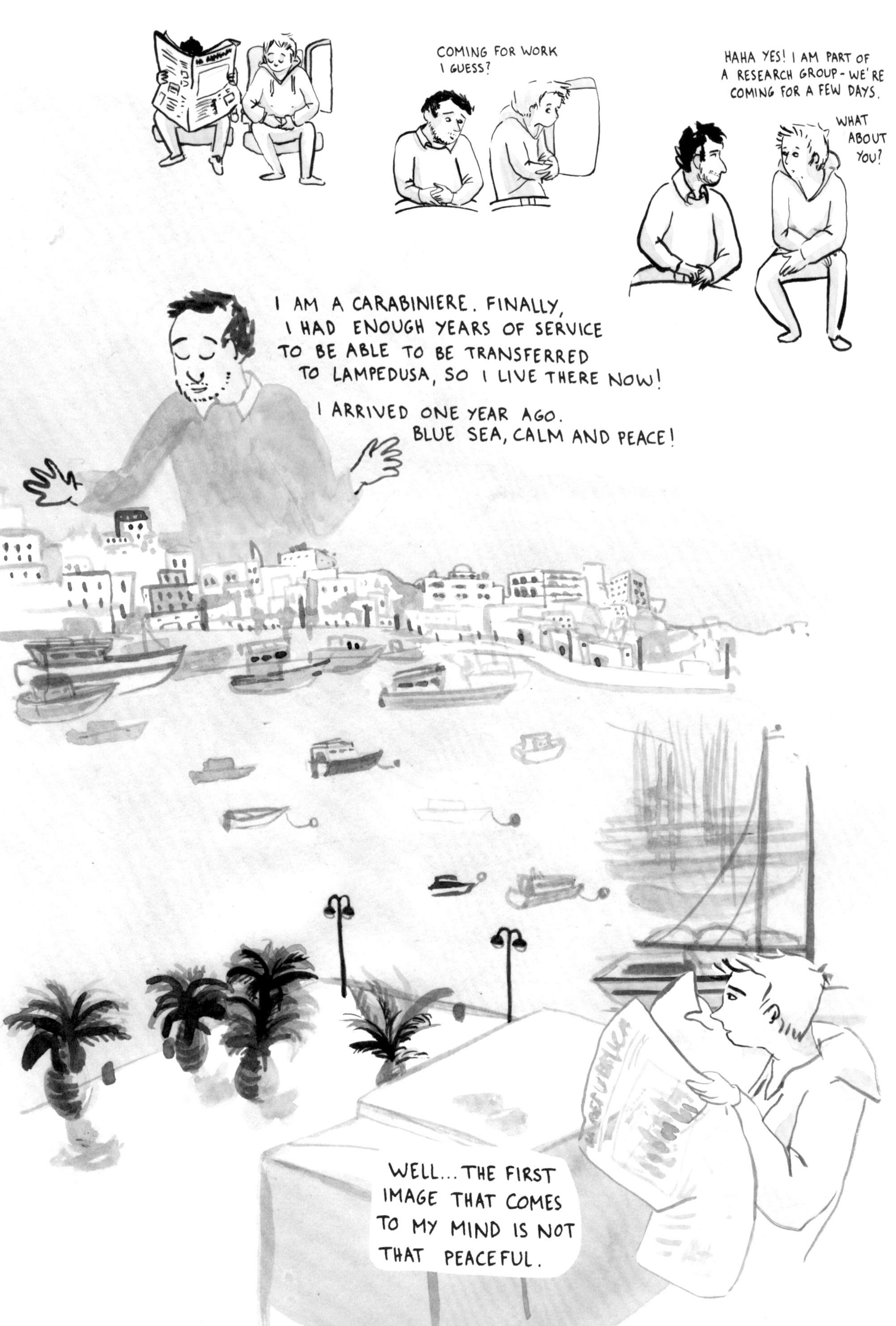

COMING FOR WORK I GUESS?
HAHA YES! I AM PART OF A RESEARCH GROUP - WE'RE COMING FOR A FEW DAYS.
WHAT ABOUT YOU?
I AM A CARABINIERE. FINALLY, I HAD ENOUGH YEARS OF SERVICE TO BE ABLE TO BE TRANSFERRED TO LAMPEDUSA, SO I LIVE THERE NOW!
I ARRIVED ONE YEAR AGO. BLUE SEA, CALM AND PEACE!
WELL... THE FIRST IMAGE THAT COMES TO MY MIND IS NOT THAT PEACEFUL.

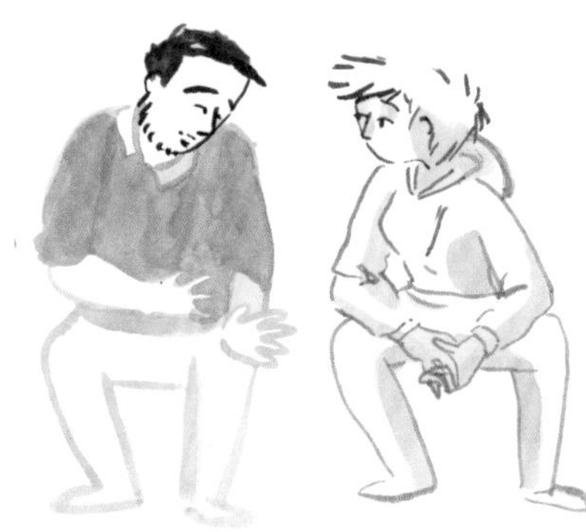

EVERYTHING IS ORGANIZED FOR HANDLING MIGRANTS. THE ISLAND IS REALLY CALM. YOU WILL SEE, THERE ARE SO MANY POLICE, ARMY, AND NGOs FOR THIS MINUSCULE ISLAND, EVERYTHING IS UNDER CONTROL.

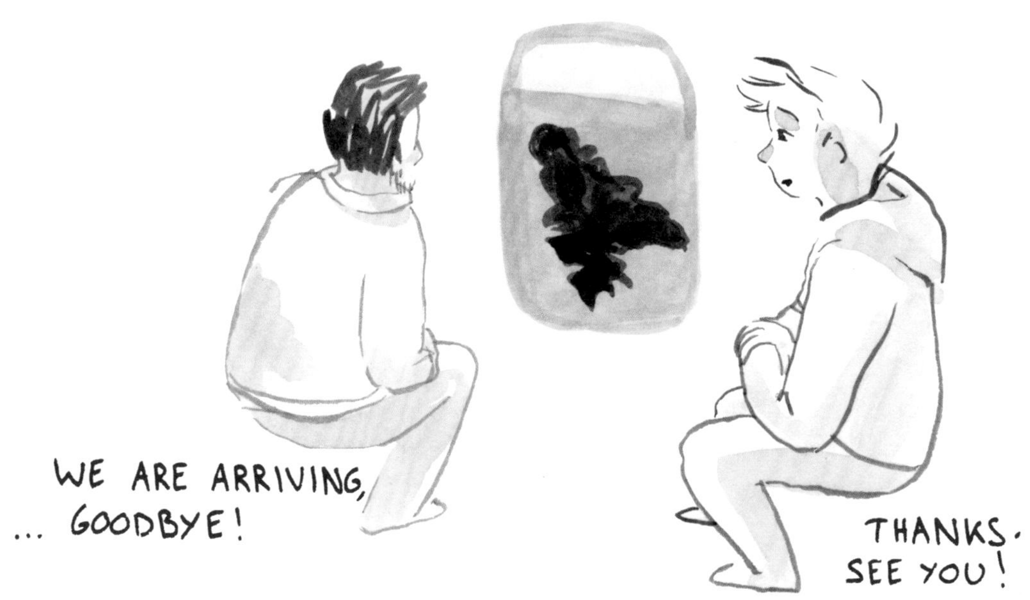

WE ARE ARRIVING, ... GOODBYE!
THANKS. SEE YOU!

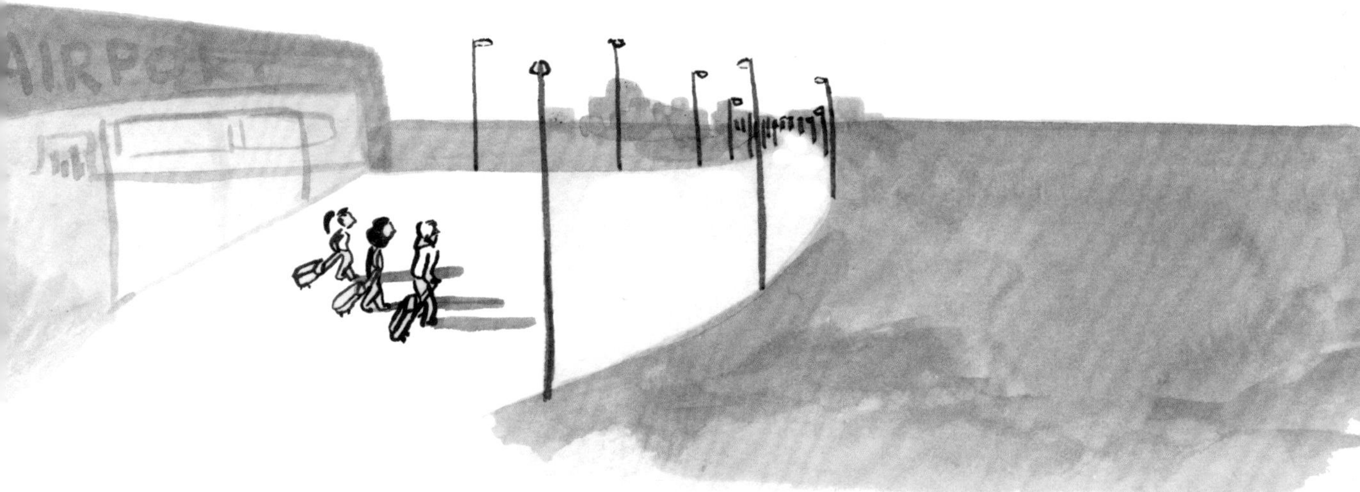

AIRPORT
LET'S DROP OUR BAGS OFF AT THE HOUSE AND GO FOR A WALK!

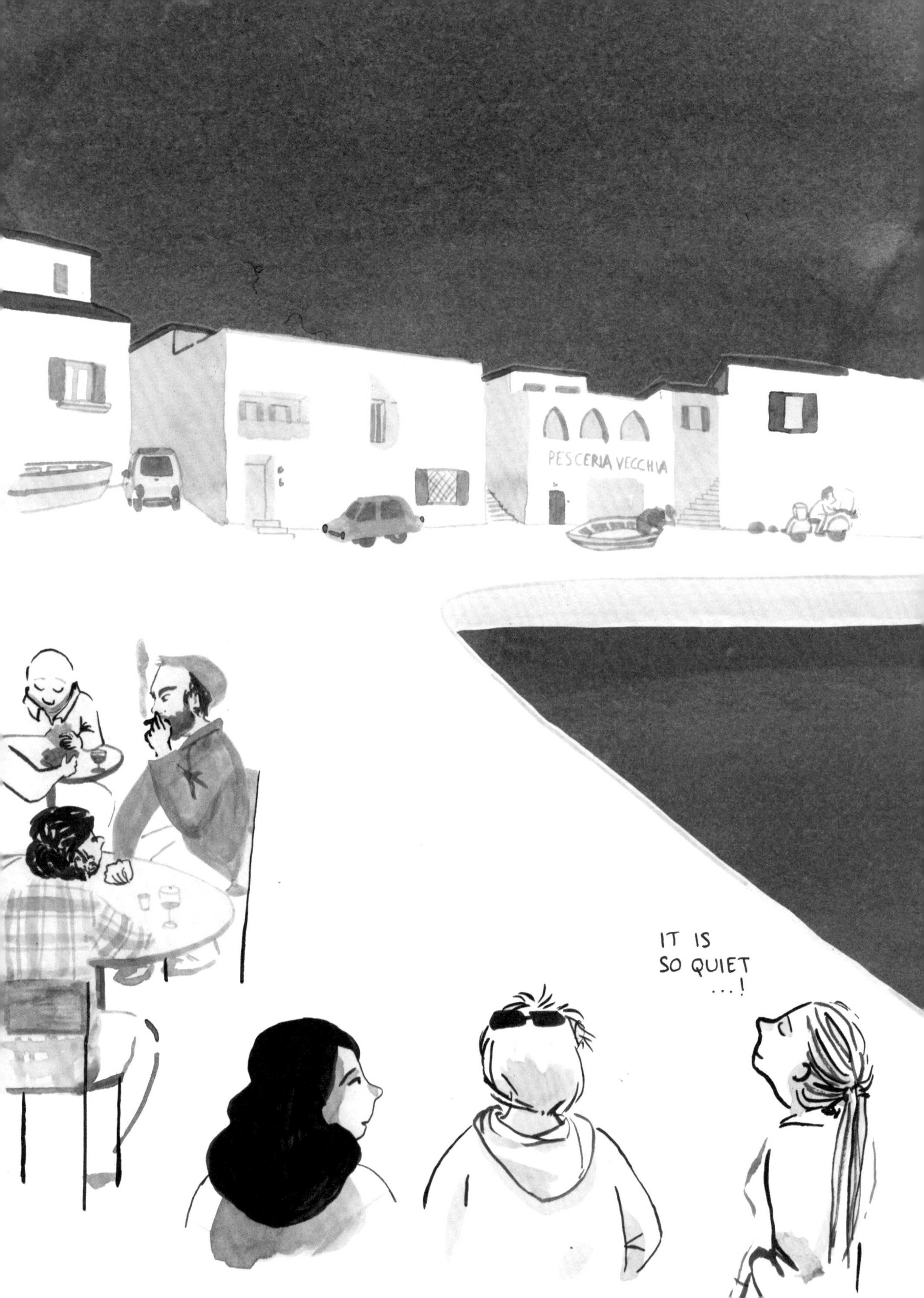
PESCERIA VECCHIA
IT IS
SO QUIET
...!

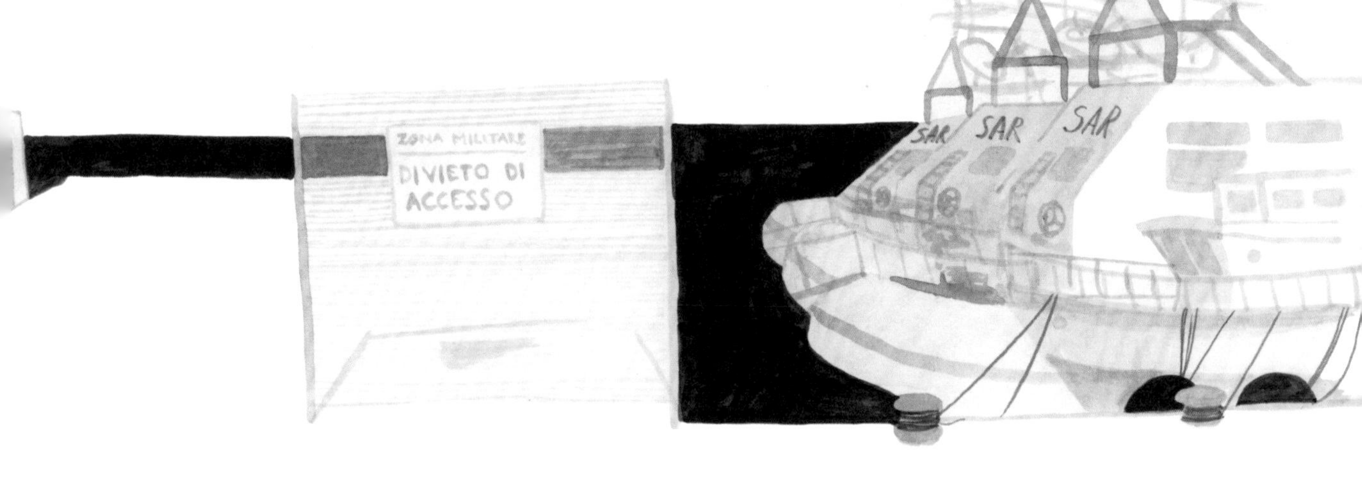

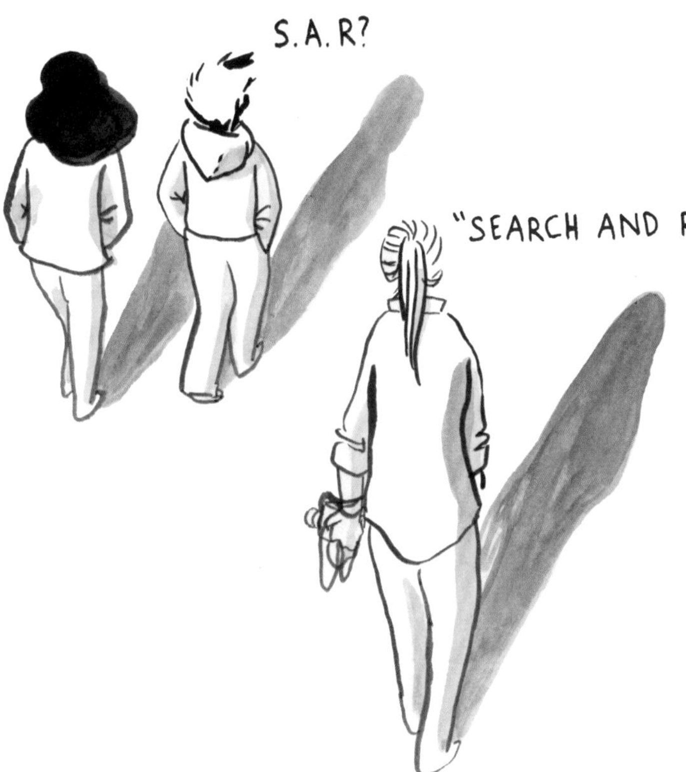

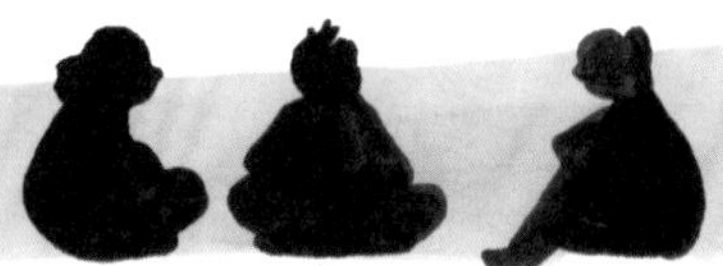

CAN YOU IMAGINE BEING SURROUNDED BY THESE DARK WATERS? NOT A SINGLE LIGHT, ONLY THAT DEEP CRUSHING DARKNESS ALL AROUND YOU...

MIGRANT PROTEST 1

BY EMILIE JOSSO

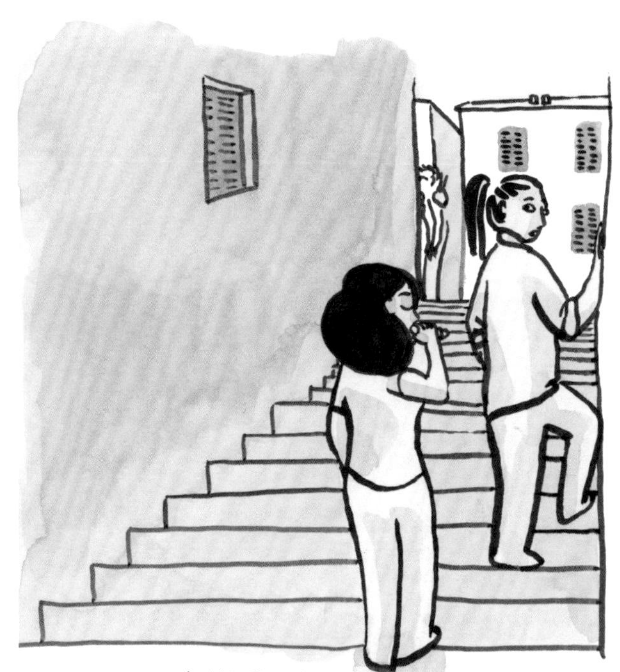

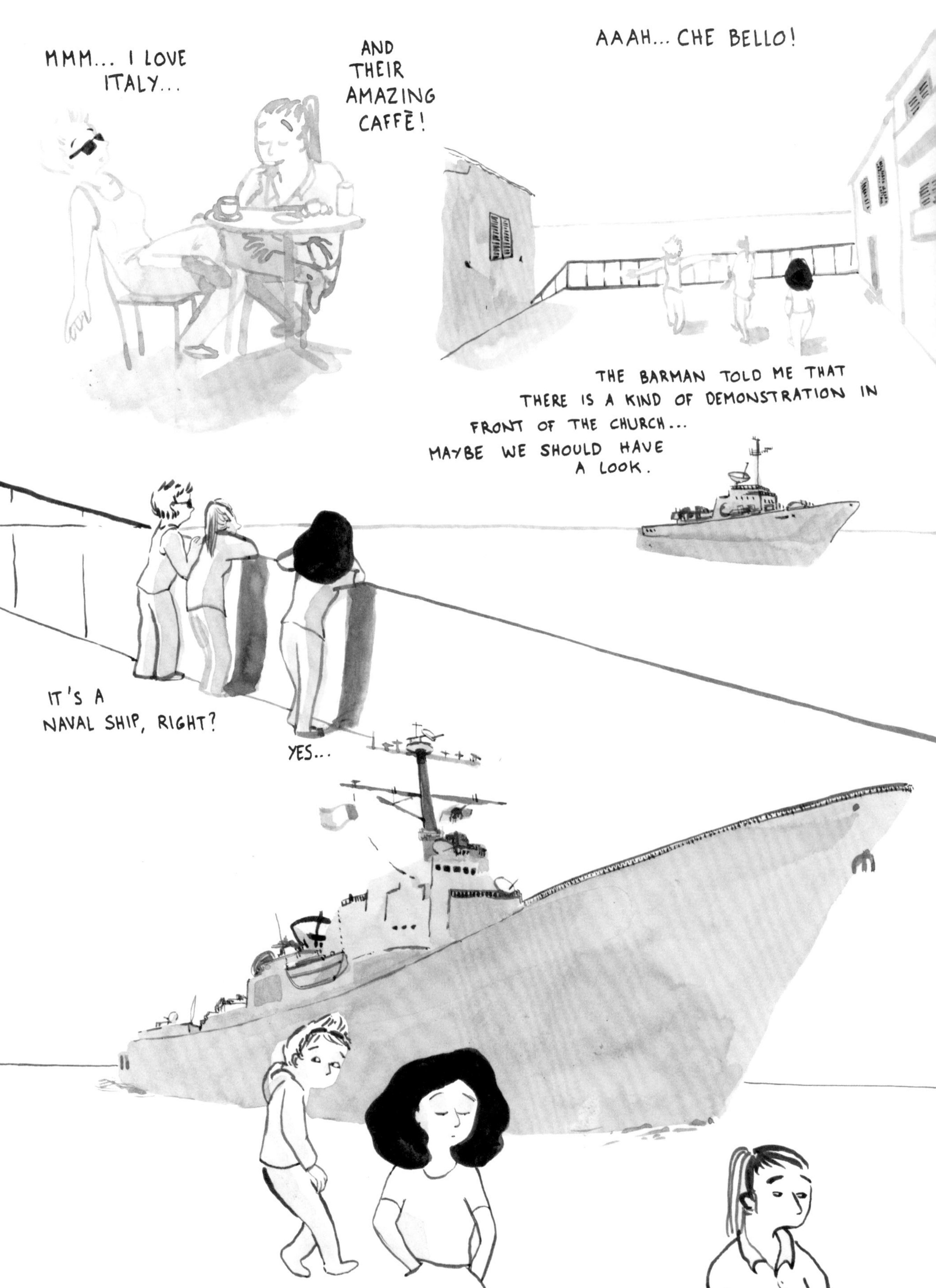

MMM... I LOVE ITALY...
AND THEIR AMAZING CAFFÈ!
AAAH... CHE BELLO!
THE BARMAN TOLD ME THAT THERE IS A KIND OF DEMONSTRATION IN FRONT OF THE CHURCH... MAYBE WE SHOULD HAVE A LOOK.
IT'S A NAVAL SHIP, RIGHT?
YES...

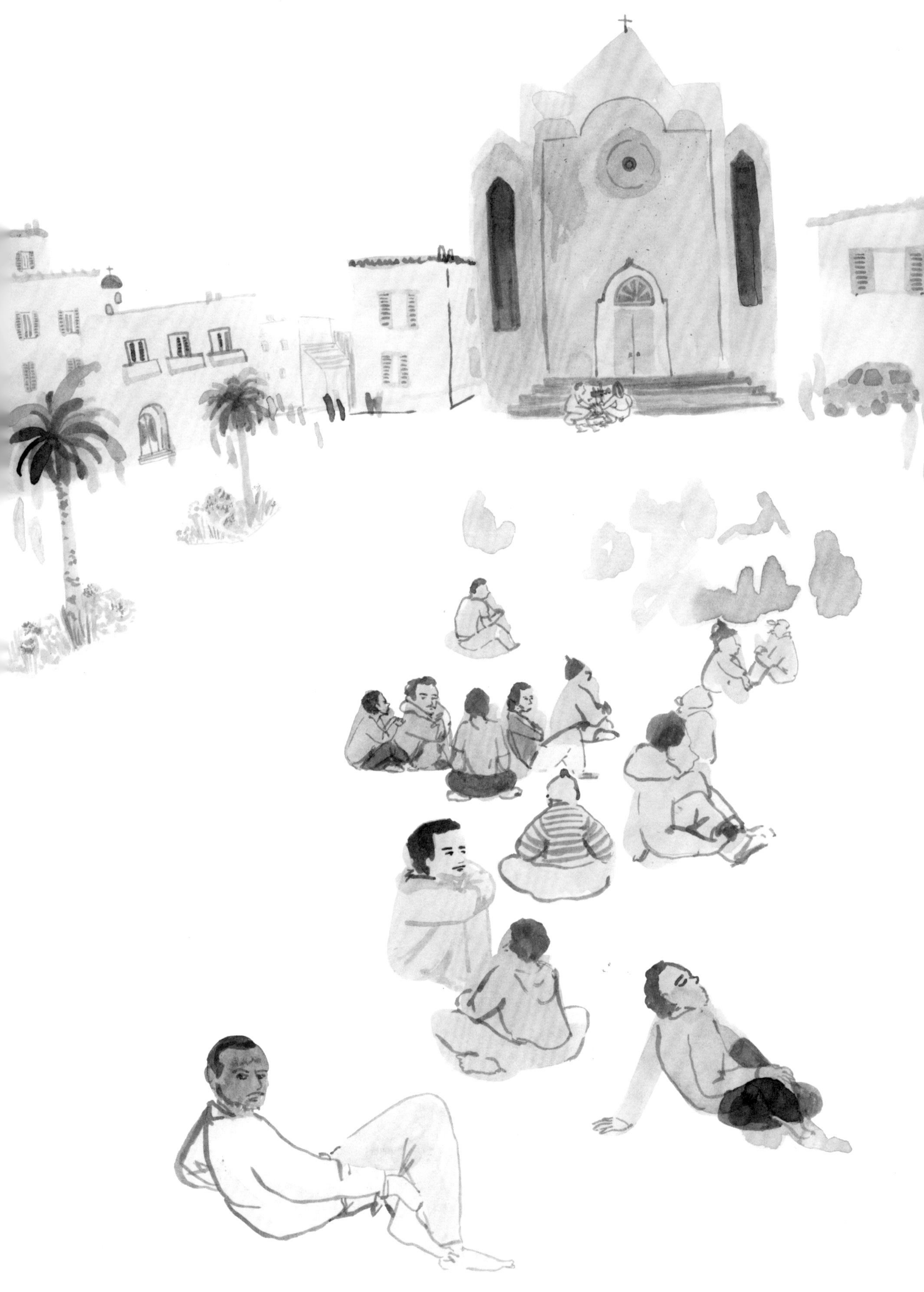

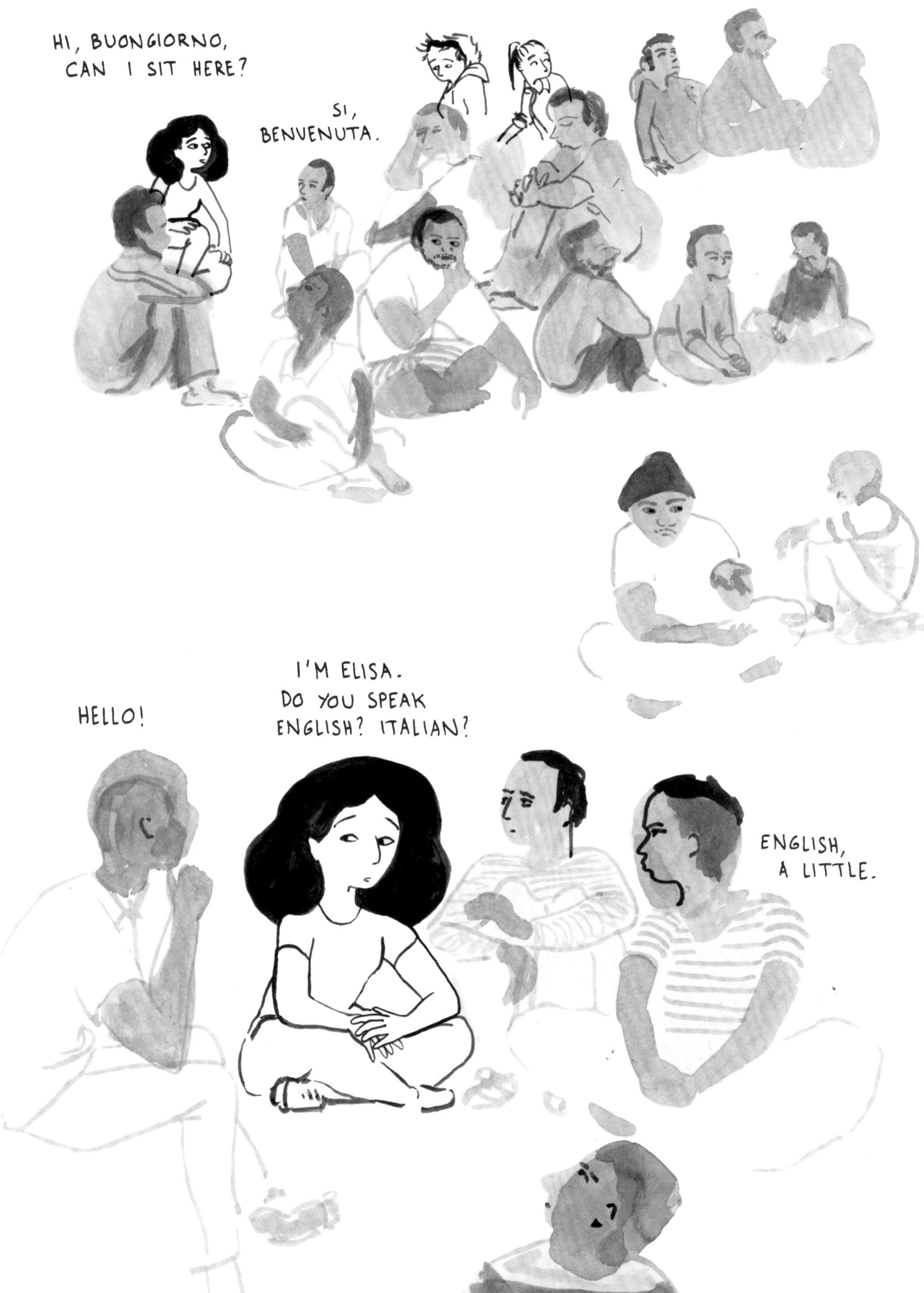

HI, BUONGIORNO, CAN I SIT HERE?
SI, BENVENUTA.
HELLO!
I'M ELISA. DO YOU SPEAK ENGLISH? ITALIAN?
ENGLISH, A LITTLE.

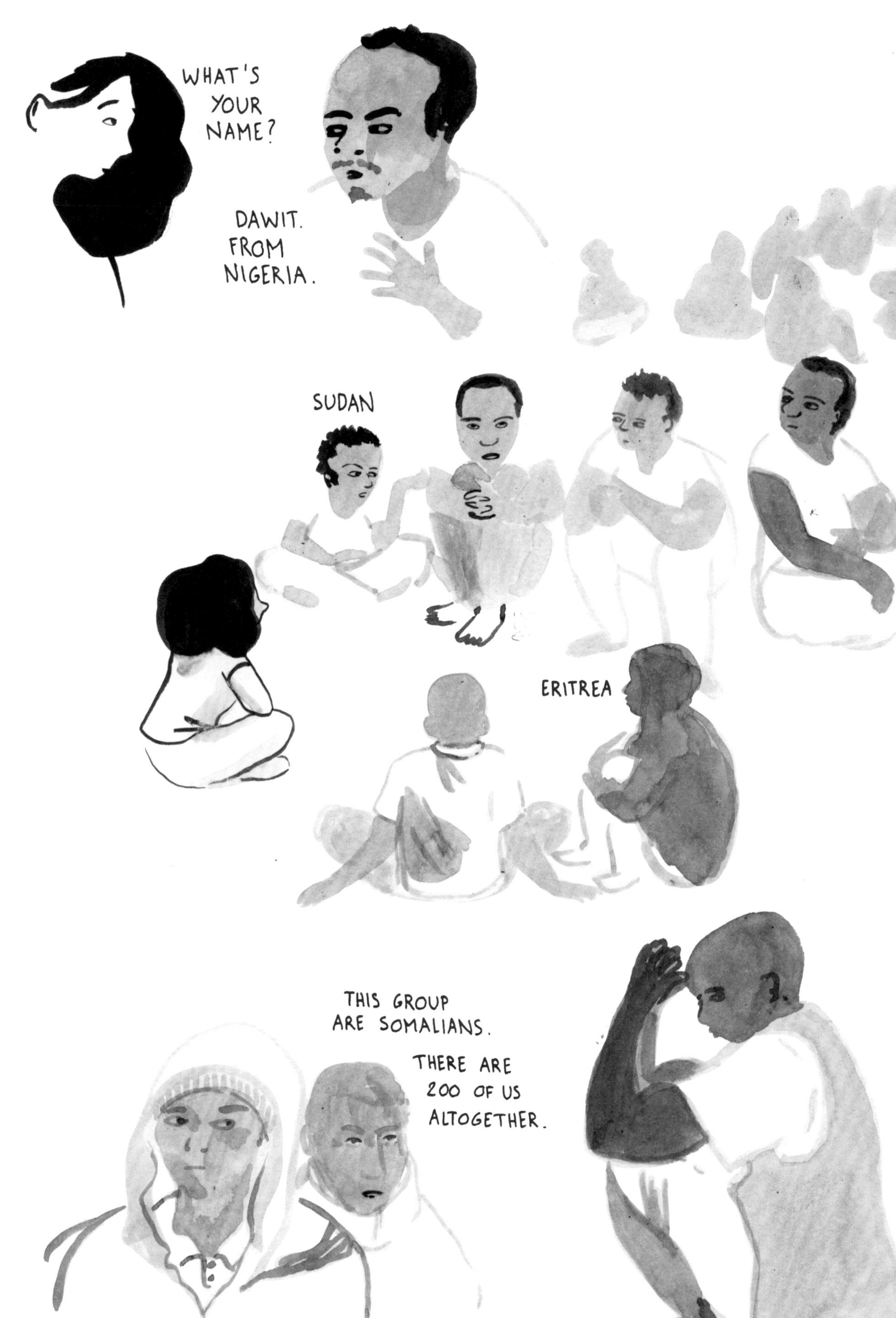

WHAT'S YOUR NAME?
DAWIT. FROM NIGERIA.
SUDAN
ERITREA
THIS GROUP ARE SOMALIANS.
THERE ARE 200 OF US ALTOGETHER.

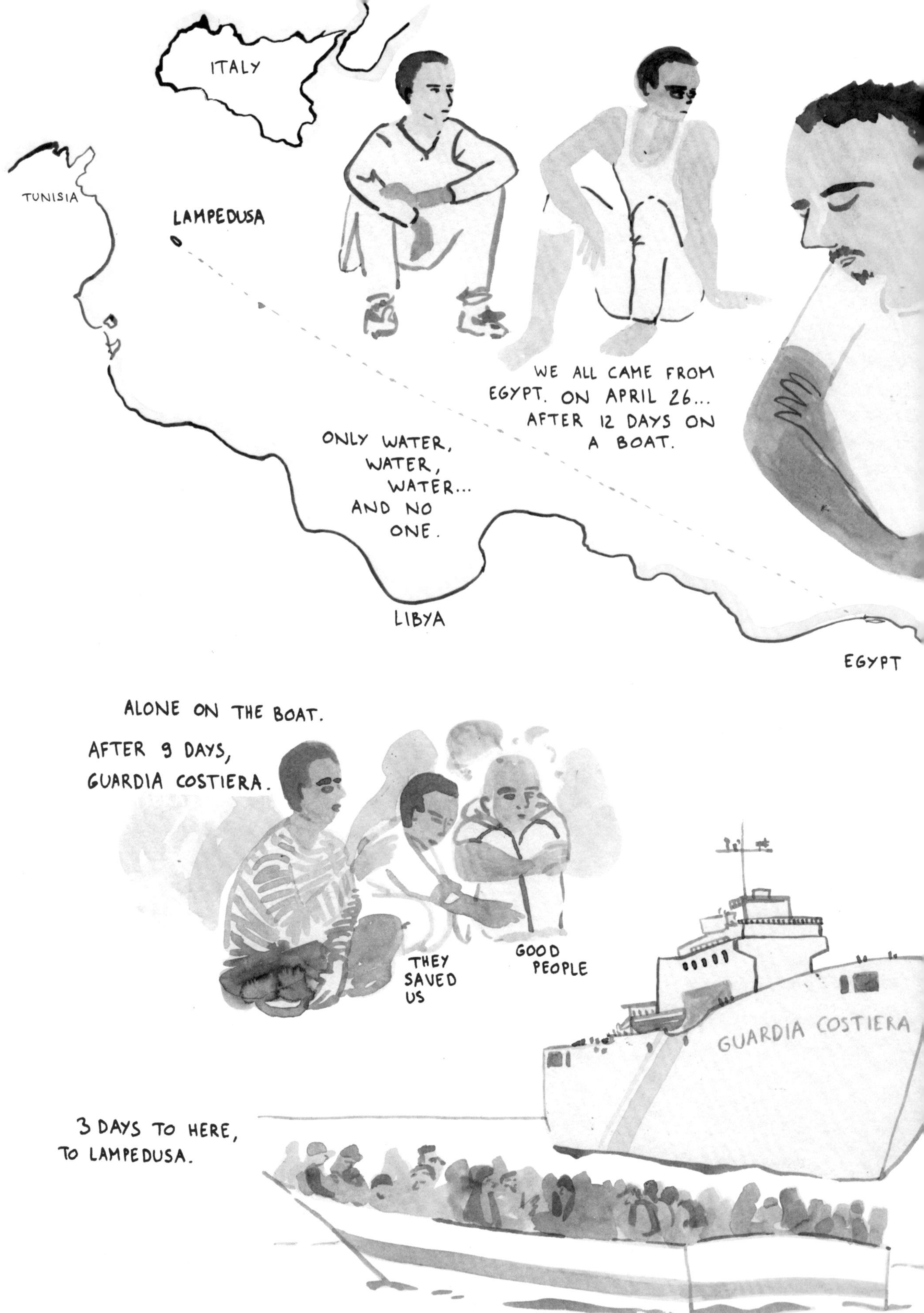

ITALY
TUNISIA
LAMPEDUSA
WE ALL CAME FROM EGYPT. ON APRIL 26... AFTER 12 DAYS ON A BOAT.
ONLY WATER, WATER, WATER... AND NO ONE.
LIBYA
EGYPT
ALONE ON THE BOAT.
AFTER 9 DAYS, GUARDIA COSTIERA.
THEY SAVED US
GOOD PEOPLE
GUARDIA COSTIERA
3 DAYS TO HERE, TO LAMPEDUSA.

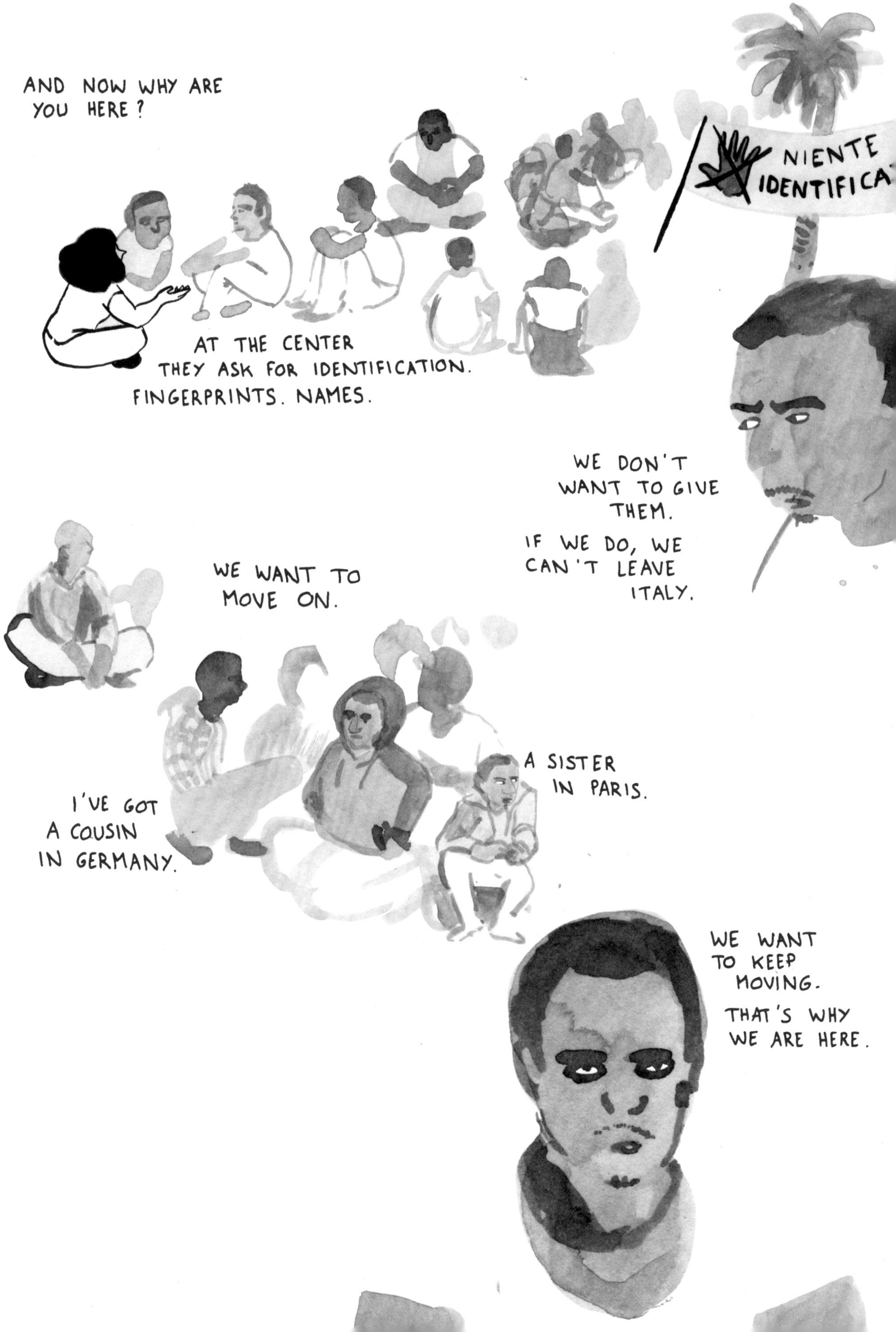

AND NOW WHY ARE
YOU HERE?

AT THE CENTER
THEY ASK FOR IDENTIFICATION.
FINGERPRINTS. NAMES.

WE DON'T
WANT TO GIVE
THEM.

IF WE DO, WE
CAN'T LEAVE
ITALY.

WE WANT TO
MOVE ON.

I'VE GOT
A COUSIN
IN GERMANY.

A SISTER
IN PARIS.

WE WANT
TO KEEP
MOVING.

THAT'S WHY
WE ARE HERE.

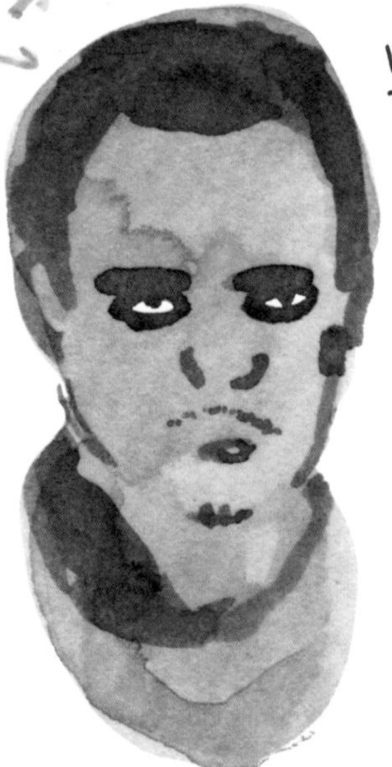

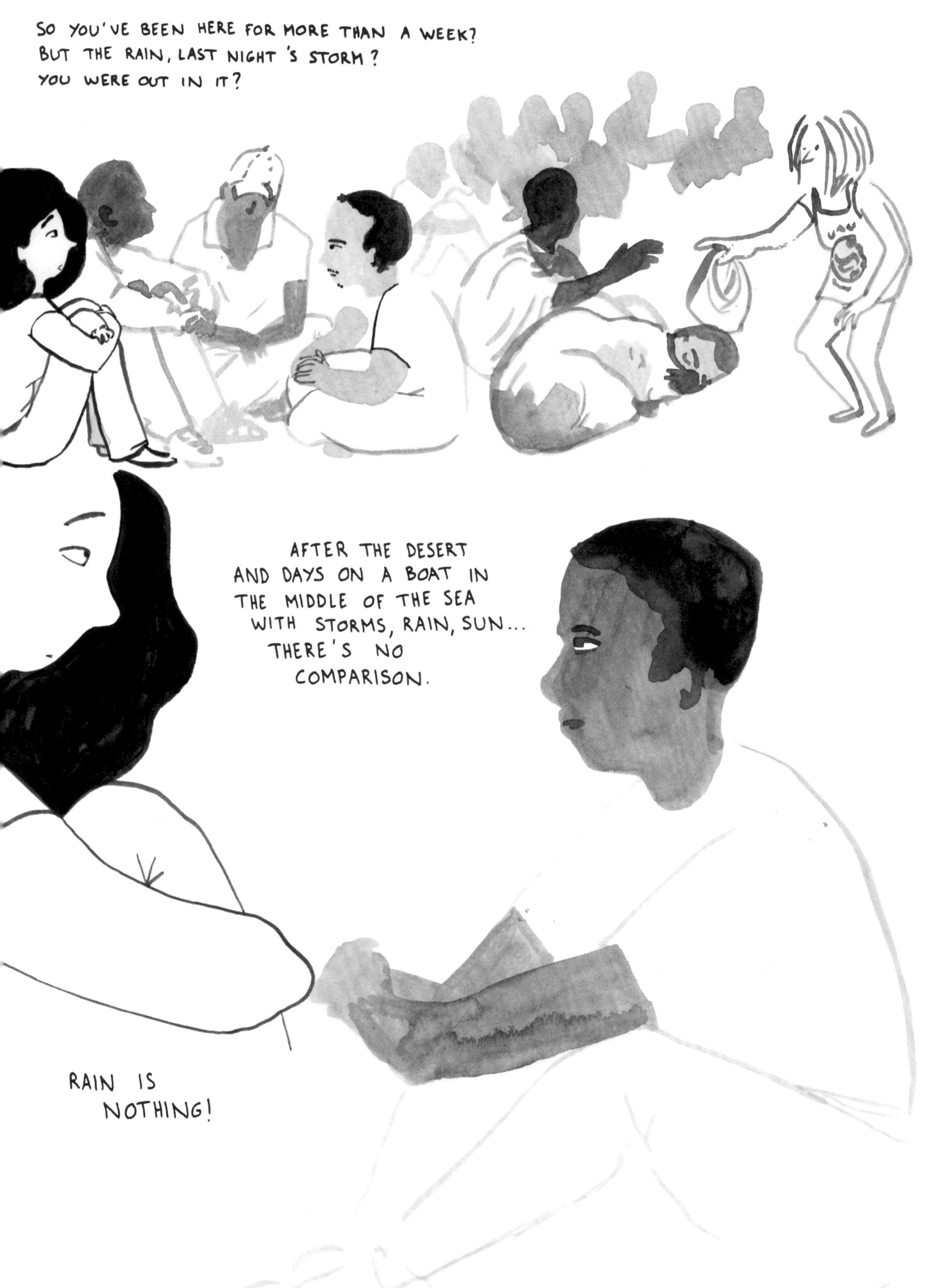

SO YOU'VE BEEN HERE FOR MORE THAN A WEEK?
BUT THE RAIN, LAST NIGHT'S STORM?
YOU WERE OUT IN IT?
AFTER THE DESERT AND DAYS ON A BOAT IN THE MIDDLE OF THE SEA WITH STORMS, RAIN, SUN... THERE'S NO COMPARISON.
RAIN IS NOTHING!

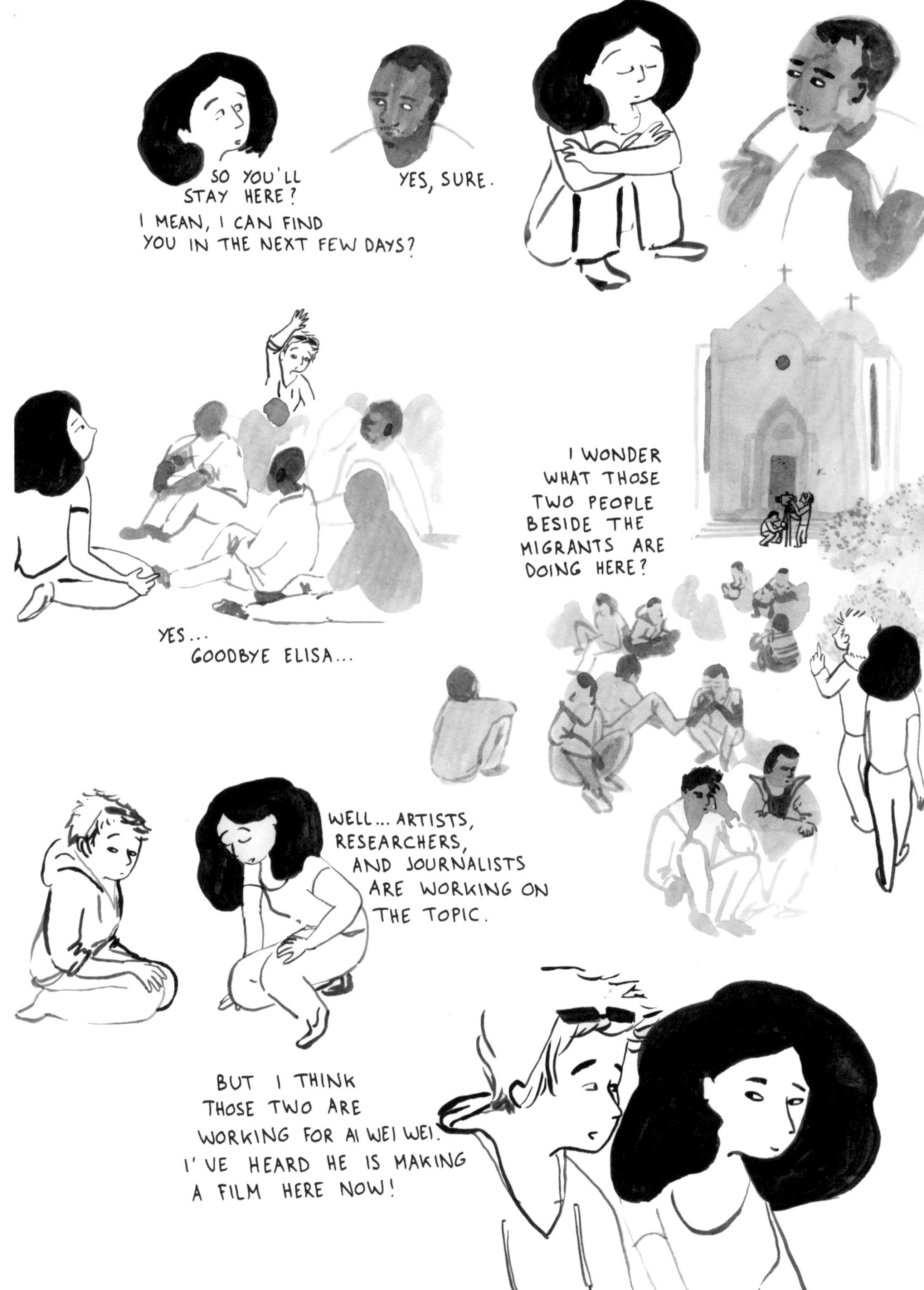

SO YOU'LL STAY HERE? I MEAN, I CAN FIND YOU IN THE NEXT FEW DAYS?
YES, SURE.
YES... GOODBYE ELISA...
I WONDER WHAT THOSE TWO PEOPLE BESIDE THE MIGRANTS ARE DOING HERE?
WELL... ARTISTS, RESEARCHERS, AND JOURNALISTS ARE WORKING ON THE TOPIC.
BUT I THINK THOSE TWO ARE WORKING FOR AI WEI WEI. I'VE HEARD HE IS MAKING A FILM HERE NOW!

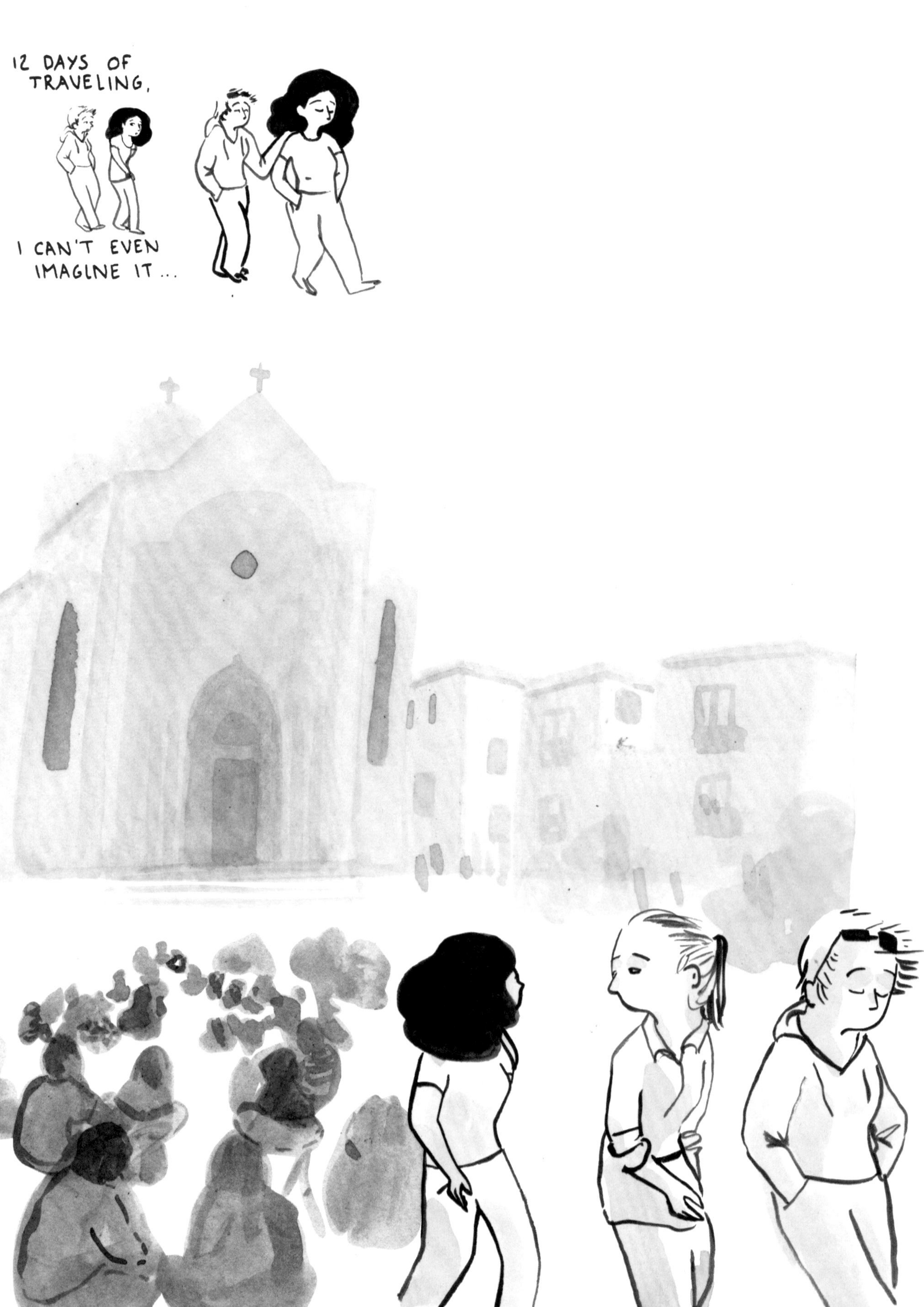

12 DAYS OF
TRAVELING,

I CAN'T EVEN
IMAGINE IT...

Jan Wenzel

"Photography is quite good. But not good enough."

The Search for New Forms of Visual Display

In the last decades, digitization has brought the world closer together at lightning speed. There is something inherently uncanny about this process. Everything is at once both there and not there. Wars are conducted elsewhere; things that define our daily lives—clothing, electronics, food—are produced elsewhere. And the crises that happen elsewhere in the world and which reverberate in the global movements of migrants are also both there and not there in our day-to-day existence.

It is often images that entangle us most intractably in the world. They reach us via the daily newspapers, Facebook, or Instagram. Writing on this phenomenon, cultural studies expert Karl Schlögel says, "The pictures we are confronted with are as new as the world looming on the horizon. [...] The images are harbingers of the new reality that we are still having difficulties arriving in."[1]

Observing the production of these images up close was the starting point in 2010 for the fieldwork carried out by the Migrant Image Research Group on its first visit to Lampedusa. Since the late 1990s, the small Mediterranean island has been regarded as a nodal point in the movement of migrants between Africa and Europe. The Italian island (which is part of Europe) has been a crucial threshold on the long refugee routes—which often involve several years on the move—marking the moment in which people become visible. "Migrants are everywhere, but they are only seen in the places where they are picked up, where their ships are captured and towed by the Coast Guard, where they are left alone and abandoned to their fate by smugglers."[2]

The pictures taken on Lampedusa are the product of different, sometimes contrasting intentions. Photojournalistic reportage; photos used by aid organizations to document their work; shots from government offices used for registration and identification purposes; images that migrants have put on Facebook to maintain contact with their family and friends—all these pictures clearly reveal varying perspectives of one and the same event, whose shorthand name in the media is "The Refugee Crisis."

Thus, an important part of the research consisted in speaking on-site with the various image producers on Lampedusa to get a sense of their role, their agenda, and their particular angle on events. Art historian John Berger writes the following in his 1975 work *A Seventh Man: A Book of Images and Words about the Experience of Migrant Workers in Europe*, an important study of images of migration: "To try to understand the experience of another it is necessary to dismantle the world as seen from one's own place within it, and to reassemble it as seen from his. For example, to understand a given choice another makes, one must face in imagination the lack of choices which may confront and deny him. The well-fed are incapable of understanding the choices of the under-fed. The world has to be dismantled and re-assembled in order to be able to grasp, however clumsily, the experience of another. To talk of entering the other's subjectivity is misleading. The subjectivity of another does not simply constitute a different interior attitude to the same exterior facts. The constellation of facts, of which he is the centre, is different."[3]

What Berger is advocating are new forms of representation and treatment, through which experiences might be communicated.

And in a certain sense the task of dismantling and reassembling formed the core of our research work. In the process, we tracked the pathways followed by the images just as much as the routes the people took. We extended the radius of our research beyond Lampedusa, traveling to Egypt to find out how events on the other side of the Mediterranean are presented, and speaking with activists from the Lampedusa in Hamburg group, with Kwadjo Anabisa and Andreas Listowell, who have become part of the group's public face in the political sphere—they are now no longer simply "arrivals" but "co-creators."

An important methodological approach has been to use drawings to obtain a view of photography from the outside. In Paula Bulling, Mohamed and Haitham El-Seht, and Emilie Josso we found four illustrators who were to become part of the research team. They expanded the possibilities of how events and the photographic practices organized around them could be visually represented. Now more than ever, the photographic image needs drawing and illustration as a counterpart. The act of translating reality, the quanta of interpretation, stylization, and imagination inscribed in every sketch may make drawing, in the current historical moment, a more trustworthy medium, a means of representation that is more suited to the complexity of the world today than photography.

"Photography is quite good. But not good enough." David Hockney used this formula to express his skepticism toward photography in an interview in 2004. "I believe that we must learn to break free of it. [...] For many decades we have learned to see as though we were a camera. Because we only look at reality with cameras, digital devices, and smartphones, we are beginning to see like a camera. We only see images that look like the pictures we are familiar with from these photographs. With these lighting effects, these shadows, these features. It is my belief that we must relearn how to look, how to see, how reality actually is. We must learn to overcome the SLR in our eyes."[4]

Photography, as a nineteenth-century medium of representation, an imaging process from the first industrial revolution, emerged at the same time as the railway and the mechanical loom. The promise of facticity and veracity won it the trust of viewers for just under two hundred years. This is now dwindling with digitization and the ubiquity of the photographic image. The question, then, of what kind of corrective photography needs in the twenty-first century has, from the outset, been a factor in how this publication evolved. As viewers, all of us who live in the world of rapidly streaming images are tasked with learning to read pictures, and this means that we need to be conscious of the conditions under which photographs are produced.

In this respect, the book addresses two themes: it speaks of a continued interest in photography, its different practices and image producers, and it also entertains an inquisitive desire to progress beyond photography to find new forms of representation more in line with the reality of the twenty-first century: what are needed are ways to convey the world in visual form. Modes of representation that are sufficiently nuanced—technical imaging processes and their applications only manage this to a limited extent—to record how reality is composed in a particular location; modes of representation that are tailored to the complex modern-day montage of a globalized world, that connect the transport routes of raw materials with the movements of refugees, the blurring of work boundaries with the transit of goods. And it needs forms of display that appeal to our imaginative faculties: photographs bring us the facts of the world in visual snippets, but we must have imagination and empathy to piece together the mosaic of the world into experience. This may be one result of these seven years of research: the polyphony and mutual illumination of photography and drawing appear to be an extremely productive path along which to travel in search of new forms of representation.

1   Karl Schlögel, *Planet der Nomaden* (Berlin, 2006), p. 17.
2   Ibid., p. 26.
3   John Berger and Jean Mohr, *A Seventh Man: A Book of Images and Words about the Experience of Migrant Workers in Europe* (Harmondsworth, 1975), pp. 93–94.
4   "Die Fotografie ist am Ende," interview with David Hockney, Spiegel Online (December 5, 2005), http://www.spiegel.de/kultur/gesellschaft/interview-mit-david-hockney-die-fotografie-ist-am-ende-a-389005.html.

Frankfurter Allgemeine

ZEITUNG FÜR DEUTSCHLAND

Freitag, 4. Oktober 2013 · Nr. 230 / 40 D 2   HERAUSGEGEBEN VON WERNER D'INKA, BERTHOLD KOHLER, GÜNTHER NONNENMACHER, FRANK SCHIRRMACHER, HOLGER STELTZNER   2,20 €   D 2954 A   F.A.Z. im Internet: faz.net

Dutzende Tote bei Flüchtlingsdrama vor Lampedusa

jöb./nbu. ROM/BRÜSSEL, 3. Oktober. Mindestens 133 Flüchtlinge sind am Donnerstag vor der Küste der süditalienischen Insel Lampedusa ertrunken, nachdem ihr Schiff in Brand geraten und gesunken war. Das meldete die Nachrichtenagentur Ansa unter Berufung auf die Küstenwache. Unter den Opfern waren auch zwei schwangere Frauen und vier Kinder. 151 Menschen konnten bis zum Abend gerettet werden. Mehr als 200 würden noch vermisst, teilte der Leiter der lokalen Gesundheitsbehörde, Antonio Candela, mit. Die Bürgermeisterin von Lampedusa, Giusi Nicolini, sagte unter Tränen, die Leichenkammer der Insel sei zu klein für die vielen Toten. Deshalb müssten die Opfer in einem Hangar am Flughafen aufgebahrt werden. Vor seinem Abflug nach Lampedusa sagte Innenminister Angelino Alfano: Dies „ist nicht nur ein italienisches Drama." Es betreffe ganz Europa. Italiens Senatspräsident Pietro Grasso forderte, Italien und Europa dürften nicht länger die Augen vor dem Unglück der Migranten verschließen. In Italien müsse über alle politischen Grenzen hinweg ein offeneres Immigrationsgesetz geschaffen werden. *(Fortsetzung Seite 2.)*

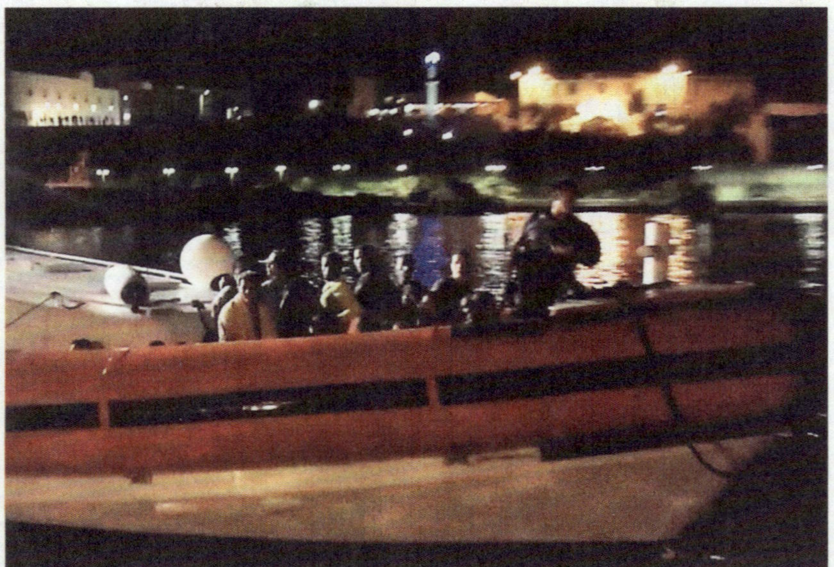

Gerettet: *Vor Lampedusa geborgene Schiffbrüchige an Bord eines Bootes der italienischen Küstenwache*   Foto AFP

Das Projekt

Von Reinhard Müller

Am Tag der Deutschen Einheit zeigte sich Angela Merkel gewohnt bescheiden: Nicht nur Europa, nein, die ganze Welt schaue jetzt auf Deutschland. Damit wird auch die Latte vor dem an diesem Freitag beginnenden Sondierungsgespräch mit der SPD recht hoch gehängt. Erwartet die Welt eine bewährte, aber eher bleiern-bräsige große Koalition oder ein ebenso buntes wie riskantes Experiment? Nicht ohne Grund verdichten sich nun im Bund wie auch im Labor Hessen die Anzeichen, dass Schwarz-Grün ernsthaft als eine Möglichkeit der Regierungsbildung ins Auge gefasst wird.

In den Führungszirkeln beider Parteien gibt es – ungeachtet der erwartbaren Breitseiten aus Bayern – keine unüberwindbaren Berührungsängste. Kontakte wurden immer gepflegt; zudem haben die Grünen auch konservative Wurzeln – der Kern ihres Programms ist die Bewahrung der Natur. Es spricht Bände, dass ein grüner Spitzenmann kurz vor der Wahl als größten programmatischen Unterschied zur Union spontan das Betreuungsgeld nannte. Solche Differenzen sollten sich überwinden lassen. Nun sind die Erfahrungen in den Ländern überschaubar und nicht gerade nachhaltige Erfolgsgeschichten. Irgendwann freilich ist die Zeit reif.

Der Traum führender Politiker aus CDU und Grünen, Wirtschaftskompetenz mit ökologischem Sachverstand ganz neu zu verknüpfen – Klimaschutz steht ja in der Tat weltweit auf der Agenda –, kann aber nicht ohne die Parteivölker verwirklicht werden. Nun ist die Basis beider Seiten in guten Teilen durchaus in ähnlichen Milieus zu Hause, aber es stecken doch unterschiedliche (Welt-) Anschauungen hinter den bürgerlichen Fassaden. Die Grünen haben für einen klaren Politikwechsel, für Umverteilung, für mehr Staat gekämpft. Das macht sie nicht zu einer Verbotspartei – auch die vom Gegner geschickt aufgebauschte Forderung nach einem Veggie Day kann dafür nicht herhalten. Aber sie wollen eine Umkehr. Beim grünen Leib-und-Magen-Thema Energie hat die Kanzlerin diese Umkehr freilich mit ihrem immer noch quietschenden U-Turn so rasend vollzogen, dass manchem Grünen die Spucke wegblieb. Doch bei aller Bedeutung der Basis: Zunächst haben es die Parteioberen in der Hand, ein Projekt „reif" zu machen. Man sieht zu Beginn der Gespräche mit den alten Kumpeln von der SPD: So schlecht ist die Lage der vermeintlichen Pyrrhus-Siegerin Merkel nicht.

Heute

CDU-Führung: Schwarz-Grün ist eine echte Alternative

„Gesellschaftliches Klima spricht dafür" / Zustimmung und Skepsis bei den Grünen

ban./Lt. BERLIN, 3. Oktober. Bundeskanzlerin Angela Merkel (CDU) hat „faire Sondierungsgespräche" mit der SPD an diesem Freitag und mit den Grünen am nächsten Donnerstag in Aussicht gestellt. Es gebe „eine gemeinsame Verantwor- Göring-Eckardt Beachtung, die im Gespräch mit der Zeitung „Die Welt" angab: „Wir sagen nicht von vornherein, das wird nichts mit der Union." Die Grünen gingen „ernsthaft in die Gespräche". Aus den Bundesländern meldeten sich bei den Grünen sei nicht eine einzige schwarz-grüne Landesregierung vertreten. Auch eine große Koalition im Bund habe im Bundesrat keine eigene Mehrheit, hieß es dazu in der CDU, weshalb auch ein Bündnis aus Union und SPD dort auf Stimmen von Lan-

Die Macht am Rhein

Von Reiner Burger

Nordrhein-Westfalen ist das Schlüsselland für die politische Mehrheitsbildung in Deutschland. Das hat schon mit seiner schieren Größe zu tun: Im bevölkerungsreichsten Bundesland gibt es die größten Landesverbände der Parteien. Eine Volkspartei, die in einer Bundestagswahl zwischen Rhein und Weser (deutlich) schlechtere Ergebnisse als im deutschen Durchschnitt erzielt, hat keine packen. Viele Straßen- und Schienenwege müssen dringend saniert werden, damit Nordrhein-Westfalen wirtschaftlicher Kraft-Raum Deutschlands bleibt. Nach dem Aufbau Ost muss es in den kommenden Jahren eine Erneuerung West geben. Als Industrieland ist Nordrhein-Westfalen zudem dringend darauf angewiesen, dass die Energiewende endlich umfas-

Photographs from Everyday Life

Italian relief organization I Girasoli
on the use of images

PHOTO STORY: LISA BERGMANN

I Girasoli (The Sunflowers) is a non-profit relief organization that assumes guardianship of underage migrants and helps them through the various agencies so that they can attend school and find vocational training. While waiting for the outcome of their asylum applications, the youths receive food and shelter in shared accommodation in Mazzarino in Sicily. The relief organization has been in existence for ten years and has already offered support to over 550 young people. I Girasoli works with a concept whereby the refugees are taken back to their place of arrival in Italy after a specified period so that they can look at it with fresh eyes.

The photographs taken by the staff of I Girasoli document the everyday experience of the youths on their visits to the authorities as they attempt to extend their residency permits and apply for passports. In 2010, the Migrant Image Research Group visited I Girasoli and spoke with staff members Cettina Nicosiano and Michele Liuzzo.

A lot of young people escape from extreme situations of armed conflict. Many of them have an idealized view of the West as a place with no corruption, where everyone's rights are respected. The longing for freedom, for work, and for the recovery of one's dignity—I see a bit of this in all the kids that arrive here and get taken in by us.

We try as much as possible to create a life that comes close to family life and that offers the affection that the kids were probably lacking for several years during their long period in transit. We also want to provide these minors with knowledge about what Italy is like and what difficulties they can expect. We try in any way we can to provide the teens with a school qualification that is recognized in Italy—in particular, vocational training. The idea is that when they leave here, they will be able to build a life in Italy.

When they arrive in Mazzarino, they have to get through the hearing with the territorial commission to recognize their legal status in Italy. So the first step of our work involves listening to their stories. There is an intervention by our psychologist, who seeks to understand the trauma they suffered while travelling, together with our lawyer, with the intention of keeping the minors calm enough to deal with the interrogation by the commission. What follows is really the most difficult situation, and a trauma that the kids have to overcome—the waiting in uncertainty for some form of documentation.

We notice that nowadays, as a consequence of the restrictions imposed by the Italian government and the Treaty of Friendship between Italy and Libya, nobody arrives directly from

Africa anymore. The route has changed. It now either crosses Syria and then goes on to Turkey or starts in Egypt and leads across Syria, also ending in Turkey. When people reach Turkey, they have to choose between continuing to Greece and trying to travel right across Europe.

Before the Berlusconi government, our work was easier, but we still try to resolve some of the problems the minors face. Before, there were no refoulements to Libya or Greece, as just happened this morning, despite the European directive that, due to human rights violations in Greece, there should be no refoulements.

North Africans are not recognized as asylum seekers. So people coming from Tunisia, or Algeria, from the Maghreb coast, or from Egypt, they will all be considered by the Italian government as illegals who come for the sole purpose of seeking work. So even an Egyptian who has political problems in his country will not be able to apply for asylum.

Depending on your country of origin, you have the right to choose whether or not to ask for asylum—even if you are applying for reasons that have been established as valid by the Geneva Convention, like persecution due to race, ethnicity or religion.

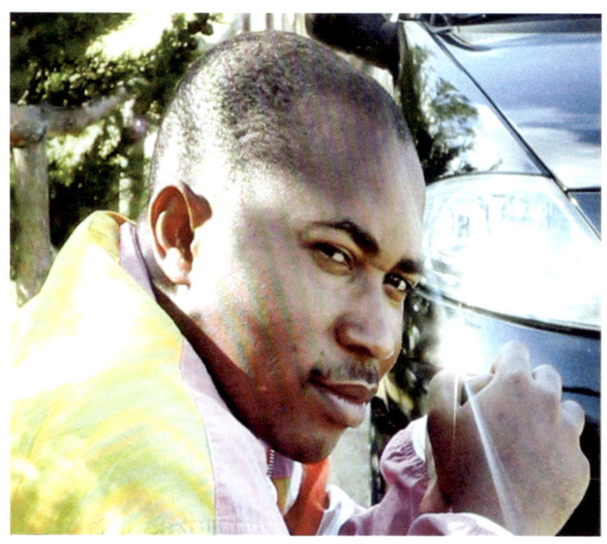

←   This is a Nigerian who now lives in Pisa. His application was refused and he was not granted refugee status. He was given a study permit, because he was still at school. When he turned eighteen, he had to renew his residence permit, because he had an employment contract. The labor union that was handling his application made a mistake in the procedure and as a result he is facing deportation from Italy. The Italian immigration quota decree stipulates that you have to apply from abroad if you want to come to Italy to work. If you are already in the country, you cannot apply for a work permit.

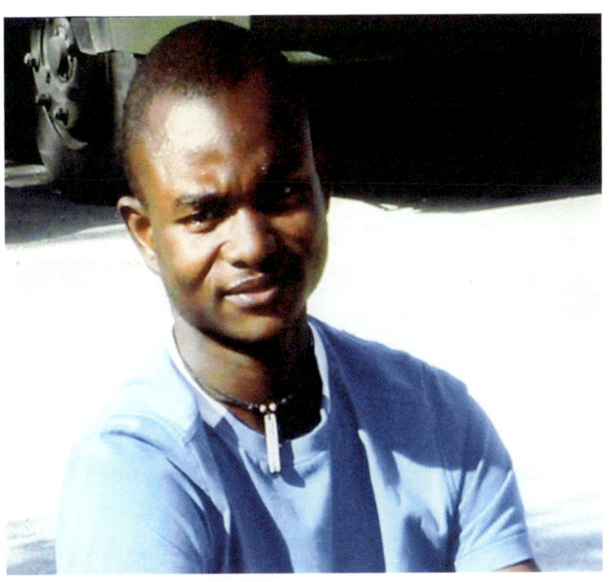

← Daniel received a notice of rejection too. He works in the agricultural sector with a regular employment contract. In order to renew a residence permit, you need a passport. To obtain a passport at his embassy is extremely difficult, above all because he has dual citizenship. He was born to a Ghanaian mother and a Burkinabe father. He had to apply for his passport at the Ghanaian Embassy, which made a mistake with his name. So he ended up with a residence permit in one name and a passport in a different name and with a different nationality. As a result he has major difficulties renewing his residence permit.

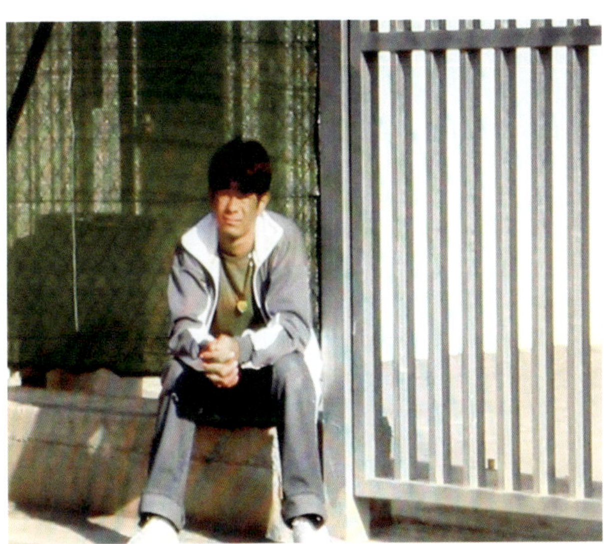

← This is Ali, a young Afghan, who arrived by way of Greece in a truck. He was accommodated in the Mazzarino camp and then found work at a construction company operating in the region of Milan. After six months his job ended and he got a place in a reception project in Udine. He stayed for six months in Udine and attended a vocational training course; today he works at a marble manufacturing company.

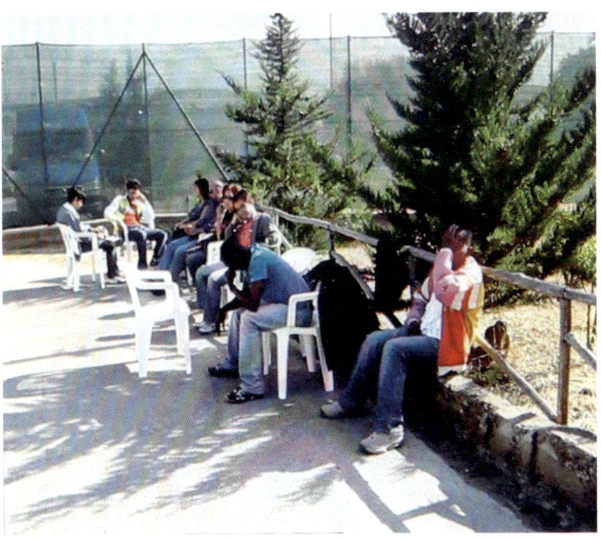

← Here we are in the C.A.R.A. center, the reception camp in Syracuse. These youths are waiting to be examined by the regional commission. The tension that has built up before facing the commission is clearly evident in the photo. The commission is composed of the prefect of Syracuse, an official from the police department, a civil society member nominated by the local administration, and a representative from the Office of the United Nations High Commissioner for Refugees (UNHCR).

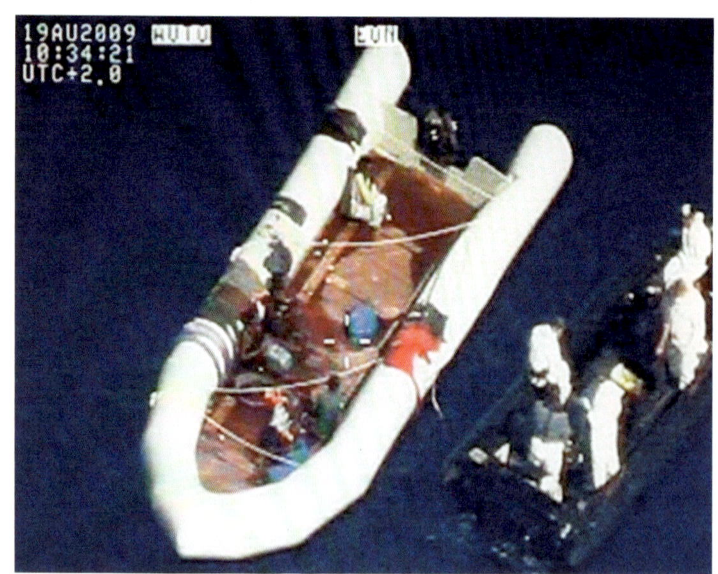

←   This image was taken from an Italian airplane on August 19, 2009. It shows a rubber boat with five people on board, Eritreans, with a boat from the Maltese Maritime Squadron next to it, passing them water and fuel. To begin with, there were seventy people on board, but after twenty days of drifting in the Mediterranean, sixty-five people had died and there were only five left. But still these five people weren't rescued by the Maltese or the Italian navy. When it was published, this picture caused quite a stir in Italy.

Two of these Eritreans, after arriving in Lampedusa, were sent to us. They had to overcome the trauma of witnessing people dying next to them. We organized for the five of them to meet again here in Mazzarino and swap experiences.

We came to an agreement with the Salesian Institute of Marsala, Sicily, to give the kids the possibility to go to the sea in the summer. It's a structure almost like a hostel, so for a week we were able to go on holiday with everybody. In this way they experienced new things and met people other than those from our little village, but they also encountered the sea as a place of relaxation and joy rather than of risk and danger. Prior to this, many of them tried to avoid any open water, which they perceived as a force of nature. For some of them, it was the first time that they had had a swim in the sea.

Arrival and Return

Photos as a way to remember for Andy Joseph Smith

PHOTO STORY: LISA BERGMANN

Andy Joseph Smith from Sunyani, Ghana, was taken as an underage asylum seeker from Lampedusa to Mazzarino, Sicily, where he was brought to I Girasoli. The Sicilian relief organization found him a place on a vocational training specializing in tourism—a few months later I Girasoli went with him on a day trip back to Lampedusa.

After a year of voluntary social work Smith began working as a carer for the elderly, and he is now a member of the I Girasoli staff. The Migrant Image Research Group spoke with him in 2010. Andy collects images on his Facebook account. Like many other refugees he uses Facebook as a means to share photos of himself and his surroundings with his family and friends, allowing them to participate in his new life.

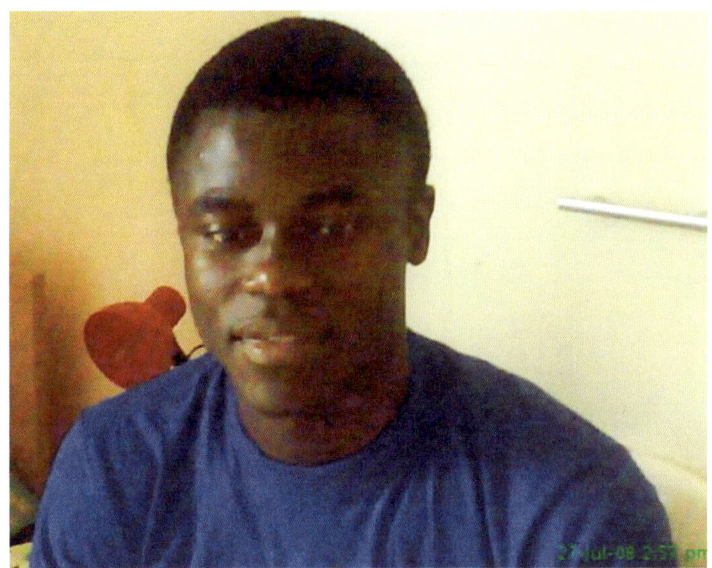

↑   SMITH: This is a picture taken during the first days in Mazzarino. This was with the guys from I Girasoli. They told me how things work in Italy—that I might stay here for six months or a year and still not get any documents. I thought of all the things I had been through, all the problems I had faced, and then, in the end, maybe I wouldn't get the documents … so I was quite upset. And while I was listening to all these explanations, they took this picture of me.

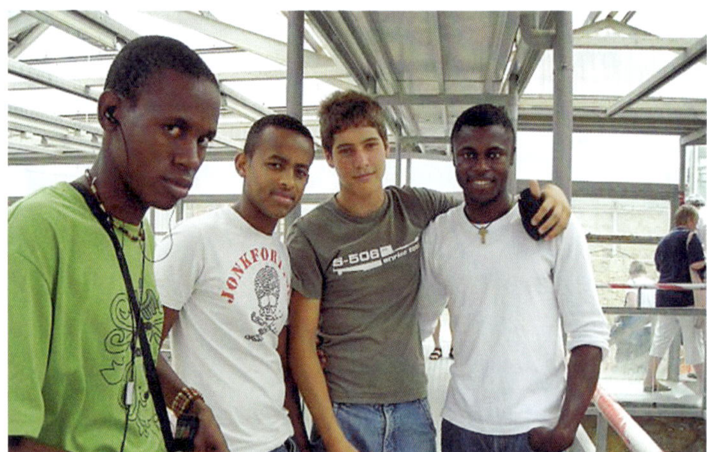

← This is a picture which reminds me of when I had the necessary composure to do what I wanted to do. It was taken after completing the exam for admission into the tourism management program, so I was content and relaxed.

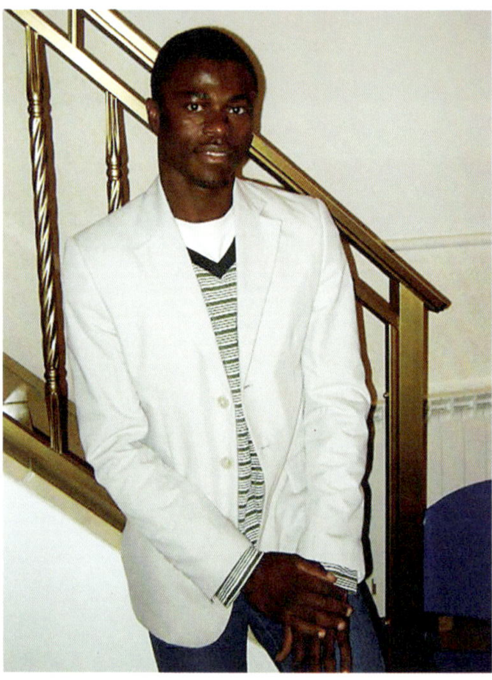

← Q: *You look elegant here!*
SMITH: Elegant, but with some problems … It's the moment I was notified that my application for asylum had been rejected. So at that instant I was a little … but we are still humans even if we have problems.

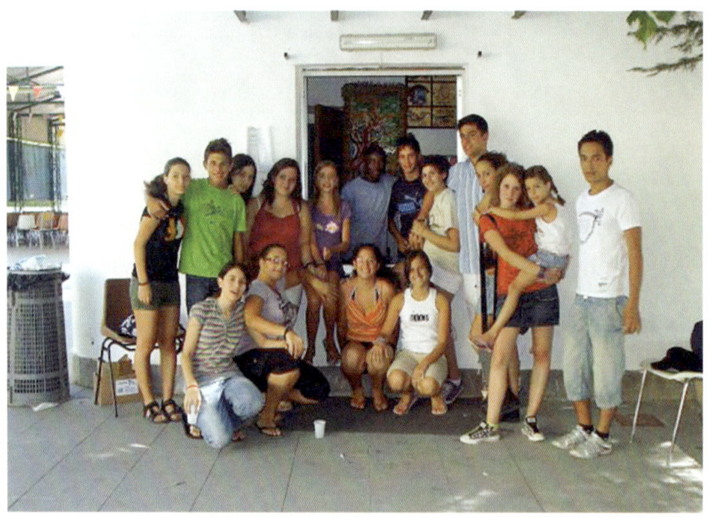

← NICOSIANO: These are Salesians, who take in groups for worship and prayers. It's an "oasis of spirituality," and for the last two summers, some of the boys like Joseph, Noufou, and Abdi stayed on to work at the Don Bosco Institute there.
SMITH: This is a photo that we took together with all the guys working there. Alessio, Veronika, etc. We were quite happy together.

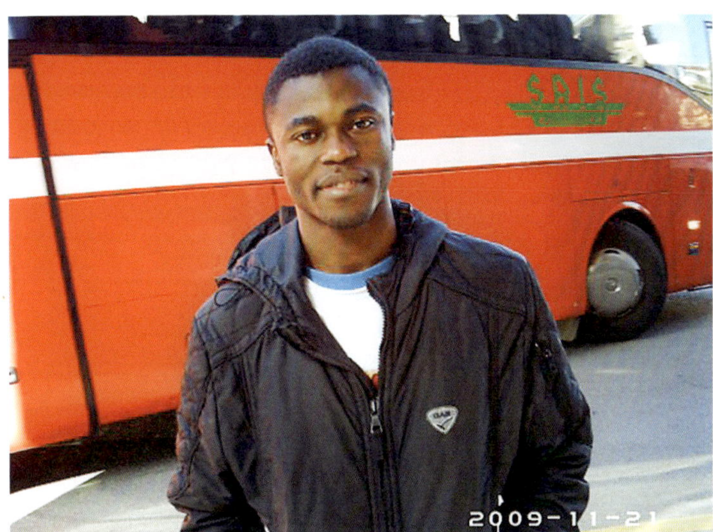

← This is in Palermo.

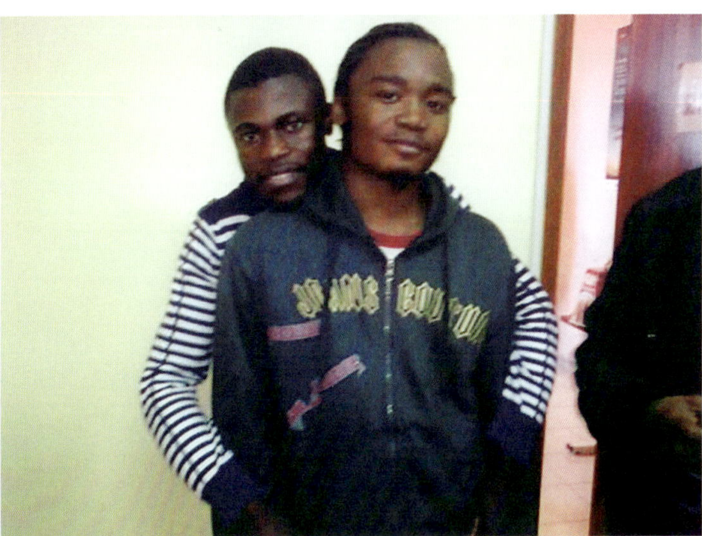

← With my friend Isaac.

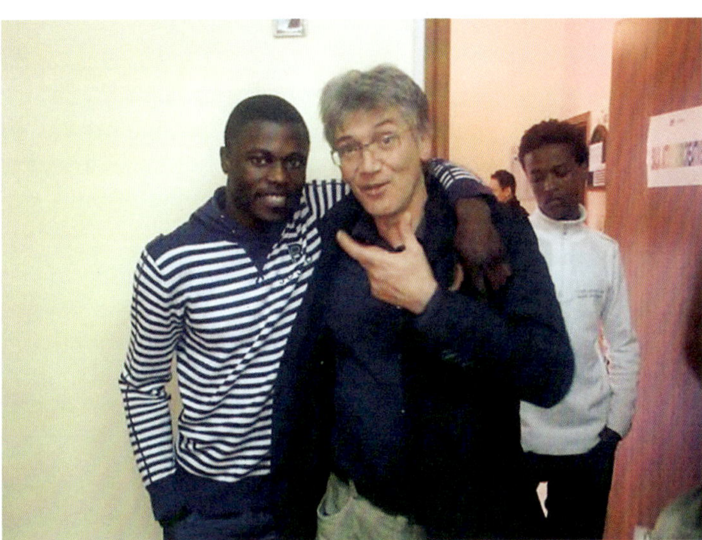

← Here I am with Michele.

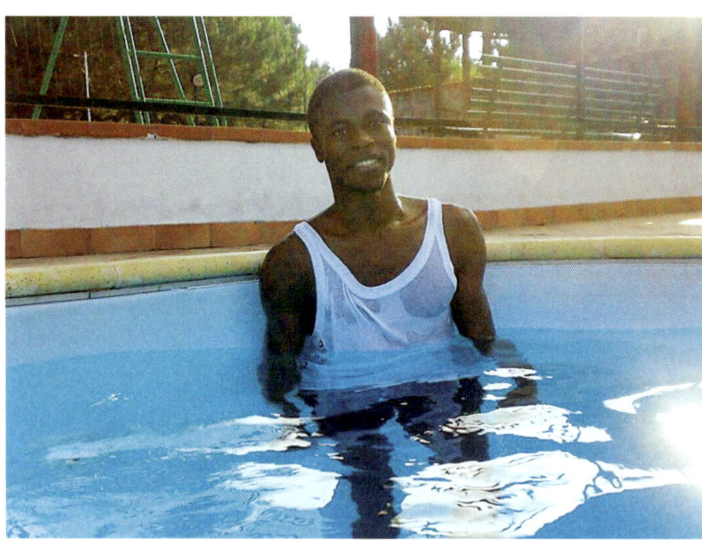

← NICOSIANO: Joseph in the swimming pool …
SMITH: I always say, "I hate swimming," but the guys would say, "No, no, no, come on!" As I didn't want to, I got in with my clothes on.

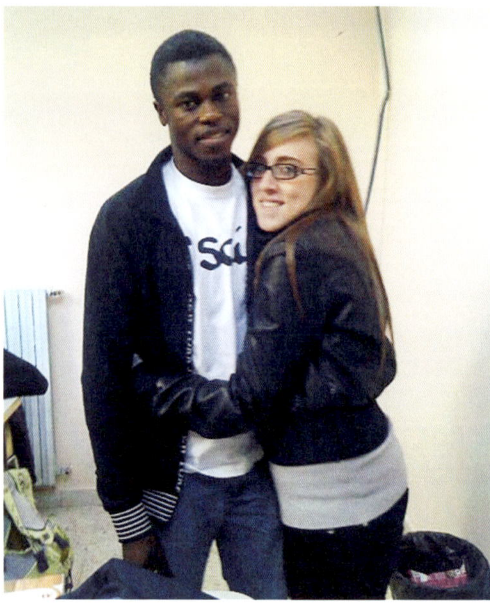

← Here I am at school. This is my classmate, her name is Francesca.

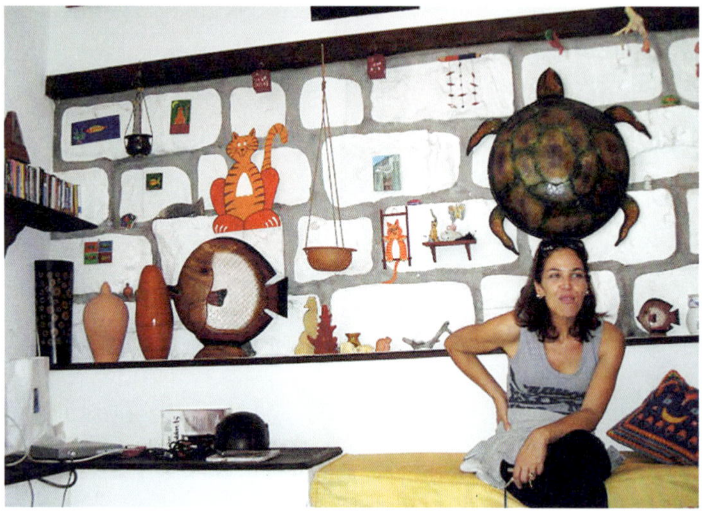

← Here, on Lampedusa … at Paola's house. The first day when we arrived to work as volunteers at Legambiente, the Italian environmental association.

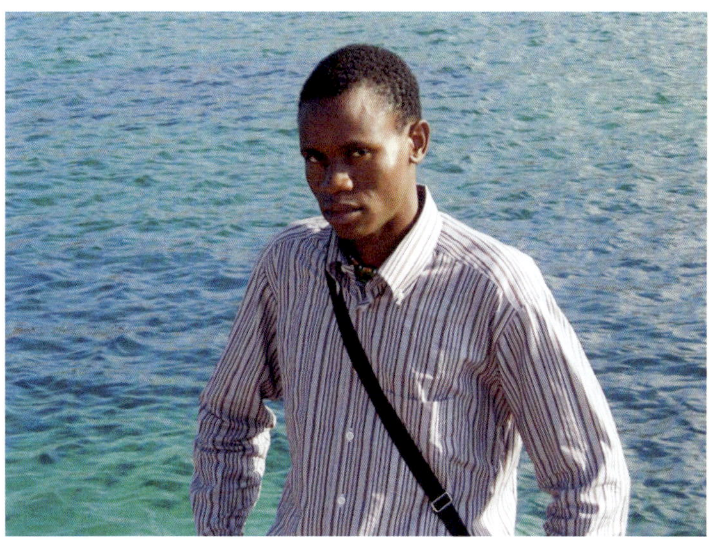

← SMITH: This is my best friend. His name is Noufou Yabré from Burkina Faso. He is a fine man, I adore him.
NICOSIANO: How did it feel returning to Lampedusa—from the opposite side, not from the Mediterranean Sea but from Italy? Going there this time with your documents?
SMITH: It was beautiful! I was so calm because once you have your documents, you are independent and you can travel and do whatever you like.

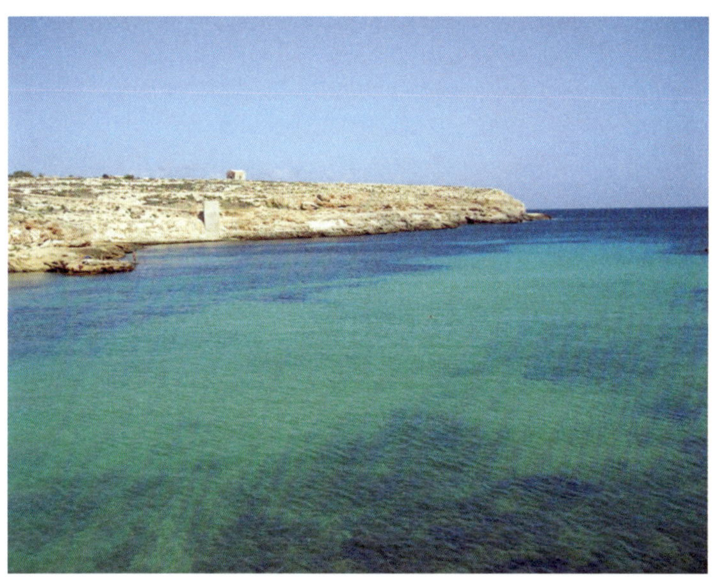

← Paola said to me, "You remember this place?" and I said, "No, I don't," and Paola said, "How can you not remember …? It's the place where they left you the first time you arrived on Lampedusa from Africa." And I said, "Yeah, right." When I arrived I was confused and I didn't remember. But here I was calm and kind of happy so I had to take a picture. For me, Lampedusa is a very important place because it saved many people. I always want to return there.

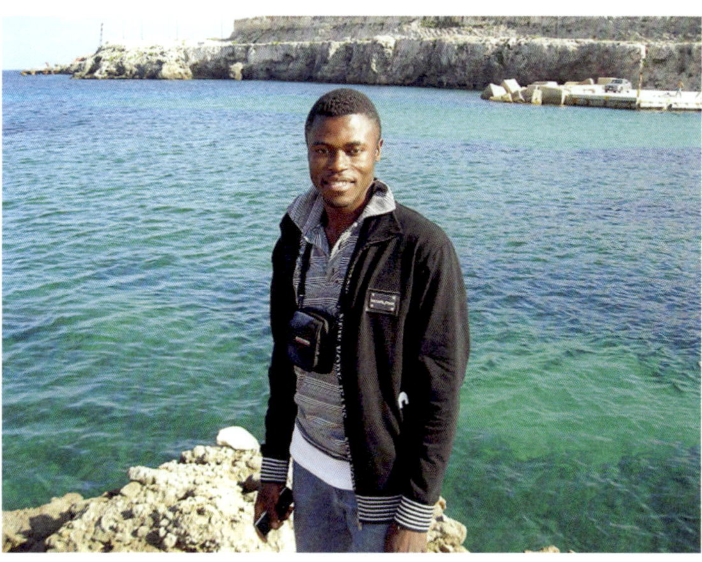

← We went for a walk here.

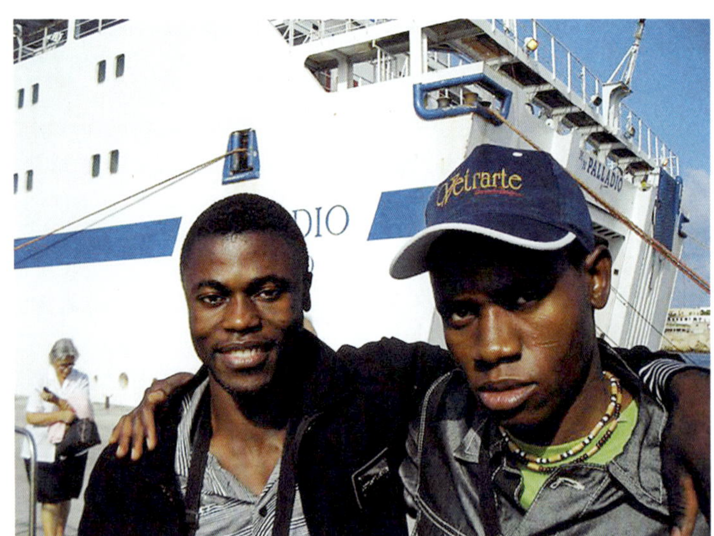

← The last day on Lampedusa, when we had to leave.

Q: When you returned to Lampedusa, did you gain any new impressions? Are they different from the old ones? Do you have a new image now of Lampedusa?

SMITH: I can say that now my memories are more beautiful. I had a nice experience on Lampedusa, because I did volunteer work with Legambiente and it always reminds me of Lampedusa.

NICOSIANO: The youths looked after the Isola dei Conigli because the turtles go there to lay their eggs. They make sure that the other visitors respect nature.

SMITH: All the things I did as a volunteer helped me a lot. Before, I was shy, and speaking in public was difficult for me. The experience with Legambiente really helped me.

NICOSIANO: I think we are all travelers in life. Even if you think you have completed your journey, when you return to the place where you were before, you've changed—maybe you have become better, have achieved other things, so this place will never be the same to you. The journey never comes to an end.

My Private Photographs

Noufou Yabré on his arrival
and stay in Italy

PHOTO STORY: LISA BERGMANN

When Noufou Yabré reached Lampedusa, he was immediately brought to the Center for Identification and Expulsion (CIE) and held there for several days. As a result he had no information about where he had landed. After that he came straight to Mazzarino and was taken to I Girasoli, a non-profit relief organization for underage migrants. He took part in a group trip back to Lampedusa in 2009. The visit was the first time he got to see something of the island. Like most of the youths from I Girasoli, he speaks several languages and dialects. He has completed his training in tourism management in Italy. The Migrant Image Research Group spoke with him in 2010.

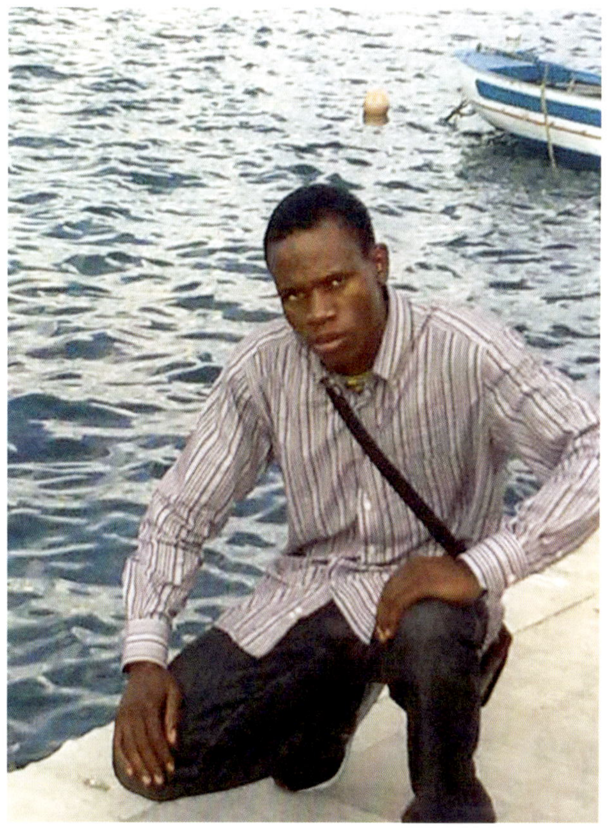

↑   Q: *Where are you here in this picture?*
YABRÉ: On Lampedusa.
    Q: *Was it when you came back there?*
YABRÉ: Yes, when I came with Cettina Nicosiano and my colleagues.

Q: Lampedusa was the first place you landed in Italy?
YABRÉ: Yes, in 2008. But this picture here is from one year ago. I was very happy because my life was saved at Lampedusa. I had never traveled by sea before. This was the first time. I didn't think I would have the chance to return to this island freely. I took this photo to always remember.

Q: What happened when you reached Lampedusa after crossing the sea? Did someone take you to a reception camp?
YABRÉ: Yes, some policemen.

Q: So you saw nothing of Lampedusa?
YABRÉ: No. I was in the camp, wasn't I? I had never spent thirteen days being idle. I was happy, in the sense that I was finally safe after two days at sea, but I wasn't very pleased. I had never in my whole life been in a camp before, like a prison.

Q: Why did you want to come to Italy?
YABRÉ: Italy is a part of the world, isn't it? I wanted to learn about other places.

Q: But did you already know what things were like in Italy?
YABRÉ: No.

Q: Who convinced you to come?
YABRÉ: The world is full of states, right? In Italy I can walk freely.

First I went to Libya. If you work in Libya, it is very difficult. On your way home you have to hide. Even if you take a taxi, you have to be careful. The police do not ask you if you have an ID card. Even if you tell them you have one, they grab you anyway and put you in jail. So all the foreigners who live there have a very hard time.

Q: How long did you stay in Libya?
YABRÉ: Five months.

Q: And did you work there?
YABRÉ: Yes, but it was terrible. I worked off and on. One day yes, one day no.

Q: Why did you leave Burkina Faso?
YABRÉ: I was a student and it was summer vacation. There were five of us that wanted to go on holiday. We said, "Let's go to Niger," which is close to my country, "let's go have a look. When school starts again we'll come back." So we left and reached Niger. But it was hard to return. I was a minor and didn't have a passport, which would have made it easy to return. It was better to go forward. So we continued our journey to Libya. When we got there, things really went from bad to worse. We couldn't do anything and we were stuck. I went to our embassy and said I wanted to return. But since I was a minor, I couldn't get a passport. If they could help me to return, I thought to myself, I would wait.

Q: Did you know about the agreement between Libya and Italy, the Italian Bossi-Fini Law, which was signed in 2002?

It provides for the deportation of migrants to the last third country they have visited and for their imprisonment, notwithstanding human rights violations reported by some unstable North African states. In other words, you were in big danger.

YABRÉ: Yes, then there was the moment when my friends told me, "There is a boat here that will go to Italy. If you want to come, come. We're going." I said, "We were planning to return and now you are thinking of going somewhere else?" We were not thinking that some people go and die at sea …

"We will just go." – "But you don't know!" – "We're going!" Then we departed, like that. Now it would be easy to travel, because I have papers.

Q: What did you feel when you got your papers?

YABRÉ: I was very happy. Because without papers you are illegal. It's terrible.

Q: In the newspapers, on television, they show this problem with the boats, the illegal immigrants on Lampedusa.

Do you think they represent this in a correct way?

YABRÉ: There are laws, that is what they show. But, in my opinion, some of the laws are wrong.

For example: A friend of mine was on a boat with eighty people—only five of them survived. From Libya it doesn't take more than one day to arrive in Europe by sea, either in Malta or Italy. It took them more than twenty days, and it is not true that no one saw them drifting. So many boats go to fish in the Mediterranean. But people did not want to save them. Only five of them reached Lampedusa, seventy-five are dead. For me, this is not right.

Q: What do you think when they talk about migration to Europe on TV?

YABRÉ: Local people say, "Immigrants come to take away our jobs." But that is not true. We are productive too—we help their prosperity. When someone works, he pays taxes, he doesn't steal. We produce wealth for the community too. Last year, in the province of Reggio Calabria, there was the incident in Rosarno.

Q: What happened?

YABRÉ: Rosarno is a town where there are many farms, especially orange groves. During the harvest time many migrants arrive there from all over Italy. They live in very poor conditions, abandoned houses, a sort of ghetto camp.

Last year there were some young migrant workers walking down the street and someone shot at them. They were very angry about this and a revolt took place. They held a demonstration to claim their rights. In these places there is a gangmaster system—both in Rosarno and in Foggia. The man in control may get thirty euro a day from the producer, but the migrant worker only gets fifteen euro. The rest is kept by the gangmaster, but what is more, the migrants are treated like slaves and made to work for hours and hours. They live in abandoned lodgings or out on the field, without drinking water, without a shower, in very dire conditions.

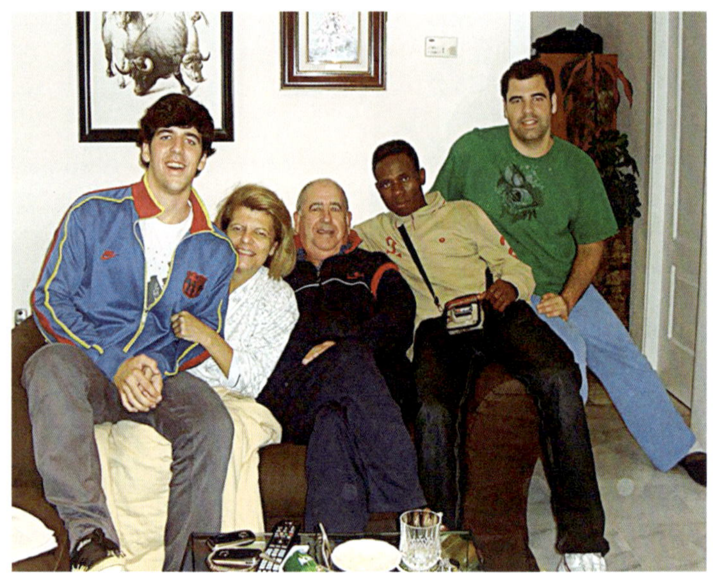

← Q: *Where are you in this picture?*
YABRÉ: Seville in Spain.

    Q: *Did you go there on an exchange with I Girasoli?*
YABRÉ: No, with my school in Piazza Marino, near Mazzarino. This is my "twin", his parents, this here is his brother. I took this picture to remember the moment. I was so happy. I was happy because I as an African coming from far away have had the chance to do these things.

    His parents were great with me, they treated me as if I were their son. From that I have learned that difference is the basis on which you can construct true equality.

Estelle Blaschke

Networked Images

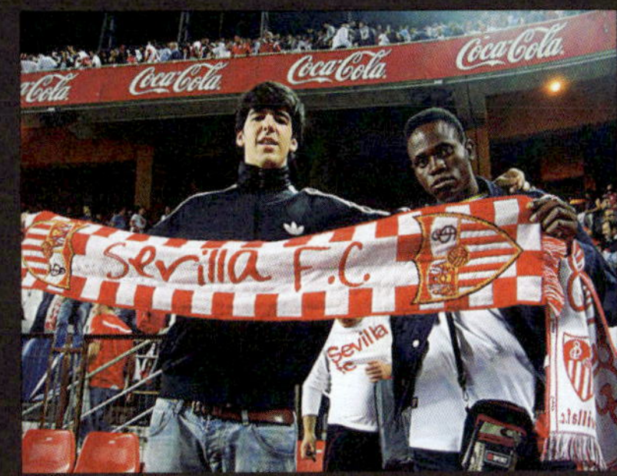

Some of the phenomena associated with digital photography can be traced back to historical trends within photography itself. Vernacular photography has always been an important driving force in photographic production and an indicator of the medium's social significance. Photographs were and still are images in motion: they circulate and transcend geographical and cultural borders. *Cartes de visite*, studio photography, the Polaroid, and the photo booth were all precursors of the selfie culture. The world has been flooded with images many times before, and the act of manipulating and appropriating images is not an innovation that came in with digital photography—it has simply been made easier, faster, and more versatile by the use of these new technologies.

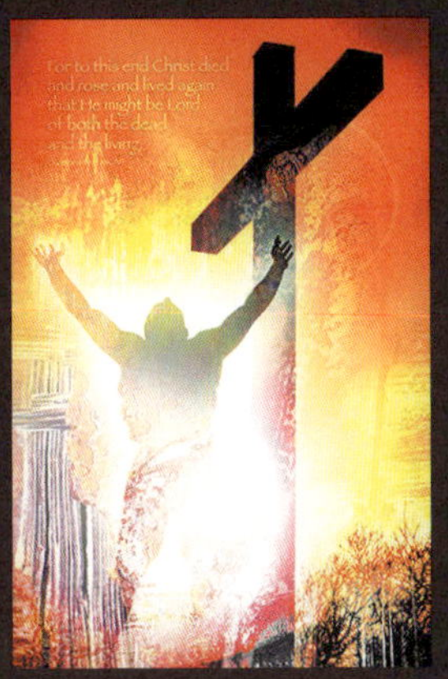

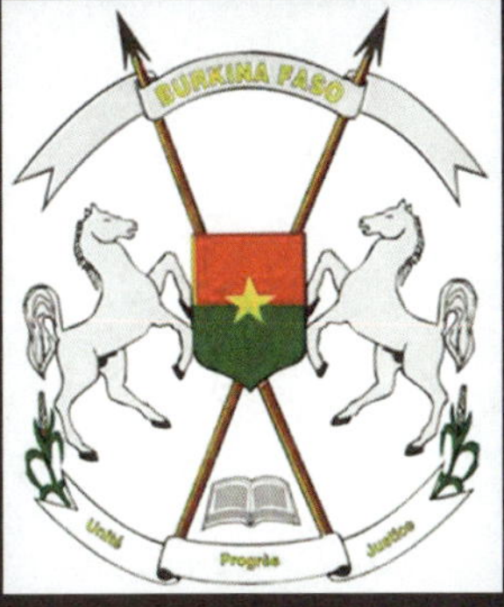

What has, however, been fundamentally changed by digital photography and the launch of smartphones and social media platforms is the status of the image as a "networked image."[1] Photographs are no longer just a representation of the world but a hybrid form combining image content and metadata. They consist of a binary code, tags, geodata, technical details, comments, and hashtags. Digital photography has not so much introduced new image motifs and genres but has instead created *image infrastructures*. Images today are defined by their "fluidity"[2] and the possibility of their being shared and commented on. They are shot, posted, and edited; they migrate or disappear; they are grouped into fragile formations in timelines or folders.

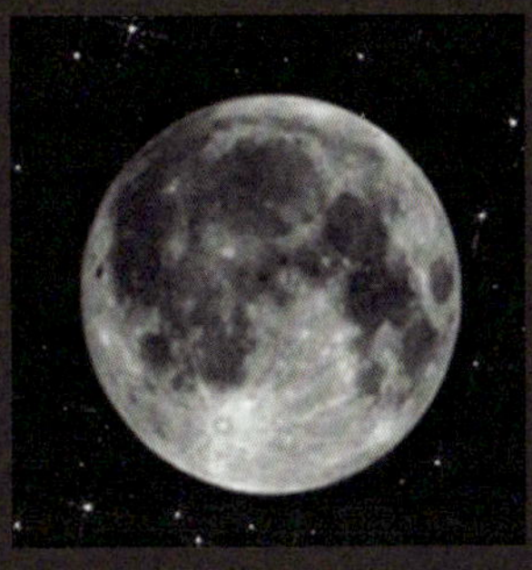

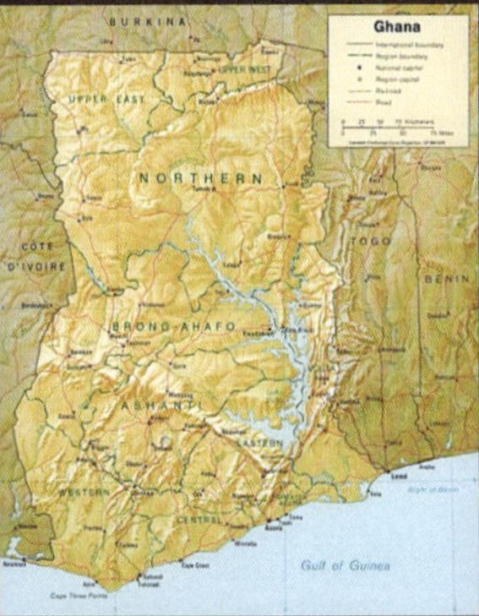

The photos by Andy Joseph Smith and Noufou Yabré exist in the parallel universe that is Facebook. They circulate on their personal accounts among friends, family members, and acquaintances: access to them is therefore limited. Noufou Yabré with a soccer scarf in the stadium in Seville; the two of them upon their arrival on Lampedusa; a stock image of praying hands holding a rosary in front of an opened Bible; a theatrical illustration of the resurrection of Christ; pictures of a toucan and a sea turtle; a map of Ghana; the coat of arms

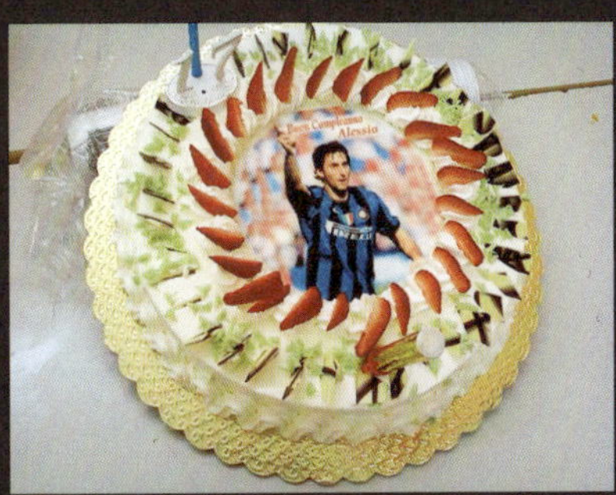

of Burkina Faso; a full moon; a birthday cake with the picture of a soccer player on top. A hodgepodge of pictures that Smith and Yabré, at a certain moment in time, have regarded as important or possibly identified with (for example, the portrait, the map, and the religious motifs), or have simply deemed interesting or beautiful.

If in the early years of digital photography and digitization the number of pictures in the digital format was still considered limited and limitable,[3] social media platforms such as Flickr, Facebook, and Instagram and the spread of smartphones soon made this initial assumption appear increasingly absurd. The fluidity produced led to an unprecedented proliferation of images, and perhaps even more importantly to the emancipation of the producers of images. Today, images can be taken by anybody, copied by anybody, and (to some extent) published by anybody. The hierarchies established by the cultural industry that once clearly separated amateurs and professional photographers have become more porous or have shifted altogether. Although photography, since its invention, has been a medium for the democratization of the gaze, no other device has contributed to this democratization more than the smartphone, as the French historian André Gunthert has remarked.[4] Through the smartphone and the circulation of images on Facebook and similar platforms, users are transformed from consumers into producers.

In this case too, Smith and Yabré are both the producers and editors of their images. Through their private use of Facebook they create their own "image": an image that is radically different from the representation of migrants in the mass media. Instead of preserving distance from the "victim" being photographed, the image here is an intimate one, part of a practice that can scarcely be distinguished from that of other Facebook users—the representation of the self or of a fictional persona. Facebook also facilitates the exchange of information (and, increasingly, self-promotion and product advertising). For Smith and Yabré it provides an opportunity to report on their life from afar, to communicate with other refugees, and also to participate in a global pop-cultural phenomenon.

However, the fact that the digital production of images is connected to the production of data and that these platforms are primarily modes of commercial distribution means that the information and images can potentially be instrumentalized and controlled. The posting of personal messages and images is of particular significance for a company like Facebook. With the help of the data that are collected, product advertisements can be specifically targeted and algorithms developed like the DeepFace system, which is able to automatically recognize faces in the welter of images. Even though the development of the facial recognition system is still in its infancy, the potential uses of these algorithms, as well as the general creation of a "digital footprint," can easily be made to serve political ends, and—especially in the case of refugees and people without residence permits—this can have unpredictable consequences.

1   Daniel Rubinstein and Katrina Sluis, "A Life More Photographic," *Photographies* 1, no. 1 (2008), pp. 9–28.
2   André Gunthert, *L'image partagée: La photographie numérique* (Paris, 2015), p. 11.
3   Estelle Blaschke, *Banking on Images. The Bettmann Archive and Corbis* (Leipzig, 2016), p. 166.
4   Gunthert, *L'image partagée* (see n. 2), pp. 71ff.

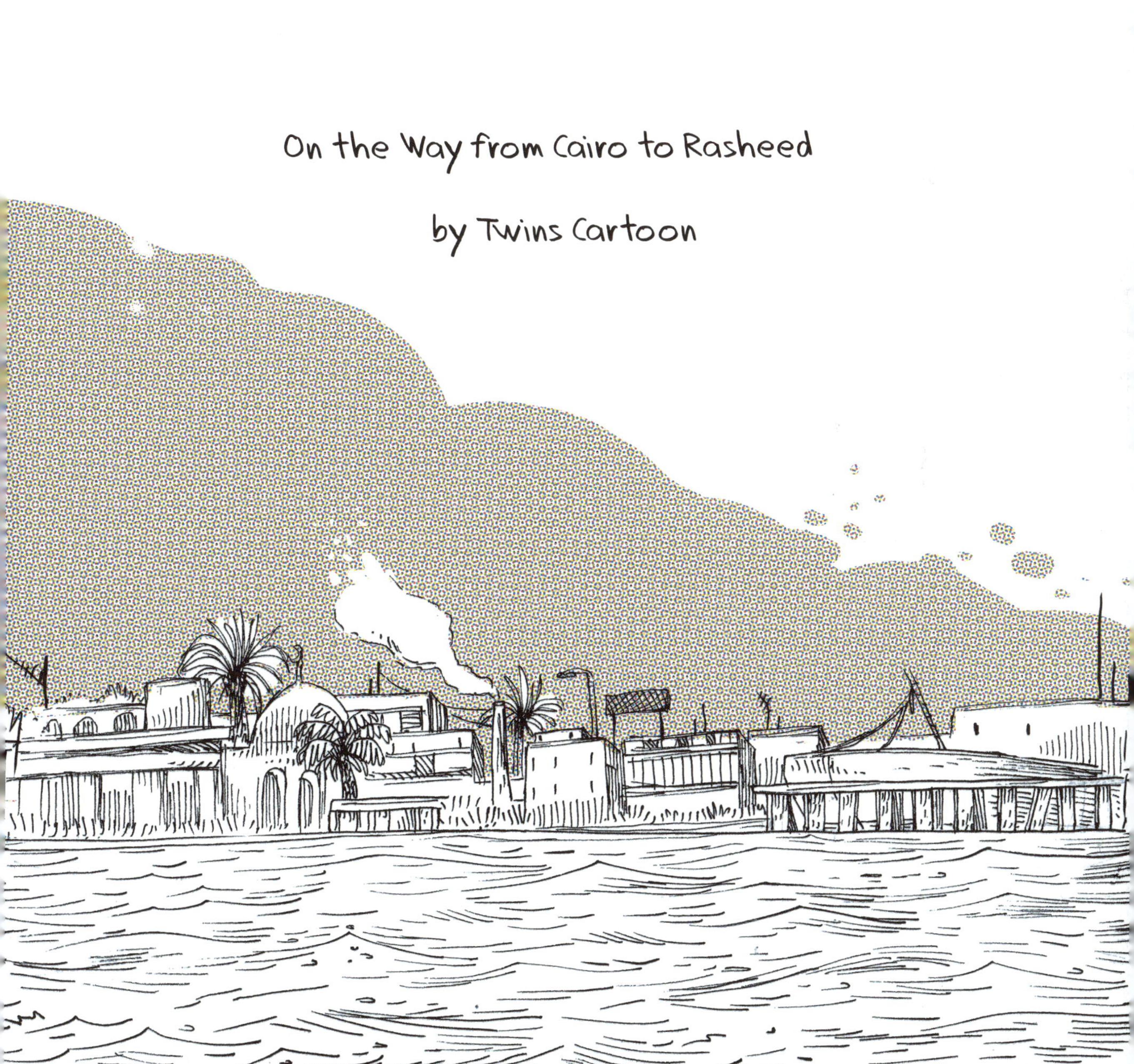

On the Way from Cairo to Rasheed

by Twins Cartoon

Talaat Harb Square, Cairo

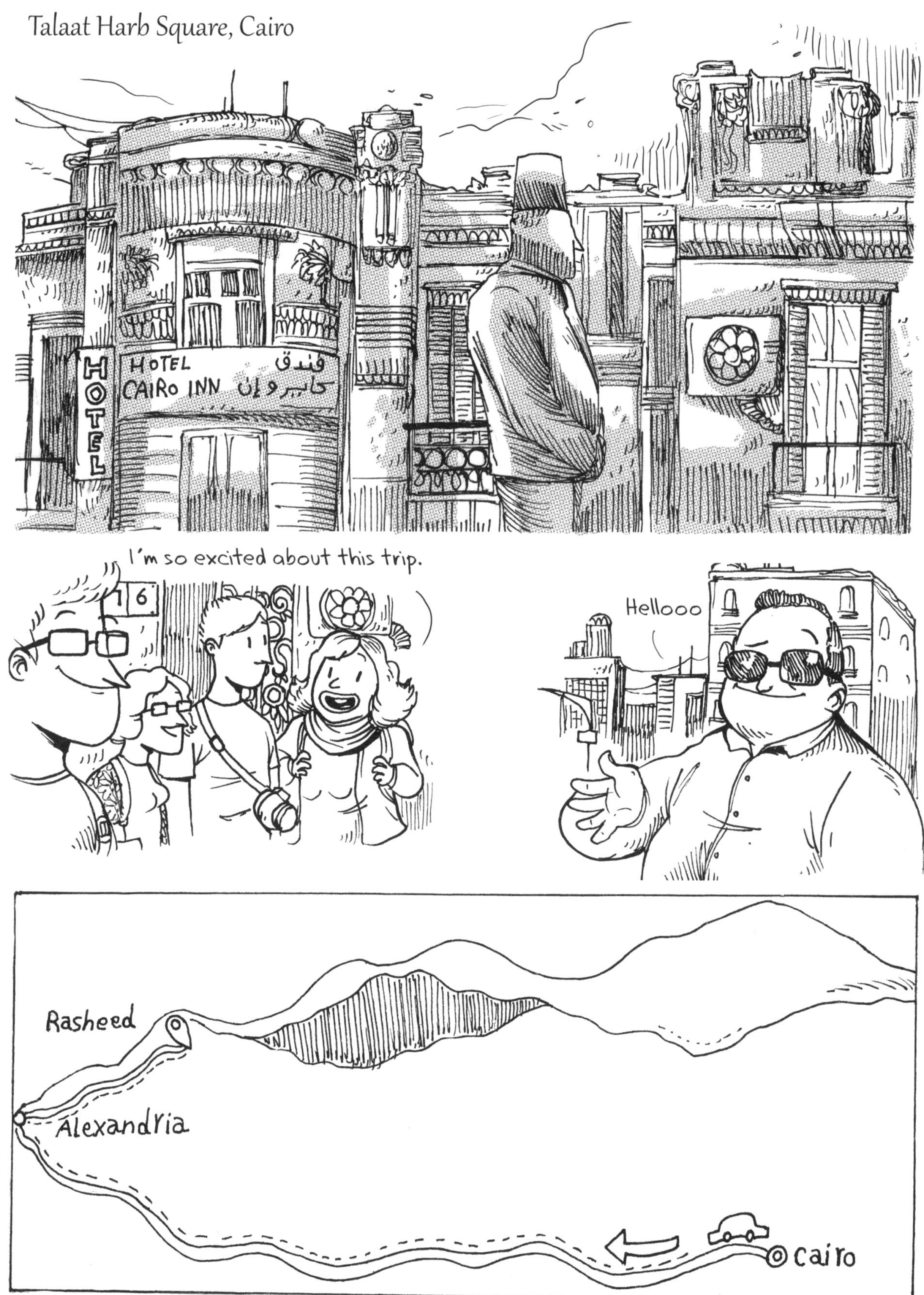

HOTEL
HOTEL
CAIRO INN
HOTEL
I'm so excited about this trip.
16
Hellooo
Rasheed
Alexandria
Cairo

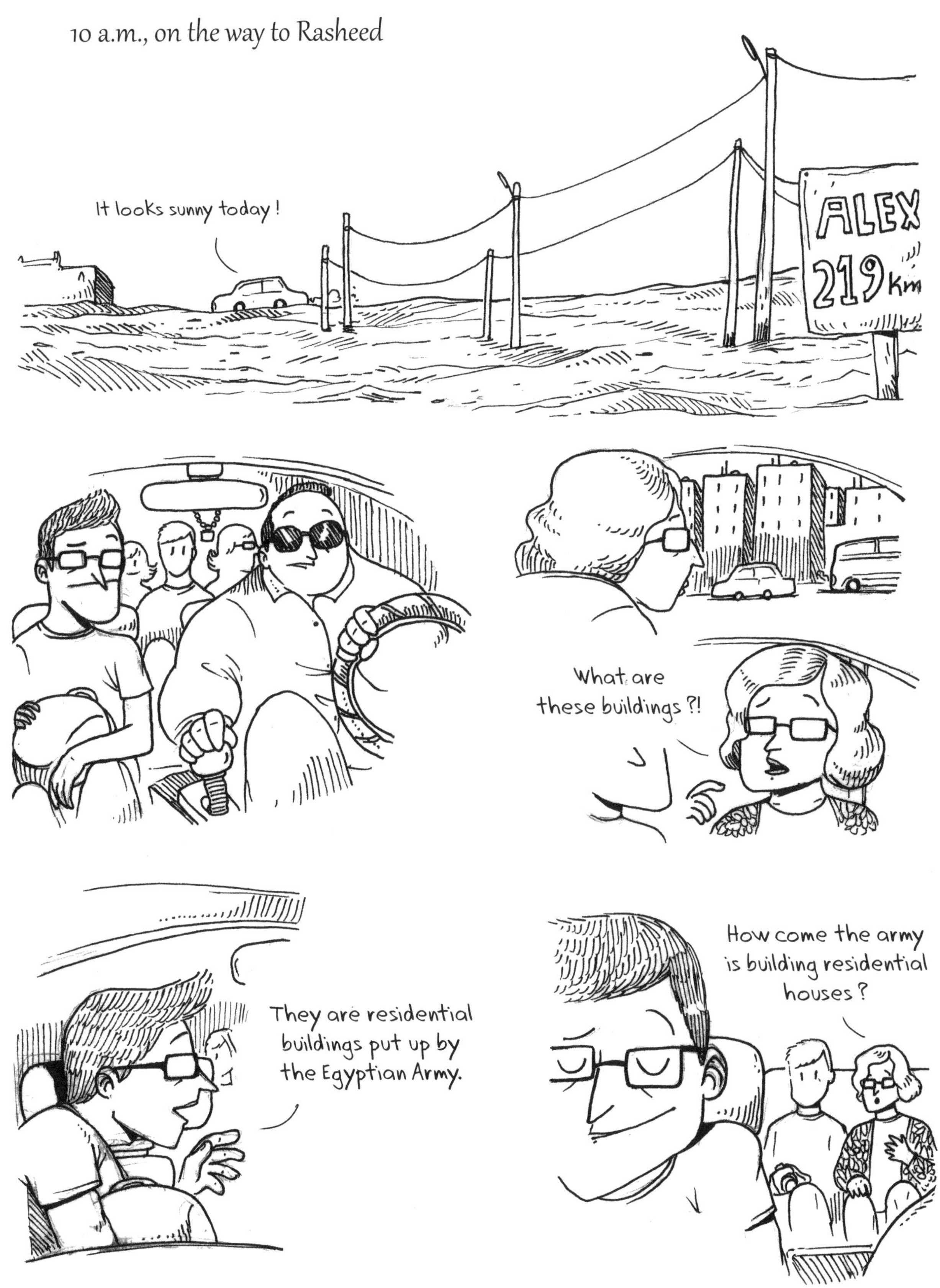
10 a.m., on the way to Rasheed
It looks sunny today !
ALEX
219 Km
What are these buildings ?!
They are residential buildings put up by the Egyptian Army.
How come the army is building residential houses ?

These things happen in Egypt. The army can build houses quicker than other companies and it can make sure that the buildings are finished on time.

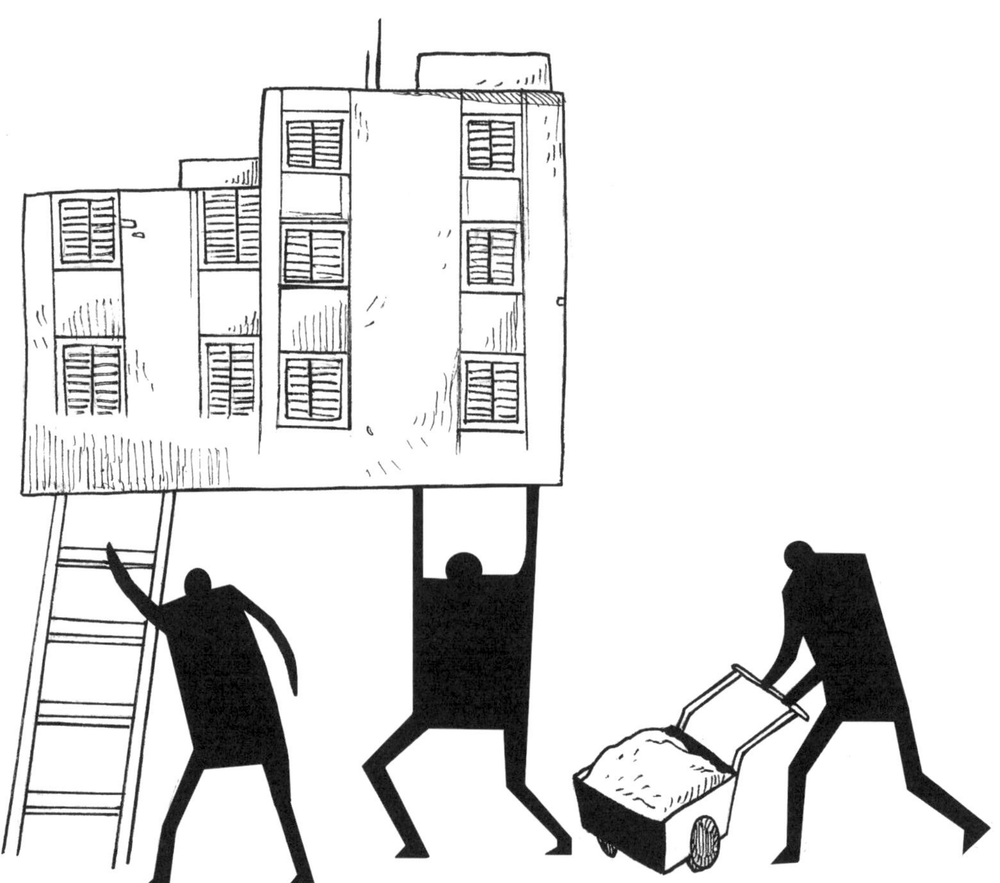

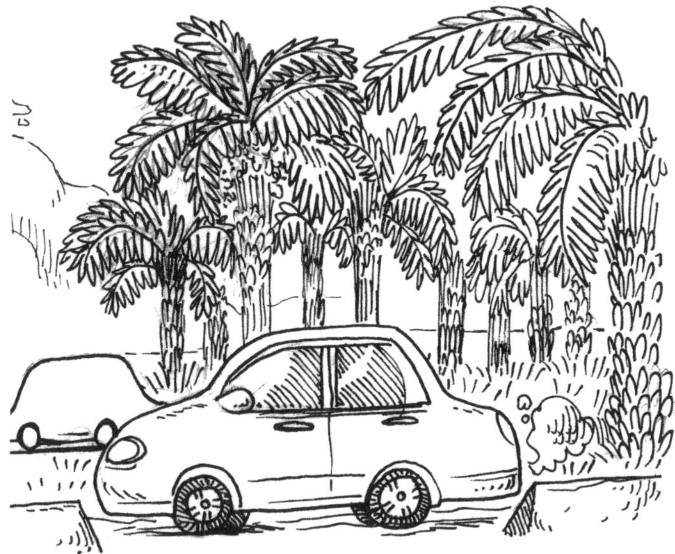

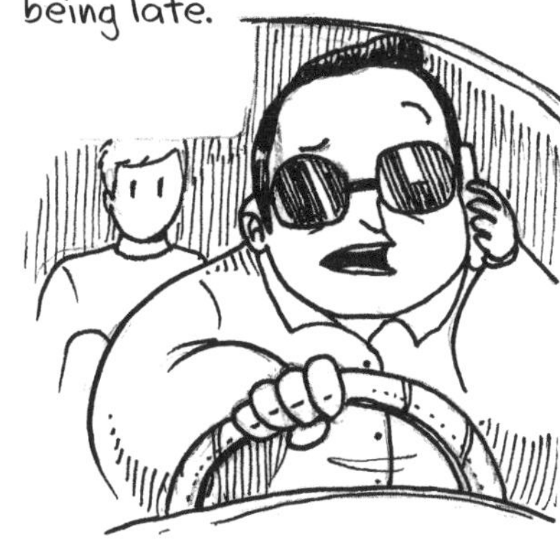
- We've arrived, Osama. We're waiting for you
- OK, I will be over there in five minutes, sorry for being late.

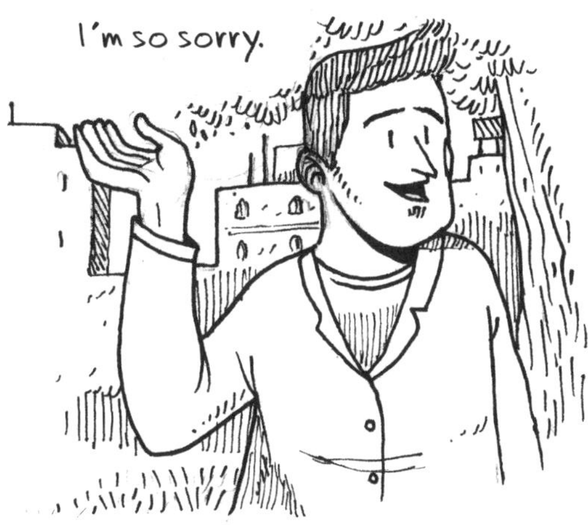
I'm so sorry.

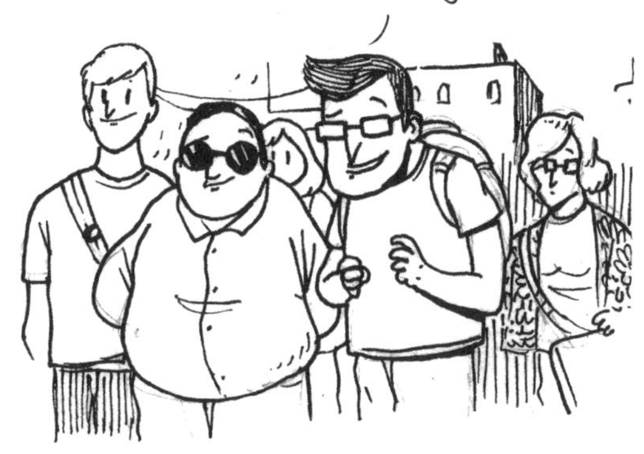
No need to apologize! Thanks for coming.

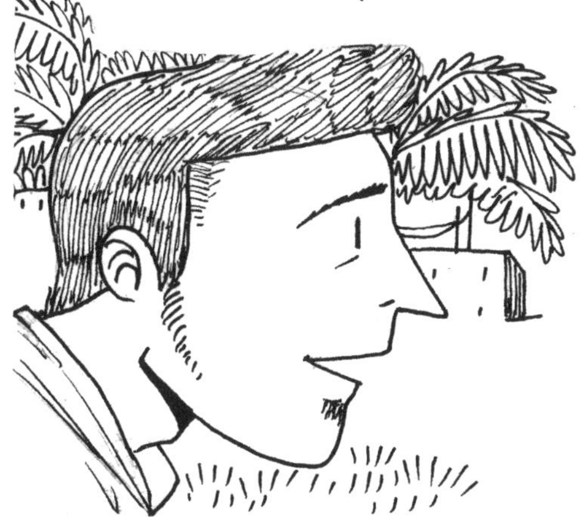
It was out of my control.

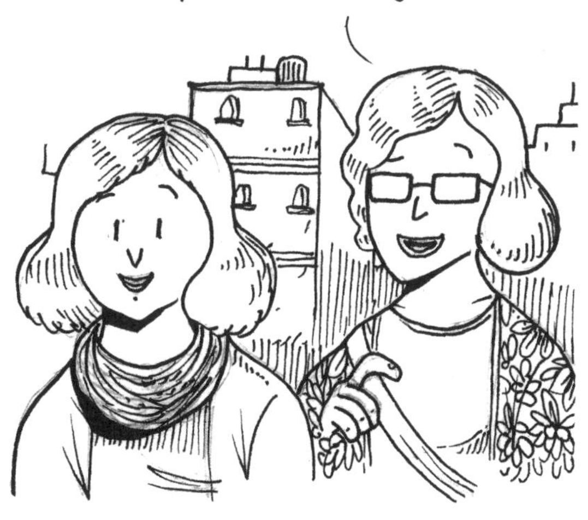
It's our pleasure that you will be our guide.

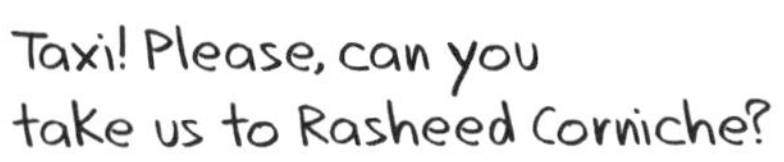

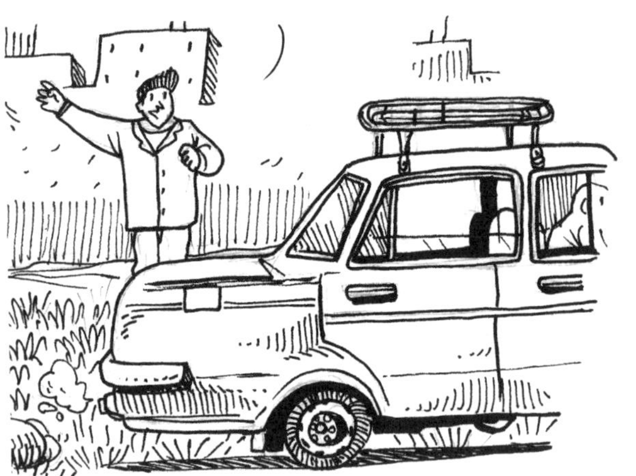

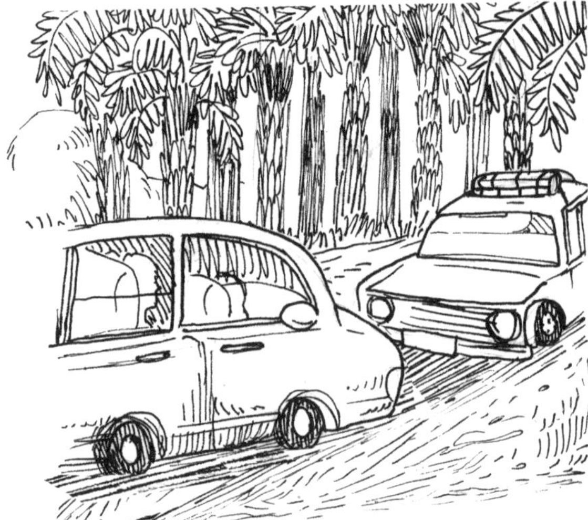

Osama points to the place where the Nile and the Mediterranean meet.

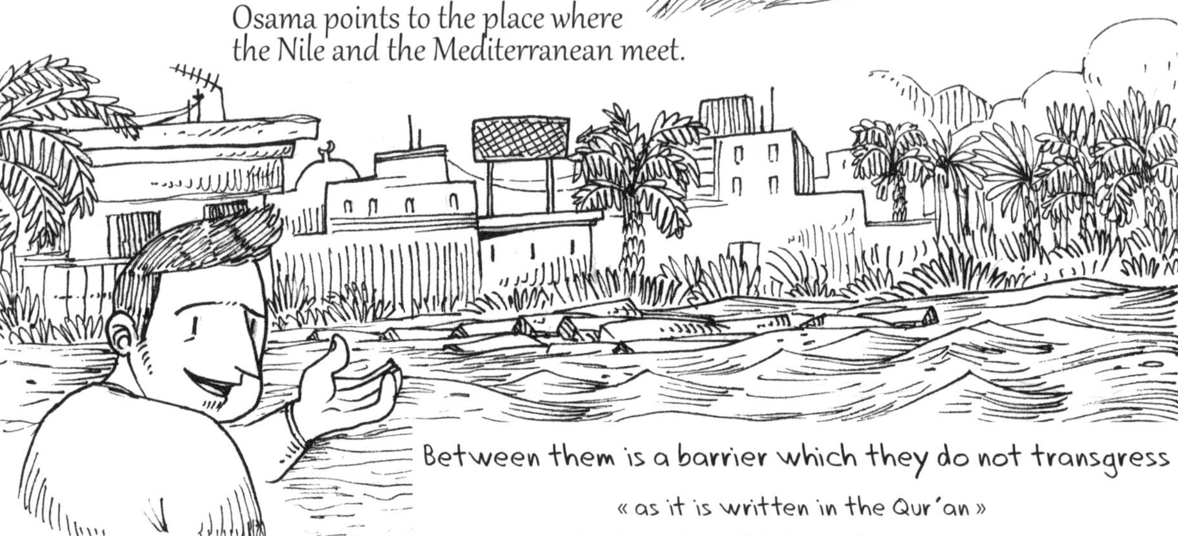

Captain Bouchard, a French officer in Napoleon's Egyptian army, discovered the Rosetta Stone in 1799. He realized that the stone could be used to decipher hieroglyphics for the first time. After their defeat by the British, however, the French were forced to abandon the stone, which was subsequently transported to the British Museum in London.

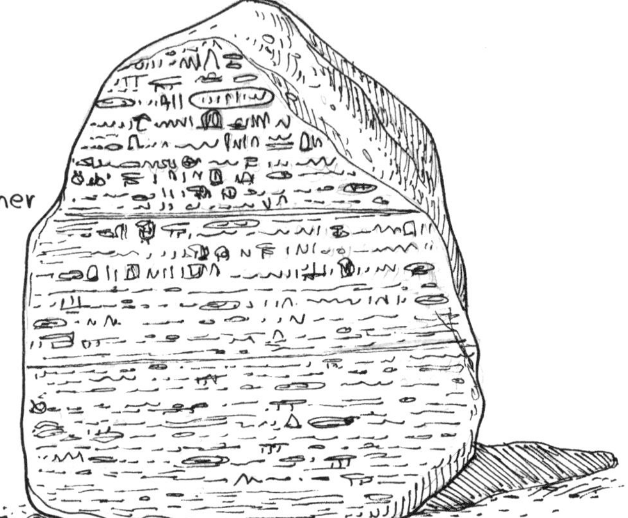

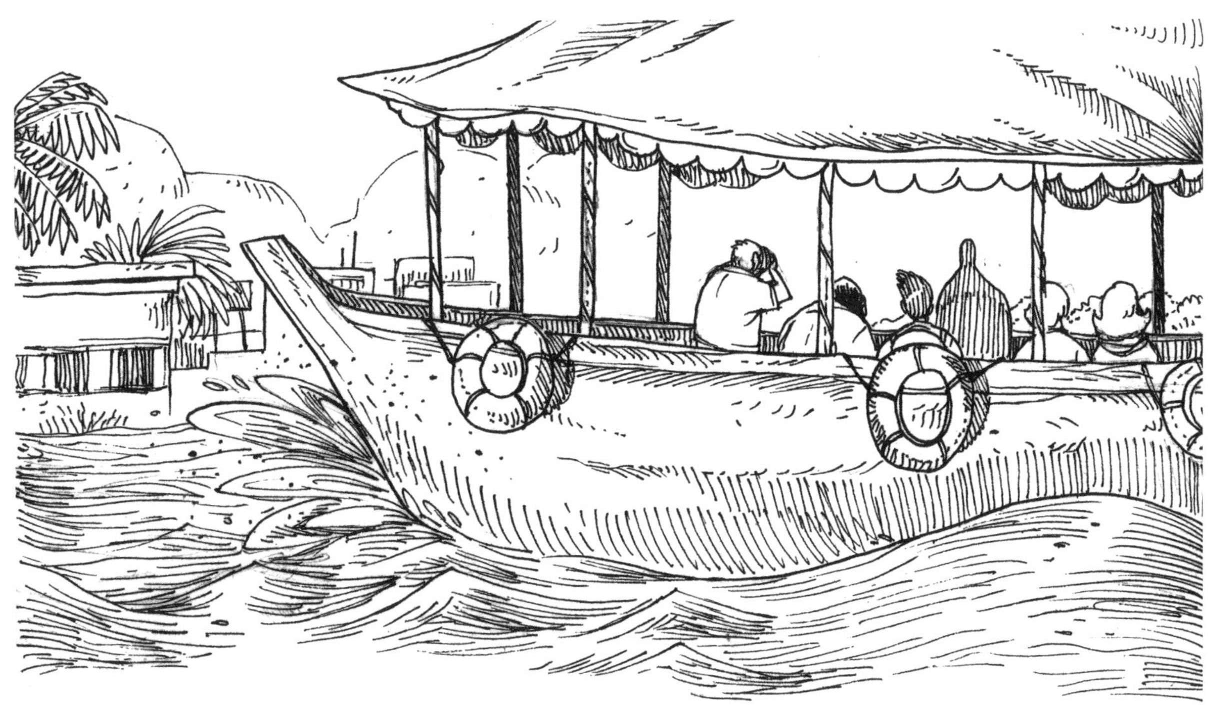

- Osama, what are these
boxes in the river for?

-They are fish boxes. Fishermen put
small fish inside, and feed them
over a short period. The fish
grow fast and the fishermen
make a quick profit instead of
following the traditional
fishing process.

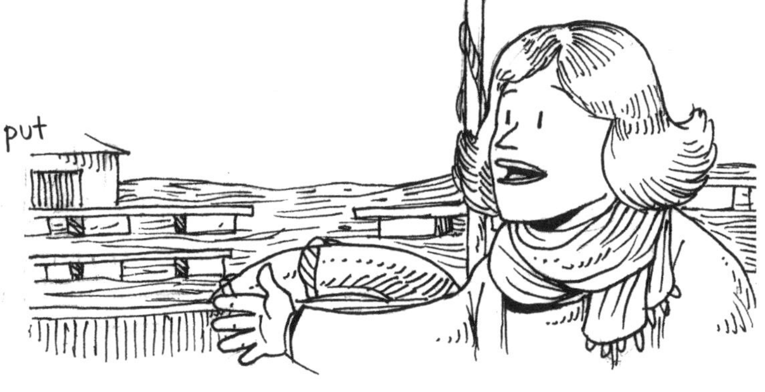

Osama's novel is inspired by
fish boxes located in the river,
but he added the linguistic dimension.
His book is referring to recent
events that have occurred
on Green Island.
The fishermen put small fish inside
of the boxes. The smugglers do
a similar thing, they put a lot of
migrant people in places like
the fridge inside of a boat,
and they also make the most
profit out of it. Fish and
people have the same destiny.
They are going to die.

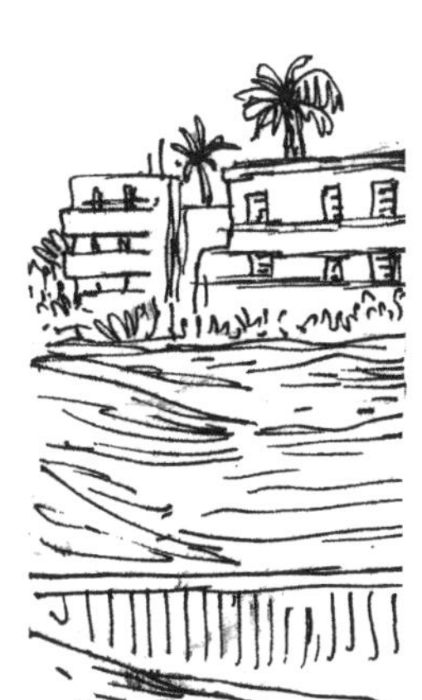

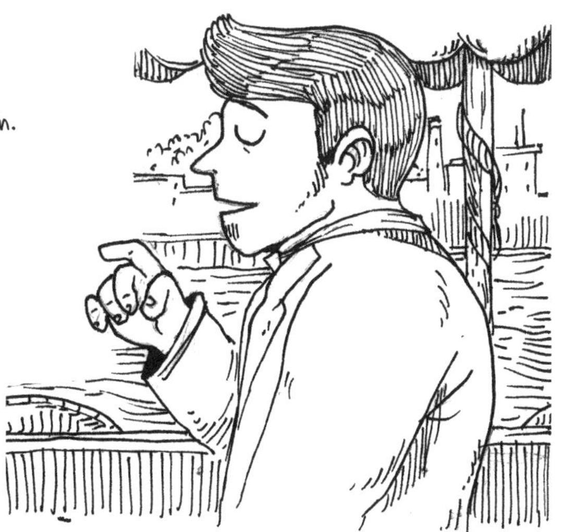

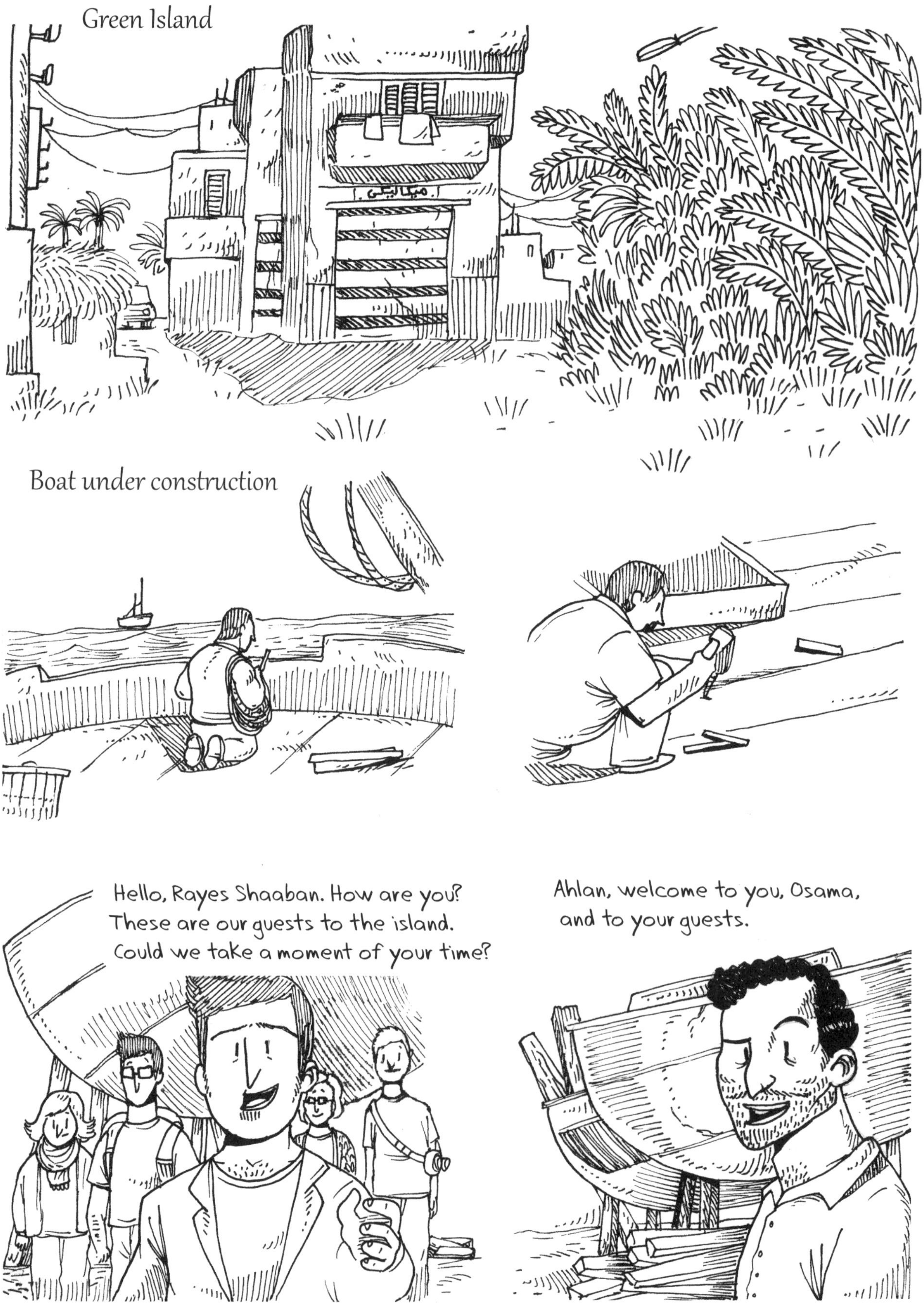

Green Island

Boat under construction

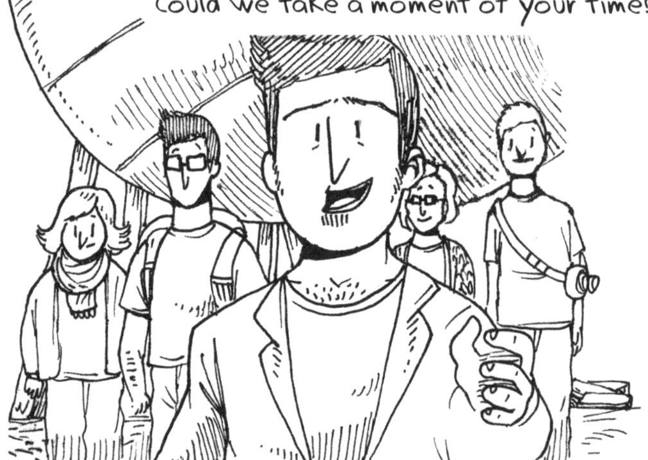

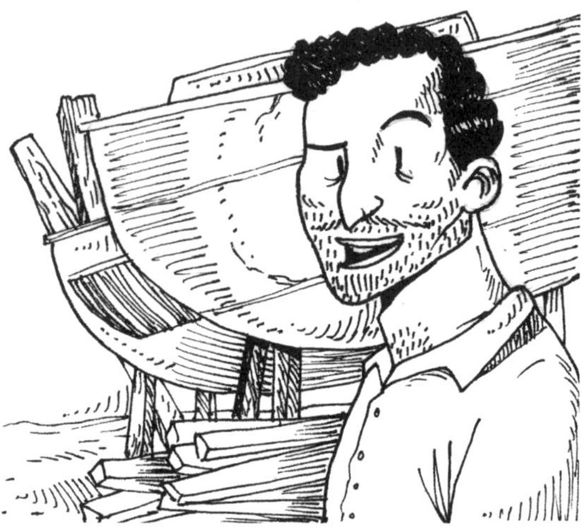

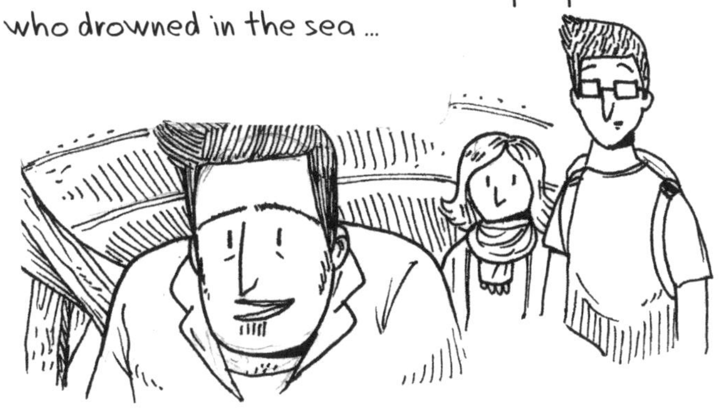

Oh, Rayes Shaaban, could you tell us how much it costs to build a fishing cutter like that? Who do you sell it to and how much does it cost in the end? Also about people who drowned in the sea ...

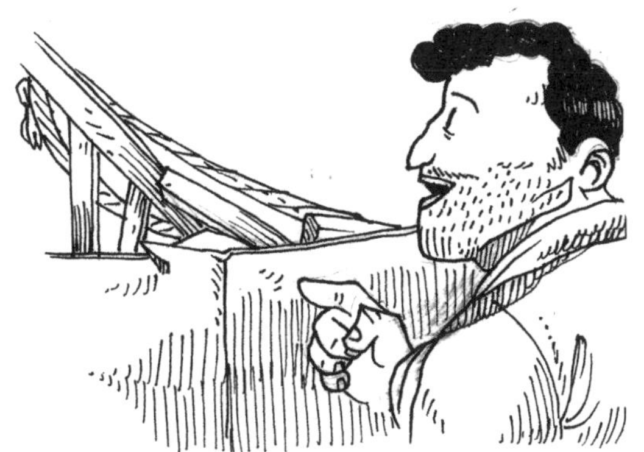

Osama, I know you're here because of the accident that happened a couple of days ago.

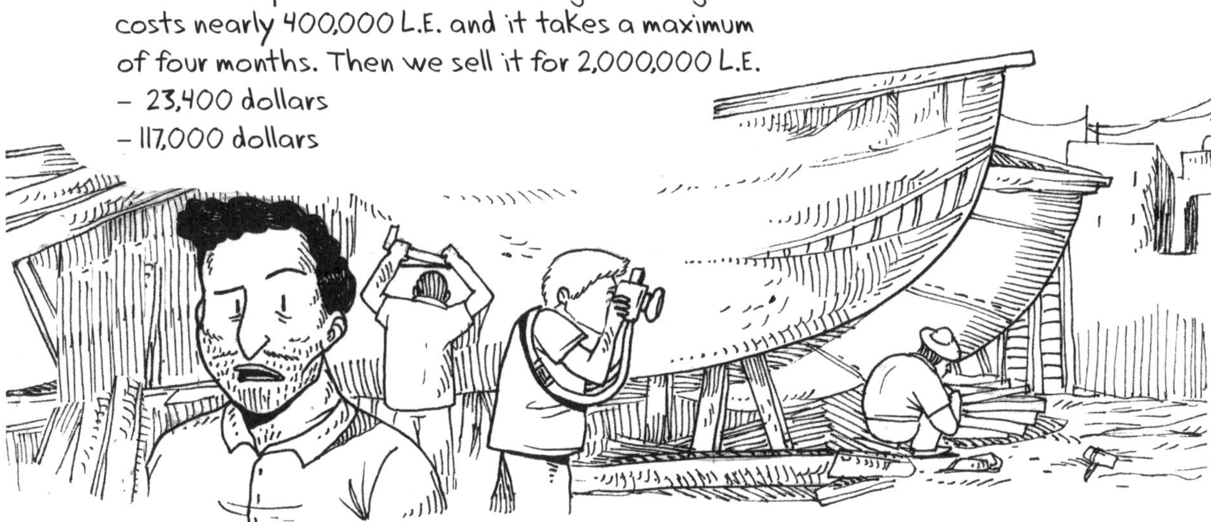

The whole process of constructing a fishing boat costs nearly 400,000 L.E. and it takes a maximum of four months. Then we sell it for 2,000,000 L.E.
– 23,400 dollars
– 117,000 dollars

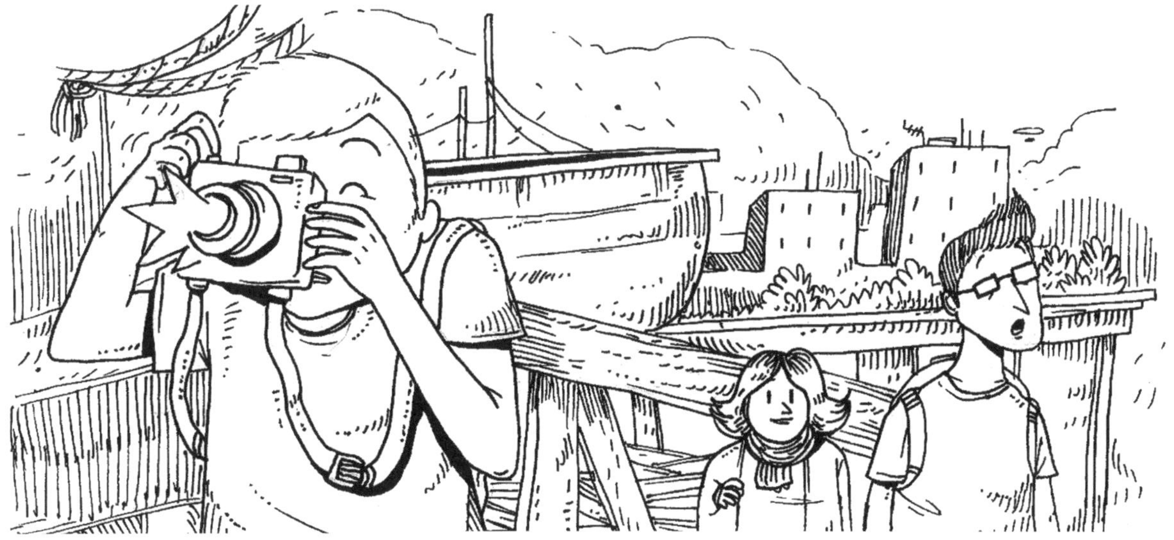

Who will buy these boats?

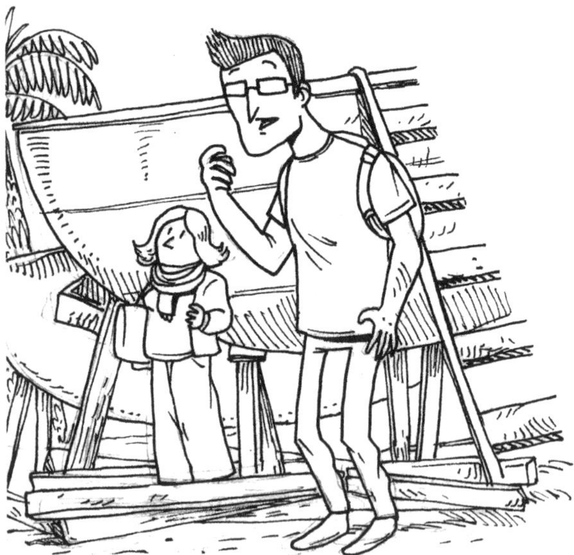

– The lucky ones, O Pascha.*

Behind Shaaban while he was talking to us:
There was a group of workers
working under a blazing sun
and I noticed one of the workers
looking at me and smiling, I felt that
he wanted to tell me
something.

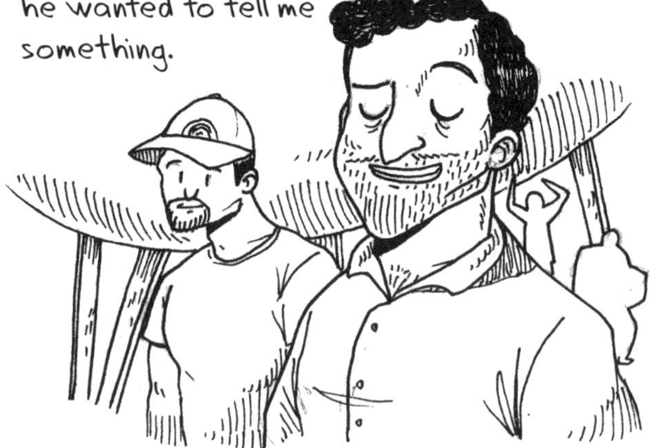

I withdrew quietly and told Shaaban that I would take a tour with Andi to
shoot the boat construction process but I basically went off to talk with
Ghazal, one of the workers.

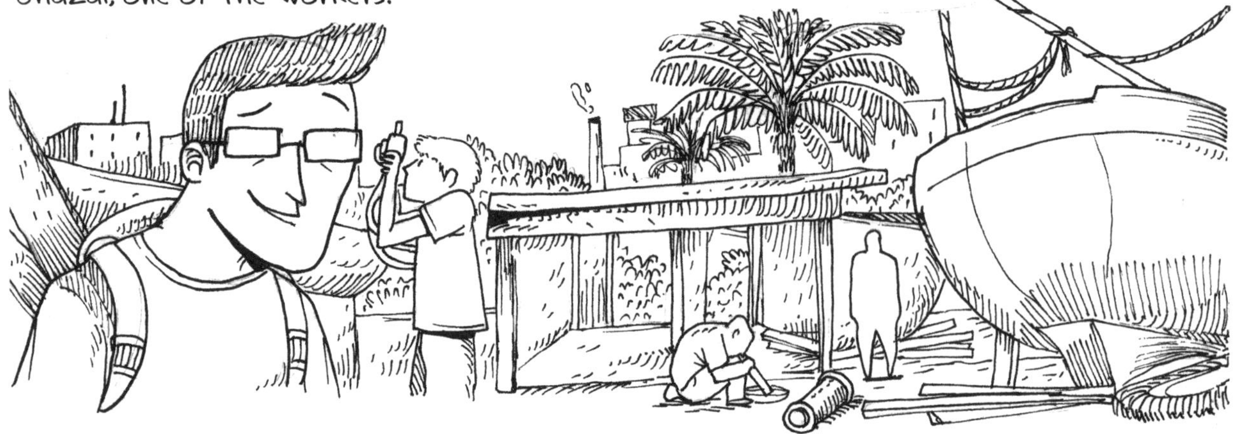

Ghazal is a good-looking man in his thirties,
with open features, a strong body, and light brown eyes.

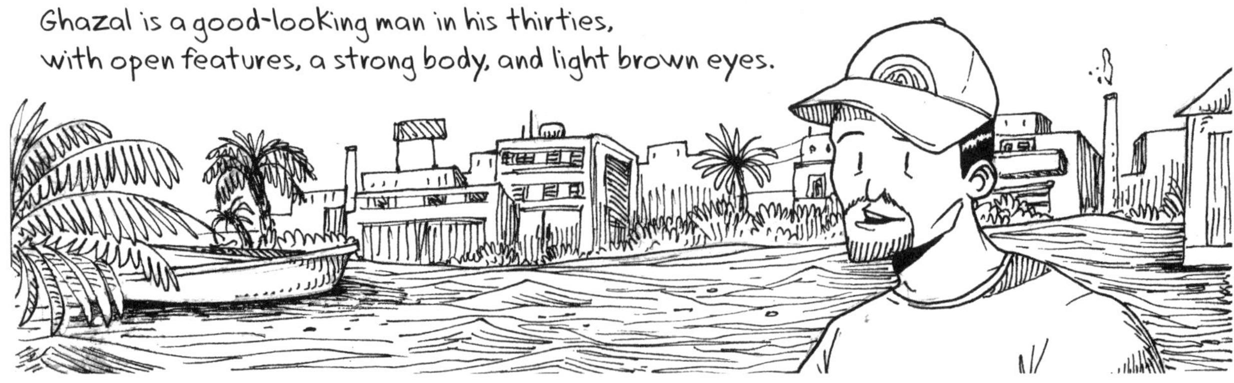

* Pascha: title of a Turkish officer of high rank. After the Ottoman Caliphate, Egyptians used it to
mean officers, it's also a slang word among Egyptians.

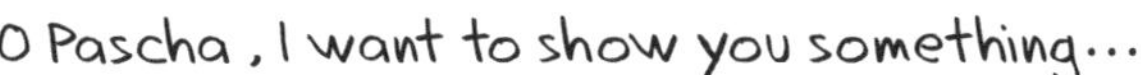
O Pascha , I want to show you something…

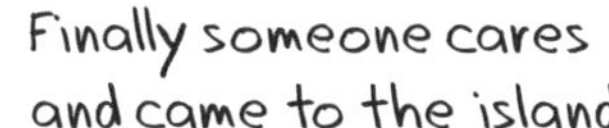
Finally someone cares
and came to the island

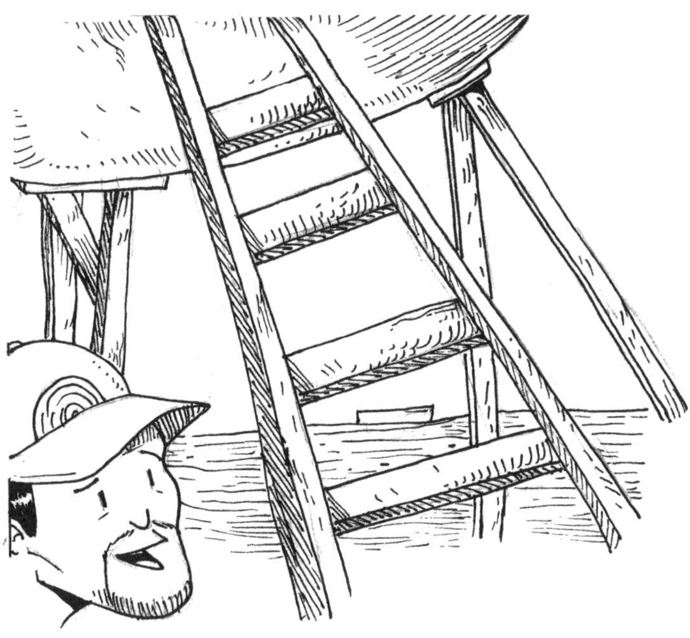

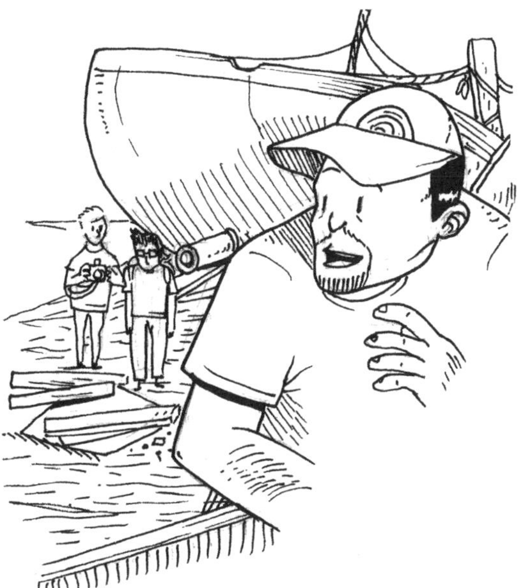

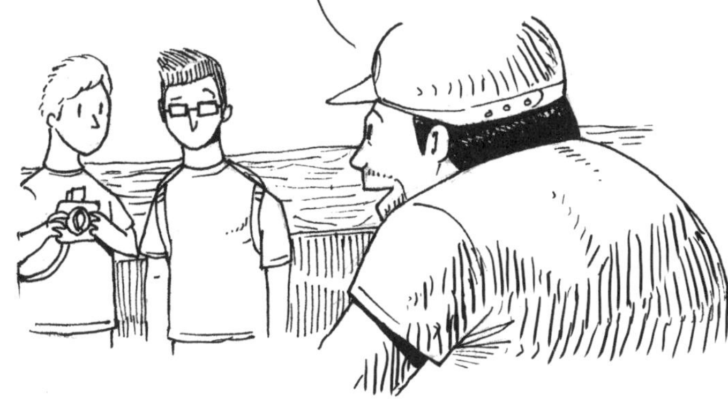
to ask about these people who drowned or just
to ask about their poor families?

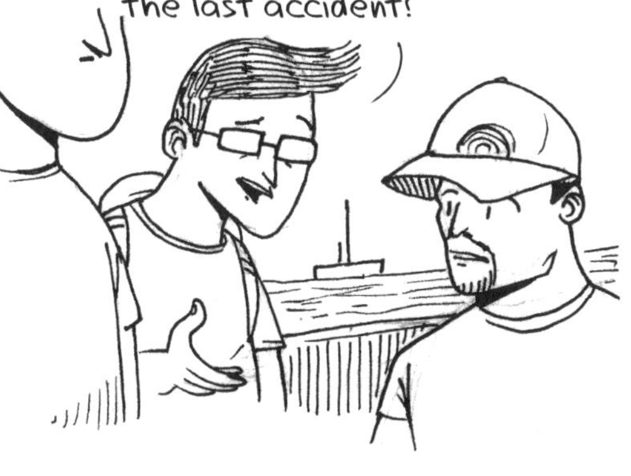
Did any of your people drown in
the last accident?

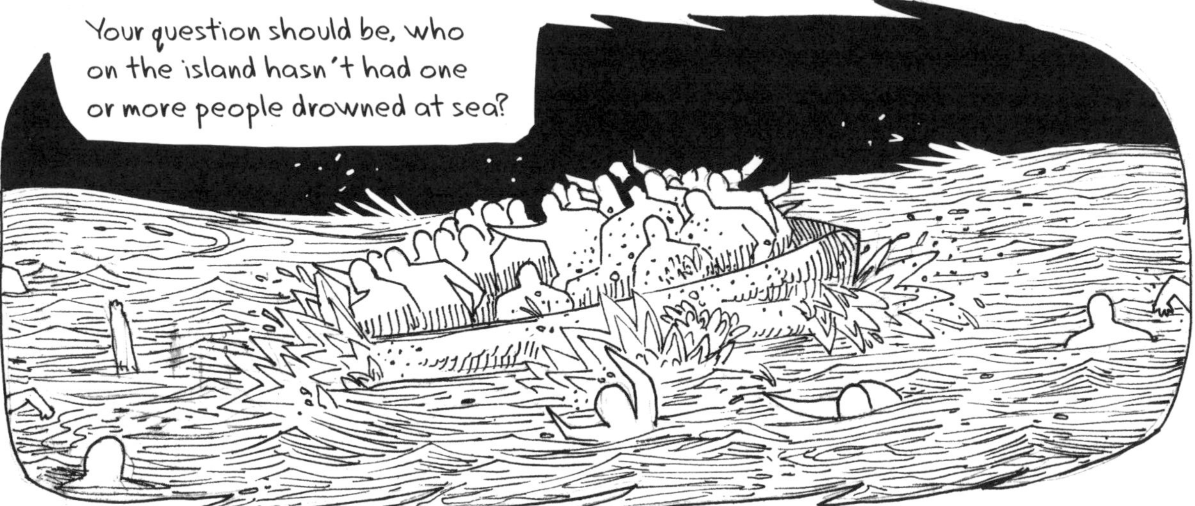
Your question should be, who
on the island hasn't had one
or more people drowned at sea?

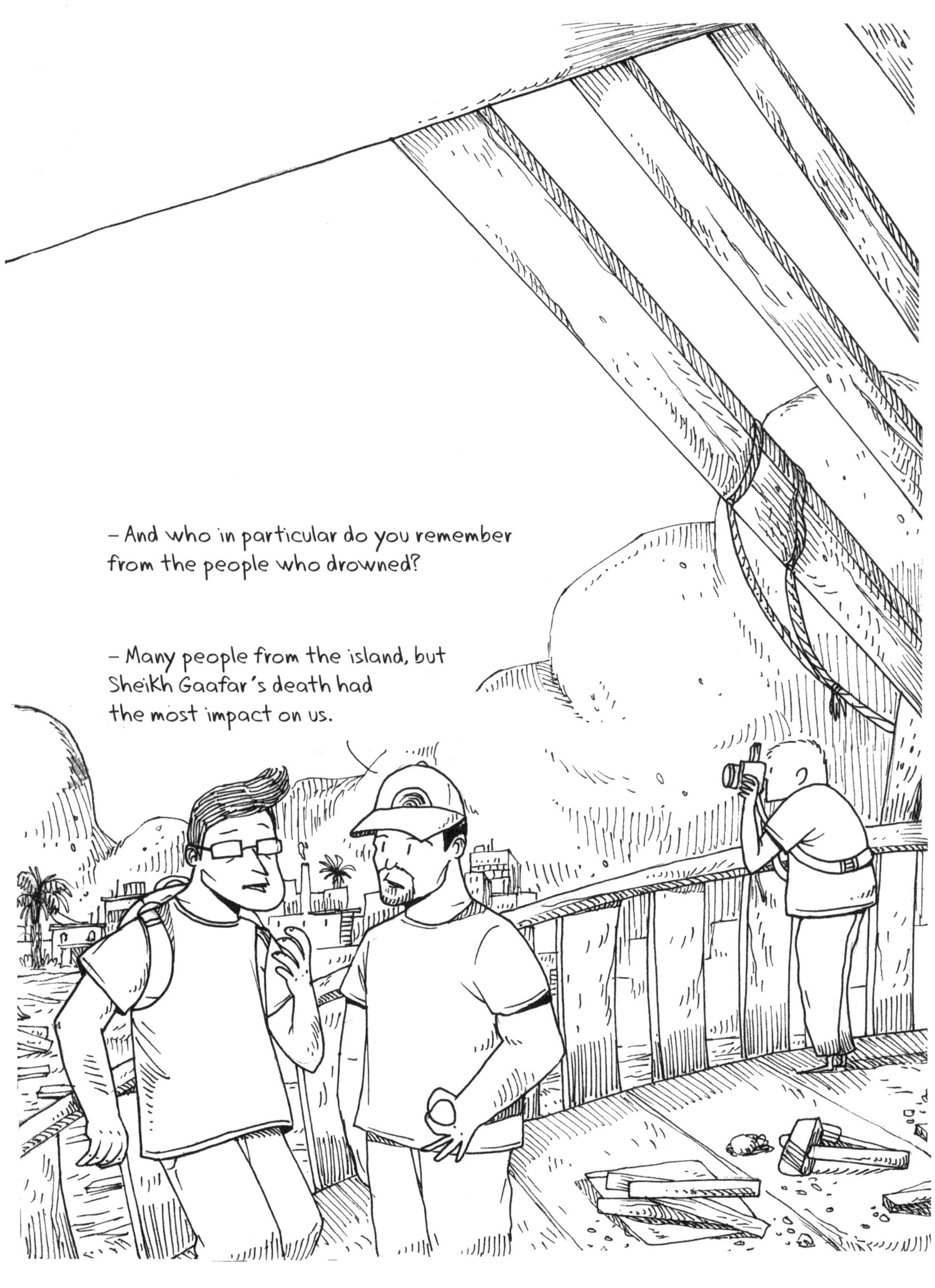

- And who in particular do you remember from the people who drowned?

- Many people from the island, but Sheikh Gaafar's death had the most impact on us.

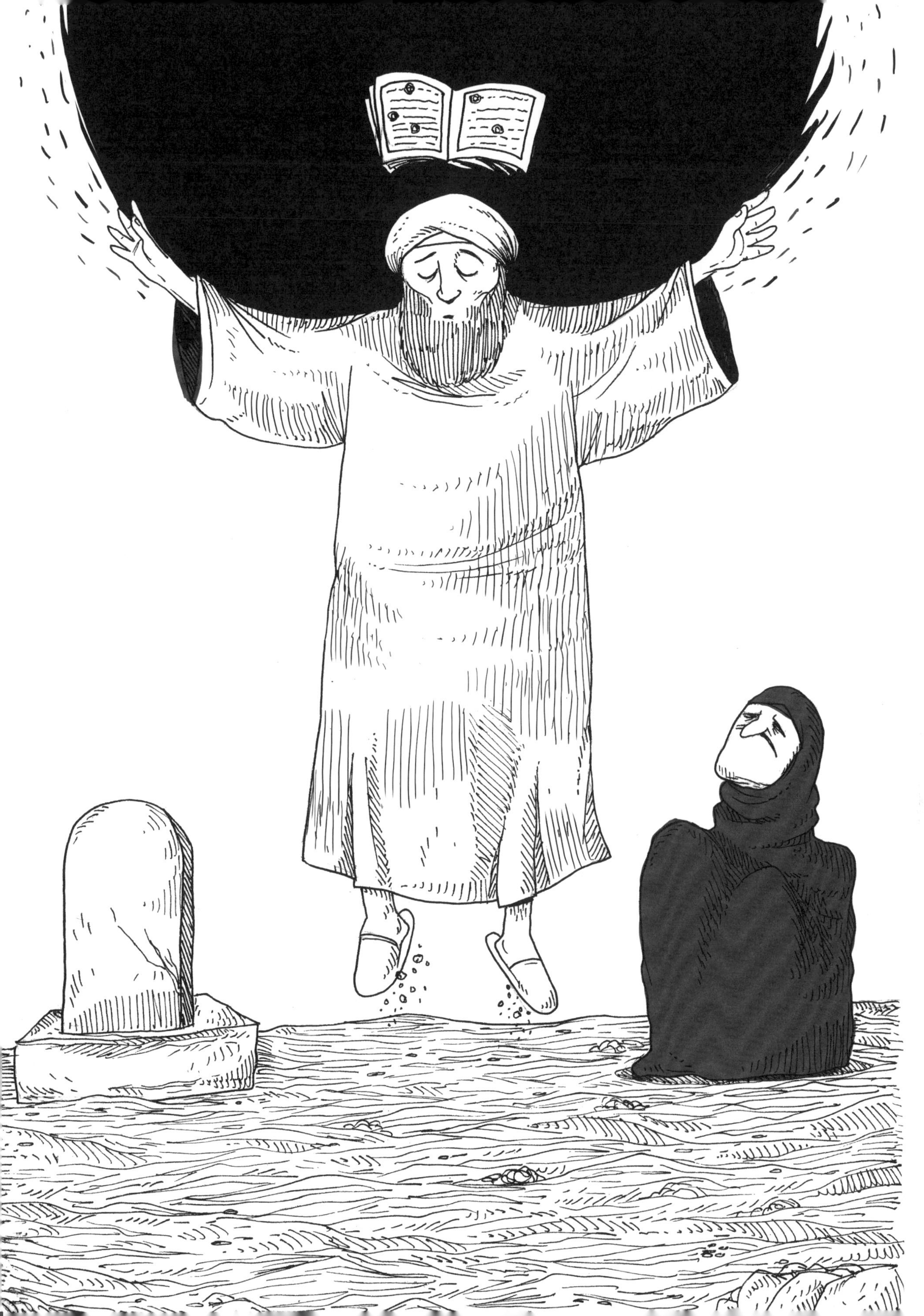

Gaafar was sheikh of the zawya, the small mosque where we pray. He was such a religious man. Quite honestly, we never saw him commit a sin like many people from the island when they didn't have a good life. He took the boat with the others, although he was always saying that this is the land of righteousness and over there "in Europe" is the land of the misguided. He lived with his sick mom who doesn't have anyone else now that he's gone. He was thirty-eight but he didn't have money to marry because he could barely afford the medicine for his sick mother from his work at the mosque.
His salary came from the Ministry of Endowments. After Asr prayer he was Imam of the small mosque which I talked about. He went with the boat like the other people from the island.

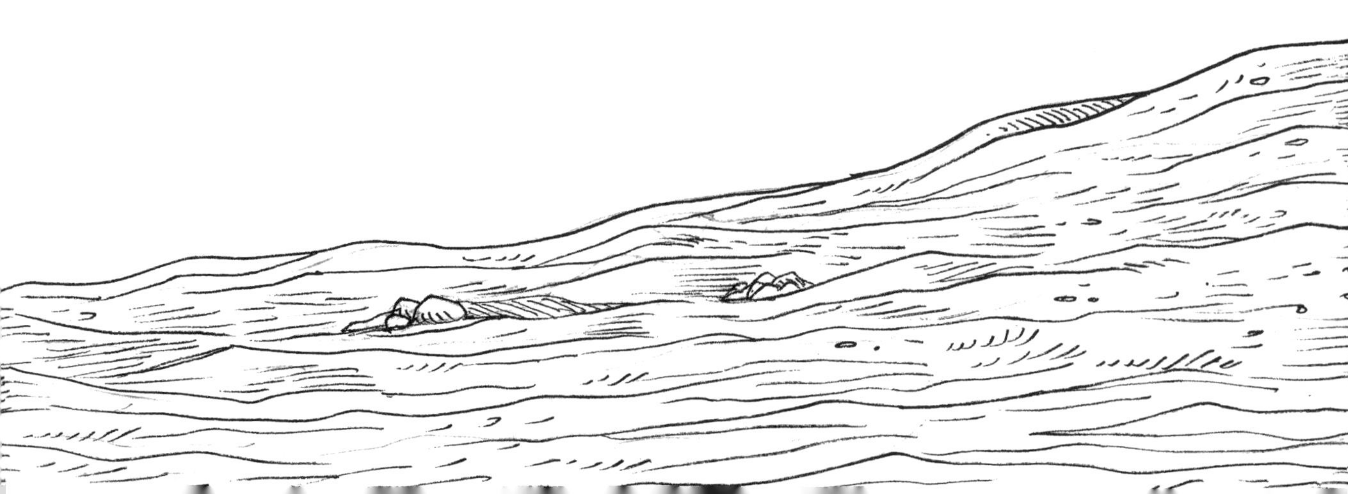

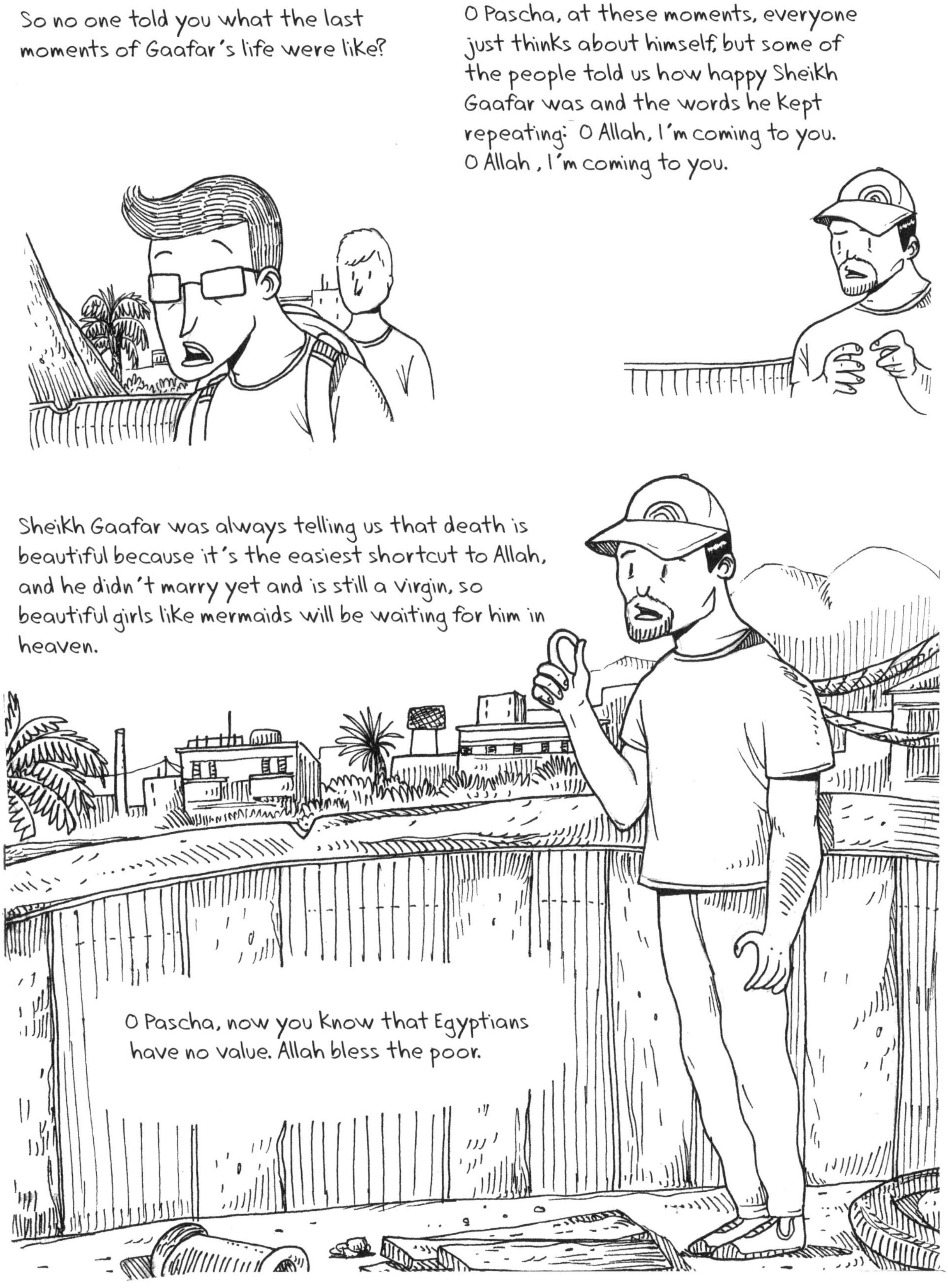

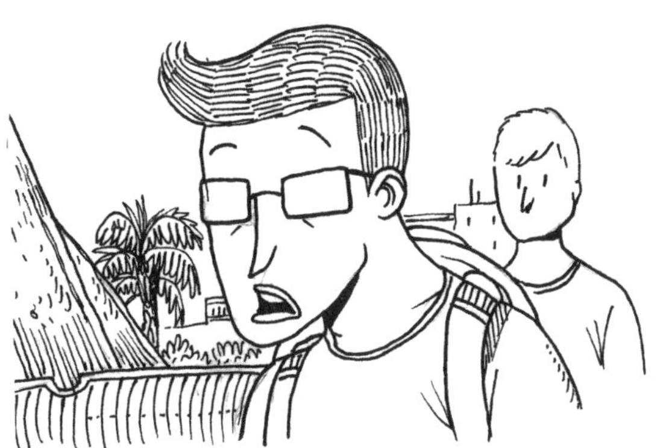

So no one told you what the last moments of Gaafar's life were like?

O Pascha, at these moments, everyone just thinks about himself, but some of the people told us how happy Sheikh Gaafar was and the words he kept repeating: O Allah, I'm coming to you. O Allah, I'm coming to you.

Sheikh Gaafar was always telling us that death is beautiful because it's the easiest shortcut to Allah, and he didn't marry yet and is still a virgin, so beautiful girls like mermaids will be waiting for him in heaven.

O Pascha, now you know that Egyptians have no value. Allah bless the poor.

On November 3 , 2016 , there was a currency crash in Egypt .
The Egyptian pound lost almost half its value against the euro and dollar.

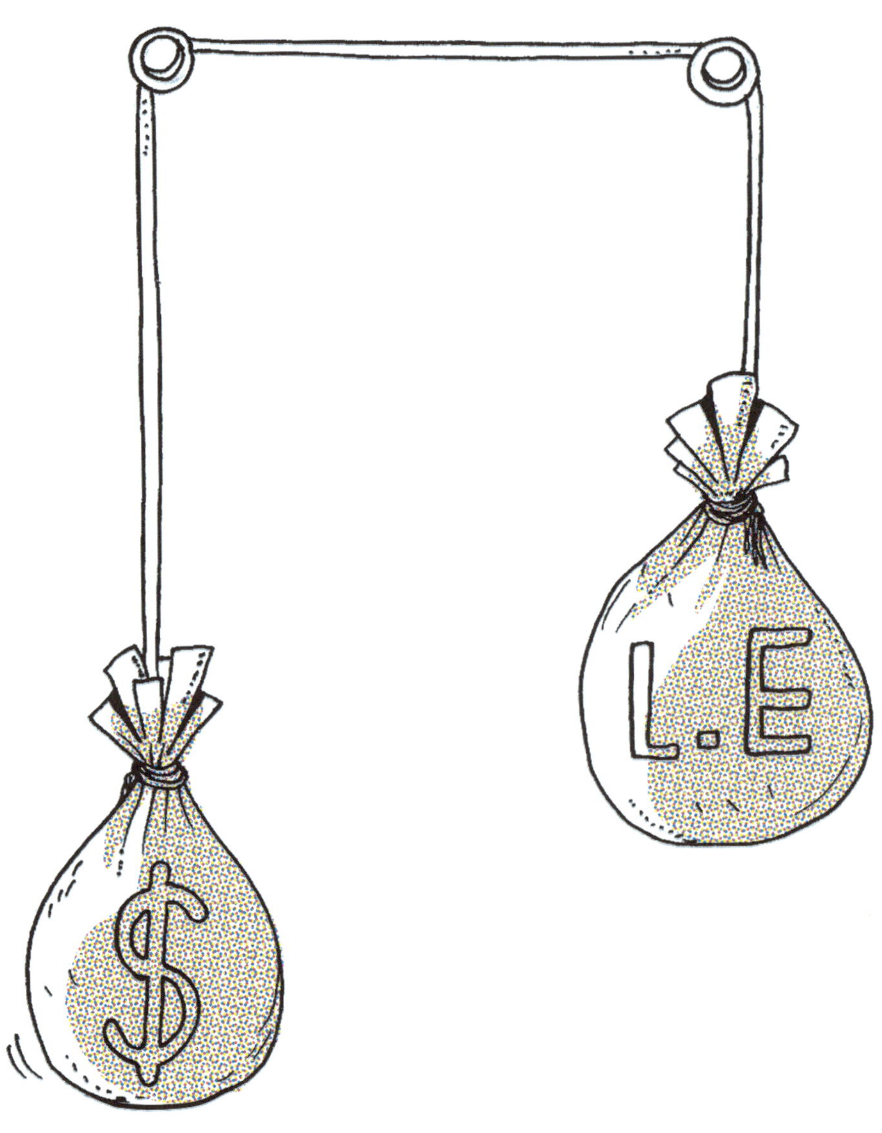

-Which revolution?!

- Any of them Shaaban , take your pick.

- O Pascha, life doesn't let me think about such things,
at least before 2011, the January 25 Revolution.
Libya was the only hub for people who
took boats or illegal migrants as you like to call them.

- Rayes Shaaban, why is Libya no longer the only way for them?

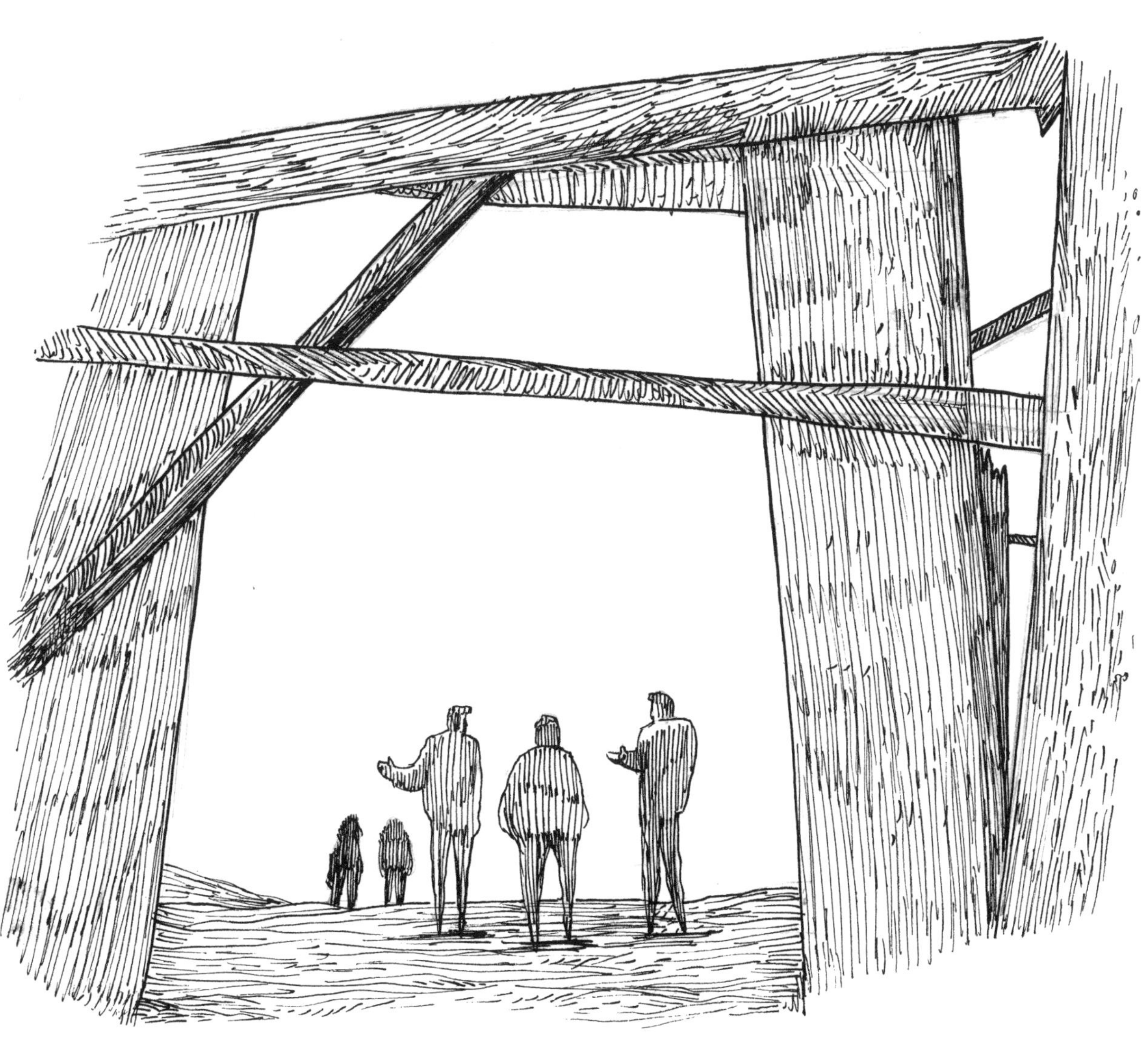

For many reasons. One of the most important reasons is ISIS and other terrorist groups who are based in the deserts. Also Egyptian workers who got kicked out from the Gulf area did not return to Egypt but instead tried to go to Europe. Social circumstances also forced young people to choose Europe as the only destination. So Egypt became a hub after Libya was ruined.

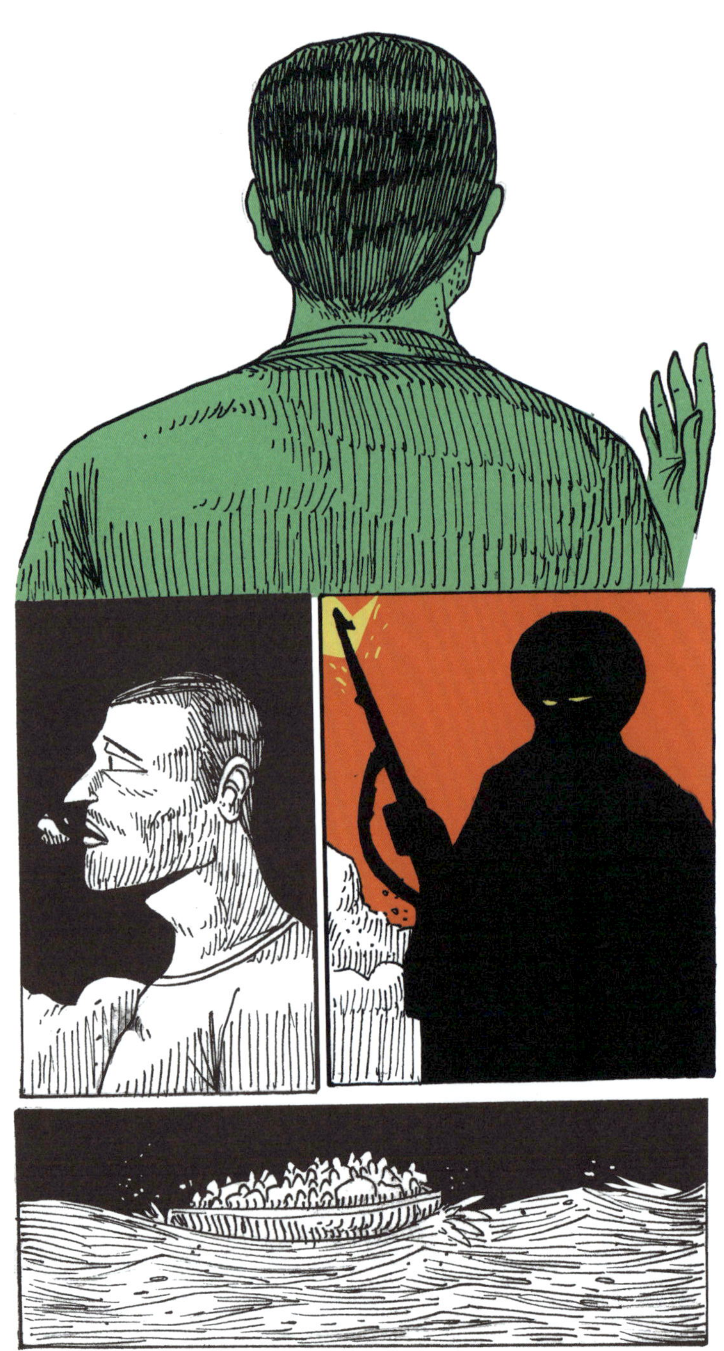

The January 25 Revolution in Egypt came with many hopes after the Jasmine Revolution in Tunisia. Everyone had one goal and that was to bring down the tyrannical regime and create economic reform in just three words: bread, freedom, social justice. Sadly all this gradually changed. The people who started the revolution are now in jail and the regime's stakeholders are the beneficiaries.

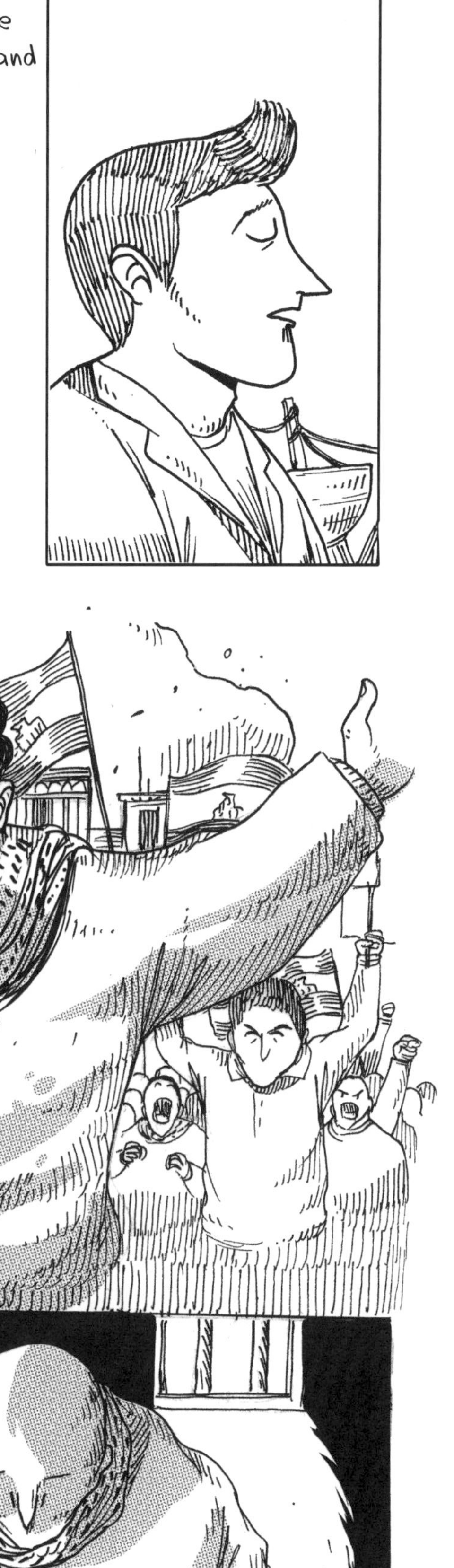

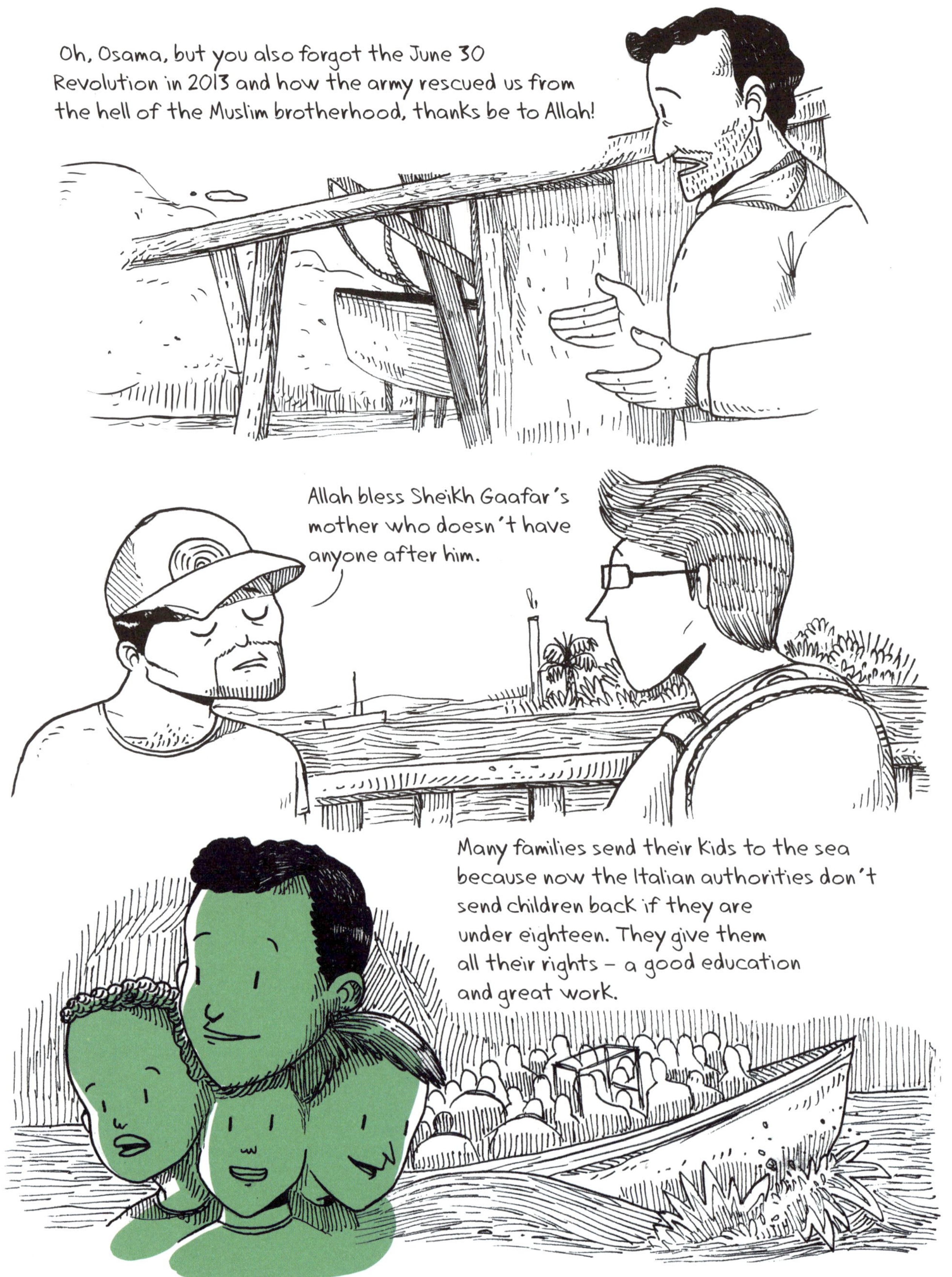

Oh, Osama, but you also forgot the June 30 Revolution in 2013 and how the army rescued us from the hell of the Muslim brotherhood, thanks be to Allah!

Allah bless Sheikh Gaafar's mother who doesn't have anyone after him.

Many families send their kids to the sea because now the Italian authorities don't send children back if they are under eighteen. They give them all their rights – a good education and great work.

Did anyone from the press come here and cover the accident, Ghazal?

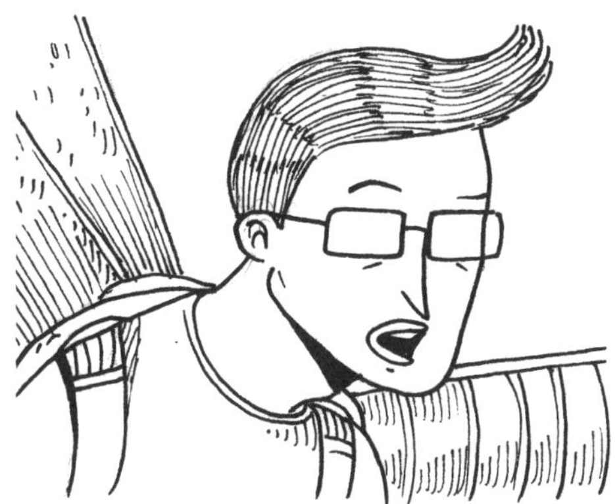

O Pascha, it's not the first time that it happened here but maybe because this time there were a large number of dead people from Egypt.

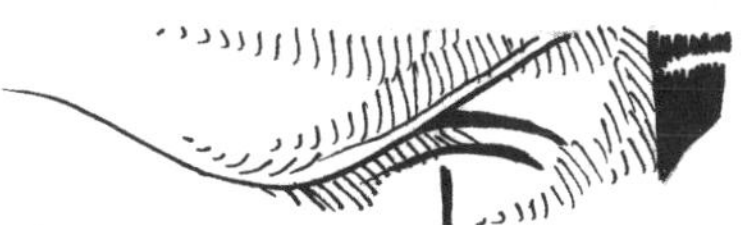

Egyptian journalists don't care, the foreign journalists care more!

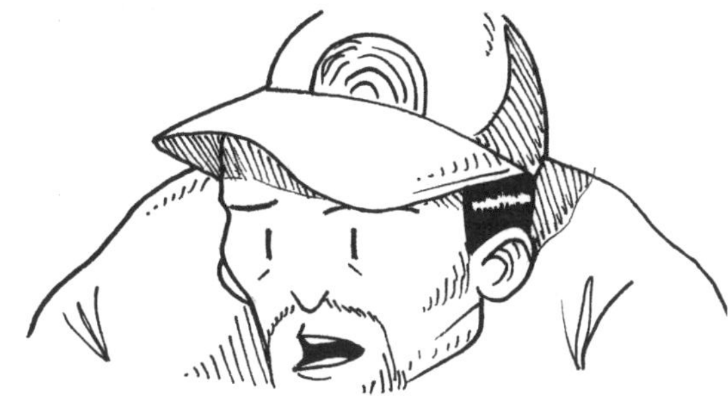

Reports in the words of Hani Mustafa, a journalist from Al-Ahram Weekly:

Egyptian newspapers don't usually publish news about boats of illegal immigrants sinking – even if Egyptians are involved – and mostly don't send journalists. They quote international news agencies like Reuters or AP and a succession of European newspapers, and in their news coverage they use impassioned headlines like "death flight" or "moments of terror" and rarely address the matter as a humanitarian issue or give it the lead as the main headline.

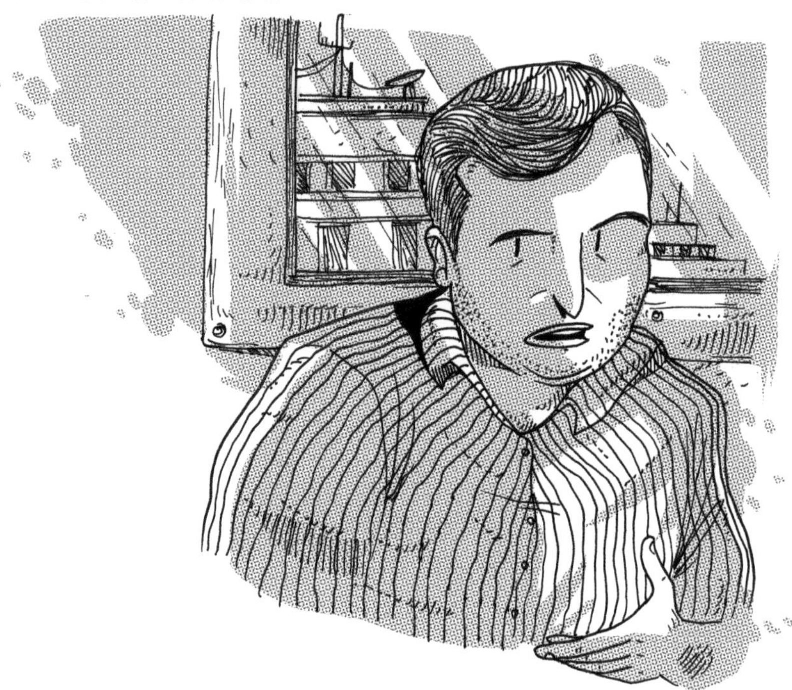

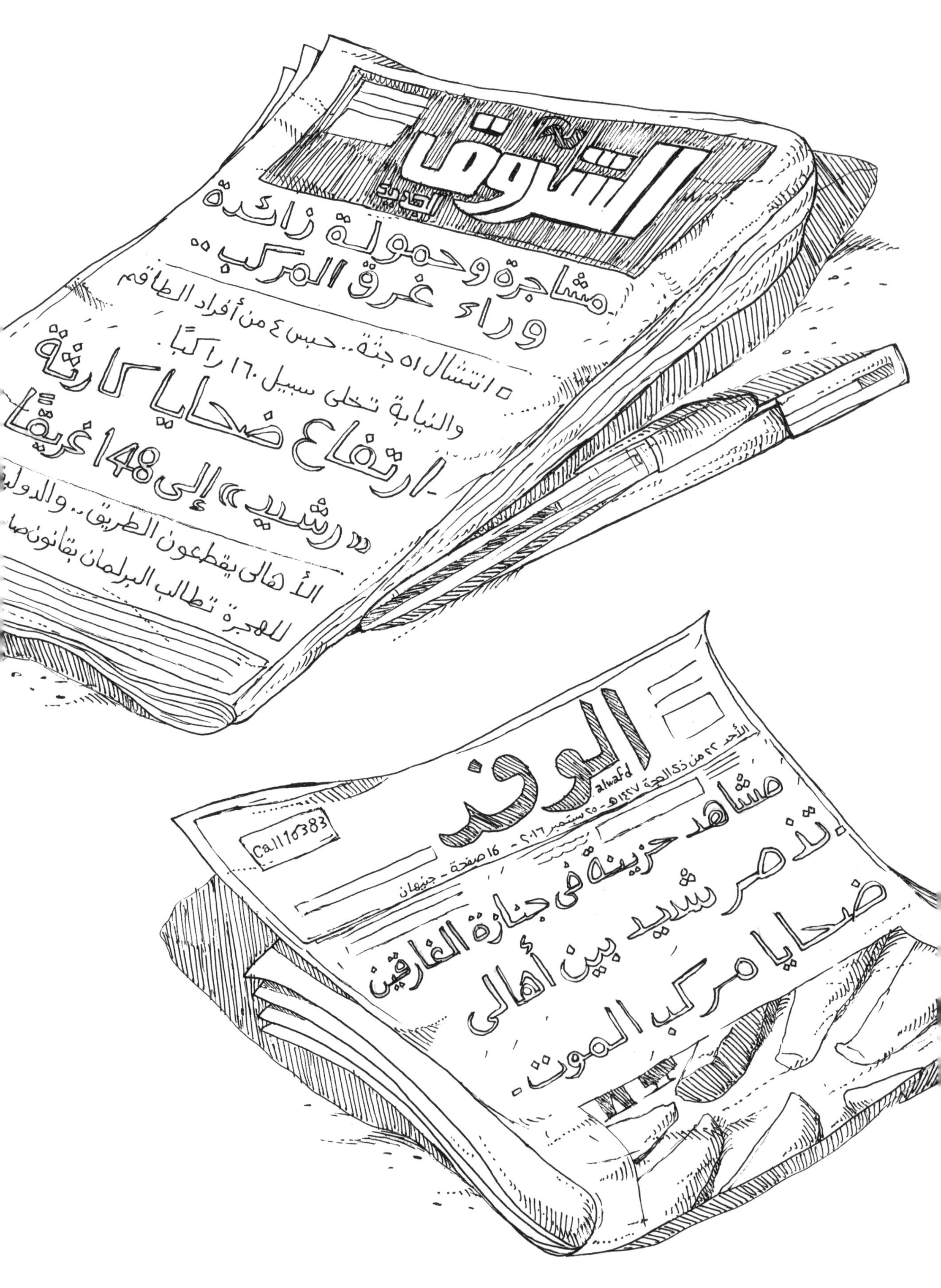
الشروق الجديد
مشاجرة وحمولة زائدة وراء غرق المركب
انتشال ٥١ جثة.. حبس ٤ من أفراد الطاقم
والنيابة تخلي سبيل ١٦٠ راكبا
ارتفاع ضحايا كارثة "رشيد" إلى ١٤٨ غريقا
الأهالي يقطعون الطريق.. والدولة
تطالب البرلمان بقانون صارم
للهجرة
الوطن
alwafd
الأحد ٢٢ من ذي الحجة ١٤٣٧ هـ - ٢٥ سبتمبر ٢٠١٦
١٦ صفحة - جنيهان
Call 16383
مشاهد حزينة في جنازة الغارقين
تزمر شديد بين أهالي ضحايا مركب الموت

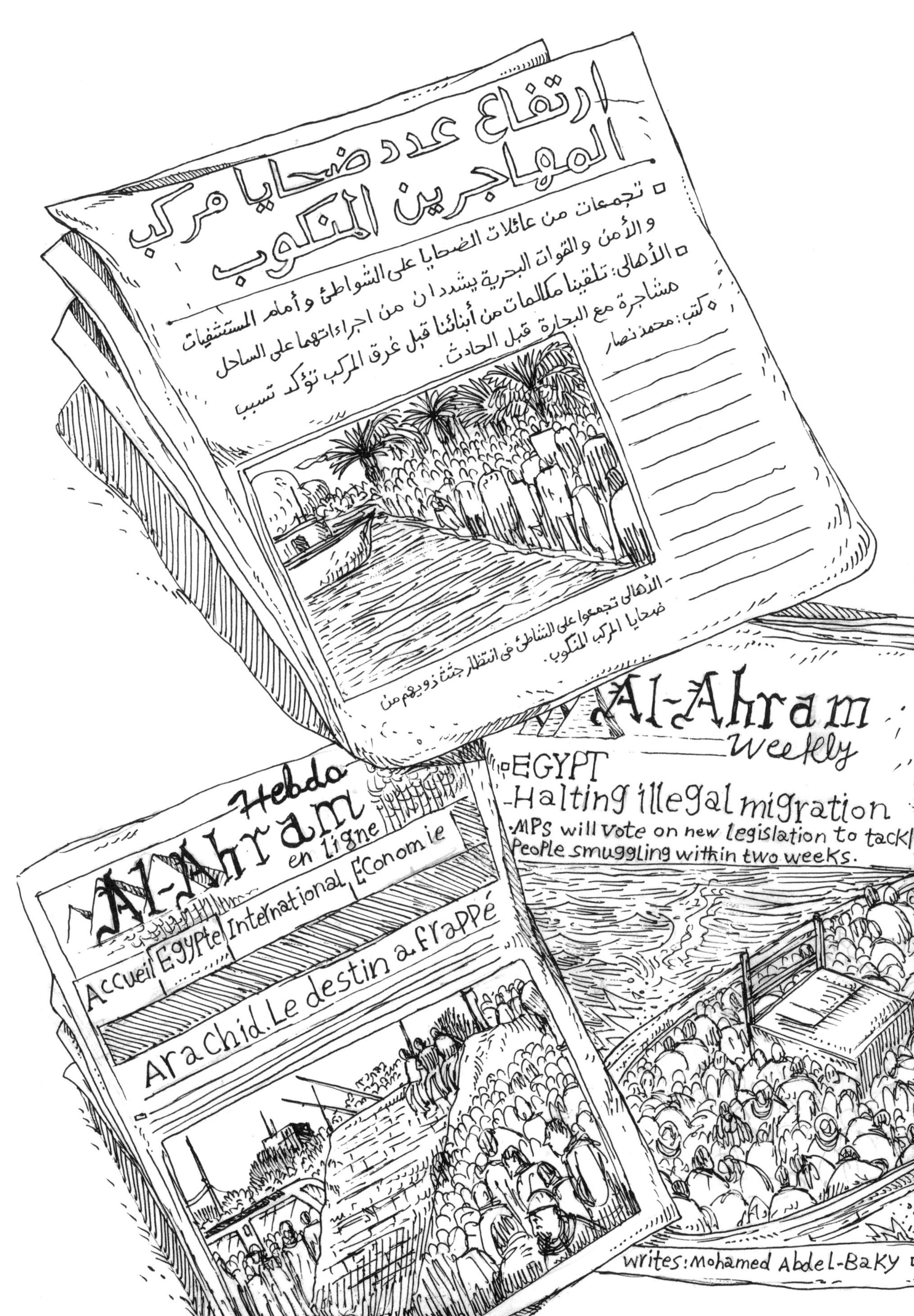
ارتفاع عدد ضحايا مركب المهاجرين المنكوب
تجمعات من عائلات الضحايا على الشواطئ والأمن والقوات البحرية يشددان من اجراءاتهما على الساحل
الأهالي: تلقينا مكالمات من أبنائنا قبل غرق المركب تؤكد تسبب
مشاجرة مع البحارة قبل الحادث.
كتب: محمد نصار
الأهالي تجمعوا على الشاطئ
ضحايا المركب المنكوب في انتظار جثث ذويهم من
Hebdo
Al-Ahram
en ligne
Accueil Egypte International Economie
Arachid. Le destin a frappé
Al-Ahram
weekly
EGYPT
Halting illegal migration
MPs will vote on new legislation to tackle
people smuggling within two weeks.
Writes: Mohamed Abdel-Baky

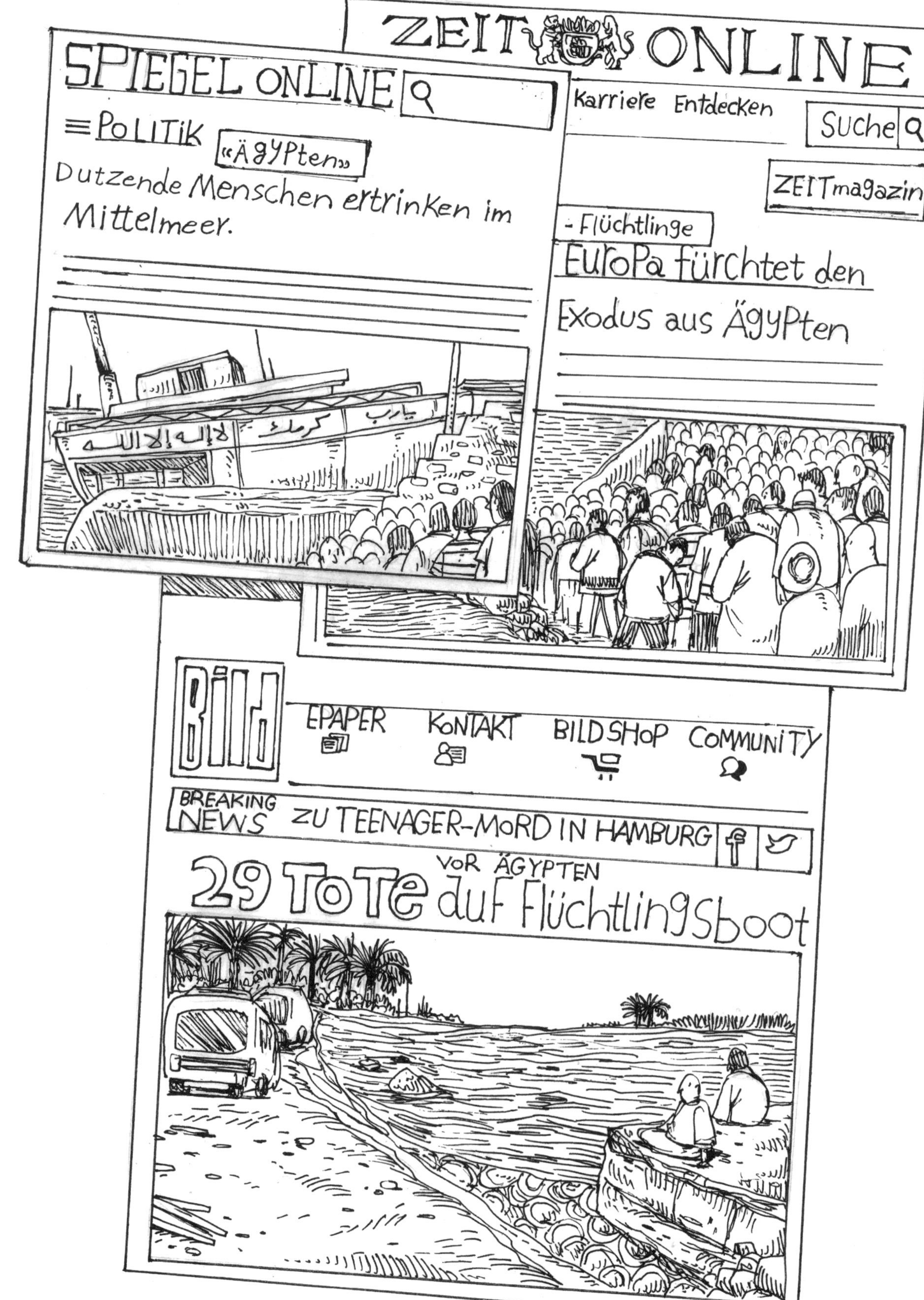
SPIEGEL ONLINE
POLITIK
«Ägypten»
Dutzende Menschen ertrinken im Mittelmeer.
ZEIT ONLINE
Karriere Entdecken
Suche
ZEITmagazin
- Flüchtlinge
Europa fürchtet den Exodus aus Ägypten
Bild
EPAPER
KONTAKT
BILDSHOP COMMUNITY
BREAKING NEWS ZU TEENAGER-MORD IN HAMBURG
VOR ÄGYPTEN
29 TOTE auf Flüchtlingsboot

And what about smugglers? Who is taking the migrants out to sea? How do they get them?

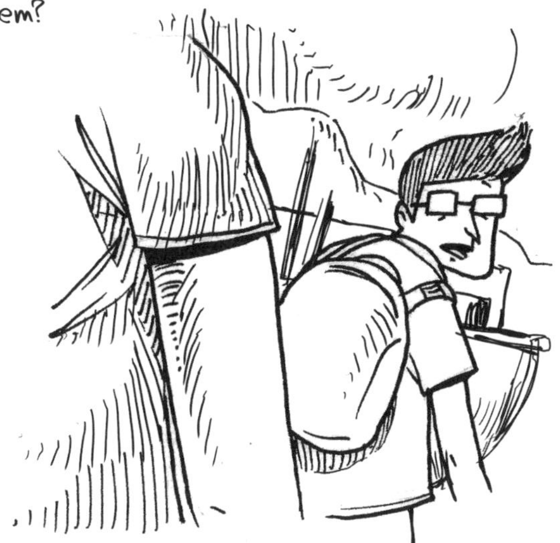

There are many of them – you can find them everywhere.

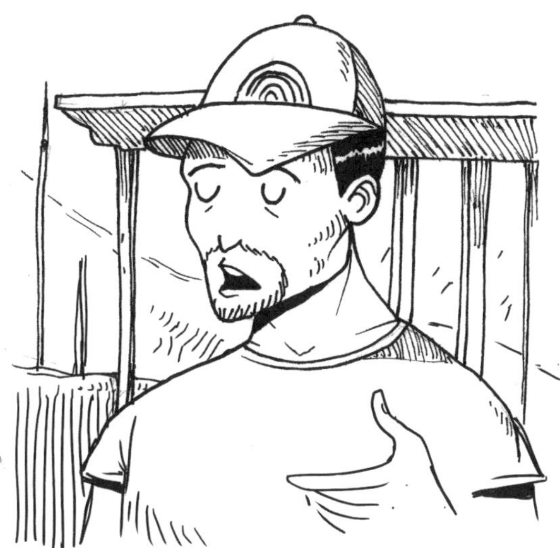

Their employers are well known: they are people with a lot of power in this country. Smugglers come to poor fishermen with fishing boats who have problems getting their papers processed. So the smugglers take advantage of the difficult situation of poor fishermen who have debts. They offer to buy their boat without registered papers. Any fisherman who refuses this deal will be forced by the smugglers to sell his boat.

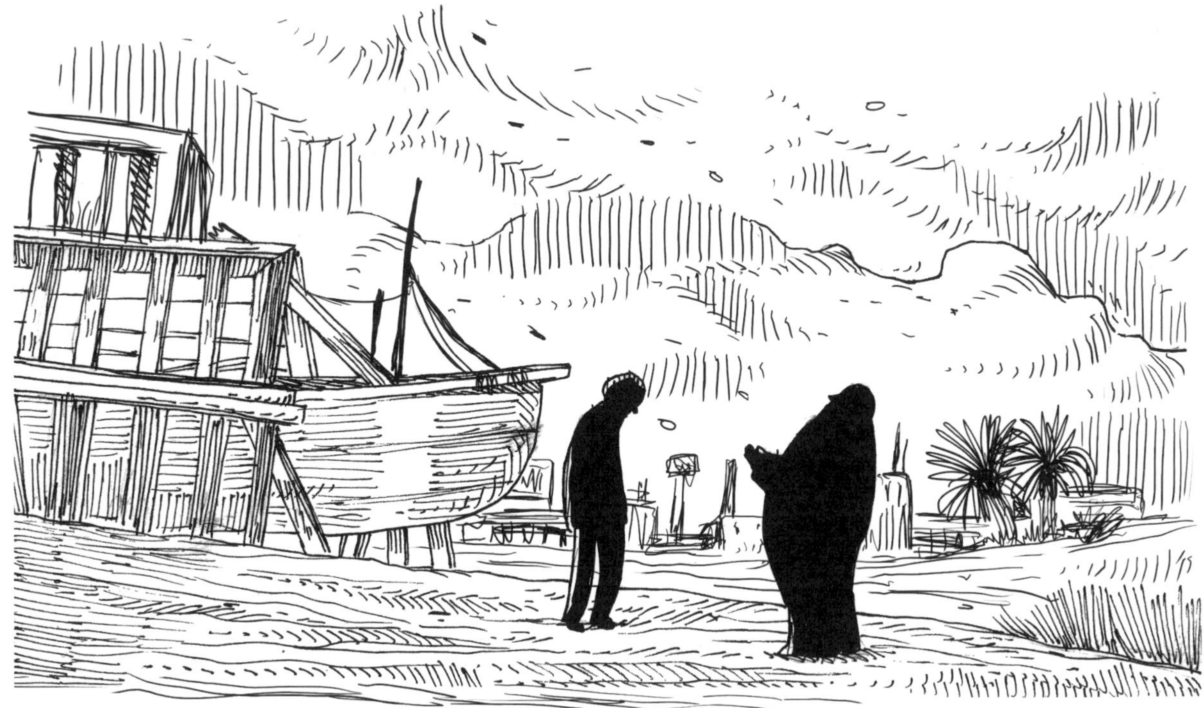

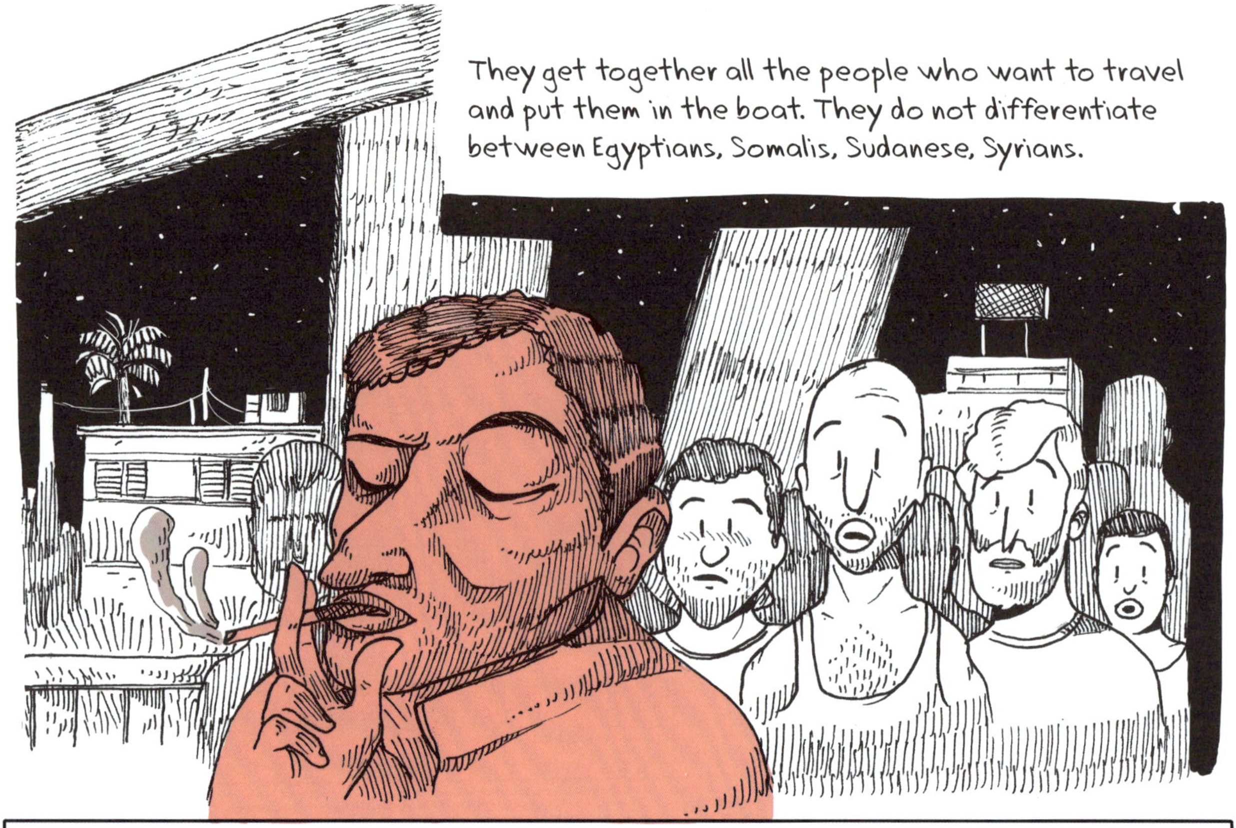

They get together all the people who want to travel and put them in the boat. They do not differentiate between Egyptians, Somalis, Sudanese, Syrians.

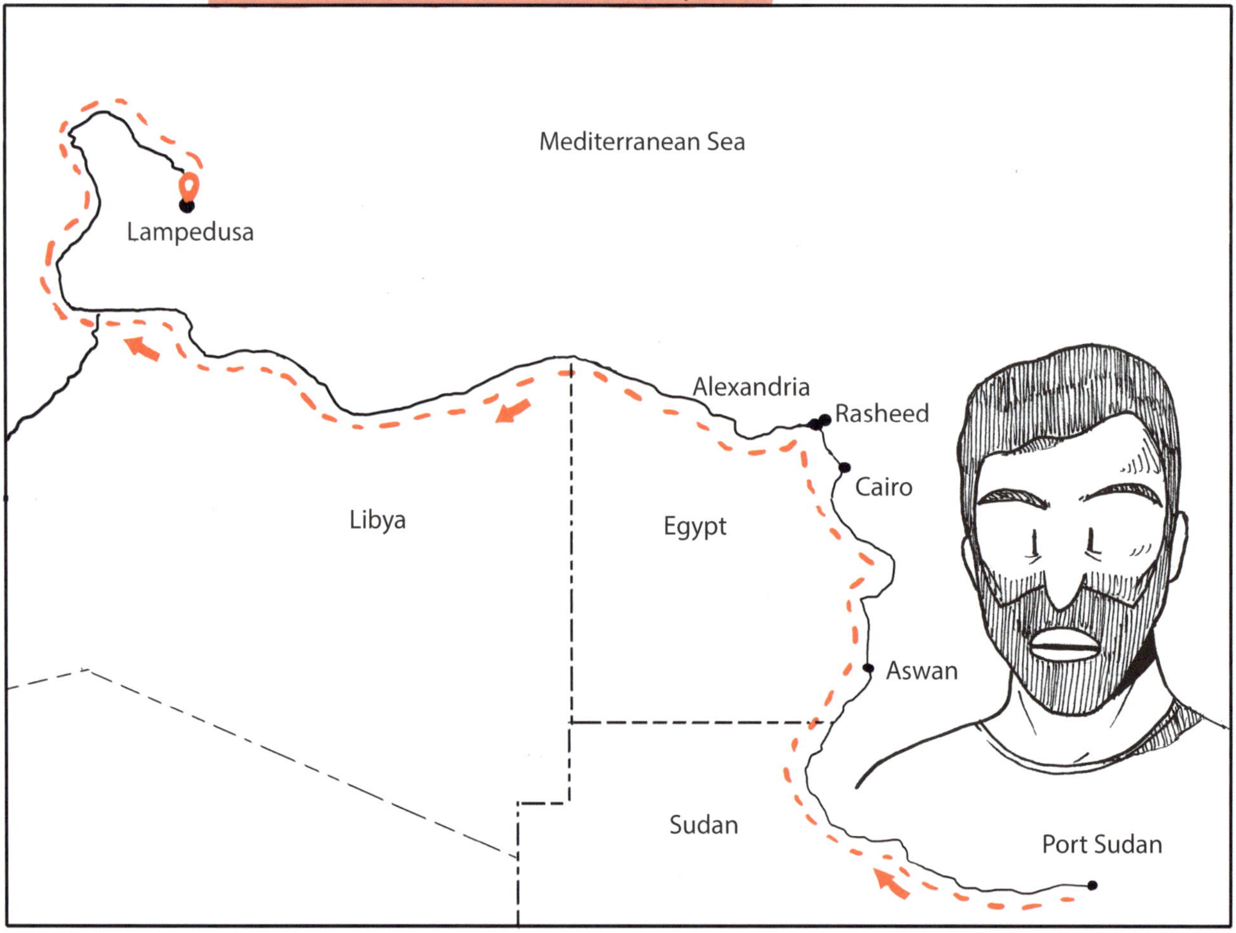

Mediterranean Sea
Lampedusa
Alexandria
Rasheed
Cairo
Libya
Egypt
Aswan
Sudan
Port Sudan

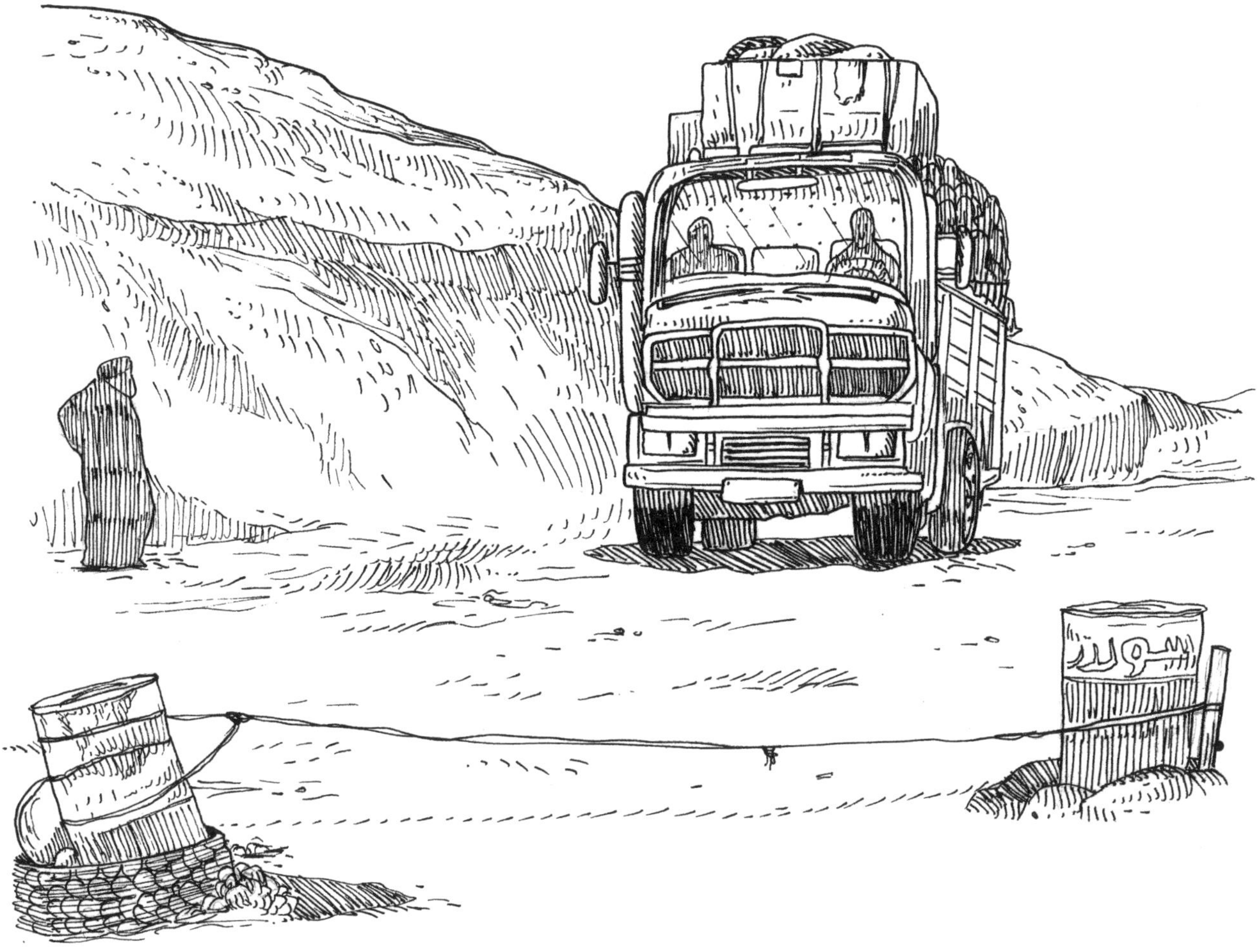

- The most important thing
is their profit...

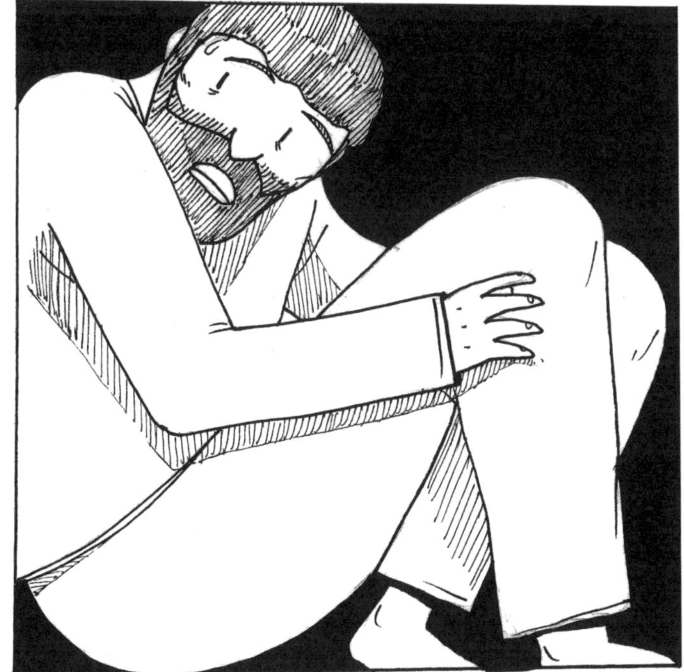

– Do you know, Ghazal, how much they pay for
the smugglers and where the smugglers take them?

– It depends. If the person who wants to travel is an Egyptian and from the island he will pay
50/50, around 15,000 L.E.* Then when they get safely across to the other coast in Italy, they
pay the rest of the money – 15,000 L.E. If they are Egyptian but not from the island, they
will pay the whole 30,000 L.E. **in cash before they leave, but if they are African or Syrian,
they pay around 3–4,000 dollars. But also it's good that they sometimes have mercy on the
Syrians, who only pay 2,000 dollars. It's enough that war destroyed their land and they lost
all their money and family. Mostly the smugglers take them to Lampedusa in Italy.

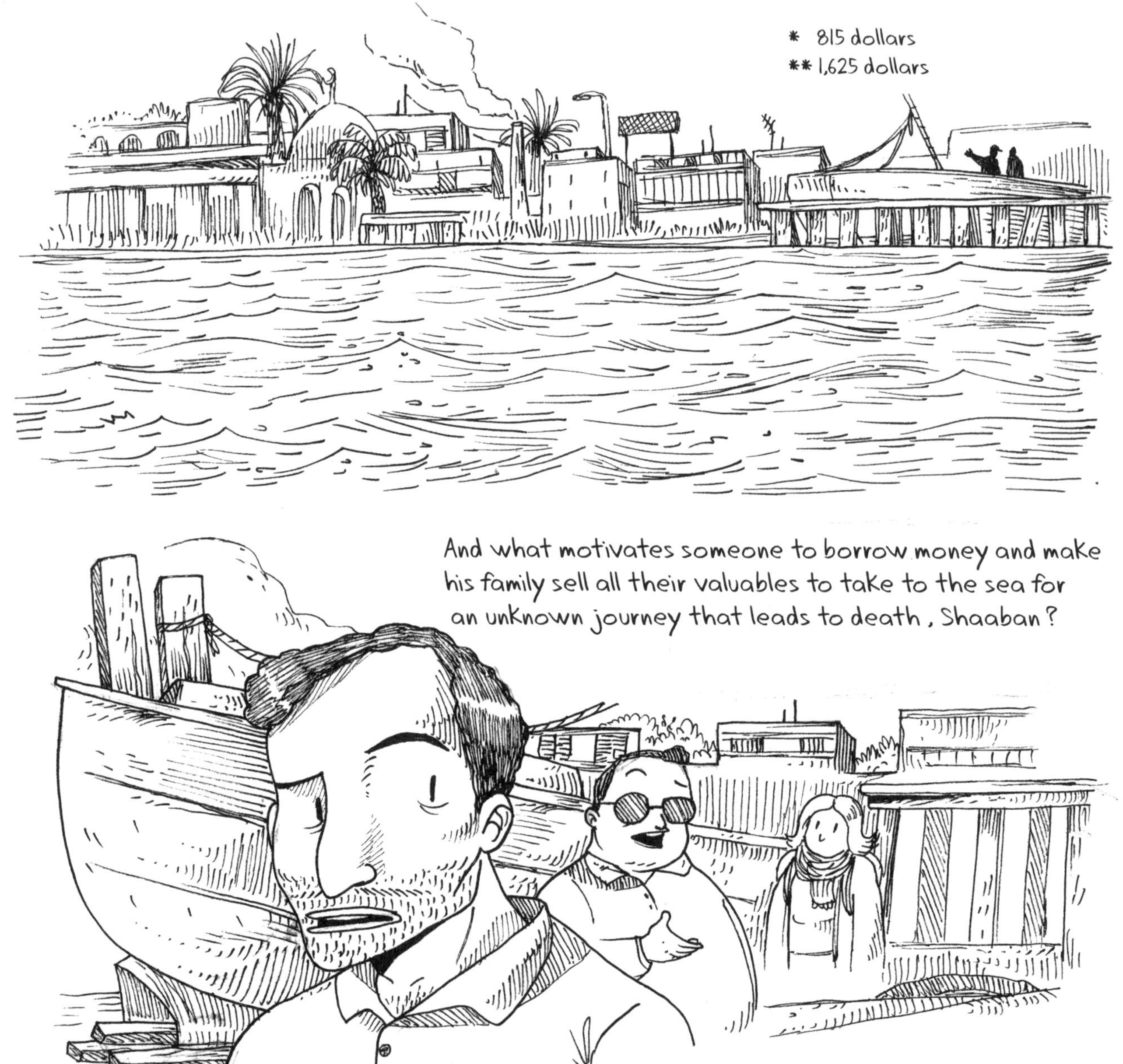

And what motivates someone to borrow money and make
his family sell all their valuables to take to the sea for
an unknown journey that leads to death, Shaaban?

O Pascha, what can a person do if he is unemployed and doesn't have money? Look at the people who returned from Italy and who are building new houses or marrying or starting a new project!

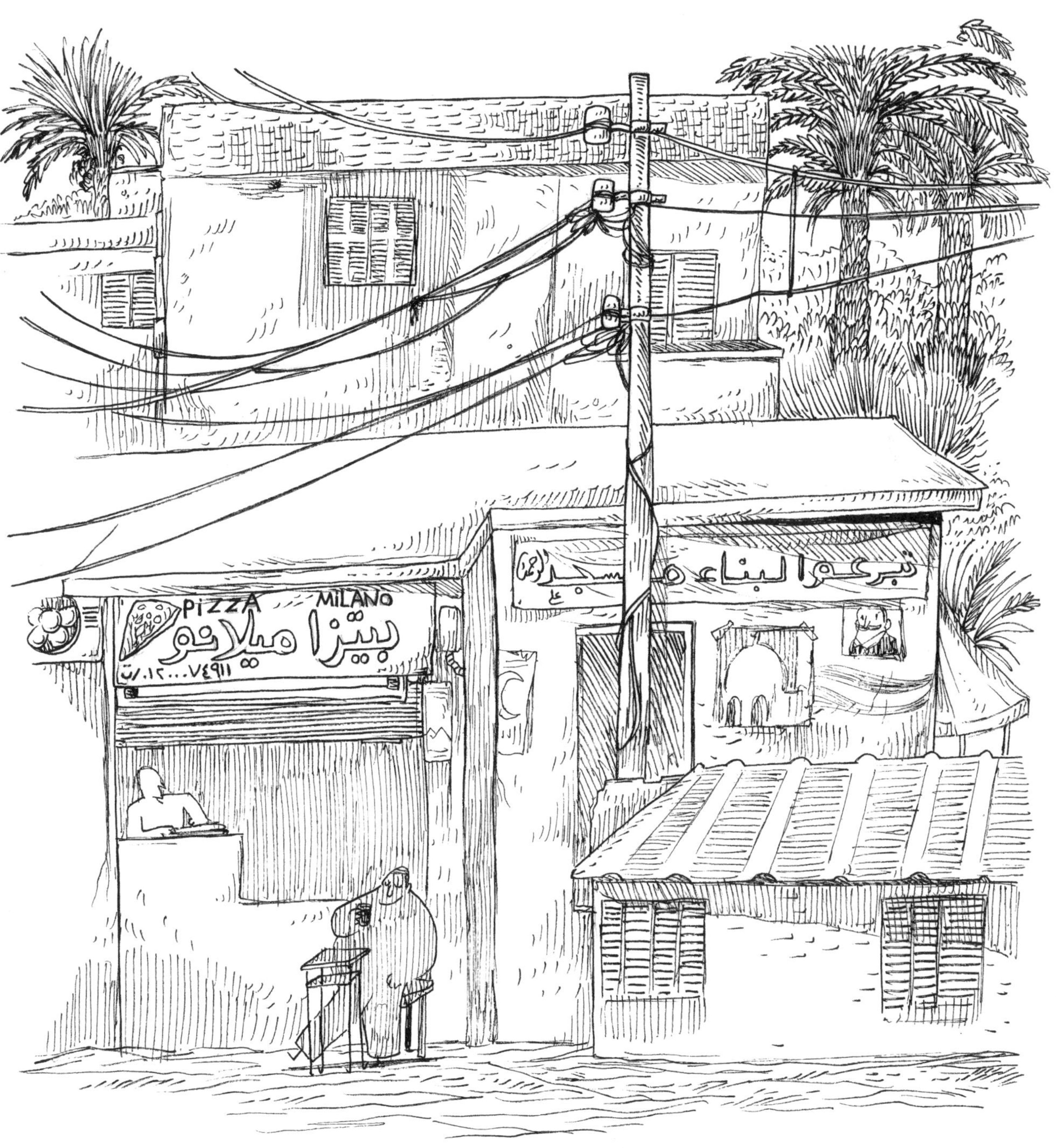

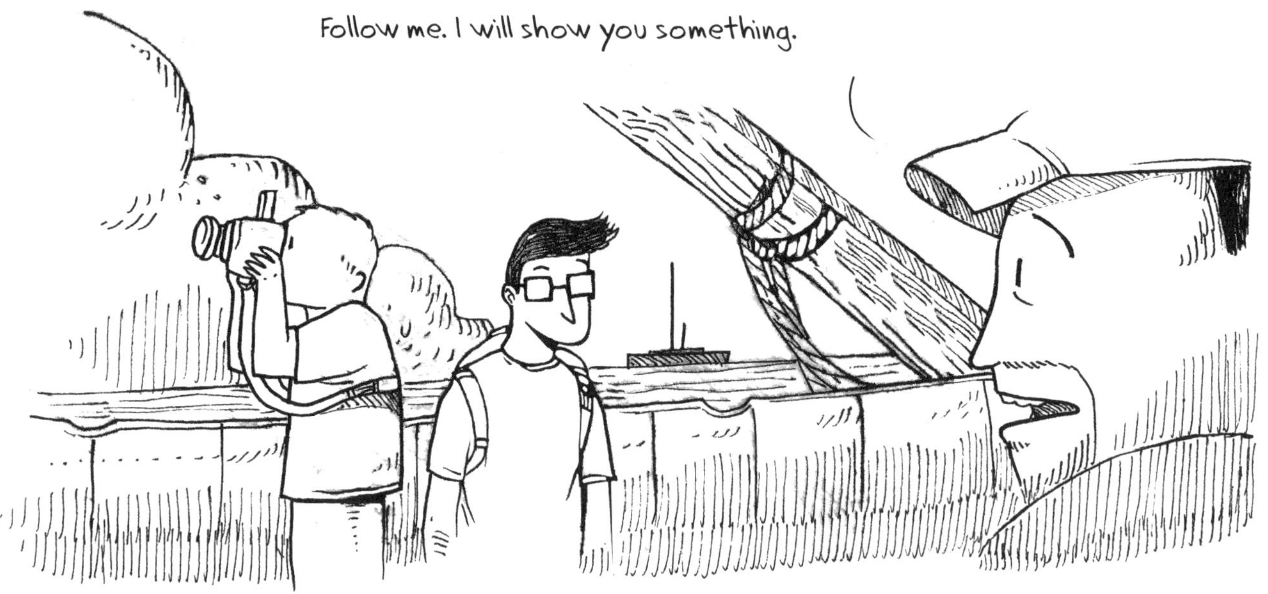

– What is this, Ghazal?

– It's the fridge that any fishing boat should have. The fishermen put fish and ice inside. But when the smugglers buy the boat they misuse this space. They take people who want to migrate to Europe and put them in this hidden place, so they are out of sight of the coastguard. The fridge has capacity for only 25 people. The smugglers put 200 people in the fridge and close the top over them.

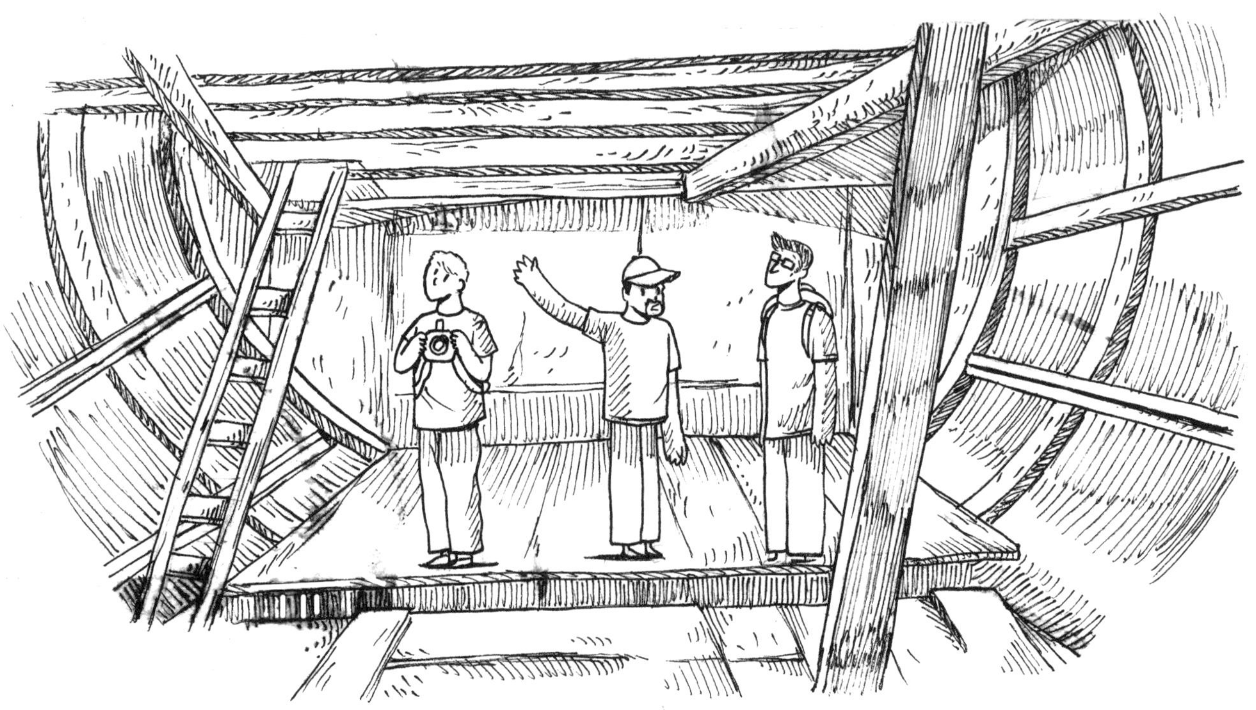

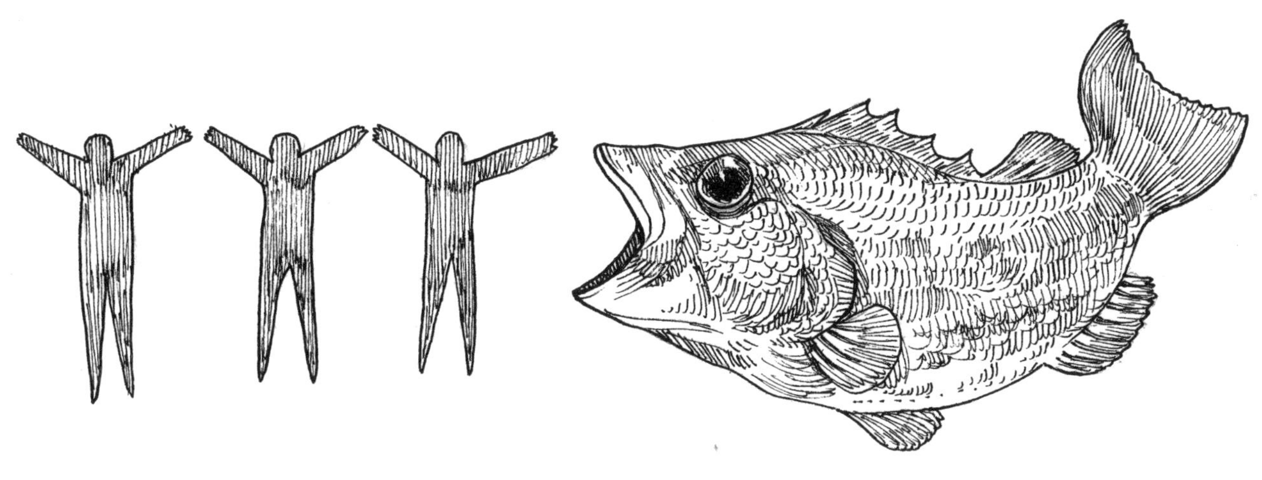

In the past we were eating fish, now the fish eat us!

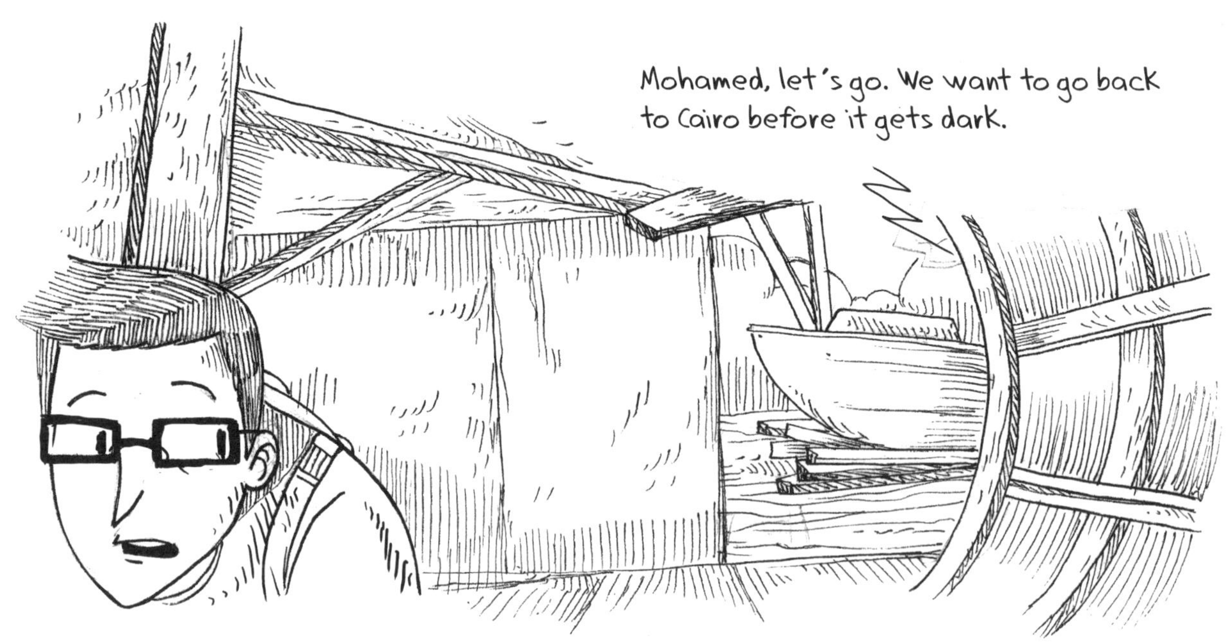

Mohamed, let's go. We want to go back to Cairo before it gets dark.

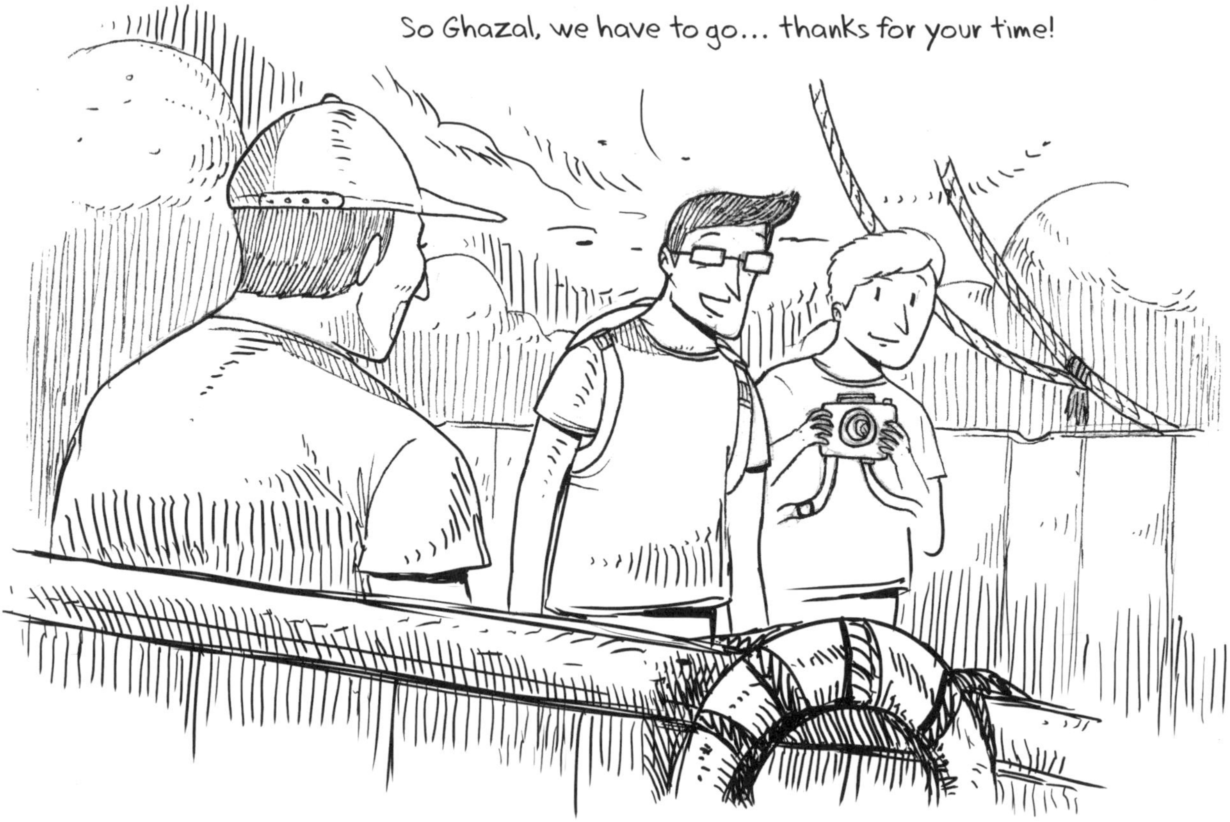

So Ghazal, we have to go... thanks for your time!

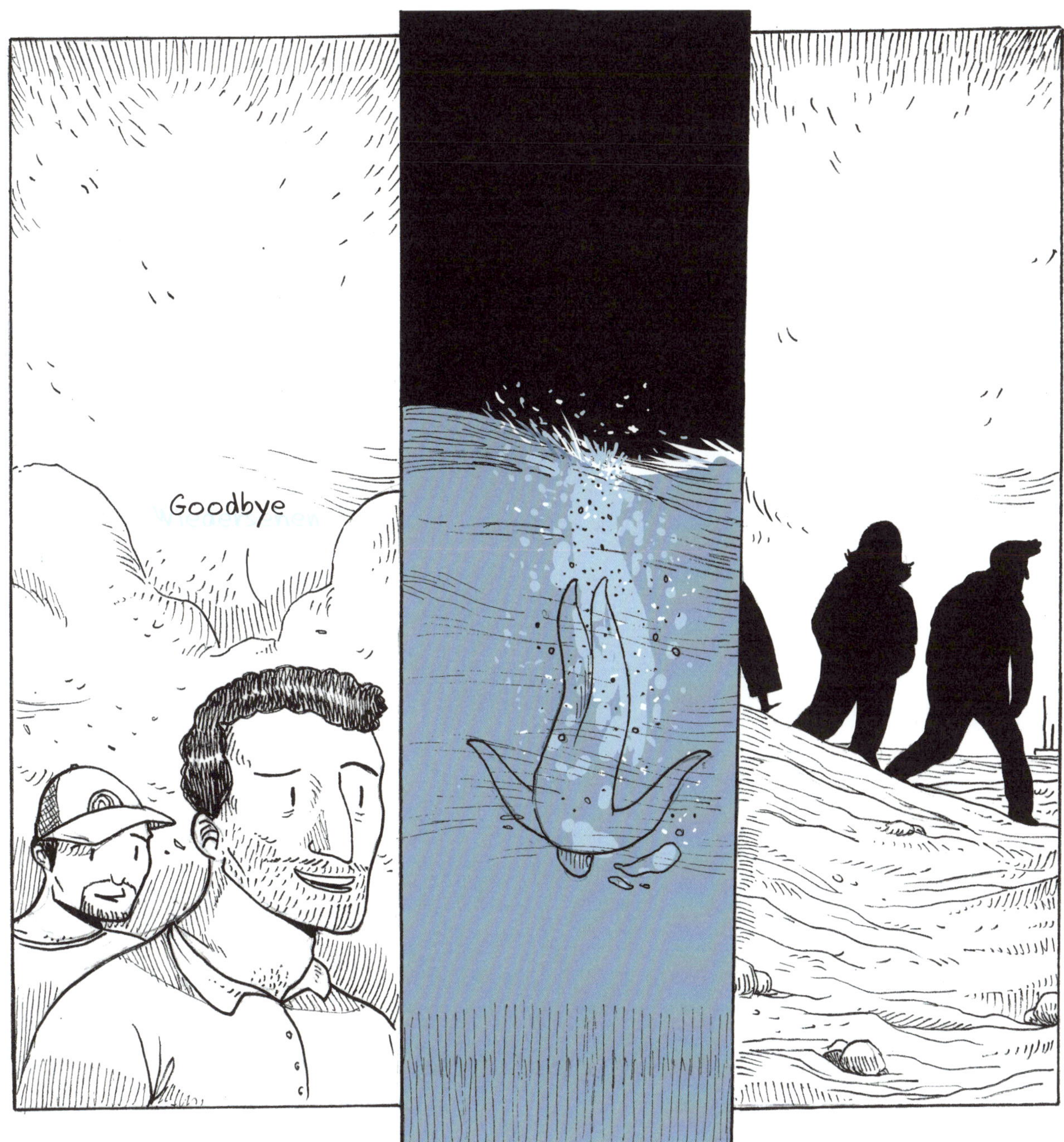
Goodbye

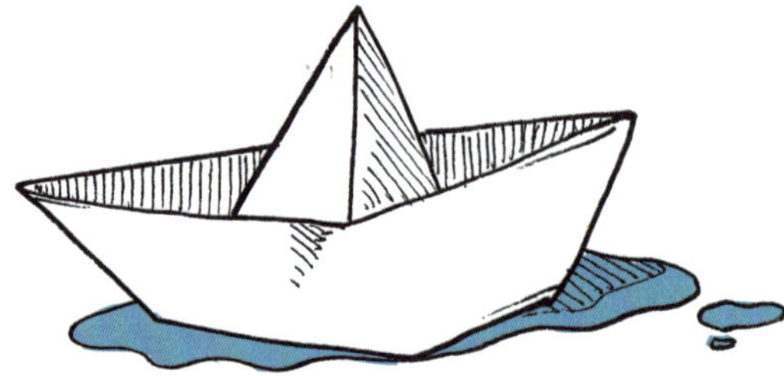

A Question of Perspective

Hani Mustafa, layout editor of the Egyptian *Al-Ahram Weekly*, on Western image sources

Al-Ahram Weekly is published by *Al-Ahram* and it comes out every Thursday. The newspaper was established in English in 1991, the same year that Hani Mustafa finished his studies in the Journalism Department of Cairo University's Faculty of Mass Communication, and started working for *Al-Ahram Weekly* where he is an executive. Ninety percent of the edition is distributed in Egypt for foreigners living in the country. Mustafa's work with newspaper pictures includes selecting images as well as layouting and supervising the pages. In 2016 we visited him in his office in downtown Cairo. Before entering *Al-Ahram's* high-rise building in Al-Galaa Street, we were checked by security. The interview was conducted by Anne König, Andreas Langfeld, and Karolina Sobel.

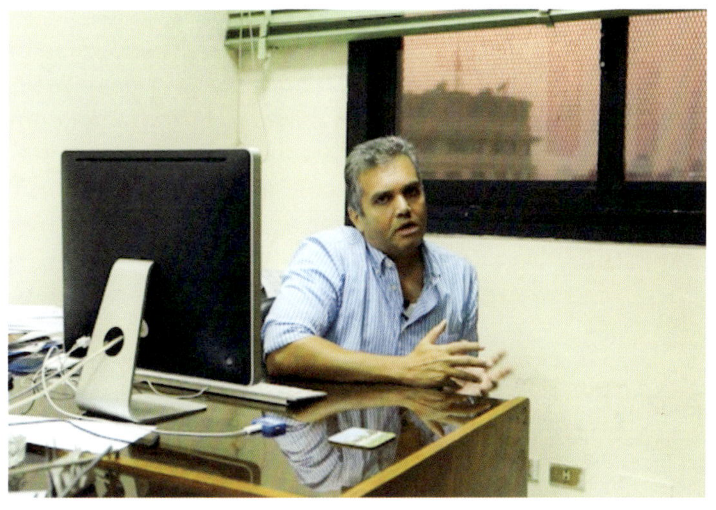

Q: *How do you organize the editing process?*
MUSTAFA: Choosing the photographs that are going to be published is a team process.

Q: *How has this ongoing topic of migration been represented by images in your newspaper?*
MUSTAFA: It has been a tragic situation for a couple of years now. Boats sinking in the Mediterranean and people dying is tragic. This became a top priority. There is politics in the background. If we talk, for example, about Syrian migrants—they are representative of the conflict in Syria, and people from there are dying in large numbers, like on the boat. It is very difficult not to have images of these people or images of the wreckage of the boat in our minds or not to put them on the front page.

Q: When did Egypt become the transit country for migrants?

MUSTAFA: It was possible to see the flow of migrants in the 1990s. I think it started with the economic collapse. Because of its location, Egypt turned into a transit country for migration from Africa, for African and Syrian migrants. Egypt and Tunisia became a passage channeling the flow from Africa to the northern Mediterranean. The flow of African migrants goes from south to north because of economic problems: in the process, it passes through Egypt.

Q: But what about migration as a more general phenomenon in Egypt?

MUSTAFA: Migration in Egypt occurred in the 1960s among middle-class professionals, like physicians, engineers, and dentists, hoping to improve their standard of living. There were economic reasons for migrating to Western countries like America and Canada.

Later, in the mid-1970s, migration shifted to middle-class groups in the Persian Gulf—this was caused by the "oil economy." It was favorable for people to work in similar cultures and get a better job.

Q: What are the sources of the images in Al-Ahram Weekly? *Where do you choose your pictures from?*

MUSTAFA: *Al-Ahram* has contracts with AP, Reuters, and AFP for news and photos. They are the more relevant sources for the topic of illegal migration. The source is the same pool of images as for the Western media. There is a department of staff photographers and MENA, the Middle East News Agency based in Egypt. They report on government events.

After preparing the edition, we look to see what our colleagues—for example, at the *Daily Telegraph* or *Observer*—are publishing, because we are working in the same language. We try to present an event or photo from a different angle. We don't use images that were published before by other colleagues, because they have been seen before. We try to be different by cropping or choosing another photo. We always try to choose a different angle. There are pictures which are clichéd. Not in a negative way. For example, the picture of Alan Kurdi, the Syrian boy who died while migrating. It is an iconic image. We published it as well but not as a front-page image. We couldn't ignore it.

Q: In Rasheed, on September 21, 2016, a tragedy happened in which more than 170 young people from Egypt died in the Mediterranean. Your newspaper reported on it as well. Why did you chose this image for the front page?

MUSTAFA: The front page shows migration from an Egyptian perspective. Egyptian citizens are grieving. The image comes from AFP. It shows the grief—probably the people there are relatives, waiting for the bodies or belongings of the refugees.

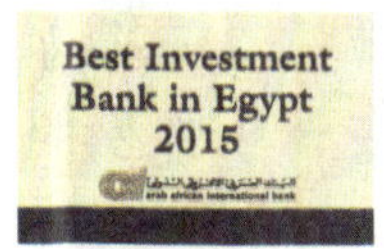

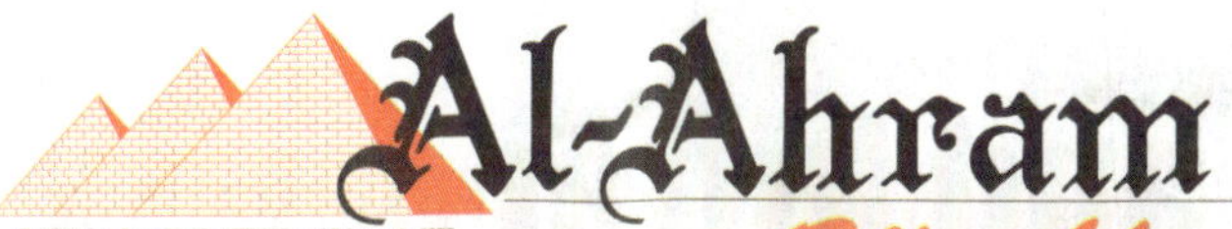

No. 1313   الأهرام ويكلي   ISSN: 1110-2977   29 September – 5 October 2016   weekly.ahram.org.eg   LE 5

Victims by proxy

Syria has become the major arena for the ongoing Russian-US standoff, writes **Bassel Oudat**

After the truce collapsed — or more accurately the blueprint for a truce that the Russians and Americans were hammering out — the Aleppo front exploded.

Aleppo remains a strategic goal for all local, regional and international stakeholders in the Syrian conflict. It is the main and strongest front of the opposition and has long served as a gauge of the balance of forces.

A week ago Russian aircraft launched an intensive wave of assaults against the eastern sector of the city which is controlled by the Syrian opposition. The bombardment was so fierce hospitals in the city were unable to cope with the casualties and civil defence units announced they were unable to rescue people from beneath the rubble of collapsed buildings. UNICEF reported that the city's main water station was struck, compounding the humanitarian disaster by cutting supplies of potable water to nearly a million people.

The sequence of unfolding events offers an insight into what is happening behind the scenes between Russia and the US. Organisations involved in documenting violations of the truce recorded more than 300 breaches during the first days of Eid Al-Adha, 95 per cent of them the responsibility of the regime. The Russians and Americans simultaneously announced the collapse of the truce, marking the breakdown of an agreement that could have been the beginning of a solution to the Syrian crisis.

US-led international coalition air forces subsequently bombarded Syrian army camps in Deir Al-Zor in eastern Syria. "By mistake", the Americans claim, but if so who supplied the false intelligence? Over 100 Syrian soldiers and members of affiliated militias were killed, most of them from Palestinian factions that support Al-Assad. The Russians were furious. Moscow refused to believe it was a "mistake" and regarded the attack as American provocation.

The US-Russian agreement had provided for the entry of humanitarian aid to areas of Aleppo besieged by regime forces. Ambiguous statements from Washington suggesting the truce was still intact led the UN to approve the dispatch of an aid convoy to areas controlled by the opposition. Russian aircraft bombarded the convoy before it could reach its recipients. Moscow denies targeting the convoy though airspace over the targeted area is entirely controlled by the Russians and the Syrian regime. Most Syrians saw the strike as a message addressed to Washington in retaliation for bombing the Syrian army camps at Deir Al-Zor.

Opposition forces then advanced in Hama, the governorate next to Aleppo, where they achieved some victories. Meanwhile, the Russians and Americans exchanged recriminations over who had undermined the truce in language that sometimes contained thinly veiled threats.

That was when the assault on Aleppo — the most ferocious aerial bombardment to date in Syria — began. The Syrian opposition has accused Russia and the Syrian regime of pursuing a scorched earth policy, levelling everything in preparation for a ground offensive.

On Sunday the Security Council convened to discuss the military escalation in Aleppo. The session quickly turned into a trial of Moscow's role in Syria. Russia and the Syrian regime were accused of committing war crimes. The US described Russian actions in Syria as barbaric. For the first time since the Syrian crisis erupted five years ago UN Secretary-General Ban Ki-moon accused Russia and the Syrian regime of committing war crimes. In another precedent, UN envoy to Syria Staffan de Mistura held the "Syrian government" responsible for the latest military assault against Aleppo.

The Security Council session drove home the extent of the gulf that now exists between Russia and the US over Syria.

Since the beginning of the Syrian revolution the US administration's approach to Syria has been reckless, ambiguous and cavalier. The Russians have taken full advantage of this, pursuing their strategy confident Barack Obama would not challenge them politically or militarily. Russia strengthened its role in Syria until it could use the Syrian question to pressure the US and Europe on other issues seen as crucial by Moscow. In doing so it encouraged the Syrian regime to persist in pursuing a murderous military solution without making any concessions.

The fracas between Moscow and Washington raises the question as to whether Russia now has the upper hand.

"When the Syrian revolution began in 2011, Moscow was almost on the fringes of events," says Fayez Sara, a member of the Syrian opposition coalition. "There were at most 40 Russian soldiers in Syria and they were stationed at the Tartus naval base on the Mediterranean coast. Today the situation could not be more different. The Russians have a huge military force in Syria, a large naval base in Tartus, an airbase in Khmeimim and another at Bassel Al-Assad Airport near Latakia. Russian troops in Syria now number in the thousands and Russia's involvement in the Syrian conflict is a central plank of Moscow's foreign policy. The disputes between it and the US have escalated to a dangerous level."

As well as being directly embroiled in warfare in Syria Russian diplomacy has pursued two courses that are "contradictory in form but complementary in function," says Sara.

"On the one hand Russia has assumed the management of its allies, primarily Iran and the Al-Assad regime. On the other, it is trying to participate with the US in international efforts to resolve the Syrian question and turn those efforts to its own advantage and to the advantage of the Syrian-Iranian alliance. Given the levels of international collusion, silence and regional acquiescence Russia is unlikely to hesitate in using more of its military and material capacities to win the war. But in doing so it is ignoring the Soviet experience in Afghanistan, one of the causes of the collapse of the Soviet Union. Although Syria is not Afghanistan and circumstances there are different the amount of regional and international intervention in the Syrian issue does not work in Moscow's favour. Instead of winning the war in Syria, it risks losing the war and the price it will pay increases the more it embroils itself."

Russia and the US appear to have definitively parted ways over Syria leaving the civilian population to wonder what will happen next. Who will stop the catastrophe?

Syrian opposition member Walid Al-Bunni believes the "Russian-Iranian bombardment will continue until the US and Russia decide enough blood has been shed and come to terms on outstanding issues between them."

He warns that there will be no let-up in the ferocity of fighting during the remainder of the Obama administration and things could easily grow worse.

"The Russian aerial assaults will grow more brutal in the hope of gaining as much territory as possible before the next administration comes into power in Washington. Russia will try to resolve the Syrian question militarily and put an end to the Syrian opposition entirely in the few remaining months of the current administration in the hope that, when the new administration arrives, it will find no one that it can call an opposition and will be forced to work with Russia to fight the Islamic State, the Nusra Front and associated organisations. It will also find that the Al-Assad regime, thanks to Iranian and sectarian militia support on the ground and Russian air cover, will have imposed its control over Syrian territory."

This scenario can be altered under one condition, argues Al-Bunni — "if the current US administration agrees to conclude a comprehensive agreement that covers not only Syria but other outstanding issues, from Ukraine and NATO missiles to US and European sanctions against Russia."

He does not anticipate such a possibility. "The Obama administration does not want to encumber its successor with agreements that will circumscribe its own international policies."

6&8

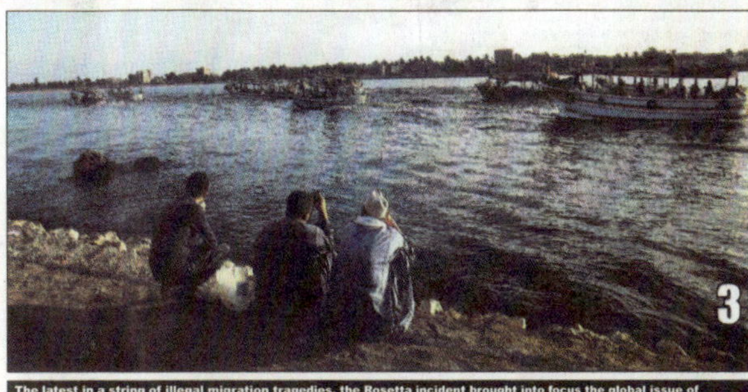
The latest in a string of illegal migration tragedies, the Rosetta incident brought into focus the global issue of north-south inequality once again, framing it in an Egyptian context as never before. When a fishing boat reportedly carrying 500 migrants, both Egyptian and not, capsized off the coast of the idyllic port, an alarm sounded for both the Egyptian authorities and the population. Looking out from one of two points where the Nile meets the Mediterranean, as the relatives of still lost migrants in the picture do, one now sees "the death boats" at the heart of the coastal vista. *(photo: AFP)*

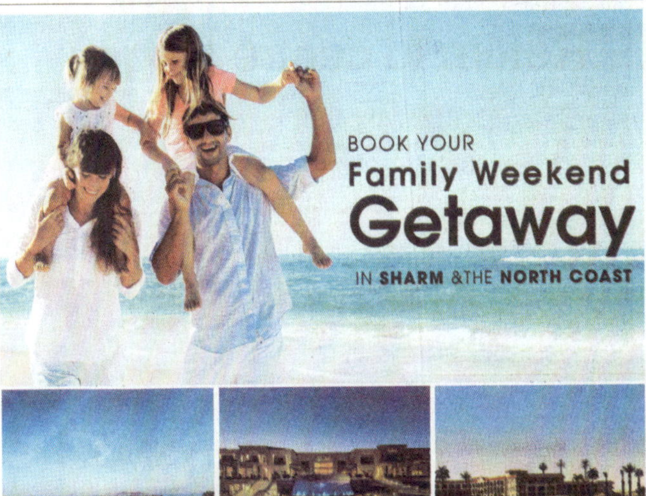

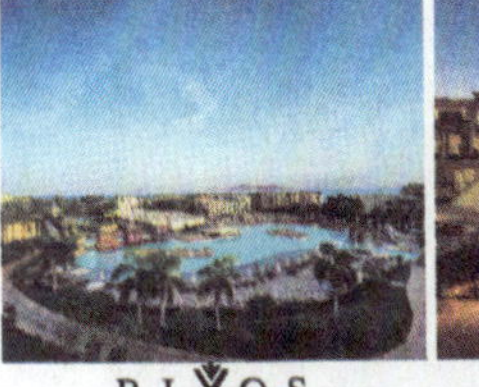

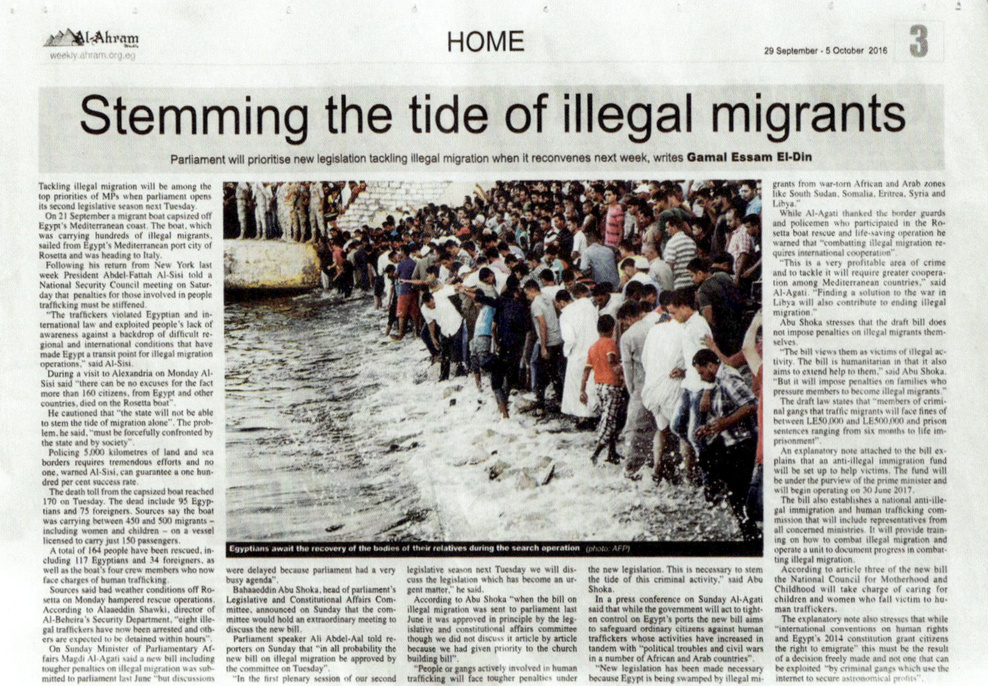

Stemming the tide of illegal migrants

Parliament will prioritise new legislation tackling illegal migration when it reconvenes next week, writes **Gamal Essam El-Din**

Tackling illegal migration will be among the top priorities of MPs when parliament opens its second legislative season next Tuesday.

On 21 September a migrant boat capsized off Egypt's Mediterranean coast. The boat, which was carrying hundreds of illegal migrants, sailed from Egypt's Mediterranean port city of Rosetta and was heading to Italy.

Following his return from New York last week President Abdel-Fattah Al-Sisi told a National Security Council meeting on Saturday that penalties for those involved in people trafficking must be stiffened.

"The traffickers violated Egyptian and international law and exploited people's lack of awareness against a backdrop of difficult regional and international conditions that have made Egypt a transit point for illegal migration operations," said Al-Sisi.

During a visit to Alexandria on Monday Al-Sisi said "there can be no excuses for the fact more than 160 citizens, from Egypt and other countries, died on the Rosetta boat."

He cautioned that "the state will not be able to stem the tide of migration alone". The problem, he said, "must be forcefully confronted by the state and by society".

Policing 5,000 kilometres of land and sea borders requires tremendous efforts and no one, warned Al-Sisi, can guarantee a one hundred per cent success rate.

The death toll from the capsized boat reached 170 on Tuesday. The dead include 95 Egyptians and 75 foreigners. Sources say the boat was carrying between 450 and 500 migrants – including women and children – on a vessel licensed to carry just 150 passengers.

A total of 164 people have been rescued, including 117 Egyptians and 34 foreigners, as well as the boat's four crew members who now face charges of human trafficking.

Sources said bad weather conditions off Rosetta on Monday hampered rescue operations. According to Alaaeddin Shawki, director of Al-Beheira's Security Department, "eight illegal traffickers have now been arrested and others are expected to be detained within hours".

On Sunday Minister of Parliamentary Affairs Magdi Al-Agati said a new bill including tougher penalties on illegal migration was submitted to parliament last June "but discussions were delayed because parliament had a very busy agenda".

Bahaaeddin Abu Shoka, head of parliament's Legislative and Constitutional Affairs Committee, announced on Sunday that the committee would hold an extraordinary meeting to discuss the new bill.

Parliament speaker Ali Abdel-Aal told reporters on Sunday that "in all probability the new bill on illegal migration be approved by the committee on Tuesday".

"In the first plenary session of our second legislative season next Tuesday we will discuss the legislation which has become an urgent matter," he said.

According to Abu Shoka "when the bill on illegal migration was sent to parliament last June it was approved in principle by the legislative and constitutional affairs committee though we did not discuss it article by article because we had given priority to the church building bill".

"People or gangs actively involved in human trafficking will face tougher penalties under the new legislation. This is necessary to stem the tide of this criminal activity," said Abu Shoka.

In a press conference on Sunday Al-Agati said that while the government will act to tighten control on Egypt's ports the new bill aims to safeguard ordinary citizens against human traffickers whose activities have increased in tandem with "political troubles and civil wars in a number of African and Arab countries".

"New legislation has been made necessary because Egypt is being swamped by illegal migrants from war-torn African and Arab zones like South Sudan, Somalia, Eritrea, Syria and Libya."

While Al-Agati thanked the border guards and policemen who participated in the Rosetta boat rescue and life-saving operation he warned that "combatting illegal migration requires international cooperation".

"This is a very profitable area of crime and to tackle it will require greater cooperation among Mediterranean countries," said Al-Agati. "Finding a solution to the war in Libya will also contribute to ending illegal migration."

Abu Shoka stresses that the draft bill does not impose penalties on illegal migrants themselves.

"The bill views them as victims of illegal activity. The bill is humanitarian in that it also aims to extend help to them," said Abu Shoka. "But it will impose penalties on families who pressure members to become illegal migrants."

The draft law states that "members of criminal gangs that traffic migrants will face fines of between LE50,000 and LE500,000 and prison sentences ranging from six months to life imprisonment".

An explanatory note attached to the bill explains that an anti-illegal immigration fund will be set up to help victims. The fund will be under the purview of the prime minister and will begin operating on 30 June 2017.

The bill also establishes a national anti-illegal immigration and human trafficking commission that will include representatives from all concerned ministries. It will provide training on how to combat illegal migration and operate a unit to document progress in combatting illegal migration.

According to article three of the new bill the National Council for Motherhood and Childhood will take charge of caring for children and women who fall victim to human traffickers.

The explanatory note also stresses that while "international conventions on human rights and Egypt's 2014 constitution grant citizens the right to emigrate" this must be the result of a decision freely made and not one that can be exploited "by criminal gangs which use the internet to secure astronomical profits".

Egyptians await the recovery of the bodies of their relatives during the search operation *(photo: AFP)*

↑ From the same edition, this image comes from AFP. It depicts another angle on the same subject. It is more dramatic. When we think about the front page, the images have to be simpler, to catch the viewer's eye. Those two photographs are good pictures. But the first image shows the grief. The choice of different images has something to do with the editor and the treatment of refugees as a problem. We are thinking about these people, about those who lost relatives.

We use the Mosaic Group. Mosaic is a source for all the agencies, which allows you to choose from a specific agency and select from the pool of images on the topic. Checking with the keywords "illegal migrants," we see resources from all over the world. Mosaic always uses current news: it allows you to look at the last two or three days. The keywords are in captions and it shows all the images connected with this topic.

Q: But if you search for some images from a week or a month ago? How do you that?

MUSTAFA: It's not possible. I can only look back two or three days.

Q: What images are shown when you use the caption "migrants and Egyptians"?

MUSTAFA: Unfortunately, there are only images about migration. Another source is just Google Search. If we are looking for iconic images, we just google them. For world issues, Mosaic and Google are our sources. For Arabic and local issues we send photographers. Our local photographers don't cover the topic of migration. The agency pictures often have a better quality than our local photographs.

(Mustafa shows an image folder from the last *Al-Ahram Weekly* issue) These are all the photos that we chose from and that were published on our homepage. Every image is in both color and black and white in the folder shown.

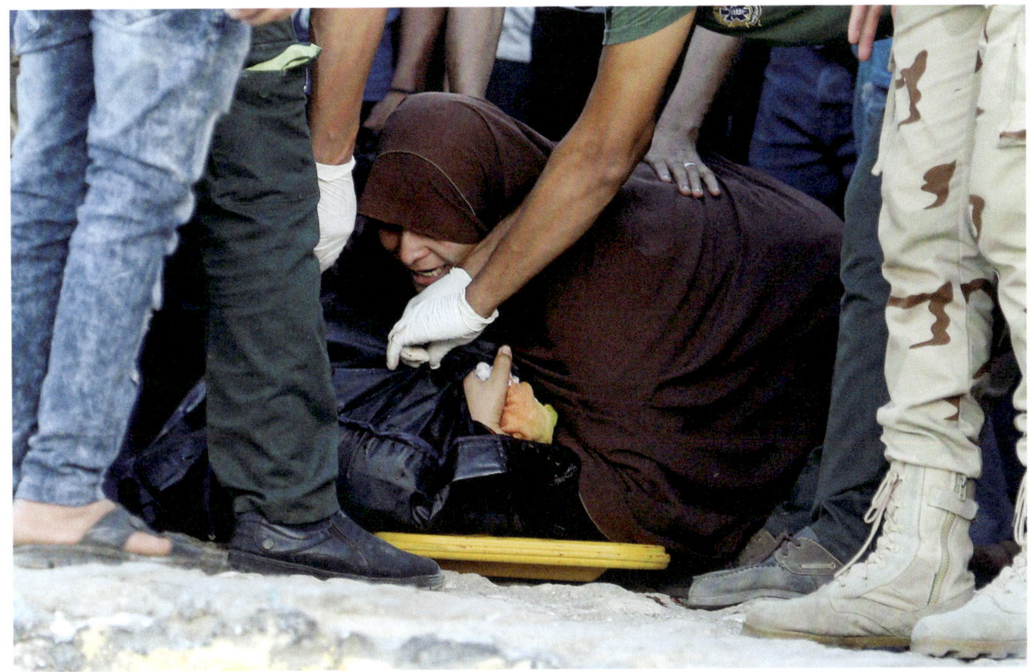

↑   This picture deals with migrants. (Mustafa reads out the caption) "An Egyptian mother grieving beside the body of her son, who was on the migrant boat that capsized off the coast of Rasheed on September 21, 2016."

The photo is too dramatic for the front page, so we decided to publish it on the website. It is a very good photo. It shows the grieving but it would have been too dramatic for the front cover.

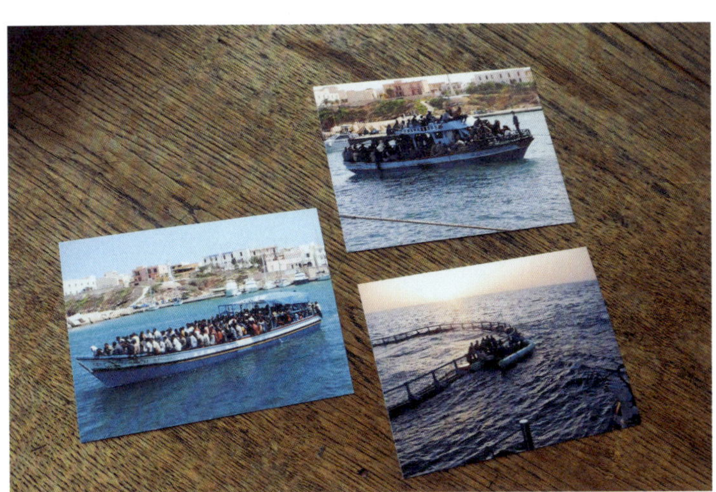

←   (The Migrant Image Research Group shows Mustafa some images from Lampedusa from the Red Cross folder) These pictures are ordinary. They are not catchy enough to be published—they don't have any action.

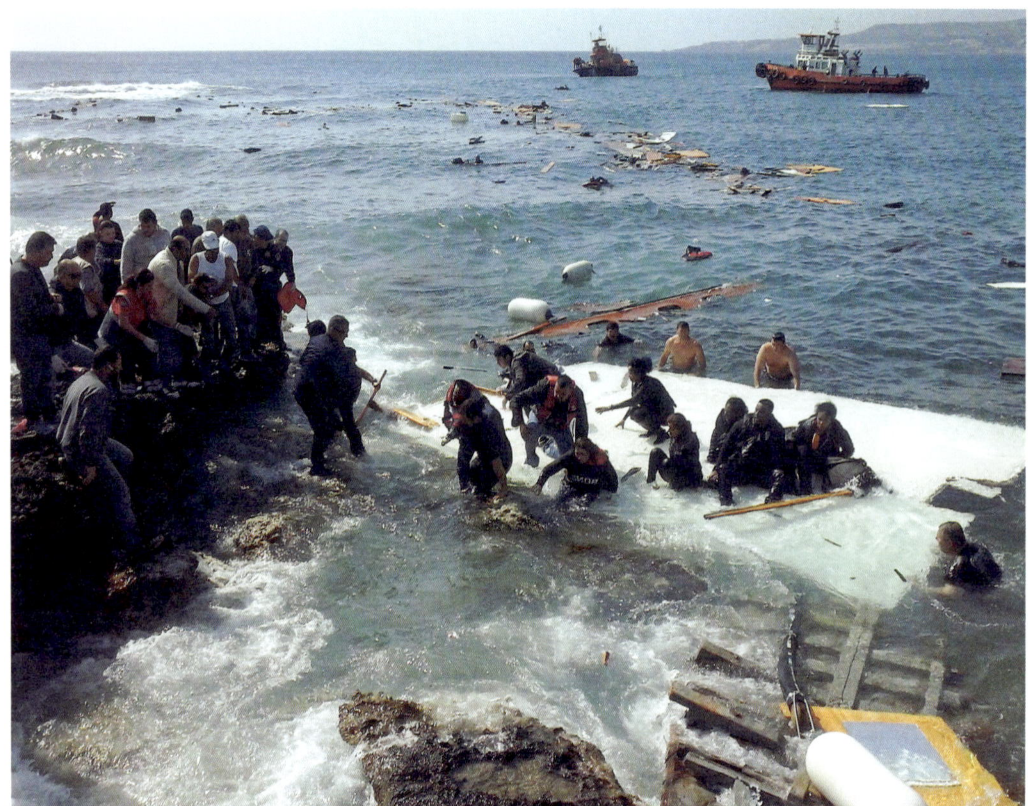

↑ (Mustafa shows the website of *Al-Ahram Weekly*)
Some time ago we published images reporting on illegal migration. We find all these published images on Google on the topic of illegal migration. This image has action. It is dramatic.

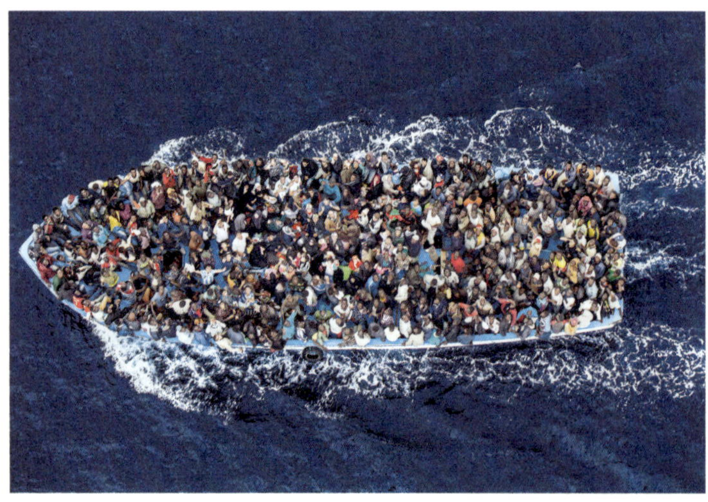

← This one is unique because it has no action at all. However, the boat didn't sink and it shows the people on the boat. It is an iconic photo.

MIGRANT IMAGES

BY EMILIE JOSSO

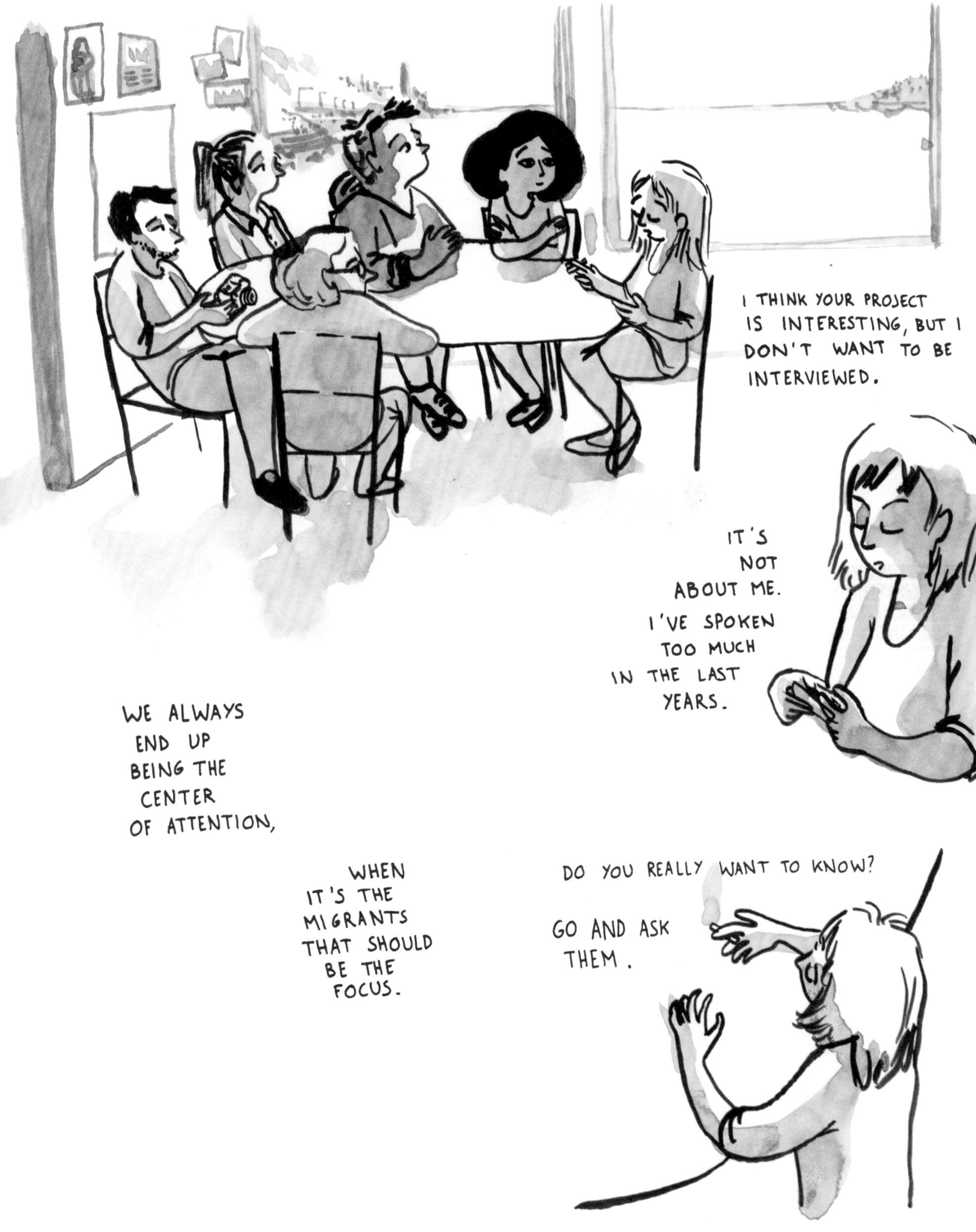

I THINK YOUR PROJECT IS INTERESTING, BUT I DON'T WANT TO BE INTERVIEWED.

IT'S NOT ABOUT ME. I'VE SPOKEN TOO MUCH IN THE LAST YEARS.

WE ALWAYS END UP BEING THE CENTER OF ATTENTION,

WHEN IT'S THE MIGRANTS THAT SHOULD BE THE FOCUS.

DO YOU REALLY WANT TO KNOW?

GO AND ASK THEM.

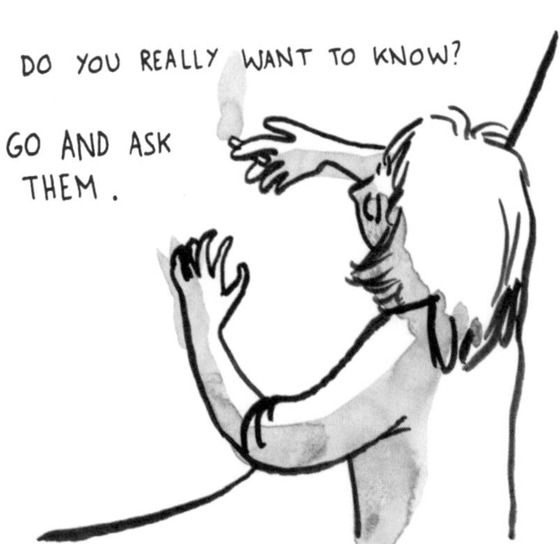

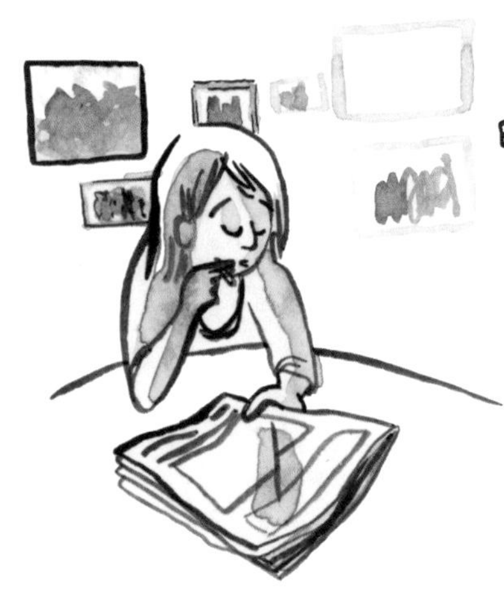

BUT I ADMIT
THAT THIS ANALYSIS
OF THE USE OF
PHOTOGRAPHY
IN THE MEDIA IS
VERY INTERESTING.

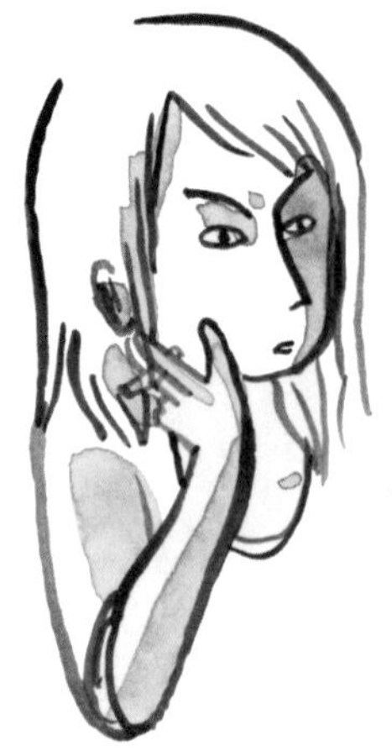

YOU KNOW,
SOME PEOPLE
REALLY KNOW
ABOUT IMAGES...

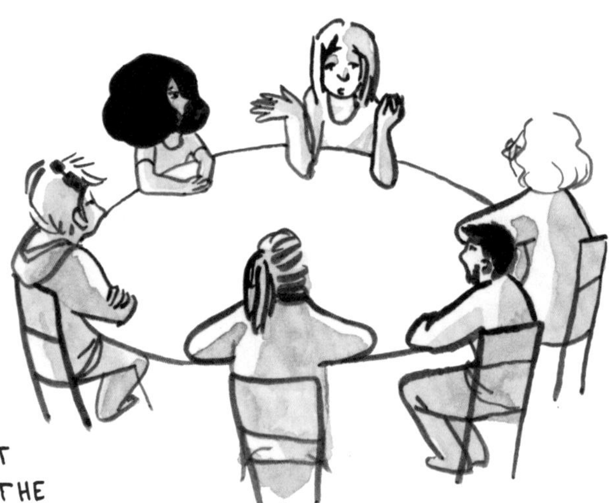

WE UNDERSTAND
PEOPLE'S MINDS
AND EMOTIONS

AND CURRENT
TRENDS ON THE
ONE HAND,

AND IMAGES
ON THE
OTHER.

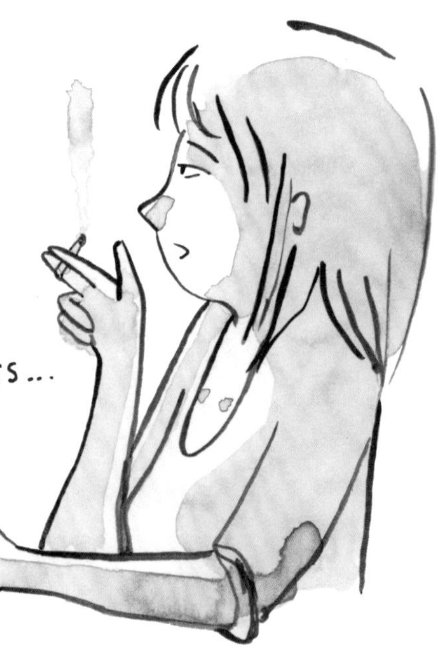

I AM OBVIOUSLY
TALKING ABOUT
ADVERTISEMENTS...

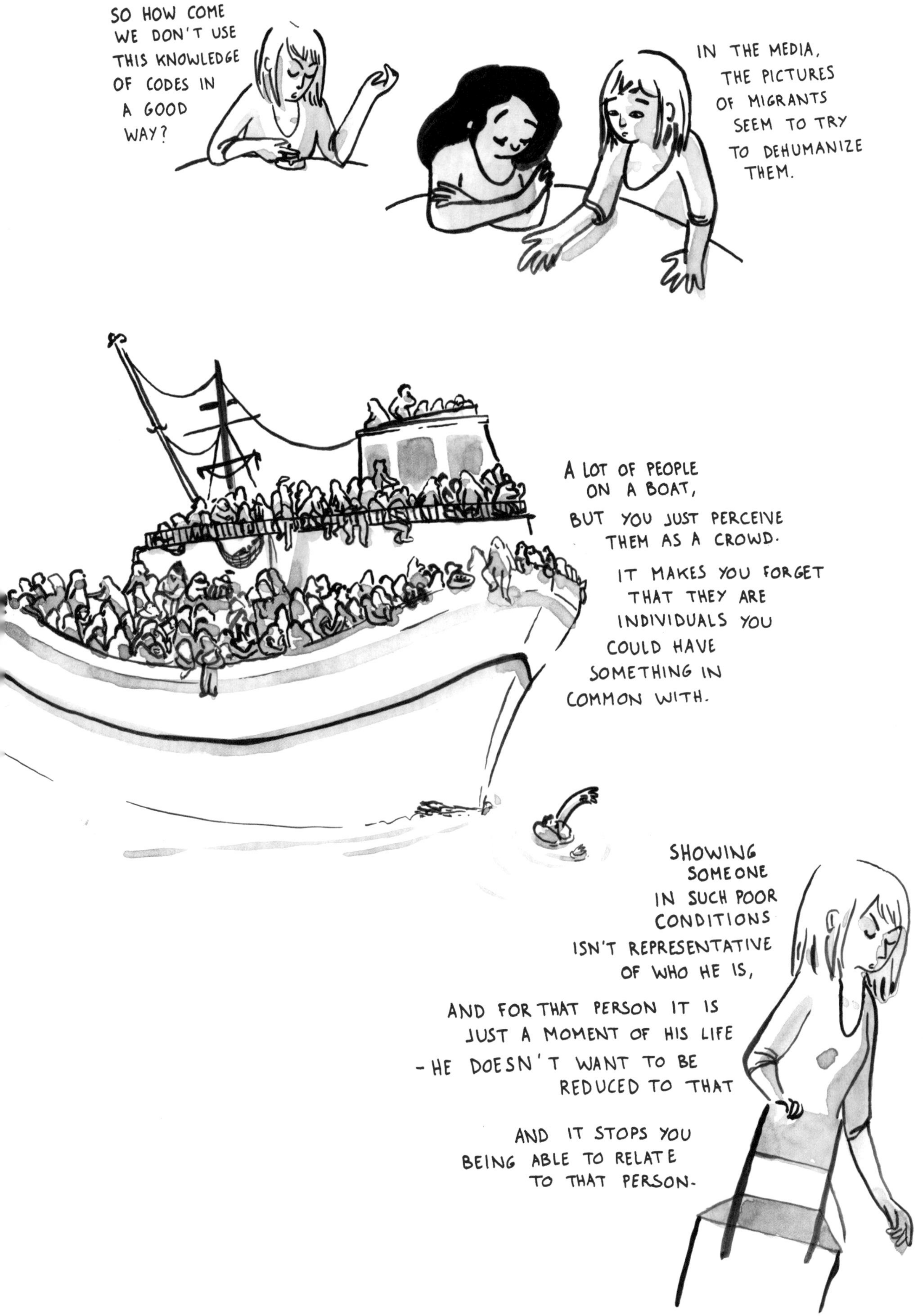

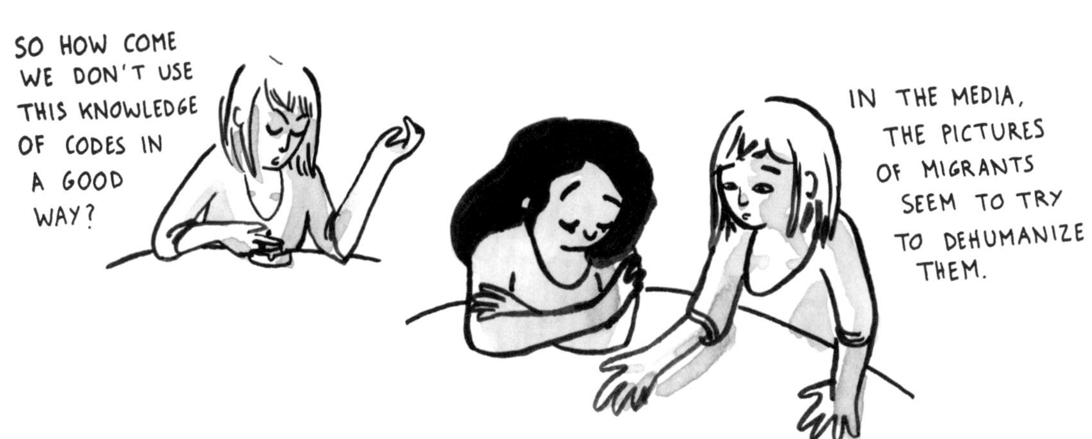

SO HOW COME WE DON'T USE THIS KNOWLEDGE OF CODES IN A GOOD WAY?
IN THE MEDIA, THE PICTURES OF MIGRANTS SEEM TO TRY TO DEHUMANIZE THEM.

A LOT OF PEOPLE ON A BOAT, BUT YOU JUST PERCEIVE THEM AS A CROWD.
IT MAKES YOU FORGET THAT THEY ARE INDIVIDUALS YOU COULD HAVE SOMETHING IN COMMON WITH.
SHOWING SOMEONE IN SUCH POOR CONDITIONS ISN'T REPRESENTATIVE OF WHO HE IS,
AND FOR THAT PERSON IT IS JUST A MOMENT OF HIS LIFE - HE DOESN'T WANT TO BE REDUCED TO THAT
AND IT STOPS YOU BEING ABLE TO RELATE TO THAT PERSON.

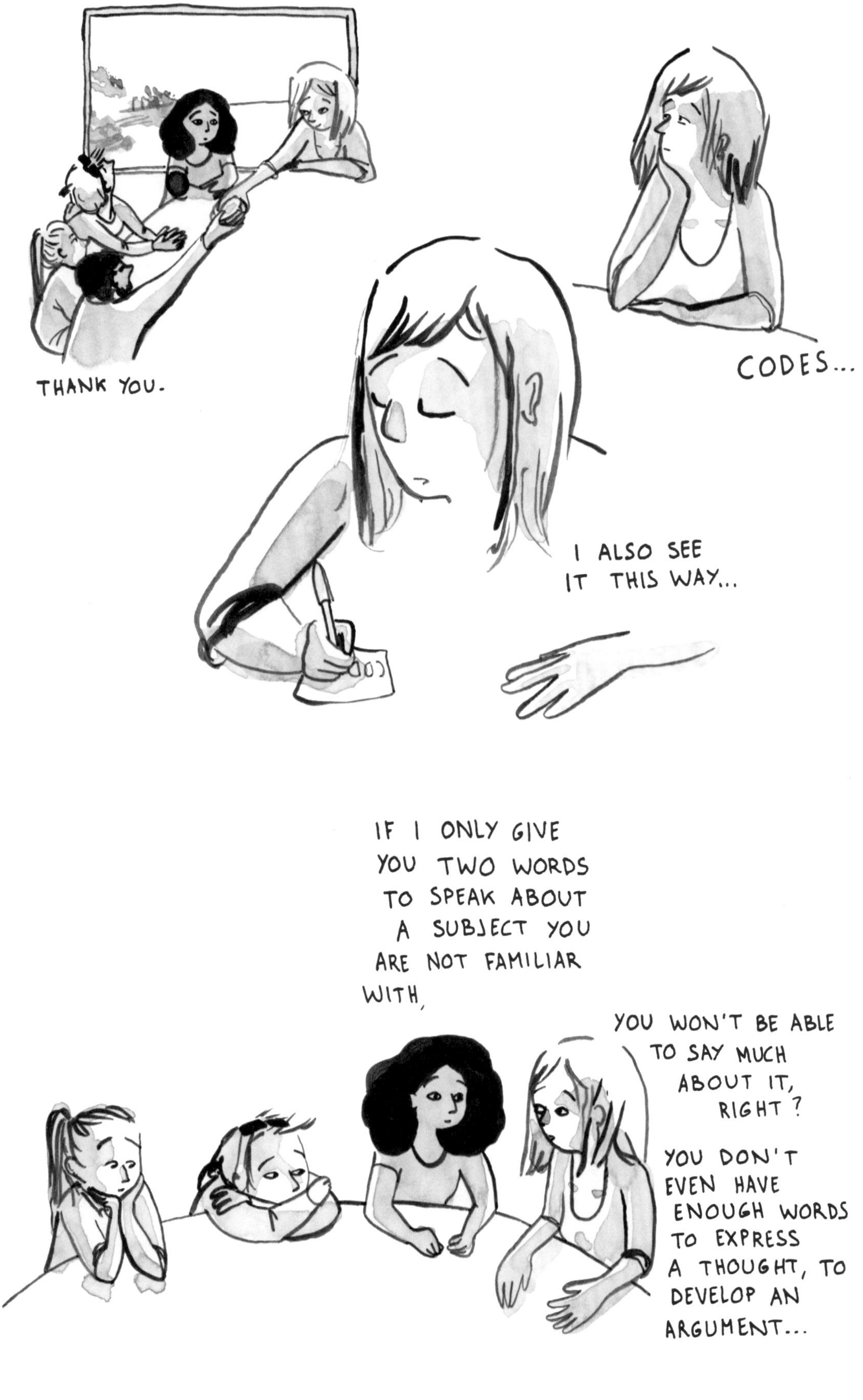

THANK YOU.

CODES...

I ALSO SEE
IT THIS WAY...

IF I ONLY GIVE
YOU TWO WORDS
TO SPEAK ABOUT
A SUBJECT YOU
ARE NOT FAMILIAR
WITH,

YOU WON'T BE ABLE
TO SAY MUCH
ABOUT IT,
RIGHT?

YOU DON'T
EVEN HAVE
ENOUGH WORDS
TO EXPRESS
A THOUGHT, TO
DEVELOP AN
ARGUMENT...

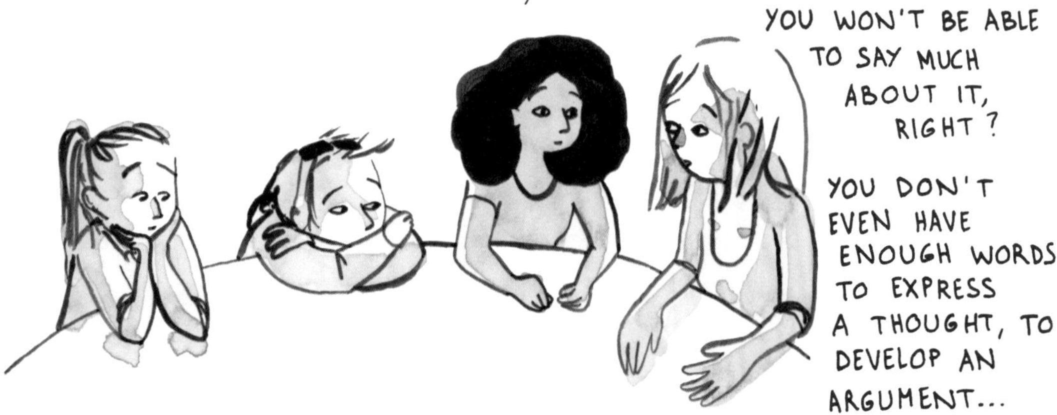

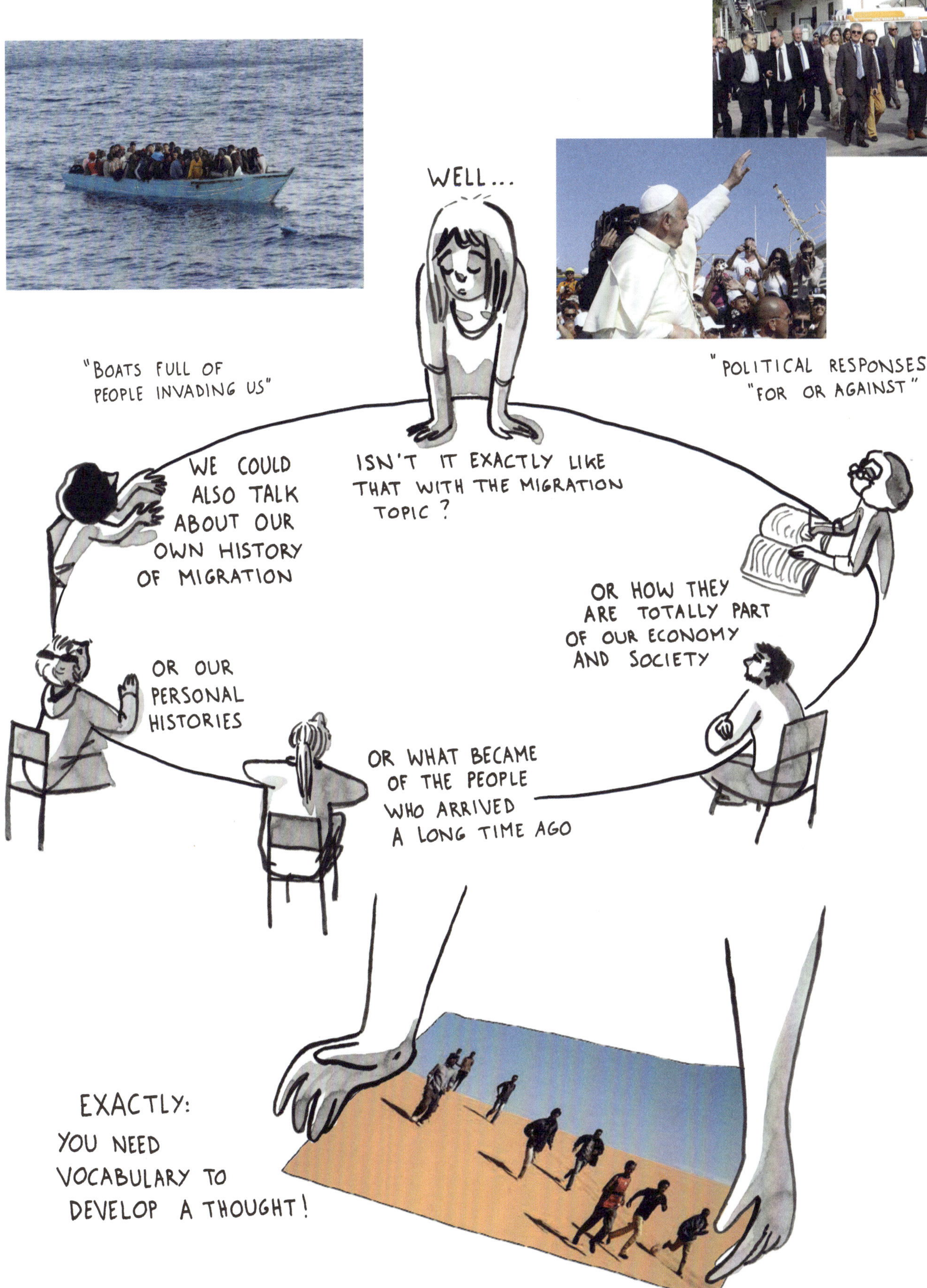

"BOATS FULL OF PEOPLE INVADING US"
WELL...
"POLITICAL RESPONSES"
"FOR OR AGAINST"
ISN'T IT EXACTLY LIKE THAT WITH THE MIGRATION TOPIC?
WE COULD ALSO TALK ABOUT OUR OWN HISTORY OF MIGRATION
OR HOW THEY ARE TOTALLY PART OF OUR ECONOMY AND SOCIETY
OR OUR PERSONAL HISTORIES
OR WHAT BECAME OF THE PEOPLE WHO ARRIVED A LONG TIME AGO
EXACTLY: YOU NEED VOCABULARY TO DEVELOP A THOUGHT!

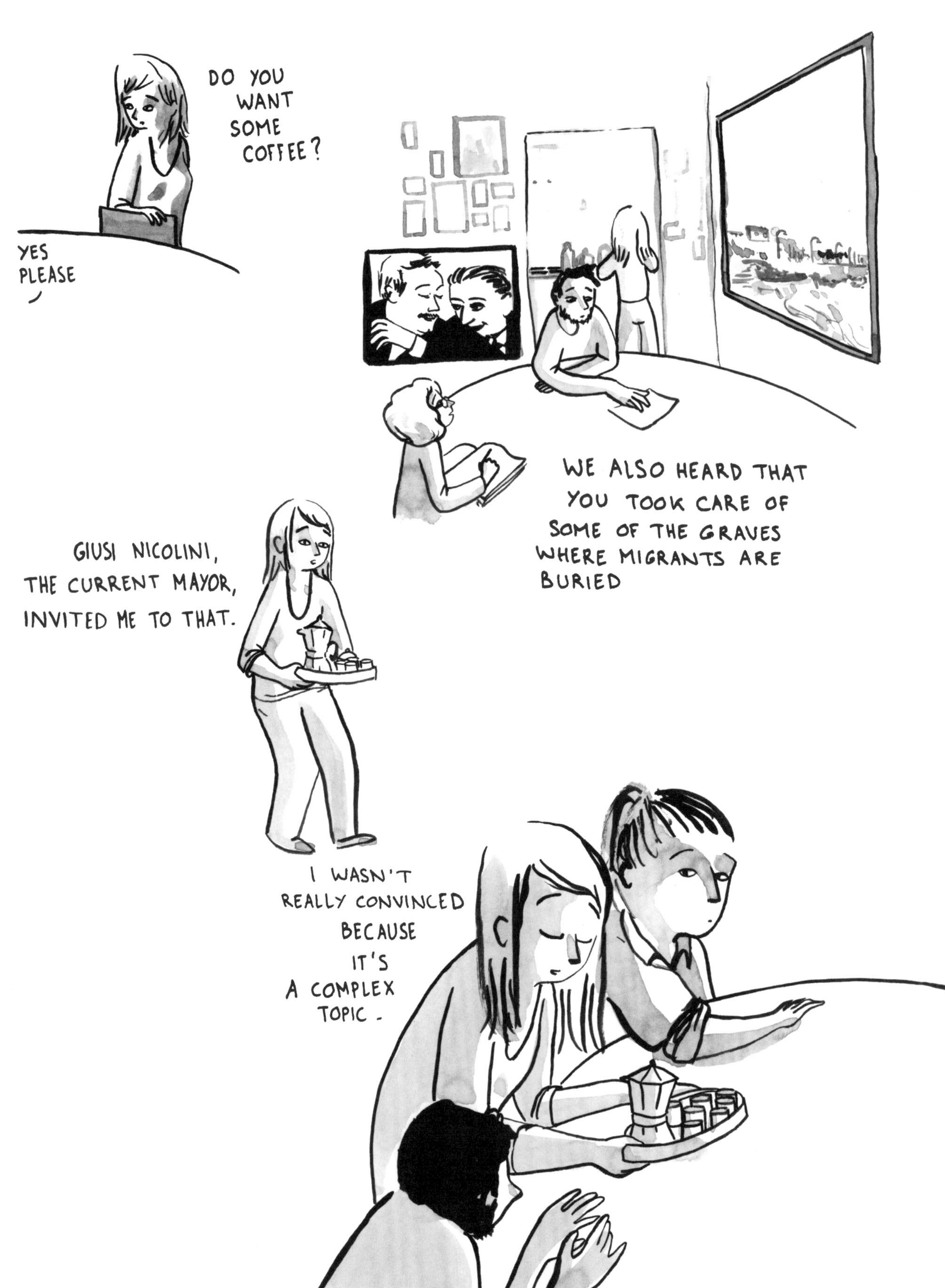

DO YOU WANT SOME COFFEE?
YES PLEASE
WE ALSO HEARD THAT YOU TOOK CARE OF SOME OF THE GRAVES WHERE MIGRANTS ARE BURIED
GIUSI NICOLINI, THE CURRENT MAYOR, INVITED ME TO THAT.
I WASN'T REALLY CONVINCED BECAUSE IT'S A COMPLEX TOPIC.

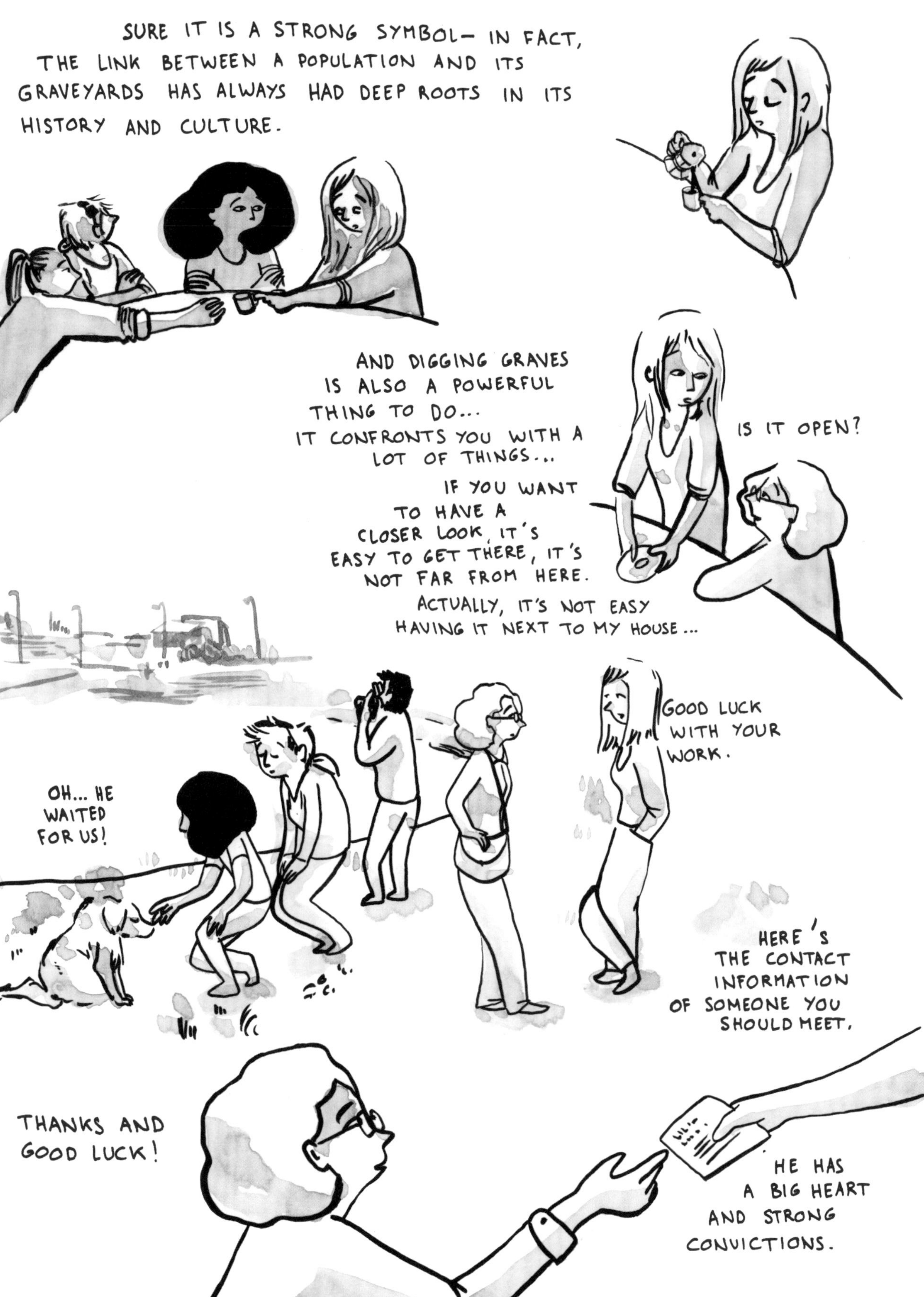

SURE IT IS A STRONG SYMBOL— IN FACT, THE LINK BETWEEN A POPULATION AND ITS GRAVEYARDS HAS ALWAYS HAD DEEP ROOTS IN ITS HISTORY AND CULTURE.
AND DIGGING GRAVES IS ALSO A POWERFUL THING TO DO...
IT CONFRONTS YOU WITH A LOT OF THINGS...
IF YOU WANT TO HAVE A CLOSER LOOK, IT'S EASY TO GET THERE, IT'S NOT FAR FROM HERE.
ACTUALLY, IT'S NOT EASY HAVING IT NEXT TO MY HOUSE...
IS IT OPEN?
GOOD LUCK WITH YOUR WORK.
OH... HE WAITED FOR US!
HERE'S THE CONTACT INFORMATION OF SOMEONE YOU SHOULD MEET,
THANKS AND GOOD LUCK!
HE HAS A BIG HEART AND STRONG CONVICTIONS.

Entering Two Words— "Immigrants" "Lampedusa"

Giovanna Calvenzi on the logic of searching for images and programmed layouts in newspapers

PHOTO STORY: ELISA CALORE

Giovanna Calvenzi started her career as a professional photo editor for *Amica*, a weekly fashion magazine, in 1985. Prior to that, she taught the history of photography on the professional course at the Società Umanitaria after taking a degree in literature. In 2013 the Migrant Image Research Group met her in her office in Milan, where she explained to us that at first she did not have a specific interest in photography. When the interview took place Giovanna Calvenzi was working as a image consultant for San Paolo periodicals. In January 2016 she started a new job at *Donna Moderna*. The interview was conducted by Elisa Calore and Valeria Malito.

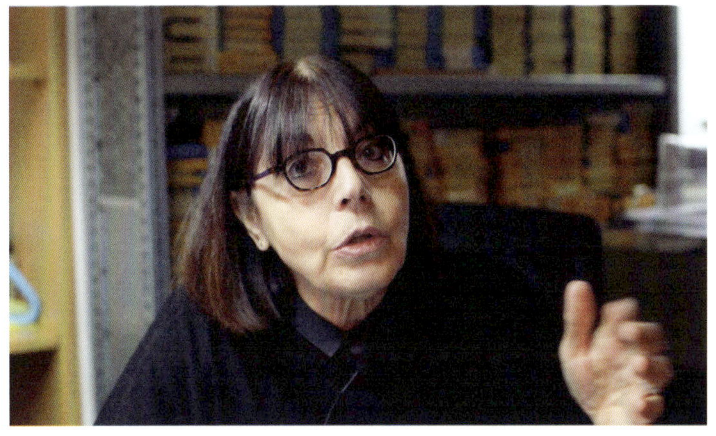

Q: How did you get into photography, even though you were not interested in it at first?

CALVENZI: While I was at college, I worked as an assistant for three different photographers. When I submitted my CV to teach at the Umanitaria, they thought I knew something about photography. They hired me and I spent the whole summer getting ready to teach. Then *Amica* called me, and I began to write and work as a photo editor. I have done photo editing for many periodicals: *Amica, Max, Sette, Vanity Fair, Specchio, Sportweek,* a supplement of *Gazzetta dello Sport*… Now I am an image consultant for the San Paolo periodicals group. Being a photo editor means concentrating on the visualization of news, creating the image of the periodical in agreement with the editor and the art director, producing shoots or coordinating research to find shoots that have already been done. So, in substance, the photo editor is the person who takes care of all the photographs that appear in a newspaper or magazine.

Q: Have you ever worked on the topic of migration?
CALVENZI: In my area of personal interest, I concentrate on the history of contemporary photography. I work on exhibitions and books, and I did see and monitor this type of issue. In the publications I work for today, this is a theme that could easily fit into current events coverage. For this interview I looked at the main national agencies to see how the problem of immigration on Lampedusa and the arrivals and landings there have been approached over time. I decided to check with the European agencies—the English Reuters, French AFP, and Italian ANSA—entering two sets of words, "immigrants lampedusa" and "landings immigrants lampedusa," in Italian and English, because Getty, for example, is bilingual, while Reuters is only in English. Then I checked the production agency Contrasto. The photographs start from around 2003 and more or less continue until today. In ANSA there are also a few photos from 1996 and 1998, which are scanned.

I think the first large-scale landings were in 1996, because almost all of them include 1996 in the image data, so that must have been a truly important year. The number of photographs varies, as does their quality, depending on whether you submit "landing" or "immigrants." If you key in "landing" in Reuters you get 85 photos, while if you key in "immigrants" you get 341. They range from 2002 to 2012, with a few in 1998. The numbers are pretty close: AFP has 1,447, Getty has a few more.

Let's start with Reuters. In the case of the online agencies, the fundamental thing, though it might seem banal, is to decide what you are looking for. Reuters is an English site and you can search it only in English. So if we write only "Lampedusa," we also get a lot of tourist-type images, which in our case are not of interest. To avoid such results, we input "landing lampedusa."

Q: Do magazines have an annual subscription?
CALVENZI: Depending on the publication. All the Italian daily newspapers subscribe to ANSA, Reuters, and AFP, and they can have subscriptions with other agencies, known as contracts. Actually the agencies upload their entire worldwide output on the server of the newspaper every day, and the newspaper selects what to publish.

Q: What about the texts that accompany the photos?
CALVENZI: The texts are inserted by the agency, and they have to work for an international audience, so they are very concise, very objective, and they should contain all the fundamental information.

Q: Can we have a look at the French AFP production?
CALVENZI: Getty is an Italian distributor that represents the French national agency AFP in Italy. I put in "AFP" as a keyword to see how the French have analyzed the problem.

Q: Is the information provided by the agencies similar?
CALVENZI: All the agencies offer the same type of information. They always put the name of the photographer and the name of the agency. Thanks to digital cameras, we are also able to discover other information, like the type of camera, the exposure times, the stops … To read the information, I have to download the picture, open it with Photoshop, and check the info file.

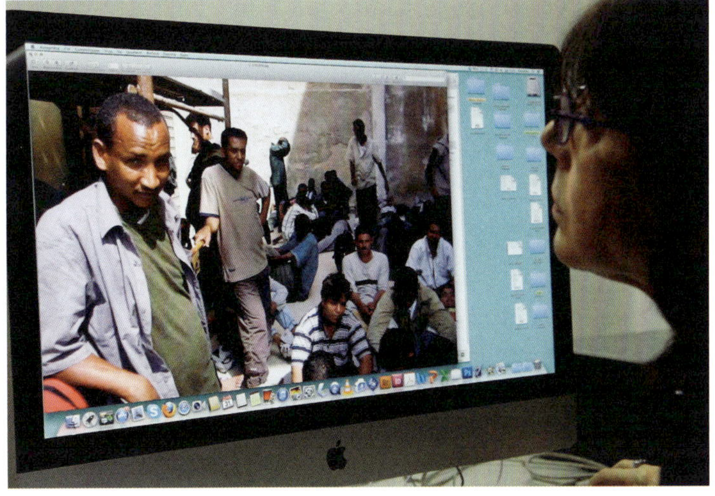

← In this case, we read that it is an AFP photo, with a number, that it was done by staff, and in this case there is the name "Franco Lannino." If it was done by a member of the staff, it is one of the photographers who works in-house. The photo was shot on March 2, 2009, simultaneously downloaded, and modified. We also find the camera info, number of pixels, and initial resolution.

One interesting thing is to look at Contrasto, an Italian agency for production and distribution. It distributes in Italy for Magnum and other agencies, German, Swedish, Danish, etc. If you search just in Italian, you find only Contrasto because in Italy Reuters and Getty are mainly distributors. We put "Lampedusa" … The logic of searching images is to know more or less what each individual agency has, because it helps you to choose the search terms. At Contrasto, the photographers are mostly photojournalists, so you do not need to write "migrants"; "Lampedusa" is enough and you get 791 image results. I haven't signed in, I am entering the site as a normal citizen, without a password. There are 212 photographs, and you can see the names of the photographers. Salvatore Esposito is the one who did the whole first part of the work, the pictures from April 2011. Then comes Emiliano Mancuso, and then Francesco Cocco continues.

Q: At Contrasto, the photographs seem almost more "artistic," in black and white ... They look really different.
CALVENZI: There is a substantial difference in the concept of the international agencies. Reuters is an agency with a high level of quality, while ANSA for many years documented events, although on an aesthetic level they didn't take the same kind of care. This can be seen more clearly, perhaps, in the case of a theme like soccer. In Italy, soccer is photographed in a very simple way: capturing the play, isolating one figure. In English photography, soccer is a social phenomenon: you see the fans, the field—there are very interesting areas where photographers can work ... The photographers who work for ANSA, Reuters, or AFP have to work for the whole world, because these agencies are big commercial containers, and even when their photojournalism is socially engaged, they have to sell worldwide ... As for the style of Contrasto, let's call it "linguistic excess," though this is not really the right term. Their photographs can appeal to a certain audience, but not to everyone. The theme of language is very complex. If we want, there is a definition by Walker Evans, which even dates back to the 1930s. The documentary language is the one the photographer uses, taking a stance of empathy with respect to reality, but without any stylistic intervention. If you remember Walker Evans's way of working, it has a sense of the most absolute objectivity, obviously using that term with all kinds of reservations. Whatever his subject was, he just stood in front of it without trying to create formal balances. He stood there with a large-format camera, absolutely still.

In the language of photojournalism, from the 1970s on, we have seen the presence of the photographer, and his declaration of intent, become an almost everyday phenomenon. Just consider two photographers from the 1950s, Henri Cartier-Bresson and William Klein. Cartier-Bresson is intentionally objective, and I insist on this term, which is a convention in photography, because objectivity does not exist in photography. In any case, he put himself in such a position that the subject he photographed was not aware of his presence, so he did not interact with the reality he was photographing.

During the same period, William Klein interacted extensively with the reality he photographed, so if he came into this room and took our picture, he would do it with a wide-angle, coming closer and we would have to react to his presence. Cartier-Bresson's narrative is the hardest, because you have to reach great heights of composition and graphic expertise, you have to make a perfect study of the use of the light ... The language of photojournalism starting from the 1970s has been enriched with all these components that have to be skillfully utilized, because photos have to be sellable.

Q: What kind of relationship do the photographers have

with the agencies? Do they sign yearly contracts? Or are the photographers contracted job by job?

CALVENZI: There are very different situations, case by case. We should say that in 2013 the situation is evolving, but previously there were agencies like Grazia Neri, or like the old Contrasto structure, that had photographers who had a totally exclusive relationship with the agency. Those who worked with Contrasto or Grazia Neri gave the agency a percentage and, at the same time, the agency produced their features, paying expenses up front and, above all, making the contacts with the periodicals, in order to have guaranteed minimums, to have certainty of publication in advance of the work. Then Grazia Neri closed, after having been one of the most important agencies for years; this agency helped to create the photography market, and the rules of the game for the photography publishing market.

Contrasto has also started to break the structure down, so it has photographers who are independent, who can work freelance on their own and also work for Contrasto. They can have clients with whom they nurture ongoing relationships managed on their own. Or there are situations in which a newspaper needs something and calls Contrasto, which then contacts the photographer and has the assignment done. There are photographers who are only distributed, which is true for Contrasto and for an agency formed after Grazia Neri, called LUZ. In short, the market has broken up, after being practically run by those two. I'm talking about photojournalism—gossip is something different: it has its own very particular rules and there are agencies that specialize in this sector ...

Q: Can you explain to us how you read photos?

CALVENZI: Being a professional, I instinctively think with the mind of the newspaper or magazine I am working for at the moment. So right now, working for Gruppo San Paolo, the idea is always to be on the side of the persons photographed, to have an ethical level that comes to the fore, without sensationalism.

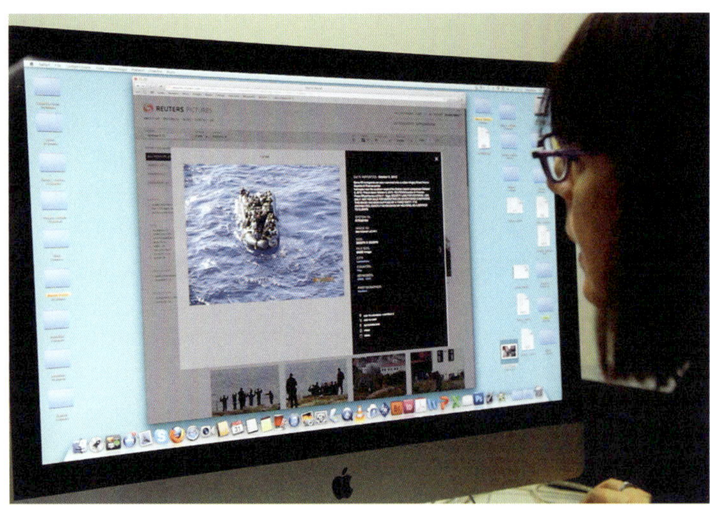

← This is a type of image that is often seen, which works for everything and everybody. It is a type of photography that always works, because it sums up the whole situation. There is everything here, so this is a photograph that I would download, in any case, and definitely use. On the other hand, if you worked for *Panorama* or *Espresso*, certain aesthetics and visual forms of sensationalism are obligatory.

↓ I'm thinking of photographs like this one here, where there is a gesture …

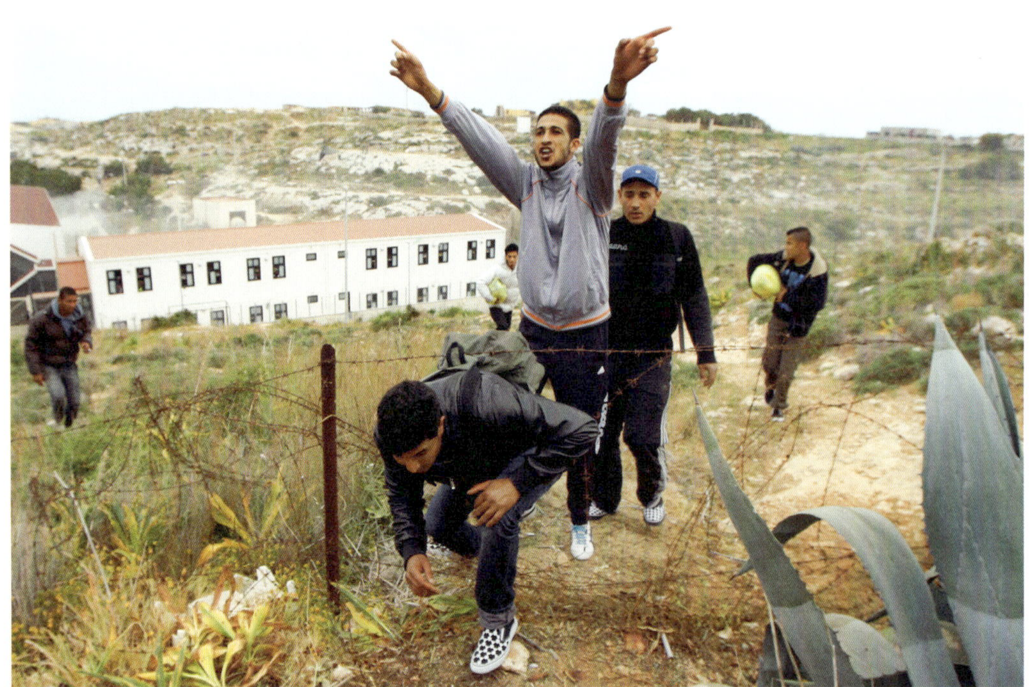

Q: *In your view, why is there no focus on the figure of the photo editor in daily newspapers?*
CALVENZI: It just doesn't exist. The normal practice is for the journalist to choose the image to go with his or her piece. Already, this idea of "going with" says a lot, because the text has to stand on its own; it is not supposed to need photographs. I can only talk about the *Corriere*, which is the only newspaper I know from the inside—there are already programmed layouts. Sometimes the person in charge of the page puts in the photographs, sometimes the journalists do it themselves, but if you have a fantastic photograph that is horizontal, and they

have left you a vertical space, it is going to get cropped …
in other words, there is no culture of photography, no
respect for it.

   Q: Yes, it is almost a question of filling in a diagram …

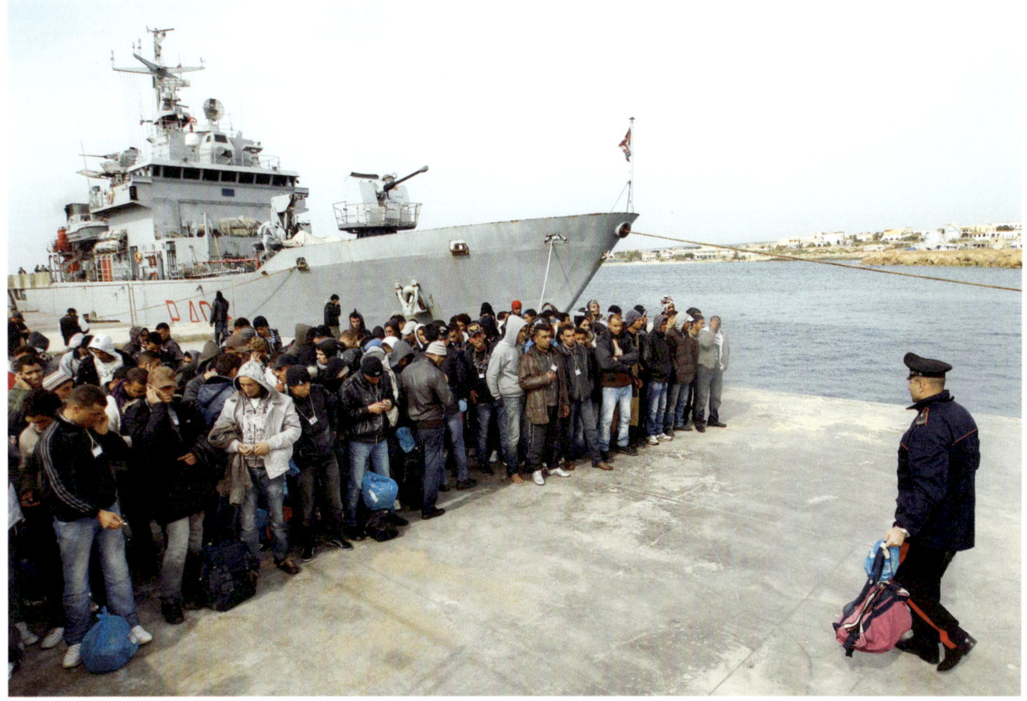

↑   CALVENZI: This one, for example, might interest me …
This has characteristics everyone can interpret as they please.
In any case, there is this sensation of waiting, of hope, you
might say, though it is not particularly dramatic: this guy is
making a phone call and the Carabiniere has picked up the
backpacks of the people who had lost them and is bringing
them to their owners. So it is a situation, almost, from everyday
life, a bit sad but not particularly desperate.

   *Q: Logically, depending on the way the picture is cropped,
you could eliminate parts and it would change the interpretation of what is happening in the image …*

CALVENZI: In photojournalism, the most correct way to
proceed is to crop nothing. I always try to respect the work.

   Q: No exploitation of images for other purposes …

CALVENZI: Now I want to see if we can get into ANSA …
"immigrati lampedusa." This is the leading Italian agency, the
one that covers all social phenomena. Their website is a bit
complicated—it always has been—but that is because they
do not rely on online searches, but only on subscriptions. Just
look at the difference between the Reuters page and the
ANSA page. You can immediately see the different approach:
simpler images, they don't have the same quality as those of
Reuters, unfortunately.

Q: Can we see an example from the Magnum agency?
CALVENZI: Yes, it's an interesting case because this is a cooperative agency where the photographers are members. It has been in existence since 1946 and continues to work in the same way. If I enter the search term "lampedusa," let's see what happens. Well, there's a project from 2011. This is the whole feature done by Patrick Zachmann. Maybe because it was at night, these are also more dramatic shots. When you look at this photo, you can sense the suffering of arriving in a country that is not your country, not knowing what will become of you. You don't know if they will accept you; maybe you haven't had anything to eat for a week. These things are narrated here, and not in other images, and that depends on the skill of the photographers. The approach is always less like newspapers, more for magazines, more narrative, more in-depth. Magnum has this characteristic of always having defended what was called engaged photojournalism: namely photojournalism where it is the photographer who chooses.

Q: They are more "authorial" …
CALVENZI: The concept of "authorialism" is a neologism that I don't like … To become a member of Magnum, you have to demonstrate to the other members of the cooperative that you have the necessary formal and qualitative journalistic characteristics. They want to know that you are capable of narrating, effectively and forcefully, the story you set out to tell.

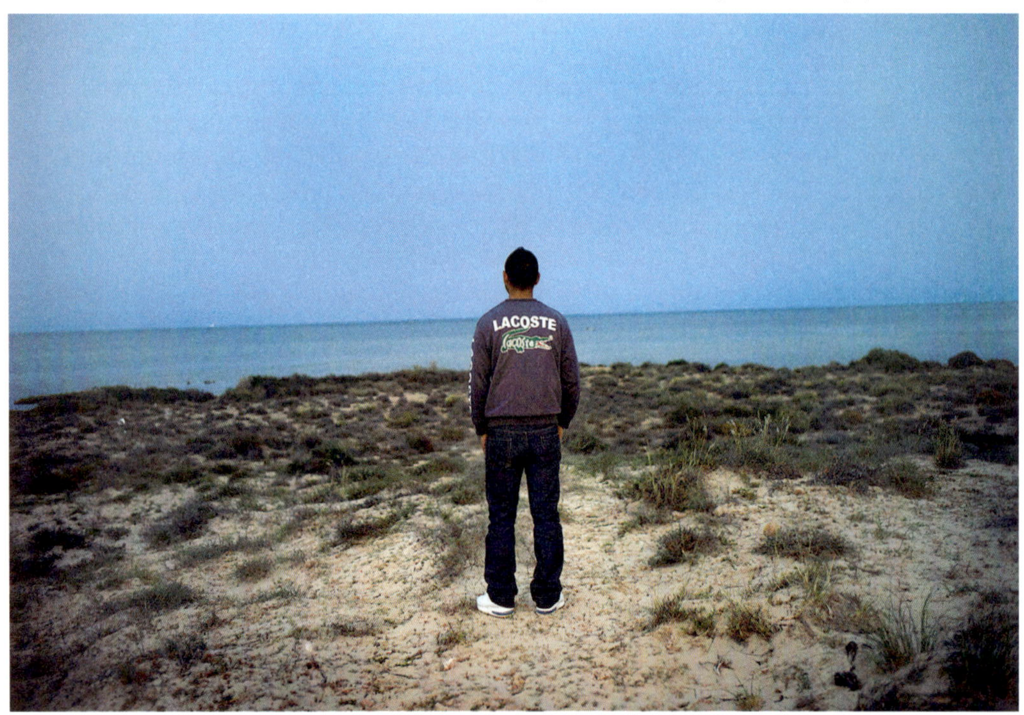

↑   Here, for example, one of the substantial differences can be seen in the work of Patrick Zachmann. Zachmann is in Tunisia together with this young man of nineteen, who is waiting for a boat that will take him to Lampedusa. Then Zachmann follows the young man to Lampedusa. A photographer from a traditional agency would be there, on Lampedusa, only when the boat arrives, and only if there were victims or a clash with the police ... Zachmann is narrating a human story, the dramatic story of a young man who leaves Tunisia for Lampedusa. So it is a very different conception of journalism, a considered and committed narrative, instead of just a documentation of the event.

Q: Do you think it is possible to speak about trends?
CALVENZI: Absolutely. You do notice that there are recurring themes, almost always in the area of photojournalism. There was the year of the gypsies, then the year of the East, the year of the bombs ... There was the moment of Syria, of Gaza, of Mali ... Or just look at the Arab Spring last year. Everyone went to see the Arab Spring.

Q: I read somewhere that now there is the problem that all the journalists and photographers are freelance.
CALVENZI: But, at least in Italy, there are no longer any employee photographers. For example, Paolo Pellegrini is insured by the magazine when he travels, though he is still not an employee but an independent photographer. Many American publications still have a lot of in-house photographers, hired employees, but computers and the Internet have changed the way people work. I believe that your discourse on photography is very important because it preserves a whole series of things that would otherwise vanish. I also think that this speed, this ease of access, is creating an entire realm of useless photography, but opportunities do still exist for great photography, real photography, for those who work with integrity. I am convinced that we are living through a period of great interest, because all these different types of expression can coexist.

LOCAL PERSPECTIVE, GLOBAL VISION

DAILY SABAH

WEDNESDAY
OCTOBER 5 / 2016
TL 3.00

www.dailysabah.com

Turkey offers lifeline to freed Syrian town of Jarablus as new aid trucks arrive

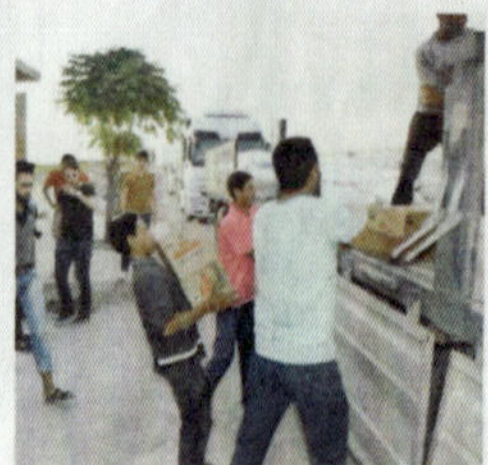

The people of the northern Syrian town of Jarablus have been given a helping hand by Turkey's governmental and non-governmental organizations (NGOs), which continue to deliver humanitarian aid trucks arriving in the reawakening town

YUNUS PAKSOY – JARABLUS, SYRIA

▶▶ **AS DAILY** life in the northern Syrian town of Jarablus returns to normal after the Turkey-backed Free Syrian Army (FSA) liberated the town from Daish terrorists in Operation Euphrates Shield, the government and non-governmental organizations (NGOs) continue to deliver humanitarian aid to the people of Jarablus. Daily Sabah traveled to the town in northern Syria to learn more about developments in the region. On Monday the Justice and Development Party (AK Party) youth branch brought two trucks of humanitarian aid to Jarablus being the "voice of the oppressed in Syria." Tens of thousands of people fled Jarablus two to three years ago because of Daish terror and many adults had feared they too would be in danger if Daish were to seize their town. In addition, hundreds of teenagers also fled the town as they faced forceful recruitment as child soldiers. Even though tens of thousands of people used to live in the northern Syrian town, the Daish siege of the area brought a sharp decline in the population. Prior to the launching of Operation Euphrates Shield on Aug. 24, only 1,500 people still lived in Jarablus. *PAGE 9*

MOSCOW HALTS PLUTONIUM PACT, U.S. SUSPENDS SYRIA TALKS *PAGE 10*   ASSAD FORCES DESTROY A MAJOR HOSPITAL IN ALEPPO *PAGE 10*

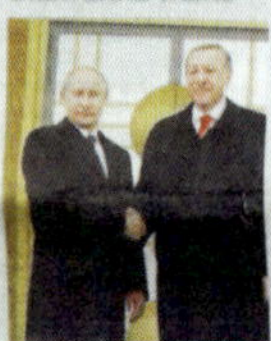

ERDOĞAN, PUTIN TO MEET IN ISTANBUL

RUSSIAN President Putin will meet President Erdoğan on Öct. 10 for the first time in Istanbul since the jet downing crisis. The Russian leader's visit is expected to focus on several issues such as the Turkish Stream and lifting some restrictions *PAGE 8*

PEGIDA protest signals polarization in Germany

THE LATEST protests by xenophobic PEGIDA in the German city of Dresden against Chancellor Angela Merkel during the Unity Day on Monday exhibited polarization within the German society as anti-immigrant and anti-Muslim sentiments have been on the rise. *PAGE 11*

7,000 foreign fighters left for Syria, Iraq since 2013

ACCORDING to a report released by the Paris-based Center for the Analysis of Terror, nearly 7,000 foreign fighters from Europe have joined terror groups in Syria and Iraq since 2013. Nearly 70 percent of those terrorist fighters come from either France, the U.K., or Germany. *PAGE 9*

WEATHER IN ISTANBUL

| WEDNESDAY | Partly Sunny | | 26/18 |
| FRIDAY | Sunny | | 24/15 |

WEATHER IN ANKARA

| WEDNESDAY | Partly Sunny | | 20/07 |
| FRIDAY | Sunny | | 22/01 |

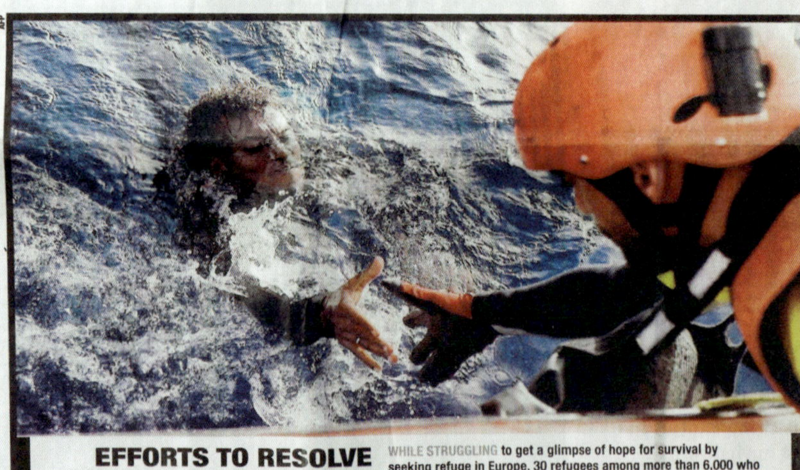

EFFORTS TO RESOLVE REFUGEE CRISIS SINK IN MEDITERRANEAN AGAIN

WHILE STRUGGLING to get a glimpse of hope for survival by seeking refuge in Europe, 30 refugees among more than 6,000 who tried to reach Europe on about 40 boats were found dead off the Libyan coast on Monday, one of the highest numbers in a single day, Libyan and Italian officials said. *PAGE 10*

Growth takes hit, expected to pick up pace in 2017

▶▶ **THE 2016** growth expectation has been revised to 3.2 percent, having been initially announced as 4.5 percent, Prime Minister Binali Yıldırım said in a press conference in which he announced the new Medium-Term Economic Program for the period of 2017-2019 yesterday in Ankara. Yıldırım pointed out that that this figure was twice as much as the world average. The prime minister noted that 3 or 4 percent growth rates would not be their aim "as global problems affect the Turkish economy as well." "We will increase our growth rates in the 2017-2019 term. This is our essential target," Yıldırım added. This year's forecast for inflation remained unchanged at 7.5 percent, whereas Yıldırım said that the expectation for 2017 is 6.5 percent and for 2018 is 5 percent. *PAGE 5*

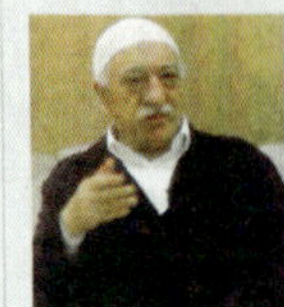

Justice minister: Coup plotter Gülen searching for new safe haven

▶▶ **JUSTICE** Minister Bekir Bozdağ said yesterday in a press meeting that he has gained intelligence that members of the Gülenist Terror Group (FETÖ) are searching for a suitable country to shelter their leader, Fetullah Gülen, in. Speaking to journalists before the Justice and Development Party's (AKP) group meeting at the Turkish Grand National Assembly (TBMM), Bozdağ said Turkey sent a detention request to U.S. authorities expressing their concern that Gülen might possibly flee to another country, to which the U.S. replied that they will respond to the request as soon as possible. "We didn't receive any response yet. U.S. authorities have not requested new information and a file," Bozdağ said. *PAGE 8*

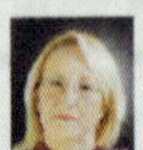

BERIL DEDEOĞLU

REFERENDUM IN COLOMBIA AND LESSONS FOR EUROPE

REFERENDUMS should not turn into instruments for violating universally accepted human rights and fundamental freedoms. *PAGE 13*

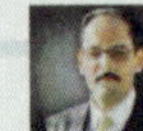

İBRAHIM KALIN

THE WEST FAILS TO UNDERSTAND THE COUP AND ITS AFTERMATH

MANY IN Europe and the U.S. continue to fail to understand the magnitude of what happened on that fateful night and what followed afterwards. *PAGE 12*

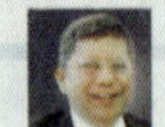

İLNUR ÇEVIK

US WANTS TO PROMOTE PYD, STALL TURKEY

TURKEY has told the U.S. over and over again that it does not want YPG personnel west of the Euphrates River in northern Syria. *PAGE 13*

Why This Photo?

Italian photo editor Renata Ferri on the process of selecting images for a reportage

PHOTO STORY: ELISA CALORE

Renata Ferri works as the editor-in-chief for *IO Donna*, the women's weekly magazine of *Corriere della Sera*, and for *Amica*, a monthly women's magazine published by RCS (Rizzoli—Corriere della Sera). Prior to this she was at Rizzoli, where she started in 2005, and for almost fifteen years she was production director at Contrasto, the biggest photo agency in Italy. The Migrant Image Research Group met her in her office in Milan in 2013. The interview was conducted by Elisa Calore and Valeria Malito.

Q: How would you define your position at RCS?
FERRI: First of all I've got a contract as a journalist and I am lucky enough to be editor-in-chief, which carries a certain weight because magazines tend to have a strong pyramid structure, with a clear hierarchy. Your position lets you assert your thinking or your image and allows you to participate in orchestrating the publication and its process of creation. When I arrived, the newspapers and their magazine supplements were very far behind, so I suddenly found myself having to manage an image that was, let's say, not essential. It needed to be reduced, simplified … The publishers still want a very simple, very direct, very clear image in terms of content, which in itself is not such a bad thing. The bad part is that, besides this, they want an image that is a bit complaisant, a little reassuring. These supplements, basically, were created in the years in which there was a lot of investment in print advertising. Especially in the 1990s, when women's magazines were started precisely with this aim of combining women's fashion and lifestyle coverage with more in-depth content on current events. Advertisers were willing to invest, so it was no longer the containers, like *Amica, Marie Claire*—i.e., the classic fashion monthlies—that had the publicity but also these supplements, with their function of mixing up different kinds of content: they were created with this mission. For images to exist in the same container, they had to be more attractive … like an implicit demand for images taken from reality, but with content and form we might call "designed" … conforming to certain geometric rules and governed by formal and stylistic constraints …

Q: Can you tell us about your experience as a photo editor dealing with images on the topic of migration to Lampedusa?

FERRI: When we decided to do a story on the island of Lampedusa, we looked for someone who was there, but in the meantime the first signs were appearing of what was to become the "Arab Spring." In just a few days, as it turned out, they had closed the CPT [temporary detention center], and there were no new migrants arriving. The boats were not coming, because the whole Arab coast was exploding, starting with Tunisia. In the end, I found a photographer, a reporter, called Massimo Di Nonno. I knew him: he is from Molise, but he has been living in Milan for a few years. I asked him, "What are you doing, you're the only one who stayed on in Lampedusa?" and he said, "I stayed here on purpose. Everyone left, after two days I was left alone on the island. I was just thinking about leaving myself." Because the revolution was breaking out over there, the boats were no longer operating, obviously. The migrant trade was having problems, armies, police, revolts, so everything had come to a halt. He told me, "I was just thinking, what am I doing here? The CPT is closed, there are no boats." I said: "Look, it seems that some boats are actually on their way, so let's see what we can do … precisely because everything is exploding over there, some people are escaping, and something will happen … What we want to do is not so much the story of migrants landing. I know it is hard, but we would like to try to meet one of them so that they can tell us how they left, when, why, what they were expecting from this voyage. It won't be the first time this has been done, but it will be the first time in a historical moment in which the situation is changing." The amazing thing about this encounter with the person we were looking for, whose name was Walid, aged twenty-five, was that we were able to photograph him in a rare moment, because we could not enter the immigration center, so we had to take our pictures outside. Massimo hit it off with him right away, and they started to converse.

Q: What about the text?

FERRI: We didn't have a journalist on the island; we had to send one. But from the moment he arrived to the moment he left, after entering the CPT, we lost track of him and we couldn't meet with him any more. So I asked Massimo not only to take the pictures but also to ask some questions. He recorded the conversation on his mobile phone, a sort of interview, asking the questions in French, and his new friend replied in his own language: his age, where he wanted to go, where his family was, etc. Then we transcribed the text and managed to obtain an image of Walid.

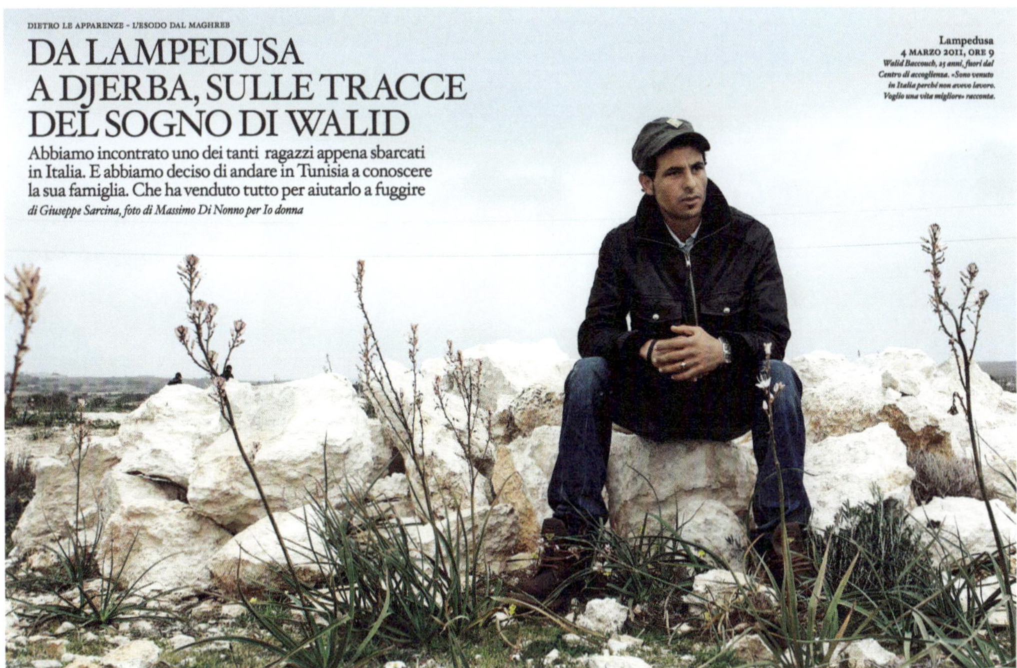

[*IO Donna*, March 19, 2011. Headline: From Lampedusa to Djerba, following the trail of Walid's dream. We met one of the guys who had recently landed in Italy. We decided to go to Tunisia to meet his family. They sold everything to help him escape. Caption: Lampedusa. March 4, 2011, 9 am: Walid, 25 years old, out from the immigration center. "I came to Italy because I have no job, I want a better life."]

↑   *Q: Why do you think your article was different from others on the same topic?*

FERRI: What we wanted to do was to move from this encounter on Lampedusa to what was happening in Tunisia to understand why he left his family just at the moment when there were all these suggestions of revolt and therefore of change. After a few days, Walid departed and Massimo went from Sicily to Tunisia to meet Walid's family, together with journalist Giuseppe Sarcina, a foreign correspondent for *Corriere della Sera.*

Q: Can we analyze the photographs of Walid?

FERRI: Yes, let's start by asking three simple questions.

1. Where there is no text, would these images be capable of telling a story on their own? Absolutely not! Where there is no text, no caption, they would narrate nothing.

2. Do they convey an emotion, apart from the context? Sure.

3. Is this an emotional image that raises questions? The only question is to understand where we are and what is happening.

But these are questions we ask when faced with any image that is not part of a project we know about, that has not been explained, that has no caption. A photograph is undoubtedly not exhaustive, but it has a role—in this case—of documentation and illustration, where the connection … well, this is a very felicitous case in which the text is very closely connected with each individual image—we might say they go hand in hand. The image of Walid corresponds to our questions and the answers he gave us in his little recording in Arabic.

La casa dei Baccouch è un "bunker
della povertà": tre piccole stanze per sette
persone, la cucina ridotta a un ripiano
con un fornelletto. "Facciamo fatica a pagare
l'affitto di 150 dinari (75 euro circa)" dicono

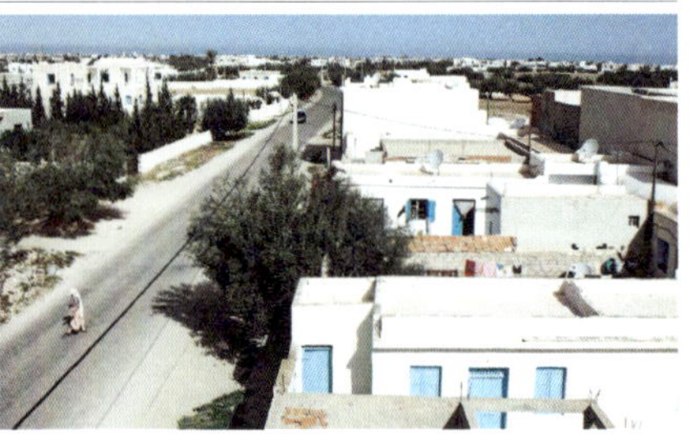

Djerba

In primo piano, la casa dei Baccouch, una costruzione tipica dell'isola: bassa, bianca, con porte e finestre colorate di azzurro. A poca distanza c'è la parte turistica dell'isola, con alberghi di lusso e ristoranti.

QUALCHE MAGLIETTA, due o tre paia di pantaloni, i calzini appallottolati. Il mobiletto di legno con i due cassetti lunghi e stretti contiene agevolmente tutto ciò che Walid Baccouch ha accumulato nei suoi primi 25 anni di vita a Djerba. La notte tra martedì 1 marzo e mercoledì 2 è salito sul barcone dei clandestini vestito al suo meglio: giubbotto nero in pelle, jeans, scarponcini di tela e braccialetto di cuoio. Ce l'ha fatta, o meglio: pensa di avercela fatta. Ora è a Lampedusa, dove ha incontrato il nostro fotoreporter a pochi metri da un buco nella recinzione del "Centro di primo soccorso e accoglienza". «Sto bene, sono venuto in Italia perché non avevo lavoro: voglio costruirmi una vita diversa e voglio aiutare la mia famiglia». Le sue parole, registrate venerdì 4 marzo, sono quanto di più personale e, nello stesso tempo, quanto di più universale si possa oggi ascoltare non solo a Djerba, ma a Gabes, Zarzis, Medenine, Tatouine, in tutti i villaggi e le cittadine della Tunisia meridionale, dove i ragazzi come Walid - siano essi manovali o ragionieri, contadini o esperti di computer - di fatto **non hanno alternative al "bar dei disoccupati"**: tre ore di "seduta" la mattina e tre ore il pomeriggio.

La famiglia di Walid abita a qualche chilometro da Houmt Souk, lo sperone di Djerba, un'isola circondata da un mare colorato con lo stesso smalto azzurro usato per le porte e le finestre delle case, basse e bianche. Se non fosse per i mobiletti, la stanza di Walid sarebbe

[Caption: March 6, 12 pm, Djerba. Low, white house, with window frames painted blue. The part of the island for tourists, with luxury hotels and restaurants, is nearby.]

"Che ci stava a fare mio nipote qui? A morire
di fame?" chiede la zia. "So che attraversare
il mare è pericoloso, ma qualcosa doveva
pur inventarsi. Ho messo insieme i risparmi
perché potesse pagarsi il passaggio sulla barca"

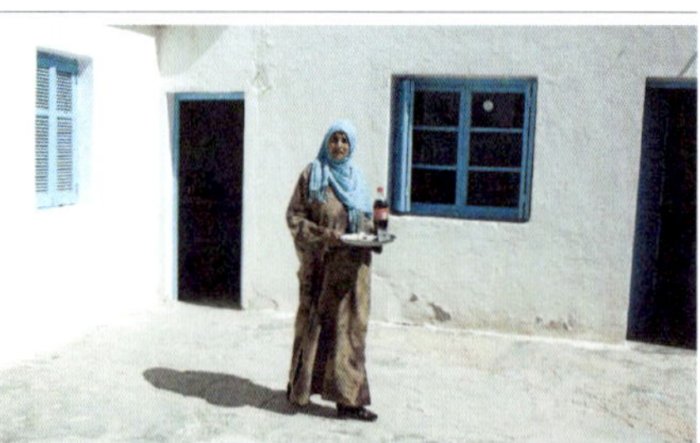

Djerba
6 MARZO 2011, ORE 12.30
Mabrouka Baccouch, 40 anni, zia di Walid, porta al giornalista e al fotografo ospiti una Coca Cola e qualche wafer. Li ha pagati 3 dinari, l'equivalente di una cena a base di cous-cous e fagiolini.

niente di più che una comoda cuccia: due sottili materassi sistemati per terra, una stuoia di lana grezza. Fine. Ma tutta la casa dei Baccouch è "un bunker della povertà", uno dei tanti disseminati in una delle regioni a più forte vocazione turistica. Al di qua del cancello (azzurro, naturalmente), tre piccole stanze vuote (per sette persone) si affacciano su un patio di una decina di metri quadrati, con i fili per la biancheria e una piattaforma scoscesa in cemento: è il pozzo per la raccolta dell'acqua piovana. La cucina si riduce a un ripiano con un fornelletto e una bombola a gas. Niente doccia, niente tv. Uno spazio per la preghiera musulmana. La pulizia è impressionante, l'ordine assoluto. È evidente che le donne passino la giornata a lavare, sfregare, rassettare.

Beshir Baccouch, 55 anni, **non si rade dal giorno in cui suo figlio è partito**. La moglie Aisha (47 anni) non è in casa e così nessuno degli altri 5 figli, salvo Najhla, 22 anni, testa bassa e mani sul velo. All'inizio non è neanche ammessa alla conversazione. Barche, immigrazione, Lampedusa: per i tunisini del Sud questa è una storia maschile, di giovani uomini, di predatori senza donne, senza una fidanzata, una moglie (la compagna è esclusa di ufficio).

I Baccouch sono in affitto: 150 dinari al mese (circa 75 euro). Poco? «Per noi è tanto, facciamo fatica a pagare» dice Mabrouka, la sorella di Beshir, accorsa a sostituire la cognata e a fare gli onori di casa. Sbuca dalla cucina con un vassoio: una bottiglia di Coca Cola, un piattino con qualche wafer. Costo: 3 dinari,

[Caption: March 6, 12.30 pm, Djerba. Mabrouka Baccouch, 40 years old, Walid's aunt, brings her guests, the journalist and the photographer, a Coca Cola and some wafers. This offering cost her 3 dinars, the price of a dinner of couscous and beans.]

La camera da letto ha soltanto due sottili
materassi sistemati per terra e una stuoia
di lana grezza. La pulizia e l'ordine sono assoluti:
è evidente che le donne trascorrano
la giornata a lavare, sfregare, rassettare

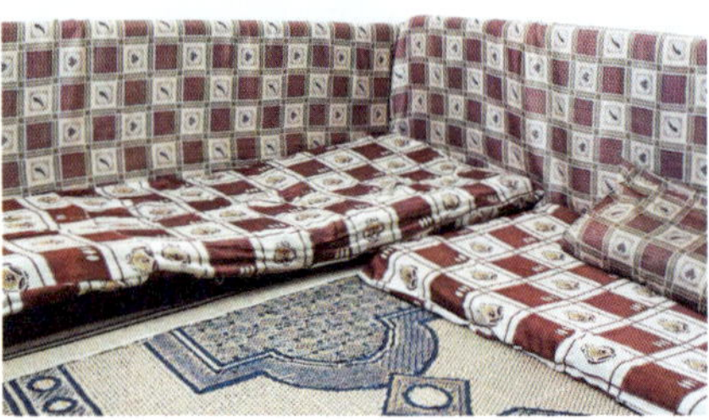

Djerba
6 MARZO 2011, ORE 13
Il letto che Walid ha lasciato. Ha cinque fratelli, ma il suo vero punto di riferimento è lo zio trentacinquenne, Taieb Baccouch: fa l'agente di viaggio e guadagna l'equivalente di 400 euro al mese.

l'equivalente di una cena a base di cous-cous e fagiolini. Forse per questo ci sono solo i bicchieri per gli ospiti. Beshir, il capofamiglia, intanto, sta raccontando la sua vita di muratore a cottimo, una sequela di lavoretti malpagati. Sempre incerti, precari come gli ultimi incisivi che gli restano in bocca.

Al di là del muro della casa Baccouch, invece, i soldi girano e rigirano in circuiti chiusi: un gruppetto di imprenditori alberghieri, ristoratori, noleggiatori di auto e poco altro, fino a pochi mesi fa legato per vie traverse al **clan affaristico-parassitario della famiglia di Leila Trabelsi**, la moglie di Ben Ali, il presidente-dittatore rovesciato il 14 gennaio. Ventitré anni di saccheggio sistematico hanno lasciato in eredità un'economia fasulla che scoraggia l'iniziativa imprenditoriale e che quindi non può avere il dinamismo necessario per far crescere l'occupazione.

Taieb Baccouch, 35 anni, è lo zio e il punto di riferimento principale di Walid. Lavora come agente di viaggio, guadagna 800 dinari al mese (circa 400 euro), guida una Renault Clio modello familiare e si sposerà il prossimo 28 marzo (tutti invitati). Taieb rappresenta lo spartiacque tra le ultime due generazioni di giovani che convivono tra le stesse palme, ulivi ed eucalipti, ma con prospettive radicalmente diverse. «Mio nipote riusciva a lavorare al massimo uno o due giorni al mese. Metteva insieme giusto i soldi per il caffè e le sigarette». La signora Mabrouka, 40 anni nascosti sotto l'hijab colorato, invece, non sa niente dell'Italia e neanche della

---

Beshir non si rade la barba dal giorno
in cui il figlio l'ha lasciato, però è consapevole
che per lui non c'erano alternative
al "bar dei disoccupati", dove i giovani passano
tre ore la mattina e tre ore il pomeriggio

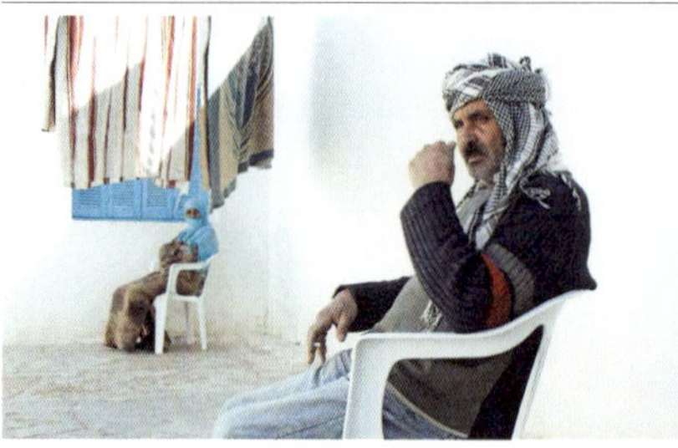

Djerba
6 MARZO 2011, ORE 13.30
Beshir Baccouch, 55 anni, e, sullo sfondo, la sorella Mabrouka. Pure la figlia Najhla, 22 anni, sogna di lasciare la Tunisia. «Anch'io vorrei lavorare e, se potessi, andrei in Europa», ci confida.

Francia. E, a quanto pare, non le importa granché. Sa solo, e comunque pensa, che lì ci possa essere un futuro per Walid. E ragiona con una logica difficile da aggirare: «Che ci stava a fare qui? A morire di fame? So che attraversare il mare è pericoloso. Ma qualcosa doveva pur fare, o no? Io l'ho incoraggiato a partire. Ho venduto delle cose, ho messo insieme i miei risparmi per dargli 200 dinari (100 euro circa) per pagarsi il passaggio sulla barca». Per la cronaca: i "passeur", i trafficanti di immigrati, da ultimo hanno rialzato i prezzi. Ora **chiedono 2.500 dinari (1.250 euro) per un biglietto per Lampedusa**, sola andata.

Finalmente anche Najhla si convince a uscire dalla sua tana psicologica, che qui chiamano tradizione. All'inizio con qualche frasetta di circostanza, «Sì, mio fratello mi manca, è partito perché non c'è lavoro: eccetera) guardando suo zio Taieb. Poi, piano piano, le battute si fanno sorridenti.

Fin dove arriva l'orizzonte di una ragazza di Djerba? La regista tunisina Moufida Tlatli ha ambientato proprio da queste parti il film *La Saison des Hommes* (2000), il racconto di una donna dell'isola che passa la vita ad aspettare il ritorno del marito, immigrato in Francia. Ma Najhla, quando ormai è arrivato il momento di salutare, finalmente lascia il segno: «Anch'io vorrei lavorare e se potessi anch'io vorrei andare in Europa. Inshallah. È bella l'Italia?». •

Altre immagini su iodonna.it

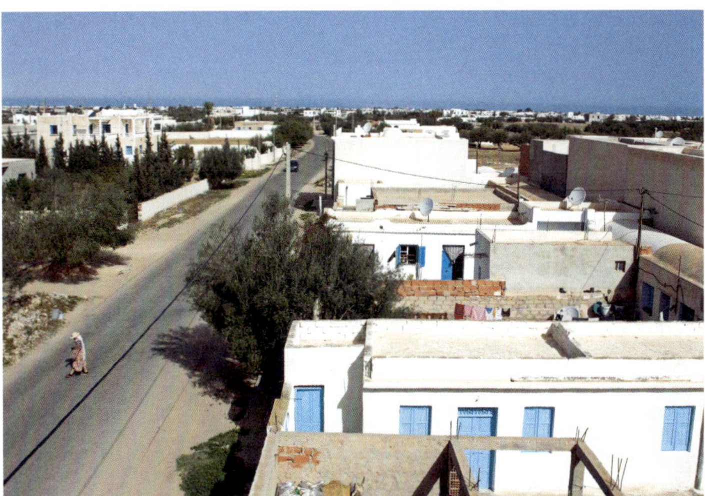

← The photograph of his neighbor-hood in Djerba shows us where he came from, what he is leaving behind.

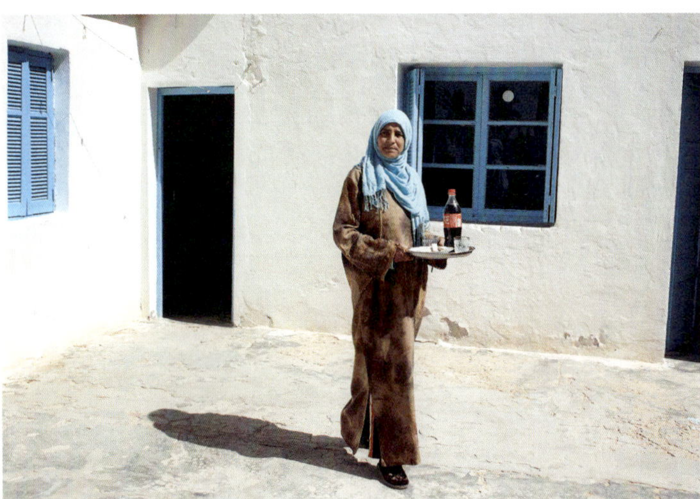

← The photo of his aunt, who is a key figure, which is then explained in the text by …

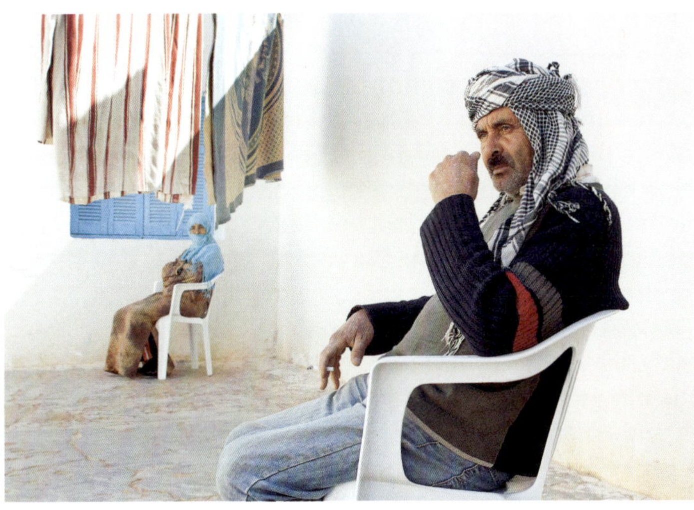

← … the uncle in particular. She is the person who welcomes our team, then Walid's father and sister talk about their dream of going to Europe, which everyone dreams of because there is no future in their country, no hope, no work. Now if I don't read the caption, if I don't read the text, what does this image convey? What can I learn from it? How does it reach me? As the photo editor, I try to respond to the magazine's needs, to respond to very clear questions—i.e., to know that we are talking about Walid, and to see his face. The standard request might be that the subject is looking at the camera, so that we have a clear view, which I think is a bit beside the point. The picture should at least be succinct and illustrative, very simple, easy to grasp, never dramatizing reality. I am completely in agreement with not being overly dramatic, because I think lots of bad photography, over the last twenty years, has turned every situation into a catastrophe, a massacre.

Q: So, let's get into the mechanism of how a publication functions. How does it work?

FERRI: The photographer sends low-res pictures, which I use to do a pre-edit of the images. There is generally no information in these low-res pictures. Then we ask for the high-res versions, with a caption. The caption often serves as a starting point: the journalist then writes a longer caption—straightening out the original, one might say. Usually the captions arrive in English.

Q: Does the magazine do postproduction?

FERRI: There's always postproduction! I try to make sure that no one removes things. But there is always a need to improve the image, to change the light to suit the magazine, to … post-produce. We make adjustments on the files, depending on what kind of paper we are using. There are color profiles, and not everyone has the parameters of our paper. For us, for example, the blacks tend to open up, and we have to close them. So there is a technical person who only works on this.

Q: And what about the editing?

FERRI: There is this need to make everything extremely simple … as if you had to give viewers as many tools as possible to help them understand the image. A synthesis is sought, a monstrous, excessive simplification in which you have a subject in front of you, you explain it, and on the next page you have another subject from the same story: the pictures tend to be arranged in an order that is not particularly dynamic so that the readers won't get lost. On an aesthetic level, there is a need for great stillness, for formal beauty, according to a particular criterion of beauty …

Q: Are the photographs commissioned?

FERRI: Yes, we commission and buy them, but they remain the property of the photographer. When a production is done for a newspaper, a minimum embargo time is required. I normally ask for a three-month embargo period, in which the picture cannot be published in other magazines. Six months for Italy and three months for other countries.

Q: How does the process of selecting photos work?

FERRI: Analyzing photo by photo, to understand why this has become the image of the hospitality of Walid's aunt—i.e., why this image and not this other one, or why not the rest of the family—is very complicated. There are many people making the decision. You pick an image, for the opening of the article, which might be this one, but actually you offer several alternatives. Why does this one get chosen? Because there is space to insert the title, it has all the space needed to let the image breathe, as we say. There is the subject, not at the center, because that would be hidden in the fold of the two-page spread, but slightly off center, which works best on the page. There are other little subjects that influence this. There is also a morphology of the territory, which speaks of an island … You can get into the picture. Even if we read nothing, if we don't read the article, there is a header, a very long caption. But if we don't even read that, this image would still give us the idea that we are on Lampedusa, and that the man is a migrant from a boat … it is quite recognizable, the island at least. We photographed Walid on March 4. In the meantime, the photographer sent me the pictures, it was quite clear they were from Lampedusa. When the pre-selection arrived—seven or eight images already chosen by the photographer … from about fifteen, let's say, not very many, because the situation was difficult with the police there, the CPT … back here you can see the facility where they take them, they let him out for a minute, and the photographer took fifteen shots, very fast. He sent me seven or eight, and I called him back and said, "OK, we have our portrait," and then he left. On March 6 he was already in Djerba, at the home of Walid's family.

Q: With the journalist?

FERRI: Yes, with the journalist. They met in Djerba, the writer was already there because he was covering what was happening on the North African coast—he was already in Tunisia. The photographer took a lot of photographs because I wanted to see if there was something more to bring out—other stories, another image, other angles. I wasn't sure: that is, I trusted him, but I wanted to see more from the viewpoint of the editing that would be right for the magazine. I brought all the results to show to the editor, the deputy editor, the art director. In this case, the writer wasn't there, because he was a correspondent, so he was elsewhere, but when there is an in-house journalist, we look at more or less the whole job together, and normally a decision is made about the opening picture, the picture that tells the story best.But let's say that partly due to the pace of the work, which can be pretty frenetic, and partly due to bad Italian manners, there is always a sort of rank pulling … certain opinions dominate.

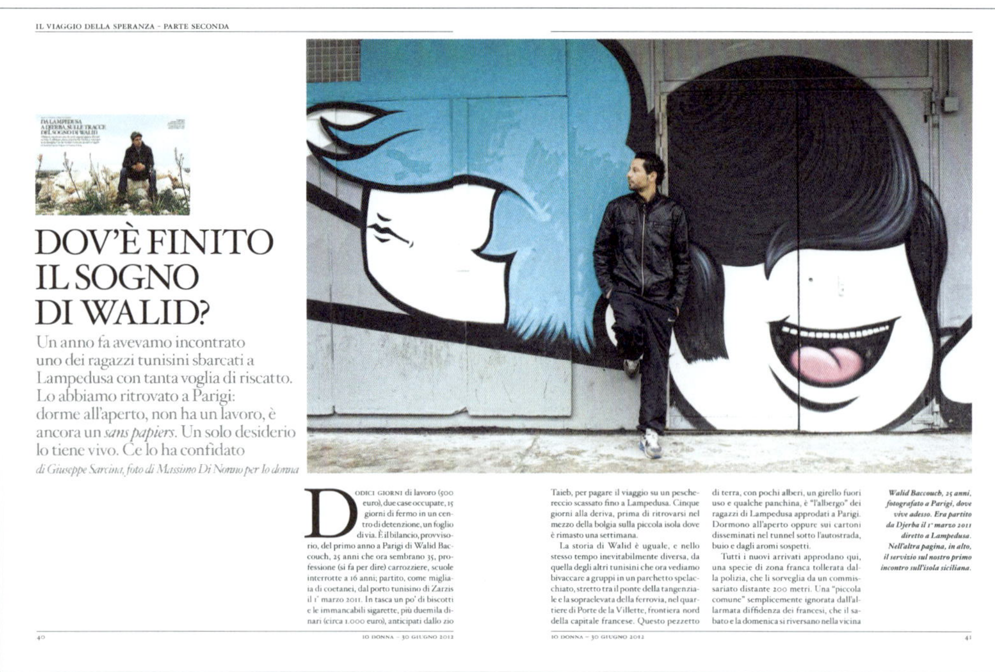

DOV'È FINITO IL SOGNO DI WALID?

Un anno fa avevamo incontrato uno dei ragazzi tunisini sbarcati a Lampedusa con tanta voglia di riscatto. Lo abbiamo ritrovato a Parigi: dorme all'aperto, non ha un lavoro, è ancora un *sans papiers*. Un solo desiderio lo tiene vivo. Ce lo ha confidato

di Giuseppe Sarcina, foto di Massimo Di Nonno per Io donna

DODICI GIORNI di lavoro (500 euro), due case occupate, 15 giorni di fermo in un centro di detenzione, un foglio di via. È il bilancio, provvisorio, del primo anno a Parigi di Walid Baccouch, 25 anni che ora sembrano 35, professione (si fa per dire) carrozziere, scuole interrotte a 16 anni; partito, come migliaia di coetanei, dal porto tunisino di Zarzis il 1° marzo 2011. In tasca un po' di biscotti e le immancabili sigarette, più duemila dinari (circa 1.000 euro), anticipati dallo zio Taieb, per pagare il viaggio su un peschereccio scassato fino a Lampedusa. Cinque giorni alla deriva, prima di ritrovarsi nel mezzo della bolgia sulla piccola isola dove è rimasto una settimana.

La storia di Walid è uguale, e nello stesso tempo inevitabilmente diversa, da quella degli altri tunisini che ora vediamo bivaccare a gruppi in un parchetto splacchiato, stretto tra il ponte della tangenziale e la sopraelevata della ferrovia, nel quartiere di Porte de la Villette, frontiera nord della capitale francese. Questo pezzetto di terra, con pochi alberi, un girello fuori uso e qualche panchina, è "l'albergo" dei ragazzi di Lampedusa approdati a Parigi. Dormono all'aperto oppure sui cartoni disseminati nel tunnel sotto l'autostrada, buio e dagli aromi sospetti.

Tutti i nuovi arrivati approdano qui, una specie di zona franca tollerata dalla polizia, che li sorveglia da un commissariato distante 200 metri. Una "piccola comune" semplicemente ignorata dall'allarmata diffidenza dei francesi, che il sabato e la domenica si riversano nella vicina

Walid Baccouch, 25 anni, fotografato a Parigi, dove vive adesso. Era partito da Djerba il 1° marzo 2011 diretto a Lampedusa. Nell'altra pagina, in alto, il servizio sul nostro primo incontro sull'isola siciliana.

40   IO DONNA – 30 GIUGNO 2012   IO DONNA – 30 GIUGNO 2012   41

↑   One year later Massimo Di Nonno went to Paris to meet Walid again. As you see, the summary and the photo help the reader to remember the first episode of Walid's story. Here we see Walid still well dressed, in front of a mural in Paris. It is not so easy to identify the city, but given the quality of the graffiti we are definitely not on Lampedusa, and we are not in Tunisia.

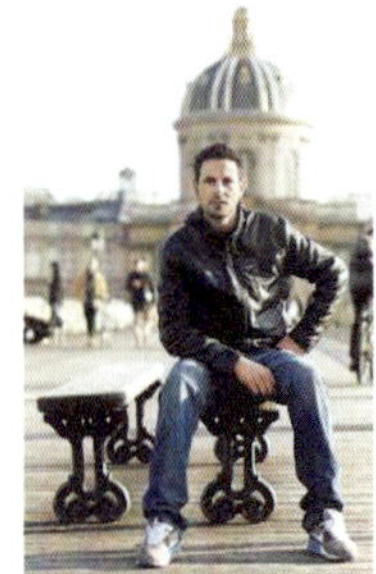

...a delle Scienze e dell'Industria", ad ...rare la grande sfera argentata del ...tarium. Walid vorrebbe diventa...ne uno di quei giovanotti che vede...re un passeggino o tenere per mano ...nzata. «Cerco un lavoro, poi troverò ...agazza, mi sposerò e avrò la mia fa...a»: un programma modesto e linea...? D'altra parte un suo concittadino, ...a si è unito al gruppo, ci è riuscito. ...ama Arafat, ha 28 anni, è arrivato a ... nel 2001, fa il panettiere, ha moglie ...ese) e due figli. E allora perché lui ...at) sì e io (Walid) no? Ma perché, ver...da rispondergli, è cambiato tutto, ...e ne sei accorto? In un intero anno ...sso insieme solo una dozzina di gior...avorative nei cantieri a trasportare ...e mattoni dalle 8 alle 19 per 40 euro.

In un anno ha messo...

su cui contare. Le vecchie comunità tu...sine sono troppo occupate a blindarsi ...loro ghetti storici (gli *arrondissement* 92... e 94) per accogliere i nuovi giovani. Il g...verno di Tunisi, esaurita la retorica sui ...gli emigrati" da riportare in Patria, se...plicemente non si occupa di loro.

ALLA FINE LA VERA SORPRESA viene d... le autorità francesi. Nonostante le p... re dei cittadini sotto assedio covate ne... periferie dove Marine Le Pen, leader de... destra xenofoba, ha fatto il pieno di vo... i *flic* (i poliziotti) si muovono con pragm... tismo. Tre-quattrocento metri alle spa... dei giardinetti-dormitorio, nel quartiere ... Seine-Saint-Denise, i *sans papiers* tunisi... marocchini, senegalesi e ivoriani si sono ... filati negli appartamenti sfitti delle gra...

←   It already suggests the metropolis, and in the image on the next page, a single after a two-page spread, we see Walid sitting on a bench with a beautiful church behind him, in Paris.

At this point there is not much doubt about where we are. Were there still any uncertainty, this little image, which is a bit like a postcard, tells us we are in a European capital where there are churches, for someone who comes from a land of minarets …
so it can be a cliché, at times, a very iconic image. That is just what you need to sum up the idea that he is there, and so on, that he is on a bench in the center of the city …

PHOTO AGENCY CONTRASTO ROME

BY EMILIE JOSSO

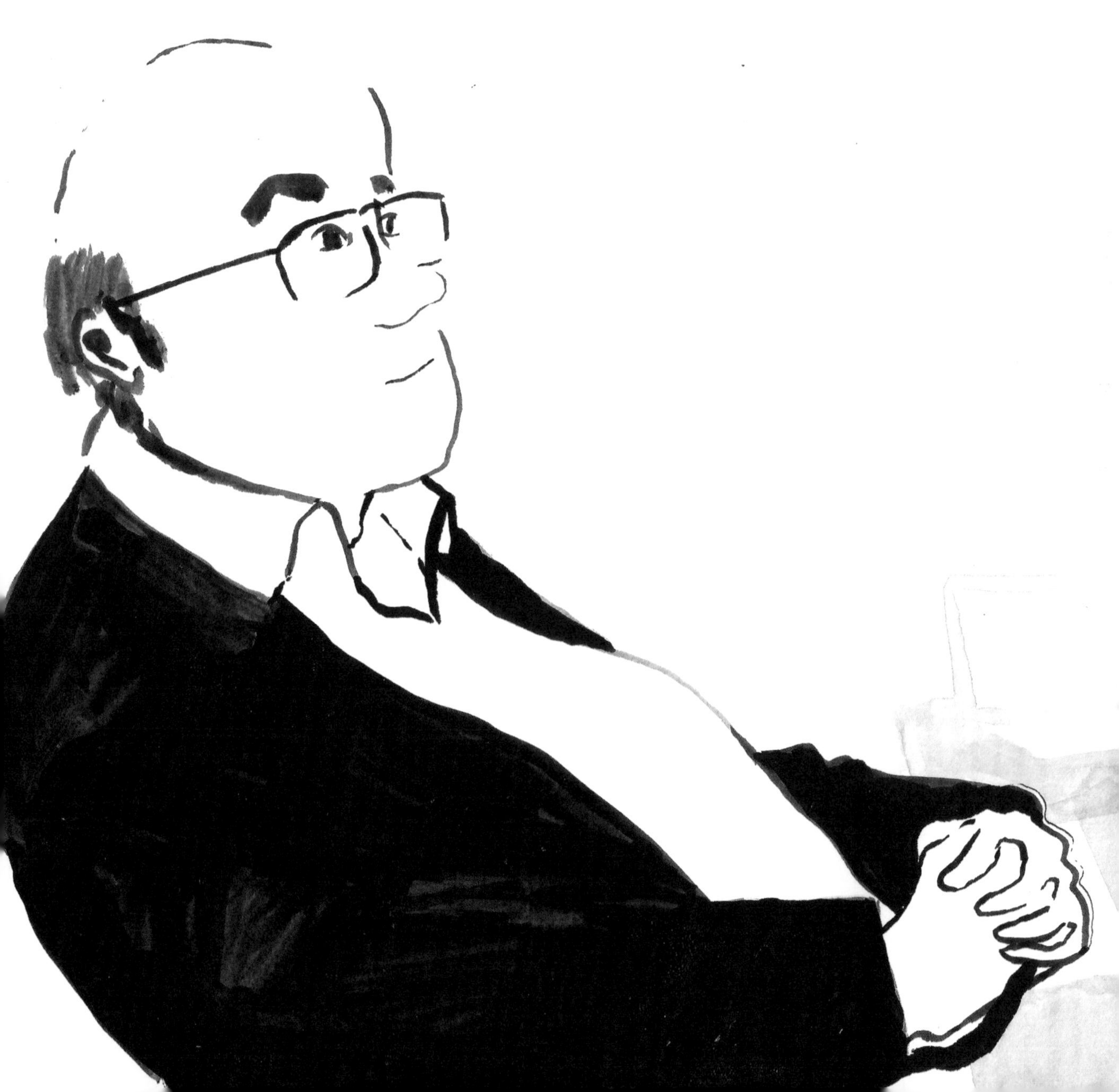

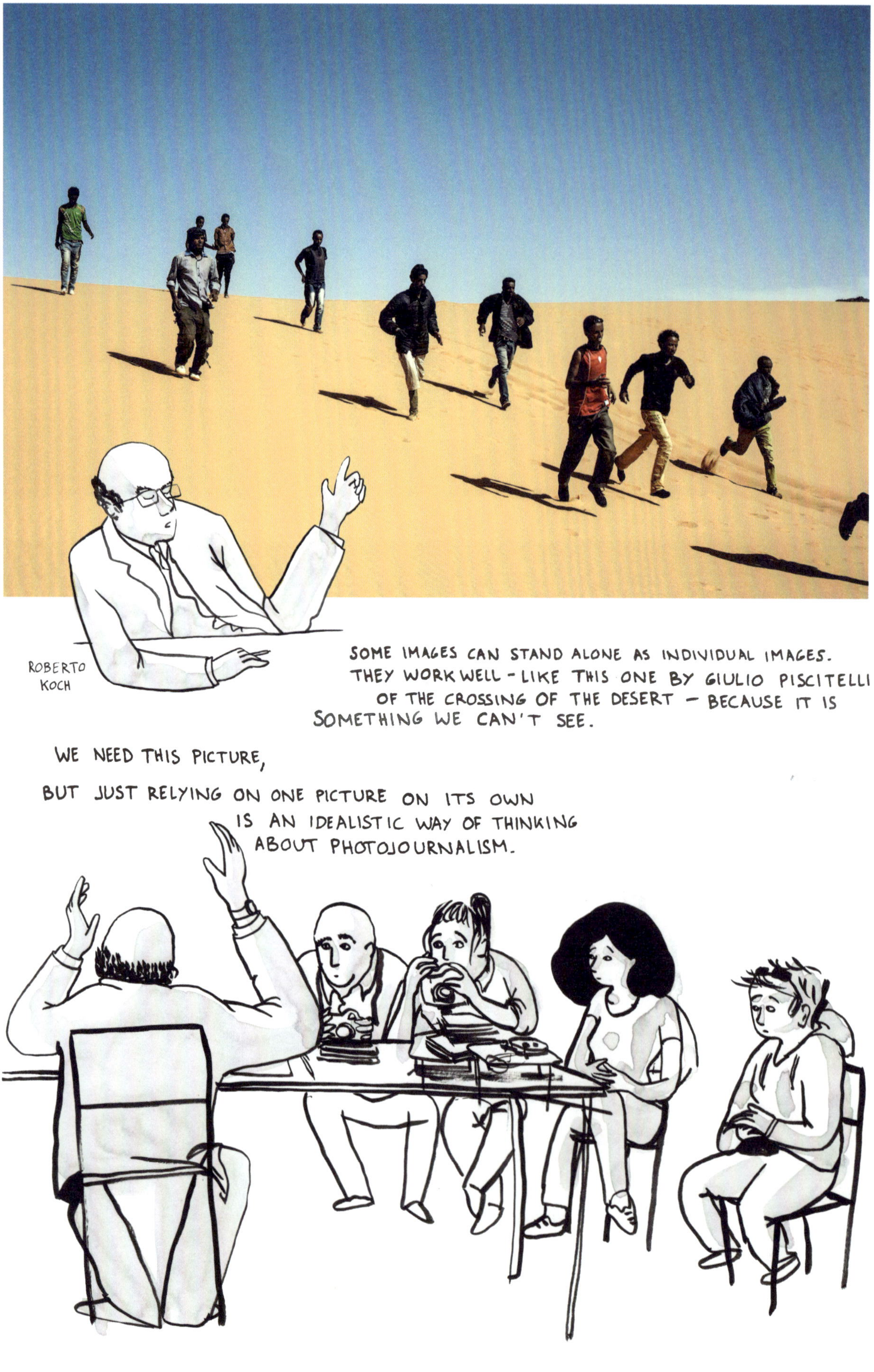

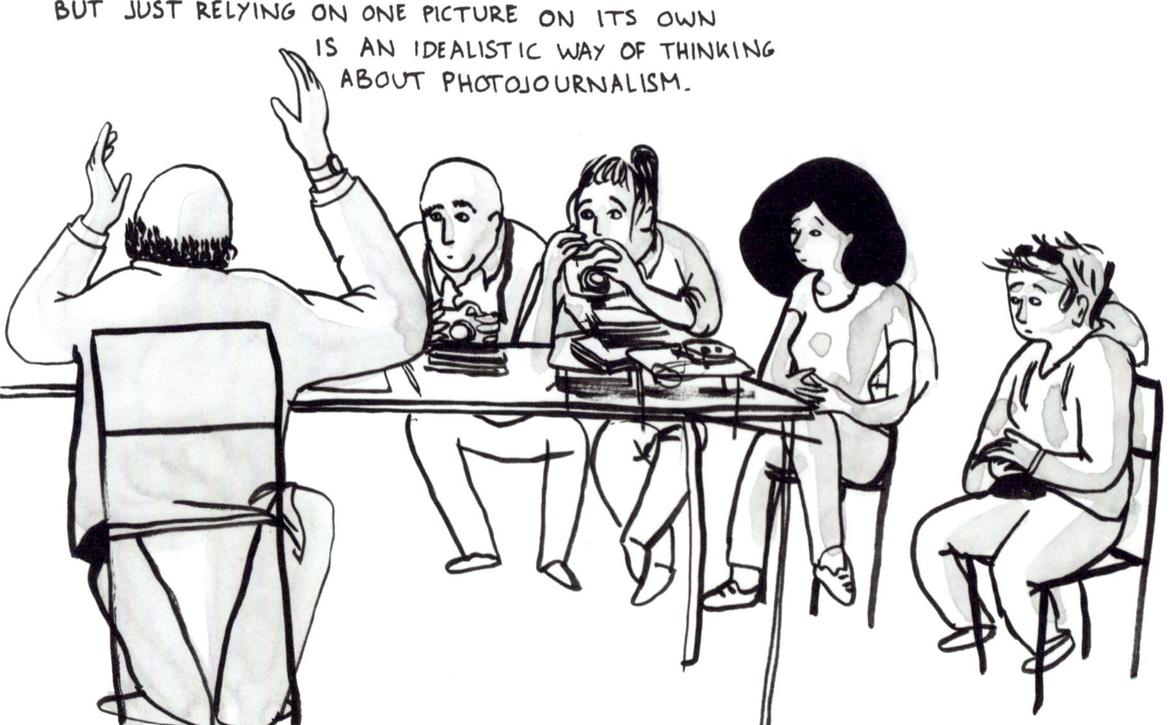

SOME IMAGES CAN STAND ALONE AS INDIVIDUAL IMAGES.
THEY WORK WELL — LIKE THIS ONE BY GIULIO PISCITELLI
OF THE CROSSING OF THE DESERT — BECAUSE IT IS
SOMETHING WE CAN'T SEE.

WE NEED THIS PICTURE,

BUT JUST RELYING ON ONE PICTURE ON ITS OWN
IS AN IDEALISTIC WAY OF THINKING
ABOUT PHOTOJOURNALISM.

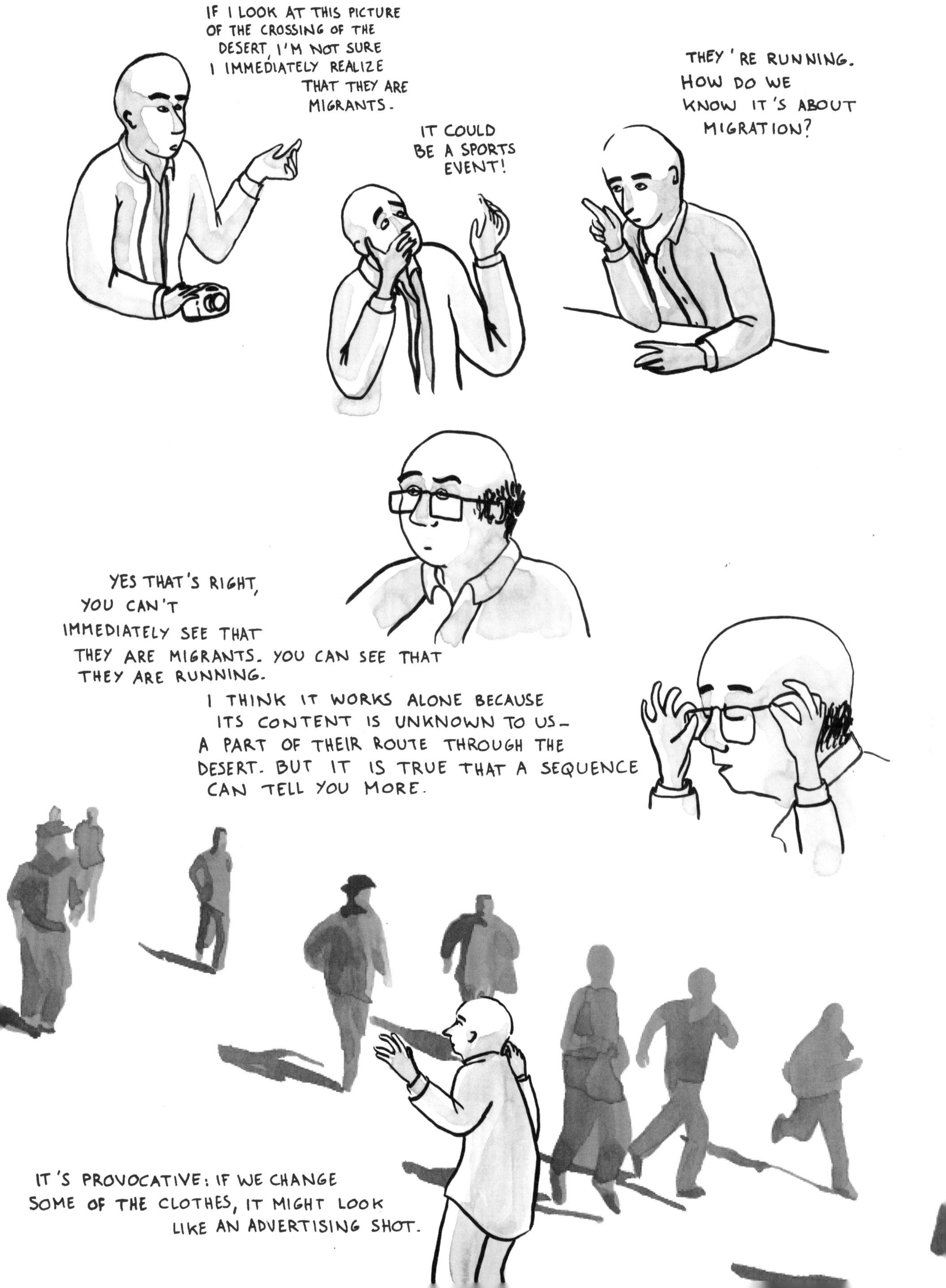

IF I LOOK AT THIS PICTURE OF THE CROSSING OF THE DESERT, I'M NOT SURE I IMMEDIATELY REALIZE THAT THEY ARE MIGRANTS.
IT COULD BE A SPORTS EVENT!
THEY'RE RUNNING. HOW DO WE KNOW IT'S ABOUT MIGRATION?
YES THAT'S RIGHT, YOU CAN'T IMMEDIATELY SEE THAT THEY ARE MIGRANTS. YOU CAN SEE THAT THEY ARE RUNNING.
I THINK IT WORKS ALONE BECAUSE ITS CONTENT IS UNKNOWN TO US— A PART OF THEIR ROUTE THROUGH THE DESERT. BUT IT IS TRUE THAT A SEQUENCE CAN TELL YOU MORE.
IT'S PROVOCATIVE: IF WE CHANGE SOME OF THE CLOTHES, IT MIGHT LOOK LIKE AN ADVERTISING SHOT.

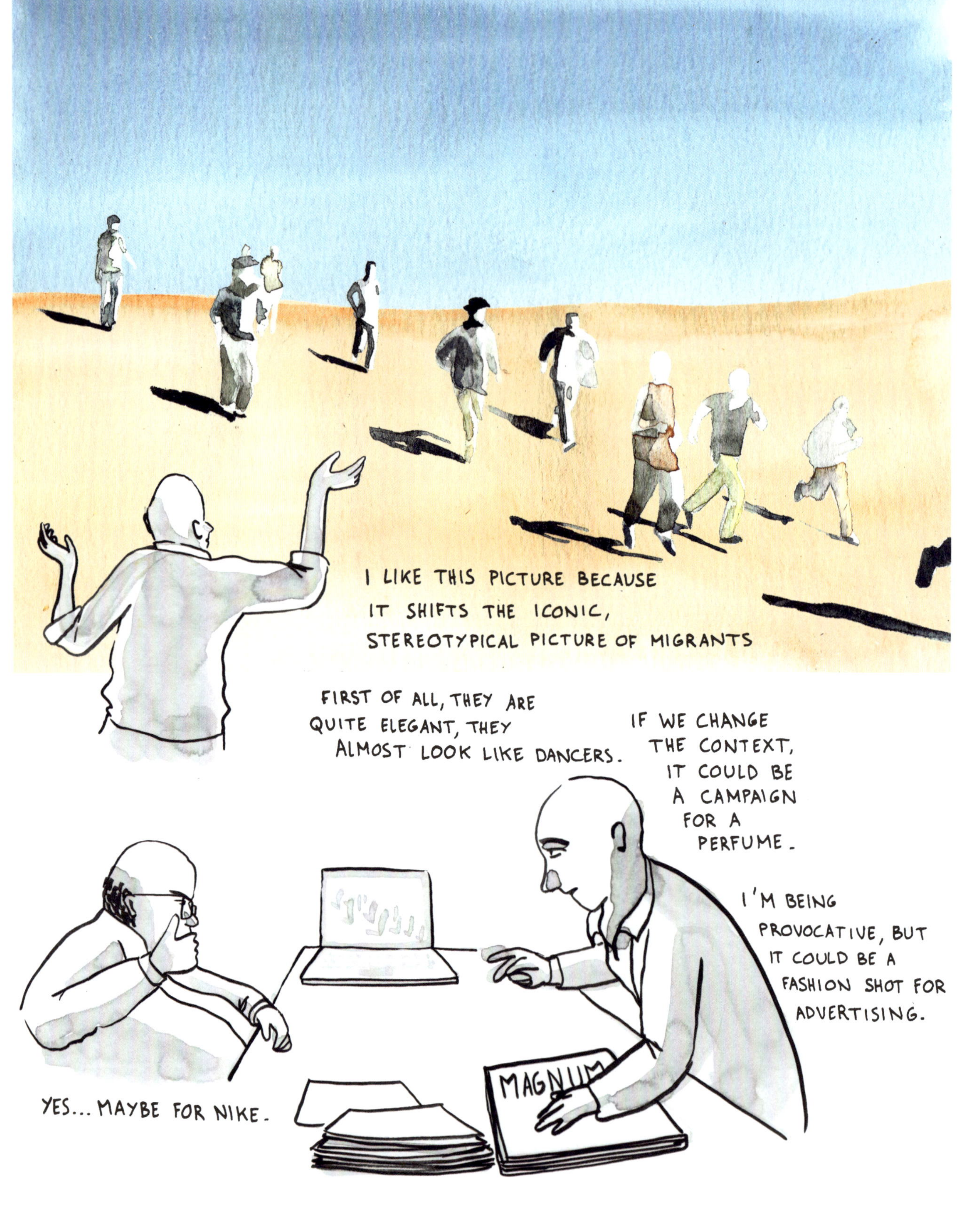

I LIKE THIS PICTURE BECAUSE IT SHIFTS THE ICONIC, STEREOTYPICAL PICTURE OF MIGRANTS
FIRST OF ALL, THEY ARE QUITE ELEGANT, THEY ALMOST LOOK LIKE DANCERS.
IF WE CHANGE THE CONTEXT, IT COULD BE A CAMPAIGN FOR A PERFUME.
I'M BEING PROVOCATIVE, BUT IT COULD BE A FASHION SHOT FOR ADVERTISING.
YES... MAYBE FOR NIKE.
MAGNUM

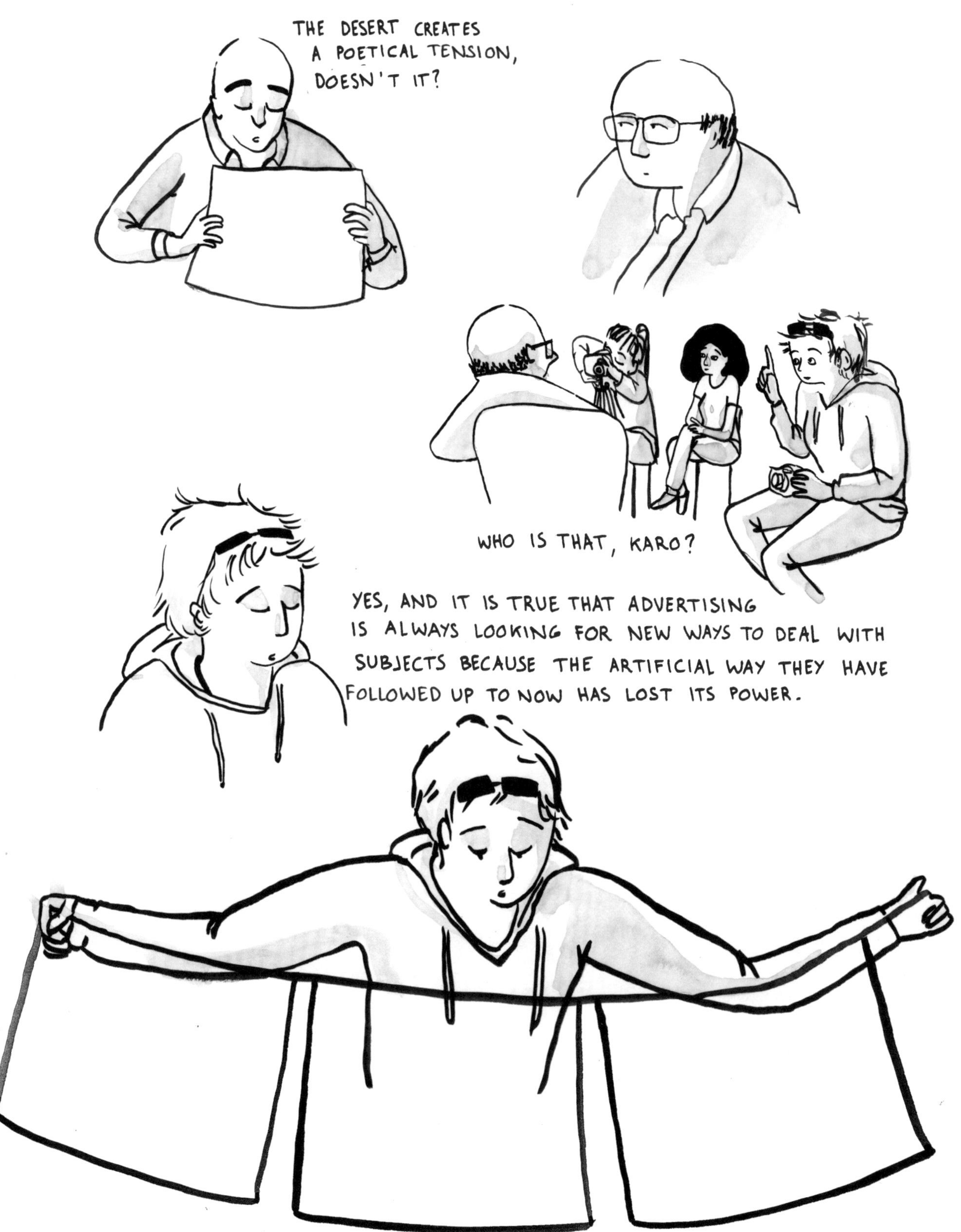

THE DESERT CREATES A POETICAL TENSION, DOESN'T IT?
WHO IS THAT, KARO?
YES, AND IT IS TRUE THAT ADVERTISING IS ALWAYS LOOKING FOR NEW WAYS TO DEAL WITH SUBJECTS BECAUSE THE ARTIFICIAL WAY THEY HAVE FOLLOWED UP TO NOW HAS LOST ITS POWER.
BUT YOU WON'T FIND THIS PICTURE STANDING ALONE— IT'S THE PHOTOGRAPHER'S DECISION TO KEEP IT IN A SEQUENCE.

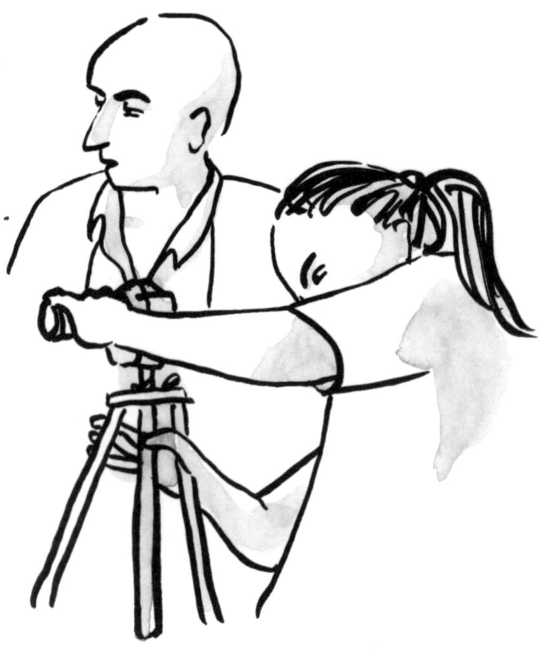

I JUST WANT TO SAY THAT TO ME WHAT I'M SAYING IS A COMPLIMENT. I LIKE IT WHEN A PICTURE NEEDS MORE TIME TO BE DECODED.

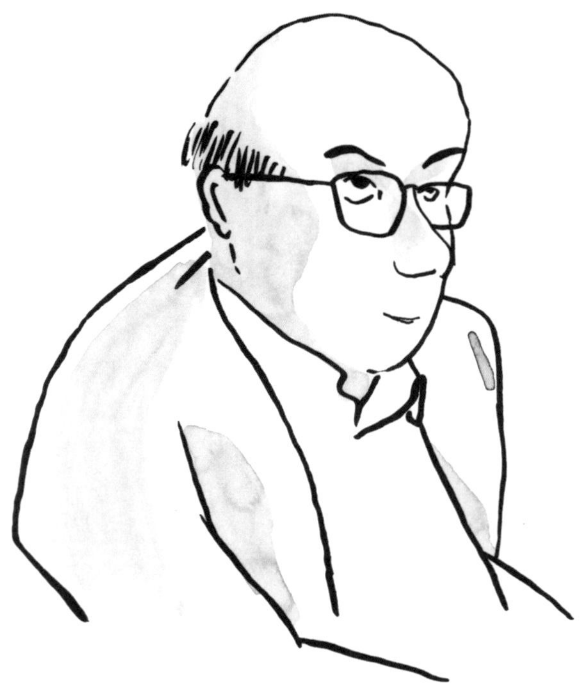

I TOTALLY AGREE.
OF COURSE, THE VISUAL COMPOSITION AND THE AESTHETIC ASPECT OF THIS PICTURE ARE QUITE STRONG, BUT CREATING A STRONG PICTURE FROM A REAL STORY IS ONE OF THE GOALS OF GOOD PHOTOGRAPHERS AND, INDEED, OF PHOTOJOURNALISTS.

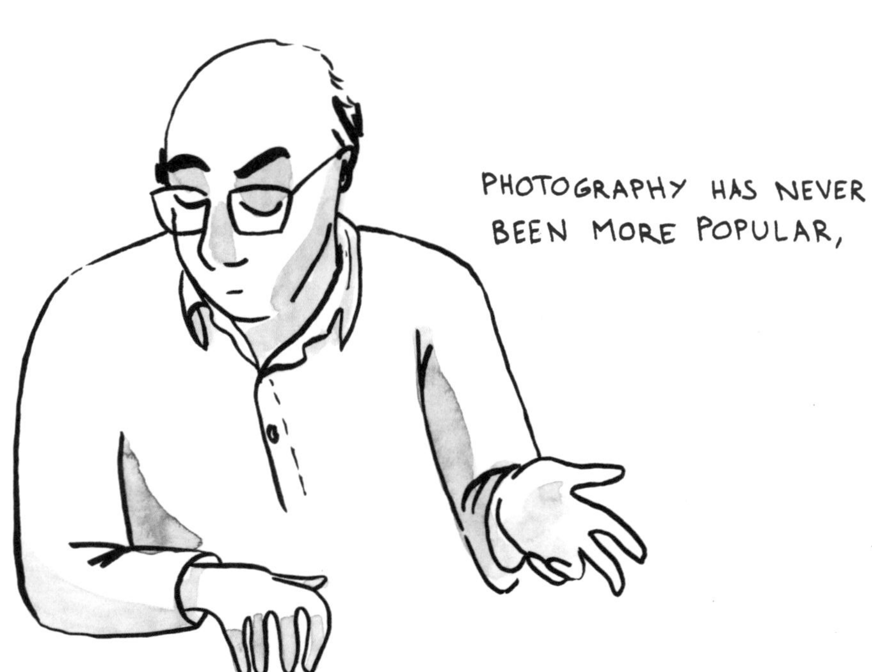

THIS IS A KEY TO THE SITUATION OF PHOTOJOURNALISM TODAY. ON THE ONE HAND, IT LOOKS LIKE THE WORLD IS REJECTING PHOTOJOURNALISTS;
PHOTOGRAPHY HAS NEVER BEEN MORE POPULAR,

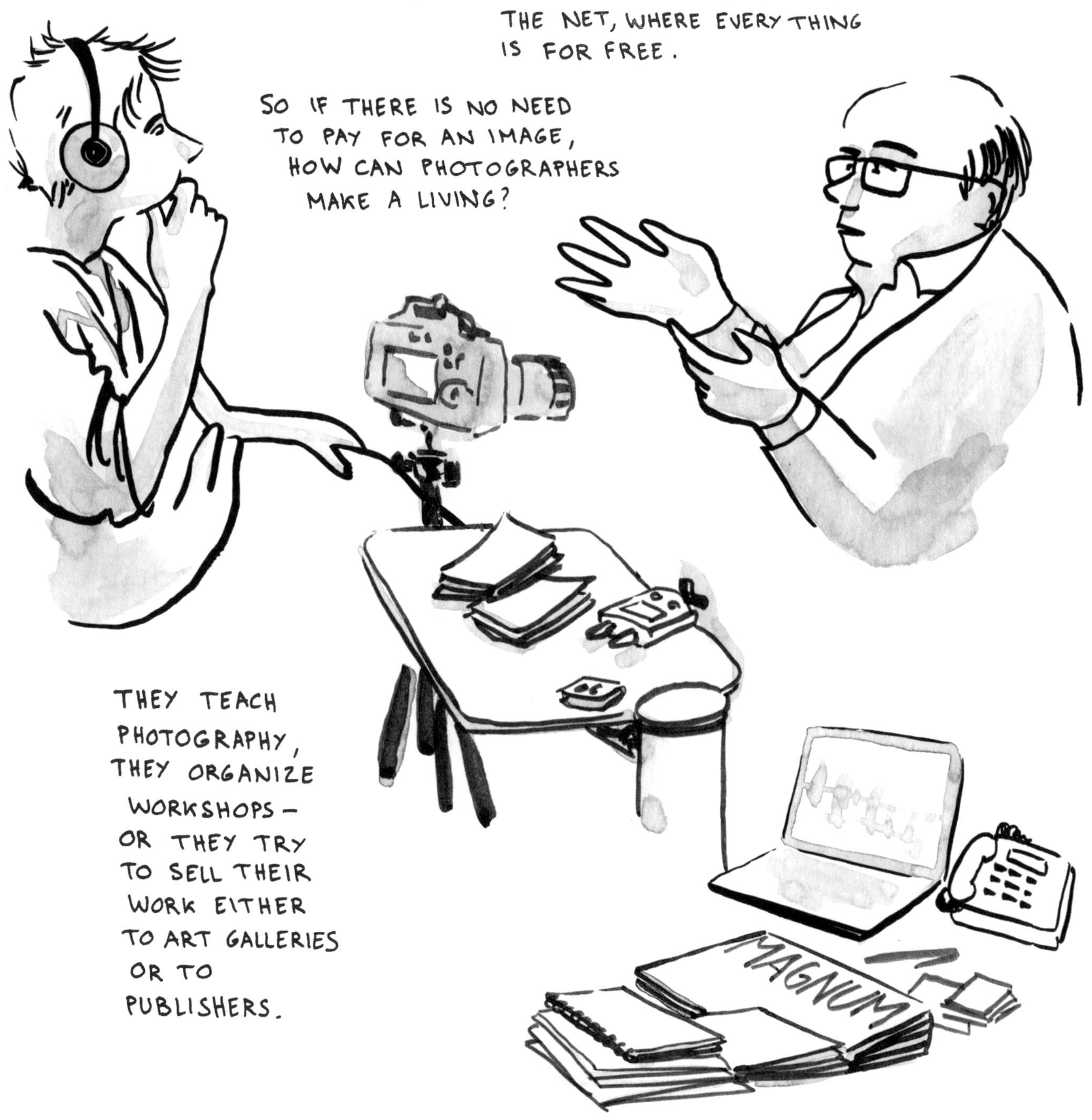

BUT THIS DOESN'T MEAN THAT PHOTOGRAPHERS ARE MORE RESPECTED THAN BEFORE.
AT THE SAME TIME, THE ROLE OF THE PHOTOGRAPHER IS BEING QUESTIONED EVERY DAY.
IT'S GETTING MORE AND MORE DIFFICULT FOR PHOTOJOURNALISTS TO GET PAID FOR THEIR WORK, BASED ON THE IDEA OF THE NET, WHERE EVERYTHING IS FOR FREE.
SO IF THERE IS NO NEED TO PAY FOR AN IMAGE, HOW CAN PHOTOGRAPHERS MAKE A LIVING?
THEY TEACH PHOTOGRAPHY, THEY ORGANIZE WORKSHOPS — OR THEY TRY TO SELL THEIR WORK EITHER TO ART GALLERIES OR TO PUBLISHERS.
MAGNUM

The following email exchange took place between Anne König and Giulio Piscitelli, who took the photograph.

2017-06-02 12:27 GMT+02:00 Anne König

Dear Giulio,

I'm the publisher at Spector Books, and we are preparing a book about Lampedusa. We bought one image by you from Contrasto to include in the book. It's the photo where the refugees are running through the desert.
Unfortunately, Contrasto didn't send us so much information about the photo and there are a couple of questions we would like to ask you: Where exactly was the photo taken? What is the name of the region you were going through?

Thanks for your help.
With best regards,
Anne König

2017-06-02 13:01 MESZ Giulio Piscitelli

Dear Anne,

Thanks for your email, I'm sorry that the agency didn't gave you enough info.
By the way: The picture of the dune was taken on May 2014 in the Libyan Sahara desert, a few kilometers from the border with Sudan, approximately 200 km from the Kufrah Oasis.
The people in the picture were traveling from Khartoum, the capital of Sudan, and had been on their way for 3 days.
I hope this info is sufficient. If you need more help, I will be at your disposal.

Best,
Giulio

2017-06-02 14:21 GMT+02:00 Anne König

Dear Giulio,

Thanks for your prompt reply! That helps a lot.
May I ask how you met these people? Did you already know them in Khartoum? Did you travel together with them?
Why were they running through the desert?
Do you know that your image didn't make it into any of the

German newspapers? It's really well known in Italy. I'm curious if you know why it didn't reach other countries apart from the one I mentioned.

Have a nice day,
Anne

2017-06-02 15:52:07 MESZ Giulio Piscitelli

Hi Anne,

The picture is part of a report on the smuggling of refugees from Sudan to Libya that I did for *Vanity Fair*, I was traveling with a local militia group that controls the border and after a day of patrolling, we met three cars with 80 people (women, men, and small children) on board stuck in the desert due to some problems with the engines; we helped them by giving them water and food because they were almost dead from dehydration after many days in the direct sun; after that, the militia escorted them to Kufrah Oasis, where they received first aid, but probably later they were caught and smuggled again (unfortunately, despite our efforts to contact the UNHCR and other NGOS, no one came to give a hand to these people). In the picture the refugees are running to reach the car when the engine restarted after the repair.
I published part of my entire project on immigration with *Stern* (from time to time I collaborate with them), but not this image unfortunately, I don't know why—it's just one case. Did the agency show you the entire project? If not, you can take a look at the different chapters developed in the last seven years in more than fifteen countries, describing the routes and the system of "welcoming" in Europe, a work that in some ways is still ongoing: in fact, I recently started working on the refugees crisis in Iraq, which in my project represents a good metaphor for the reason why many people are leaving their countries: https://giuliopiscitelli.viewbook.com/from-there-to-here

I wish you a nice day too and I'm at your disposal in case you still need me.

Best,
Giulio

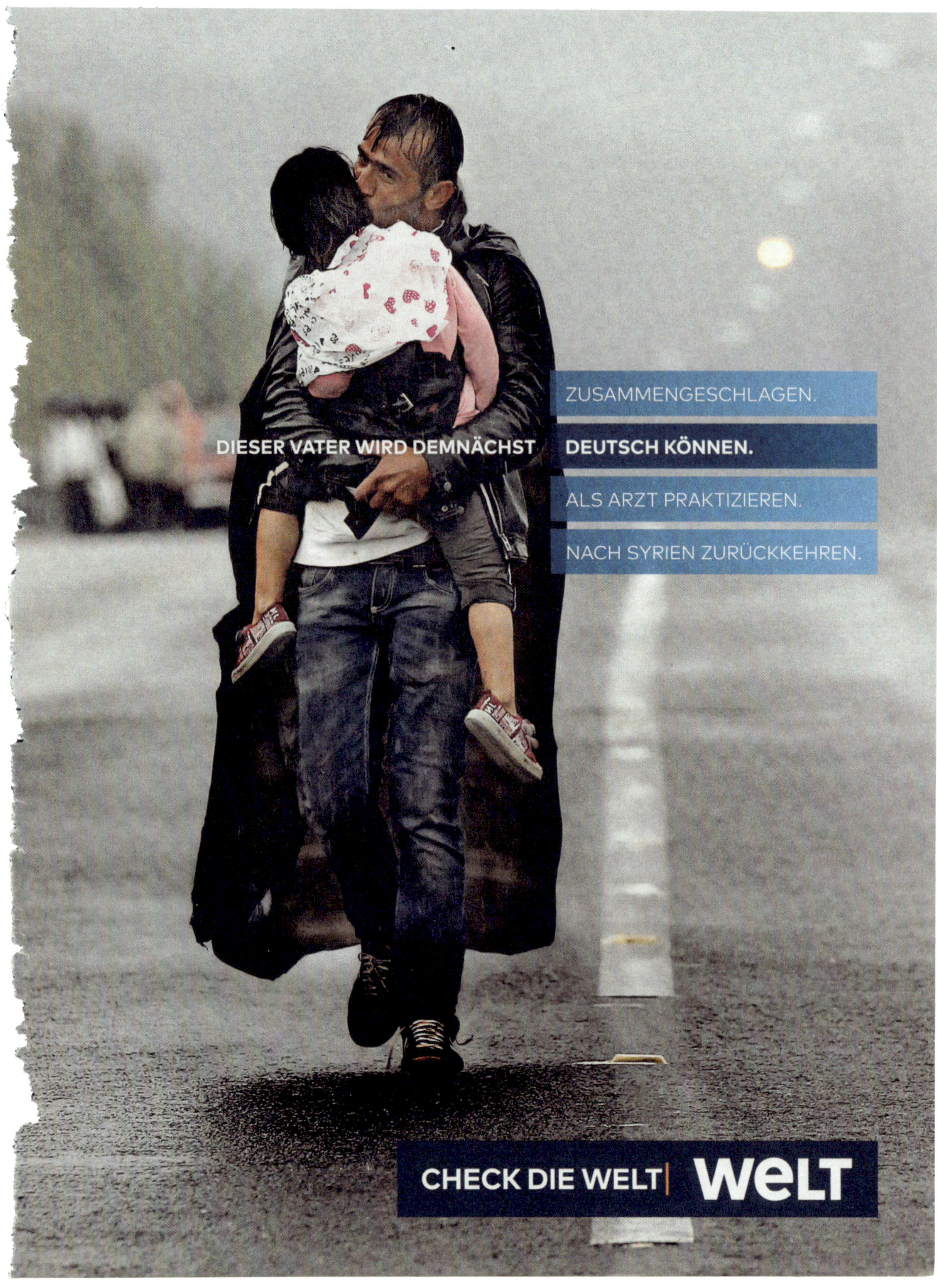

[This father will soon: Be beaten up. Be able to speak German. Practise as a doctor. Go home to Syria. — Check the world.] Advertisement for the German daily *Die Welt*, 2016

The Dangerous Journey

Italian photographer Alessio Genovese on the beginning of the Arab Spring

At the beginning of the Arab Spring Alessio Genovese, who specializes in Arabic and Islamic studies, traveled to the Middle East to make a photographic record of the revolution in Tunisia and the situation facing political refugees there. The Italian and foreign press published his photographs, while NGOs used them to illustrate the issue of integration. In 2011 the Migrant Image Research Group visited Genovese in his apartment in Trapani. His reportages shed light on the dangerous journey undertaken by refugees culminating in their arrival at the Identification and Expulsion Center (CIE) on Lampedusa. The photographs date from spring 2011, when the Lampedusa CIE became so overcrowded that new camps had to be opened on the Italian mainland and in Sicily, including one in Trapani.

Genovese was commissioned by the Sicilian Region to produce a report on the arrival of migrants on Lampedusa and the sit-uation in refugee camps in Sicily. The report was published in the pages of the online edition of the newspaper *La Repubblica* in April 2011. The interview was conducted by Valeria Malito, Filippo Baracchi, and Laura Morcillo.

What we see is a selection of about twenty pictures I presented at the international photo competition *Picture of the Year*. At the moment we are in the top twelve.

The idea in this series of pictures is to study the phenomenon of Tunisia and understand the country by looking at the various consequences triggered by the fall of the regime of Zine el-Abidine Ben Ali: from the destabilization that the mili-tias (which are still active in some parts of the country) and the former members of the SD party—the sole ruling party at the time of Ben Ali—tried to create to the waves of mass emigration.

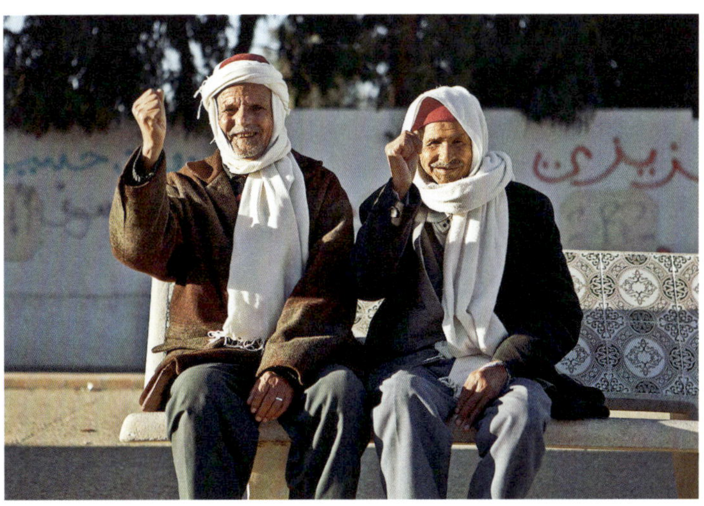

↑　These are two supporters of the revolution.

I analyzed the consequences of the revolution over the course of a year. There are two factors supporting the revolution. The intention of my work is to show that there were people close to Ben Ali who wanted Tunisia to be destabilized. There are some regions where it is still very dangerous to live.

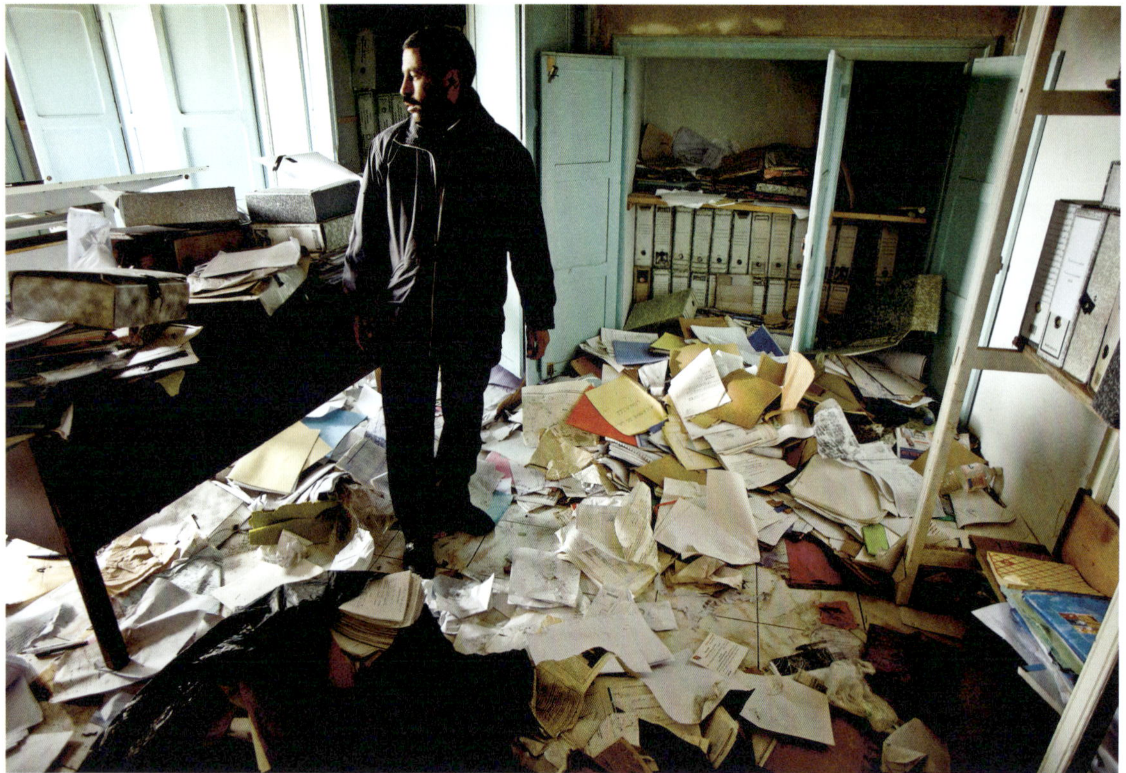

↑   This is a state archive. The regime systematically destroyed any type of information about the local population. They destroyed the state apparatus in the various provinces of the country. They did this to show that the country is unstable without Ben Ali; and there is a second, much more worrying aspect, which is the physical elimination of the people who were moving the revolution forward.

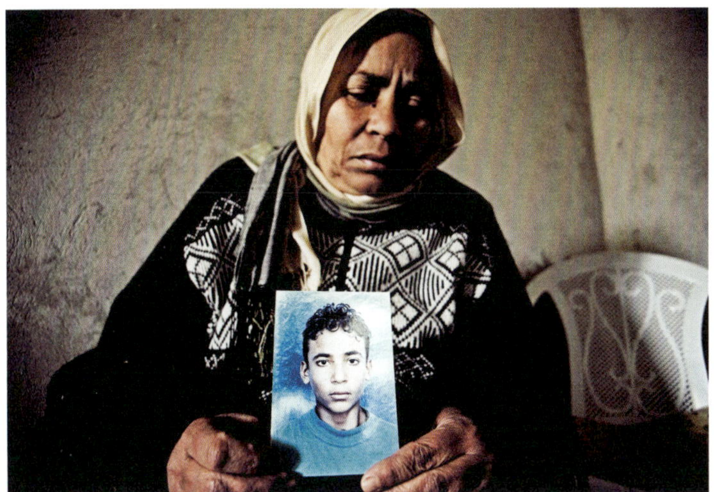

← This is the mother of a sixteen-year-old kid that was killed by the former chief of police in one of the provinces in the south of Tunisia. He was chief of police at the time of Ben Ali; when the regime fell he became chief of the militias. This is the game they played during this period.

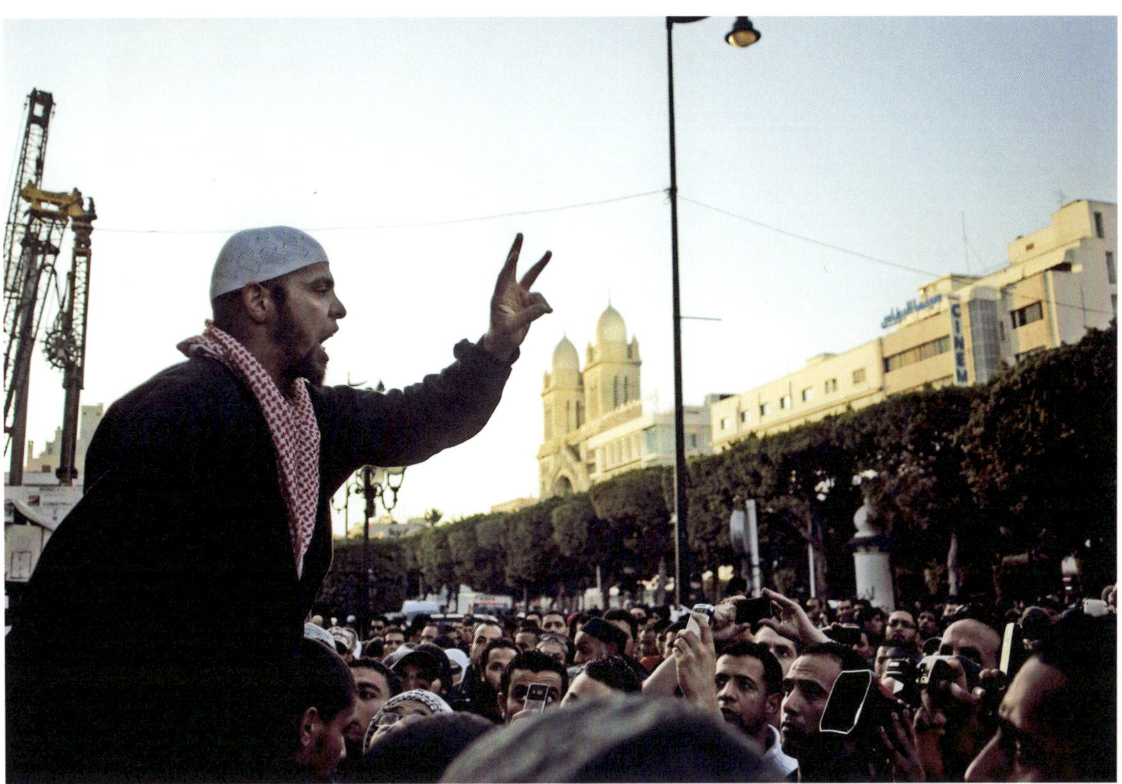

↑ This is Tunis. You can see three symbols in it: this is the Christian cathedral; this is a Muslim community; and this is the symbol of advancing modernity—skyscrapers springing up like mushrooms all over the city.

↑ This is during the January curfew in Tunis.

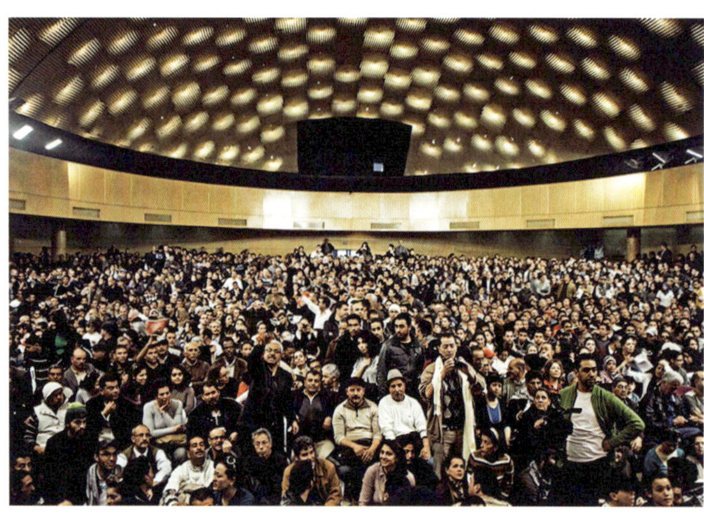

← This is the first official assembly of the 14th of January Front, which unifies all the left-wing opponents who until that day could only meet secretly.

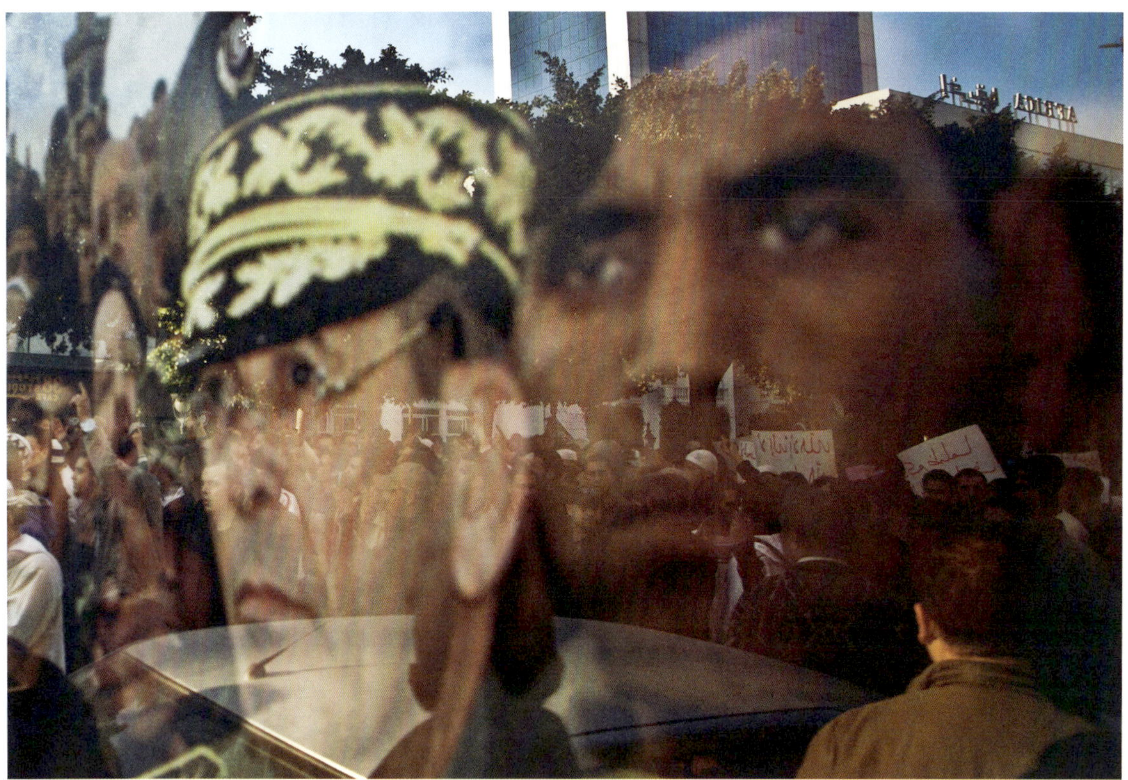

↑   This is still Tunisia. It is a Muslim demonstration. Now, after Ben Ali, Muslims are expanding into all the areas that the state prohibited for years.

←   Still Tunisia, praying.

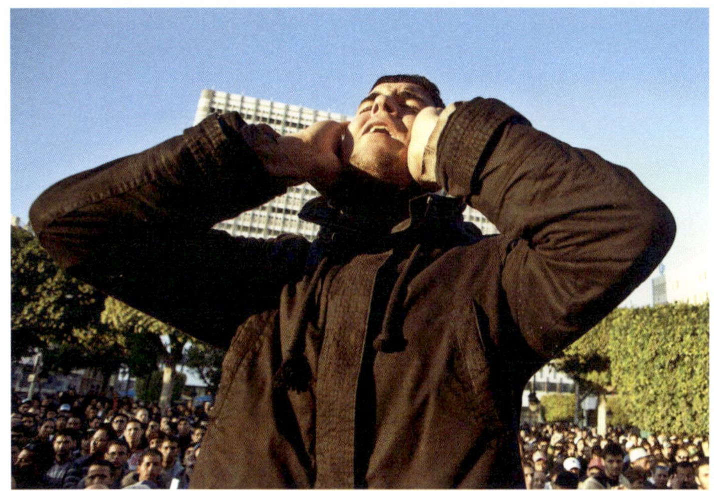

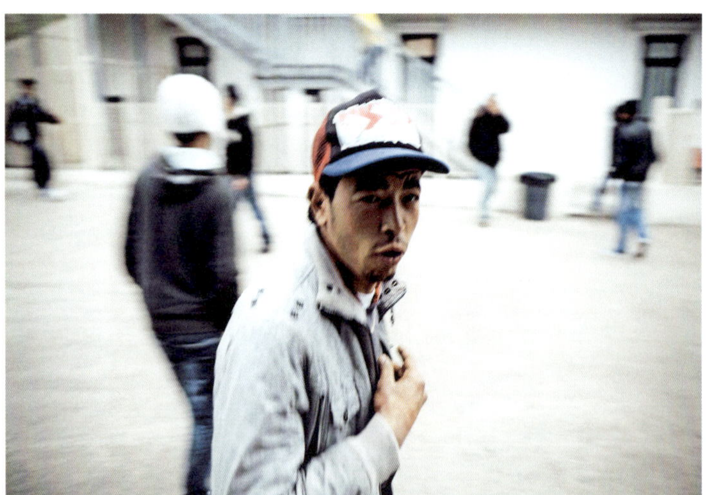

← Lampedusa in March, if I remember rightly. This is inside the center on Lampedusa, showing the people who remained from the first wave of Tunisian migrants between February and March.

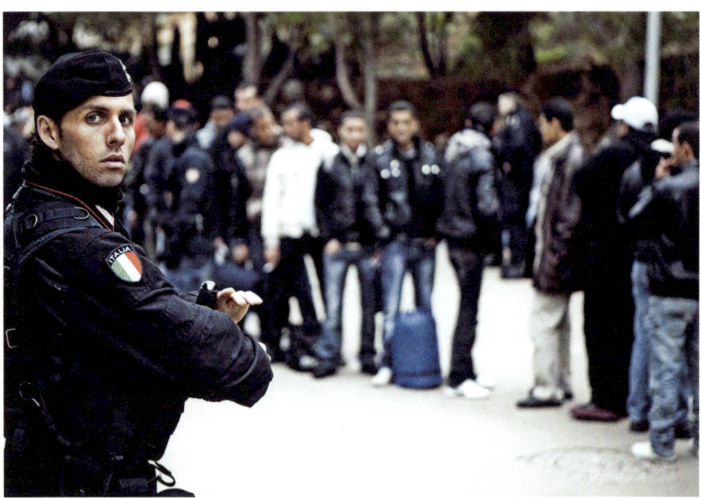

← This is how the authorities organize the transfers; on Lampedusa the migrants get a number.

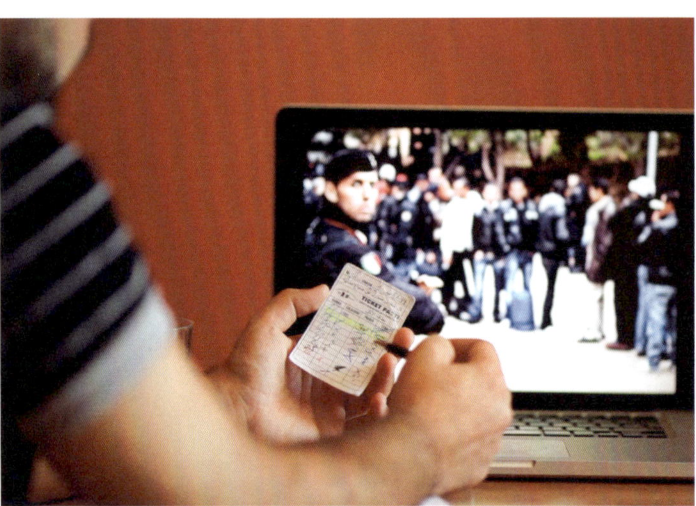

← This is a card from a guy who left yesterday. They gave him number twenty-eight of landing number one on May 6, 2011. They do this kind of registration directly on Lampedusa and from there people are transferred. On April 5, Roberto Maroni and Silvio Berlusconi succeeded in concluding a treaty with the temporary government in Tunisia to arrange forced repatriations for everyone arriving after that date. Those who arrived before this received temporary residence permits. The *Adhan*, the call to prayer from the minaret, was prohibited; this happened at the time of Ben Ali. It's like stopping people ringing the bells in Italy—it's the same thing.

This guy was repatriated twice in two weeks: he arrived on Lampedusa, they put him in an airplane, told him he was going to Milan, and after some hours he found himself in Tunis. So he took a boat back to Lampedusa—that was on May 6.

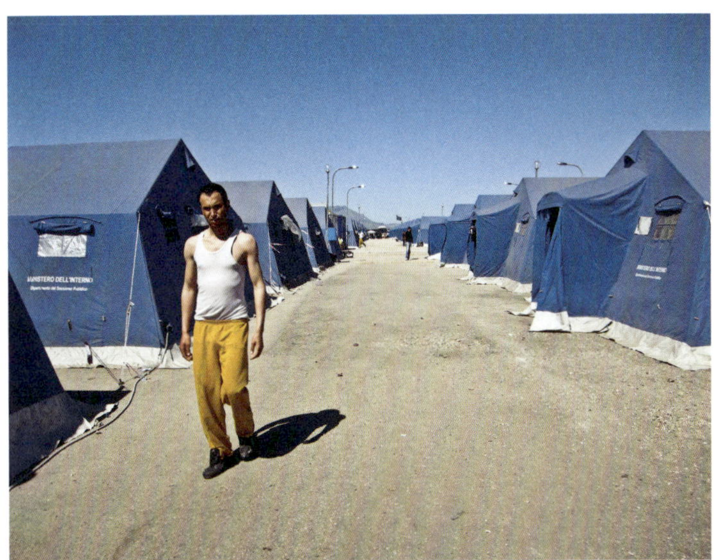

← This here is the CIE of Chinisia (Trapani), built for emergencies. The Italian government, or rather the Minister of the Interior, has built these centers as real, modern-day concentration camps.

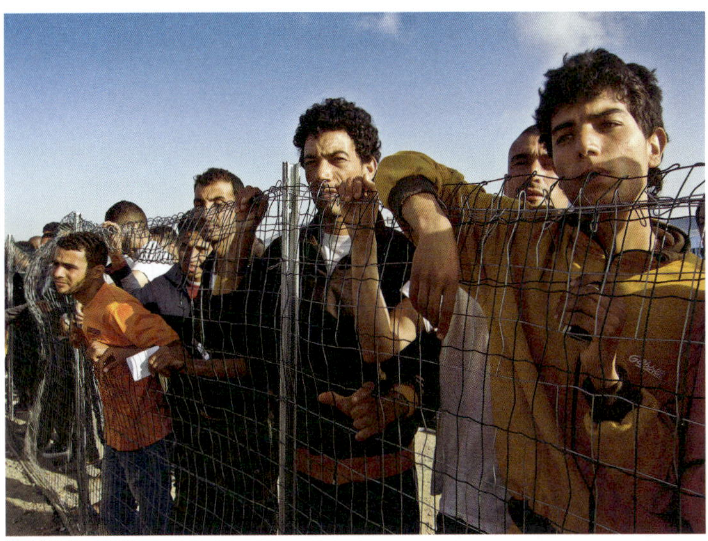

← These guys arrived before April 5, so all of them received temporary permission to stay. I managed to sneak into this center, passing myself off as a cultural mediator to do a photographic reportage. This is still inside the tent city. As you can see in the pictures there are minors and thirty-some-things—the average age is twenty-five—and many of them go to France. Some of them wanted to make a trip around Europe and then return to Tunisia for the elections, which should have taken place on July 25 but were then postponed to October.

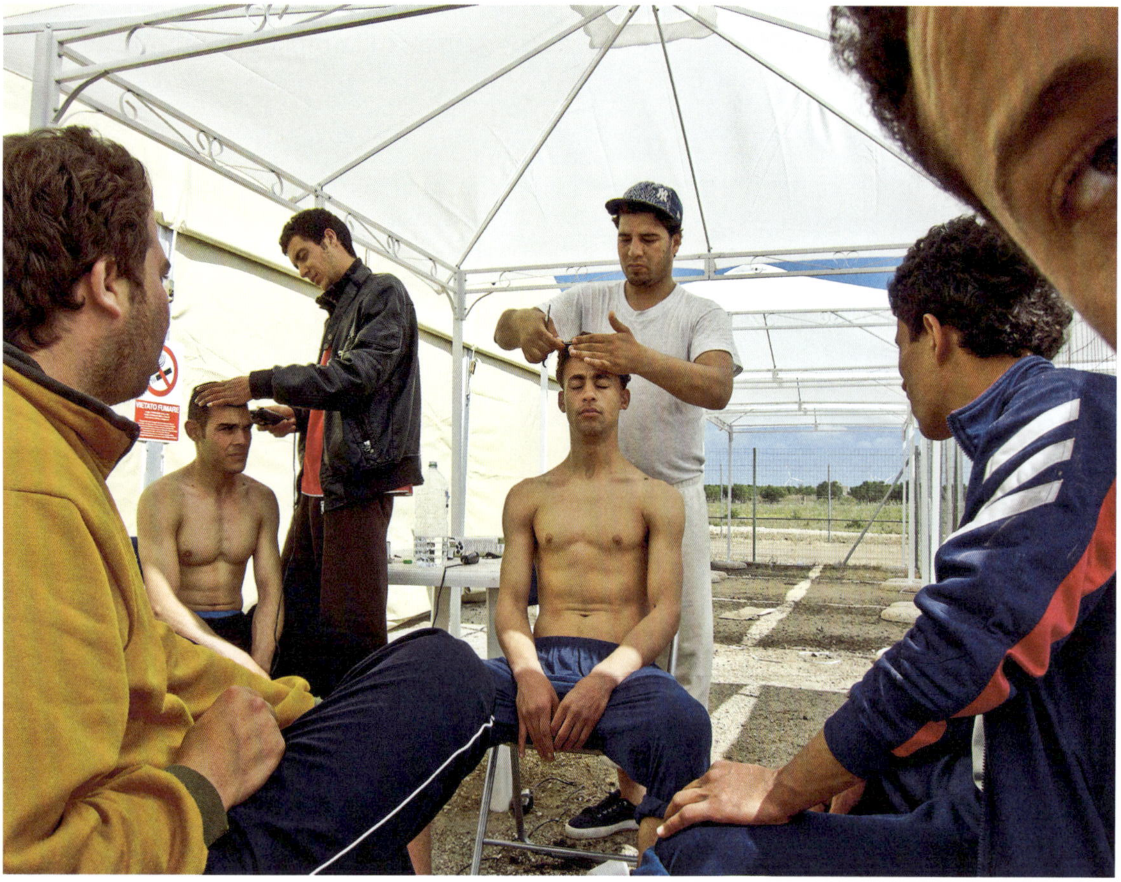

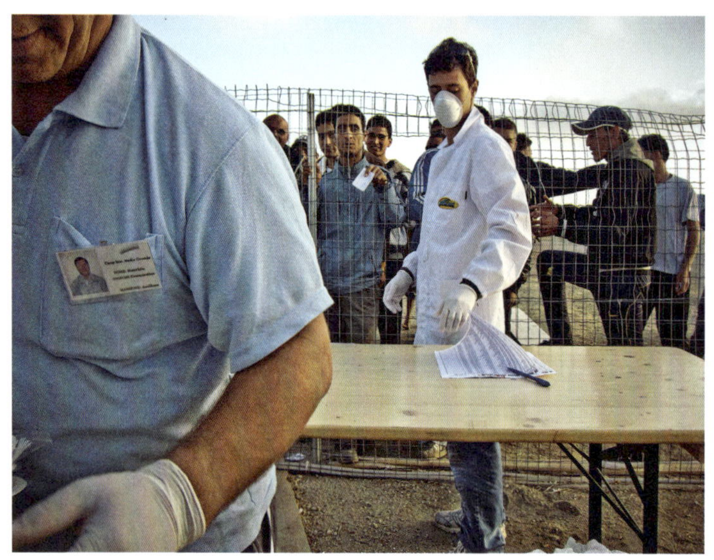

↑   This is still inside the camp. People stayed there for a month. They procured some combs for basic personal care. Here we see some people getting haircuts.

← This shows the meals being dis-tri-buted. At that time it was called CAI—Center for Reception and Identi-fica-tion—and all of the arrivals were to receive a permit for seven months. This was the fence that separated the Tunisians from the workers. Here is how they distributed the meals, but today they use containers, each about fifteen meters high with a counter. Migrants are like animals in a cage.

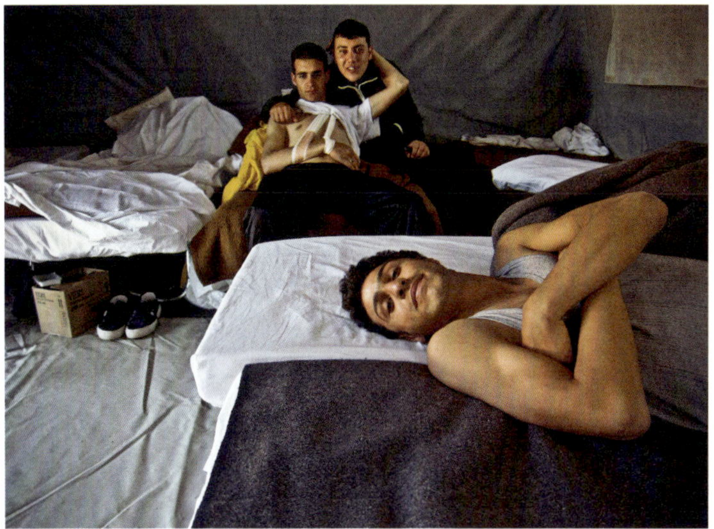

← This is inside the tent city in Sicily. The people are all very young. Bilal is the one with the bandaged arm. The majority of those who came to Italy during the days of the revolution actively participated in the uprising; over the years they had been oppressed, became disillusioned, and were then forced to flee. One time they made a concerted attempt to get close to the parliament, before the Tunisian police arrived on the scene and laid into them.

They shot at their legs and knees; Bilal and his friend were beaten with rifle butts and had their shoulder blades smashed. When Bilal arrived on Lampedusa, no one examined him, no medics or anything. Then he got locked up in this center I visited—it wasn't until a month later that an orthopedist finally came to examine him. He was prescribed some painkillers and that was it.

Anyone who has been in a Tunisian prison has learned how to mutilate himself as a form of protest, to find a way out. In an attempt to escape, many of them cut themselves. They cut horizontally; they learn how to do it. Many of them swallow pieces of iron or glass.

There have been many such incidents here in Italy, of the kind that happened to a kid a few months ago at Santa Maria Capua Vetere. Some of the people arriving in Italy apply for their voluntary repatriation when they see the other people there and the conditions they live in. Italy denies them this possibility and at that point people remain locked up in the center, stuck in the Italian bureaucracy, waiting for the Italian law.

الأديان لا تتعارض مع مفاهيم الولاء وحب الوطن

المشاركون في مؤتمر «تحديات المواطنة ودولة القانون»:

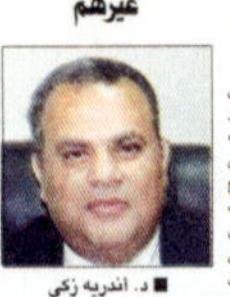

■ جانب من فعاليات المؤتمر

■ تحقيق ـ شادية يوسف

هل تتعارض الأديان مع مفاهيم المواطنة والولاء وحب الوطن؟ وإذا كانت الرسالات السماوية في مجملها تمثل دعوة إلى الحب والمؤاخاة الإنسانية ونشر الخير والتعايش بين البشر، فلماذا نجد واجبا من كثير من أبناء المجتمعات على اختلاف انتماءاتهم فيقتل ويدمر على أساس الدين والعرق واللون؟ وإذا كان أهل الديانات والأعراق المختلفة قد نشأت عبر تاريخ الإسلام حكومات إسلامية بدءا من المدينة المنورة التي تأسست على دستور مكتوب يعترف بحقوق المواطنة لجميع المكونات الدينية والعرقية للسكان، فمن أين تأتي مقولات ودعاوى التنظيمات الإرهابية التي تقتل وتدمر باسم الدين.

رجال الدين الإسلامي والمسيحي وخبراء الحفاظ الدين والاجتماع، المشاركون في مؤتمر «تحديات المواطنة ودولة القانون» الذي نظمته الهيئة الإنجيلية بمشاركة عدد من كبار علماء الأزهر والقساوسة يؤكدون أن الأديان لا تتعارض مع مفاهيم المواطنة والولاء والانتماء للوطن، وما يتخصص من حقوق وواجبات في الجماعات التكفيرية أكثر من تساء في الإسلام.

مال وإعلام

وأرجع د. محيي الدين عفيفي، ارتفاع وبروز الخطاب المتطرف في السنوات الماضية إلى ما يصاحبه من زخم إعلامي ودعم مالي، وقد ركز هذا الخطاب على المسحات من الناس، ومن ليس لديه حظ ثقافي واسع لبيع مشاعرهم وترغيب مفاهيمهم وعيهم.

■ د. محيي الدين عفيفي
أمين مجمع البحوث الإسلامية:

المتشددون يكفرون المسلمين ويعادون غيرهم

■ د. أندريه زكي
رئيس الطائفة الإنجيلية:

العيش المشترك ليس شعارا إنما هو واجب وفرض على الجميع

الحفاظ على مقومات الدولة

ويقول الدكتور محيي الدين عفيفي، الأمين العام لمجمع البحوث الإسلامية: إن قضية المواطنة من الهادي الحديثة المهمة بالنسبة للدول في عالمنا المعاصر.

رفض التدخل الأجنبي

الولاء والأمانة

غياب الرؤية

اختلاس المال من صاحب العمل تحت دعوى التمييز بين العمال.. حرام

ارتفاع عدد ضحايا مركب الموت إلى ١٧٨ قتيلا واستمرار البحث عن مفقودين

■ كتب ـ أحمد الأترجي ـ البحيرة ـ إمام الشفعي

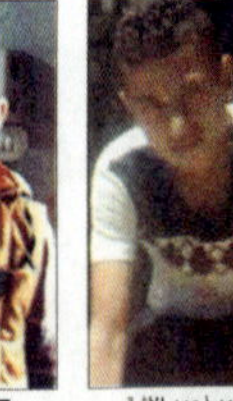
■ عبده غزال فرج

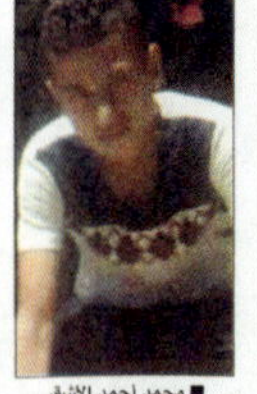
■ محمد أحمد الأشقر

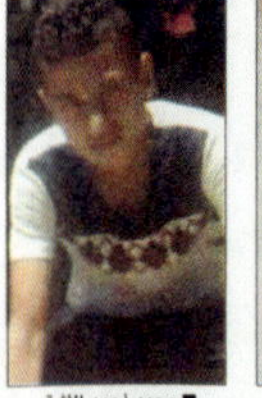
■ أحمد هلال الأشقر

سمسار الموت ينشر صورة أموال الضحايا على فيس بوك

■ كتبت ـ رانيا رفاعي

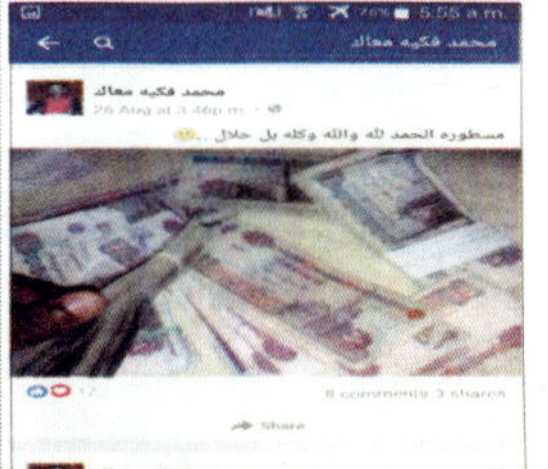

تشييع جثمان طالب الثانوي ضحية المركب المنكوب

■ المنصورة ـ نرمين عبد المجيد الشوادفي

حبس سيدة اقتحمت مطعما بسيارتها فقتلت اثنين وأصابت ٣ آخرين

■ المنصورة ـ إبراهيم العشماوي

.. وإصابة نقيب و٣ مجندين في انقلاب سيارة شرطة بنويبع

■ جنوب سيناء ـ هاني الأسمر

مصرع ضابط شرطة وإصابة ٣ آخرين إثر انقلاب سيارتهم ببور سعيد

■ بورسعيد ـ خضر خضير

الحبس ثلاث سنوات لمتهم بـ أحداث الإسماعيلية

■ كتبت ـ سميرة على عياد

تسريب زيت بـ صلاح سالم.. مازال لغزا أمام الشرطة!

■ كتب ـ محمد صبري

■ كتب ـ حاتم محسب

■ كتب ـ محمد كمال

Bad News Makes for Good Photos

Maurizio Seminara on his ambivalent work as a photojournalist on Lampedusa

PHOTO STORY: LISA BERGMANN

Maurizio Seminara is an Italian photojournalist who moved to Lampedusa in 2006 to document migration on the island. For almost ten years he presented his photos via Image Forum, an image databank catering to international news agencies and publishers. In an interview in 2010 he explained how his photos come into being, how they are distributed, and why certain images sell well. When the Migrant Image Research Group went back to the island in 2016, it was not possible to meet with him again. He became the assistant to Giusi Nicolini, the mayor of Lampedusa, until the last communal elections in June 2017.

The interview in the journalist's home office on Lampedusa was conducted by Lisa Bergmann, Armin Linke, Valeria Malito, Laura Morcillo, and Chris Spatschek.

I arrived on Lampedusa in 2006 when I accepted a contract from Sky TG24. Mauro Seminara is the signature I use for my photos and videos even though my full name is Maurizio. I have been working in journalism on Lampedusa for four years—initially only for the Sky channel in Italy. I moved to Lampedusa to document the "phenomenon of illegal migration," which was the description on the contract. For two years, up until the middle of 2008, Sky TG24 continuously broadcast video images of the landings on Lampedusa. After two years, we broke off the contract with Sky, and my company, MAS Media, was born, based in this small but cozy little study. My work expanded and Sky is now my client. When you cover the only news topic on Lampedusa, you end up being part of the news.

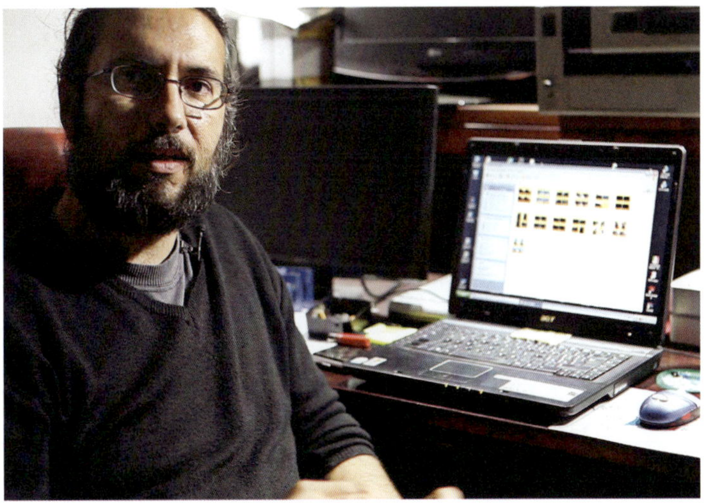

I started out as a photographer, then I was moved to video journalism before going back to taking pictures—I now mainly work with Agence France-Presse (AFP) as a photographer and provider of audiovisual services. A little for everyone, from the regional news to RAI. My images go to Sky, Mediaset, or those who show an interest in what Lampedusa has to offer in terms of a record, mainly of illegal immigration, of course.

At first I followed the phenomenon by simply documenting it here on Lampedusa. After initially trying to suppress my curiosity, it was inevitable that I would begin following illegal immigration as a phenomenon in some broader way—looking for news even outside Lampedusa, in Italy or in North Africa, getting acquainted with the how and why.

Q: *In the archive, roughly how many images do you have on the subject?*

SEMINARA: On my computer, there are twelve thousand pictures divided into four hundred folders, which means four hundred days of work. I can show you some pictures. I can try to pass on this know-how, if I can, with a few visual stories. I will go through the images a little at random, because there are two or three years of work here.

I remember things as I look at the photos. In most cases there remain impressions that are striking even if you're used to documenting everything from murder to the ships landing. But there are things that leave a particular impression.

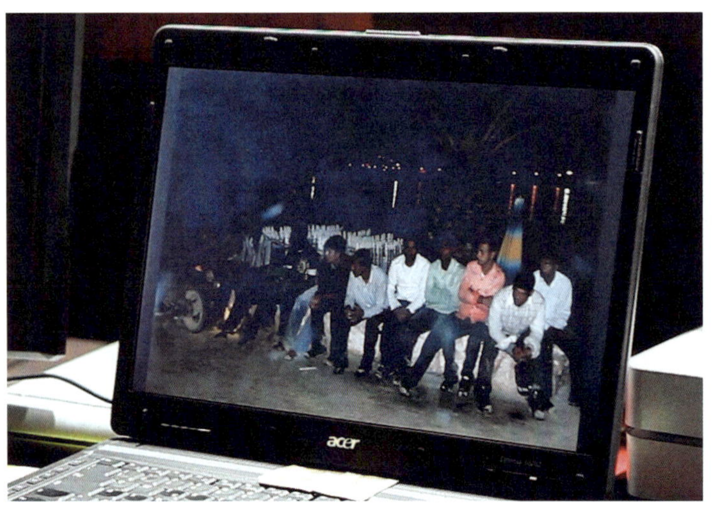

← For example, this is an image of a landing. I arrived around four or five in the morning on the beach of Guitgia. This is the main beach, more within reach of the island, where each year the O'scia music festival is organized by Claudio Baglioni—an event that was born eight years ago, with the aim of sensitizing the public to the topic of migration.

Eight years on, this event has forgotten its origins and is now funded by the Italian Ministry of the Interior—in other words, by the same ministry that, in the same year it funded the event, turned away migrants at sea, forcing them to return to Libya with consequences that have been written about in the newspapers.

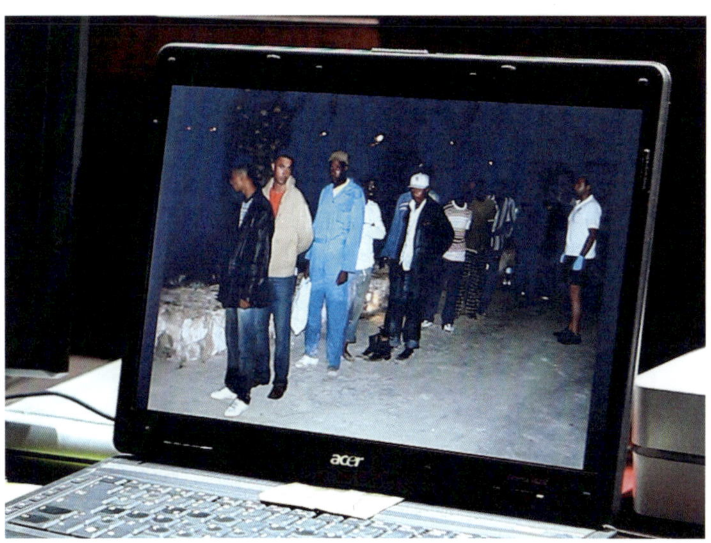

← These people arrived on the beach at four in the morning and immediately tripped the alarm, starting the usual procedure. The police and coast guards arrived. The police because the people were already on the ground and so are of relevance to the judicial police, and the coast guard for the recovery of the boat and for all coastal and offshore operations. They were lined up ready to be counted and transferred, waiting for the bus from the Centro di Accoglienza, the reception center.

This is one of the more unusual events. This type of landing almost represents an exception because at that time the people would usually be intercepted at sea and taken ashore by a coast guard from a military boat. The whole process took place in a contained zone.

So some boats got past the authorities, and people found themselves stranded on the beach. This is what officials were trying to avoid at all costs so as to also avoid an uproar on Lampedusa by the Lampedusans—there was a strong fear among the population of the risk such news would pose to the tourist industry.

Sometimes it was less risky working in this context; there was less pressure. At other times, for a week you might be given a hard time if you went to the bar to get a coffee. This is why living on the island as a reporter becomes suffocating. Remember, the island covers $25\,km^2$ with six thousand inhabitants, so you are always meeting the same people.

Q: As a photographer, you are given the blame for creating a negative image of the island because you photograph immigrants on a beach that is dedicated to tourism?
SEMINARA: Yes. If it were not for me, if I did not live on Lampedusa and were not working there, neither the television news nor the newspapers would get these images. In most cases, news of this type, deprived of its visual power, would not make it onto the page. Because of me, the whole of Italy sees dramatic news about Lampedusa in the newspapers every day, and this coverage can be annoying and may influence tourism on the island.

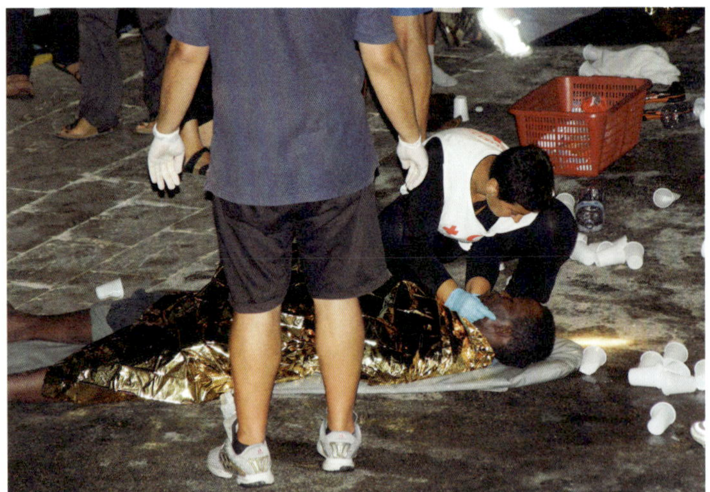

← Q: *What are these aluminum covers?*

SEMINARA: They are called thermal blankets. It is simply the material they are made of, plastic with a chrome surface. When wet clothes are removed and this is put on, it prevents loss of heat from the human body. So it allows the body to recover its own temperature.

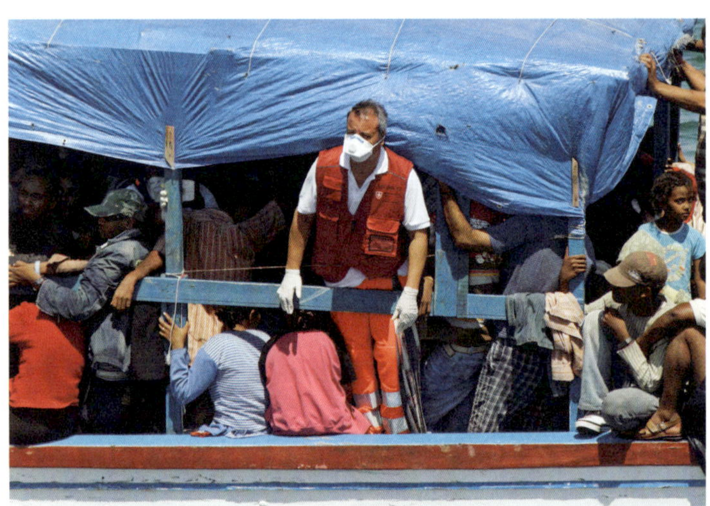

← Q: *And the fact that the operators wear gloves or respirator masks?*

SEMINARA: Thanks to some journalists, this has come to be seen as something evil. It gets underlined by some people as a racist gesture. But clearly that is not so. Among these unfortunate people are many who have suffered a long period of hunger and made a long and dangerous journey where they certainly cannot afford to drink mineral water or wash regularly. Then they find themselves abandoned in a little house in Libya where hygiene is nonexistent and they commonly arrive with scabies. In some cases someone arrives who has tuberculosis. They might not be aware they are carrying the disease, they do not have the means to go to the doctor, they do not know that this cough is not just a cough. But operators are likely to be infected. So they have to protect themselves at least in the first stages. After that the people are visited by a doctor and have the opportunity to wash.

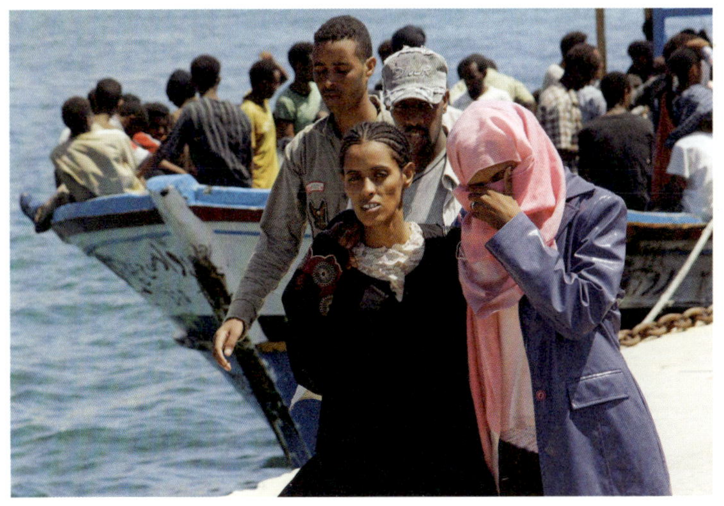

← *Q: Earlier there was a picture of a girl passing the camera. She seemed to lift a hand in order to cover her face from a possible photo. Could that be the case?*
SEMINARA: Yes, many or even most Eritreans are afraid of being photographed. They are in a more delicate situation than the Maghrebi or other ethnic groups, meaning the Eritrean government will search for them and demand that they are repatriated.

In some cases, they will come to a bad end in prison; in other cases, they will do some time in jail and then be enrolled again in the Eritrean army. So Eritreans are literally political refugees—there is an association for protecting Eritreans, who recently presented a dossier revealing that there are Eritreans collaborating with the authorities in almost all countries, including Italy, and playing a double game. "I am Eritrean, hello." You turn to someone from your own country, but instead this person relays your full name and location in Italy to the government in Eritrea. It is natural that people are afraid of being photographed.

In other cases, it is because of modesty. Before arriving in Italy, people have a different outlook on this trip. Which is a little like that of the Italians who emigrated to the United States in the early 1900s. When they arrived, before disembarking, they put on their best clothes, combed their hair, and gave themselves a more dignified look. For these migrants it is the same. They set off with the most beautiful and valuable clothes they have. They do not know that as soon that they come ashore, they will lose everything.

They don't get their shoes back, and their clothes are thrown away because they are given clothes at the Centro di Accoglienza. But people have this vision of how things will be.

When they land, they realize that the arrival was different from the journey they had imagined. They are dirty, smell of gasoline—because on board the gasoline spills onto them—and have no shoes. They are battered. It is a question of dignity: they do not want to be photographed in this condition.

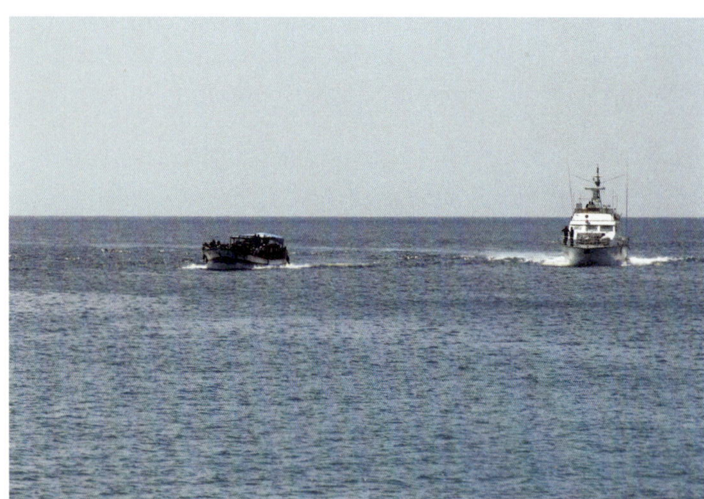

← This is another ordinary circumstance. The guard with the motor boat. At the most, he will recover another boat or two with migrants.

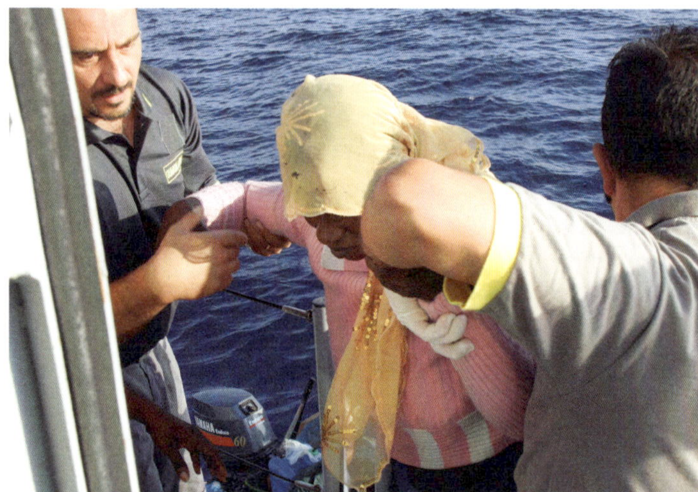

← This is from a sequence of photos— in such cases I take an average of four or five shots per second, because you see someone who has a particular expression, who is afraid, perhaps was already afraid of the sea … who is afraid to go up to the edge of the boat he arrived on. You can see the fear of crossing the gangway of the motor boat. There is the evident cynicism of the reporter looking for a sensational incident.

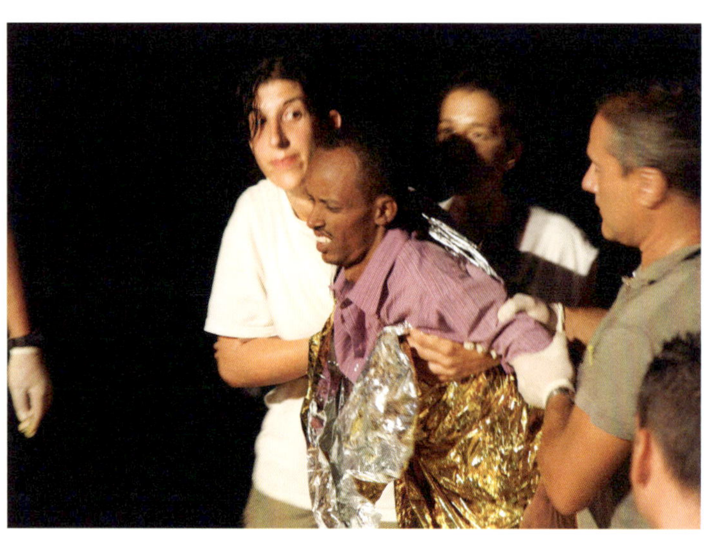

← This photo is less sellable, for a very banal reason: it doesn't look good when printed on newsprint paper, which is unsuitable for creating definition, except perhaps for rendering black. Maybe it's also too artistic a style for a newspaper—you can generally find these kinds of images published in magazines or at least on glossy paper.

And those are the cases where something strikes me. At that moment I stop taking journalistic photos and start shaking off the dust on some photography techniques I know. I have my doubts about suggesting them to the agency. In this case, yes, I sold some of them, others maybe not—anyway, you don't care about all the details being visible. It's the details that make the pictures easier to sell because they contextualize them—taking the picture in such a way that you can clearly see the Medici Senza Frontiere (MSF) emblem on these white T-shirts. Or if we're talking about soldiers, then it is about seeing the escutcheon on the shoulder or arm. Here you don't pay attention to that. Here you isolate the expression of suffering and accentuate the chaos.

I don't remember what you call this technique. Nowadays with Photoshop, you cut out the main object, apply a motion blur or a movement or some blurring effect to the background, and reinsert the main object.

At that time, you did these things at the moment of capture and you could add hardly anything during the developing. You had other tricks during the developing and printing phase. Combined with the camera moving forward, it is almost like a theatrical performance.

You should take this kind of photo using the flash—that way you get a shorter, reduced exposure time, and you don't get a motion blur on your main object. But you increase the time of exposure a bit and follow the movement of your object … it isn't easy to do but if you give it one or two tries, you should be able to manage it. It's that 1/50th or 1/60th of a second that allows you to catch the object in a stable position, so the object emerges with more detailed contours, while everything else moving behind gets blurred.

It's a technique often used in car and motorbike magazines. Even if the car is moving at only ten kilometers per hour, you capture it with an exposure of 1/250th of a second, increasing the time in a manner that creates this "striping" effect behind its rear, which gives the impression of high speed. This adds additional value to the motorbike they have to advertise.

But here you won't show the speed, you'll show the chaos. If I had to imagine this photo as a short video clip, I would imagine the man moving at natural speed with his facial expression and his gasp. And behind him, as if in slow motion, the slowed-down chaos with the audio. An audio like this, with him shouting, "H-o-l-d h-i-m!" and her, "C-o-m-e o-n." It is slowed-down confusion because you focus only on him.

Q: It's as if these photography techniques enabled you to report two different psychological levels. In this case it's about the migrant. The two levels of focus become two levels of perception as well, with different, unsynchronized focuses.

SEMINARA: Yes, and fundamentally my idea of photographic technique is this: the prodigy of the snapshot, of the fraction of a second, when you succeed in immortalizing things as you see them. Video, on the other hand, or the photographic sequence, with fifteen to twenty-five pictures per second, has a higher degree of realism.

Maybe photography allows you to distort, to interpret, or to report in a different manner. If you master the photographic technique, you can narrate on more levels.

There is a difference from photos you use in a newspaper that have nothing artistic about them, no photographic technique, but just serve to portray a topic in the clearest and sharpest way possible. However, in this picture it is possible to perceive the tension, the fear of the subject that has been arrested and is being brought to the car.

If you manage to find a way to valorize what you see, you ensure that a single picture, exhibited and seen by other people, is able to convey ten percent of the hundred percent that you experienced.

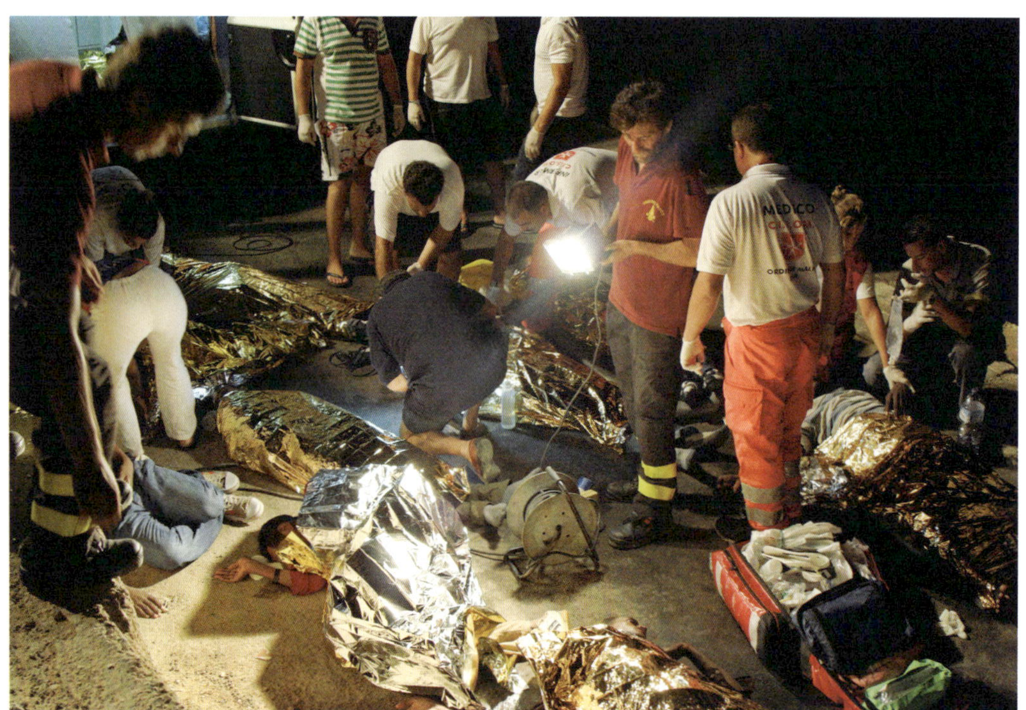

↑   In my opinion, the same applies to this photo—it's obviously taken with a different technique, but the concept is the same. In the scene you see pure chaos with a lot of people lying on the ground, wrapped in thermal blankets. Everyone is busy all around with the lights accentuating only certain aspects.

Evidently, in this scene there are good reasons for this beautiful theatrical lighting. If you could take photos saying, "Stop, one moment, I'll change the position of this floodlight. Give me another one over here," and so on, okay. But doing this in reportage is a bit more complicated. In a fraction of a second you have to realize how to take advantage of the given situation without adding anything, without making what you are capturing artificial.

In this case here, the good luck for me as a photographer in this situation was the halogen floodlight set up by the firefighters and aimed at the location in order to allow the medics to get a better view of what they were doing.

Therefore the situation was all low light, with this powerful contrast. I only had to find the best shot to highlight it.

Like this one. Here I was searching for the beam of light on the location. I was looking for contours. These are minor characters with a dash of light, a marginal light. That's the main scene.

One thing I never liked and which I often see are shots at eye level. I don't do that, not even when I'm working with video. It's a banal perspective, too realistic. If I change this axis and place the camera fifty centimeters above the ground, everything gets a completely different effect.

Q: You are searching for a kind of Caravaggesque picture, aren't you?

SEMINARA: I adore Caravaggio. Also this reverse effect. I was standing on a bench; you can see a small piece of it out of focus. So between my street-level view and the man's view was a difference of, say, one meter, one meter twenty. In addition, the camera was elevated to push him even more to the ground.

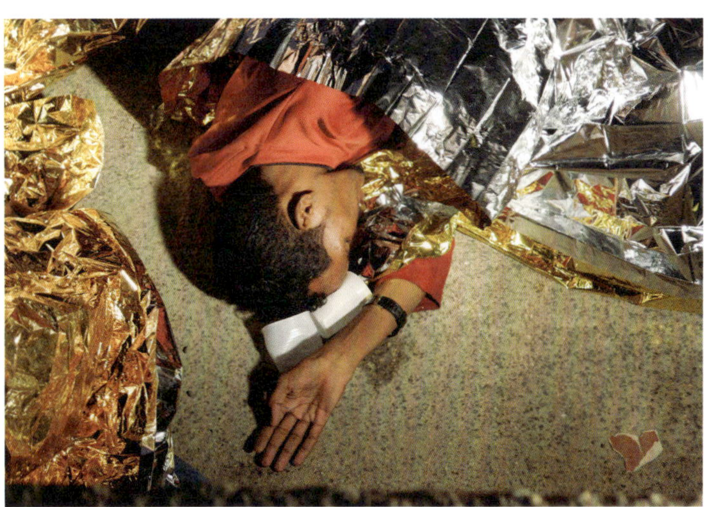

← I cannot describe this photo to you. The detail of the hand and then all this around. Do you know the typical Italian Easter eggs? Joyful, colorful, with shiny paper, all gold and silver—everything around this man constitutes a contrast to the situation he is in.

Q: It looks like an object from NASA.

SEMINARA: Yes, but it's exactly the thin material with all these wrinkles that reminds me of pannetoni and Easter eggs … usually a dying person—at least it seems as if he is dying—is not covered in wrapping paper.

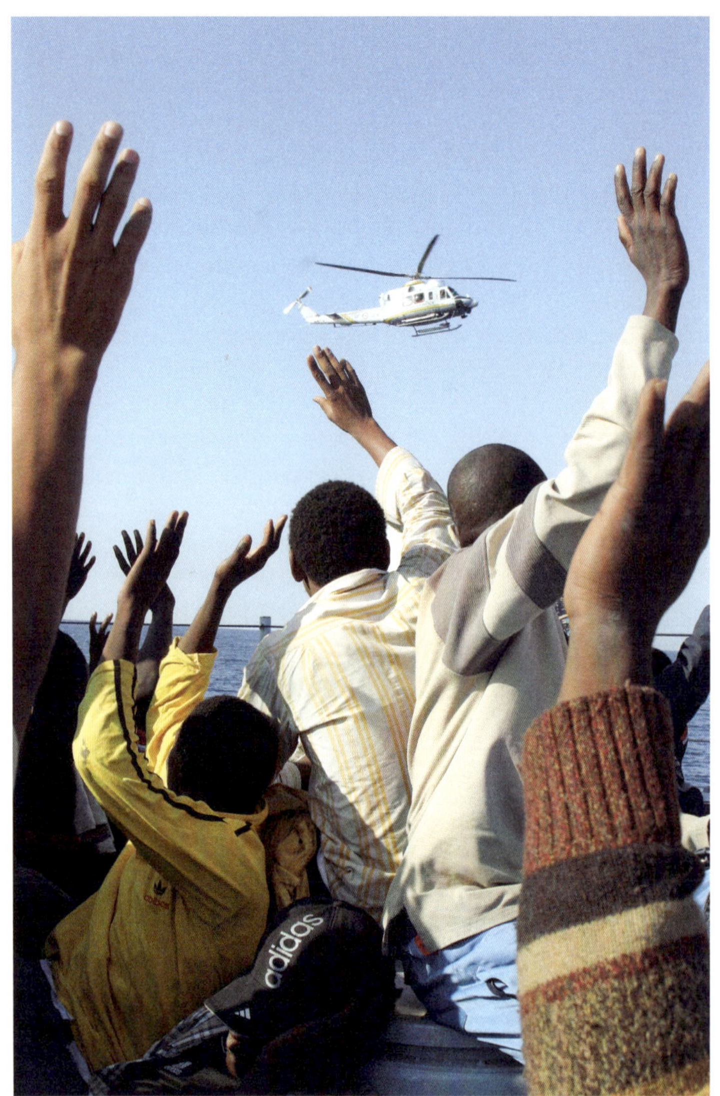

← This is a beautiful moment. This was the helicopter of the Guardia di Finanza, the Italian finance and border police who discovered them. Their boat had an engine breakdown. They had just gotten on board when the helicopter requested the okay from the ship to leave. As soon as they understood that the helicopter was leaving, all of them waved their arms to say goodbye, to thank him.

AFP has only one rival, which is Reuters; and Reuters has only one rival, which is AFP. All the rest are minor photo agencies. In practical terms, AFP has customers in the United States, in China, and all over the world. Among all the customers of AFP it's possible that someone, for some reason, is looking for a striking picture and then after a year searches the AFP archives he has subscribed to and picks out this photo.

All of the photos are published. Generally, there are good editors at AFP, so when a photo is published and brought into circulation, the picture is sold for sure.

> Q: Once you have sold a picture to AFP, do you also get a percentage, do you make a one-off sale, or do you have a monthly contract? How does the mechanism work?

SEMINARA: There are various mechanisms, various agreements. Theoretically, the most profitable method is when you keep the royalties, and every time your photo is published, they have to respect your copyright.v

I prefer the way I do it with AFP: I hand over a package of pictures with the copyright, the pictures become theirs, and they do whatever they want with them. Why discover one day that the *Chicago Tribune* published one of my photos on the front page and didn't pay 100 euros for the copyright? If you give me some extra money, you can use the pictures forever, and I don't care any more.

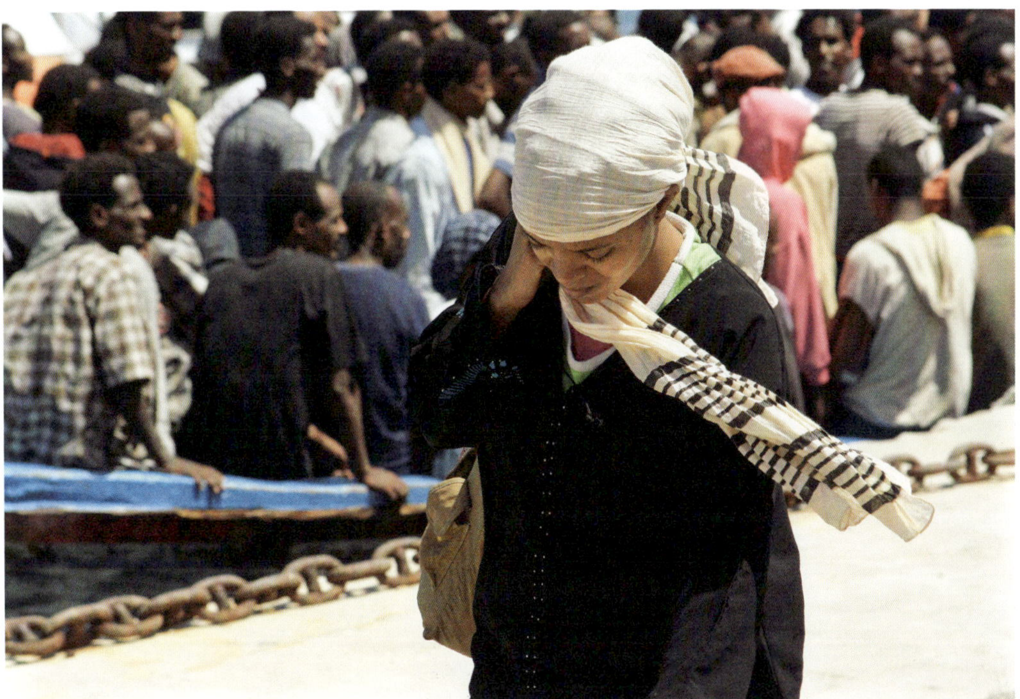

↑   This is a photo I like a lot. It's not so much what it evokes; it's more the composition of the picture. In the end, technically speaking, the basis of this kind of photography is the ability to compose the picture, to balance it, and to harmonize it for the viewer.

I liked the gentle passing of the wind on her foulard and the soft blur creating a single background with the people evidently still on the boat she had got off—her stunned gaze turned down, intense. All in all it matched.

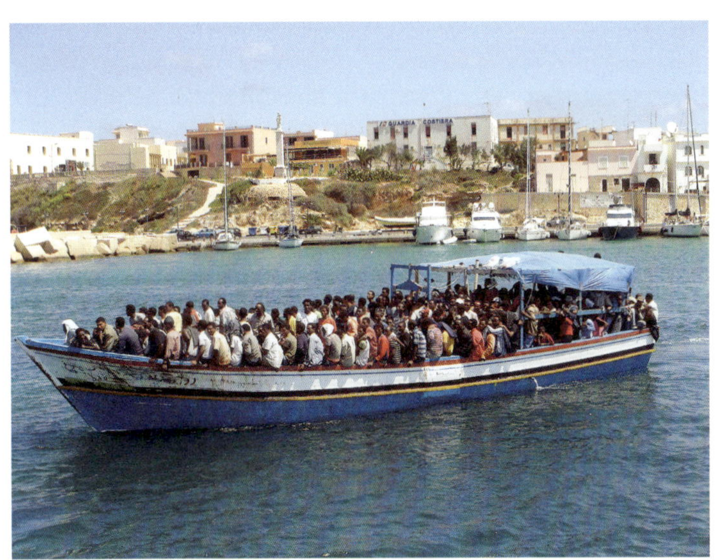

←   These are the tasty pictures that are preferred by the newspapers and often get printed immediately. Evidently, these are the ones which show a boat crammed with people in a more elementary, more simplistic manner.

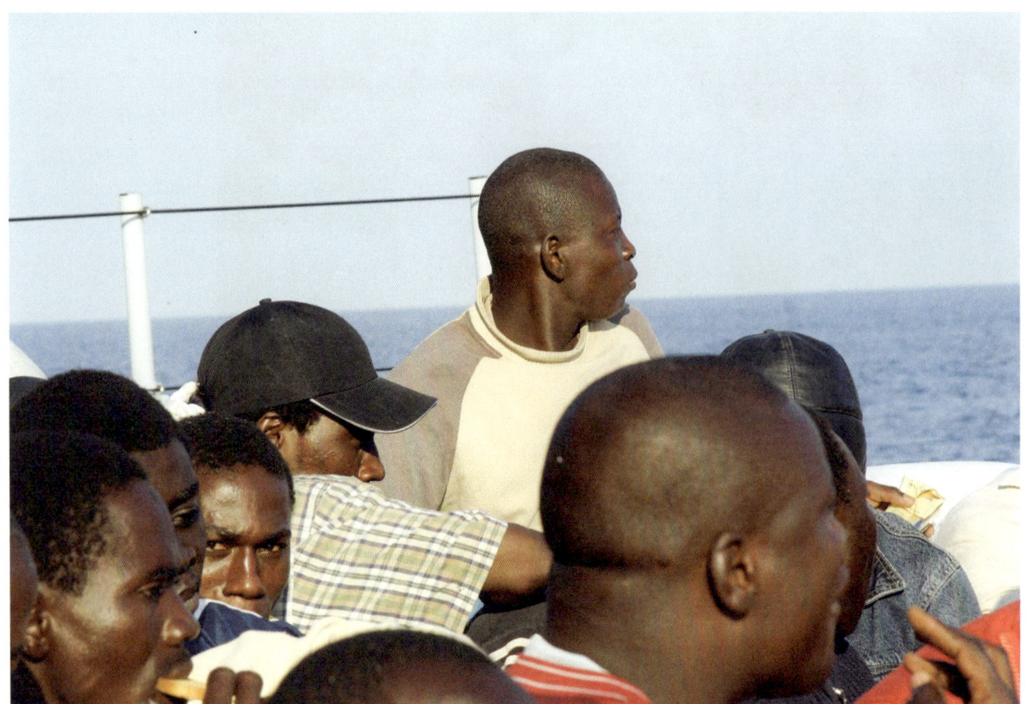

↑   Here you see another one of those pictures I took because I liked it. It was bought, and I have also seen it published a few times; it is not particularly useful without a nice title, a nice caption, because in this picture you see only a few people of color. If you don't mention it, you don't know what the situation is. From the photograph, you cannot tell that they are on board a patrol boat; you don't know that they are headed to Lampedusa; that they are looking back and that behind them, where they are looking, is the rubber boat they came on, being towed by the patrol boat. But it is very intense in its expression.

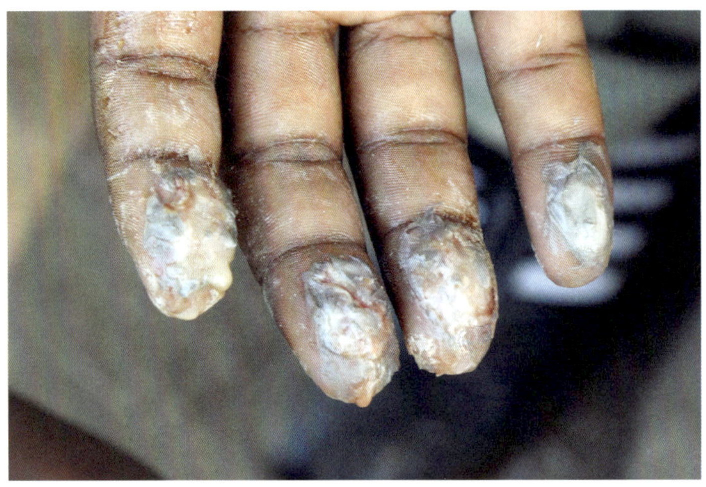

←   These are scorched fingertips, burned by the motor. Normally the magazines publish this kind of picture in half-page size. It is a striking detail often accompanied by descriptions of misery.

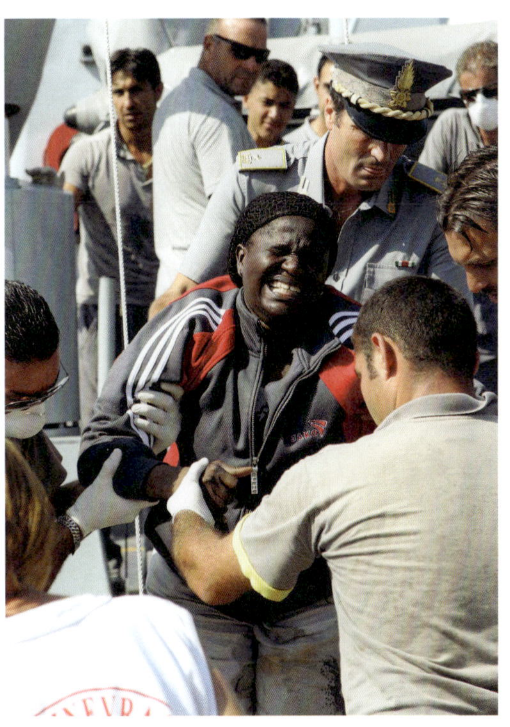

← How did this picture come into being? You are there at a few meters' distance observing who gets on board the patrol boat of the Guardia di Finanza. And you see clearly that the first ones to get off the boat are the more battered ones. Now it's your lens's turn, near the gangway. You start taking pictures and make the first click. And then, when you finally get an unobstructed view, you see that they are about to push this woman down the gangway, that's when you begin to shoot. It's broad daylight, and you capture the intense light with the photosensitivity set to 800 ASA.

It has to be at least 1/250th or 1/500th of a second; you take five pictures a second. Why do you take all these pictures? Because with these five you have your margin of error, and there will be one in which coincidentally all of the subjects have the good or bad facial expression you want.

The captain, directed to accompany her with a certain gentleness, bites his lip; the petty officer behind him stands still and stops the others. It looks like a particularly tricky moment. These people are busy pulling her up; and in the center the expression of particular suffering at that moment.

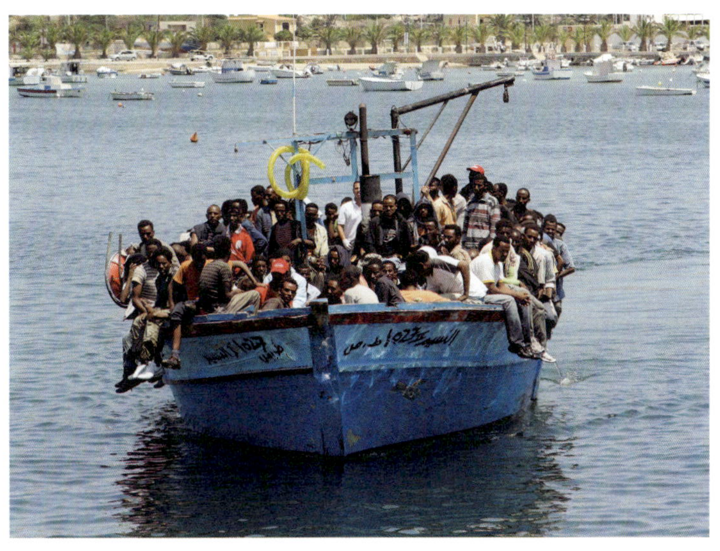

← This was the most published image last year. In the last year, or in the last two—it became the emblem, the front-page picture with titles like "Illegal immigration." Why do you think this is the case? You can clearly see that the boat, which you can tell by its name is Arab … that so many people are on board—so many, that many of them are sitting with their legs outside, off the boat. It's full of colors, it's intense. It explains the concept of an old and unsafe boat, a boat of hope. It already makes up the headline by itself—it doesn't need long explications of numbers, times, and types of boats.

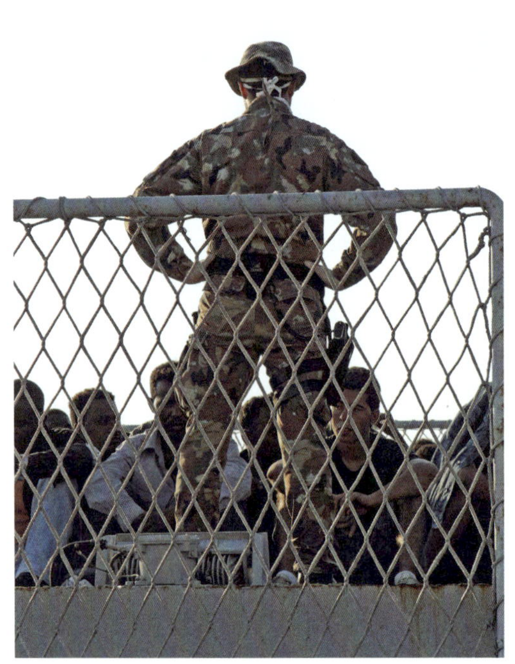

←   This one here is a bit more of a straightforward cynical search for a picture. Right now I can't remember, but maybe a meter more or less in that direction there was the gap between the one fender and the other. But I was looking for that one.

This grid is not made of steel, but anyway it makes a particular impression seeing these people, sitting there with their humbled facial expressions, behind a bit of latticework which seems to be a prison, intensified by this man in camouflage uniform, standing with his hands in his belt, making him look severe, and with a large part of his pistol visible.

These are easy to sell. These are the ones you are looking for, waiting for the moment. From the ones we have seen now in our two pages of selections, we have two contrasting types of photograph: one that lets you earn money, and one in which you rediscover the reason why, when you were only twelve years old, you already had a passion for photography and why you began to follow photographers and to learn.

Q: *How are your relations with institutions like Médécins Sans Frontières (MSF) or the International Organisation of Migration (IOM)? The other time you told me that at times they are also alert to what you take photos of.*
SEMINARA: Everyone stays a bit alert to this; in military areas this is for military reasons, and for NGOs and nonprofit organizations it's a question of protecting their rights.

Generally, the police are on the alert when they see me approaching a jerrycan aboard a rubber boat, so they immediately send me away because maybe I was taking a macro picture of the jerrycan's labels, on which you can read that they are Libyan products.

Relief workers stop you because the moment they receive the passengers, they all become potential asylum seekers; and as potential asylum seekers, their pictures have to be protected. It could be dangerous for them to find themselves on the front page of a newspaper.

But this is a conflict between a humanitarian organization and journalism per se. For them, at this moment, he is a potential asylum seeker; for us, he is news, and according to the rights enjoyed by the news, I take a picture, and that's it.

Actually it has never been regulated as a professional ethic; the "Carta di Roma" has never been applied, which should avoid these specific situations concerning migration. Certainly it's applied scrupulously by the press when it comes to the protection of minors. When there is the probability that one of the people is a minor when a picture is actually published, the image is disguised with a blur that covers the face.

For us, the idea of not taking photos of their faces is unthinkable, because in this case you would have nothing to take a picture of.

Q: *You told us about the nongovernmental organizations, how they are worried about not being photographed at work and about them as institutions.*

SEMINARA: The nongovernmental organizations live from public or private funding. The more visibility they gain, the more credibility they get in the eyes of the people, and the more popular they become, so people are more willing to say, "I will donate five euros too."

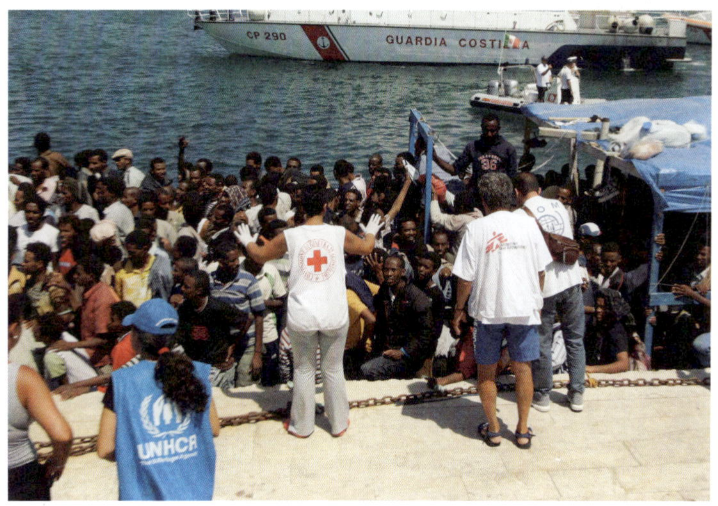

← So while you are taking photos, you have to make sure that some jacket—a vest with the name of a humanitarian organization printed on it—doesn't push its way in front of you. The same goes for the military units.

Just like any enterprise, the military units need to increase their budget in any way possible. So when the patrol boat of a military unit is always on the front page, is always present in the TV news, you can see that they are working well. If they work well, they will also be financed in the future. Maybe the year after, two more boats will be sent to strengthen the division. So for them, too, it's important to be seen. Also for them it's important to be continually present, to have an image come back of the kind they seek to provide.

In a word, everyone criticizes the camera lenses, and at the same time everyone goes looking for them. "And you are?" "We are from RAI." "Ah, RAI. If you like, there is this person willing to give you an interview." Generally this is the effect of the TV or of the press.

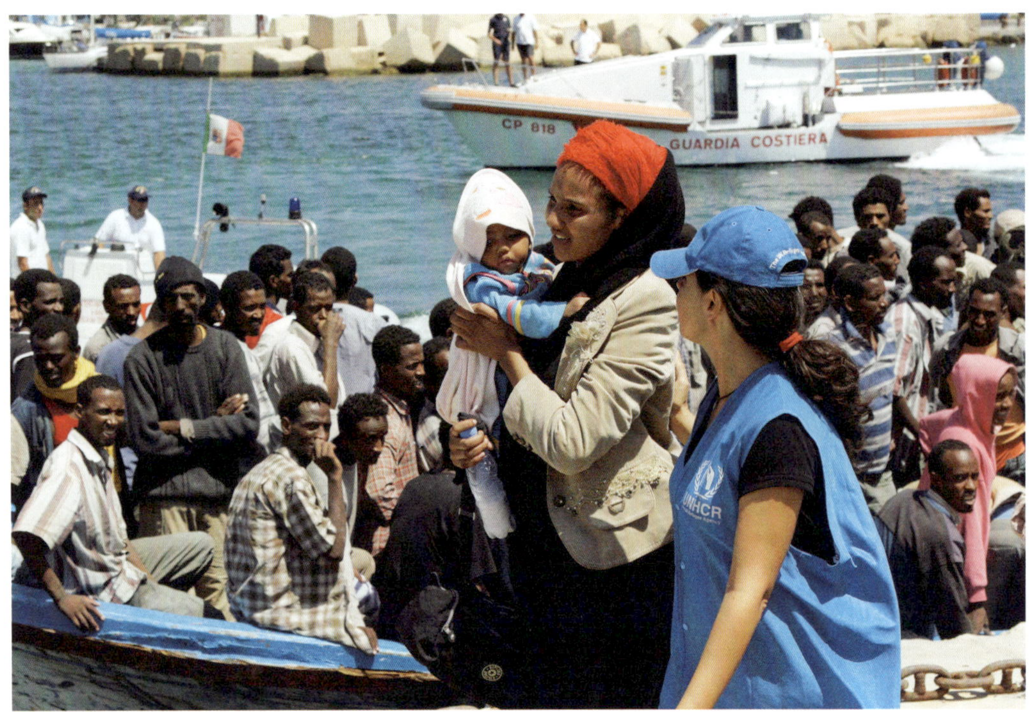

↑   A mother with her child, that is how to sell it …
Q: *The other time you told me some details of Yamaha outboard motors not being approved in Italy.*
SEMINARA: What I was interested in was that not everything
is so unpredictable. I think that's a thing that anybody can
understand with a minimum of effort. Not taking a picture for
journalistic but for investigative purposes. Normally the police
take pictures, or if they are far away offshore, the police ask
the captain of the port's office or whoever operated the rescue
mission for pictures of the boats.

They are interested in the type of boat, if there is a registration number on the boat, and, for the rubber boats, what kind
of outboard motor they used.

That's the moment you realize that in the course of the year
2008 something like—let's take a random number—a hundred
rubber boats arrived and ninety of them had the same identical motor, the same brand, the same model, the same production
line, and probably the police were able to see that the serial
number, the registration number of the motor was consecutive.

Even a child would ask the question, "Did the Libyan
traffickers become organized on an industrial scale?"

Someone accumulated a big stock of motors, directly from
the manufacturer of that brand. This means that brand X
supplied these people with a stock of two hundred identical
motors.

If this was true, it would be enough to send an official letter
to ask the manufacturer of this brand, who has a base in Italy,
just like many Japanese manufacturers have an Italian brand X

… to ask the manufacturer for a copy of the receipt and you would know who they supplied these motors to.

It will turn out that they have been supplied to the boatyard of Tom, Dick, and Harry in Libya. Okay, you go there to investigate and you're already only one step away from the bosses of the organization.

We are facing the basic logistical system, and sometimes you're more surprised by what is not done than by what actually is done. The artist and activist Giacomo Sferlazzo can also tell you that the boats are not searched, but sometimes it happens that you find an identity card. In this case I could say, "All the passengers are lined up here, let's see who looks like him? Him! Is this you?"

Perfect, one job less to do. We only take the fingerprints, because we already know what you call yourself, your name, your surname, nationality. But maybe it's okay that you waste two or three months identifying these people. Two or three months means at least 30 euros a day for accommodation and food in a migrant reception center, plus all the incidental expenses.

Who cares, gentlemen, it's the European Union that pays, which paid in this case … and now the EU pays Libya directly, so that they stop people over there.

Italy has some police instructors in Libya. Italy does not only instruct the state police, but presumably also Libyan intelligence too; that means that the Libyan secret service is monitored by the Italian secret service. This was confirmed by the Italian-Libyan friendship treaty signed two years ago. It covers the movement of migrants to a marginal extent—the fundamental thing is the gas pipeline from Algeria; instead of going directly to Sardinia, it has to pass through Libya to arrive in Sicily.

So it's necessary to spend many billions. It's fundamental in this treaty that Italy does not only sell weapons to Libya but also that Italy instructs and supports the construction of buildings in which Libyan engineers can gain Italian know-how and start producing weapons autonomously.

If that's the way it is, the simplest deduction that we can make is that we have our secret services over there.

If the Italian minister has to face a problem, an illegal migration flow, he does not rely on his own secret service in the country of provenance. That means that the police here have the possibility of knowing how many boats are leaving. This is a more serious fact than it seems to be, because our discourse is based on the arrival of the boats, while the more dramatic aspect deals with the boats that do not arrive here.

Someone in Italy knows exactly how many victims the Strait of Sicily has claimed, how many shipwrecks have occurred, but they won't ever publish these facts.

We are talking about information which is difficult to publish, because it's an arbitrary assertion. I say, there was a boat out at sea that never arrived and must have been shipwrecked. But this argument is way too easy to contradict. You're inventing this. Prove it. How can you tell?

Q: There are different kinds of newspapers—you said that in detail—different typologies, different types of publishing speed. Does this function as a filter for you as a producer of images?

SEMINARA: Yes, this is an aspect related to the time frame. A newspaper preferably wants to close the page and needs to have the layout of the page finished by 6 or 7 pm.

When the news is big—"Stop the Presses!" news—even at midnight you will stop the printing presses, change the news, and then continue the print run. A newspaper generally publishes articles with two or three columns, four with a picture—that is the maximum. In four columns it's not possible to go into more depth; that's why the photo needs to be purely informative.

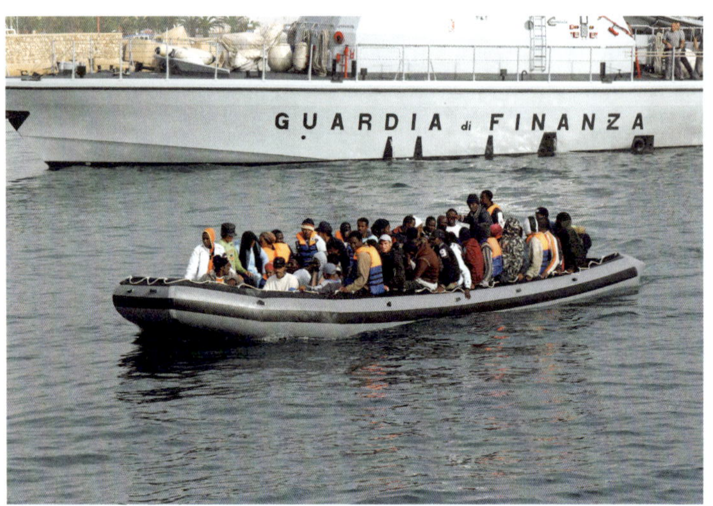

←   This is a photo for a newspaper. The rubber boat is in the foreground, you can see that there are many people on it, and behind it, there is a boat with an enormous signboard saying "Guardia di Finanza." This one says everything. It includes the basic rule of journalism—what in English are called "the five Ws": who, what, where, when, why. It's all there, it's perfect.

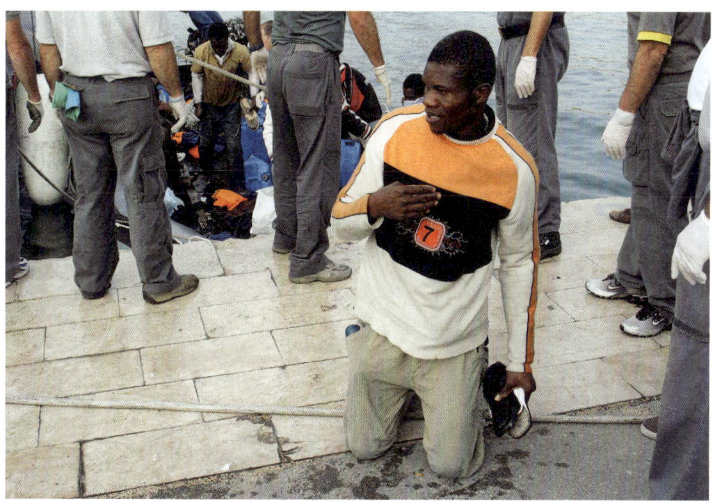

← This is a picture for a magazine, portraying someone who just set foot on shore: the first thing he does is to cross himself. Obviously this is less meaningful for a newspaper. These are more or less universal images. Magazines use pictures like that and then go on using these types of more intimate pictures.

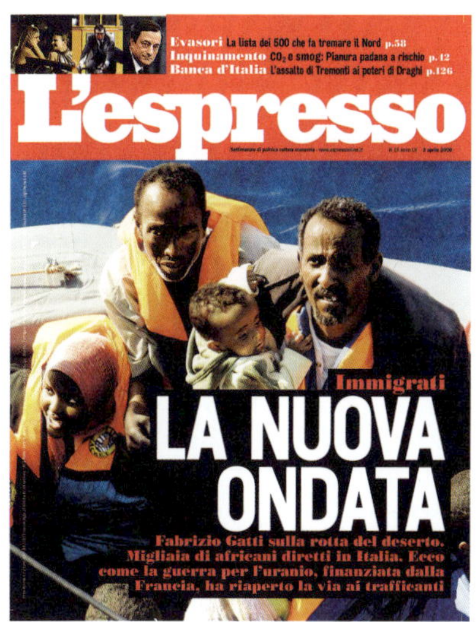

← This picture, which was published on the front page of *L'Espresso*, was taken about six months before the article inside was written. When Fabrizio Gatti did his reportage in the desert on the route to Libya, the editors decided to use my picture on the front page, entitled "Immigrants: The new wave," instead of one of the pictures taken by Fabrizio Gatti in the desert. He went to Niger, succeeded in following the caravan on the route to Libya, got on one of those trucks, and went all the way together with other migrants. Theoretically, this image sells itself—the colors, the facial expression of the man here with the child in his arms, ready to get on board. This, in the editor's opinion, was a much better comment—in a somewhat deceptive way—on the new wave of immigration. Better than the one taken by Fabrizio Gatti in the desert.

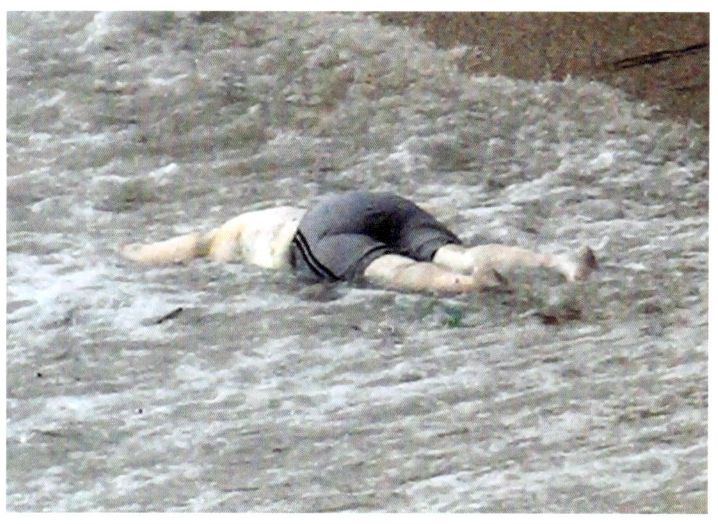

← These are the more intense images; they are scoops. Normally a dead body on the beach or on the street does not remain there for hours. Journalists don't have time to get there from wherever they may be. Anyway, when I took this picture, maybe it was the third night in a row that I didn't get a wink of sleep—that night I was out hunting. When you got a picture like that, that day you struck gold, with a maximum of cynicism in relation to what such a picture represents. This one was at the discretion of the editors; some of them do not like to show a photo like this on the cover, because it is also visible to children at the kiosk. But there were others who made a front page out of it, with the full-size picture. It was immediately published by the newspapers, because at that time they talked about how many corpses arrived; it was published in periodicals and in follow-up stories. If someone does a special on the victims of the Strait of Sicily, they may buy it from the agency, even if it dates back to June 2, 2008.

Q: It is also a testimony. It's a question that I, as a photographer, often ask myself. I think you have to be cynical because otherwise no one else can document the event, which has a historical value.

SEMINARA: This is where we return to the discourse of the humanitarian organizations and the documentary aspect. In their opinion it's not right. But in reality you know that what you're doing is the right thing to do.

But in between there is a moment in which the person behind the lens sees what is happening. And the most serious thing that can happen to you when you do this job is that you identify with that person, even if it's only for a moment. Thinking that if you were the subject, who probably only wants to be left alone, maybe as a reflex response you would take a shoe and throw it in the direction of the camera.

You know that you are violating people's privacy; you try to examine, to extract, and to tell everybody about what is in their facial expressions.

There is a bit of cynicism involved, not a nasty kind of cynicism in the sense that it's only fair that the public should have the opportunity to understand that these aren't evil black invaders coming to our continent—that they are some poor devils who arrive with these looks on their faces. That they thank God for having made it.

But at that moment you don't have the magazine in front of your eyes. At that moment you're there, you can smell their odors, you can feel their fear, their desperation—at that moment it's difficult.

Let's go a step further in exploring this aspect. Here I tried to digitally reproduce the effect of the Delta 400—this way you can see pictures in black and white.

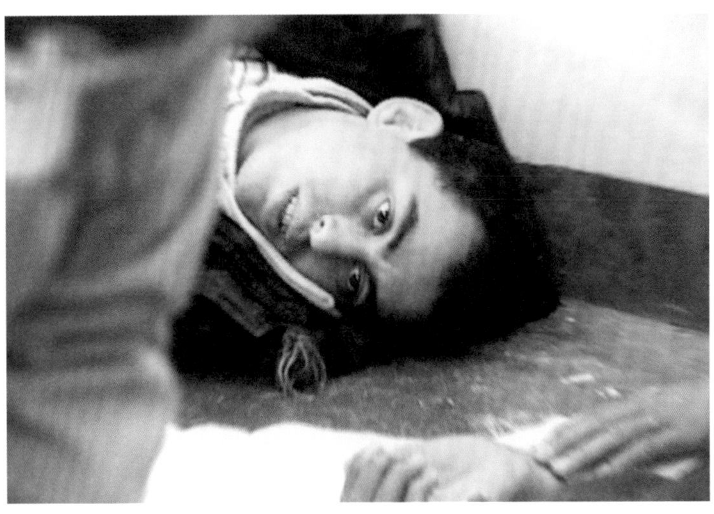

← This man wasn't noticed at first. There are situations in which you find yourself as a witness in very close proximity to remarkable emotional intensity, or even a nervous breakdown, as in this case here.

In this specific case you're there on the bridge of a ship in close contact. You perceive the odors, the moaning, the tears, and you take a picture like this one. That means you enter the person's privacy, and for a moment when you take the pictures, you stand still and ask yourself whether what you're doing is humanly correct.

It's clear that the pictures have a power, that they are intense, and your identity as a photographer prevails, you can't help but immortalize this moment.

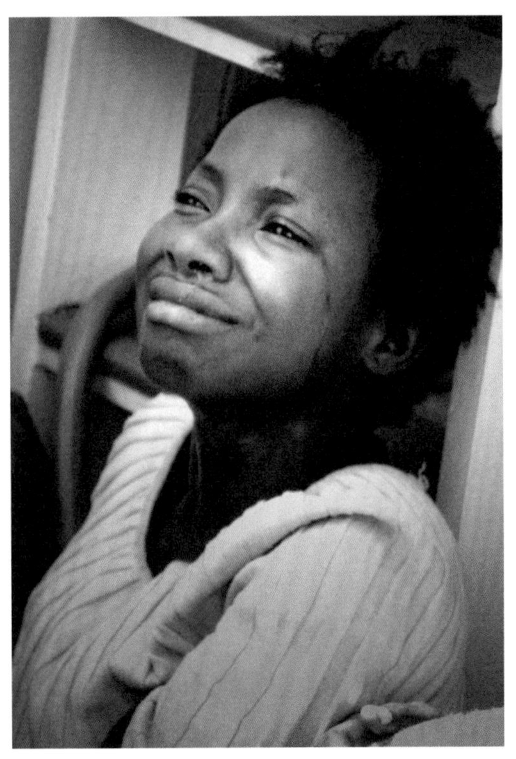

← These are expressions of emotion that are difficult to find; here you have weeping, desperation, tears still pouring down the face, but at the same time you can see a smile coming through. This woman especially looked up at the sky, like before—it's her, it's the same person. She was thanking God, you can see her gratitude, her joy at having made it. But then there is the nervous breakdown, the fear of desperation, of everything she has been fortunate to overcome. When you take pictures like that, for a moment you are in doubt: Am I being invasive? In other words, am I going too far into the private sphere of this person? At the very end, when you want to create a news report, you could probably also keep more distance. This is the threshold of cynicism and the question is, am I being cynical or is taking these photos okay?

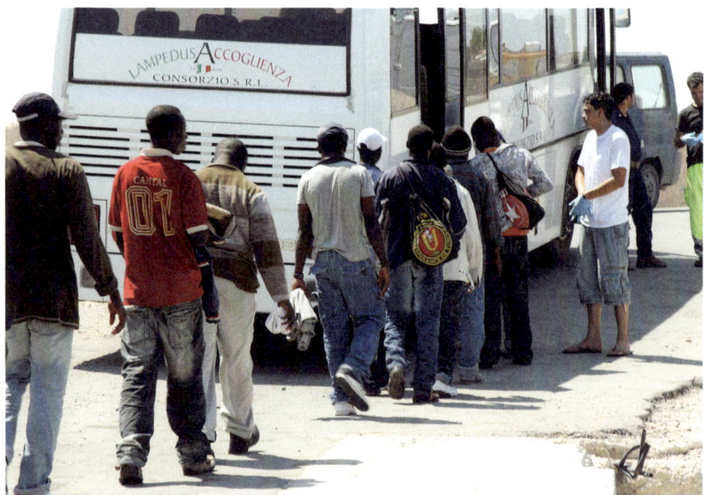

← Let's take a look at the camp. We begin with the arrival at the quay. They just arrived with the patrol boat, disembarked, and got on the bus.

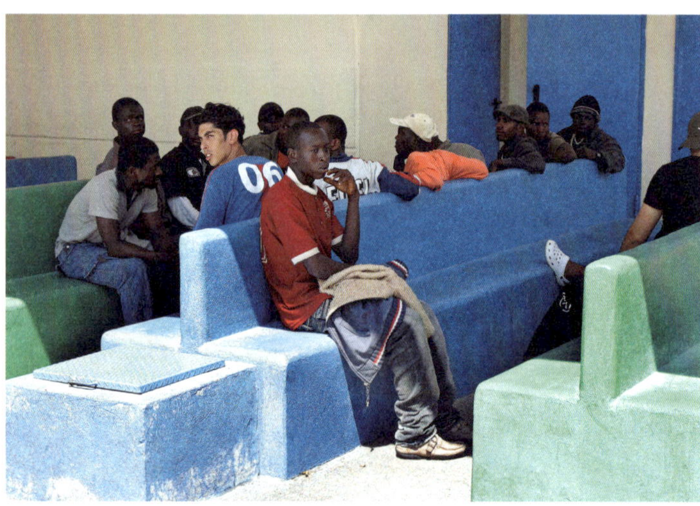

← They arrived at the reception center, sitting and waiting, the waiting area for the identification process; there are some cement benches, the colors are soft, but the seating is hard. That was the period of continuous arrivals. Having just arrived, that group was waiting for the filing process, the mug shots, the fingerprints, the personal search, etc.

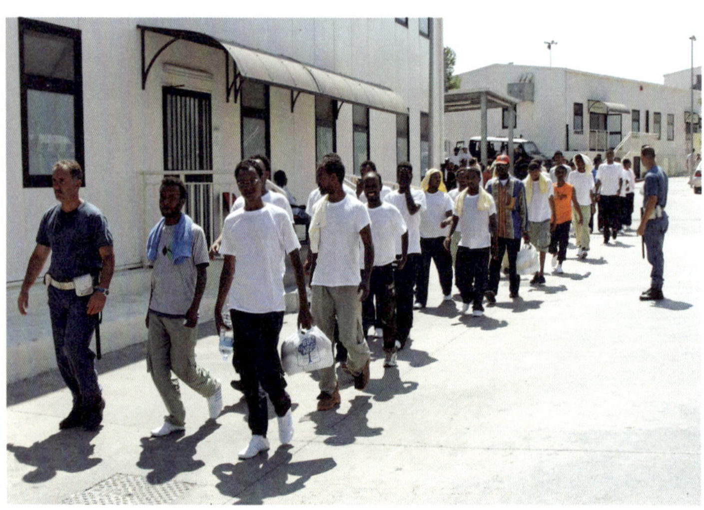

← Here we have a group which was about to be transferred. The people were going to be sent from the immigrant reception center on Lampedusa to temporary accommodation centers, to identification and expulsion centers situated all over Italian territory. With their bags, with some clothes they gave them. As you can see, they are all wearing the same kind of shoes; all of them have the same kind of pants. These things have been provided by the reception center.

These people are leaving, these ones have just arrived. Among them there are probably some who know each other, who waited together in Libya before they could leave. Maybe they didn't leave at the same time, but their journey was the same.

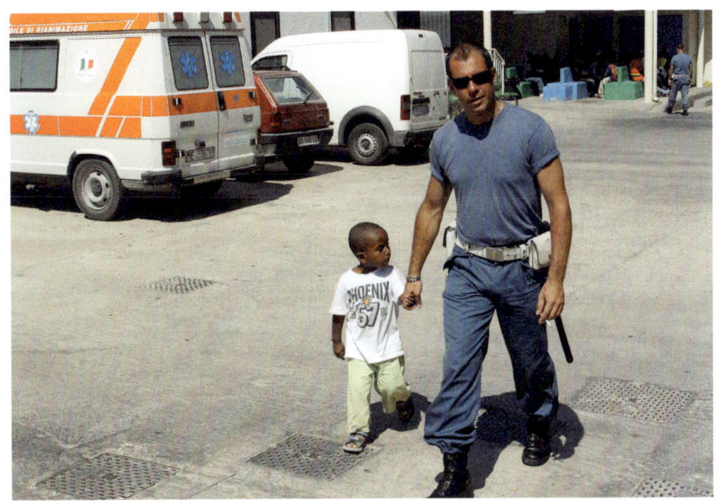

← In 2010, one could see very different pictures from Lampedusa. At that time, the state police were playing with the children and carrying them around. In my opinion, these are beautiful photos to show, although they are more difficult to sell; I don't think that many pictures of this kind have ever been published because it's not big news to see that everything is nice here, that the foreign children play with our soldiers.

Bad news sells better; people want drama, collapsing houses or mass murder. That's the principle of news, and crime news is the main pillar in terms of copies sold. So the nice news is usually put on the last pages, in the form of small articles. The newspapers prefer classic headlines like "Lampedusa center on the verge of collapse" because it exceeded its capacity—even if such phrases have now become hackneyed. There were 800 places and about 1,200–1,500 people came—as many as 2,000 ended up here.

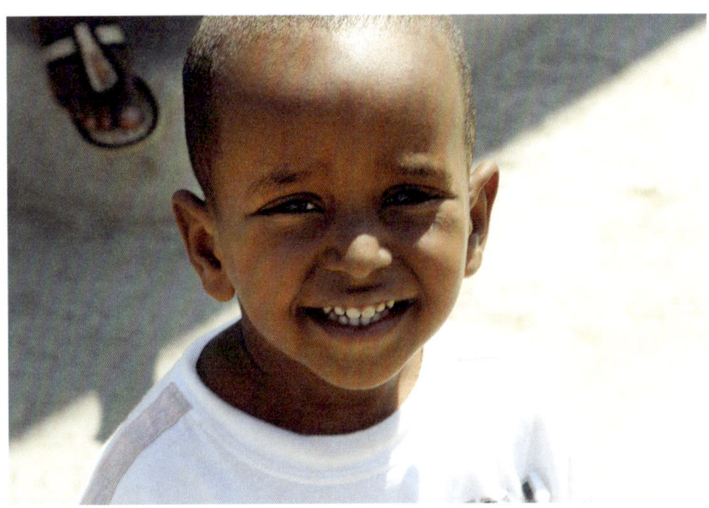

← And this child was a nice headline for the cover; a picture, however, in which children laugh, joke, and are fine, and even play with our soldiers does not meet the criteria of the media, of the news—it's not proper news.

Q: Why isn't there anybody reporting on the positive sides, maybe in a more committed kind of newspaper?

SEMINARA: Probably because we are not used to it any more. This should be the normality and crime news the negative exception. In theory, it should be that way. The opposite happens— it becomes the exception to report on a smiling person without any problems.

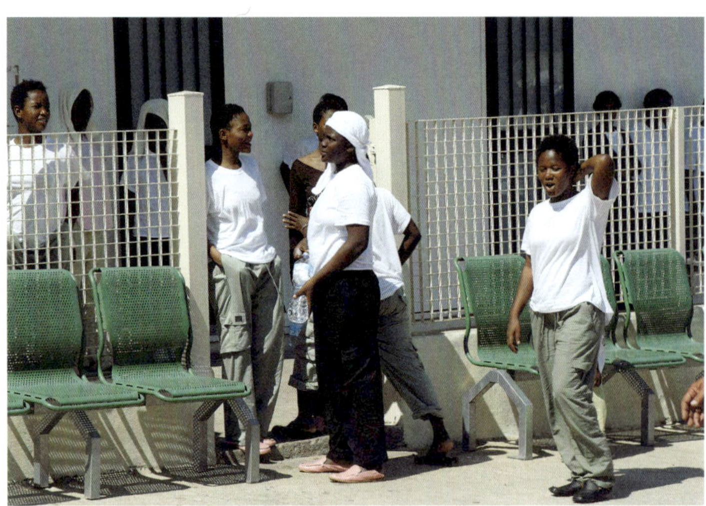

← This was the environment of the women. In my opinion it is a picture that describes the situation quite well. What you imagine from the outside is cells. Everyone in his own room, soldiers operating strict control.

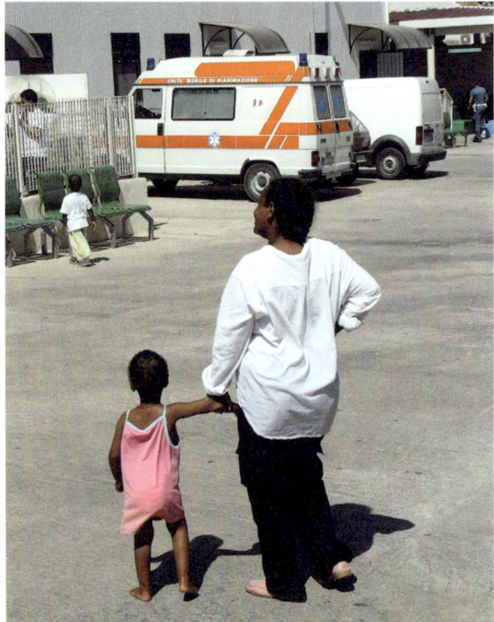

← Instead it's like a little village, or like a community; the mother going for a walk with her child, while she's talking with her neighbor.

In this case, I do mention and stress that because in the everyday life of "Drama of Lampedusa," "Invasion," "Lampedusa on the verge of collapse," "New wave on Lampedusa" etc., etc., all that was pretty much the exception in the dramatic context reported by the newspapers. Maybe also the moments of serenity these people here experienced should have been reported.

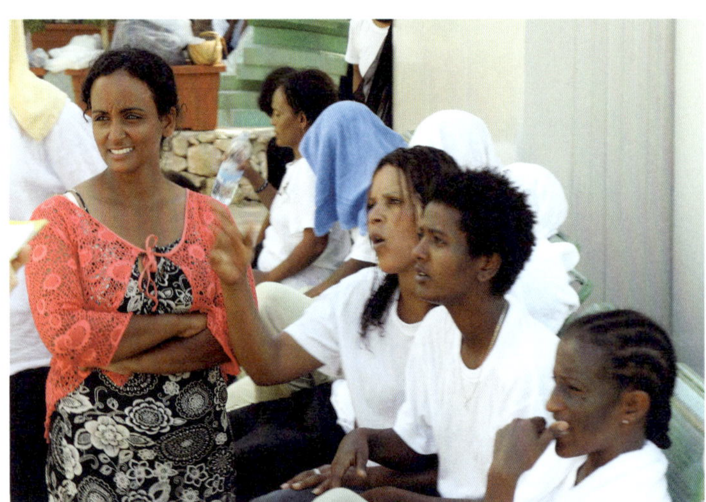

← This could be another way to report a drama. Of these women probably five or six were raped before they left, before they could embark themselves, before arriving in Italy. But here you can find a smile on their lips, or at least a calm, composed facial expression.

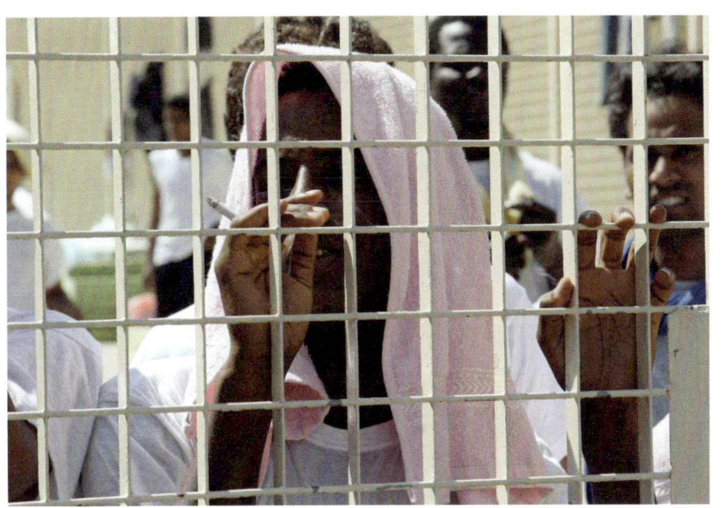

← Here we are being misled. In reality this picture is about a person calmly smoking his cigarette at the gate—you can see that in the sequence— a cigarette taken out of a pack that was given to him as one of his daily benefits by the people at the reception center. If you look at it as a picture per se, with that steel wire in front of it, with those hands clutching it. Well, I want to tell a story; but it is obvious that this photo will be sold to a newspaper or a magazine, which then publishes and uses it as a picture showing detention, a picture of the "wave of blacks locked inside the reception center." If you look at it objectively and without comment, you see a certain serenity in their faces. As I'm not satisfied with this kind of facial expression—because it seems almost too serene and peaceful to me—I look for something where you cannot see the faces, where you don't see facial expressions.

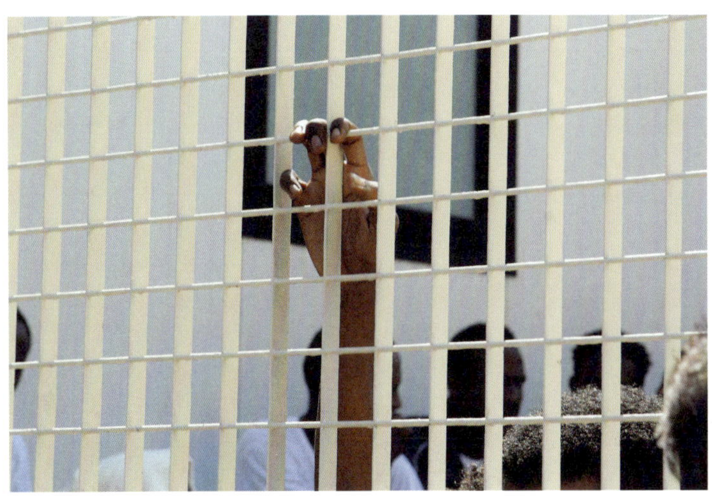

← I'm looking for the clenched hand, clutching the iron bars, so that you cannot see the expression in the face of whoever has his hand there. And actually this picture has been sold many times, because it suggests something even more dramatic.

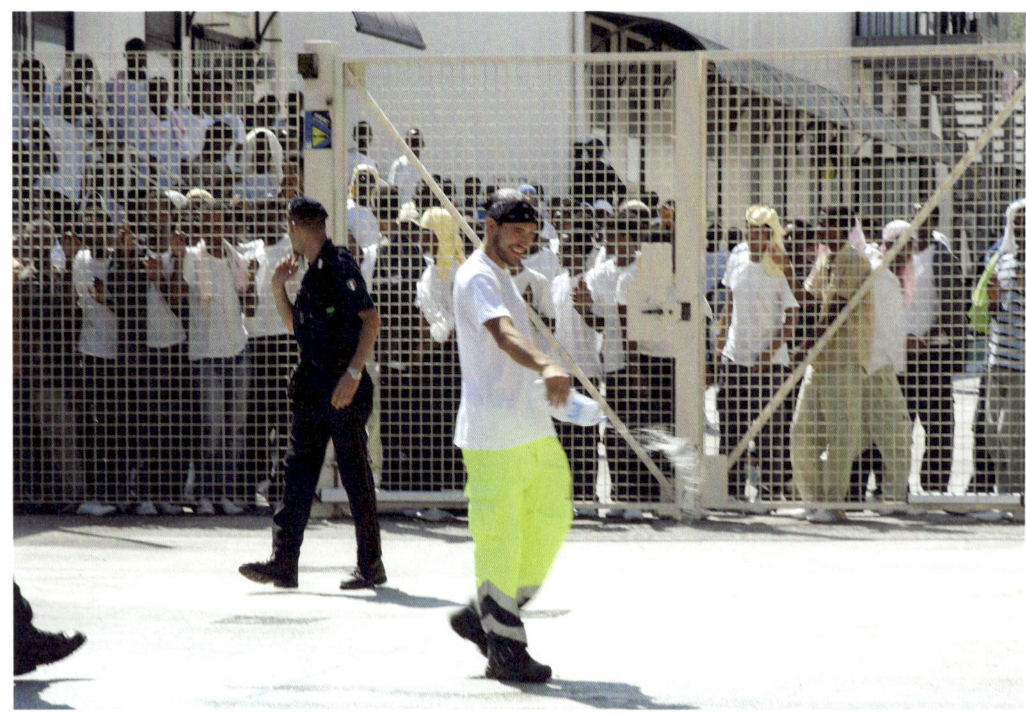

↑   This was one of the more tense moments, moments of conflict between some of the men behind this gate. The actual camp in the reception center is the area behind this gate. The majority of the migrants stayed here, because it was the area for men. On the other side were the women and minors. At that moment they were calling the ones who were about to be transferred, and that obviously created some tension. They knew that they were being called but did not know where they would be sent. The tension arose from the fact that they were afraid of being repatriated, and so it was necessary to put two more soldiers in front of them.

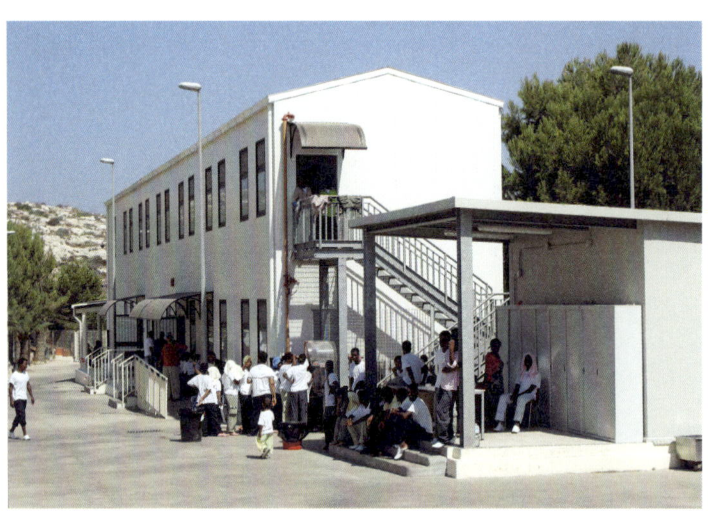

←   The first building on the left is the one which houses the infirmary on the ground floor with two examination rooms and a well-equipped pharmacy; above is the accommodation. At the entrance behind this building, you'll find the offices of the humanitarian organizations. This porch with the cupboards was the distribution zone for the benefits—from here people received new shoes for their rotten ones, and extra cigarettes for daily distribution.

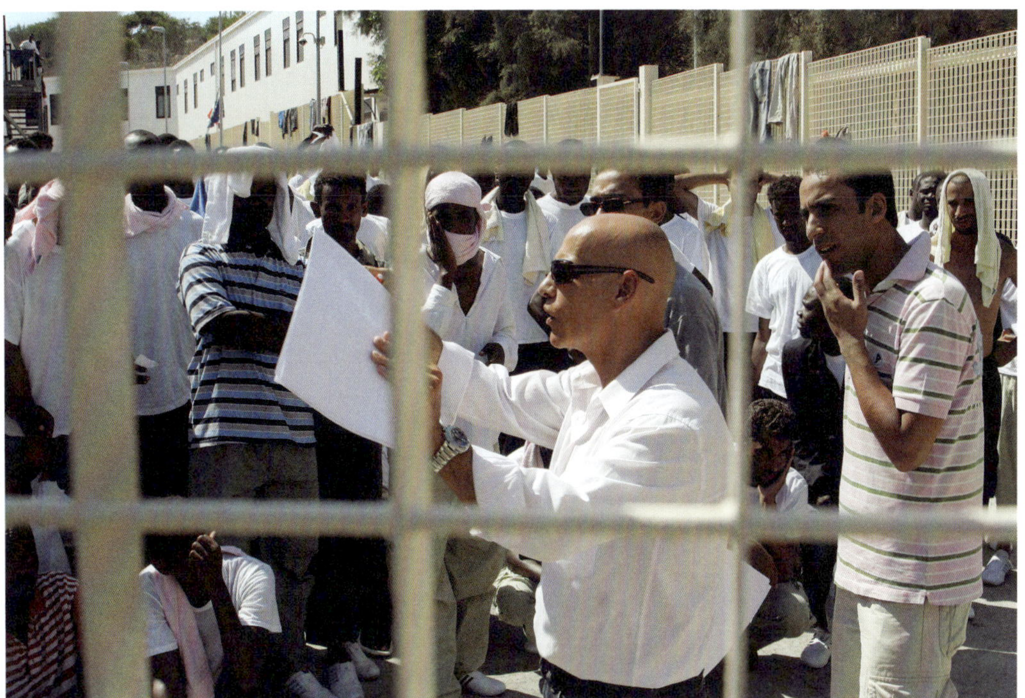

↑   There has been a moment of tension, a mix-up between two of the inhabitants; one of them was afraid of being transferred and did not want to go, and it ended up in a brawl. In Africa, the Ethiopians and the Eritreans probably hate each other; the Libyans are notorious racists and cannot stand people of color; the Muslims do not have a high regard for the Christians, and so on. Difficulties unite people during the trip—even if there are Muslims and Christians on the same boat, they help each other and they show solidarity. This atmosphere lasts until they arrive at the camp. After some days, they forget about the fear and gradually form ghettos of individual ethnic groups; and in some cases even minor incidents can spark something off. Even if there is a cultural mediator—who is also a police inspector—translating and trying to resolve the situation, a minor incident is enough to trigger a dispute between a Somali and an Egyptian, for instance.

What went well, what attracted all of the newspapers, was the moment the center was overcrowded. You are there and emphasize in a negative way who sleeps outside, who eats outside, and so on. By our standards it probably seems unacceptable, considering what people have been through—what they experienced in the years before in order to make it through half of Africa and get on a boat to come here. But when it's hot, sleeping in the shade of a tree is optimal. You can describe everything on the basis of how you want people to interpret it. It is enough to leave something out and stress something else.

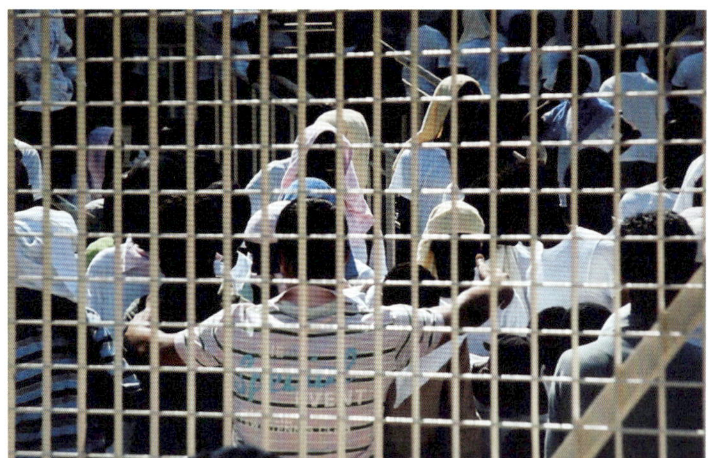

← Let us go back to the more commercial part. The better you succeed in portraying an unlimited mass of people packed behind a metal gate, the more likely someone will buy and publish the picture.

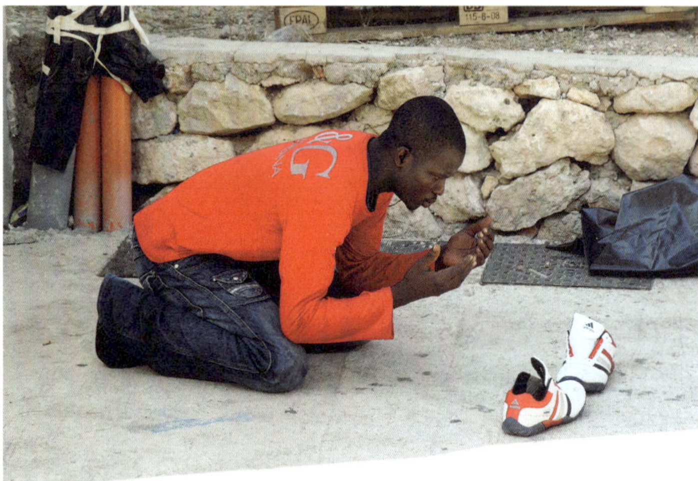

← This man here is in the area for those who are about to be transferred. He took off his shoes according to the Muslim custom. He is praying and he probably did not have a bottle of water at hand to complete the ritual act which includes washing the feet before the prayer.

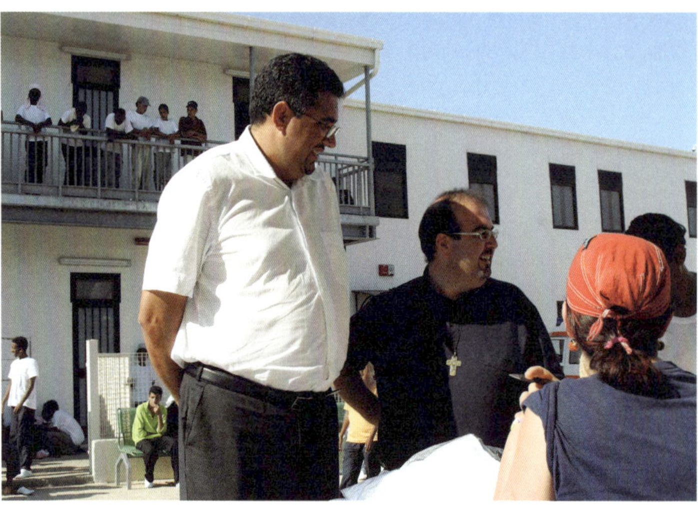

← This is the mayor of the island at that time. He often went looking for publicity at the center. Here you see him together with the priest of the island, who used to celebrate Mass for the Christians in the center.

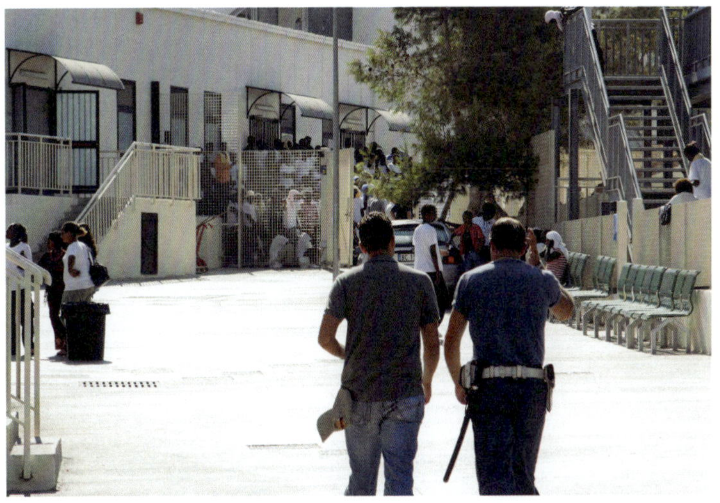

← That building there is the one that went up in flames when there was the revolt in the reception center. This occurred when the atmosphere and the rules changed. The decision was made to turn the CSPA Center for Rescue and Reception into a CIE, and the length of stay for the migrants was also extended. A contrasting view, seen from above—the village is here, so the entrance is in this direction, and this is the camp.

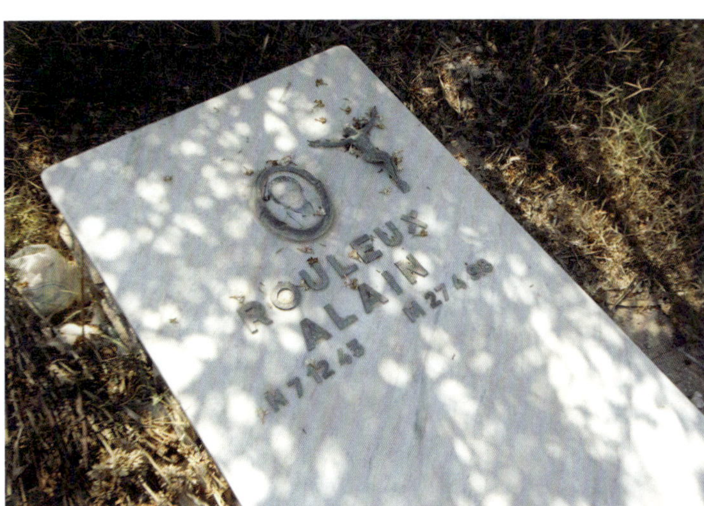

← He was one of the first to arrive and be identified, maybe because at that time he traveled with his passport. It was in 1998, so before the real upsurge in migration.

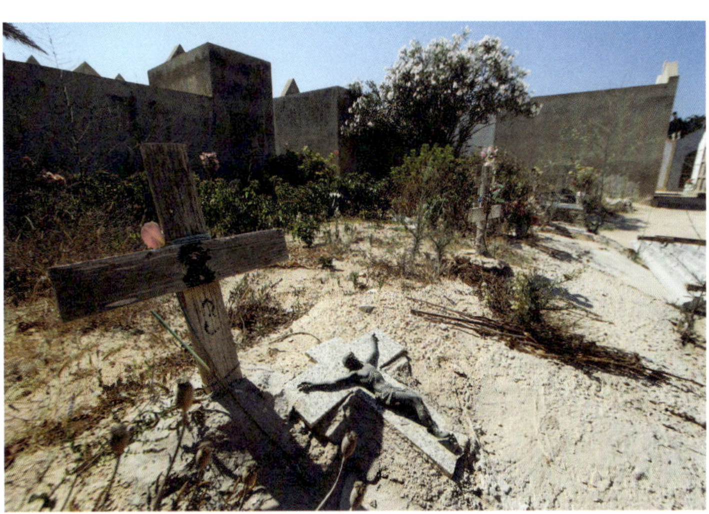

← Then the others arrived. Two pieces of wood with a number on them. These are migrants who died at sea, buried in the Lampedusa cemetery. As you can see, the area where they are buried just underground is not well cared for. Look, there's some garbage, two rotten flowers, and on top of all this there is the cross. When you consider that they were buried in the Lampedusa cemetery, people assumed—for their convenience—that the dead people were Christians. Otherwise, the cemetery would not have been able to admit them. But it is very likely that there is a Muslim lying under here.

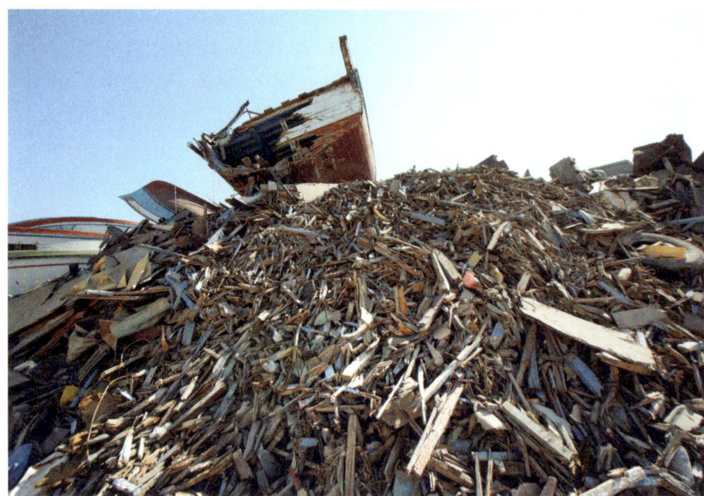

← The boat cemetery, at that time.
Q: What has happened with the cemetery?
SEMINARA: At this point, there are five or six boats left, the only ones that survived. All the rest went up in flames, they deliberately set them on fire, and nothing remained of this bunch of boats.

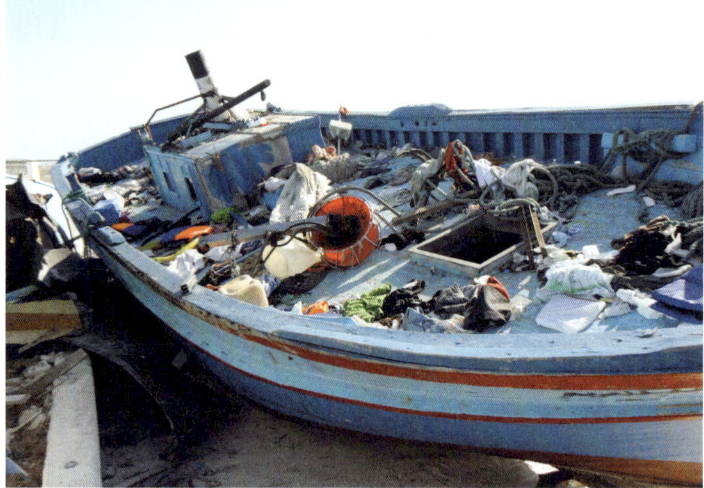

← I think these pictures date back to the time before the first fire. The whole area was destroyed twice.
Q: What was the reason for the fires?
SEMINARA: Financial interests.

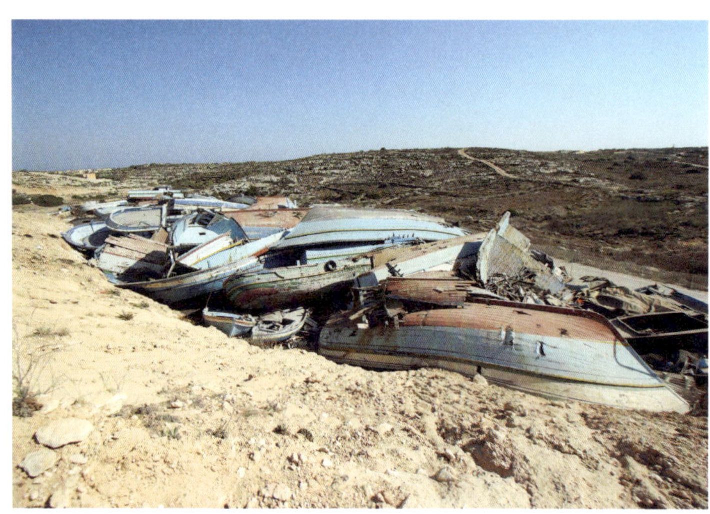

← This one was taken from above. There is one boat on top of the other, and these were boats of 15, 16 meters each. Even if they seem to be small when seen like this.
Q: The procedure with the boats is to decommission them. Why can't they be reutilized?
SEMINARA: Italian law does not permit selling these boats by auction, as is possible with confiscated scooters or cars. They are classified as the confiscated vehicles of the mafia or of a terrorist, and therefore it's not possible to resell them.

Among them there are boats that, before they were thrown there by a crane, were in perfect condition with an excellent motor; with a good starting price at the auction, some fishermen probably would have bought them.

If they had bought them, first of all they would have given money to the Italian state, and at the same time the state would have saved money; because then there wouldn't have been any boats to transport, to shred and dump.

But this is what has always happened. The boats were piled up that way and then destroyed, sometimes with a shredder, and in this case, because of the size of the planks, with the shovel of a simple excavator. Then they are collected in areas like this.

Q: *And the motors of each boat?*
SEMINARA: In contrast to street vehicles, which have a document with a registration number relating to the body and not to the motor, the registration number for boats is inside the motor. So, in theory, the hull could be sold, but not the motor. The outboard motors of the rubber boats, though—which weren't stored here but in the captain of the port's office up until a particular date—were sold by auction. So they were sold, and the hulls were not. It's one of those things that don't make a lot of sense and are therefore hard to explain.

On board there are still the lifejackets they were wearing when they arrived, their clothes, the bread they had, and the cans with food for the trip.

On it you could find everything—imagine what's still inside. We got up to three, four, five hundred boats. One time, the storage area was so packed that they created another one right next to it. An area that was then closed. There was a decision from the regional administrative court that obligated them to restore it to its former condition. Without permission they entered a protected area and devastated it.

But so many boats arrived that they did not know where to put them; so, for some years the boats were neither dumped nor transported to another place. At that time, when I was not on the island, I received the news that "the area has been set on fire." They are now beginning to put the boats there again.

Frankfurter Allgemeine

ZEITUNG FÜR DEUTSCHLAND

Freitag, 27. Mai 2016 · Nr. 121 / 21 D 1   HERAUSGEGEBEN VON WERNER D'INKA, JÜRGEN KAUBE, BERTHOLD KOHLER, HOLGER STELTZNER   2,60 € D 2954 A   F.A.Z. im Internet: faz.net

Gauck beklagt Ängstlichkeit der Deutschen

moja. LEIPZIG, 26. Mai. Bundespräsident Joachim Gauck hat auf dem Katholikentag in Leipzig „eine neue Ängstlichkeit" in Deutschland beklagt. Angst vor dem Fremden sei zwar allen Gesellschaften in irgendeiner Form eigen, aber die Erfahrung zeige, dass sie oft unbegründet sei: „Angst kann sich legen", sagte Gauck am Donnerstag während einer Podiumsdiskussion. Leider werde die Angst derzeit in Deutschland von Leuten ausgenutzt, die „ihr eigenes Süppchen kochen" und „Hysterie" verbreiten wollten. Ein sprechendes Beispiel dafür seien die Zusammenkünfte in Teilen von Sachsen, sagte Gauck mit Blick auf die Pegida-Demonstrationen in Dresden. Dabei lebten in Sachsen nur sehr wenige Ausländer und Muslime. Dort, wo bereits einige Moscheen stünden, etwa in Nordrhein-Westfalen oder der Region Stuttgart, gebe es viel weniger Vorbehalte. Im Vorfeld des Katholikentags hatte eine Diskussion darüber gegeben, wie mit der AfD auf dem kirchlichen Laientreffen umzugehen sei. Der Veranstalter, das Zentralkomitee der deutschen Katholiken (ZdK), hatte vorab entschieden, keine AfD-Vertreter zu Veranstaltungen einzuladen. Noch bis Sonntag findet in Leipzig der 100. Katholikentag unter dem Motto „Seht, da ist der Mensch" statt. (Siehe Seite 4.)

Heute

Sonderzahlungen dürfen angerechnet werden

hw. BERLIN, 26. Mai. Sonderzahlungen wie das Weihnachts- und Urlaubsgeld dürfen auf den gesetzlichen Mindestlohn von 8,50 Euro angerechnet werden. Das hat das Bundesarbeitsgericht am Mittwoch in seinem bisher ersten Urteil zum Mindestlohn entschieden. Dem Richterspruch zufolge muss es sich bei den Sonderzahlungen um ein Entgelt für geleistete Arbeit handeln. Außerdem muss das Geld monatlich gestückelt überwiesen werden, nicht etwa zweimal im Jahr. Die Linkspartei kritisierte das Urteil. (Siehe Wirtschaft, Seite 19.)

Gefährlicher Fluchtweg

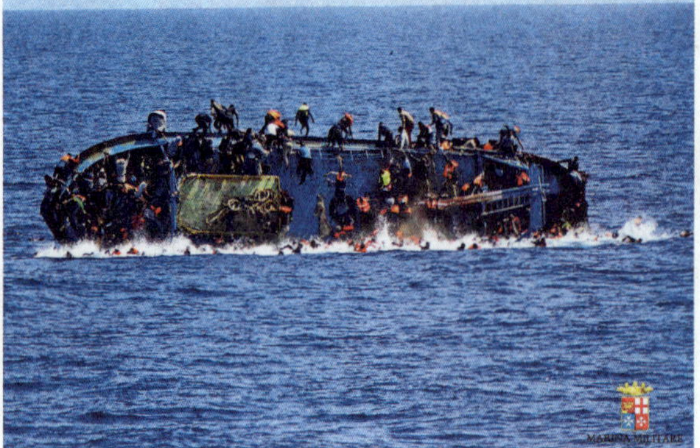

Gekentert – Bei einem Bootsunglück vor der libyschen Küste sind am Mittwoch mindestens fünf Migranten ums Leben gekommen. Die italienische Marine berichtete von einem überfüllten Boot, das in Sichtweite eines ihrer Schiffe kenterte. 500 Menschen konnten gerettet werden. Am Donnerstag kam es 65 Kilometer vor der libyschen Küste zu einem weiteren schweren Unglück. Rund hundert Flüchtlinge seien rund um ein Boot im Meer geschwommen, während 20 bis 30 Leichen im Wasser trieben, teilte ein Sprecher der EU-Marinemission „Sophia" mit. Foto AP/Marina Militare

Merkel gegen Lockerung der Russland-Sanktionen

Kanzlerin widerspricht Gabriel / Moskau lässt ukrainische Pilotin frei / G-7-Gipfel

ami./mas./sat. ISE-SHIMA/BERLIN/VILNIUS, 26. Mai. Bundeskanzlerin Angela Merkel (CDU) hält eine Lockerung der Russland-Sanktionen für verfrüht, die Vizekanzler Sigmar Gabriel (SPD) angeregt hat. Merkel wies am Rande des Gipfels der sieben wichtigsten Industrieländer (G 7) im japanischen Ise-Shima dessen Vorstoß zurück. Das bedeutete keine Punkte der Minsker Beschlüsse nicht erreicht worden, sagte Merkel am Donnerstag. „Es gibt zwar keine massiven Kampfhandlungen, aber es gibt auch keinen stabilen Waffenstillstand." Man sei bei der Ausarbeitung eines Wahlgesetzes und der Abhaltung der Lokalwahlen immer noch nicht weitergekommen.

Am Vortag hatte Russland die ukrainische Pilotin Nadija Sawtschenko im Rahmen eines Gefangenenaustausches aus russischer Haft entlassen. Dies begrüßte Merkel, gleichwohl bekräftigte sie die Haltung der G 7 zu den Sanktionen: „Eine Veränderung der Position gegenüber den Monaten zuvor ist erst einmal nicht zu erwarten." Sie setzte hinzu: „Für mich ist es jetzt im Augenblick zu früh, in irgendeiner Weise Entwarnung zu geben." Für den Abend waren Gespräche zum Konflikt zwischen Russland und der Ukraine geplant.

Gabriel hatte sich am Mittwoch für den schrittweisen Abbau der Sanktionen ausgesprochen. Zwar machte er deutlich, dass eine Aufhebung der Sanktionen nur möglich sei, wenn die Verabredungen von Minsk eingehalten würden. Doch kritisierte er den Kurs der EU, zu sagen, „erst 100 Prozent Minsk und dann gibt es 100 Prozent

Aufhebung der Sanktionen". Außenminister Frank-Walter Steinmeier, der ebenfalls eine Flexibilisierung der Sanktionsregimes anstrebt, sagte in Vilnius, sein Interesse richte sich jetzt darauf, Fortschritte bei der Umsetzung des Minsker Abkommens zu erreichen.

In Ise-Shima beschäftigen die Staats- und Regierungschefs auch der Territorialstreitigkeiten Chinas mit einer Reihe von Nachbarländern im Ost- und im Südchinesischen Meer. „Wir haben hier eine gemeinsame Haltung, dass wir friedliche Konfliktlösungen wollen", sagte Merkel mit Blick auf die angerufenen Schiedsgerichte. Mit Finanzzusagen zur Linderung der Flüchtlingskrise im Nahen Osten wurde nicht gerechnet. (Siehe Seite 2 sowie Wirtschaft, Seiten 17 und 22.)

Streik gegen Arbeitsrechtsreform lähmt Frankreich

Hollande und Valls beharren auf Reformkurs / Finanzminister Sapin erwägt Änderungen

mic. PARIS, 26. Mai. Der Protest gegen die Arbeitsrechtsreform in Frankreich eskaliert. An Donnerstag kam es zu gewaltsamen Zwischenfällen bei einer Demonstration in Paris, zu der unter anderem die Gewerkschaften CGT und FO aufgerufen hatten. CGT-Chef Philippe Martinez sagte, Präsident François Hollande diktiere dem Land eine Reform, die nicht von der sozialistischen Fraktion getragen werde. „Hollande hat keine Mehrheit mehr", behauptete der CGT-Chef. Der linke Flügel in der sozialistischen Parlamentsfraktion hat angekündigt, zu einem Misstrauensantrag gegen die eigene Regierung sammeln zu wollen. Die Nationalversammlung muss noch in zweiter Lesung über die Gesetzesvorhaben abstimmen. Martinez verlangte einen Gesprächstermin im Elysée-Palast. Die Streikbewegung hat inzwischen alle 19 Atomkraftwerksstandorte erfasst. In zwölf Reaktoren wurde die Stromproduktion zurückgefahren. Die Blockaden der Treibstoffdepots gingen unterdessen weiter. Die Polizei räumte mehrere Straßenblockaden. Viele Tankstellen blieben geschlossen oder mussten die Treibstoffverkauf rationieren. Im Bahnverkehr kam es aufgrund von Arbeitsniederlegungen vereinzelt zu Störungen und Verspätungen. Am Flughafen Paris-Orly wurden 15 Prozent der Flüge wegen Streiks gestrichen. Premierminister Manuel Valls kritisierte die von den Gewerkschaften organisierte Einschränkung der Treibstoffversorgung als „unverantwortlich". „Diese Situation kann unserer Wirtschaft scha-

den", sagte der Regierungschef im Fernsehen. Etwa ein Drittel aller Tankstellen ist von Treibstoffknappheit betroffen. Valls schloss aus, die neue Arbeitszeitregelung zurückzunehmen. Sie soll nicht mehr zurückgenommen, sondern aus Betriebsebene. Die CGT verlangt eine Rücknahme der ganzen Reform, ist aber besonders über diesen Punkt erbost. Präsident Hollande sagte beim G-7-Gipfel in Japan, Valls sage „genau das, was wir vor mir meinen". Finanzminister Michel Sapin stellte hingegen Änderungen in Aussicht. Finanzminister Schäuble sagte in Berlin, Frankreich sei nicht reformunfähig. Die Proteste seien „Ausdruck einer lebendigen Demokratie". (Siehe Seiten 3 und 8 sowie Wirtschaft, Seite 17.)

Obama zeigt Verständnis für Ablehnung Trumps

nw. WASHINGTON, 26. Mai. Barack Obama hat auf dem G-7-Gipfel mitgeteilt, viele Staats- und Regierungschefs seien „aus gutem Grund" vom Erfolg des Präsidentschaftskandidaten Donald Trump schockiert. Der demokratische Amtsinhaber sagte, viele Vorschläge des Republikaners „Ignoranz gegenüber der Welt" oder die Neigung, „das Schlagzeile für wichtiger zu halten, als zu durchdenken, was nötig ist, um Amerika zu schützen". Trump behauptete derweil, Hillary Clinton sei eine „üble Ganovin". Das belege ein Bericht des Generalinspekteurs des Außenministeriums. Er besagt, dass Clinton durch Nutzung ihres privaten E-Mail-Servers als Ministerin Regeln brach. (Siehe Seite 3; Kommentar Seite 8.)

Weißbuch: Deutschland als Gestaltungsmacht

elo. BERLIN, 26. Mai. Deutschland sieht sich künftig sicherheitspolitisch als „aktive Gestaltungsmacht" in der Welt. Das ergibt sich aus dem Entwurf des neuen Weißbuchs, auf den sich jetzt Verteidigungsministerium, Auswärtiges Amt und Kanzleramt geeinigt haben. Der Text definiert weitreichende außen- und sicherheitspolitische Interessen Deutschlands; zu denen nun neben der Einbettung in EU und Nato auch das Interesse an freiem Handel und freiem Informationsfluss weltweit, an sicherer Rohstoff- und Energieversorgung gehört. Die Idee des Verteidigungsministeriums, einen Teil der Krisenkabinett auf Dauer einzurichten, setzte sich hingegen nicht durch. (Siehe Seite 5.)

Behörden: 14,8 Prozent Migrationshintergrund

elo. BERLIN, 26. Mai. 14,8 Prozent der Mitarbeiter der Bundesverwaltung haben einen Migrationshintergrund. Das ist das Ergebnis einer Studie, die am Donnerstag im Bundesinnenministerium vorgestellt wurde. Sie basiert auf einer freiwilligen Befragung der Mitarbeiter von 24 Behörden der Bundesverwaltung, darunter 13 Bundesministerien und das Kanzleramt. Der Bund beschäftigt fast eine halbe Million Menschen im öffentlichen Dienst, 46 000 von ihnen arbeiten bei den befragten 24 Behörden; 27 000 füllten die Fragebögen aus. Im Bund sind damit mehr Menschen mit Migrationshintergrund beschäftigt als in der allgemeinen öffentlichen Verwaltung (6,7 Prozent), aber weniger als in der Privatwirtschaft (20,1 Prozent).

Hollande am Ende

Von Michaela Wiegel

„Es geht besser" – so lautet der Spruch, mit dem der französische Präsident das Ende seiner Amtszeit bestreiten wollte. Doch wieder einmal ist François Hollande von den Ereignissen überrascht worden. „Ça va mieux" taugt jetzt bestenfalls noch für Spottgesänge. Der Sozialist hatte nicht damit gerechnet, dass die Gewerkschaft CGT zum Totentanz auf die bereits totgewähnte Arbeitsrechtsreform aufspielt. „Nichts verläuft wie geplant", so überschrieb der Schriftsteller Laurent Binet sein Buch über den Einzug Hollandes in den Elysée-Palast. Von diesem Titel hat sich der Präsident auch ein knappes Jahr vor Ablauf seines Mandats nicht lösen können.

Nun sucht der Präsident verzweifelt nach einem Notausgang. Wie kann er rechtzeitig zur Beginn der Fußball-Europameisterschaft das Land befrieden? Von seinem Vorgänger im Département Corrèze, Jacques Chirac, hat er gelernt, auf Proteste mit Zugeständnissen zu reagieren. Hollande hat sich zwar auch in die Nähe des Agenda-2010-Kanzlers Gerhard Schröder gerückt und versprochen, sein Land in „eine Sozialdemokratie à la française" zu verwandeln. Aber auch diese Äußerungen haben sich als leichtfertige und voreilige Mutmaßungen entpuppt. Im Dialog mit den Gewerkschaften hat Hollandes Regierung versagt. Die CGT ist auf diese Weise zum Amoklauf gegen die Arbeitsrechtsreform aufgebrochen. Sie weiß: Wenn die Barrikaden erst einmal brennen, verzagen die meisten französischen Präsidenten.

Angesichts des Streikchaos und der umstürzlerischen Missstimmung im Volk sucht Hollande, der frühere sozialistische Parteichef, eine politische Überlebensstrategie in tradierten Haltungen. Der Präsident weiß, wie sehr sein Land vom Geist der Französischen Revolution geprägt bleibt. Der Kern des politischen Systems weist auf 1789 zurück und beruht auf ein knappes Jahr vor allem der Macht. Die politische Konfrontation spielt sich direkt zwischen Staat und Individuum ab. Vermittlungsinstanzen werden nicht anerkannt. So erklärt sich der eruptive und aggressive Charakter der derzeitigen Auseinandersetzung. Die Legitimität des Präsidenten ist schon viel zu schwach, um es mit der radikalen Minderheit der CGT-Streikenden noch aufzunehmen. Das alles zeigt, warum Reformen an das kleine Ende der Regierungszeit so gut wie unmöglich sind – erst recht in Frankreich.

Die Irrtümer Lateinamerikas

Von Matthias Rüb

Die „roten" Regierungen Lateinamerikas haben die Missstände nicht beseitigen können, die schon die Militärdiktaturen und Regime kultivierten, die sie einst stürzten: Die Sumpfblüten Korruption und Klientelismus wechselten einfach nur die Farbe. Beim Kampf um den Machterhalt waren auch den linken Caudillos alle Mittel recht, von der Verunglimpfung bis zur offenen Verfolgung des politischen Gegners. Die doppelte Lebenslüge der lateinamerikanischen Linken lautet, nur sie könne das Los der Marginalisierten verbessern und ein Machtwechsel bedeute den Rückfall in die historische Düsternis von Kolonialismus und Raubtierkapitalismus.

Jetzt rollt in Lateinamerika eine neue Welle heran. Symptomatisch dafür ist zu Tage der Niedergang des „Sozialismus des 21. Jahrhunderts". Wie sieht es dort aus? Nur wer stundenlang vor den staatlichen Supermärkten ansteht, ergattert ein Grundnahrungsmittel oder Toilettenpapier. Die Inflationsquote ist die höchste der Welt, sie dürfte bald siebenhundert Prozent erreichen. Vergangenes Jahr ist die Wirtschaft um zehn Prozent geschrumpft. In Apotheken und Krankenhäusern fehlt es an Medikamenten und Verbandsmaterial. In Staatsbetrieben und Verwaltungen wird nur noch montags und dienstags gearbeitet, um Strom zu sparen. Die Gewaltkriminalität ist außer Kontrolle. Die Hauptstadt ist eine der gefährlichsten Metropolen der Welt. Nur sechs Prozent der Morde werden aufgeklärt.

So sieht es in Venezuela aus. Dabei verfügt das Land über die größten nachgewiesenen Ölreserven der Welt. Ende der sechziger Jahre steuerte das Überschall-Passagierflugzeug Concorde neben New York und Miami auch die Hauptstadt Caracas an. Eigentlich müsste Venezuela mit seinen 31 Millionen Einwohnern heute der reichste und moderneste Staat, der vorzeigbarste Lateinamerikas sein. Stattdessen steht es vor der wirtschaftlichen und sozialen Implosion. Das Elend und die grassierende Korruption haben das Gemeinwesen zersetzt.

Verantwortung für den Niedergang trägt das sozialistische Regime unter Hugo Chávez. Der charismatische Revolutionsführer herrschte von 1999 bis zu seinem Tod im März 2013 wie ein Caudillo. An seine Anhänger verteilte er Geld und Waffen. Er enteignete manche Privatbetriebe, vor allem brachte er den staatlichen Ölmonopolisten und damit die jahrelang sicher endlos sprudelnden Einnahmen aus dem Ölexport unter seine Kontrolle. Der einstige Oberstleutnant des Heeres begnügte sich aber nicht damit, die Milliarden zu kassieren und Transferzahlungen an die Armen daheim zu verwenden. Er setzte in Venezuela wie überall in Lateinamerika jahrzehntelang nicht gehört werden und hielten Chávez' unendliche Tiraden gegen den Kapitalismus und die Vereinigten Staaten für den authentischen Widerhall ihrer eigenen Stimme.

Chávez sah sich vor allem als historischen Wiedergänger des großen Simón Bolívar, der im neunzehnten Jahrhundert nicht nur seinem Heimatland Venezuela, sondern auch Bolivien, Ecuador, Kolumbien und Peru die Unabhängigkeit erkämpfte. Hunderte Milliarden aus dem Ölexport verteilte Chávez in der Karibik und in Südamerika, um seine „bolivarische" Mission einer „zweiten Befreiung" Lateinamerikas zu erreichen – dieses Mal vom Joch des Kapitalismus und der Vereinigten Staaten. Im März 2013 starb Chávez, ohne im Zusammenbruch seines kolossalen Irrtums vom Sozialismus und vom Aufstand des globalen Südens erleben zu müssen. Chávez' Nachfol-

Die Lage in Venezuela ist symptomatisch: Die „rote Welle" hinterlässt einen Krisenkontinent.

ger Nicolás Maduro ist ein orientierungsloser Politiker, das der Kartenhaus vollends zum Einsturz bringen wird. Das ist ein Fanal für die jünger Chávez', die in den Jahren nach dem ersten Wahlsieg im Dezember 1998 in Bolivien und Brasilien, in Argentinien und Ecuador, auch in Nicaragua, Honduras und El Salvador an die Macht kamen. Auch Chile und Uruguay wurden von der „roten Welle" nach der Jahrtausendwende erfasst, doch dort herrschte bis heute gemäßigte Linke.

Für das Verebben der linken Welle in Lateinamerika gibt es ungeachtet der unterschiedlichen ideologischen „Tönung" in den einzelnen Ländern gemeinsame Ursachen: Der relative Erfolg der aktiven Umverteilungspolitik gründete auf der von China angestoßenen internationalen Nachfrage nach Rohstoffen und Agrarprodukten: Die Exporterlöse für Öl und Gas, Eisenerz und Kupfer, Soja und Rindfleisch hatten den Regierungen umfangreiche Sozialprogramme zur Reduzierung von Armut ermöglicht. Das Ende dieses historischen Booms vor gut zwei Jahren legte die Versäumnisse bloß: Das Geld der letzten Jahre war vor allem in den Konsum geflossen, wo in der Unterschicht freilich ein großer Nachholbedarf bestanden hatte. Doch Investitionen in die Infrastruktur, in das Bildungs- und das Gesundheitswesen, auch in die öffentliche Sicherheit blieben weit hinter den Erfordernissen zurück. Wirtschaftsreformen und Budgetdisziplin wurden hintangestellt.

Seit ein paar Monaten haben Argentinien und Brasilien konservative Regierungen. In Bolivien, Ecuador und Chile sinkt die Stern der linken Präsidenten. Die große Reparatur hat begonnen. Aber daraus wird noch lange kein neues Lateinamerika.

Estelle Blaschke

The Boat Is Full

In the summer of 2014, Italian photographer Massimo Sestini took a picture of a refugee boat near the Tunisian coast shortly before the people on it were taken off by the Italian Navy as part of Operation Mare Nostrum (OMN; fig. 1). *Rescue Operation* is an overhead shot of a boat crammed with people in the open sea, and it has become one of the iconic images of the refugee crisis. This image summed up similar images of refugee boats from this as well as past crises, but it also added a particular aesthetic edge to this "generic image"[1]—and provided a spectacular quality.

In 2015 Sestini's picture won second prize in the "General News" category of the World Press Photo Award (first prize went to Mads Nissen for *Jon and Alex*, the portrait of a gay couple in Saint Petersburg). Before and after this, the picture circulated on different media. The website of the World Press Photo Foundation, where the photographs that have been selected are archived after appearing in the media, includes a short text about the work and final disbandment of OMN. The description includes technical details about the camera and the settings, the geographical location of the take, and a portrait of the photographer. Like Nissen, Sestini uses a Canon. Canon is the sponsor of World Press Photo, because "at Canon, photography is more than just a business, it is part of our heritage and part of our DNA."[2]

As Sestini's self-portrayal suggests, his way of taking photographs is a high-risk business (fig. 2). The photographer is standing on the outer landing skid of a helicopter, tied to the inside of the vehicle. With one hand he is holding the flash, while taking the picture with the other. Neither he nor the helicopter can allow themself to move much during the take. In *Rescue Operation*, Sestini flies as an "embedded journalist" on a Coast Guard search-and-rescue helicopter. This job is not so very different from the work of a paparazzo, which he carries on in parallel. Renting a helicopter requires good weather, and each minute is expensive: it has to be worth it.

The myth of the professional photographer finds expression in his extreme logistical and physical commitment. Spurred on by his mission, he puts himself in danger, armed with multiple cameras, in order to produce pictures that no amateur could possibly take, and which show us the world in a way that is seldom seen. The public performance of the photographer thus becomes the guarantee that a picture like *Rescue Operation* could not have been simply taken by a military surveillance camera or by a drone. The photographer is not here just as a witness to the take. As author, he constitutes the seam between the process of creation and the journalistic and artistic uses of an image.

In the history of photography, the mobility of the device and the physical elevation of the photographer above the surface have always led to new aesthetic achievements—think of László Moholy-Nagy's architectural views, Berenice Abbott's *New York,* or Andreas Gursky's aerial takes. The overhead view produces an effect of estrangement, the third dimension dissolves, the objects portrayed are abstracted into forms and surfaces. Here the northward-bound boat is composed of a mass of individual, colored dots set against a deep-blue background. *Rescue Operation* is similar in some regards to Edward Burtynsky's *Manufactured Landscapes*, where the aesthetic of the image and the spectacle of production tend to conceal the actual contents. As with Burtynsky, Sestini's image runs the risk of being nothing more than a depressingly "beautiful" image, all the more so as it is barely possible to distinguish important details and information at mostly low resolutions or in print: people looking up with hope, some waving, some laughing for the camera, children held up high, people squeezed together, some people below deck visible behind an open hatch.

For the rhetoric of the image and its reception, however, these details are only secondary. One particular reading—its vocabulary tied

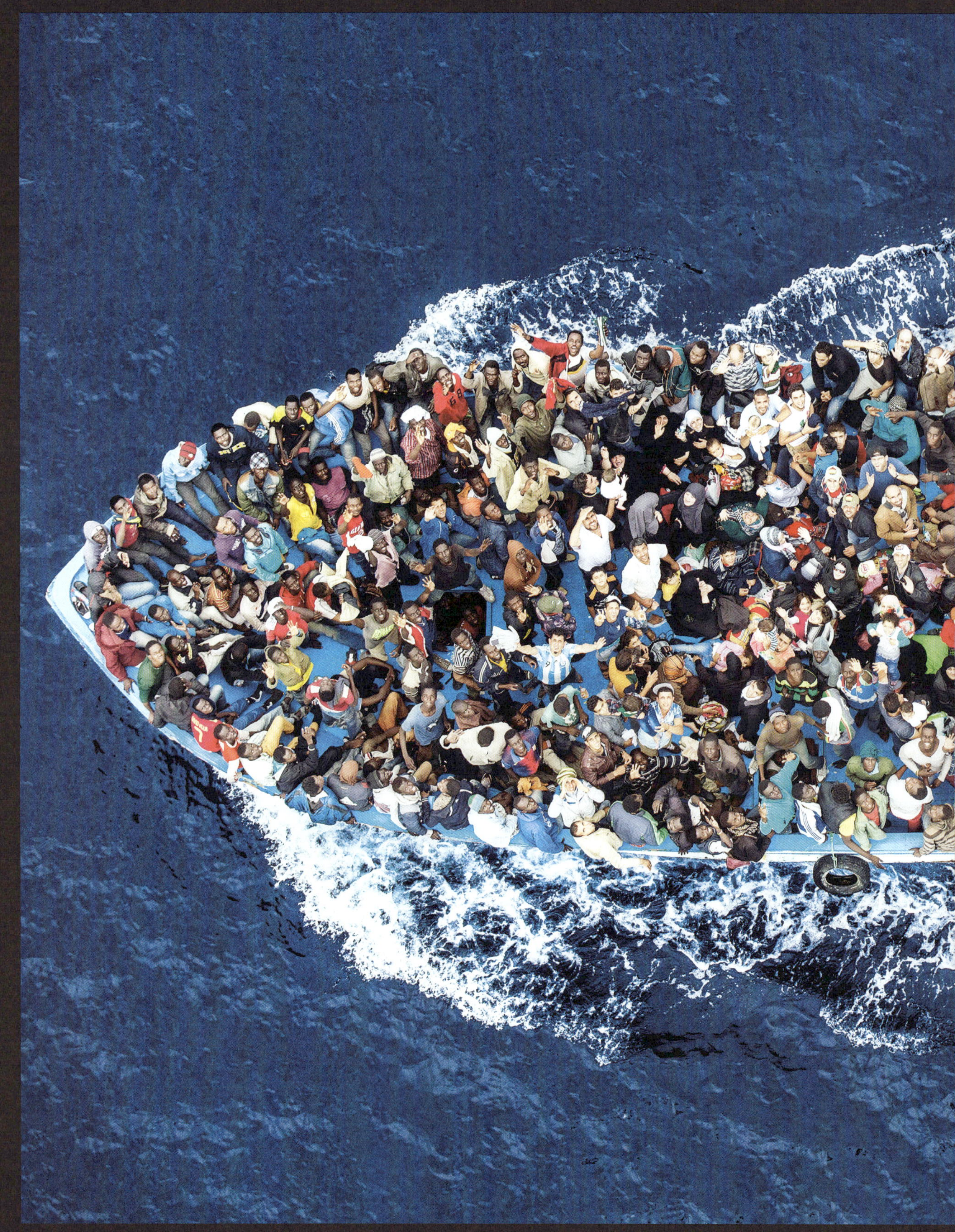

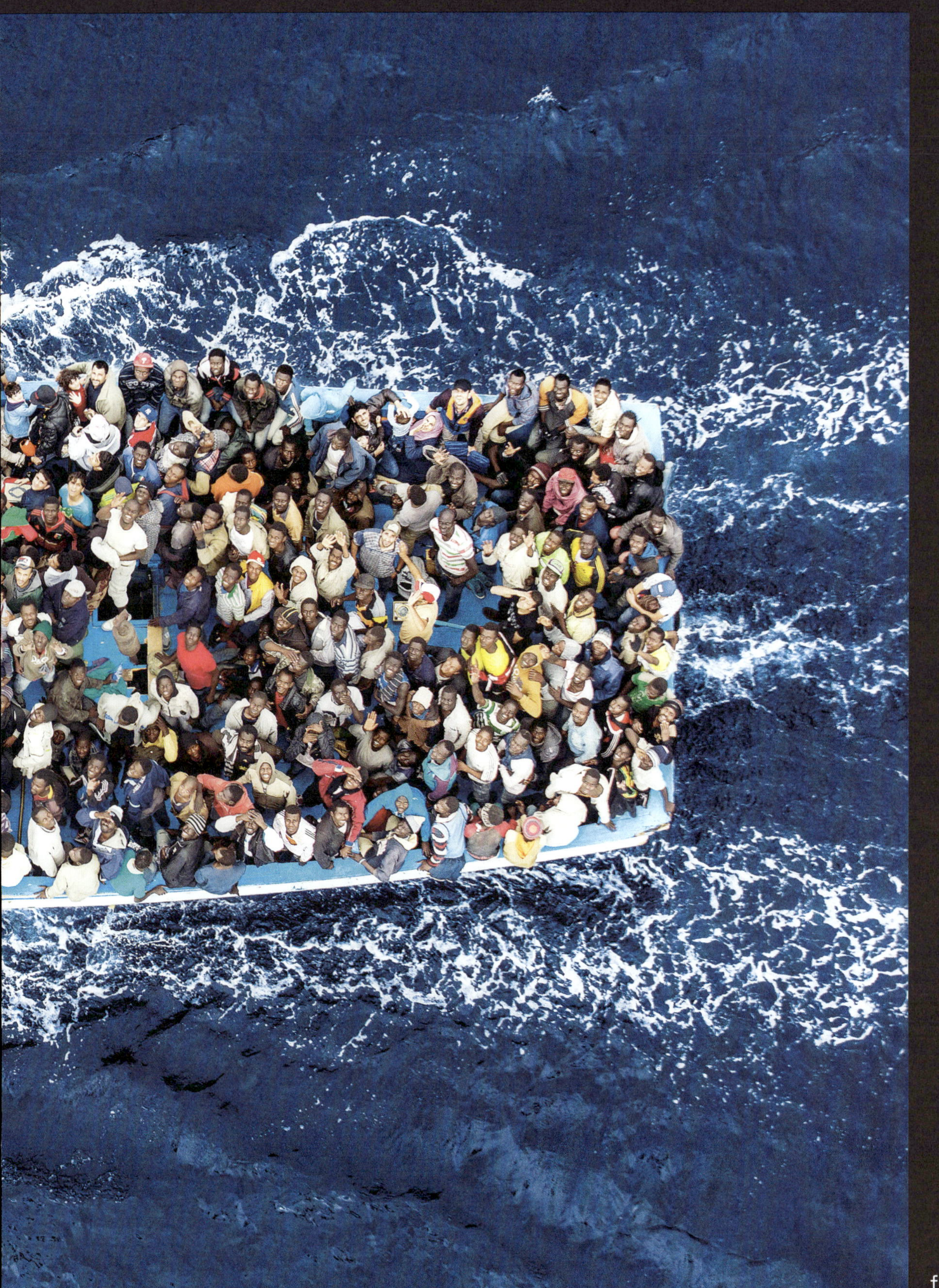

fig. 1

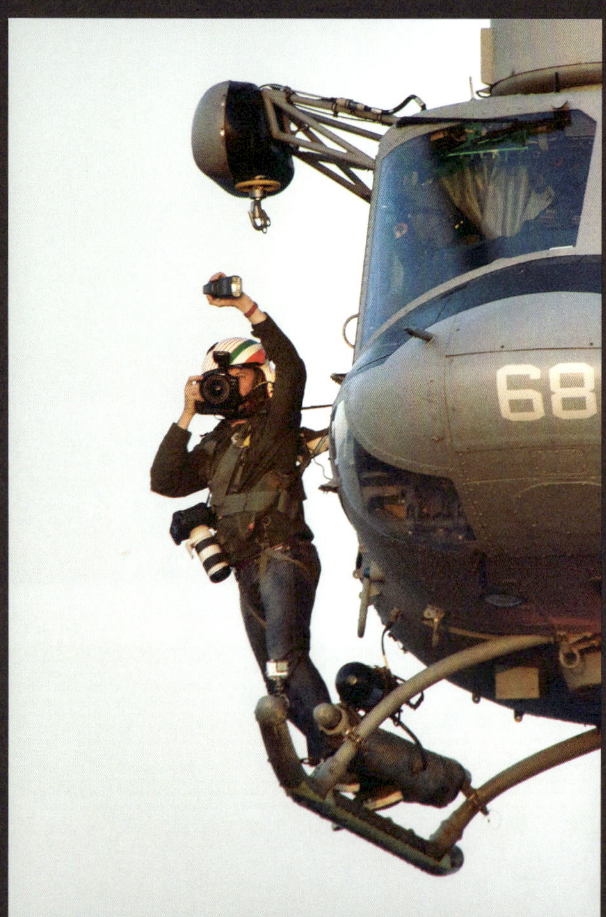

fig. 2

to a specific cultural memory—seems instead to prevail: "The boat is full." In 1942, Switzerland used this same metaphor—coined by the Minister of Justice Eduard von Steiger—to legitimize sending back Jewish refugees and closing the country's borders. In order not to sink, one has to protect oneself from the assault of refugees. At the beginning of the 1990s, the slogan "The boat is full" was back on the election campaign posters of one of Germany's political parties, the Republicans. *Der Spiegel* also put the topic—"The assault of the poor: Refugees, emigrants, asylum seekers"—on its cover, with a drawing of a boat painted black, red, and gold that is in danger of sinking from the load it is carrying.[3] "The boat is full" has subliminally entered the minds of many and resonates in all the pictures of overcrowded refugee boats as a particularly persistent association. *Rescue Operation* is no Noah's Ark; we are not all on the same boat, but instead are looking down at it from a safe distance.

AN ARCHIVIST ON LAMPEDUSA

BY EMILIE JOSSO

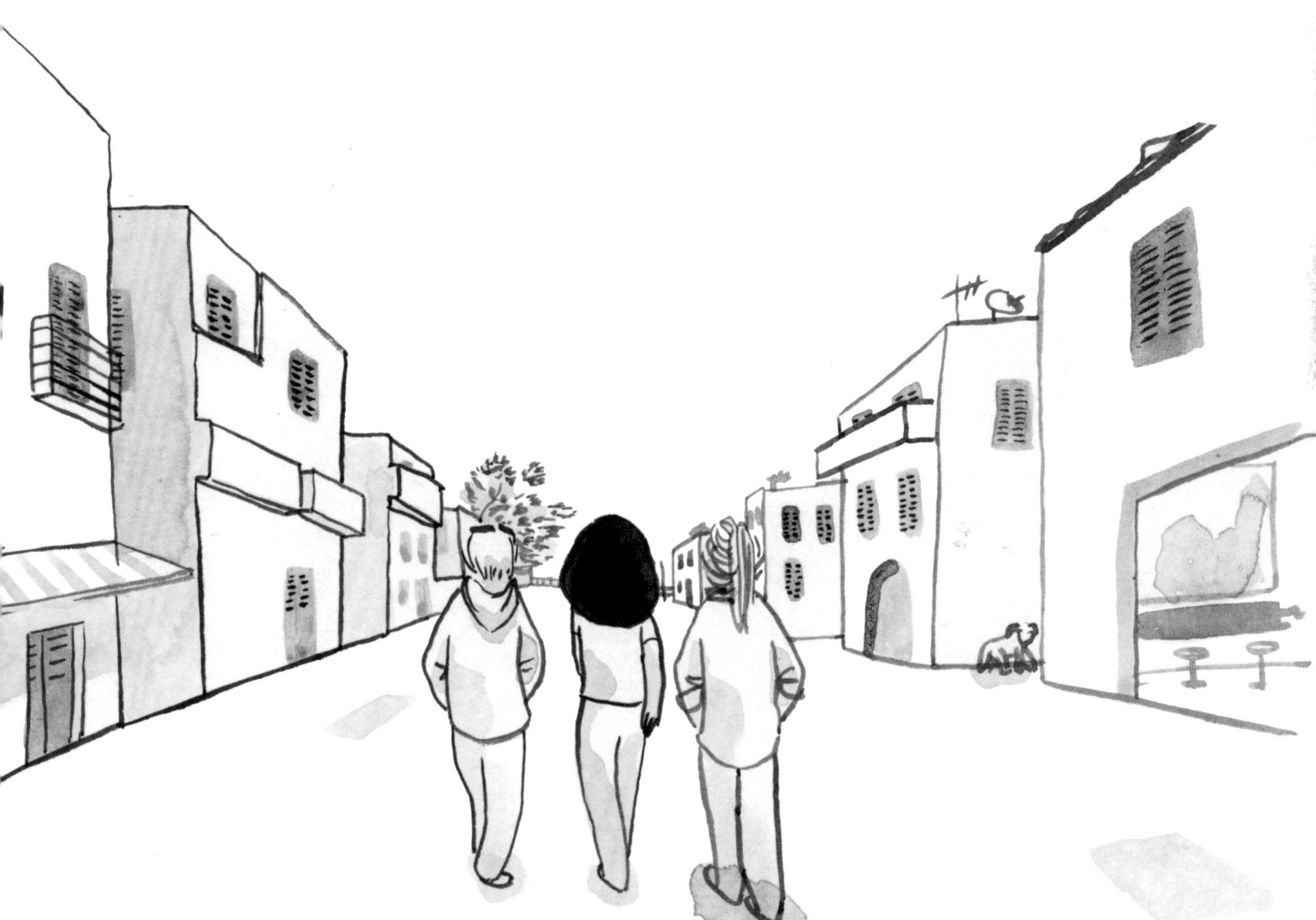

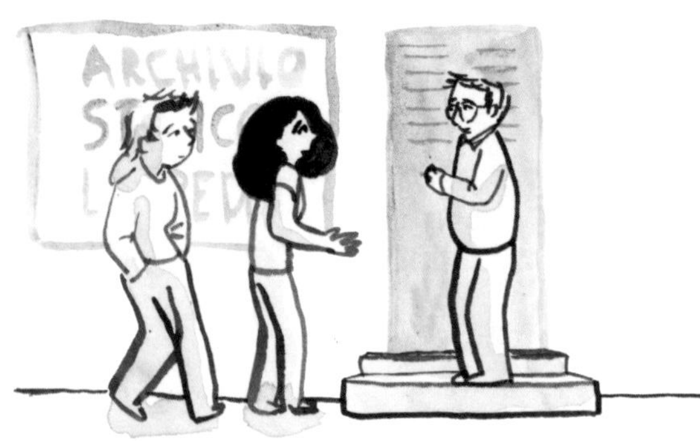

HELLO!

BUONGIORNO!
COME IN,
YOU'RE WELCOME.

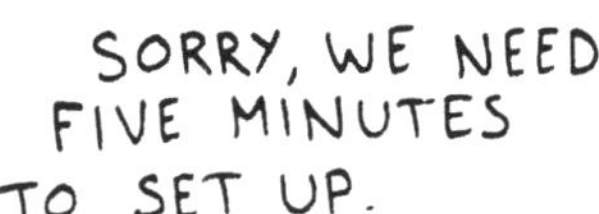

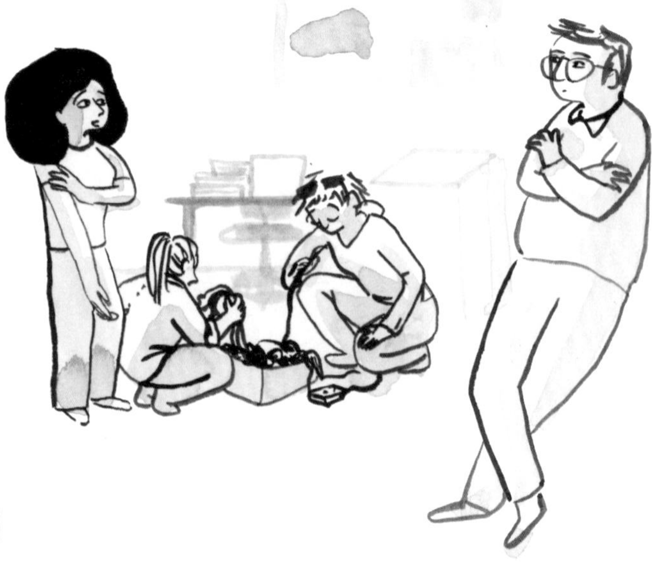

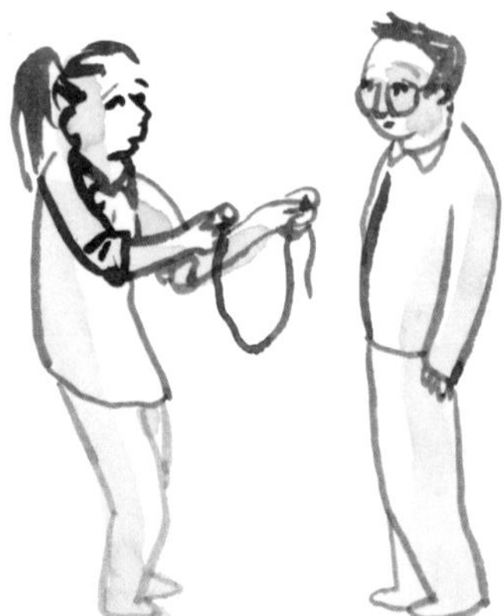

CAN I PUT
A MIKE
ON YOU?

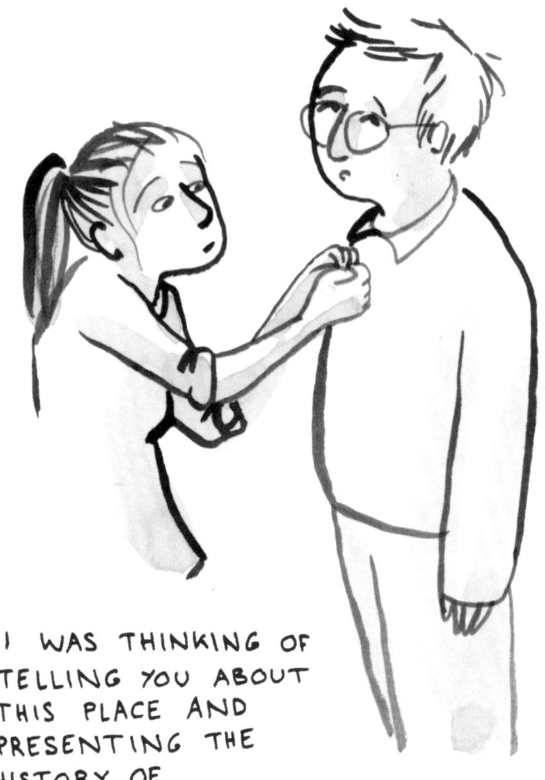

I WAS THINKING OF
TELLING YOU ABOUT
THIS PLACE AND
PRESENTING THE
HISTORY OF
LAMPEDUSA AND
THEN GOING TO TALK
ABOUT MIGRANTS HERE.

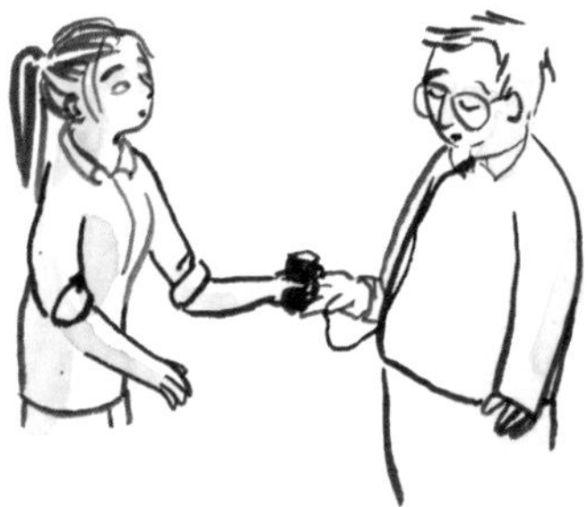

THAT SOUNDS GREAT!
COULD YOU PUT THIS
IN YOUR POCKET?

DO YOU ALREADY
KNOW WHO ELSE
YOU WANT TO MEET?

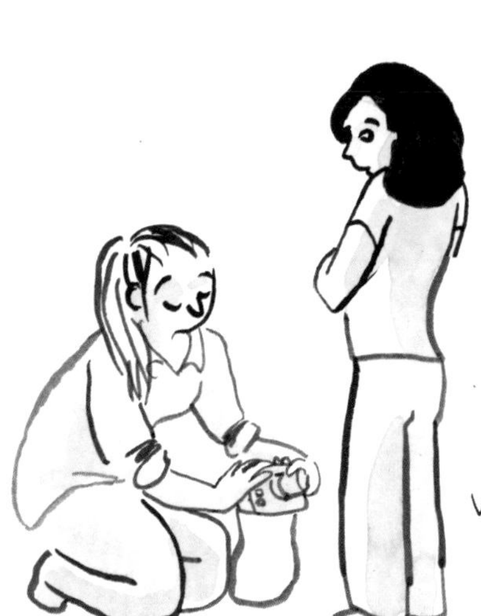

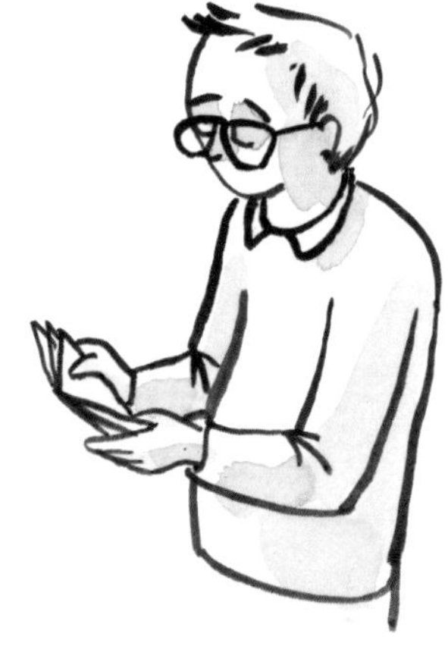

WE WOULD LIKE TO
SPEAK TO THE MARINA
MILITARE, LEGAMBIENTE,
AND ALSO TO GIUSI NICOLINI,
THE MAYOR.

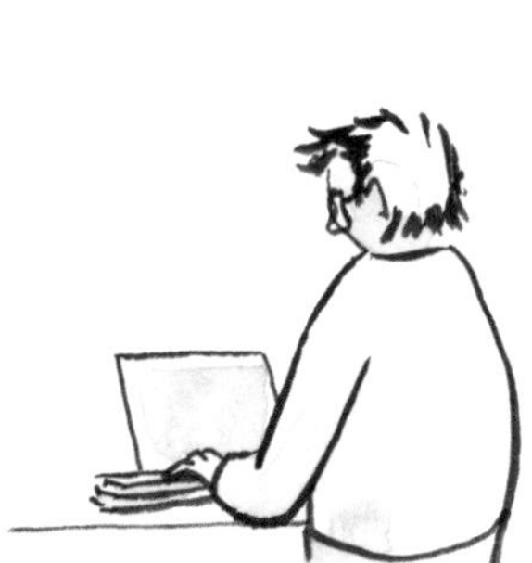

OH... REALLY?

I'AM AFRAID THAT
MIGHT BE DIFFICULT.
SHE IS RARELY HERE,
ON THE ISLAND.

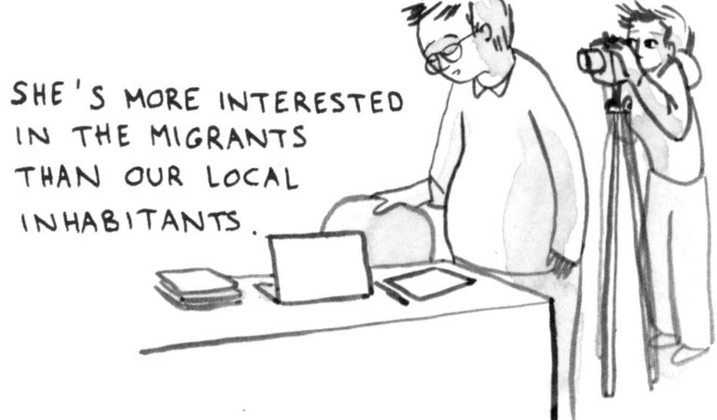

SHE'S MORE INTERESTED
IN THE MIGRANTS
THAN OUR LOCAL
INHABITANTS.

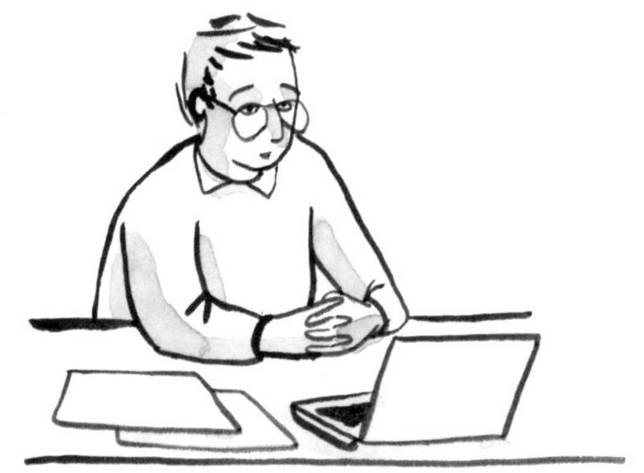

SHOULD WE START?

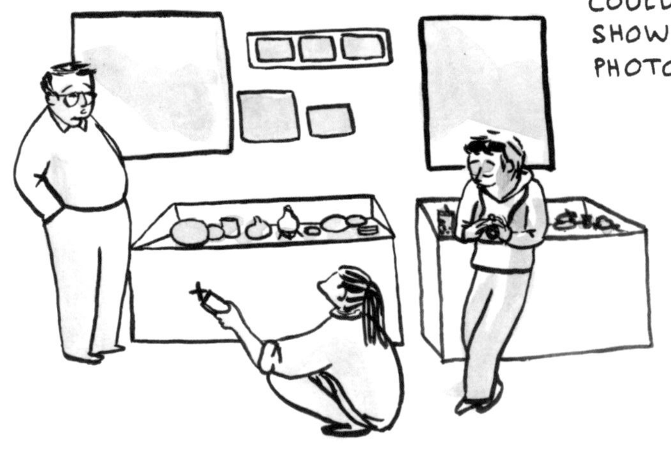
COULD YOU
SHOW US SOME
PHOTOS?

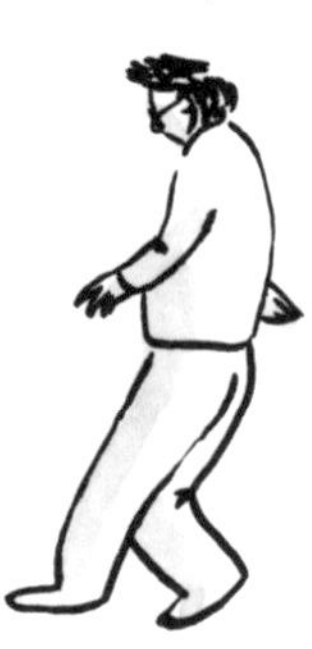
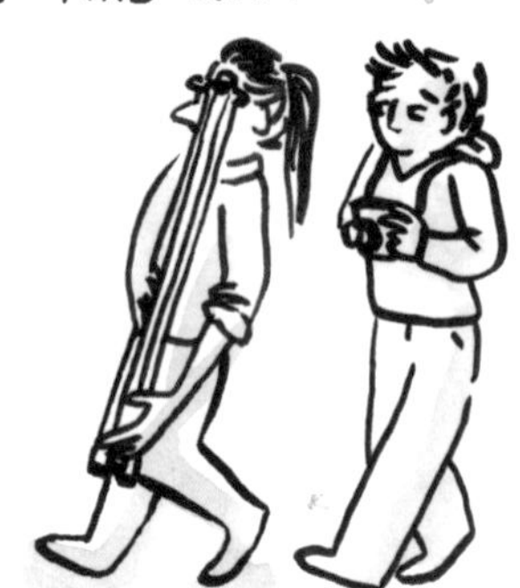
YES, COME THIS WAY.

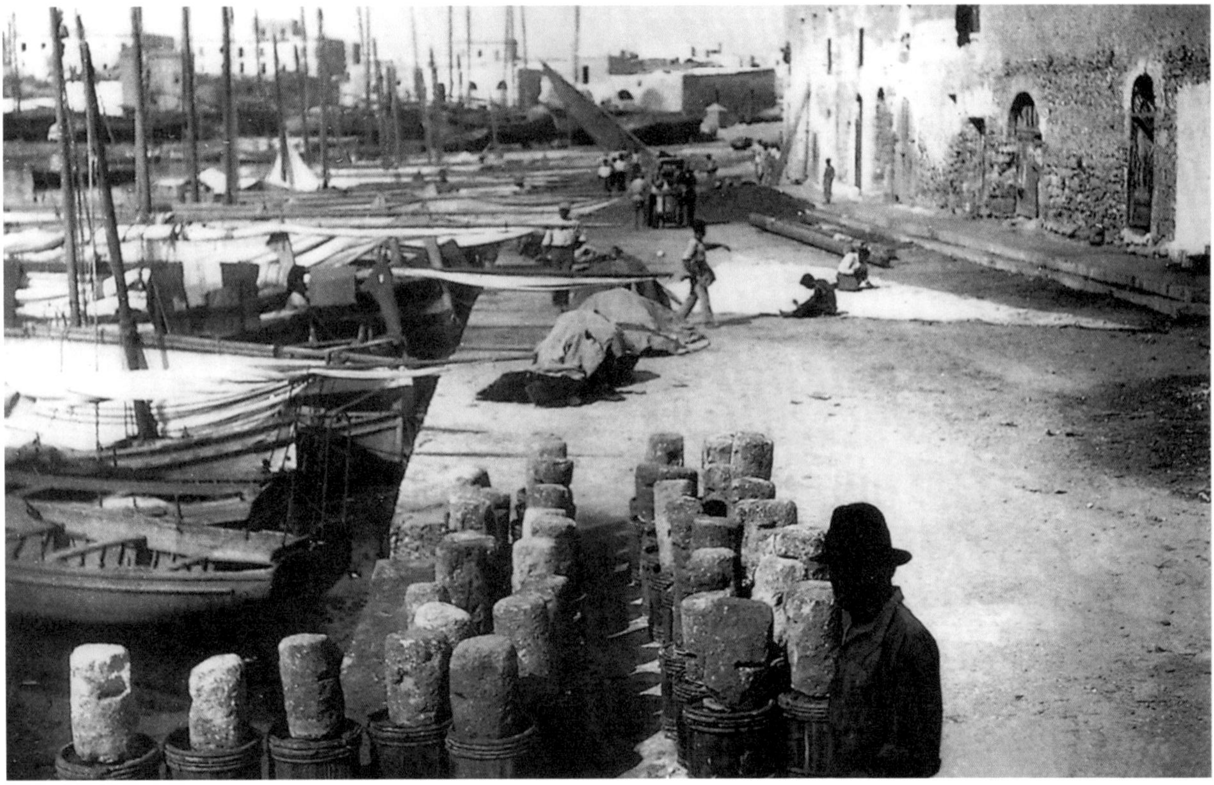

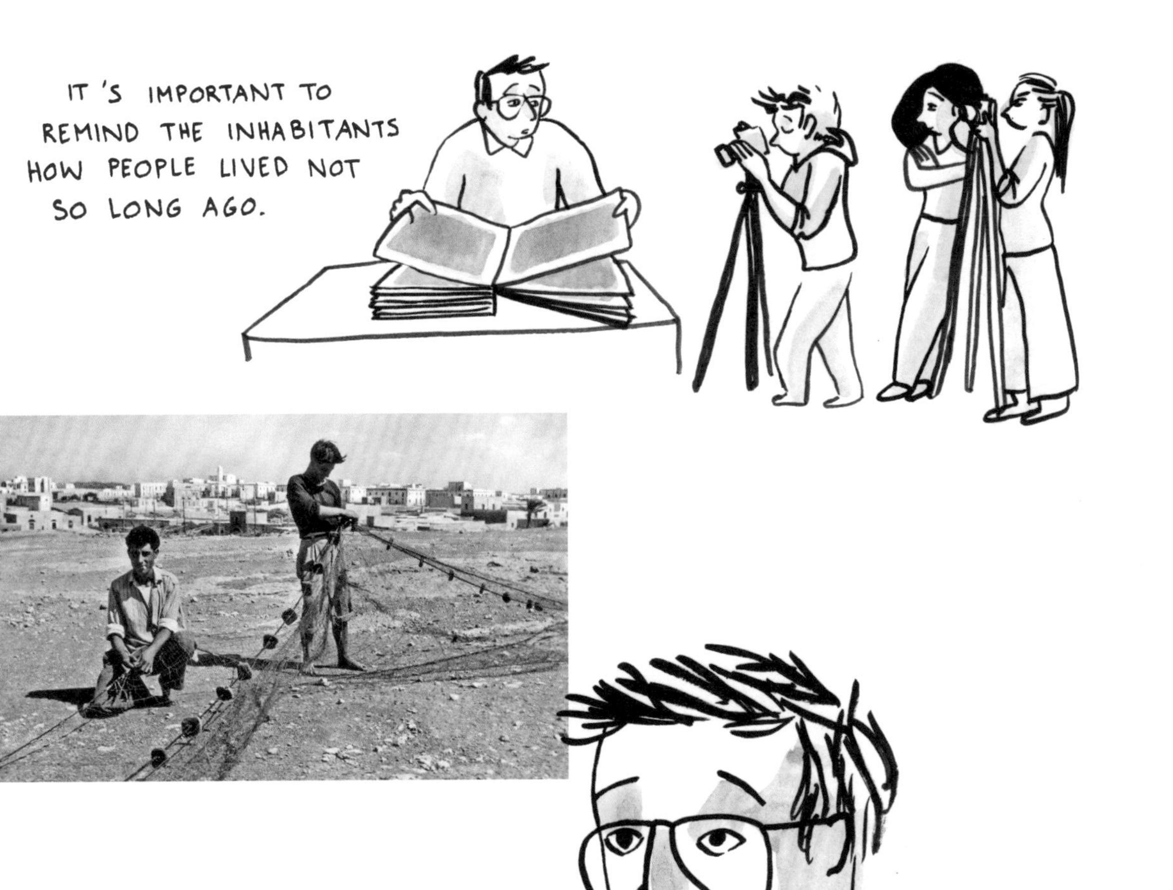

IT 'S IMPORTANT TO REMIND THE INHABITANTS HOW PEOPLE LIVED NOT SO LONG AGO.

LOSING OUR MEMORY IS LIKE LOSING A PART OF OURSELVES.

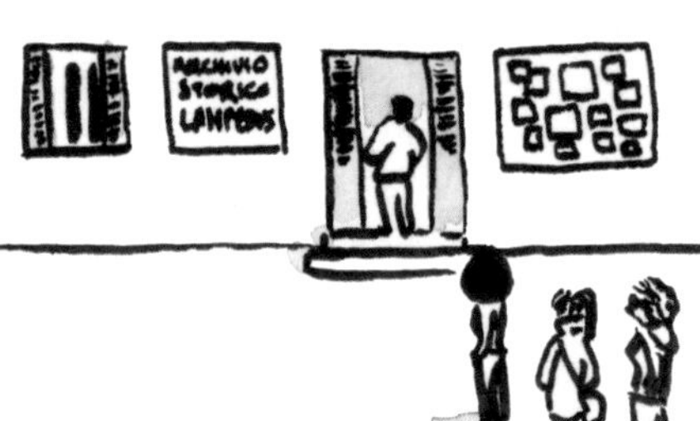

IT MAKES TOTAL SENSE THAT YOU BUILT THIS PLACE.

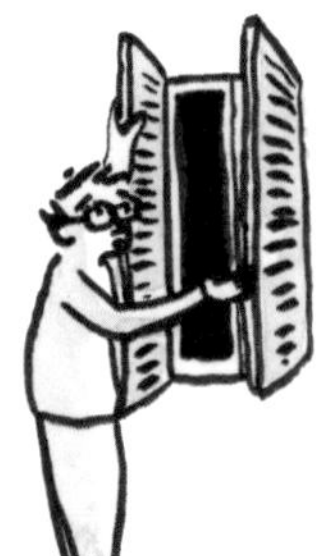

I'M HAPPY ABOUT IT, BECAUSE IT IS EXACTLY WHAT I WANT TO DO.

YOU KNOW, BECAUSE THIS PLACE CONTAINS SOME OF LAMPEDUSA'S HISTORY, IT ALSO MAKES IT PRESENT ON THE ISLAND.

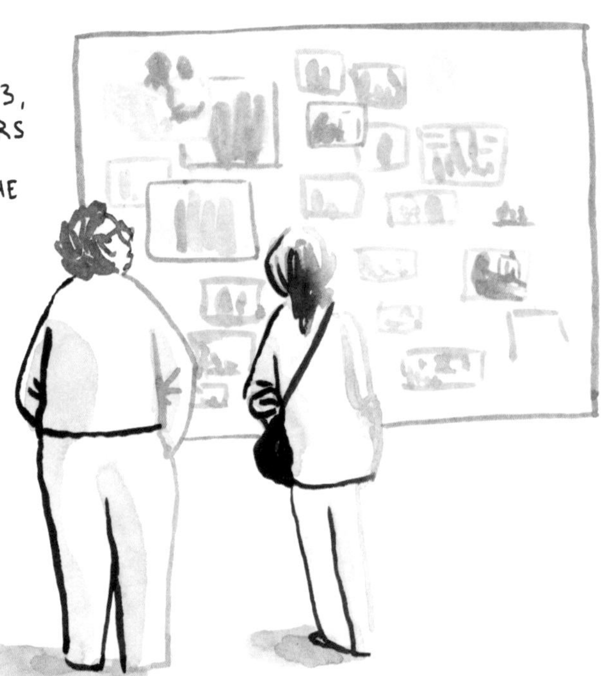

AFTER THE TRAGEDY OF OCTOBER 3, 2013, SOME SURVIVORS FROM ERITREA REMAINED ON THE ISLAND FOR SEVERAL MONTHS.

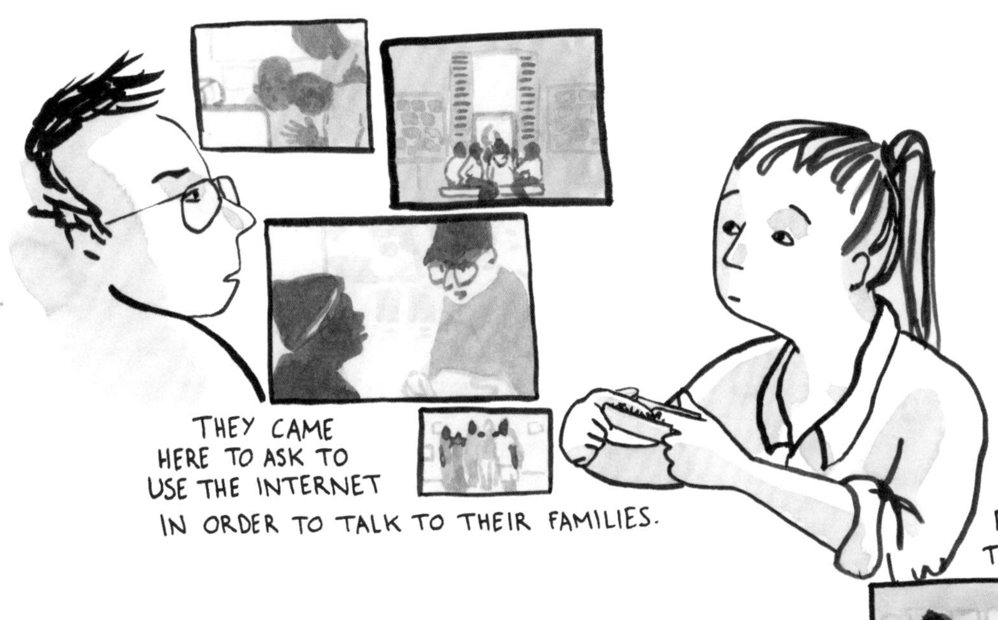

THEY CAME HERE TO ASK TO USE THE INTERNET IN ORDER TO TALK TO THEIR FAMILIES.

FRIENDSHIP BEGAN THERE.

THE TOURIST SEASON WAS FINISHED, AND THEY CAME EVERY NIGHT TO WATCH VIDEOS FROM THE ARCHIVE.

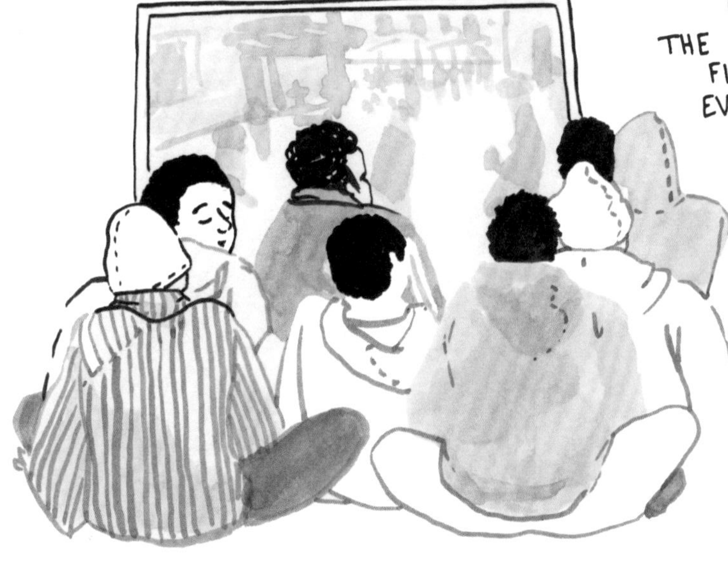

AFTER A WHILE WE HAD THE IDEA OF DOWNLOADING SOME FILMS IN THEIR LANGUAGE, OR SOME OF THEIR MUSIC, SO THAT THEY COULD RELAX A BIT.

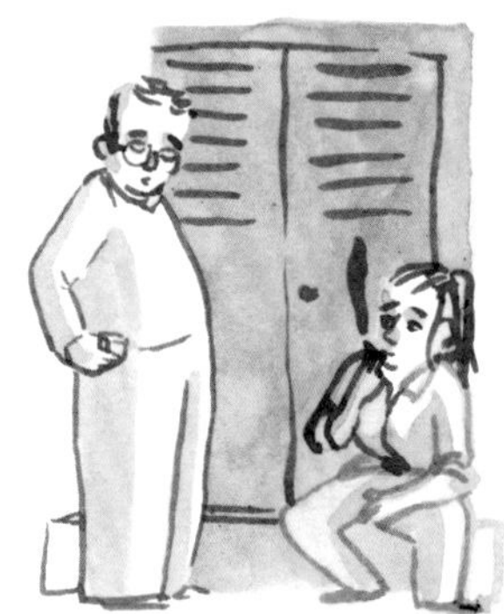

I WONDER HOW PEOPLE FROM LAMPEDUSA REGARD MEDIA IMAGES OF THEIR ISLAND.
WELL, LAMPEDUSA HAS BECOME A STAGE FOR JOURNALISTS.

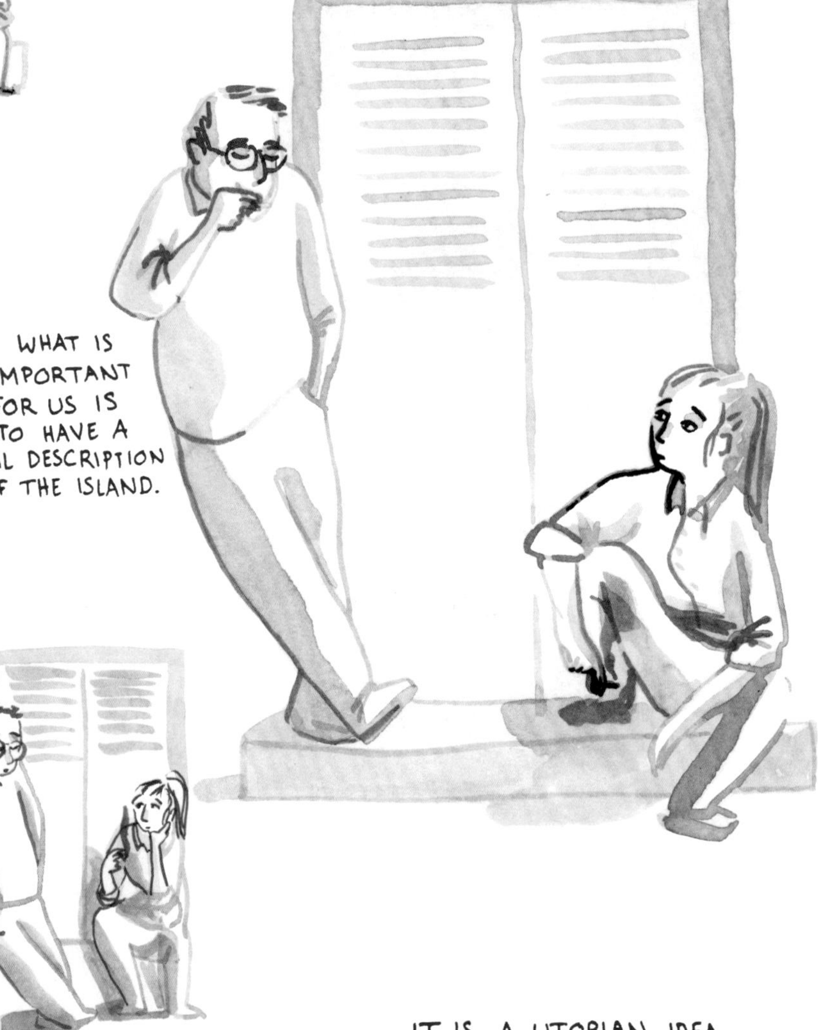

WHAT IS IMPORTANT FOR US IS TO HAVE A REAL DESCRIPTION OF THE ISLAND.
BUT THE WORK OF THE MEDIA IS TO OFFER AN INTERPRETATION. FIRST OF ALL, THE QUESTION OF WHETHER OR NOT TO TALK ABOUT SOMETHING IS ALREADY A CHOICE.
IT IS A UTOPIAN IDEA TO THINK THAT THE MEDIA COULD GIVE AN OBJECTIVE POINT OF VIEW. THERE IS NO SINGLE WAY OF SEEING THINGS — THERE ARE AS MANY REALITIES AS THERE ARE PEOPLE.

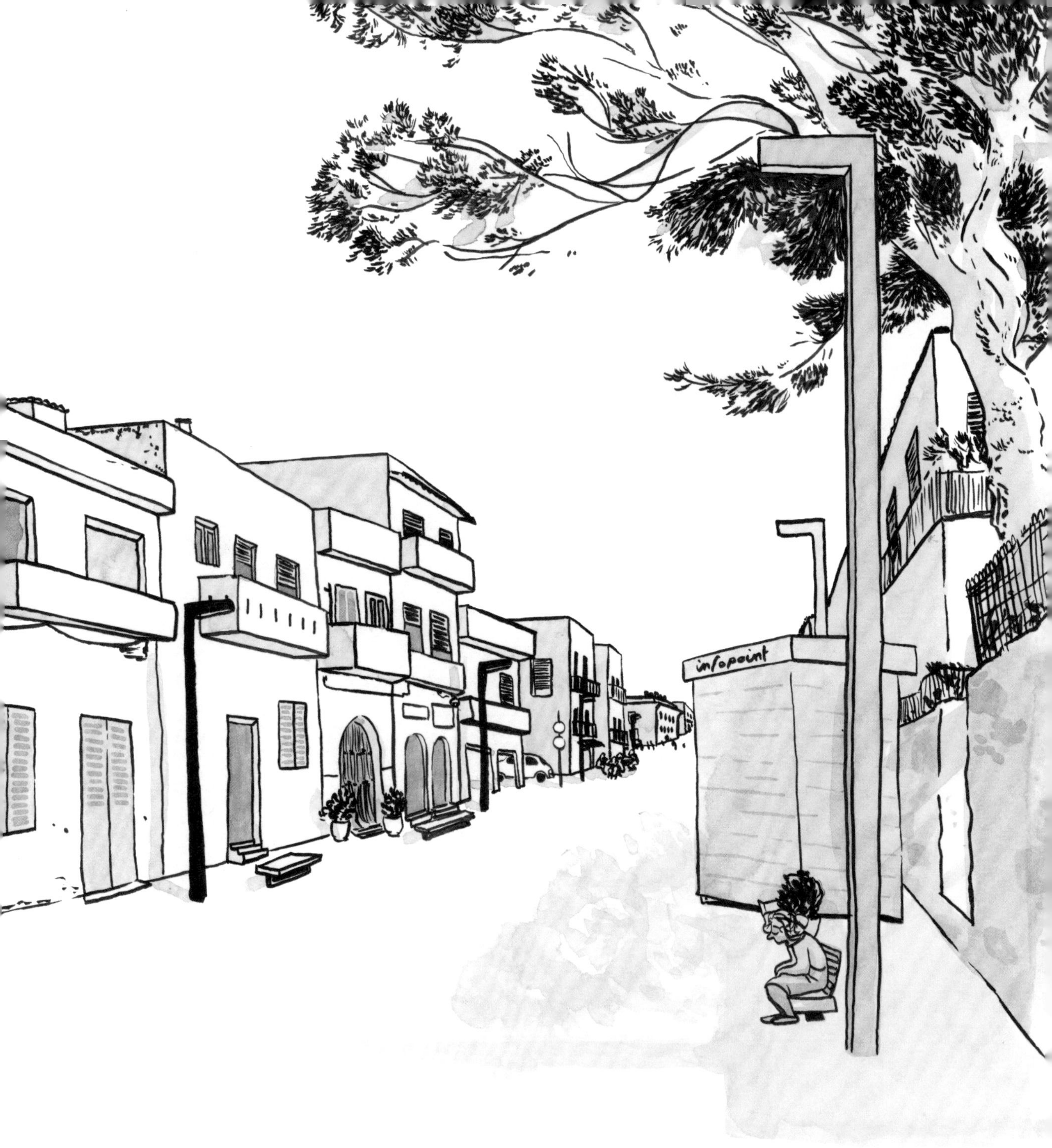

SO, COMING BACK TO THE INHABITANTS OF LAMPEDUSA, I CAN SAY THAT SOME OF US THINK ONE WAY, WHILE OTHERS HAVE A DIFFERENT OPINION. BUT I'M STILL CONVINCED THAT IT WAS FAR TOO MUCH TO CONSIDER AWARDING THE NOBEL PEACE PRIZE TO OUR ISLAND. BECAUSE WE ONLY DO WHAT SEEMS NORMAL TO US. AND WE DON'T WANT ANYONE TO TURN IT INTO A SHOW.

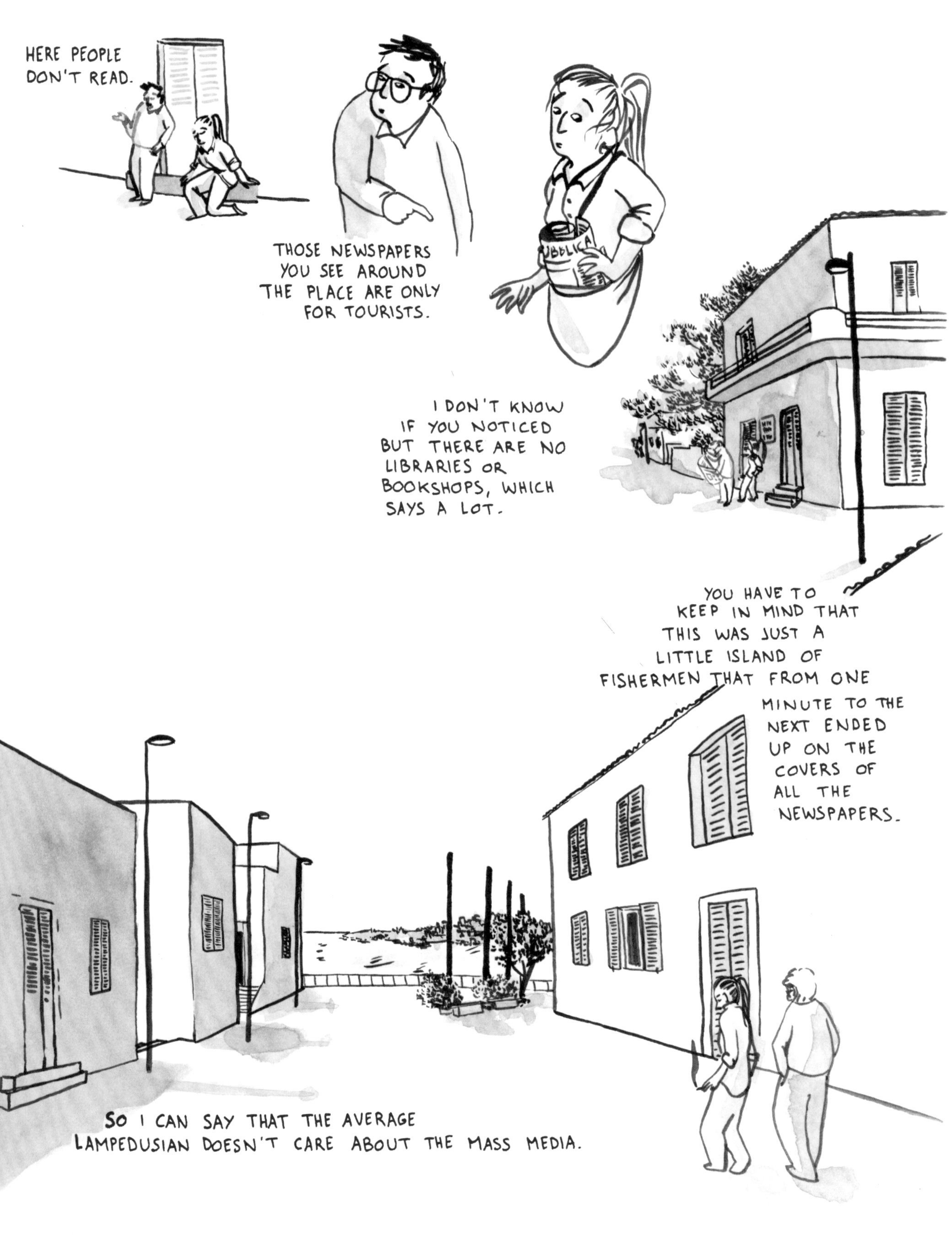

HERE PEOPLE DON'T READ.
THOSE NEWSPAPERS YOU SEE AROUND THE PLACE ARE ONLY FOR TOURISTS.
I DON'T KNOW IF YOU NOTICED BUT THERE ARE NO LIBRARIES OR BOOKSHOPS, WHICH SAYS A LOT.
YOU HAVE TO KEEP IN MIND THAT THIS WAS JUST A LITTLE ISLAND OF FISHERMEN THAT FROM ONE MINUTE TO THE NEXT ENDED UP ON THE COVERS OF ALL THE NEWSPAPERS.
SO I CAN SAY THAT THE AVERAGE LAMPEDUSIAN DOESN'T CARE ABOUT THE MASS MEDIA.

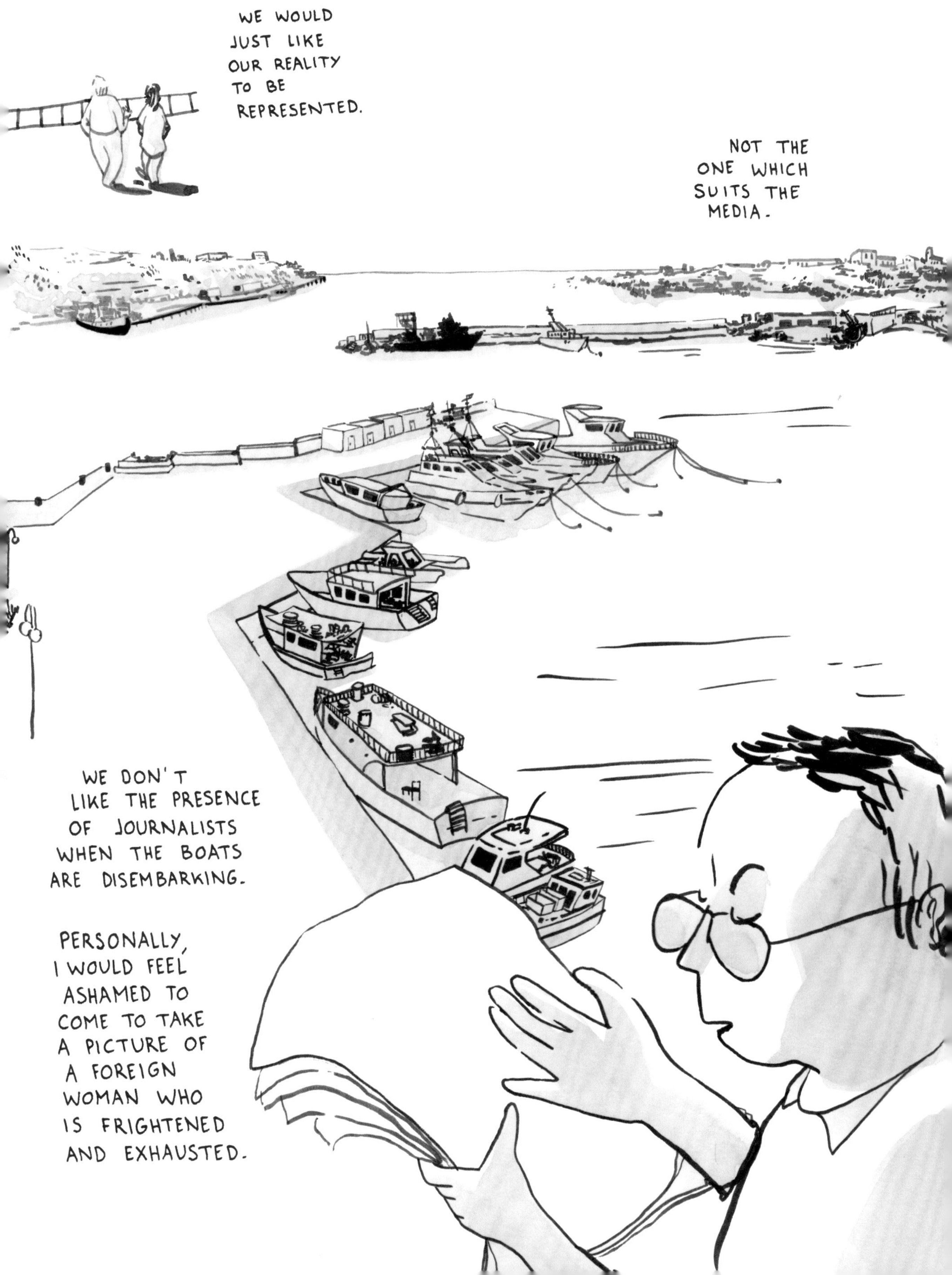

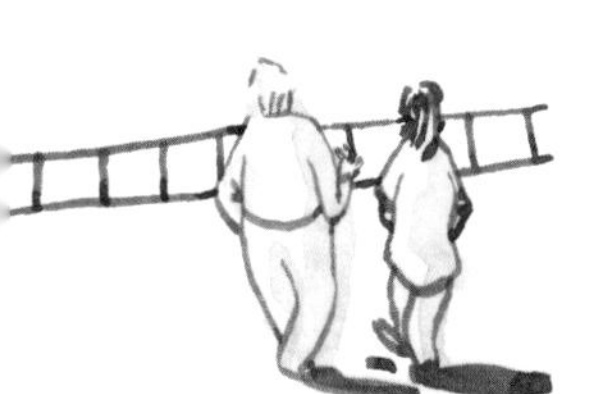

WE WOULD JUST LIKE OUR REALITY TO BE REPRESENTED.
NOT THE ONE WHICH SUITS THE MEDIA.
WE DON'T LIKE THE PRESENCE OF JOURNALISTS WHEN THE BOATS ARE DISEMBARKING.
PERSONALLY, I WOULD FEEL ASHAMED TO COME TO TAKE A PICTURE OF A FOREIGN WOMAN WHO IS FRIGHTENED AND EXHAUSTED.

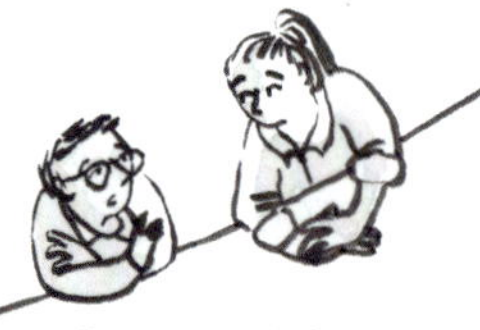

THE IMAGE CREATED
IS ONE OF EMERGENCY,
WHICH HAS NEVER EXISTED.

EXCEPT
WHEN THE
TUNISIANS
WERE ARRIVING
AFTER THE
ARAB SPRING.

WHAT
HAPPENED
HERE BACK
THEN?

THE FALL OF THE BEN ALI
REGIME ENDED THE
SYSTEM OF BORDER
CONTROL THAT WAS
IN PLACE TO HONOR
THE TREATY WITH
EUROPE.
(READMISSION
AGREEMENT)

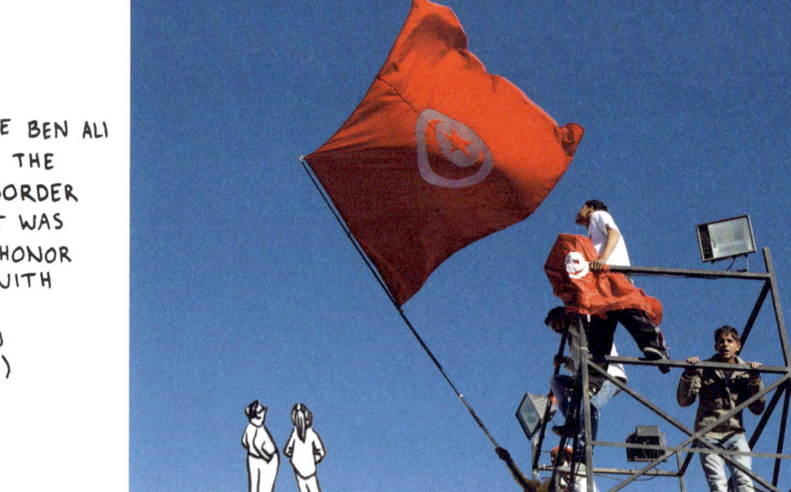

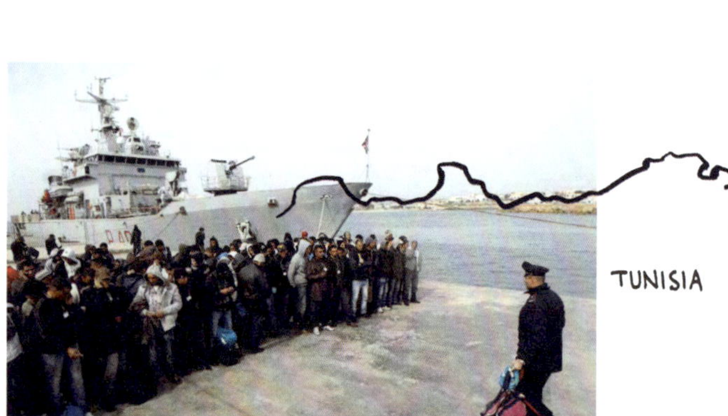

SO IN A FEW WEEKS
THOUSANDS OF
TUNISIANS
CROSSED THE
MEDITERRANEAN
AND ENDED UP
HERE

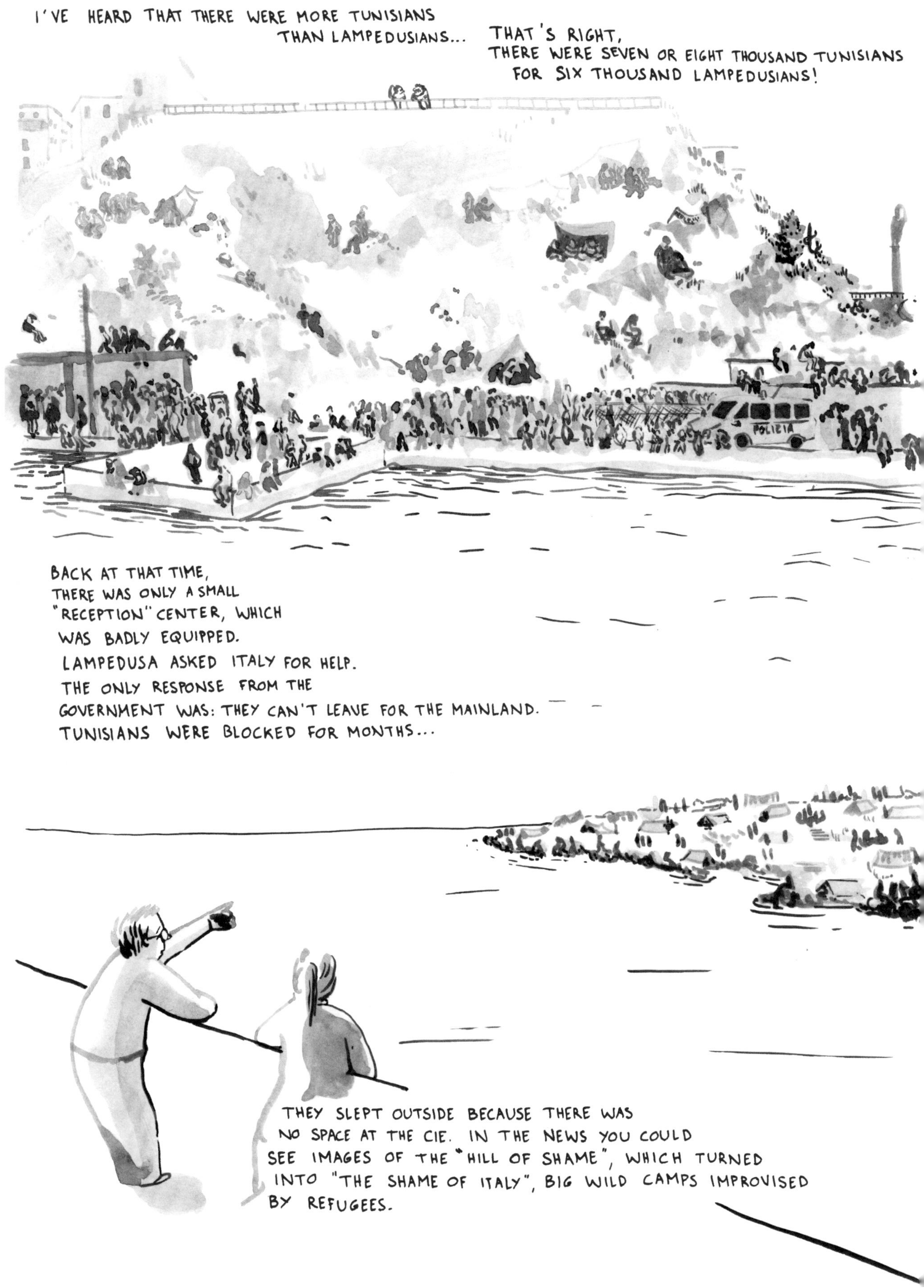

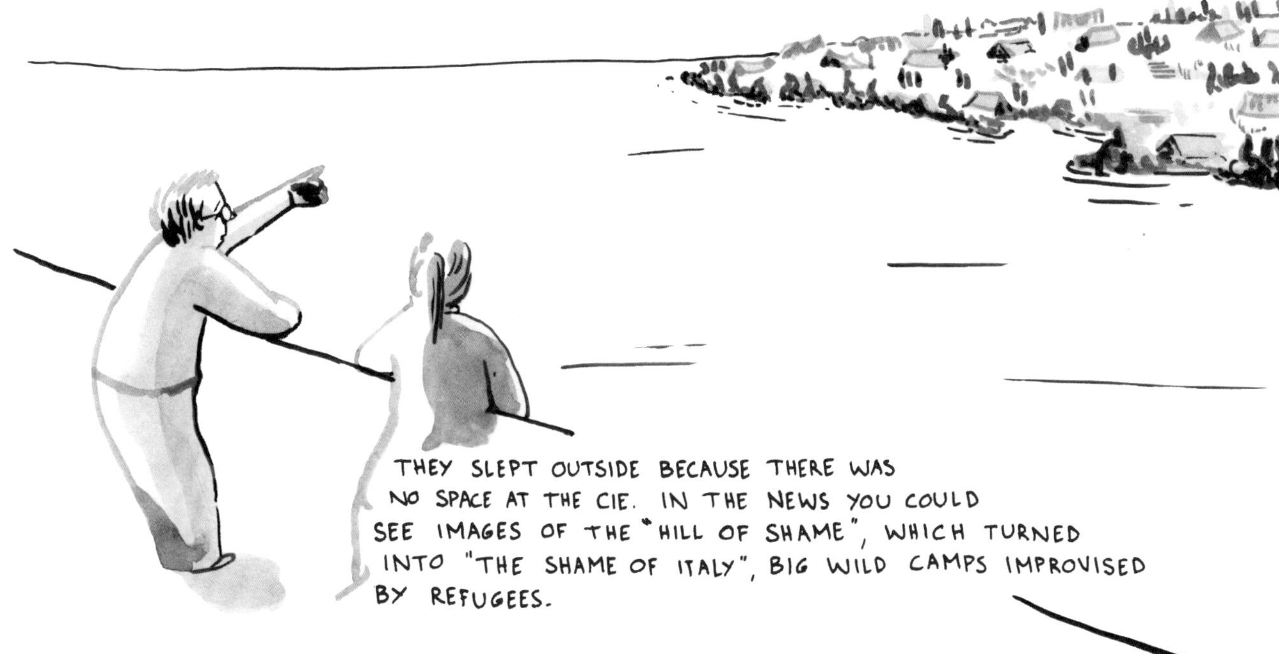

I'VE HEARD THAT THERE WERE MORE TUNISIANS THAN LAMPEDUSIANS...
THAT'S RIGHT, THERE WERE SEVEN OR EIGHT THOUSAND TUNISIANS FOR SIX THOUSAND LAMPEDUSIANS!
BACK AT THAT TIME, THERE WAS ONLY A SMALL "RECEPTION" CENTER, WHICH WAS BADLY EQUIPPED. LAMPEDUSA ASKED ITALY FOR HELP. THE ONLY RESPONSE FROM THE GOVERNMENT WAS: THEY CAN'T LEAVE FOR THE MAINLAND. TUNISIANS WERE BLOCKED FOR MONTHS...
THEY SLEPT OUTSIDE BECAUSE THERE WAS NO SPACE AT THE CIE. IN THE NEWS YOU COULD SEE IMAGES OF THE "HILL OF SHAME", WHICH TURNED INTO "THE SHAME OF ITALY", BIG WILD CAMPS IMPROVISED BY REFUGEES.

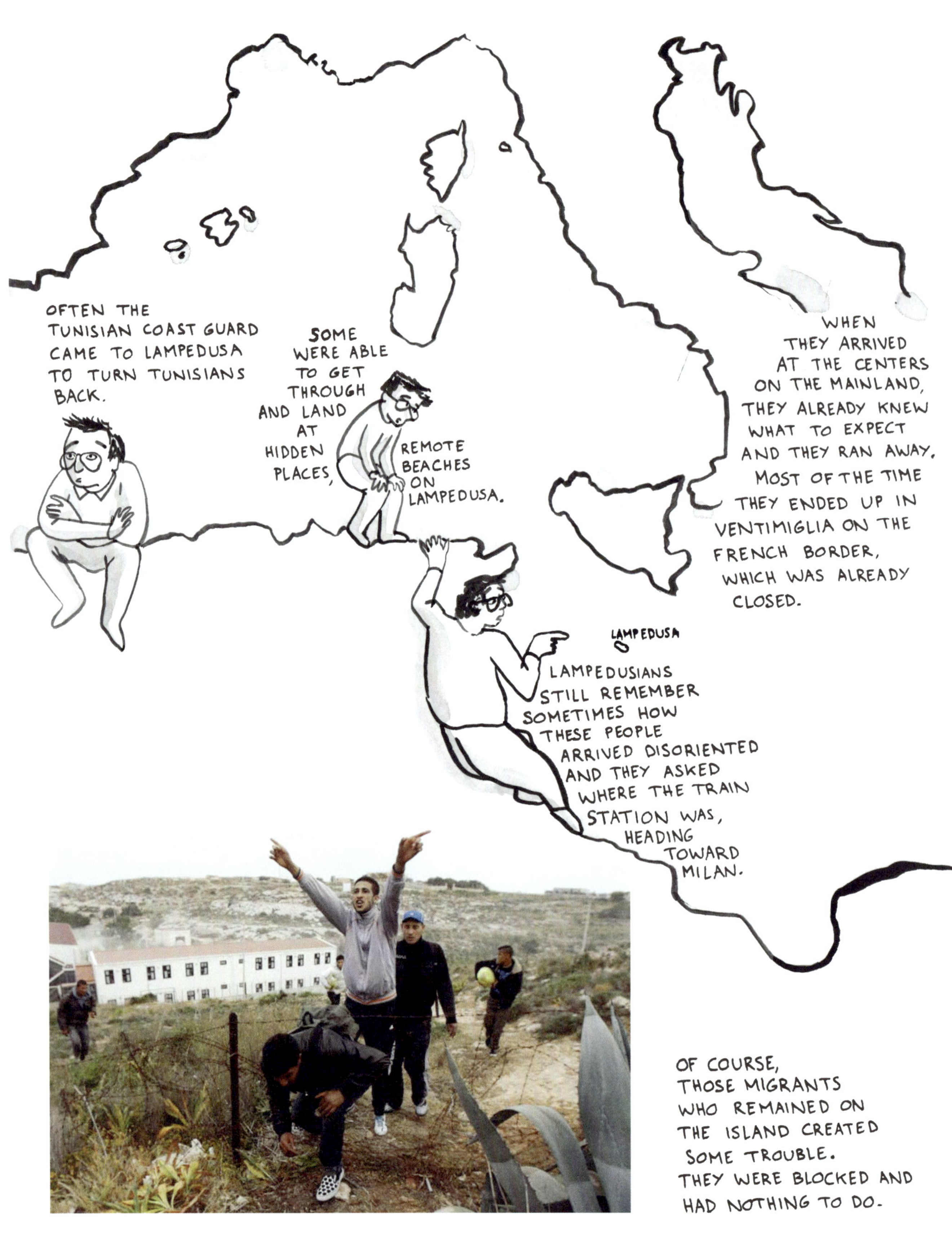

OFTEN THE
TUNISIAN COAST GUARD
CAME TO LAMPEDUSA
TO TURN TUNISIANS
BACK.

SOME WERE ABLE TO GET THROUGH AND LAND AT HIDDEN PLACES,

REMOTE BEACHES ON LAMPEDUSA.

WHEN THEY ARRIVED AT THE CENTERS ON THE MAINLAND, THEY ALREADY KNEW WHAT TO EXPECT AND THEY RAN AWAY. MOST OF THE TIME THEY ENDED UP IN VENTIMIGLIA ON THE FRENCH BORDER, WHICH WAS ALREADY CLOSED.

LAMPEDUSA

LAMPEDUSIANS STILL REMEMBER SOMETIMES HOW THESE PEOPLE ARRIVED DISORIENTED AND THEY ASKED WHERE THE TRAIN STATION WAS, HEADING TOWARD MILAN.

OF COURSE, THOSE MIGRANTS WHO REMAINED ON THE ISLAND CREATED SOME TROUBLE. THEY WERE BLOCKED AND HAD NOTHING TO DO.

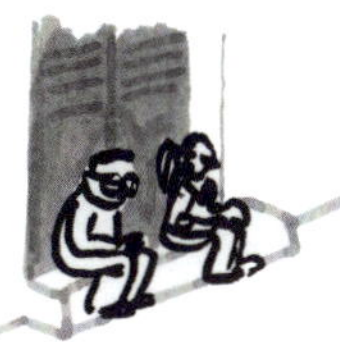

THEY ALSO
BURNED THE CENTER,
AS A PROTEST.

THE CATASTROPHIC
CONSEQUENCE WAS
THE DECLINE IN
TOURISM IN 2012.

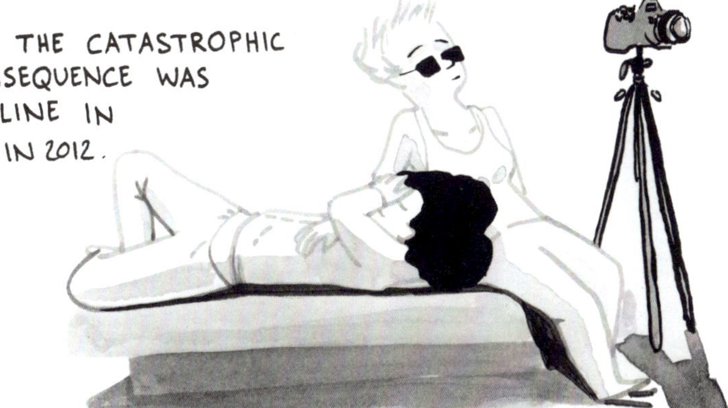

THE ISLAND BEGAN TO BE
VISITED ONLY BY JOURNALISTS,
WHO ALL RUN TO TAKE PICTURES
OF THE LAST DISEMBARKATIONS.

AFTER SOME MONTHS WE NOTICED
SOME CHANGES IN THE PEOPLE
WHO WERE ARRIVING.

THEY WERE
NO LONGER YOUNG
MEN WITH NIKE SHOES
AND CELL PHONES BUT
FAMILIES, CHILDREN,
AND TEENAGERS
WITHOUT
PARENTS

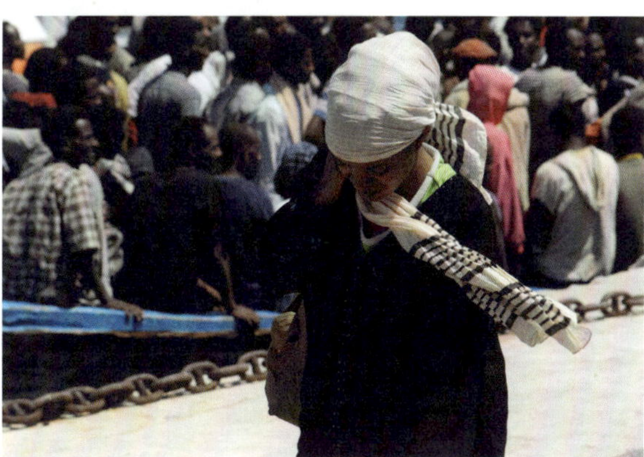

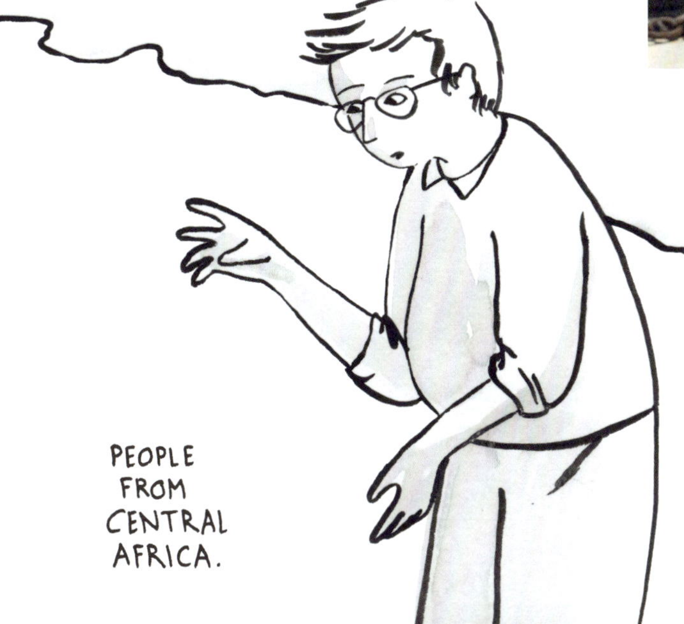

PEOPLE
FROM
CENTRAL
AFRICA.

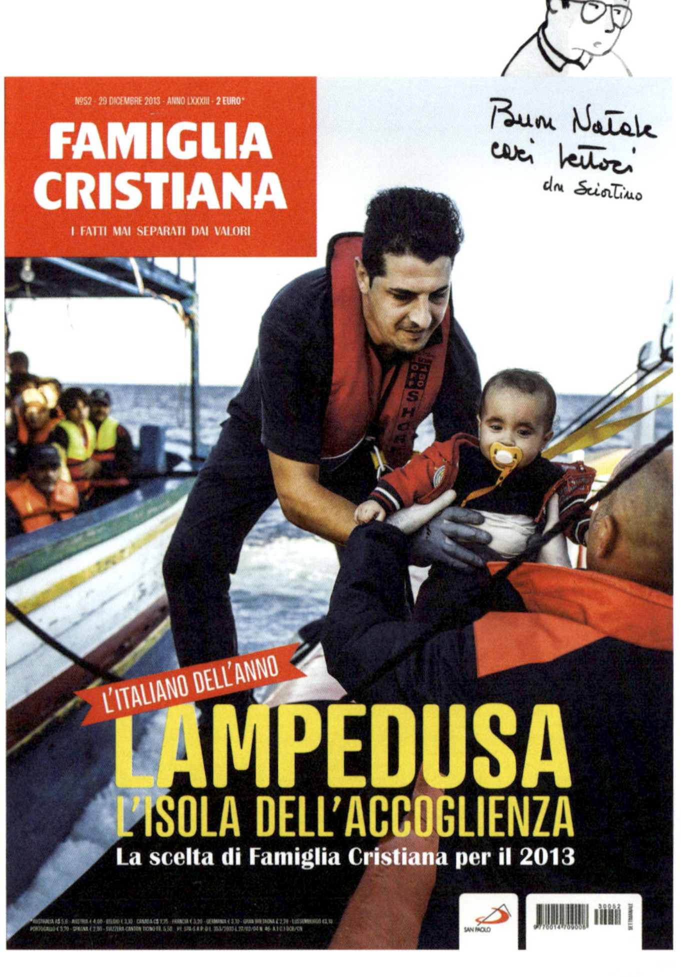

TO TELL YOU THE TRUTH,
LAMPEDUSA IS IN LESS TROUBLE
THAN ROME OR MILAN.
WE ARE PRIVILEGED COMPARED TO OTHER
BIG CITIES. WE ARE AN ISLAND IN TRANSITION.
NOBODY WILL STAY FOR A LONG TIME.
THEY MOVE ON.

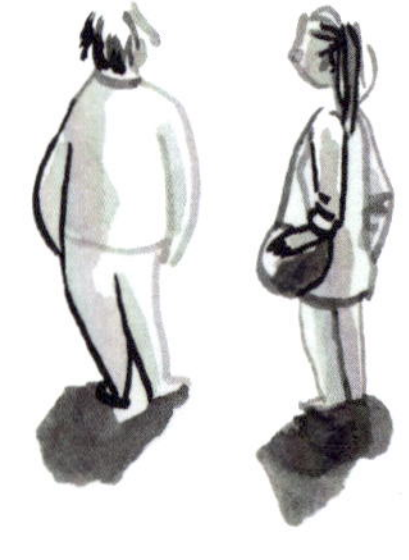

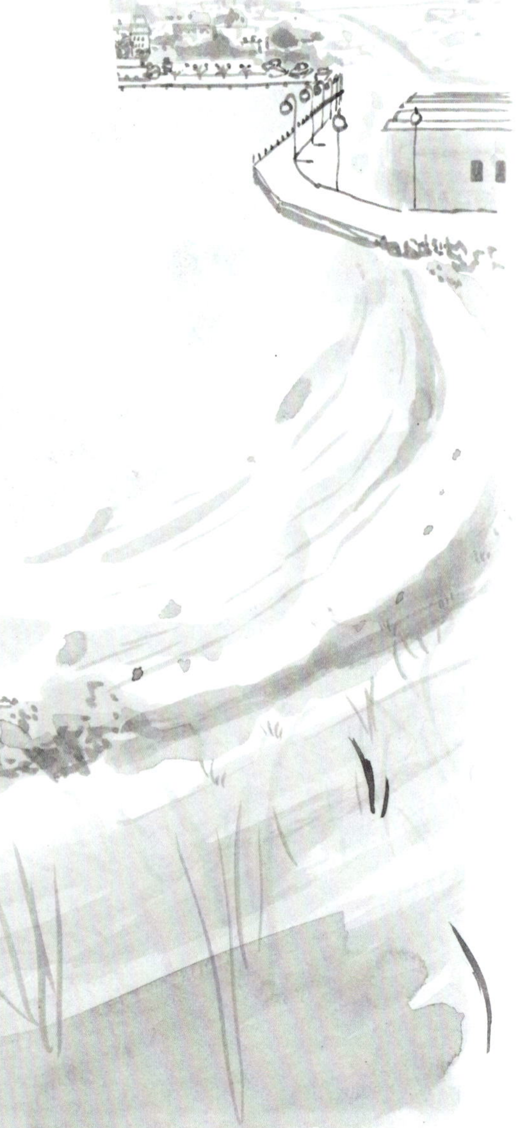

Anne König

The Pope's First Official Visit: Lampedusa

Public appearances of the leader of the Catholic Church have a strong symbolic power, and the first appearances of a newly elected pope in particular. Pope Francis chose Lampedusa as the destination for his first official visit after taking office in March 2013.

On July 8, 2013, he paid a visit to the little Mediterranean island, corroborating his intention to be the pope of the poor and of people without rights. Furthermore, the Mediterranean area has a particular meaning for Catholicism, being emblematic of the Latin culture. The fact that many African refugees came from predominantly Christian countries provided the visit with a further timely, political significance.

The four-hour stay of the pope in Lampedusa was a perfectly orchestrated event, for the symbolic power of the visit was intended to be transmitted worldwide through corresponding images. On a boat of the Coast Guard, Francis sailed the sea and threw a bunch of white and yellow chrysanthemums (the colors of the pope) into the water, praying for forgiveness. Then he returned to the land, on a sports field, where one of the refugee boats was arranged as a table and prepared to serve as an altar, and beside it stood a cross made from the wood of some of the shipwrecked boats. All the elements of the ceremony were as sober as possible. Even the wooden steering wheel decorating the home-made pulpit was not just a pretty touch by the carpenter, but a clear signal: while celebrating the mass in front of thousands of people, the pope literally took the wheel. He admonished that wealth leads to a point where "we only think of ourselves, we become indifferent to the cries of other people."

Pope Francis lamented in his address the "globalization of indifference," which makes everybody "anonymous, responsible, yet nameless and faceless" (*Süddeutsche Zeitung*, July 9, 2013). Under the cover of anonymity, everyone tries to avoid responsibility. Nobody bemoans the death of the refugees. The pope then thanked the inhabitants of the island for their determined commitment, their humanity, and their readiness to help. He shook hands with refugees, encouraged them, and kissed a baby who was handed to him.

With his visit, the Pope wanted to send out a clear message: to show solidarity with the thousands who set off daily on overcrowded boats on a dangerous journey to escape war and persecution, and to find a better life in Europe. At the same time, it was also a clear criticism of the failure of European Union policy on arrivals, in which the concerns of the refugees go unheard.

The photos taken during the pope's visit had to attest credibly to his cause.

Pope Francis is so far the only high-ranking political personality who has visited Lampedusa to show his connection to the inhabitants and the refugees. Other politicians visit the island only when it gains the global public's attention because of a particularly catastrophic event. This was the case with the former president of the European Commission, Manuel Barroso, who went to Lampedusa after the shipwreck of October 2013, to express his condolences and his sympathy in front of the many coffins. At the time, some of the inhabitants of the island booed him, shouting "murderer" and "shame." Other high-ranking politicians, such as German Chancellor Angela Merkel, have as yet not set foot on the island.

The visit of the pope might have suggested to the author of the "Petition to the Pope to end the mass murders on the sea and to open a humanitarian corridor" (December 18, 2014) that the papal nuncios should be reminded of their diplomatic power and encouraged them to grant refugees immigration visas, allowing them to come to Europe in a legal way. The petition reached the pope, but it produced no results in the Vatican.

Süddeutsche Zeitung

NEUESTE NACHRICHTEN AUS POLITIK, KULTUR, WIRTSCHAFT UND SPORT

WWW.SÜDDEUTSCHE.DE   HS2   MÜNCHEN, DIENSTAG, 9. JULI 2013   69. JAHRGANG / 28. WOCHE / NR. 156 / 2,30 EURO

Das Streiflicht

(SZ) Gesetzt den Fall, jemand möchte zur Ehre des bayerischen Löwen im Münchner Umland echte Löwen aussetzen: Wie müsste er das anstellen? Er müsste gemäß Artikel 34 Absatz 2 des Bayerischen Jagdgesetzes (BayJG) eine entsprechende Genehmigung der Jagdbehörde zu erwirken suchen. Das wäre allerdings ein vergebliches Unterfangen, da die Jagdbehörde „eine Störung des biologischen Gleichgewichts oder eine Schädigung der Landeskultur oder Gefahren für die öffentliche Sicherheit" nahen sähe und die Erlaubnis verweigerte. Gäbe es ein Löwenmanagement, wäre es dessen Aufgabe zu verhindern, dass Löwen zum Beispiel aufs Oktoberfest gehen und so der Landeskultur schaden. Ein Löwenmanagement gibt es aber nicht, weswegen man bei Problemen mit Löwen ersatzweise das Management großer Beutegreifer heranzieht. Es umfasst Luchs, Wolf und Bär, gilt also analog auch für den Löwen.

Elche sind zwar auch groß, aber keine Beutegreifer im eigentlichen Sinn. Anders als die Löwen wandern sie jedoch von sich aus in Deutschland ein, und da sie sowohl einen unermesslichen Appetit haben als auch zu zügiger Vermehrung neigen, lässt sich ein auf sie zugeschnittenes Management nicht länger umgehen. Das forderte unlängst Janosch Arnold, der beim WWF Deutschland als „Referent Großsäuger" arbeitet und sich grundsätzlich freut, dass es den Elch zu uns zieht. Man müsse nur, bei der Exotik des Zuwanderers, die Leute „informieren und mitnehmen". Dieses Mitnehmen ist gewiss nicht wörtlich zu verstehen, sondern ungefähr so, wie Cäsar seinerzeit die Römer mitnahm, als er im „Gallischen Krieg" schrieb, dass sich der Elch mangels Gelenken zum Schlafen nicht niederlege, sondern an Bäume lehne, die man, um ihn zu fangen, nur anschneiden müsse. Das ist längst nicht mehr state of science, und wenn Cäsar heute zum WWF ginge, brächte er es nicht weit, jedenfalls nicht zum Referenten Großsäuger.

Seit sich die Tiere verstärkt auf sich selber besinnen und zu neuen Lebensräumen aufbrechen, hat sich menschlicherseits eine neue Form des Managements etabliert. Natürlich hat man auch bisher schon darüber nachgedacht, wie man das Verhältnis

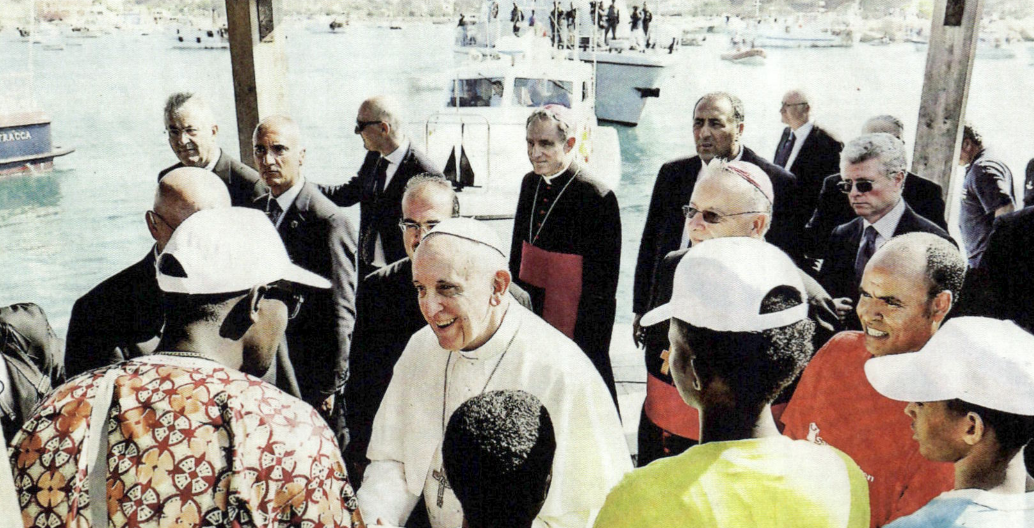

Beim Nächsten Zeichen setzen: Das gehört zum Programm von Papst Franziskus. Auch seine erste Reise war so ein Zeichen, denn sie führte ihn auf die Flüchtlingsinsel Lampedusa. Der alte Mann in Weiß, der auf die Insignien päpstlicher Pracht weitgehend verzichtet, prangerte Desinteresse gegenüber Migranten an. Der Wohlstand führe dazu, „dass wir nur an uns selbst denken, er macht uns gefühllos dem Aufschrei der anderen gegenüber". Die Abkehr von der „Globalisierung der Gleichgültigkeit" sei nötig. FOTO: T. PUGLIA/GETTY › Seite 8

Blutige Kämpfe verschärfen Krise in Kairo

Bei Gefechten zwischen Armee und Muslimbrüdern sterben mindestens 50 Menschen.
Die Salafisten boykottieren die Regierungsgespräche. Mursis Anhänger rufen zum Aufstand auf

VON SONJA ZEKRI

Gewerbesteuern steigen

Fast jede fünfte große Kommune hat 2013 die Sätze erhöht

Berlin – Zahlreiche Kommunen in Deutschland haben auch 2013 ihre Steuern für die Unternehmen erhöht. In fast einem Fünftel aller 684 Gemeinden mit mehr als 20 000 Einwohnern sind die Hebesätze für die Gewerbesteuer gestiegen. Das geht aus einer Untersuchung des Deutschen Industrie- und Handelskammertags (DIHK) hervor, die der *Süddeutschen Zeitung* vorliegt. Wie stark die Kommunen zugreifen, ist dabei höchst unterschiedlich: Besonders hoch sind die Hebesätze in Nordrhein-Westfalen, wo viele Städte wenig einnehmen, aber wachsende Sozialausgaben den Haushalt belasten. Auch bei der Grundsteuer B für Grundstücke sind die Steuersätze eher gestiegen. Dem DIHK zufolge hob ein Viertel der untersuchten Gemeinden den Hebesatz an. Viele Firmen seien in diesem Jahr deshalb mit einer doppelten Mehrbelastung konfrontiert, die teilweise sehr hoch ausfalle, heißt es in der Analyse. DIHK-Steuerexperte Rainer Kambeck nannte die enorme Spreizung zwischen Kommunen mit hohen und niedrigen Steuern „beunruhigend". TÖ › Wirtschaft

Todesurteil in China gegen Ex-Minister

Peking – Der frühere chinesische Bahnminister Liu Zhijun ist wegen Korruption und Machtmissbrauchs zu einer Todesstrafe auf Bewährung verurteilt worden. Sie kann in zwei Jahren in lebenslange Haft umgewandelt werden. Der als „Vater der Hochgeschwindigkeitszüge" berühmt gewordene Liu ist der höchste Regierungsvertreter, der seit dem Amtsantritt der neuen kommunistischen Führung wegen Korruption verurteilt wurde. DPA › Seite 8

Geringe Erwartungen

IL PRIMO VIAGGIO DI FRANCESCO

di **Serena Sartini**
Lampedusa

Il Papa ai migranti: «Chiedo perdono per chi vi ha ignorato»

*Ascolta le storie dei clandestini, bacia decine di bimbi
Ed esorta: «Il mondo abbia il coraggio dell'accoglienza»*

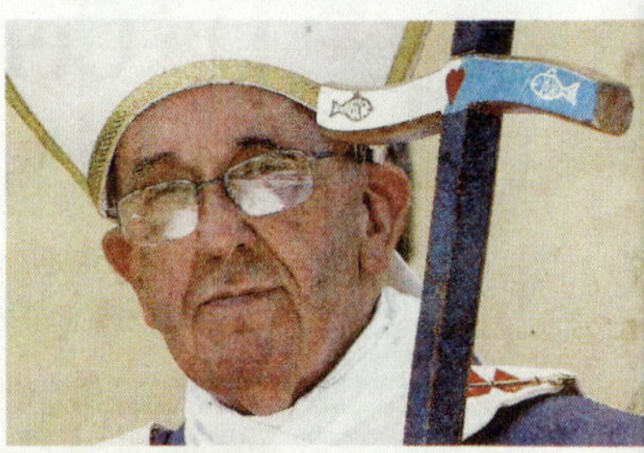

È un giorno come tutti gli altri a Lampedusa. Alle 7.40 a Punta Favarolo, nel Porto, arriva un barcone carico di 166 immigrati provenienti dal Nord Africa. «Una normalità» per l'Isola, dice il sindaco Giuseppina Nicolini. Appena un'ora dopo arriva un'altra motovedetta, questa volta della Capitaneria di Porto: a bordo c'è Francesco, primo Papa a visitare Lampedusa. I turisti sfrecciano a bordo di scooter per fare il bagno nelle calette a picco sul mare. Per molti è una tranquilla giornata di sole e mare.

Per i pescatori, invece, arriva il Papa. Lo accolgono con striscioni e foto: «Francesco uno di noi, Papa dei pescatori». Davanti a Punta Favarolo, la scritta «Benvenuto tra gli ultimi». Le bandierine con i colori del Vaticano bianco e giallo sventolano lungo il tragitto che separa il porto nuovo dall'arena sportiva. Un chilometro che il Papa percorre a bordo di una campagnola messa a disposizione da un lampedusano, tra due ali di folla. Corrono, dietro di lui, per salutare il Papa degli ultimi, per scattare una foto, per urlare «Viva Francesco». Bergoglio si ferma più volte lungo il tragitto per salutare decine e decine di bimbi, baciarli ed accarezzarli. Sembra un ingresso «trionfante» quello del Pontefice, che si lascia dietro una coda di fedeli impazziti che corre a più non posso. «Talia, il Papa» («guarda il Papa»), urla qualcuno in siciliano.

Scende dalla barca, Bergoglio, e il primo pensiero è rivolto agli immigrati. Sono 60, 40 minori, 20 adulti, tre ragazze. Il più piccolo ha 13 anni. Arrivano dalla Somalia, dall'Etiopia, dall'Eritrea. Sono cristiani, ortodossi, protestanti ma anche musulmani. Intonano per il Papa un canto religioso eritreo, di accoglienza. Il titolo dice tutto: «Fratelli del mare». Nei loro occhi c'è incredulità, sorpresa, un pizzico di emozione. Il Papa è là per loro. Una ragazza eritrea di 16 anni, tiene stretta la Bibbia tra le mani. Francesco saluta uno ad uno, ascolta le storie, si informa. Si ferma a parlare con Mahari: ha una gamba menomata a causa delle percosse subite in un carcere libico. Un altro immigrato consegna una lettera al Pontefice: dentro c'è un appello accorato. Che l'Euro-

pa, tutta, e non solo l'Italia, apra le porte a loro. Bergoglio la fa leggere ad alta voce, in lingua tigrina. Ascolta, attento.

Poi arriva all'Arena sportiva. Lo aspettano 15mila persone, attendono i suoi messaggi. Due parole segnano la giornata di Francesco a Lampedusa: perdono e indifferenza. Dal Papa un mea-culpa fortissimo che

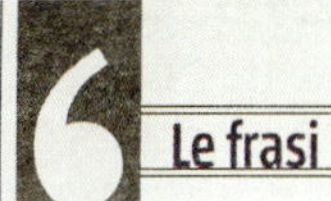

6 Le frasi

MONITO
Dio ci giudica da come trattiamo gli immigrati

DOLORE
I morti in mare sono una spina nel cuore. Chi ha pianto per loro?

riecheggia come un grido spesso inascoltato. A nome di tutte le vittime del mare. «Signore, chiediamo perdono per l'indifferenza verso tanti fratelli e sorelle - ammonisce - ti chiediamo perdono per chi si è accomodato, si è chiuso nel suo benessere che porta all'anestesia del cuore, ti chiediamo perdono per coloro che con le loro decisioni a livello mondiale hanno creato situazioni che conducono a questi drammi».

Dalla richiesta di perdono all'indifferenza il passo è breve. Si cela dietro questa indifferenza la tragedia di tanti morti in mare.

Ripete, Papa Francesco, che l'accoglienza è l'unica risposta: «Tutto il mondo abbia il coraggio di accogliere coloro che cercano una vita migliore. Lampedusa è un faro, sia di esempio a tutti. Dio ci giudicherà in base a come abbiamo trattato i più bisognosi». Torna alla mente il messaggio di Giovanni Paolo II nella Valle dei Templi. Quella volta il monito era contro i boss mafiosi, questa volta è contro tutti coloro che, nell'indifferenza, hanno lasciato morire in mare migliaia e migliaia di immigrati. Il Papa riparte, Lampedusa torna ad essere la stessa. Continua il via vai con gli scooter, continuano gli arrivi nel centro di accoglienza. Ma l'Isola non sarà più la stessa.

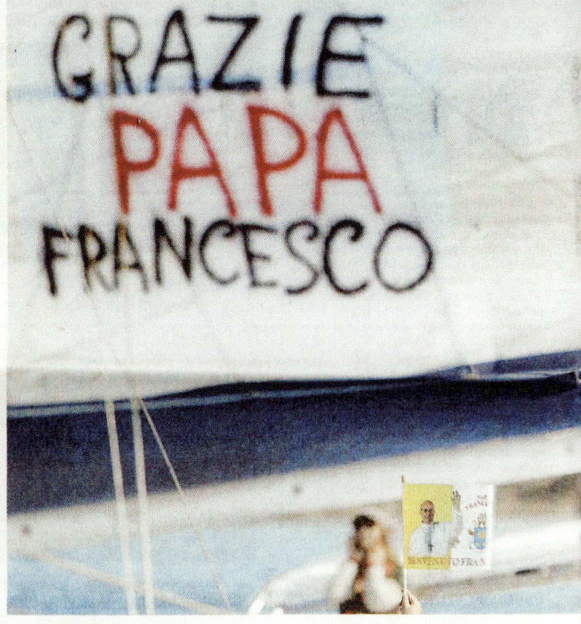

   Il messaggio del Santo Padre tra i disperati

Quel dito puntato contro la globalizzazione

Bergoglio: «Il benessere ci ha reso indifferenti, viviamo in una bolla»

Maurizio Caverzan

■ Anche Lampedusa è «alla fine del mondo». Posto di confine. Lembo estremo. Ponte tra il primo e il terzo mondo. Zattera sulla speranza o sull'abisso. Da questa «periferia geografica ed esistenziale» ieri papa Francesco ha iniziato il suo magistero itinerante, denunciando «la globalizzazione dell'indifferenza» nella quale siamo precipitati e lanciando un appello al mondo intero perché certe tragedie «non si ripetano più per favore».

Quando qualche settimana fa, ha detto il Santo Padre nell'omelia della messa celebrata davanti a diecimila persone, «ho appreso la notizia degli immigrati morti in mare, da quelle barche che invece di essere una via di speranza sono state una via di morte - il riferimento è al naufragio del 15 giugno di un'imbarcazione carica di profughi alcuni dei quali hanno tentato di salvarsi aggrappandosi alle gabbie dei tonni - «il pensiero vi è tornato continuamente come una spina nel cuore che porta sofferenza». Allora, ha continuato Francesco, «ho sentito che dovevo venire qui oggi a pregare, a compiere un gesto di vicinanza, ma anche a risvegliare le nostre coscienze perché ciò che è accaduto non si ripeta».

Durante la cerimonia il Papa ha rin-

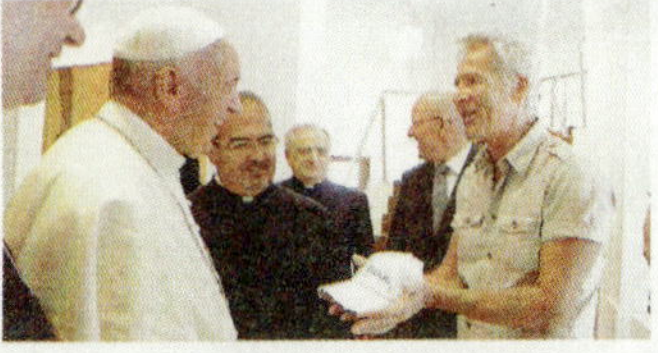

INCONTRO
Un cappellino di «O' Scià», affettuoso saluto di Lampedusa: è il regalo che Claudio Baglioni ha fatto al Papa

graziato gli abitanti di Lampedusa e Linosa per la testimonianza di solidarietà e accoglienza. Ha rivolto un pensiero «ai cari immigrati musulmani che oggi iniziano il Ramadan con l'augurio di abbondanti frutti spirituali». Ha denunciato i «trafficanti per cui la povertà degli altri è fonte di guadagno».

Per la celebrazione penitenziale aveva scelto di persona il vangelo di Matteo, con la famiglia di Gesù che emigra per sfuggire alla strage ordinata da Erode, e la Genesi, dove Dio chiede ad Adamo «dove sei?» e a Caino «dov'è tuo fratello?». Queste domande risuonano anche mentre siamo tutti disorientati, «mi includo anch'io», incapaci di custodire il nostro mondo e il nostro fratello. Ci liberiamo di ogni responsabilità come il sacerdote nella parabola del Buon Samaritano che tira dritto pensando che la sofferenza del fratello non lo ri-

guardi. «La cultura del benessere», ha proseguito Bergoglio, ci rende «insensibili alle grida degli altri». Ci fa vivere «dentro bolle di sapone» in una condizione «che ci porta all'indifferenza verso gli altri. Anzi», ha levato la sua voce Francesco, «ci porta alla globalizzazione dell'indifferenza». Per la quale, in un certo senso, siamo tutti come «l'Innominato di Manzoni, responsabili senza nome e senza volto». Ecco perché, al termine della liturgia, prima di pregare davanti alla statua di Maria, «protettrice dei migranti e degli itineranti», il Papa ha ripetuto con profonda umiltà: «Perdono, Signore».

Grande colpo di fantasia, quello di ieri è stata un gesto dal forte carattere simbolico, con Francesco primo testimone di una Chiesa che esce da se stessa, «pastore che ha l'odore delle sue pecore». È stata la visita programmatica di un pontefice deciso a situarsi sul crinale tra disperazione e annuncio cristiano, tra dimenticanza dell'uomo e salvezza di Cristo.

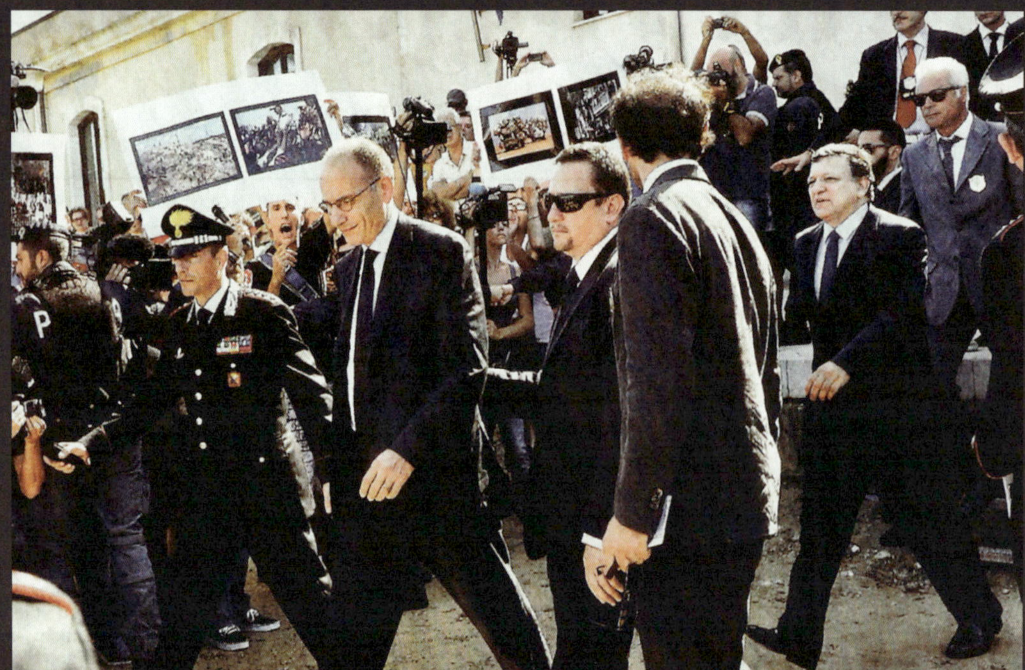

On April 16, 2016 Francis surprised public opinion with a spontaneous action that took advantage of some diplomatic regulations of the Vatican: he made a brief visit to the Greek island of Lesbos to take home twelve Syrian refugees, six of whom were children. For the moment they had to be accommodated in the Church State. The refugees had already arrived in Greece before the EU pact on refugees with Turkey came into effect, which is why they were not brought back to Turkey. The pope expressed his solidarity with the Greeks, and at the same time he criticized the European politics of isolation and the closed borders. The images of the pope in Lesbos did not find a comparable response to those of him in Lampedusa. Even the pope is able to influence the short attention span of public opinion only up to a certain point.

— *il Giornale*, printed edition, July 9, 2013, p. 10.
— *Süddeutsche Zeitung*, printed edition, July 9, 2013, pp. 1 and 7.
— *Frankfurter Allgemeine Zeitung*, printed edition, October 10, 2013, pp. 1 and 2.

Petition to the Pope

to stop the mass deaths at sea and open
a humanitarian corridor

In the face of a lack of action from the governments of the European Union, the Pope could potentially support a humane alternative to the illicit exploitation of immigrants, putting himself at the center of diplomatic action.

The Apostolic Nunciatures—i.e., the diplomatic missions that represent the Holy See in the world—could do what the EU Member States' embassies refuse to do: that is, issue entry visas so that the families, children, women, and men who flee from wars and persecution can reach safe countries using legal means of transportation rather than being forced to pay traffickers and perish by the thousands on overcrowded boats.

A humanitarian corridor provided by governments would allow those who want to apply for asylum to directly contact the embassies of European countries (in the state from which they want to escape or in its neighboring countries) without having to risk a terrible and often fatal journey.

All this would be possible simply by applying existing regulations.

The Apostolic Nunciatures also have a function of diplomatic representation, so that those who flee from persecution and war could apply to papal nuncios for an entry visa. The agreements already in effect with EU countries would permit refugees to reach the Holy See on ships, by land, or through the airports of Fiumicino or Ciampino, traveling along legal channels that would not be possible without an entry visa.

We ask Pope Francis:

1) to allow people fleeing from wars and persecutions to apply
   to the Holy See (which ratified the Refugee Convention in
   Geneva in 1951) for asylum by directly contacting the papal
   nuncios in the countries from which they wish to escape
   or those of transit, thus demonstrating to Europe that a
   humanitarian corridor can and must be built to prevent
   people from suffering and dying as they assert their right to
   asylum and survival;

2) to allow these people, when they have physically reached
   the Vatican with a temporary visa, to apply for asylum
   in other countries, contacting one of the 178 embassies
   located in the Vatican. This would also neutralize the
   Dublin Convention that limits the freedom of people to
   choose the country in which they want to seek refuge and
   reside.

Alessandra Ballerini, Leonardo Cavaliere,
Carmelo Gatani, Paola La Rosa,

https://www.change.org/p/il-papa-fermi-le-stragi-in-mare-e-
apra-dei-canali-umanitari

December 18, 2014

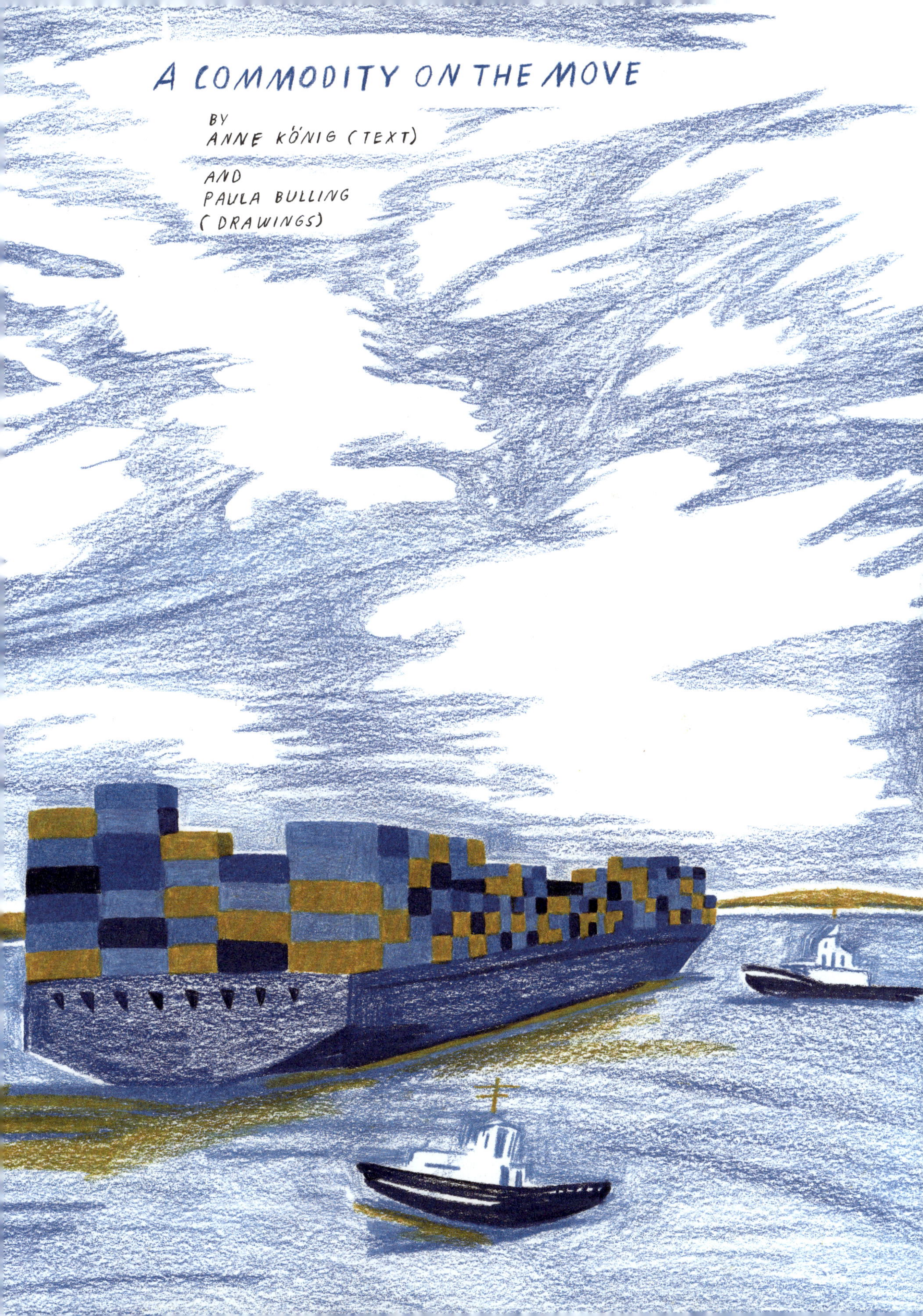

A COMMODITY ON THE MOVE
BY
ANNE KÖNIG (TEXT)
AND
PAULA BULLING
(DRAWINGS)

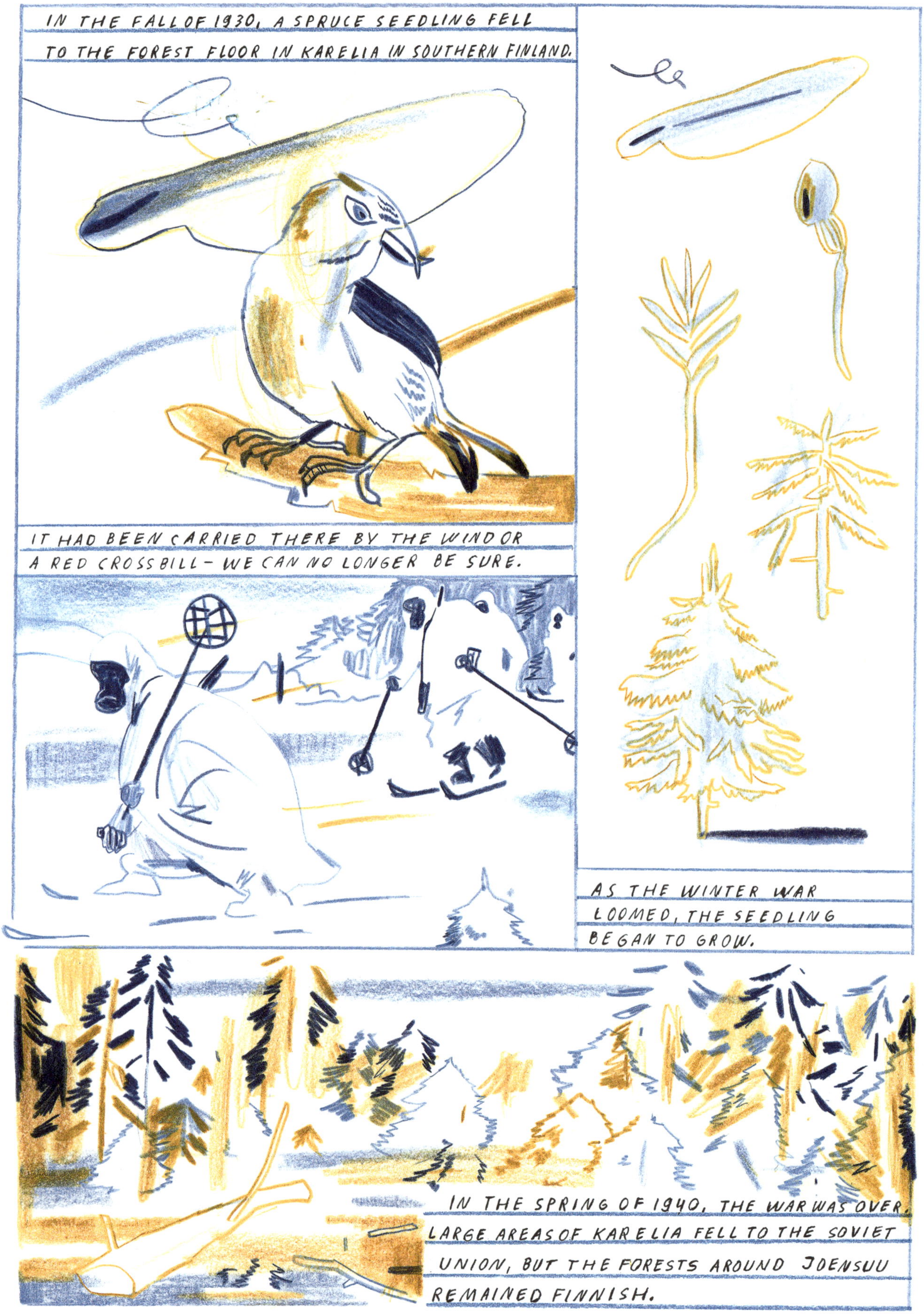

IN THE FALL OF 1930, A SPRUCE SEEDLING FELL TO THE FOREST FLOOR IN KARELIA IN SOUTHERN FINLAND.
IT HAD BEEN CARRIED THERE BY THE WIND OR A RED CROSSBILL — WE CAN NO LONGER BE SURE.
AS THE WINTER WAR LOOMED, THE SEEDLING BEGAN TO GROW.

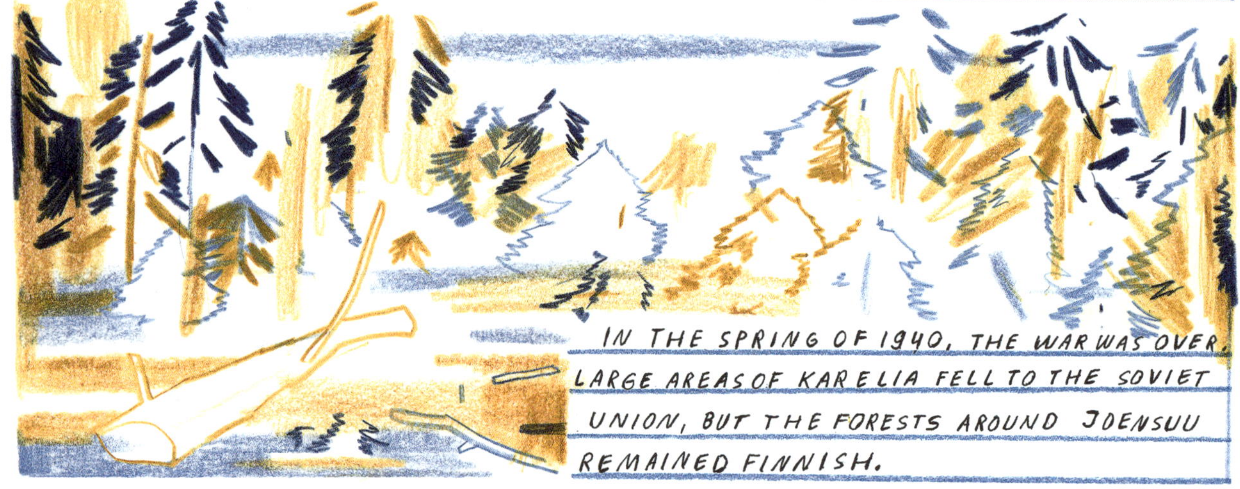

IN THE SPRING OF 1940, THE WAR WAS OVER. LARGE AREAS OF KARELIA FELL TO THE SOVIET UNION, BUT THE FORESTS AROUND JOENSUU REMAINED FINNISH.

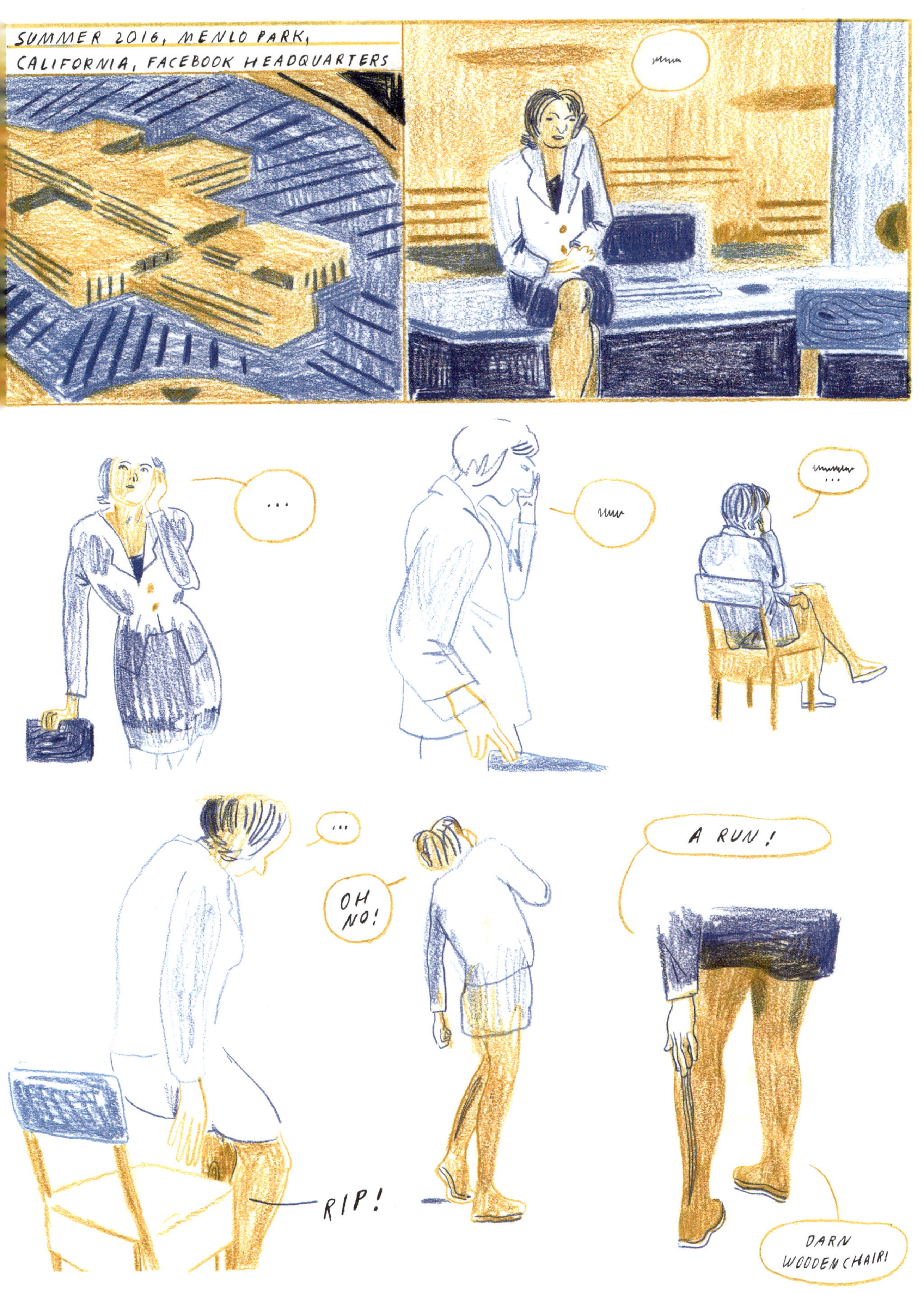

SUMMER 2016, MENLO PARK, CALIFORNIA, FACEBOOK HEADQUARTERS

...
OH NO!
A RUN!
RIP!
DARN WOODEN CHAIR!

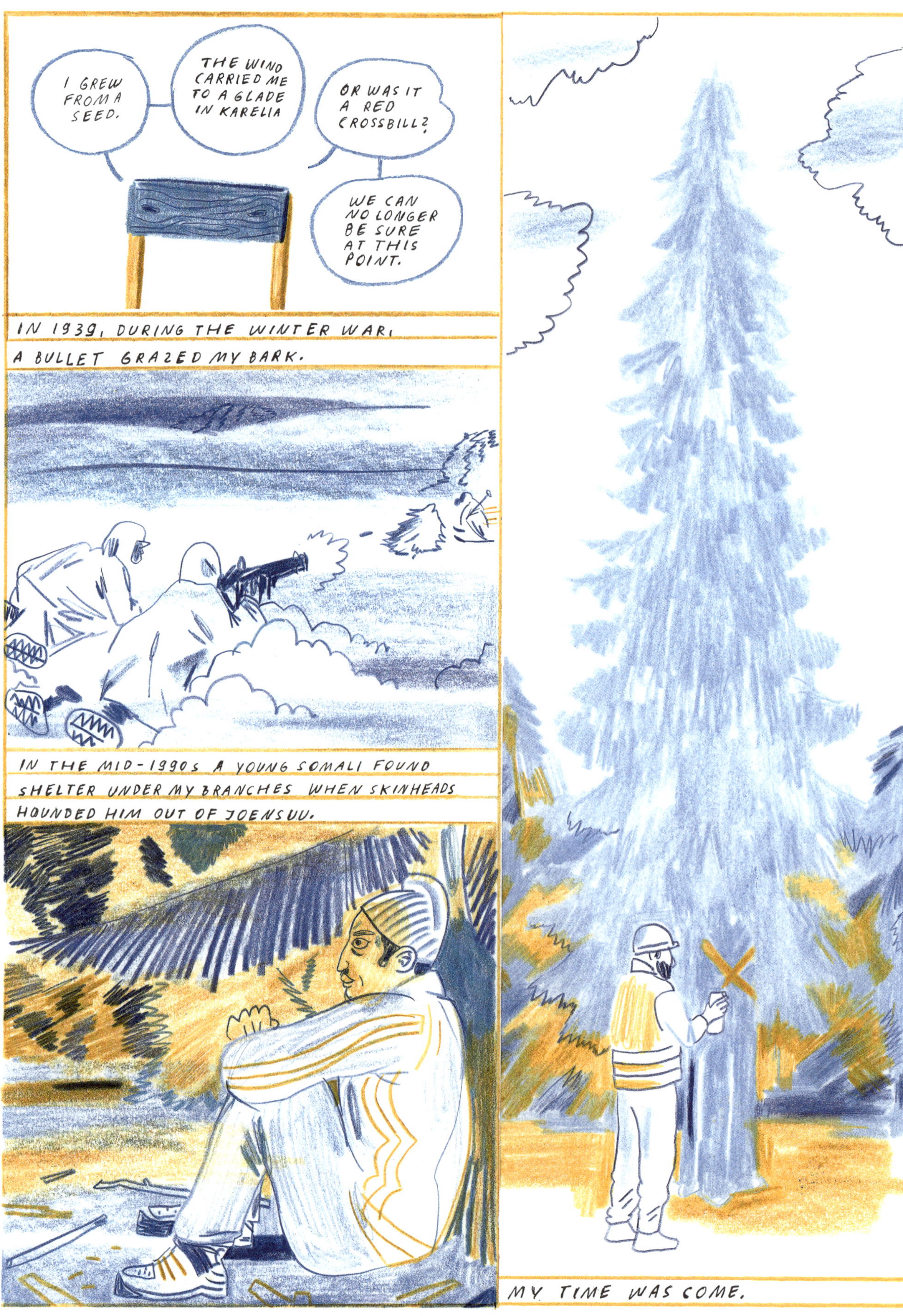

I GREW FROM A SEED.
THE WIND CARRIED ME TO A GLADE IN KARELIA
OR WAS IT A RED CROSSBILL?
WE CAN NO LONGER BE SURE AT THIS POINT.
IN 1939, DURING THE WINTER WAR, A BULLET GRAZED MY BARK.
IN THE MID-1990s A YOUNG SOMALI FOUND SHELTER UNDER MY BRANCHES WHEN SKINHEADS HOUNDED HIM OUT OF JOENSUU.
MY TIME WAS COME.

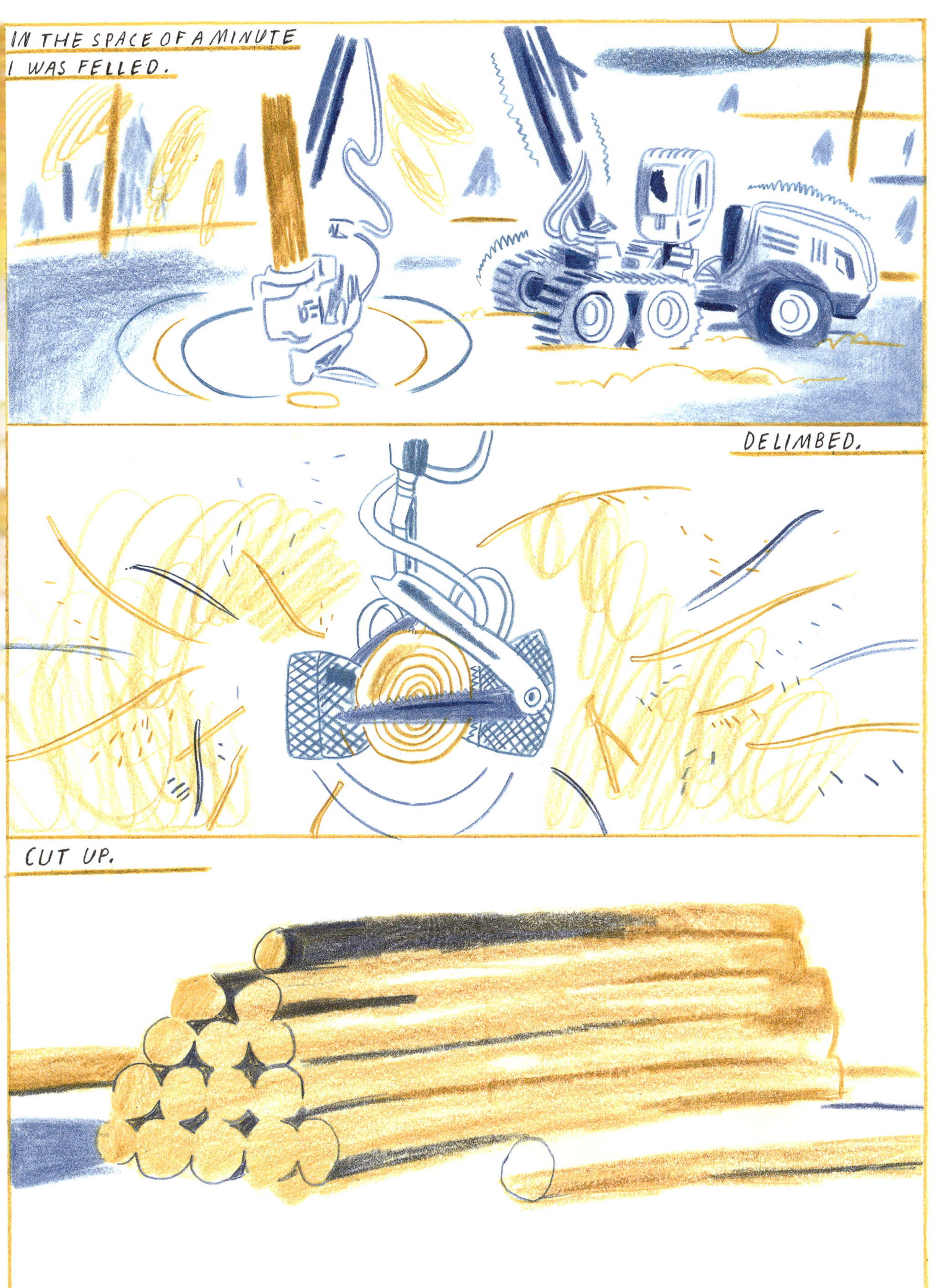

IN THE SPACE OF A MINUTE
I WAS FELLED.
DELIMBED.
CUT UP.

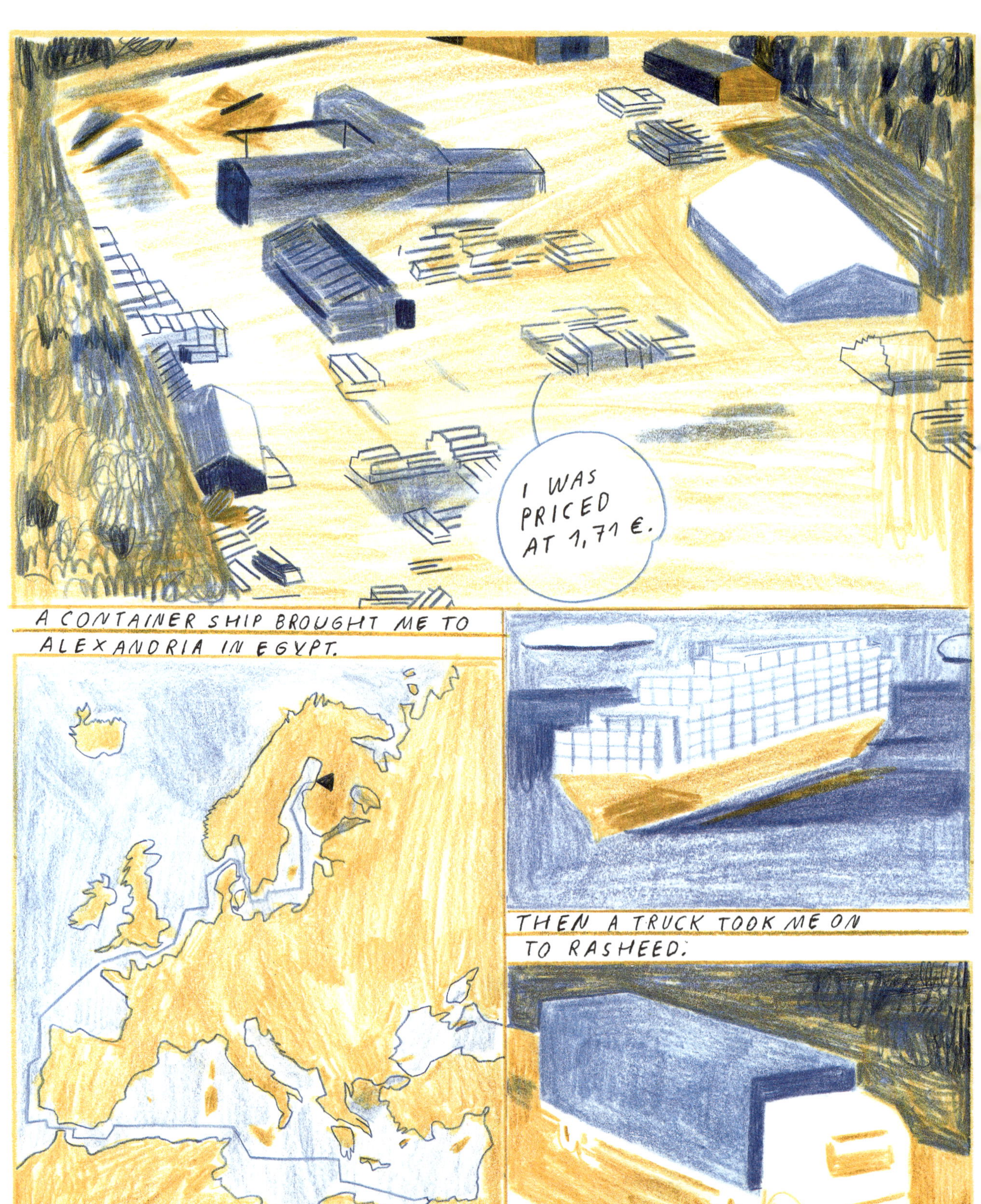
I WAS PRICED AT 1,71 €.
A CONTAINER SHIP BROUGHT ME TO ALEXANDRIA IN EGYPT.
THEN A TRUCK TOOK ME ON TO RASHEED.

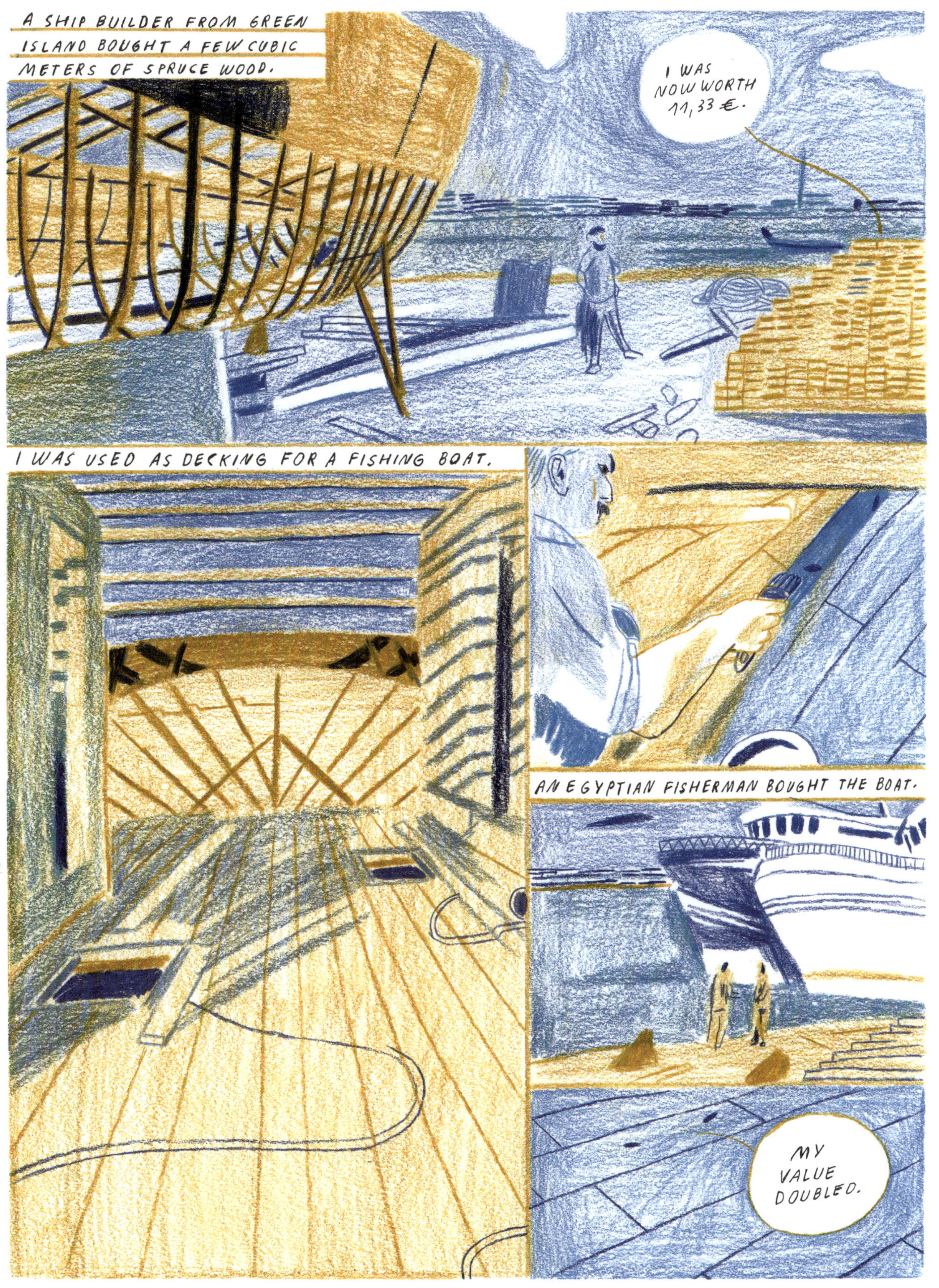

A SHIP BUILDER FROM GREEN ISLAND BOUGHT A FEW CUBIC METERS OF SPRUCE WOOD.
I WAS NOW WORTH 11,33 €.
I WAS USED AS DECKING FOR A FISHING BOAT.
AN EGYPTIAN FISHERMAN BOUGHT THE BOAT.
MY VALUE DOUBLED.

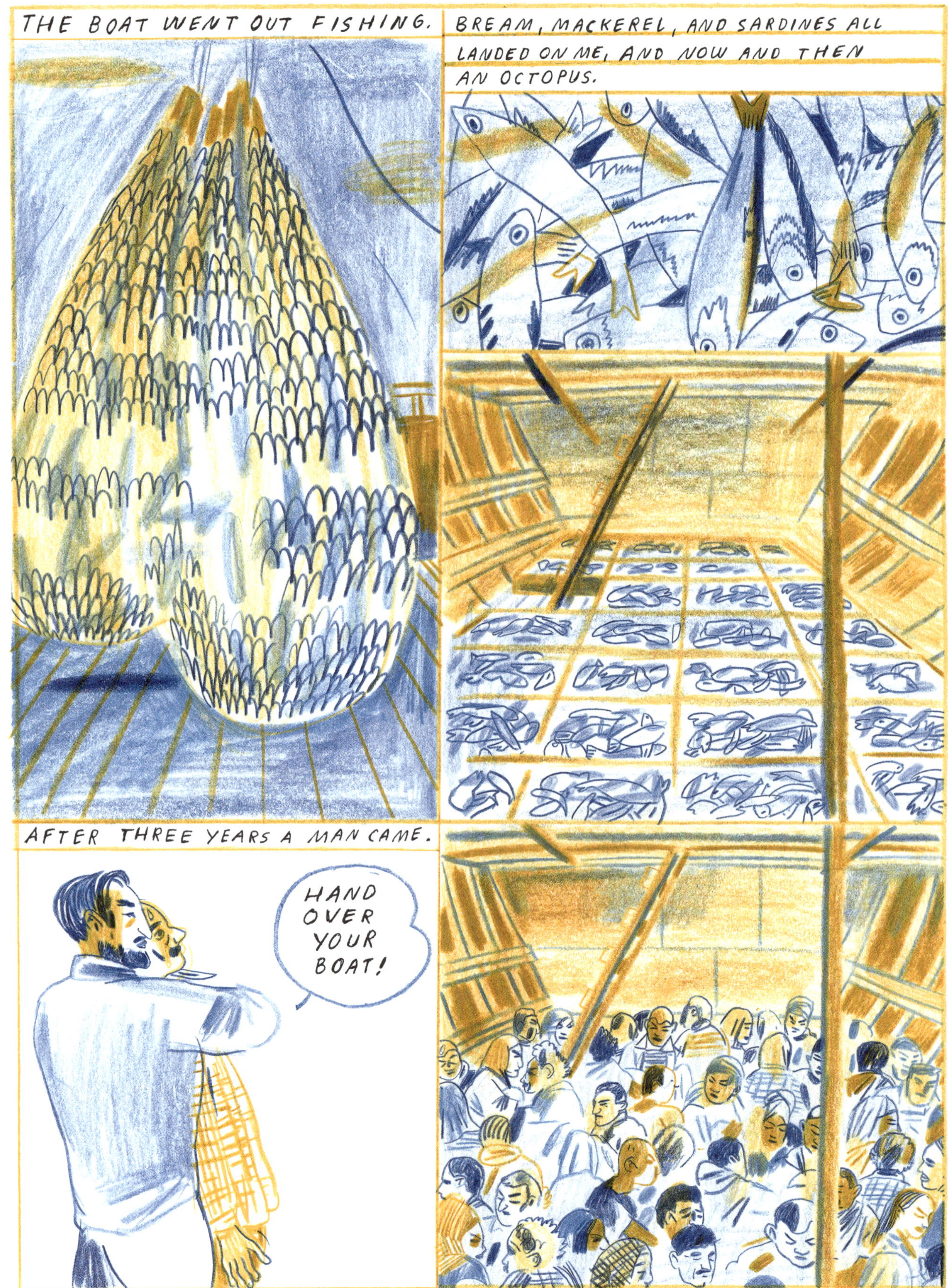

THE BOAT WENT OUT FISHING.
BREAM, MACKEREL, AND SARDINES ALL LANDED ON ME, AND NOW AND THEN AN OCTOPUS.
AFTER THREE YEARS A MAN CAME.
HAND OVER YOUR BOAT!

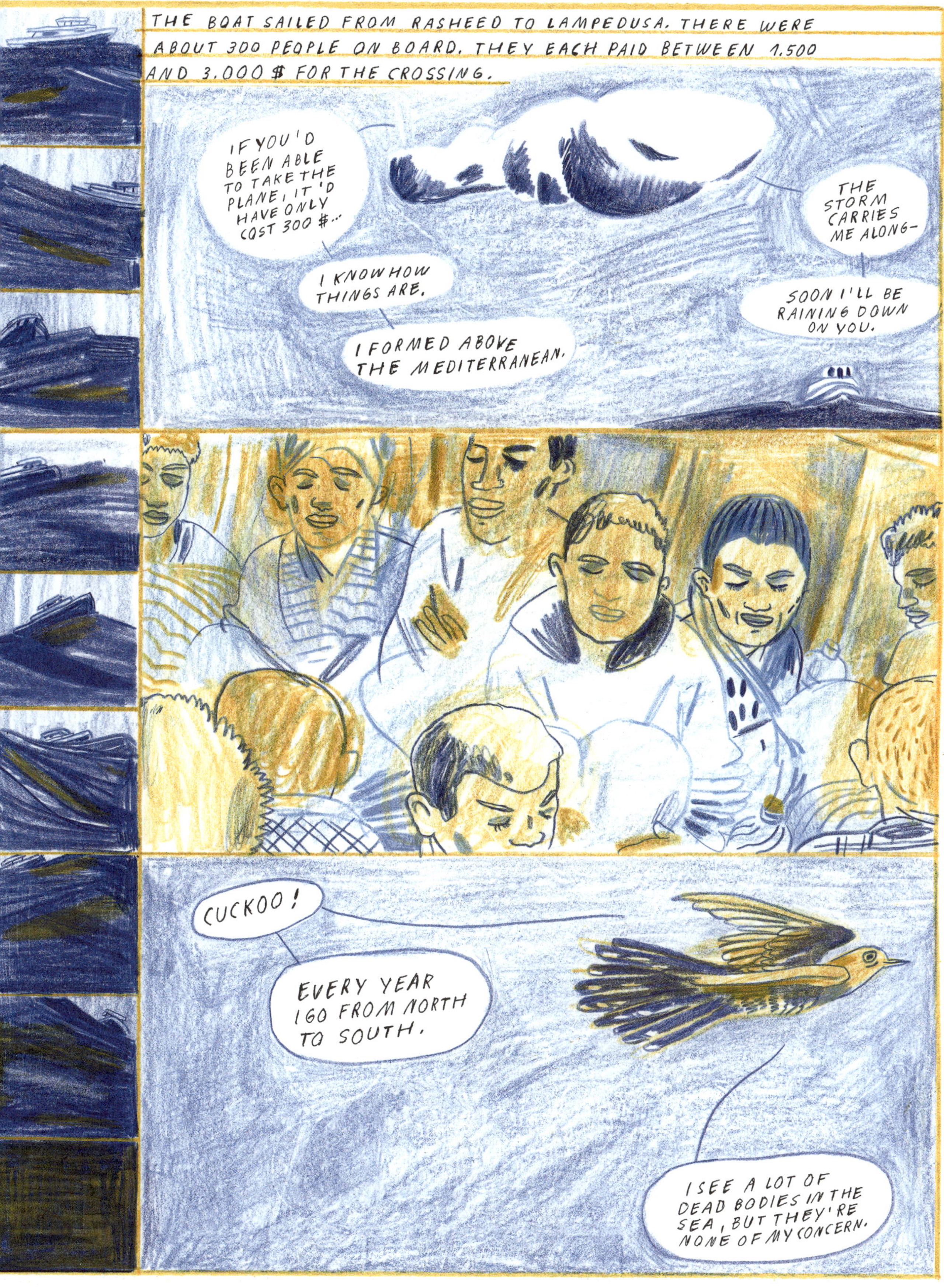

THE BOAT SAILED FROM RASHEED TO LAMPEDUSA. THERE WERE ABOUT 300 PEOPLE ON BOARD. THEY EACH PAID BETWEEN 1.500 AND 3.000 $ FOR THE CROSSING.
IF YOU'D BEEN ABLE TO TAKE THE PLANE, IT'D HAVE ONLY COST 300 $...
I KNOW HOW THINGS ARE.
I FORMED ABOVE THE MEDITERRANEAN.
THE STORM CARRIES ME ALONG-
SOON I'LL BE RAINING DOWN ON YOU.
CUCKOO!
EVERY YEAR I GO FROM NORTH TO SOUTH.
I SEE A LOT OF DEAD BODIES IN THE SEA, BUT THEY'RE NONE OF MY CONCERN.

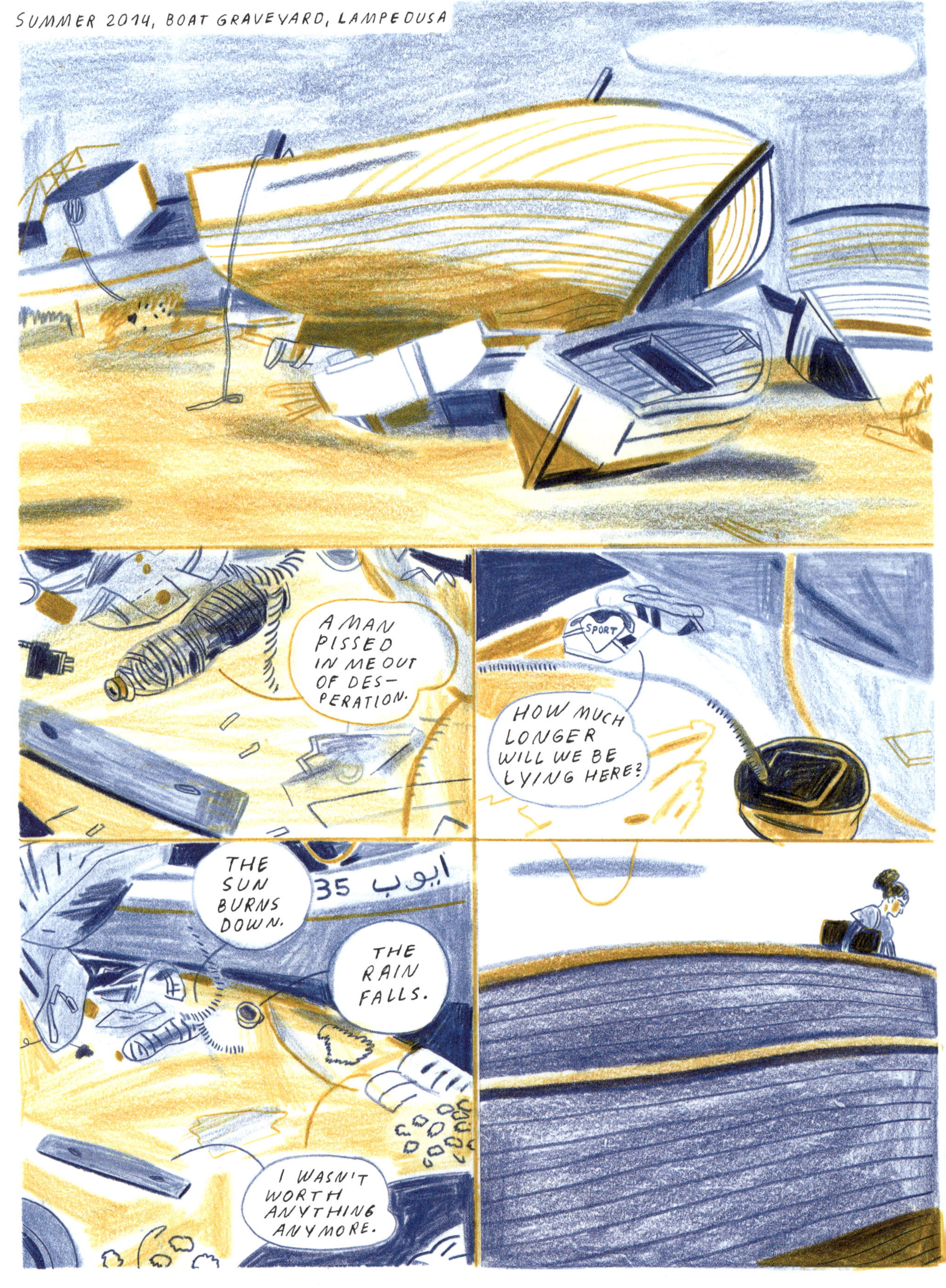
A MAN PISSED IN ME OUT OF DES—PERATION.
SPORT
HOW MUCH LONGER WILL WE BE LYING HERE?
THE SUN BURNS DOWN.
THE RAIN FALLS.
I WASN'T WORTH ANYTHING ANYMORE.

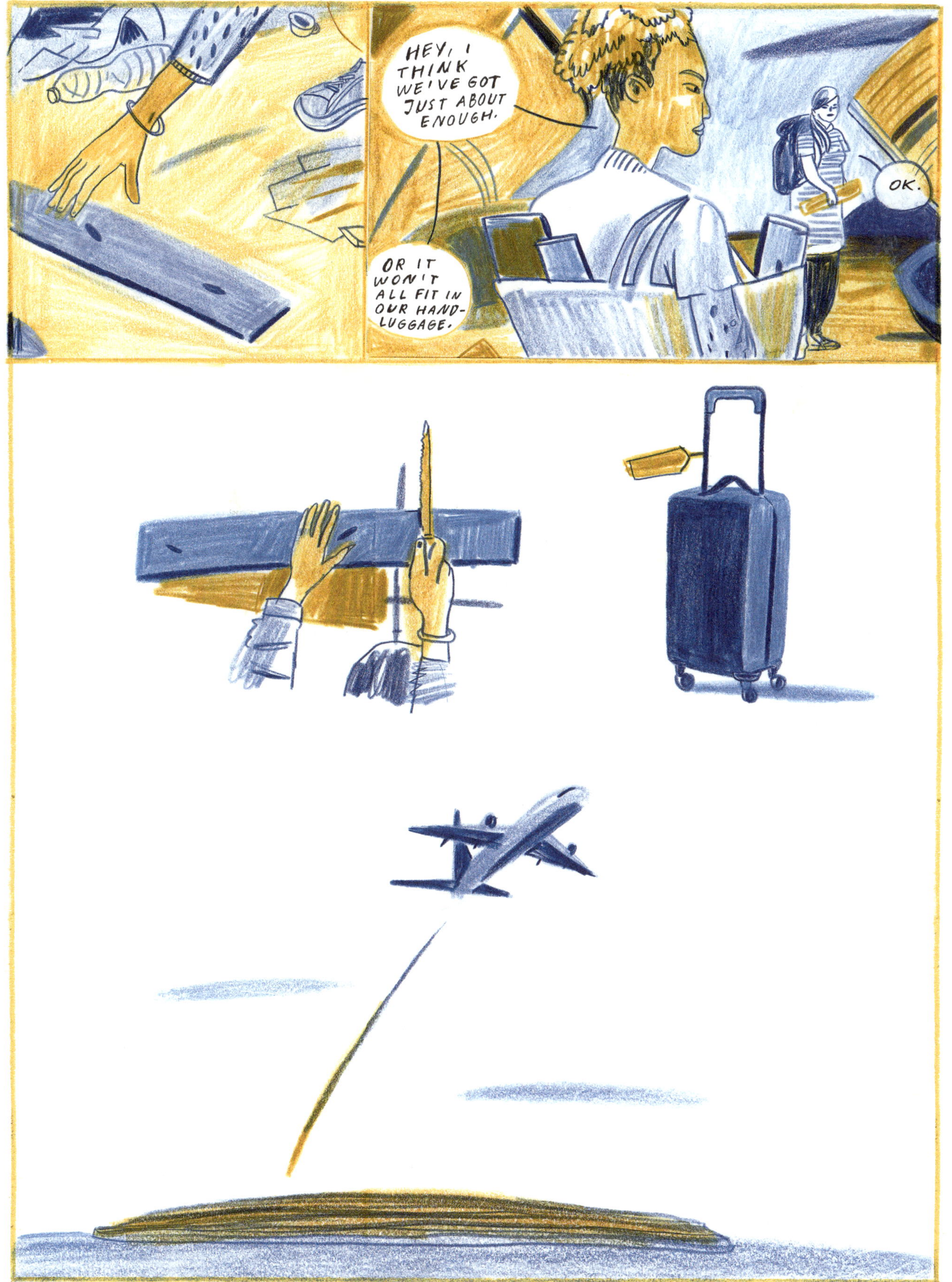

HEY, I THINK WE'VE GOT JUST ABOUT ENOUGH.
OR IT WON'T ALL FIT IN OUR HAND-LUGGAGE.
OK.

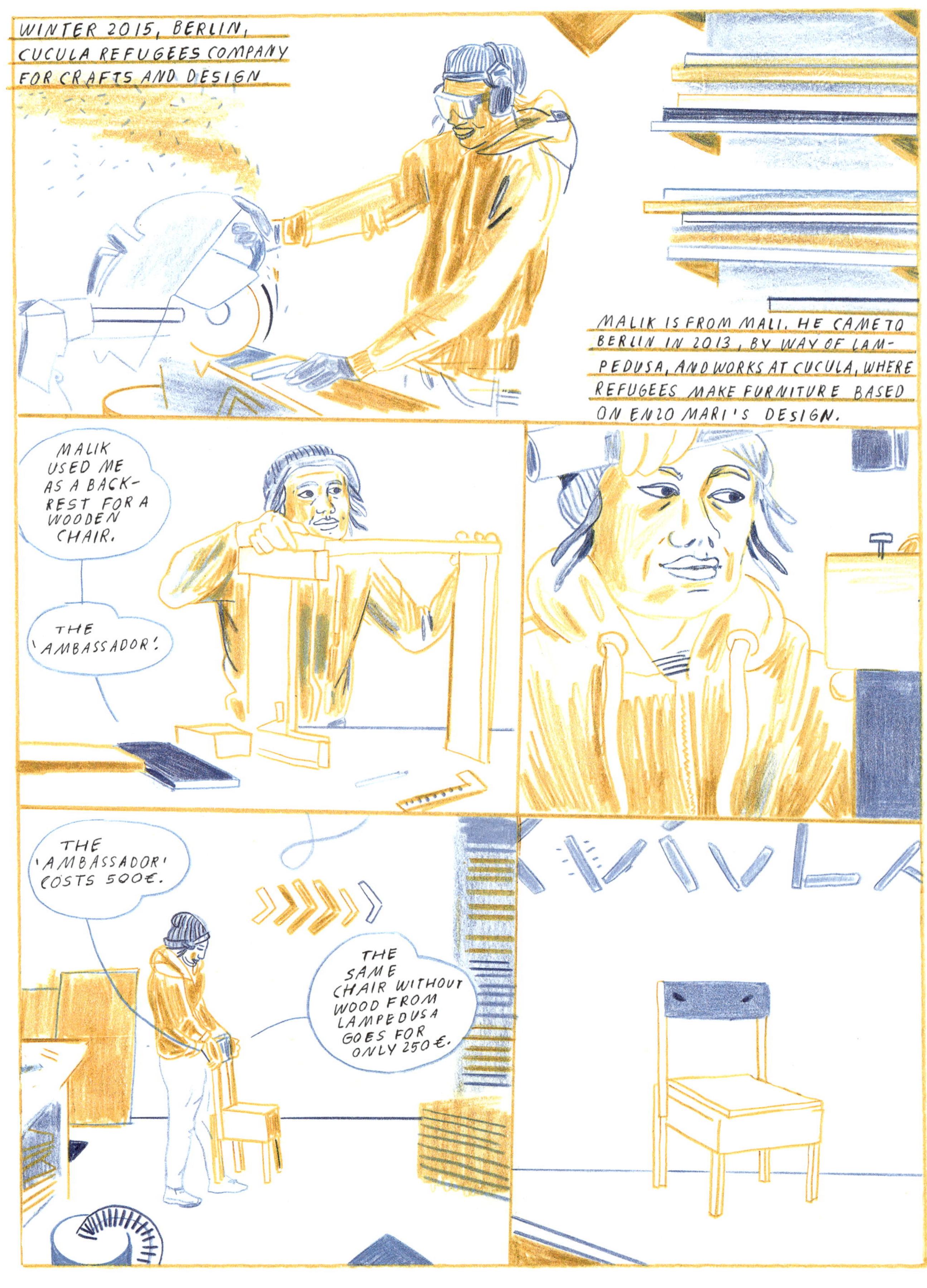

WINTER 2015, BERLIN, CUCULA REFUGEES COMPANY FOR CRAFTS AND DESIGN
MALIK IS FROM MALI. HE CAME TO BERLIN IN 2013, BY WAY OF LAMPEDUSA, AND WORKS AT CUCULA, WHERE REFUGEES MAKE FURNITURE BASED ON ENZO MARI'S DESIGN.
MALIK USED ME AS A BACKREST FOR A WOODEN CHAIR.
THE 'AMBASSADOR'!
THE 'AMBASSADOR' COSTS 500€.
THE SAME CHAIR WITHOUT WOOD FROM LAMPEDUSA GOES FOR ONLY 250€.

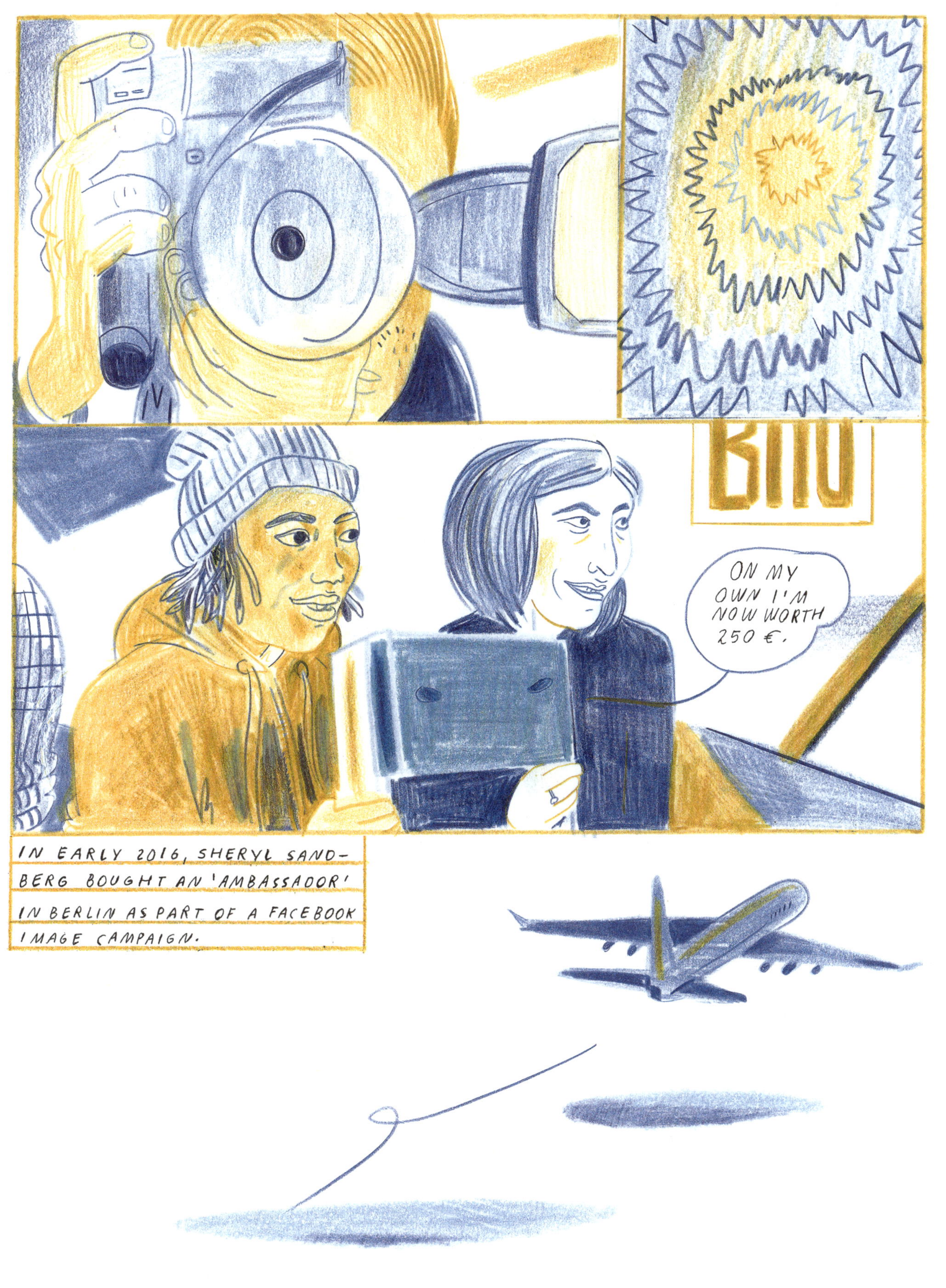

BIIO
ON MY OWN I'M NOW WORTH 250 €.
IN EARLY 2016, SHERYL SAND-
BERG BOUGHT AN 'AMBASSADOR'
IN BERLIN AS PART OF A FACEBOOK
IMAGE CAMPAIGN.

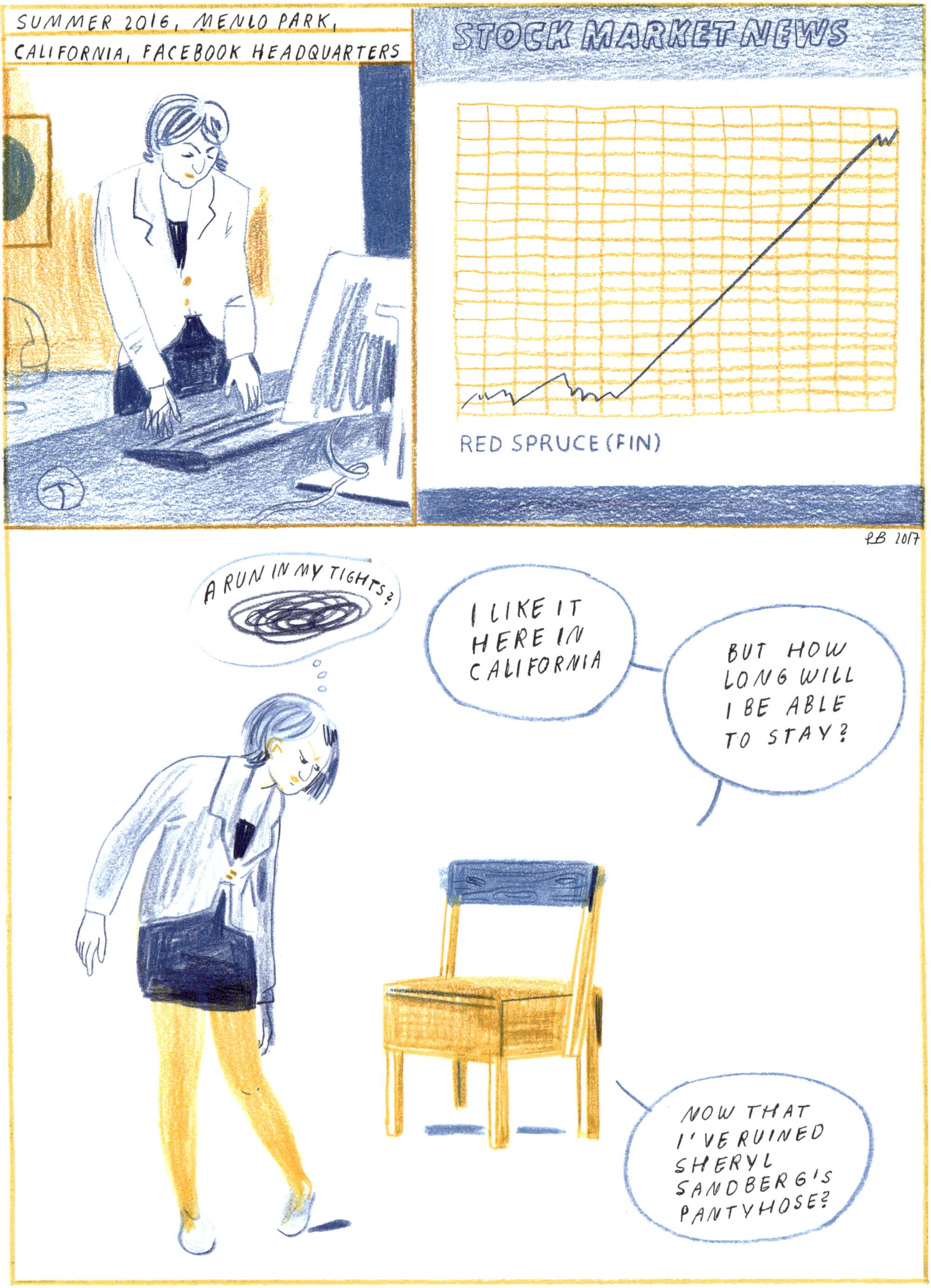

SUMMER 2016, MENLO PARK, CALIFORNIA, FACEBOOK HEADQUARTERS
STOCK MARKET NEWS
RED SPRUCE (FIN)
RB 2017
A RUN IN MY TIGHTS?
I LIKE IT HERE IN CALIFORNIA
BUT HOW LONG WILL I BE ABLE TO STAY?
NOW THAT I'VE RUINED SHERYL SANDBERG'S PANTYHOSE?

Words, Numbers, Images

At the beginning of 2015 the online edition of *Bild* showed a series of infographics outlining the routes and places of origin for refugees in the Mediterranean region. Countries are colored in gray and white, the sea is in a muted blue. Red arrows of different shapes and sizes point toward the countries of Europe and their borders: Spain, Italy, Greece, Turkey. In "Refugees on their way to Europe," published on February 11, 2015, tapering broad arrows point northward and westward from indeterminate areas of Africa and the Middle East, the color becoming more intense as the arrows taper. The numbers of refugees are symbolized by the size of the arrows, and the exact statistics are given in white ciphers framed in red. 12,783, 134,272. The message is clear: they are coming.

Infographics and statistics can do something that images and words cannot: they are radical abstractions of complex realities pared down to numbers, colors, lines, forms, and shading. They visualize big data and generate contexts. Infographics and statistics are a relatively recent invention—a response to the idea that modern science is objective. They are related to modern attempts to compress information, to make it transmittable, to empirically describe social and political conditions, and to facilitate access to knowledge.

There is usually little doubt about their facticity, reinforced by the context in which they appear, typically in the press or scientific publications and lectures. At least the first impressions leave little doubt. For Edward Tufte,[1] a statistician and political scientist, graphics are the easiest and at the same time most effective means to analyze and communicate statistical information. They seem to be made for the purpose of being consumed quickly and efficiently. They provide visual orientation, while encouraging a cursory glance. They promise to give the viewer an overview—a view over things—in the shortest possible time.

Just like images, words, or any other medium of communication, pictorial statistics are also susceptible to distortions, falsifications, and misinterpretations. But they are able to conceal them better (if this is their intention) and are, according to Tufte, highly prone to instrumentalization. They are potentially dangerous in terms of their message and effect.

The vagueness and subtle suggestiveness of dubious infographics and pictorial statistics only become evident with careful observation—if at all. Let's return now to "Refugees on their way to Europe." The most striking element is the aggressive and sharply contrasting red of the arrows. Is the color of the arrows a random choice? Of course not. According to the basic lexicon of color psychology, red is associated with attention, alertness, and danger; it also conforms to the corporate design line of the newspaper *Bild*. That the choice of color is no minor detail becomes

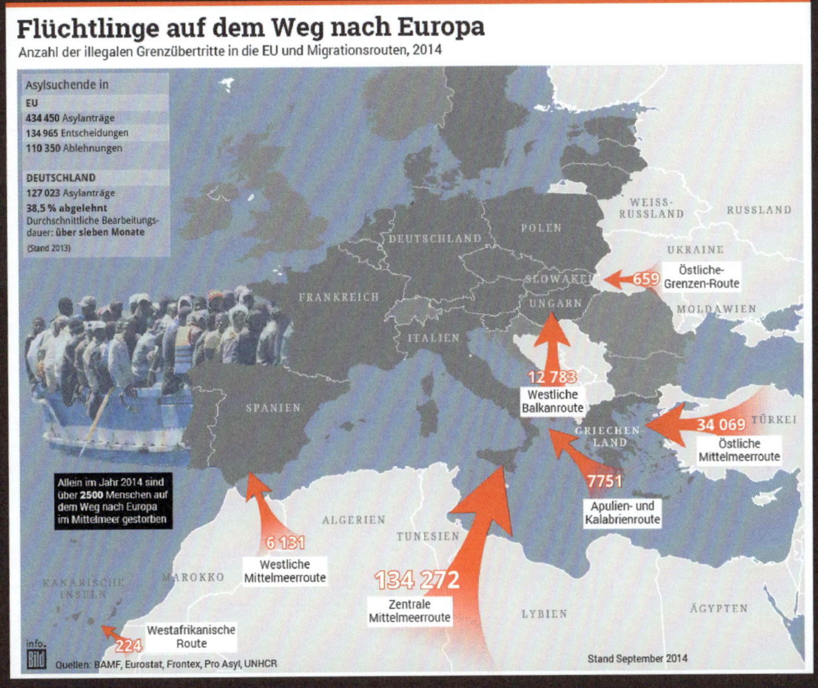

clear when we imagine a counterexample. Could the arrows have been green or yellow? Even the typographic choices appear to be motivated by underlying messages: on maps, nation-states, such as Algeria, France, or Germany, are printed in serif font and all in capitals. On top of them, the numbers and text boxes appear in sans-serif. The "traditional" order of the nation-states, which is suggested by the choice of a more "traditional" serif font, contrasts with the "new" and potentially destabilizing information.

"Refugees on the way to Europe" is supposed to show the routes of refugees and provide statistics showing the numbers of people involved. As noted at the bottom of the frame, information is based on sources from multiple institutions: the Federal Office for Migration and Refugees (BAMF), Eurostat, the statistical office of the European Union, Frontex, Pro-asyl, and the UN Refugee Agency (UNHCR). However, it is impossible to trace which data come from which sources, or what has been conflated. But how are these exact numbers arrived at, when all of the sources mentioned above offer highly detailed and complex, publicly accessible statistics that resist any easy and superficial interpretation?[2]

In addition to this, the dates are inaccurate: while the sources are dated September 2014, the text boxes in the upper left refer to data from the previous year. The sources and dates are in small print, giving the appearance of journalistic professionalism and legal hedging.

Exact numbers provide an aura of precision that is almost never questioned.[3] Is it then a matter of exact numbers here, or just of high numbers?

The numbers and arrows are accompanied by a humanizing element: a picture of a boat crowded with human beings. The semitransparent image is positioned in such a way that the boat is located on the southwestern borders of Western Europe. The picture blends with the map and the background. In the overall hierarchy of information, this picture is only secondary, but it is crucial for the overall visual effect created by the infographic. The faces of the people on the boat are not recognizable. They are mostly black males, crammed into a very narrow space. This and similar images have become a symbol of the refugee crisis. They have been produced, reproduced, and aired in the media thousands of times over, solidifying into a sort of visual cliché.

Taken together, these details produce an image whose express intention is not to make a complex reality understandable. Instead of empirically describing social and political conditions and facilitating access to knowledge, fixed opinions, prejudices, and fears are further cemented. Behind all this lies a political calculation that may come as no surprise to us. What is surprising, though, is the subtlety and the visual language—rehearsed down to the last detail—that turns the supposedly informative function of infographics into its opposite.

1   See, inter alia, Edward R. Tufte, *Visual Explanations: Images and Quantities, Evidence and Narrative* (Cheshire, CT, 1997); Tufte, *The Visual Display of Quantitative Information*, 2nd ed. (Cheshire, CT, 2001).

2   See, inter alia, Eurostat: ec.europa.eu/eurostat/ statistics-explained/index.php/Migration_and_migrant_ population_statistics; UNHCR Population Statistics: popstats.unhcr.org

3   See the interview conducted by Robin Schwarzenbach with Walter Krämer, professor of statistics at TU Dortmund, published under the title "Das ist ganz grober Unfug" ["This is utter nonsense"] in *Neue Zürcher Zeitung*, February 27, 2016.

I Lost My Spirit When They Brought Us to the Boat

Kwadjo Anabisa and Andreas Listowell recount the story of their refugee journey

In April 2015 we met two refugees from the "Lampedusa in Hamburg" group. Kwadjo Anabisa and Andreas Listowell are originally from Ghana. Andreas left his home country in 2005, when tribal conflicts broke out there. After studying for four years he had done his diploma in sales and marketing and found work in Tripoli as a management assistant in an Italian construction firm. When war broke out in Libya in 2011, the rebels thought he was a supporter of the dictator Gaddafi because of the color of his skin. They took away all his valuables, even his cell phone, and compelled him to leave the country, forcing him and Kwadjo Anabisa onto a boat across the Mediterranean. When we met in Hamburg, we showed them a selection of seventy photos that the Italian Red Cross had given to the Migrant Image Research Group in 2010. The photos were taken by people from the Red Cross documenting their work. Kwadjo and Andreas recognized some of the images and told us their story. The interview was conducted by Anne König, Ina Kwon and Andreas Langfeld.

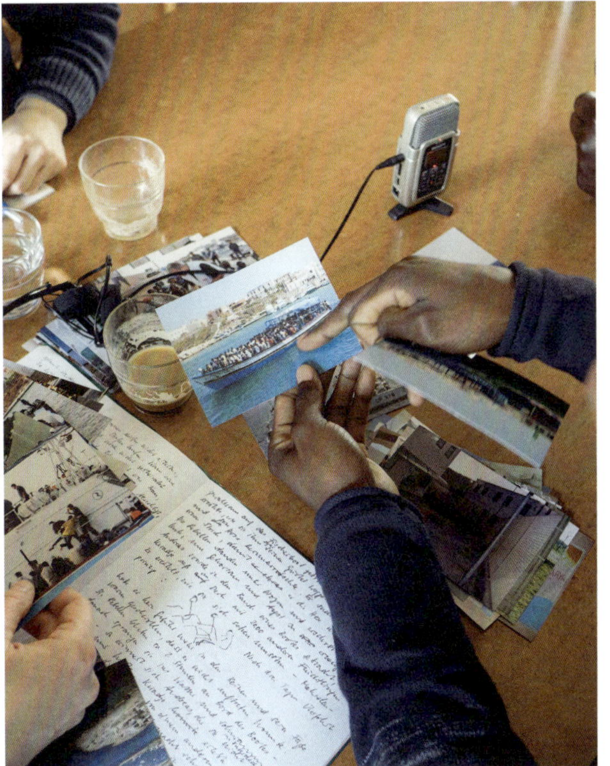

Q: What type of boat did you come on?
ANABISA: My boat was a small fishing boat. We had only one deck. It was overloaded. Normally they take a hundred people, but my boat had three hundred!

Q: How long was your trip?
ANABISA: The trip took two days from Benghazi to Lampedusa. I couldn't sleep. I kept my eyes closed because I was afraid of the water.

Q: Where were the women and children?
ANABISA: They were inside.

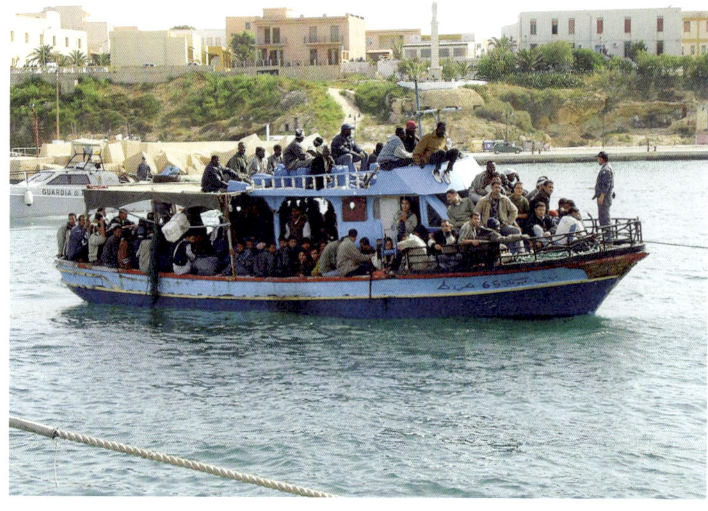

← LISTOWELL: This is the same boat I came with. On the top deck you can see people sitting there. Some are sitting here. And underneath there is a staircase. There are tables and people are arranging themselves under the tables; some are on the tables.
The people who were sitting on top had a lot of trouble, because some people wanted to jump into the sea.

Q: Because the boat was shaking so much?
LISTOWELL: Their intention was to commit suicide. If somebody wants to commit suicide, people first try to hold this person. But if somebody gets aggressive, they let him jump. Because he might affect all the people on the boat. When somebody jumped into the sea, everyone started talking and the boat was shaking. We heard the captain shouting that people should go to this or that position in order to bring the boat back into balance. We were very afraid down below because we couldn't see what was going on. We only heard the shouting.

Q: Could you choose where and how to sit?
LISTOWELL: No, no. We could not

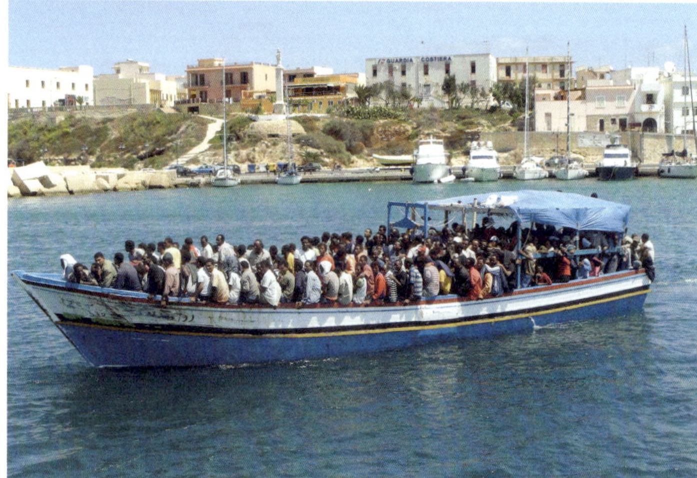

decide. The rebels pushed us.
ANABISA: They forced us to cross our legs. They pack people like this. They beat you and you cannot stretch your legs.
LISTOWELL: I lost my spirit when they brought us to the boat. There was one couple with a child. They separated the father from his wife and child. He had to go down below, and she had to sit on the top deck with her child. The man said no. And the way they beat him, I could see the blood running over his face. The family was crying and they forced them to go to the top deck. What should I say? I sat next to him. I had to sit quietly because what they did to him they could have done to me as well. And even if I sat quiet, I got some slaps from them.

I could see them taking drugs. They have to use a knife to cut the skin. The blood has to come before they can take this special drug.

Q: What's the drug called?

LISTOWELL: I don't remember. When somebody takes this drug, he doesn't feel anything any more. Therefore the rebels could kill people. The atmosphere on the boat was very aggressive. After we took off, the rebels left two hours later. They jumped into the water.

ANABISA: The rebels had guns and when they left the boat, they fired them. And then the rescue boat picked them up.

Q: Was there anybody on the boat who had a cell phone to communicate?

LISTOWELL: Nobody could get on the boat with a cell phone.

Q: When did you get a new cell phone in Europe again?

LISTOWELL: It took me two years because I didn't have money to buy one. If you get to Lampedusa, they will let you call, they will give you credit, if you still have a family …

ANABISA: Somebody will call your family and then you can speak.

Q: So you were in a queue for hours.

ANABISA: Like two hundred people. The phone call is limited. After two minutes it's finished. Then another person can call.

Q: But what if nobody answers?

ANABISA: Then you try another day.

Q: One phone call a week, two minutes. And that was on Lampedusa?

ANABISA: Manduria.

Q: So, when you arrived on Lampedusa, could you call your families?

ANABISA: I didn't manage; the phone was switched off.

Q: And you?

LISTOWELL: No.

Q: When did you get in contact with your families?

LISTOWELL: In Milan. I contacted my brother through Facebook.

Q: They didn't know where you were, if you were alive.

LISTOWELL: No.

Q: And you?

ANABISA: I went to Libya together with my mom and my dad. I don't know where they are now.

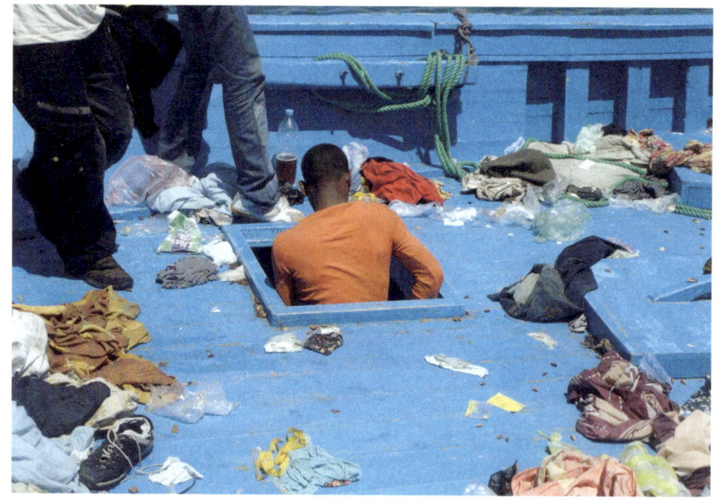

← *Q: This image was taken by a jour-nalist and not by someone from an NGO. The photographs we col-lected are meant to demons-trate and document the work of the NGOs. The press images differ from the photos we got from the NGOs. They are more catchy. We don't know who took the photos.*

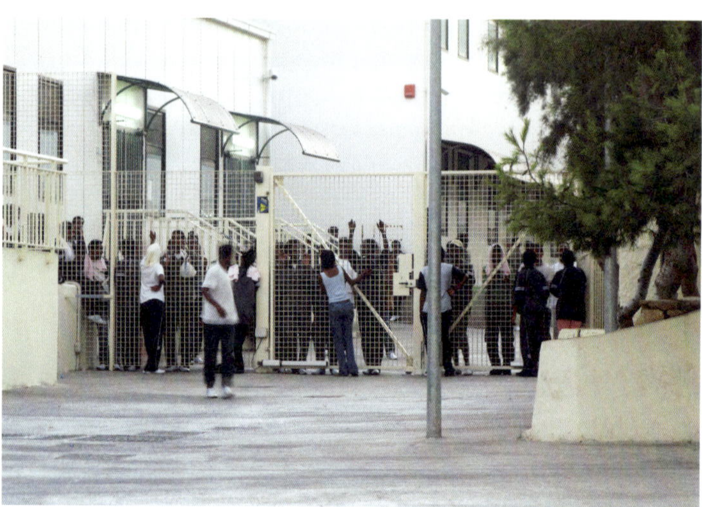

← *Q: Where is it in the camp?*
LISTOWELL: It must be on Lampe-dusa. I can see this here. You can see this route is going this way here and this is the way we came from the sea. When they took us in the bus, we went in this direction and we came to this compound. This fence is also an internal fence. There is another external fence around it and—yes, there is an-other one. They put it around the center so that nobody can run away.

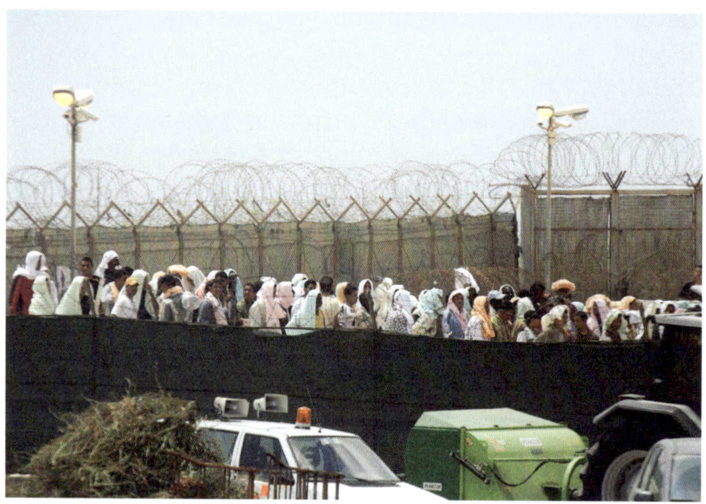

← *Q: It looks like a prison.*
LISTOWELL: When we went to Taranto, four guys were trying to escape. The police brought them back and the next day they tried again.
    Q: Why?
LISTOWELL: They didn't want to get deported. Some of them had contacts here in Europe. Italy is not the best place to have your fingerprints done—maybe they wanted to go to another country in Europe. These people tried to escape from the camp because they knew the story—if you do the fingerprinting in Italy, then everything is finished.

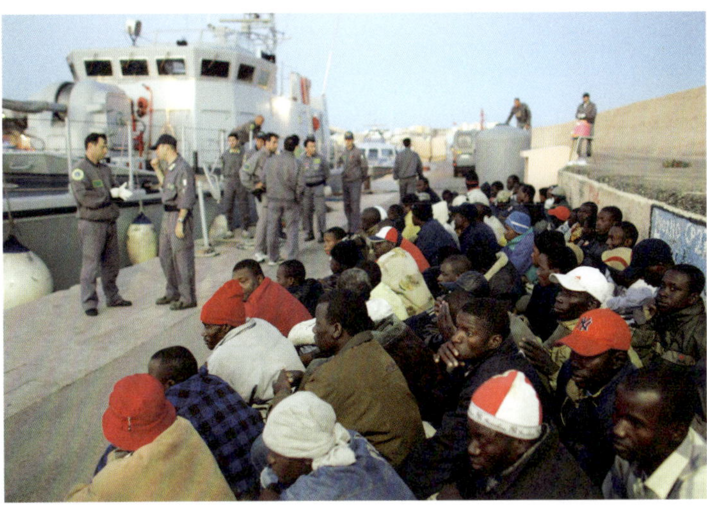

← Q: *Do you know where this photo was taken?*
LISTOWELL: Yes, it is where the boat arrives in the harbor.
  Q: *But why are they sitting outside?*
LISTOWELL: These people just arrived and they are tired. They sit on the floor so that nobody can fall over.

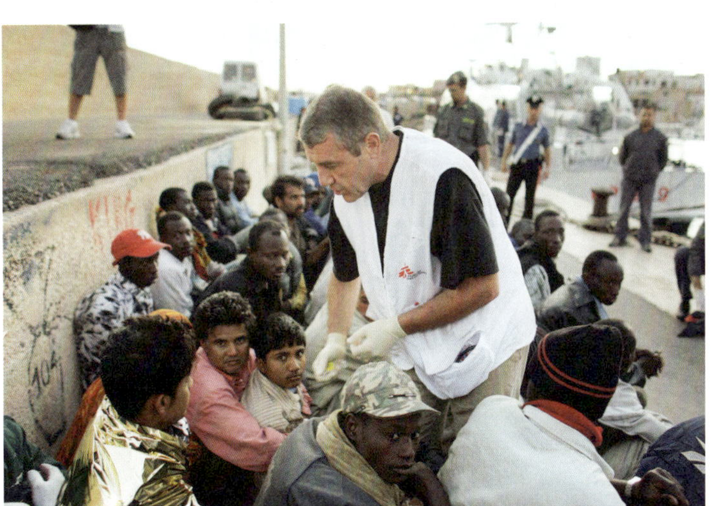

← LISTOWELL: Every day the same thing. You have to sit down. And they select those who are weak and put them in the Red Cross car, and later they call the people who are sitting down and put them on a bus.
  Q: *When you arrived on Lampedusa, did you know anything about the process of getting into Europe?*
ANABISA: Nothing.
LISTOWELL: They told us: Do this and this and this. And we did it.

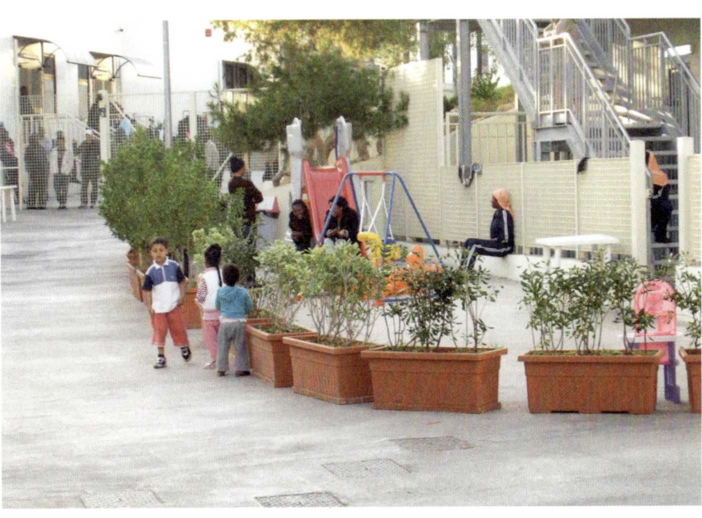

← Q: *You had a very short stay on Lampedusa. Do you remember this image here?*
LISTOWELL: I can remember this, because of this gate here. This area is like the migration office: it is where they take the fingerprints, and after you've done the fingerprints, you take your clothing and everything, and you go here, behind here, to take a shower. If they're going to transfer you, then you have to wait behind this fence, and then you come out from here and get on a bus to the ship.
  Q: *Is this the area for women and children here?*
LISTOWELL: No, it's behind here.

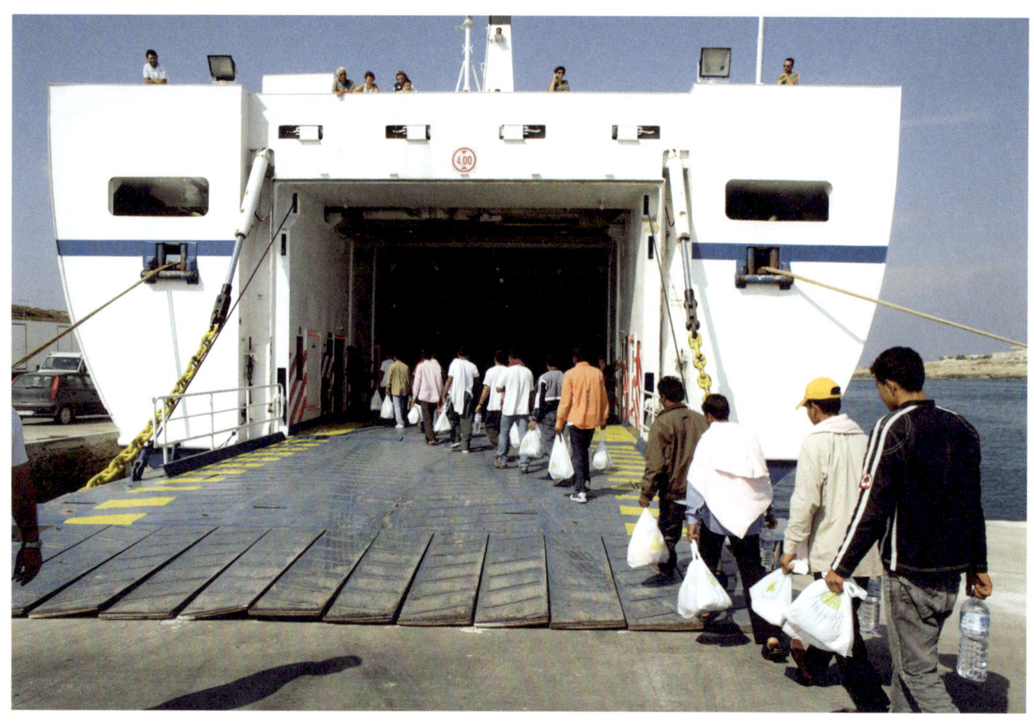

↑   Q: *What are they carrying in their white plastic bags here?*
LISTOWELL: Food and maybe the rest of the things they give to you. Like toothpaste, toothbrush, and water.
   Q: *Did you know already when you were on this ship where you would be sent to?*
LISTOWELL: No, we didn't know.
ANABISA: At first they told us they were sending us to the city.
   Q: *Was the ship full of people?*
LISTOWELL: No, there were a lot of people, but it's never full.
ANABISA: Some have bedrooms …
LISTOWELL: I was in the "Roma" room. Others were called "Napoli", "Venezia". We were sitting on chairs. It was like a church hall. If you were tired, you could lie down.
   Q: *After Taranto, they moved you to Manduria, right?*
LISTOWELL: Yes, in my case, immediately after I arrived there, I saw that it was a fucking desert. There were no trees and the sun was shining. It was a hot place at that time, a camp full of tents. In the bus we were told that we would only have to wait here for two weeks. Then they would send us to better places. My friend Collins and I decided that we were not going to sleep with six people in one tent. Three of us occupied one tent because we were just tired. The next day when the authorities came, they didn't say anything. Collins was a bit afraid. He was frightened to talk to people. He just wanted to be with me. I felt like his brother, you know. We met on the boat. He is also from Ghana. We were both afraid that they would separate us. We went to the authorities in the camp and told them that we were brothers.

Q: What did you do about your names?
LISTOWELL: They didn't ask us for our family name. They told us that we can go to Milan together. When we got there, they called my name and asked me where my younger brother was. They brought us to another place. We got one room and we stayed there two years. You can go to Milan, you can go to Naples —this is how they do the distribution. If they send you to Milan, then you go there for the asylum process. They bring you to the foreigners' office. They take fingerprints from you again, and photos of all the different parts of your body.

Q: And these are the fingerprints that count. The fingerprints on Lampedusa don't carry any weight. How long did you have to stay in Manduria?
LISTOWELL: They didn't talk to us again after we arrived there. Our group decided to stage a demonstration. The reason was this: there were some people who had arrived after us. But they were transferred before us. We found out that we—the people with yellow cards—had to wait, while the people with green cards were transported before they would put us on the bus.
ANABISA: We blocked the bus.
LISTOWELL: And the policeman was telling us we should keep it up, otherwise we would have to wait longer. During the demonstration they had to call their boss, who talked to us. We should let that bus pass. If we did that, they would make sure that the people with yellow cards would leave next. But we had to spend twenty-one days there. Our group was split, with some going to Naples and other places.

Q: How did you get to Milan?
LISTOWELL: Our group went to Milan in three buses.

Q: Where did they house you in Milan?
LISTOWELL: It wasn't too far away from the city center. I was moved to Gorgonzola for two years. The place where they make this cheese. It was a fifteen-minute drive from the main train station in Milan.
ANABISA: My place was really, really bad. I was in Brescia. In the mountains. Very cold. No bus, no transportation. We had to walk to get to the city.

Q: How long did you stay in Gorgonzola?
LISTOWELL: Two years. We went to a Guardia Costiera office, and in my group there were forty of us who were sent to this town, Gorgonzola. There was a guest house. There were forty of us who had to stay in three rooms for two years. We had to manage. The beds were like hospital beds. We were told that the community of Gorgonzola was responsible for us. We had one social worker who helped us with all these questions. Apart from that, nobody cared about us.

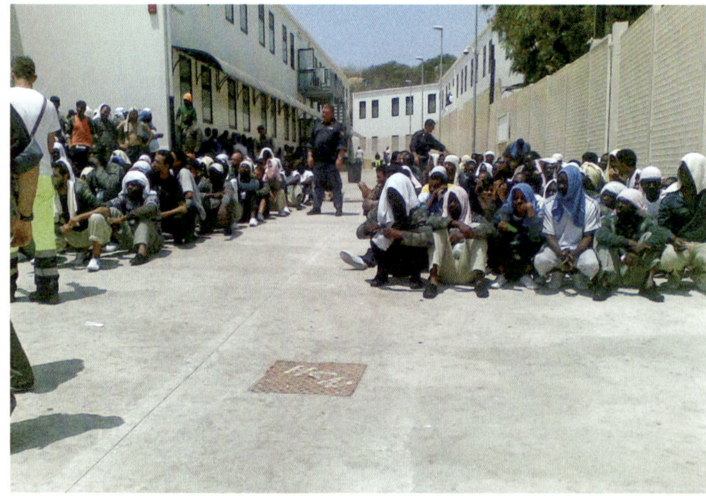

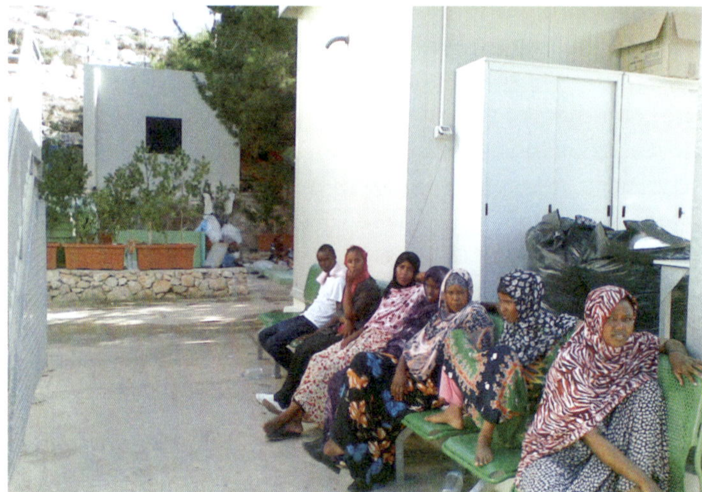

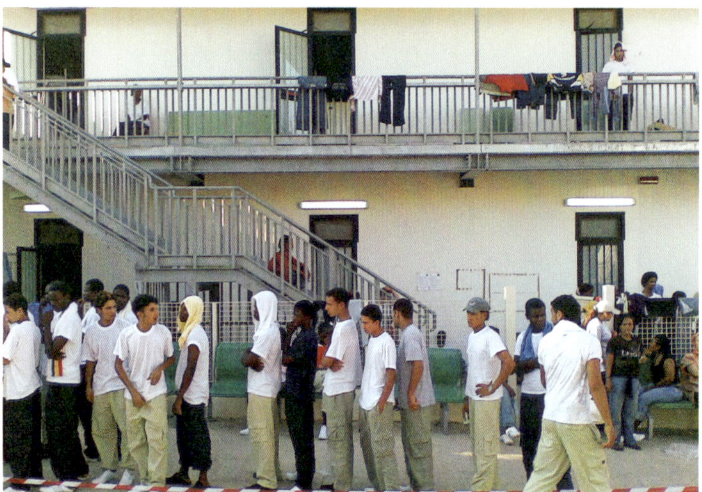

← *Q: Here are some more images from Lampedusa with a typical motif: waiting. What are these people waiting for?*

LISTOWELL: I think this is life in Lampedusa. It could happen that you are waiting, waiting—it's all about waiting. So you don't know … It's kind of a normal thing. I mean, everybody has to wait. You are waiting for fingerprints, you are waiting for your uniform, you are waiting for a towel to shower, or you are waiting for a bus … it's all waiting, waiting, waiting.

Q: And when you were in Gorgonzola?

LISTOWELL: Yes, it was also waiting!

Q: Two years of waiting.

LISTOWELL: I would eat, go out with my bicycle to the park, and sit there and read or I would go to the library. This is the life that I was living, I mean … there was someone from the church who helped me. They got me the library card and over there I could browse the Internet for free, and I could read there. I could spend as much time as I wanted. I was more or less addicted, you know, to going to the library. It was waiting, waiting, waiting.

Q: But in the library, there were only Italian books?

LISTOWELL: I learned Italian so fast. I read a lot of books, which helped my language. In Italy, if you don't learn the language, how can you talk to anyone—they won't tell you anything, the hotel manager won't give you good food, they won't give you soap or toothpaste. How are you going to complain, I mean, in what language? So I became a kind of a leader in the group. I was putting pressure on this guy, and later on he didn't like me, because he thought I was a troublemaker. Everything that he was doing was not right! He didn't give us good food, sometimes we went two weeks, one month without toothpaste. If you asked him, he would tell you tomorrow that he had forgotten. Oh, tomorrow, I forgot, you know. And it was like that, and I said no, this is bullshit, so one day we started, we led a demonstration there.

Q: *Did your protest have an impact on your situation?*
LISTOWELL: The manager decided how much money he would spend on us. He got the money, but he spent less than he should have spent. If you complained about him to the Commune, they said they couldn't do anything. The Commune told us that he is such a kind man, but he was not. He didn't do anything for us. They told us that we would have to go before our commission to tell our story, the reason we left our country and came to Europe. All this was new for us. You have to say this in front of a commission, which decides whether or not they will give you international recognition. Eighty percent of the group had their applications rejected because we were considered economic refugees. They did not accept us as political refugees because we are from Ghana, where no war is going on. We are not Libyans. We were considered to be immigrant workers in Libya —and therefore economic refugees. During our two-year stay we were dependent on United Nations money. After two years the United Nations told the Italian authorities that they could not continue to pay the money. And at this point the pressure was on the Italian authorities, and they decided to give us passports. They gave us the papers, indirectly, then they kicked us out of the camp. They gave us 400 euro. But not all of us got it. Some of us didn't get anything.

Q: *In Italy you got a residence permit, but it was impossible to find any work. In February 2013, you and Kwadjo made your way to Germany with a tourist visa, right?*
LISTOWELL: Yes, someone in the Commune asked: Where do you want to go? If you said you wanted to go to Germany, they paid the ticket from the 400 euro and gave you the balance. I used the money to get a passport, and I bought a ticket to Hamburg.

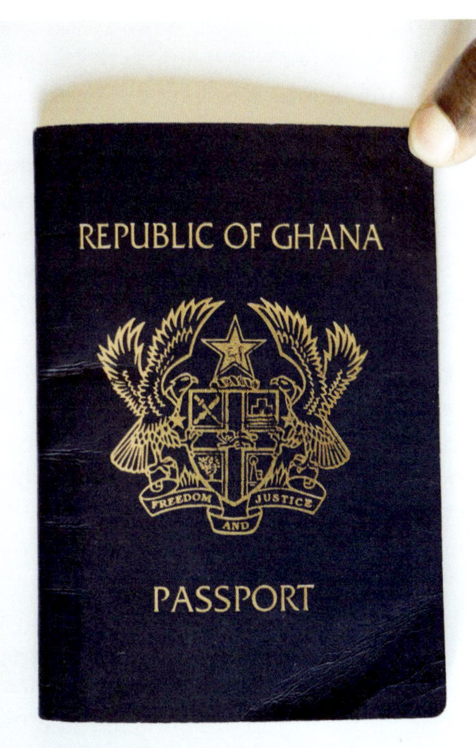

Q: *And you got the passport at the Ghanaian embassy?*
LISTOWELL: Instantly, yes.
Q: *And you still have this passport?*
LISTOWELL: I do.
Q: *And you as well?*
ANABISA: No, they gave me a refugee passport.
Q: *A refugee passport? In Ghana you had a similar passport?*
LISTOWELL: Yes, it's the same thing.
Q: *But how long did it take you to get the passport?*
LISTOWELL: Instantly.
Q: *Instantly? I mean how did they check …*

LISTOWELL: You have to go with your birth certificate that shows that you are from Ghana.

Q: *But how can you show that? I mean, if you don't have any documents?*

LISTOWELL: You have to call them, that's the reason you have to contact your family immediately, if they have to send you anything.

Q: *So, the family confirms that you are …*

LISTOWELL: No, they will send the birth certificate to you, here in Germany or in Italy. I did it in Italy.

Q: *Did you fly to Germany?*

LISTOWELL: No. I came by train.

Q: *And you?*

ANABISA: I flew to Norway and then to Germany.

Q: *To Norway? You just said where you wanted to go to and then they bought the ticket for you? No questions?*

LISTOWELL: What kind of questions? They kept us for two years. They closed the camp. There was no accommodation. If I'd stayed in Italy, it would have worked out really badly. Everybody wanted to leave.

ANABISA: I got 200 euro. I bought my ticket for 200 euro. I arrived in Germany with 5 euro left.

Q: *Why did you go to Norway?*

LISTOWELL: He wanted to start a new life!

Q: *But why Norway? Was there any rumor going round about going to Norway? How was the decision made?*

LISTOWELL: I wanted to go to Denmark. But it didn't work out. I was checking the Internet and I was really, really afraid of a racist country. I had already had my experience with racism in Italy. I found out that the Danish don't like blacks. So I checked Hamburg and it was fine. I found out that here they are more open. That was the reason I came here. Together with Collins. We were together in the guest hotel in Gorgonzola for two years. He didn't know where to go either. So I told him to go with me to Hamburg. We bought our tickets. Some of our group went to Holland or to France. They slept outside. Here we were facing the same problems as in Italy or France. But maybe it is easier to survive in Hamburg than in Italy.

Q: *Maybe you get more support here than in Italy?*

LISTOWELL: Because Italy … Who helps you? Nobody helps you. If you are sitting in the train, people get up because you're black. They are very, very racist.

Q: *It can also happen to you in Germany. Hamburg is an exception.*

LISTOWELL: Yes, but Italy shouldn't be like this. It is a country where refugees have been coming for so many years and they are still closed, you know.

ANABISA: If you speak English, then you are considered a thief.

LISTOWELL: Everybody was fed up with Italy. They didn't give us any future there, but they did give us our papers. But before they gave us the papers, they knew that they had destroyed our future by putting our hands on the machine for taking fingerprints. They knew it.

Q: What about Collins?

LISTOWELL: He is still in Hamburg. He was also desperate like I was.

Q: May I ask you how old you are?

LISTOWELL: I'm 33. Now Collins is living in a different place. He is living in Rubin Camp. He is playing in the theater as well. I call him every two days.

Q: How is he now?

LISTOWELL: Now he feels OK. People are integrated in Hamburg. We have made many friends. Collins is working in the canteen.

Q: Is there anybody who has returned home?

LISTOWELL: There were two people who went back to Ghana. They were afraid. They were frustrated and they wanted to go home. From our group nobody is living on the street at the moment. The living conditions on the streets are bad.

Q: Did you have to stay on the street?

LISTOWELL: Me?

ANABISA: I met this guy on the street. He slept in the garden. I can show you all the places in Hamburg where I stayed. I slept in the gardens.

LISTOWELL: When the *Winternotprogramm* was closed …

Q: What is this?

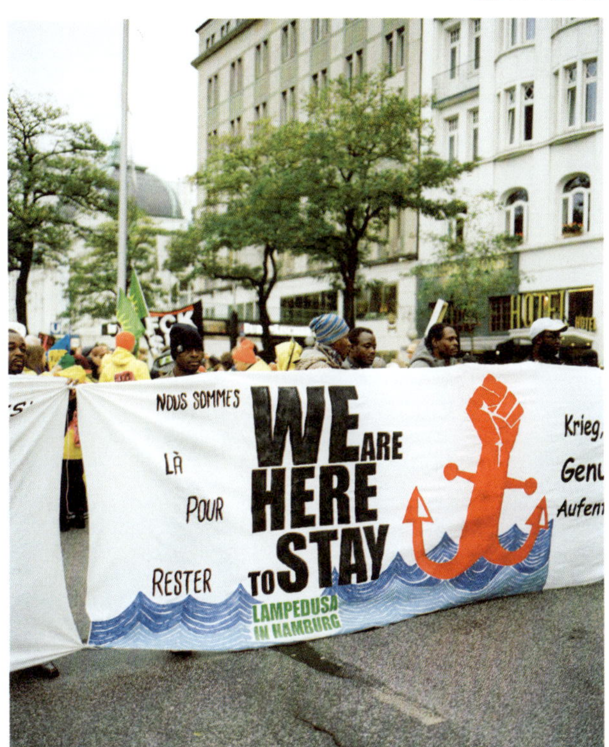

LISTOWELL: It's like—this guy, for instance. He didn't live on the street because he had the church pastor, who took three of them to stay with him. It was kind of illegal.

Q: Church asylum?

LISTOWELL: No, it wasn't that exactly. It was the decision of the church pastor to take him and the other two men in from the street. So from April till the moment when somebody took me to the church I stayed on the street. Five weeks. From April to May 2013.

ANABISA: I didn't sleep all the time in the church. Sometimes I went out to stay together with my friends on the streets, walking around.

LISTOWELL: There was a time where I felt sick. I decided not to sleep on the street any more. We were more than seven or eight hundred people alone in Hamburg. There were all these people walking up and down in front of the station.

Sometimes we were sleeping in the AStA students' union. So, we know where to get

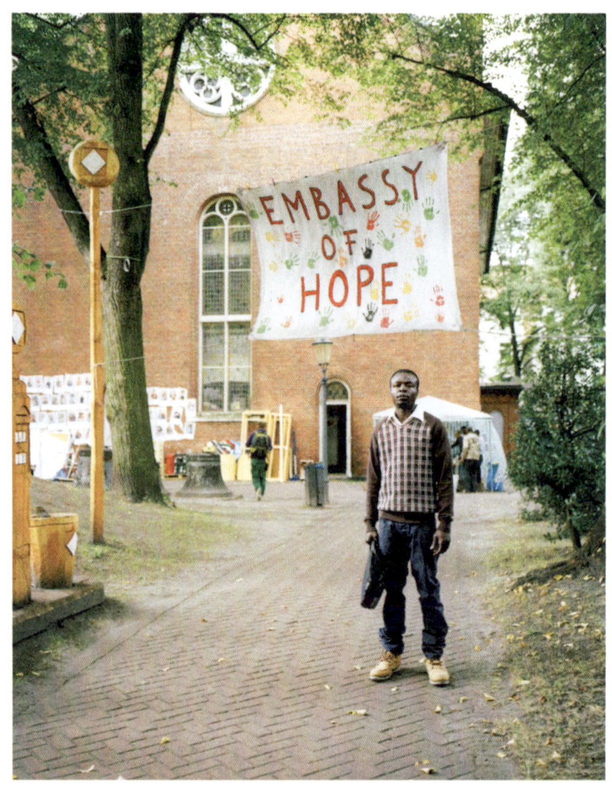

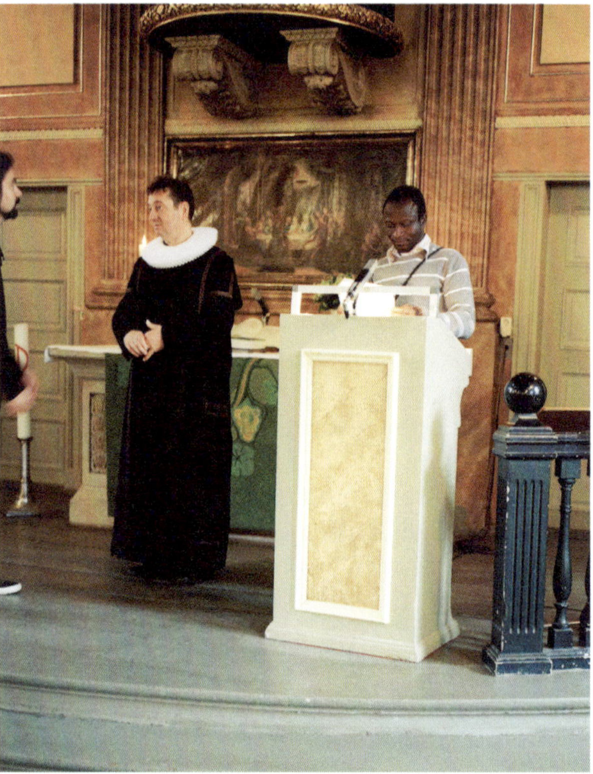

some food at Caritas. Where the homeless get it from.

ANABISA: We put our bags in the bushes because we couldn't afford a locker. Sometimes we found our bags had been opened.

When we started the protest, the first day in the town hall I was the first person who said: I won't leave this place. I want to sleep here. This place is so warm. I'm going to stay here.

Q: Then the church asylum happened to you.

LISTOWELL: We don't live on the streets any more. We live in a house. The kitchen is very big. There are two of us sharing one room. Apart from deportation, the situation is good.

ANABISA: So far so good.

In November 2013 Andreas Listowell applied for suspension of deportation. He was supported in his legal proceedings, like hundreds of other Lampedusa refugees, by the church relief organization Fluchtpunkt. In July 2016 Andreas and Kwadjo were among the first from the so-called "Lampedusa in Hamburg" group to receive a residence permit, limited to one year at first.

Interventions in the Aesthetic Regime of the Maritime Border

Charles Heller on migrating images, the disobedient gaze, and empathic ruptures

Charles Heller is a researcher and film-maker based in Geneva whose work has a long-standing focus on the politics of migration within and at the borders of Europe. In 2011, he co-founded the Forensic Oceanography research project, which critically investigates the lethal effects of the militarized border regime and the politics of migration in the Mediterranean Sea. Together with a wide network of NGOs, scientists, journalists, and activist groups, Forensic Oceanography has produced, since 2011, several human rights reports as well as maps and video animations. Heller is a co-founder of the Watch The Med platform. Today, he is a research fellow at the Centre for Research Architecture at Goldsmiths, University of London. The conversation, which traces his trajectory as an image practitioner and researcher, reflects on shifting regimes of (in)visibility at the EU's maritime frontier. The interview, which was conducted by Anne König and Lisa Bergmann, took place in the first half of 2017 over several sessions, at his home in Geneva and online.

Q: The Lampedusa project started with Armin Linke. Seven years ago, he was invited to take part in an exhibition about Lampedusa, where he refused to produce more images. Instead he traveled to the island with a team from the Karlsruhe University of Arts and Design to look for pre-existing images there. They came back with images from the Red Cross and the Italian Coast Guard as well as Facebook photos taken by the refugees themselves. So this decision not to produce more images on migration was a crucial one for the whole project, and I think it can be connected to your approach to this topic.

HELLER: I think that this moment of suspension that you described in relation to Armin's proposal, this moment of refusing to produce more images of migration and rather interrogate the production and circulation of images, is also fundamental to my own trajectory. It emerged as a necessity for me when I encountered the International Organization for Migration (IOM)'s "information campaign" in 2007, through which the IOM set out not so much to inform migrants as to deter them. In this campaign, which was funded by Switzerland and the EU and implemented mainly in Cameroon and other West African states at the time, I see a very troubled reflection of my own practice, in the sense that the videos involved the staging of a migrant's precarity, producing fictionalized representations of similar forms of precarity that I had documented myself with the aim of denouncing the migration regime that produces these conditions on a structural basis. And so this encounter led me on to stop producing *images of migration*—temporarily at least—and rather to interrogate the *migration of images* themselves, as well as the particular form of "media governmentality" that the IOM implemented.[1]

> Q: *You mentioned the idea of interrogating the production and circulation of images. What does that mean in practical terms? In your thesis you describe the image as an object, and you question image practices, drawing inspiration from a wide range of theories. But you are engaging with these theories from your specific position as a filmmaker. How does this shape your perspective?*

HELLER: When I entered this moment of crisis and suspension in my practice, I found myself asking, How are images produced and how do they circulate, what effects do they have, both in the very concrete way the border regime operates and more broadly in terms of migration policies? I was dissatisfied with some of the dominant ways of asking these questions, both within politicized art practices and in media theory, which tend to focus on the intentionality of an author, the form that his "message" takes, and how it affects a distant viewer's perception and behavior. It is not so much that I think these perspectives are simply wrong or entirely ineffective but rather that they are far too limiting, making it difficult to account for entanglements between practices related to the production and circulation of images and the forces which shape our world — particularly in the field of migration — that I was confronted with. So I tried to assemble different perspectives—emerging from both theory and practice—through which I could develop a new grammar of image politics. What I found particularly helpful were the perspectives that viewed image politics from the angle of *practice* and of *objects*, and later also of *aesthetics*. Each of these terms entails a shift in the kind of practices and processes that we can look at when we start to interrogate images. In thinking of image *practices* and *objects*, one can begin to look at images not as representations of the world that lie somehow outside of the world they represent but rather as "nodes" within the multiple practices that go into producing them, and examine the different and ambivalent ways in which they can in turn be put to use during their circulation. Images here are seen as always

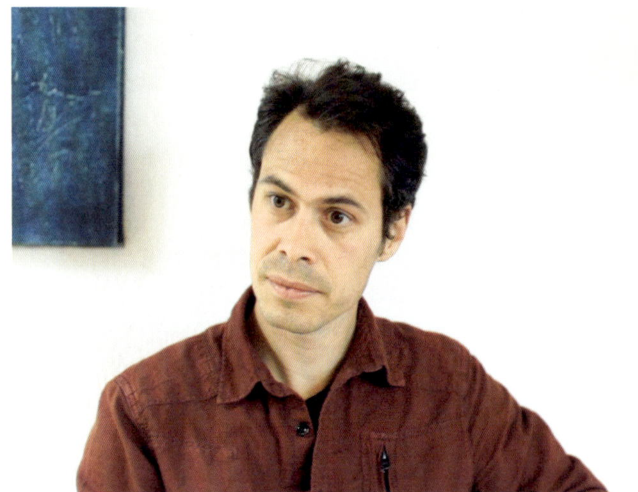

already part of the world and as shaping it in multiple ways.
To take just one example, part of my thesis focuses on the practice of photography in the Moroccan military, which systematically photographed the migrants' boats that they captured and set ablaze. Here we could see that the practice of photography was part of the very event it documented. In turn, looking carefully at the materiality of the photographs, it became possible to understand better how they were displayed and circulated and to what effect—initially in the attempt to document the work of policing they were undertaking on behalf of the EU.

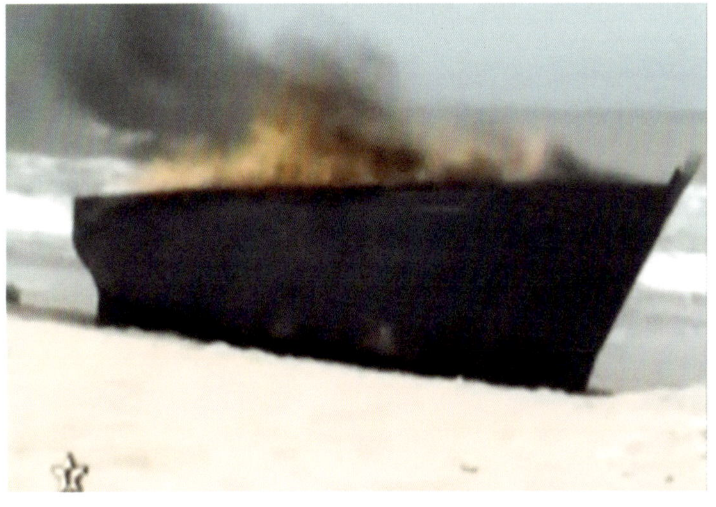

← While I sought to re-signify these images as an expression of the violence of the EU border regime in my video *Crossroads* (2006), they were extracted from my own work and published in an IOM newsletter covering anti-trafficking and anti-illegal migration activities. Rather than focusing on the "photographed event," I sought to trace the ramifications of the "event of photography" in the terms set out by Ariella Azoulay, and to examine how the image operates within the successive institutional and technological assemblages it comes to be embedded in.[2] Forging this perspective was not simply a matter of detached understanding for me but of doing better, of being able to target more precisely the politics of my aesthetic practice.

Q: Then I would say an educational program will be required to enable us to read these images properly. This analytical way of seeing an image is not something that you can develop by yourself. Media images, in particular, are an integrated part of the border regime itself, as you wrote in your thesis. The majority of the images of migration that are printed and circulated in the Western media have a negative impact, and in order to read them critically, we would need an education to allow us to read them, right?

HELLER: Yes, the representation of migration across the sea is incredibly stereotypical. Particularly since the beginning of what has been called the "migration crisis" in the Mediterranean, the international media have been flooded by images of over-crowded boats crossing the EU's maritime frontier, images that mostly either look the same or are even reused over several years, drifting from article to article—they have become "floating images," as Hito Steyerl puts it.[3] In thinking about the way these images operate through their circulation in the media and their repeated imprint on our collective visual language, the concept of "the border spectacle" coined by Nicholas de Genova has been really useful for us.[4] Through these images, the threat of illegalized migration and the securitization work of border control are simultaneously made visible and naturalized, in a circular way: if migrants are being intercepted through militarized means, it is because they are a threat; if they are a threat, then they must be policed with all necessary means. However, by focusing on the *scene* of border enforcement, the conditions that lie before (the state production of illegality through policies of exclusion) and after (the future exploitation of illegalized migrant labor) remain hidden as an *obscene* supplement. As do the structural violations that are the product of the migration regime. Here we can see more clearly the use of an aesthetic lens: an intrinsic dimension of the EU's border regime is a particular "aesthetic regime" operating across the maritime frontier shaping conditions of (dis)appearance of migration and border and relating to the way they are represented. The borders of Europe also impose boundaries on what can be seen and heard. This regime does not only operate within images that appear in the media but also operates through various surveillance technologies, which are assembled into a "scopic system" in the sense that Karin Knorr Cetina defined this term: a scope as a periscope allows you to see something further than your immediate sense of vision would allow you to.[5] This scopic system is used to detect the small boats of migrants from among large numbers of commercial vessels. To avoid detection, to travel, literally, under the radar, migrants resort to strategies of invisibilization—for example, by traveling during the night and using small boats that are difficult to detect. But when they are in distress, they do everything they can to be seen so as to be rescued: waving to boats passing by, sending out distress calls. However, when faced with their obligation to rescue the migrants, states may abandon their attempts to detect illegalized movements and instead seek not to see them at all, or at least turn a blind eye.

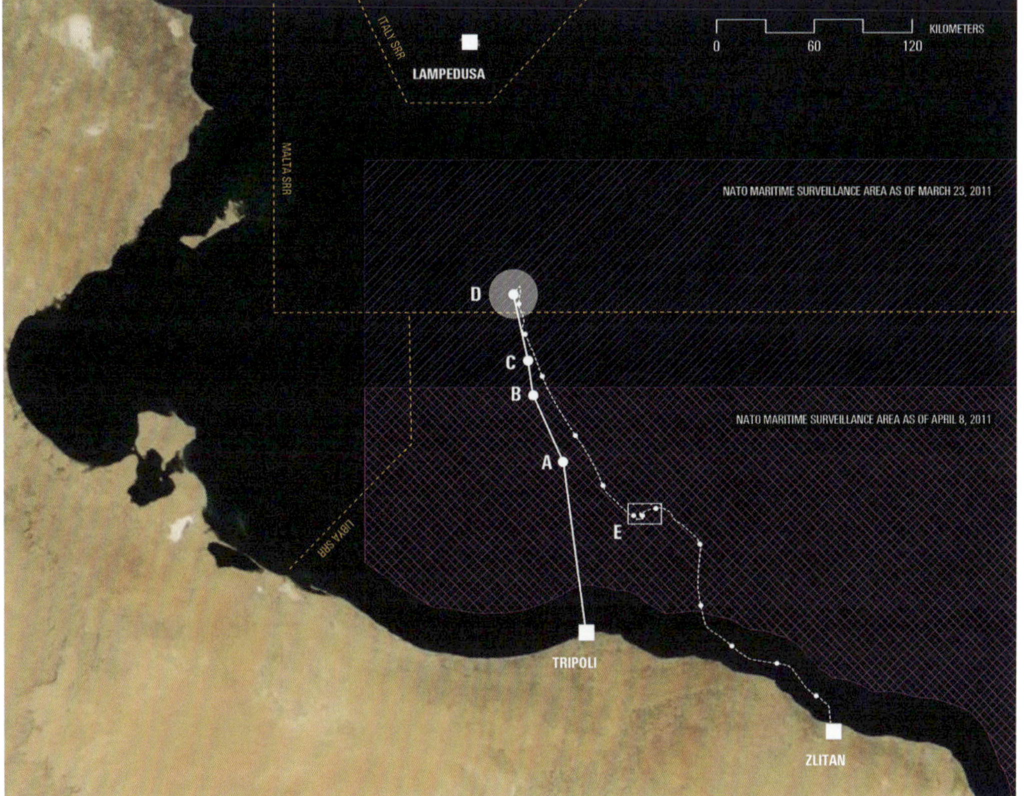

↑   *Q: This points to your Forensic Oceanography project, through which you have documented cases of non-assistance and sought to challenge the boundaries of what can be seen and heard in the Mediterranean. How did the project arise?*

HELLER: It is with this project that my own and Lorenzo Pezzani's trajectories converge. I felt that in the face of the tremendous rupture represented by the Arab uprisings, which both opened up new possibilities and led to new peaks in the number of deaths at sea, the more self-reflexive posture of my research and practice was insufficient. In addition, the Forensic Architecture project opened a new horizon of aesthetic politics by introducing us to new ways of documenting human rights violations. In this context, Lorenzo Pezzani and I initiated the Forensic Oceanography project, which sought to forge new tools to document the violations of migrants' rights at sea and understand the conditions that shape them. We initially focused on reconstructing, with technical experts and NGOs, the "left-to-die boat" case, in which seventy-two passengers were allowed to drift for fourteen days despite repeated contacts with state and non-state actors in an area closely monitored by dozens of military assets within the framework of the 2011 military intervention in Libya. This led to the slow death of sixty-three people. Based on the testimonies of survivors, and re-appropriating some of the remote sensing tools normally used for maritime surveillance, we mapped the trajectory of the migrants' vessel across the liquid geography of the sea and used satellite imagery to locate the military vessels that had abandoned the passengers to a slow death, despite having full knowledge of their condition and location. In relation to the aesthetic regime imposed by the EU's borders, we sought to put into practice a *disobedient gaze* that used some of the same sensing technologies utilized by border controllers but set out to redirect their "spotlight" from unauthorized acts of border-crossing to state and non-state practices violating migrant rights. We conceived of this gaze as aiming "*not* to disclose what the regime of migration management attempts to unveil—clandestine migration—but unveil that which it attempts to hide, the political violence it is founded on and the human rights violations that are its structural outcome."[6] While, as we will discuss later, the aesthetic regime operating at the EU's borders has undergone dramatic shifts, this imperative to critique and oppose the ever-changing conditions of (in)visibility imposed by states remains essential for me. The innovative methodology we developed for our investigation on the "left-to-die boat" case was the basis for Watch The Med, an online mapping platform designed to enable civil society to exercise a critical "right to look" at the maritime frontier of the EU, with the aim of both documenting and preventing the violations of migrant rights.

> *Q: Can you explain more precisely why 2013 saw a shift in image policy? Was it due to the catastrophe in October on Lampedusa?*

HELLER: The year 2013 is the moment when we really see the "humanitarian border"—a term proposed by William Walters—coming into being.[7] In the sense that the border regime no longer seeks to hide migrant deaths, but deaths are rather spectacularized to legitimize and deepen the border regime, justifying it through the language of humanitarianism.

This was not entirely new: Frontex had already justified the closure of the Atlantic route for mainly Senegalese migrants back in 2006 and 2007 as an act of "salvation." "Thanks to us and our collaboration with Mauritanian and Senegalese officials, we managed to close this route, and as a result we saved thousands of lives," Frontex's narrative went. But this humanitarian aspect of the border regime took on a completely new dimension in the wake of the October shipwrecks, which caused a public outcry.

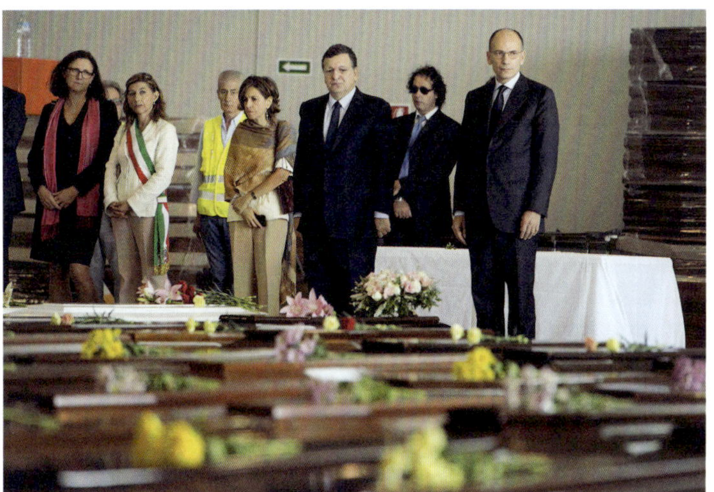

← Immediately, state officials positioned themselves in relation to these deaths: you have Manuel Barroso, president of the European Commission, traveling to Lampedusa and making a speech in front of the line of coffins of the victims of the Lampedusa tragedy. And he is not finally announcing, "We have seen the result of the European border regime and we are going to open our borders." No, of course not. Rather, he is saying, "Look, this is absolutely terrible. We need better surveillance to detect migrants. We need to crack down on migrant smugglers who are putting these people's lives at risk." So, it's a very tricky move which spectacularizes migrant deaths and foregrounds the responsibility of smugglers we all know would not exist without the EU's illegalization policies, which force migrants to resort to them, while at the same time continuing to keep the responsibility of the states and of the border regime in the shadows. I think this really marks a distinct shift in the aesthetic regime of the border and the way death is put on display, and constitutes a very tricky moment for nongovernmental actors and critical aesthetic practitioners, in the sense that foregrounding migrant deaths loses part of its transgressive edge or may even become complicit with the policies and discourse of states when these states start displaying deaths themselves.

Q: It's a good moment to come back to your analysis. You were saying that governments hide the deaths or the migration regime tries to hide them, but this does not seem to be the case any more. I don't think that a lot of thought goes into hiding anything. It is just that politics are per se not easy to see; they are not visible as such. So what is hidden is the responsibility. It's not the deaths. I mean you can see dead bodies and you know about it, but people are not aware of it. So the "spectacle of borders" you described earlier no longer seems to operate in the same way. How can NGOs and aesthetic practitioners position themselves in this context?

HELLER: Yes, the border spectacle has undergone deep changes in that, since 2013, deaths are no longer kept in the shadows. But as you correctly argue, the responsibility of EU policies in the production of illegalization and deaths at sea remains all the better hidden. This demands that we reposition our strategies, but it is challenging. One of the strategies that we've been using recently in our "Death by Rescue" report on the winding up of the Mare Nostrum operation and its lethal effects is, for example, not just using statistics on deaths at the border as a measure of the tremendous consequences of European borders but rather analyzing mortality (which is the relation between arrivals and deaths and is a measure of the danger of the crossing) and how mortality evolves in relation to shifts in EU policy.[8] So reconnecting deaths with responsibility, counting with accountability. And we also try to debunk the idea that "we have to go after smugglers to disrupt their operations so as to save migrants"—to reveal this as a lie. The only way to end all deaths at sea is to end the political and legal conditions that lead to migrants having to cross by means of clandestine strategies in the first place. But other issues arise as well. Within the EU's policies of deterrence, deaths are also implicitly used to frighten migrants, to deter them from crossing the sea, so when we denounce the lethal effects of the EU border regime, we are always also at risk of contributing to its enforcement.

I think we can draw at least two lessons here: the first is that we can never find an adequate strategy that could simply be reproduced unchanged over time. The border regime and the aesthetic regime that it imposes evolve, and we need to reposition ourselves. Second, there is no position or strategy without problems. You make strategic choices in relation to a set of problems, but you can never address them all. This should not paralyze us, however. These problems that are left unaddressed or that emerge from an evolving situation are the basis from which other shifts in our practices must emerge.

Q: Were there other shifts in the aesthetics of the border regime in relation to the 2015 peak "migration crisis"?
HELLER: Yes, in 2015 there occurred a series of other really profound ruptures, once again in the migration regime, as well as in the aesthetic regime operating at the borders. Crucially, we really see this with the collective decision, if you will, of Afghans, Iraqis, and Syrians to cross via the Aegean, when the central Mediterranean had become much more dangerous after the termination of Mare Nostrum. And here there is a real rupture in terms of image production at this moment in time, which is the product both of Syrians, in particular, being able to document their own migration trajectories with the help of smartphones, which they also use as a tool for navigation, and of unprecedented numbers of civilians on the Greek shores seeking to support migrants during their crossing and upon arrival, and filming this entire process. So the capacity of civilians to document incidents at sea has increased exponentially, taking the capacity to document migration at sea out of the exclusive hands of states.

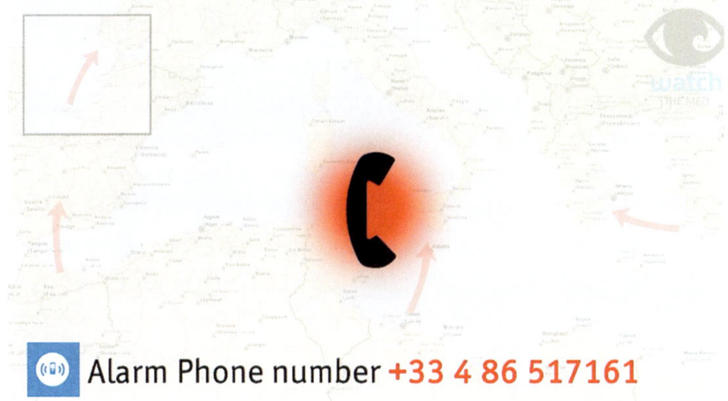

← In conjunction with this, the Watch The Med Alarm Phone project, a civilian emergency phone line operating 24/7, took off and allowed civil society to enact a form of *disobedient listening.*[9] The Alarm Phone was based on a model of practice exemplified by Father Zerai, an Eritrean priest who had been receiving phone calls for many years. Here the idea was to collectivize this kind of practice. The Alarm Phone immediately became an absolutely crucial tool both to support migrants in distress and to document violations. And it's extremely interesting that a very simple technology—mobile phones—coupled with an online phone system, could be so effective. We also see that to exercise a civilian right to look at the maritime borders, visual technologies are weak when compared to the auditory sense, the sense of active listening.

Q: Facebook works in a similar way. Warning migrants which route is safe and which they should not take ...
HELLER: You're right. That moment in 2015 is also accompanied by a multiplication of people in groups on Facebook who seek to support migration across the sea and by land by providing advice. Nonetheless, it was the people working with mobile

phones who were most effective in exercising a right to look at the sea "live," that allowed intervention at the maritime frontier itself.

Q: With the Alarm Phone project, it is no longer only about reconstructing violations but actually preventing them from happening, and supporting migrants in their movement across borders.

HELLER: Yes, this brings us back to the question of the "migration of images." One of the lessons I take from my research and practical work is that practices, like images, circulate. They can migrate from one side of the political divide on the migration regime to the other. But they can also migrate between different kinds of nongovernmental practices. The first report that we produced on the left-to-die boat made use of tools of surveillance, operating against the grain to provide accountability. It was geared to a court of law—different legal cases were filed on the basis of the report. Now, in that sense we used these tools within a particular tradition of nongovernmental politics, essentially the tradition of strategic litigation to defend migrant rights.

But what is happening with the Alarm Phone is that some of the tools that we had begun to forge through our report have been appropriated by another political tradition, which is rather what we might call the tradition of the "underground railroad." We refer to the underground railroad in the sense of the network of bases and relay stations that supported slaves fleeing from one side of the United States to the other. But today and in Europe it is more associated with the No-Border Network providing direct support for migrants' unauthorized movements. So I think what is quite fascinating here is to see that the moment you think that images and practices migrate, you also consider them somehow in terms of objects that enter novel assemblages. If you bring actor–network theory to bear on our thinking about this, you start to see that an image, a tool, or a practice doesn't do anything in and of itself. It does something depending on the particular assemblage it's embedded in. So the tools of documentation that we began to develop took on a completely different meaning and produced completely different effects in the service of the Watch The Med Alarm Phone project, which did not seek so much to document violations after the fact as to support unauthorized migration as it was unfolding.

Q: We read in your thesis that human beings and images are both unstable. They can move. I developed a story for the book. It's about a moving object and the idea behind it is that goods and trade, and also images, can move more freely than human beings. The story is told from the perspective of a piece of a wood which travels from Finland to Egypt, where it becomes part of a fishing boat, which is then stolen by smugglers, who use the boat to transport refugees. The boat with the piece of wood ends up at the boat cemetery on Lampedusa.

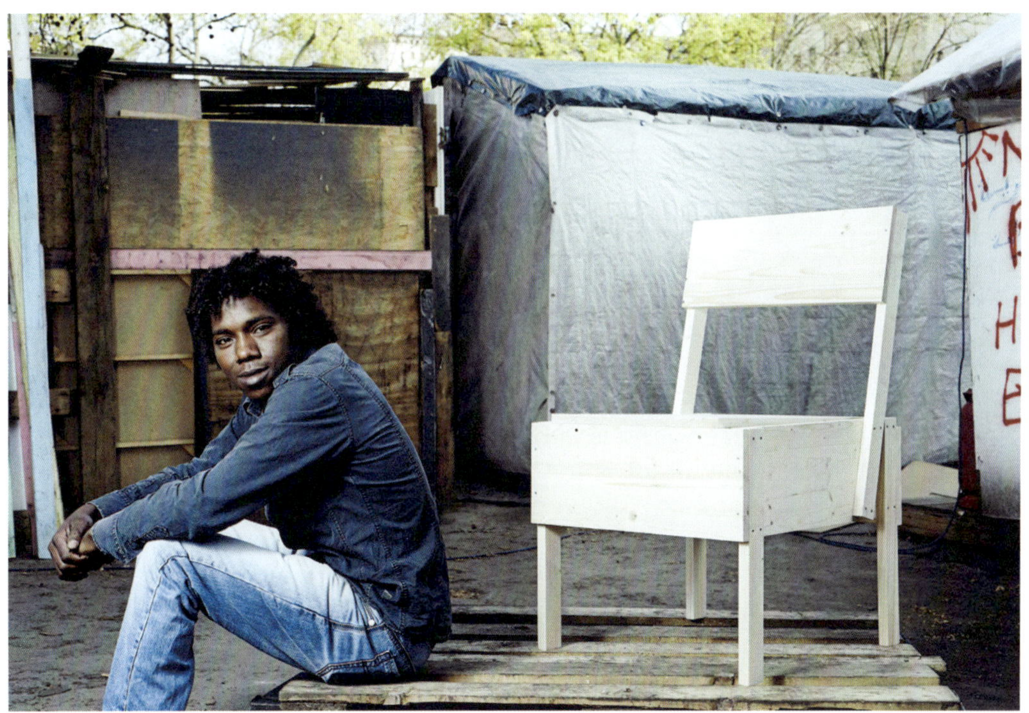

↑   *After a while the NGO Cucula from Berlin collects some pieces of the destroyed boats for their crafts and design company, where refugees who arrived via Lampedusa have built chairs based on the design produced by Enzo Mari. One day Sheryl Sandberg, the COO at Facebook's headquarters in California, visits Cucula. As part of a whitewashing campaign by Facebook, she buys a chair containing the piece of wood. She returns to California and takes the chair with her.*

HELLER: That's an amazing example of an object entering new assemblages. Images are objects too, and I think we can gain a lot in terms of practicing the politics of image making, the politics of aesthetic practice, by looking at them in this way. Also, as I tried to suggest, through the lens of aesthetics, where images and aesthetic practices operate within a broader aesthetic field that is made up of conditions of appearance, of the audibility of people and things. Finally, the lens of practice allows images to be seen not as representations, a final product, but as shaping the world in the very process of their production. Here Farocki's work on "operational images" is exemplary and inspiring.

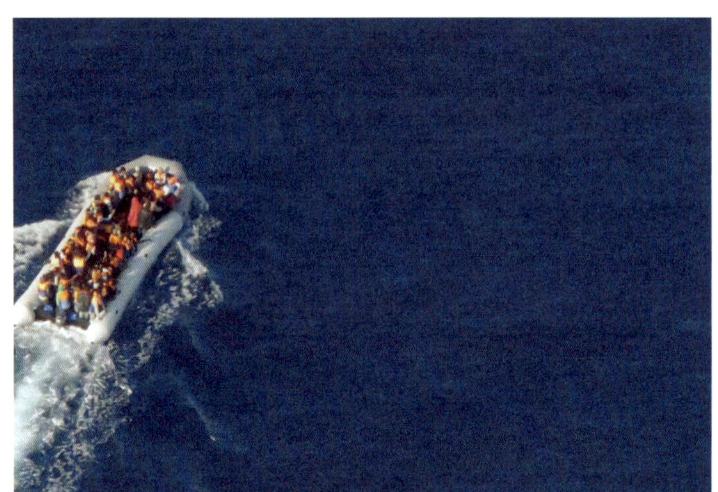

← I would like to show you one image that can be seen as an "operational image." It's an image of a boat taken from a civilian aircraft. The aim of this aircraft is not to produce an image, rather the image is part of its practice of rescue. The photograph was taken by a very recently launched civilian aircraft, the Moonbird, run by a small organization called "Humanitarian Pilots" in close collaboration with Sea Watch, a German organization. It shows one of the more than fifteen boats that were rescued during the Easter weekend, when nongovernmental rescue vessels played a leading role. This particular boat was in contact with the Watch The Med Alarm Phone. But they lost contact with it and it was not detected—it was lost. This image exemplifies many things. First, it's an example of the completely unbelievable progress that we as civil society have made over the last years in terms of our capacity to contest the monopoly that states have on images and on knowing what is going on at the maritime border. It's stunning. This was inconceivable just a few years ago.

Q: *What happened in this case? They took the picture and then the rescue organization out at sea would intervene?*
HELLER: Exactly! They took the picture and could send the picture itself and the coordinates to one of the civilian rescue boats, and the vessel was rescued. In this sense, it also exemplifies the way images are bound to practice: here, to the very act of civilian rescue at sea. Looking at image practices and the way they are involved in events immediately opens up a whole area of image politics.

Q: At first sight, the image itself is not at all spectacular. And the reason it was taken was not to document people in distress and then sell it to agencies. Quite the opposite: the photo was taken to save lives and nothing else. I see here a very fundamental difference from images taken by the media or certain organizations like the Red Cross or Mare Nostrum. They are not using photography to save people's lives in the first instance. It's about documenting their work.

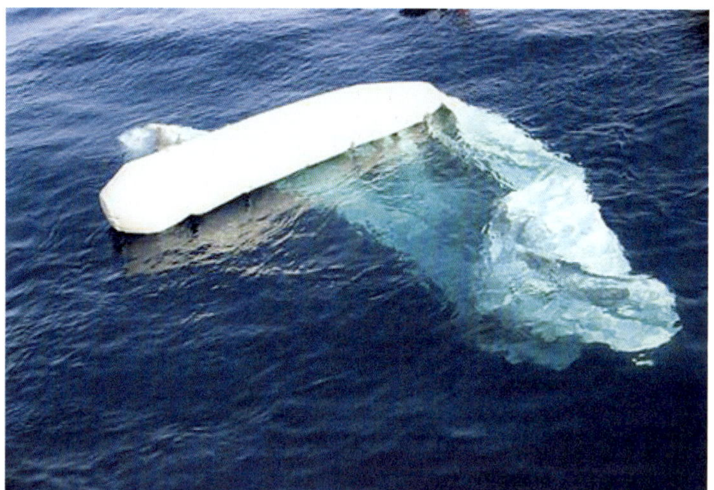

← HELLER: I want to show you one more image, if you don't mind, which is an image from just the other day (April 30, 2017). It is an image that struck me.

Q: It's a rubber boat.

HELLER: It is what's left of a rubber boat. It's an image that the small NGO vessel *Jugend rettet* took when it arrived on location. The crew had been searching for this boat since the preceding evening and in the early morning they discovered what was left of it and four bodies drifting. Now, bearing in mind that these boats carry an average of between a hundred and a hundred and fifty people, and which transport sometimes as many as two hundred, we can consider predict that more than a hundred people vanished at sea in this incident. Their deaths went unnoticed—only the *traces* of this event, recorded by the NGO, allow us to imagine what happened. But there is an extraordinary gap between the image's qualities and the event it contains traces of. This image itself is extraordinarily calm, the sea is very calm, the colors are beautiful … this turquoise. If you look at it from a distance, at first you might think it is a whale or a dolphin. It has a strange shape that you cannot immediately identify. So you have this initial sort of aesthetic and sense-oriented impression of the image. Of course, when you read the caption to the image, you realize there is a horrific story connected with the boat that the image documents. There is something in this opposition that makes the image escape the filters that are at work when we look at stereotypical images, which are identified at first glance and discarded. Here the strangeness of the image forces us to look closer, and the gap between what the image shows and the events it bears the traces of forces us to suddenly *imagine* the horrific event that unfolded. Despite our capacity to monitor the sea having evolved by leaps and bounds—both through the physical presence of actors at sea and through various aesthetic practices—as long as we have this regime of illegalization, we will have cases of death at sea. Some we are

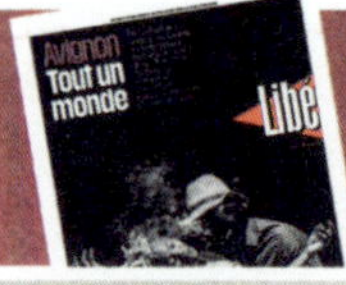

FESTIVAL D'AVIGNON
Sélection, reportages... 16 pages spéciales théâtre   CAHIER CENTRAL

Libération

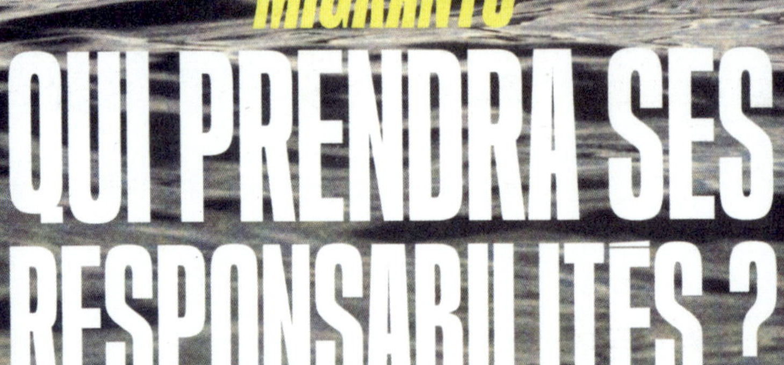

Au moins 2 200 personnes qui tentaient de rallier l'Europe ont disparu en Méditerranée depuis le début de l'année. En première ligne, Rome appelle ses partenaires, réunis ce jeudi à Tallinn, à se montrer enfin à la hauteur. **PAGES 2-5**

Le corps d'une femme, à une trentaine de kilomètres des côtes libyennes, le 21 juin. PHOTO EMILIO MORENATTI. AP

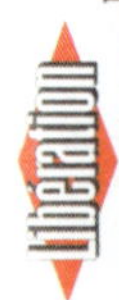

able to document, others go absolutely unremarked. The only trace they leave is that of a haunting absence for their friends and families. Currently, states are seeking to get rid of civilian rescue and oversight by criminalizing NGOs, as we have shown in our "Blaming the Rescuers" report.[10] The *Jugend rettet* vessel was actually seized on August 2 on charges of complicity with "illegal migration." I fear that with the current wave of NGO criminalization more deaths will go unnoticed.

Q: Images of deaths … Would it change anything if we could see them in the media? The problem I see is that the dead bodies are at the bottom of the sea. We have lost all connection with the number of people who have lost their lives because they are not visible any more. Where are these people?

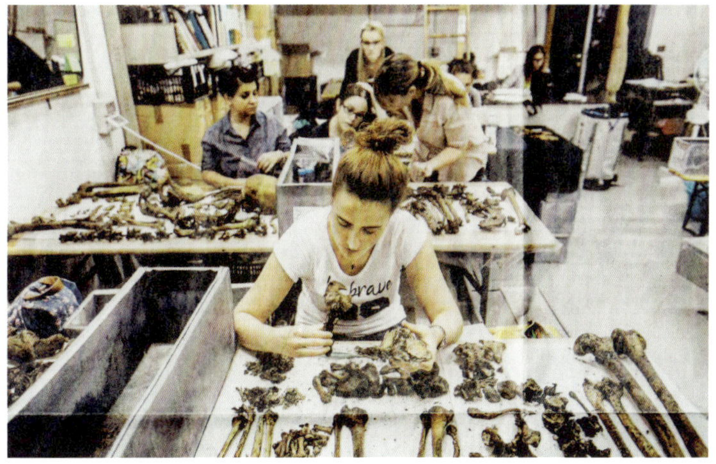

← *This is one image I found a couple of months ago in the supplement of* The New York Times International Edition Weekly, *where Italian students of archaeology in Milan are examining bones. The picture was taken in Labanof, the laboratory in Milan for forensic anthropology and odontology. Later I figured out that the caption to the photo was a bit misleading but it was one of the few images I've seen where somebody took an interest in the dead and unknown people drowned in the Mediterranean. Visual records like this are practically nonexistent.*

HELLER: It's a difficult question. I would argue for several reasons that it is not just a matter of the number of images of dead bodies. One reason is that images of migration in the mainstream press tend to be extraordinarily stereotypical, as we discussed earlier. Most photographs used to illustrate boat migration are "floating images," constantly reused precisely because they need to be immediately understood by the mainstream press's readership. However, what happens with a stereotypical image? What happens with it is that it is pre-understood. Another reason is that the border spectacle often naturalizes the conditions endured by migrants and dehumanizes the people involved, which also makes empathy with them very difficult. As a result, the reality that is portrayed in the mainstream press doesn't "hit me." So the simple presence of deaths in the media is not enough for us to truly encounter the reality of these deaths intellectually and emotionally. Finally, today we are seeing a proliferation of new levels of violence, and not only in relation to migration. Like in a boxing match, when you take one punch, it hurts, but you try to fight back. But if you take fifteen, twenty, you start to feel numb, you don't even know where to look any more. So it's not just a matter of quantity; we are dealing with stereotypicality, naturalization, and dehumanization, and the numbness that can result from the exposure to violence. All of which, in different ways, act as intellectual and emotional barriers to possible empathy with migrants. We can see these barriers at work in our own subjectivity. I work on this subject all day, every day, and I don't cry every time I see an image relating to migrant deaths. So what is needed are strategies of *rupture*, that allow a viewer to suddenly realize the reality of the violence borders have created and to feel empathy and commonality with the condition of migrants.

Q: Can you give us an example?
HELLER: One of my favorite "migration films"—listen up—is a part of the *Tatort* TV program. The *Tatort* that showed the story of a young migrant from Togo who had lost her child during the crossing, and her child had been let go in the water by one of the border guards. The morther survives the crossing and decides to find and take revenge on the guard, whom she blames for the loss of her child. You are a young mother, I'm a young father. If something like that happens to my child—I don't even want to start thinking about that—but what will I want? I may also want revenge. It is certainly an affect I can relate to. Paradox-ically, the desire for revenge is something that I can relate to much more than victimhood. And suddenly, the death of this woman's child touches me deeply, creates what we might call an *empathic rupture*. But I think it is very personal. It can de-pend on your experience, your environment, or a particular mom-ent in your life that makes you suddenly perceptive.

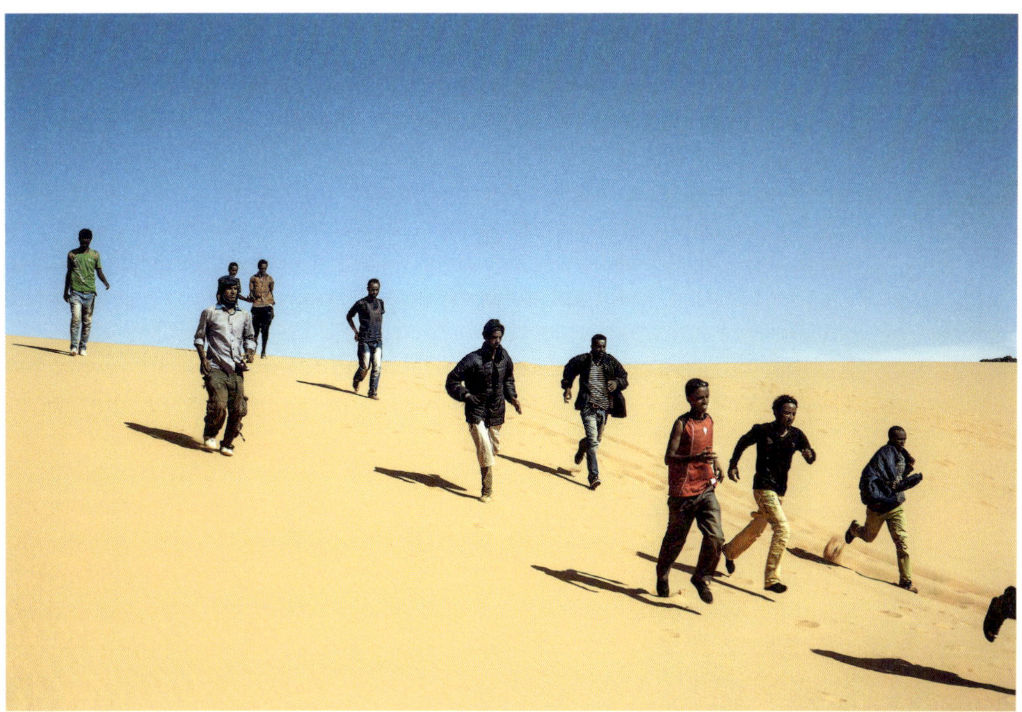

↑   Q: *This is an image that we got from Contrasto. We went to the biggest Italian photo agency in Rome. The director of Contrasto showed this image to us as another type of picture. Have you seen it before?*

HELLER: This specific picture? No, but do you mind if I look a bit closer? (Brings the computer closer to his eyes. Looks at the image) I'm curious where it is, as I cannot really identify it. The people are visibly running down a sand dune. A sand dune, which has tracks on it in what seems to be a desert area, but which is nonetheless traveled. Then those rocks. It's not quite clear what those rocks are. They could be the beginning of a coast-line—in some areas sand dunes almost meet the coast. So this is a bit mysterious for me. Also, what are the people in the image doing? They seem to be running? But it is unclear from what, or even if they are in danger. Just like this it's very banal. I think, in fact, that banality is something that I want to foreground in strategies of representing migration, precisely for the reasons we were talking about. Migration represented as a threat or as victimhood is always something exceptional, right? And our lives are mostly banal. You and me, we are not living that level of exceptionality. We are not embarking on a boat and risking our lives to seek a better life. Just think of what migrants do, with the aim of changing their lives for the better: they are ready to risk their lives. Most of us are barely capable of changing our habits or learning a new language. Neither are we subjected to the same level of arbitrary state violence. So we can relate much more to banality and simple things like that than to exception-ality. I want to give you another example. Another photographer

I met, Jörg Brüggemann, took a photo of a Syrian swimming on a beach in Greece with a lifejacket and smiling. He had arrived a day or so before and now he was using his lifejacket to have a great time at the beach. It's like if you are a migrant you can't enjoy swimming, right? In the imagined realm of migration, it is not possible, because you are reduced to this role as a victim. And so this banality, the simple joy of swimming that we all experience, suddenly connects you in a way that the exception does not. I think that these different and more subtle strategies of representation are extremely important. However, one question that we need to keep in mind and reflect on critically is, to whom are these images addressed? With what assumptions? That they should spur European citizens on to understand and reject the horrendous consequences of the European border regime so that they can push their politicians to formulate more open and progressive policies? The connections in this sequence that are often assumed are far from evident. We also risk maintaining an assumption that is at the core of our current migration regime: that it is for (European) states to decide if migrants do or do not have the right to move across borders. There is a nondemocratic dimension at the heart of all contemporary migration policies.

Q: What other urgent "strategies of rupture" might there be that you are considering for the near future?

HELLER: Today, as states increase their levels of violence in the desperate attempt to close off the Mediterranean once again, continuing to develop strategies to enable civilians to exercise the right to watch the sea and both shores of the Mediterranean remains essential. However, one great challenge I think today is to articulate the analysis of practices and accounting for specific experiences with broader global conditions. At times I am afraid that , even if we are critical of state policies, by … looking up close at the border regime, at policies and practices of the control of practices—and the migrant deaths that are the consequence of this—we risk reproducing the obfuscation of the broader systemic conditions that shape both migration and borders, which is one of the outcomes of the border spectacle. We risk losing sight of the "bigger picture."

The violence of borders cannot only be understood in terms of human suffering and deaths. There is a fundamental political injustice and violence that is perpetrated by allowing some people to travel while denying movement to others, an injustice that is both the outcome of and reproduces the fundamental inequality of the world in which we live. Conversely, even if each experience is irreducible, we can see migrants from the global South crossing borders that are denied to them as exercising their freedom and equality, demanding through their movement access to the rights and social goods from which citizens of the global North benefit—even if they are increasingly threatened today. Global domination and the resistance to it are at stake in the current *mobility conflict* unfolding in the Mediterranean.

When I say that we risk losing sight of this bigger picture, I am not advocating replacing the analysis of practices and strategies that seek to register lived experience with a grand analysis of global capitalism—rather, I am in favor of a process of *articulation*. A kind of poly-scalar and poly-temporal analysis and aesthetics is something I hope to experiment with in the future.

1   A more detailed account of this shift can be found in Charles Heller, *"Liquid Trajectories: Documenting Illegalised Migration and the Violence of Borders"* (doctoral thesis, Goldsmiths, University of London, 2015). Available at: http://research.gold.ac.uk/15069/.

2   Ariella Azoulay, "What Is a Photograph? What Is Photography?" *Philosophy of Photography* 1, no. 1 (2010): pp. 9–13.

3   Hito Steyerl, *The Wretched of the Screen* (Berlin: Sternberg Press, 2013), p. 171.

4   Nicholas de Genova, "Spectacles of Migrant 'Illegality': The Scene of Exclusion, the Obscene of Inclusion," *Ethnic and Racial Studies* 36, no. 7 (2013): 1180–1198.

5   Karin Knorr Cetina, "The Synthetic Situation: Interactionism for a Global World," *Symbolic Interaction* 32, no. 1 (2009): pp. 61–87.

6   Lorenzo Pezzani and Charles Heller, "A Disobedient Gaze: Strategic Interventions in the Knowledge(s) of Maritime Borders,' *Postcolonial Studies* 16, no. 3 (2013): pp. 289–98, here: p. 294, emphasis in original.

7   William Walters, "Foucault and Frontiers: Notes on the Birth of the Humanitarian Border," in *Governmentality: Current Issues and Future Challenges*, ed. Ulrich Bröckling, Susanne Krasmann, and Thomas Lemke (New York: Routledge, 2013).

8   "Report," *Death by Rescue*, accessed August 31, 2017, https://deathbyrescue.org/report/.

9   Charles Heller, Lorenzo Pezzani, and Maurice Stierl, "Disobedient Sensing and Border Struggles at the Maritime Frontier of Europe," *Spheres* (June 2017). Available at: http://spheres-journal.org/disobedient-sensing-and-border-struggles-at-the-maritime-frontier-of-europe/.

10   "Report," *Blaming the Rescuers*, accessed August 31, 2017, https://blamingtherescuers.org/report/.

TIME

SAVED.

One week aboard a
refugee rescue ship

BY ARYN BAKER

Migrants are pulled
from a sinking wooden
boat off the coast of
Libya on Aug. 21
Photograph by
Lynsey Addario

time.com

ANIMALS AND HUMAN BEINGS

BY EMILIE JOSSO

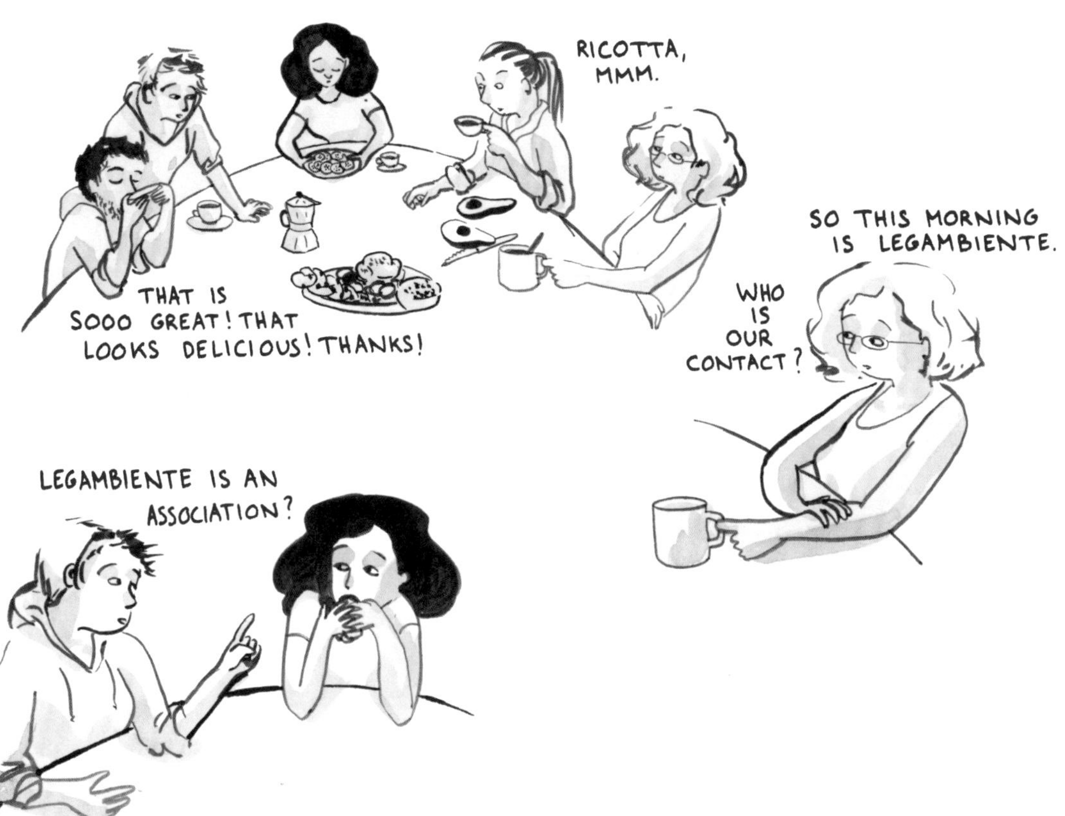

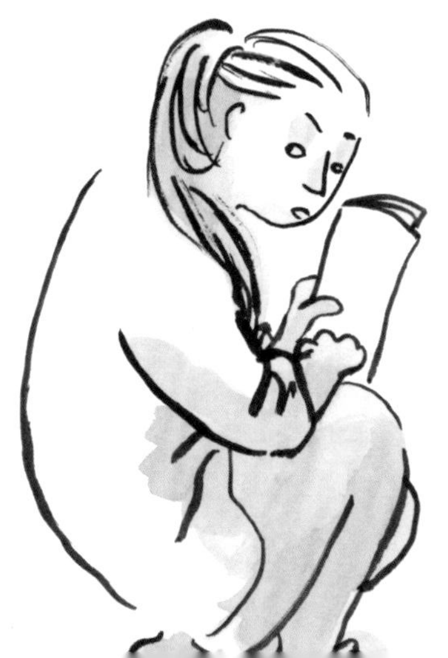

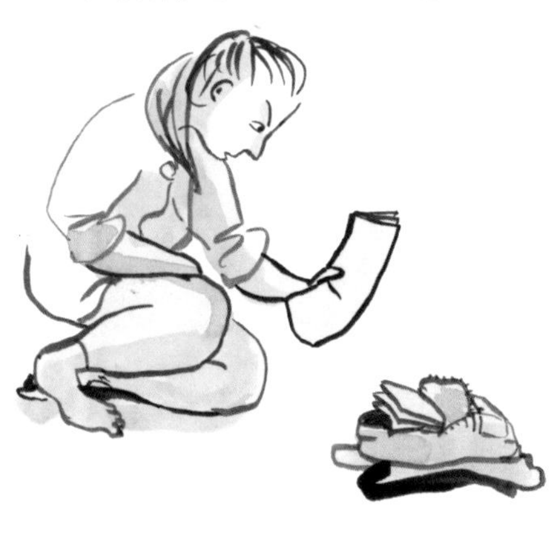

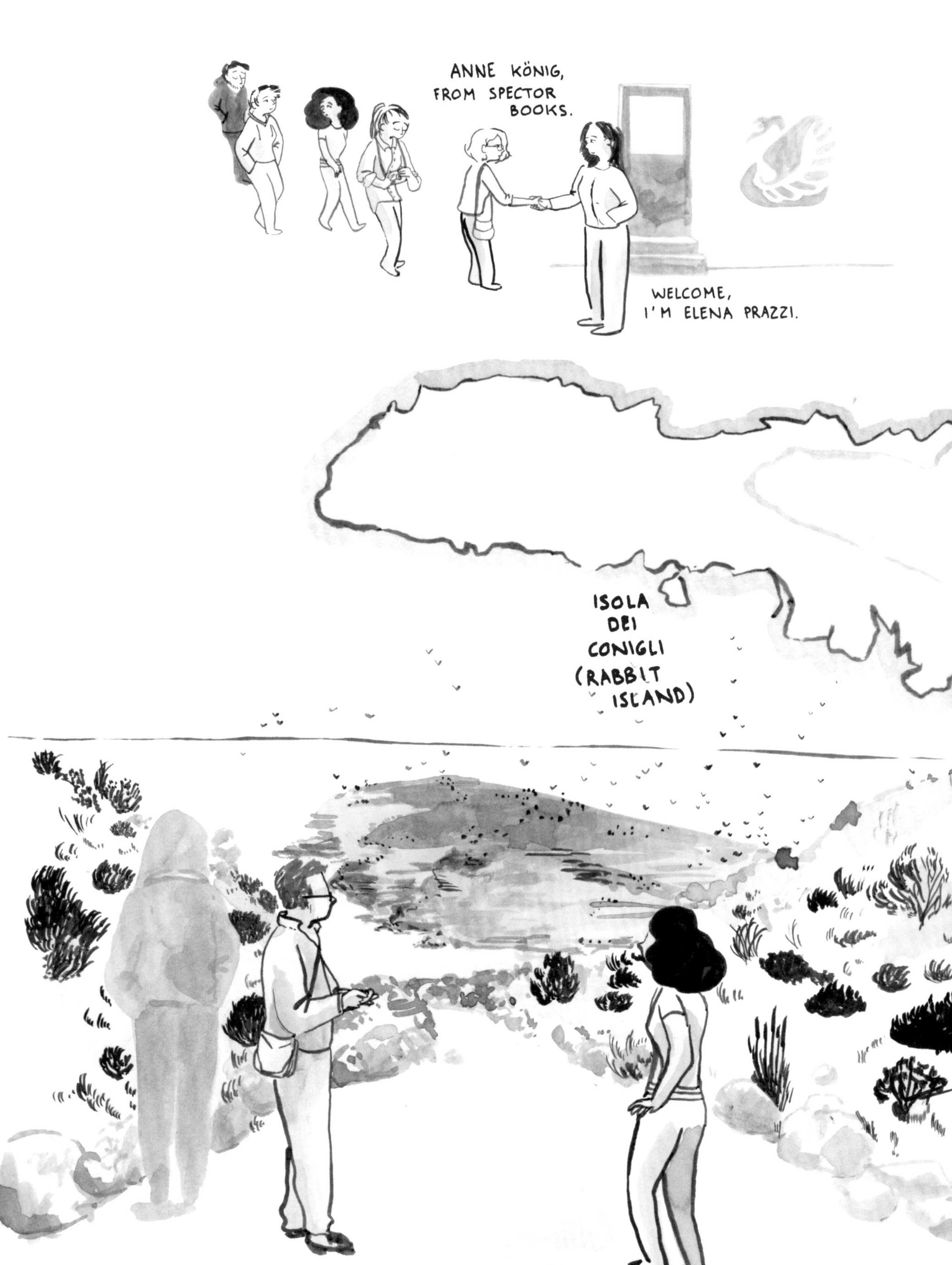

ANNE KÖNIG,
FROM SPECTOR
BOOKS.

WELCOME,
I'M ELENA PRAZZI.

ISOLA
DEI
CONIGLI
(RABBIT
ISLAND)

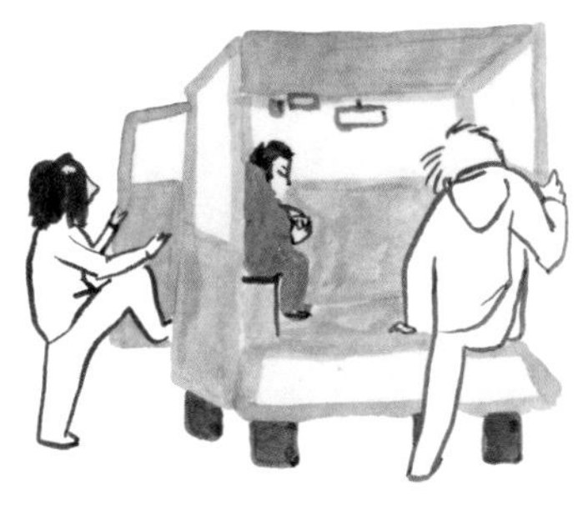

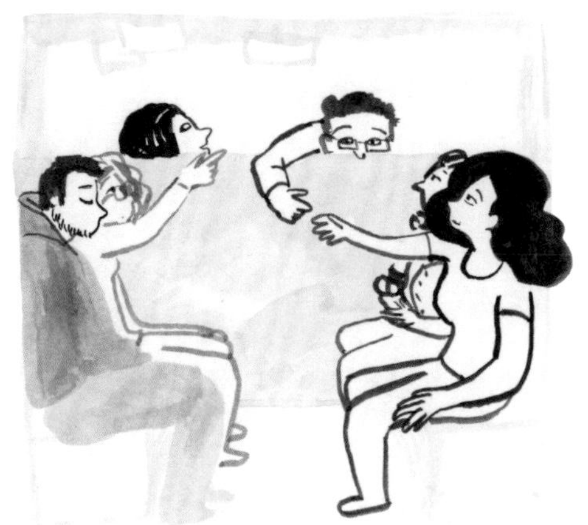

THIS IS BEPPINO.
HE ALSO WORKS
FOR LEGAMBIENTE.

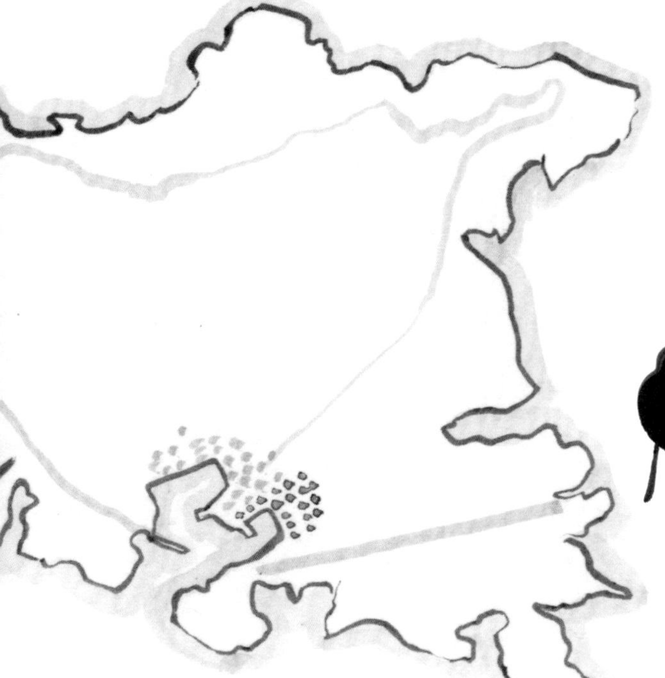

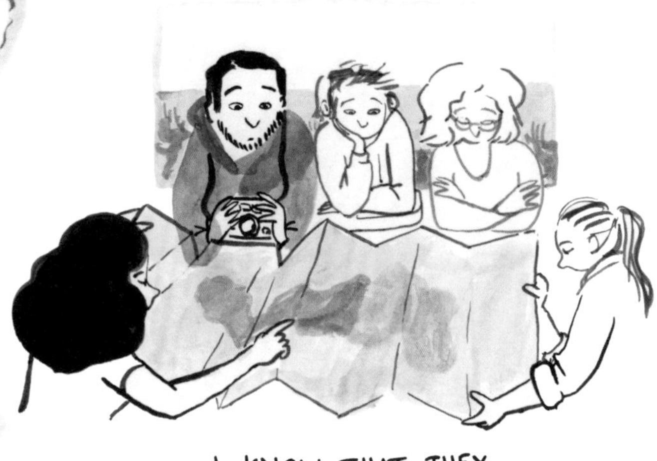

I KNOW THAT THEY
RECULTIVATED A WHOLE AREA,
THE BEACH AND ALL AROUND.

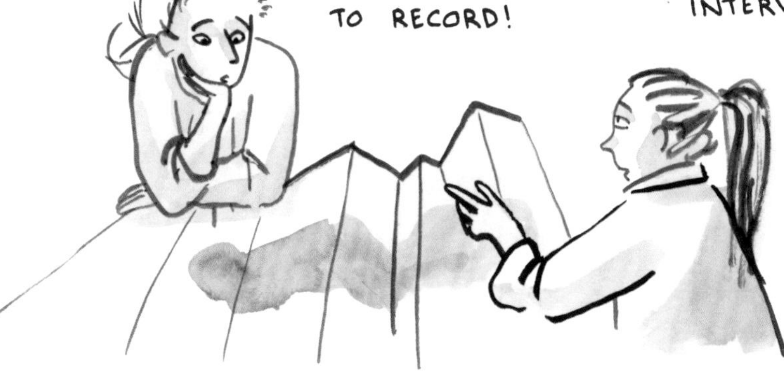

OH IT'S WINDY.
IT WON'T BE EASY
TO RECORD!
THAT'S WHERE WE
ARE GOING. I THINK
SHE PLANS TO DO THE
INTERVIEW OUTSIDE.

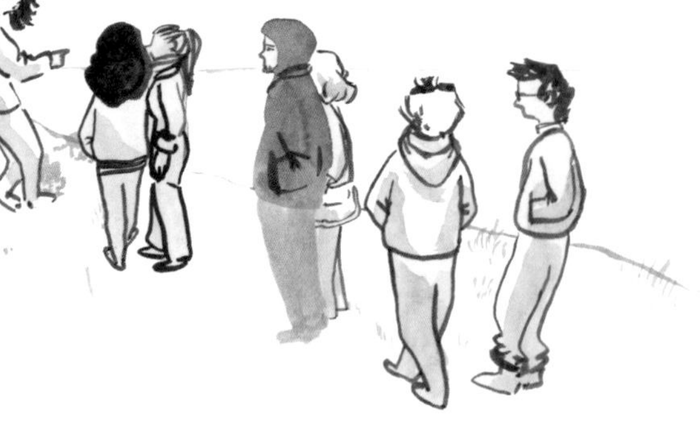

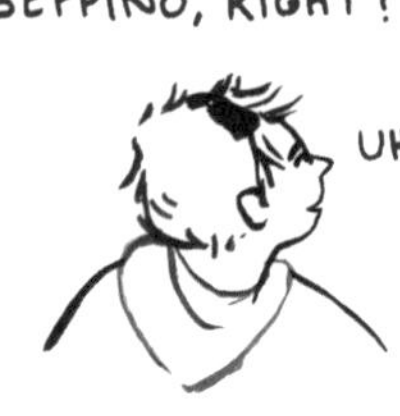

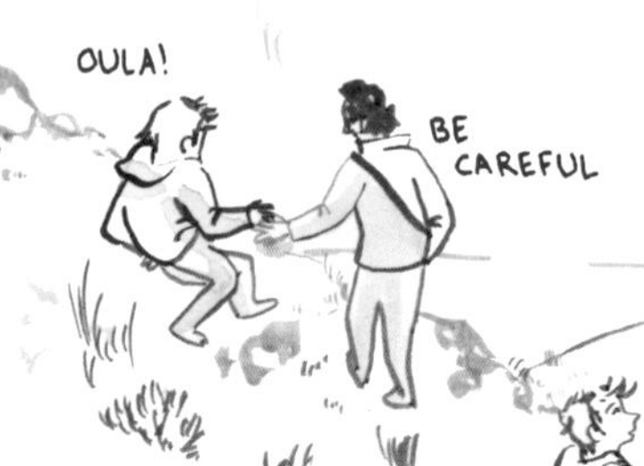

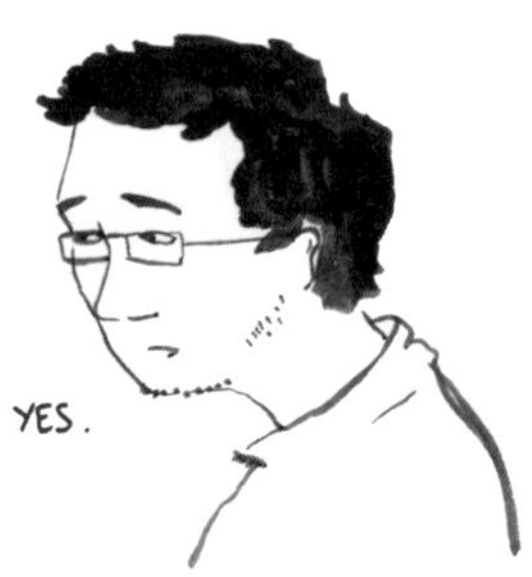

WHAT'S IT LIKE GROWING UP HERE?

WELL, YOU KNOW, THERE WAS ONLY ONE CAR
ON THE ISLAND, AND NO ROAD... IT'S SO SMALL!
I WANTED TO LIVE, DISCOVER, EXPLORE
THE ROAD!

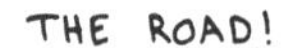

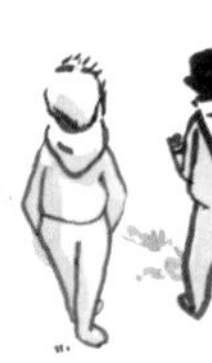

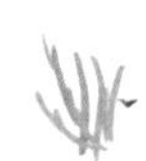

I FELT TRAPPED!

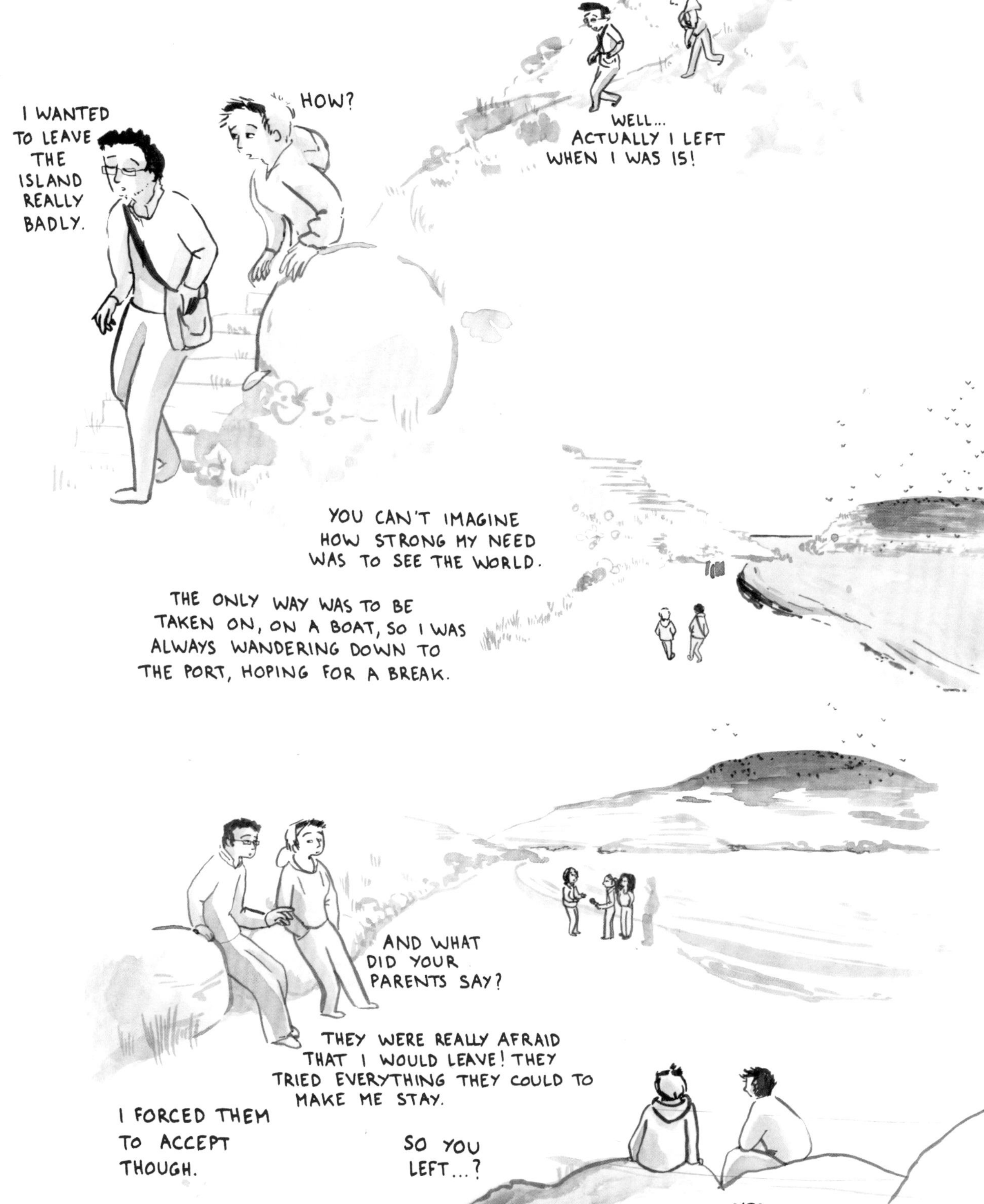
BUT YOU ARE STILL HERE...
WELL... ACTUALLY I LEFT WHEN I WAS 15!
HOW?
I WANTED TO LEAVE THE ISLAND REALLY BADLY.
YOU CAN'T IMAGINE HOW STRONG MY NEED WAS TO SEE THE WORLD.
THE ONLY WAY WAS TO BE TAKEN ON, ON A BOAT, SO I WAS ALWAYS WANDERING DOWN TO THE PORT, HOPING FOR A BREAK.
AND WHAT DID YOUR PARENTS SAY?
THEY WERE REALLY AFRAID THAT I WOULD LEAVE! THEY TRIED EVERYTHING THEY COULD TO MAKE ME STAY.
I FORCED THEM TO ACCEPT THOUGH.
SO YOU LEFT...?
YES. I GOT A JOB ON A BIG FISHING BOAT.

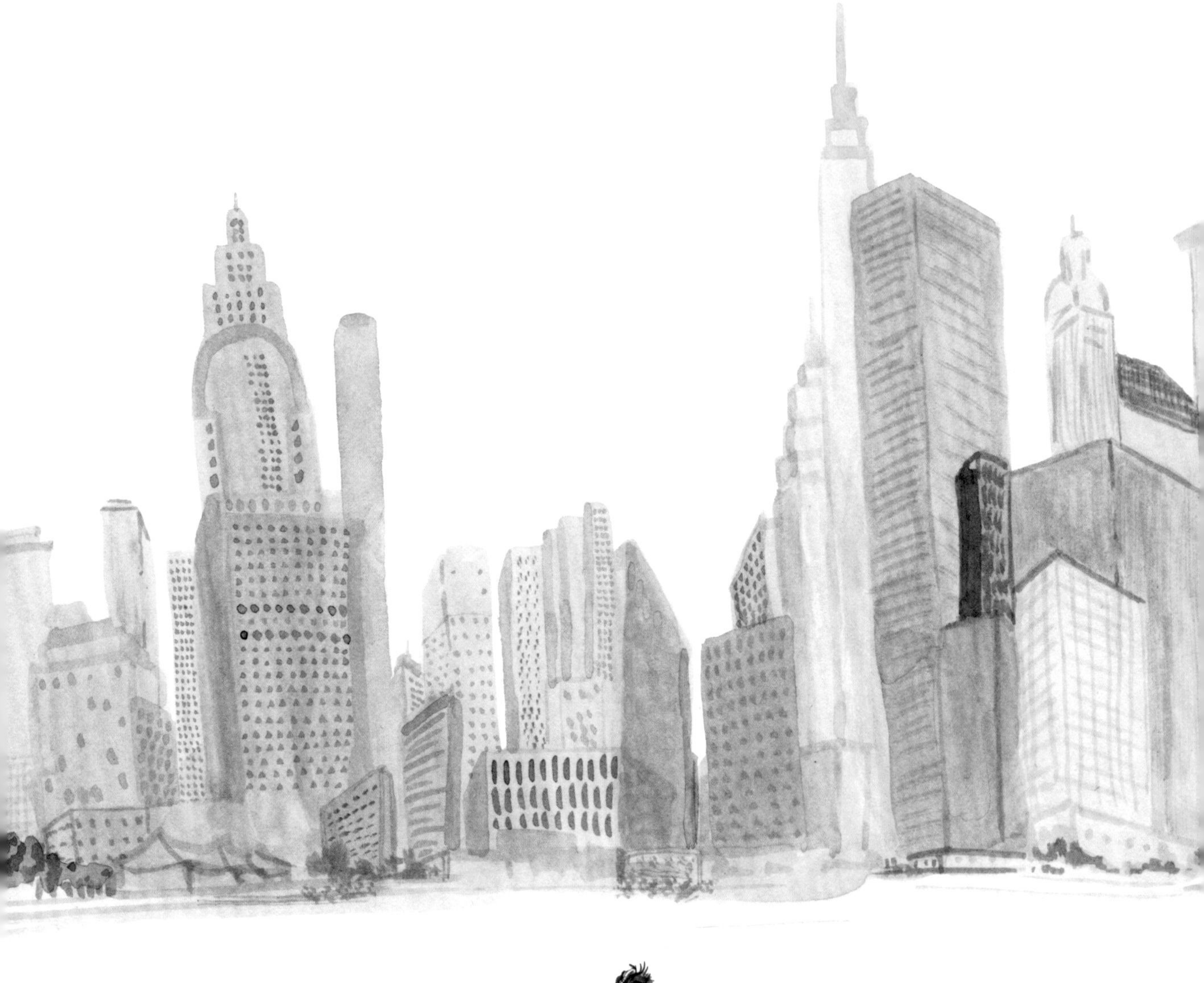

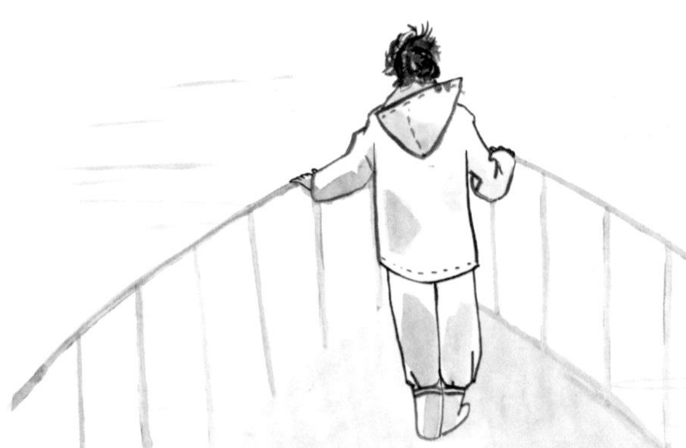

OUR FIRST PORT, AFTER A FEW MONTHS FISHING IN THE NORTH ATLANTIC, WAS NEW YORK ...

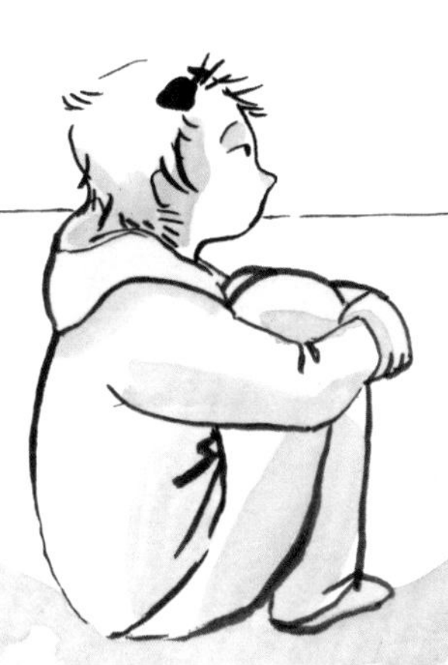
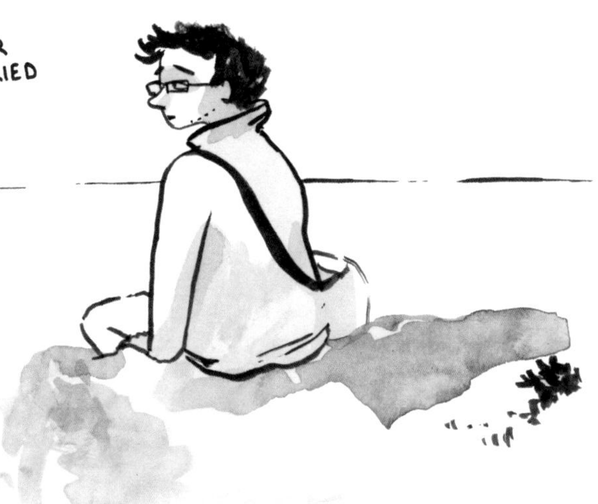

BUT I CAME BACK AFTER THREE YEARS. I GOT MARRIED AND STARTED MY OWN FAMILY HERE.

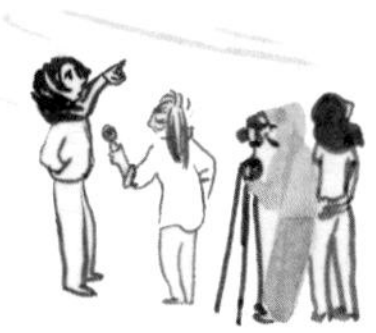

AND YOU NEVER LEFT AGAIN?
JUST ONCE TO ROME TO VISIT THE FAMILY. AND ONCE TO PALERMO TO TAKE MY MOTHER TO HOSPITAL.

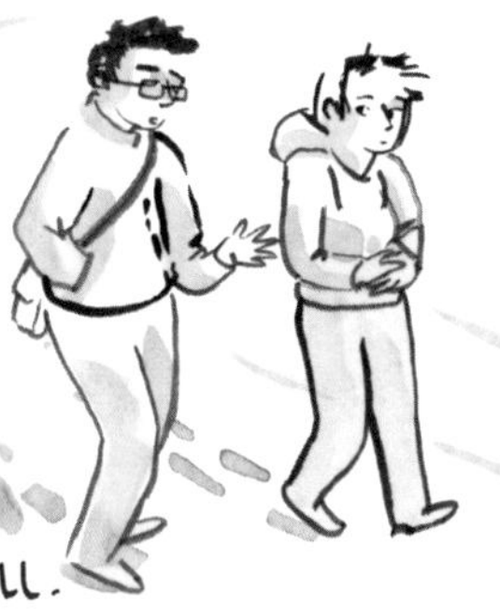

WHEN I WAS THERE, I WAS TOLD I COULD HAVE LUNCH IN THE NEXT MALL. I PREFERRED TO WALK FOR HALF AN HOUR INSTEAD OF GOING INTO THE MALL.
I'VE NEVER BEEN TO A COMMERCIAL CENTER IN MY WHOLE LIFE!

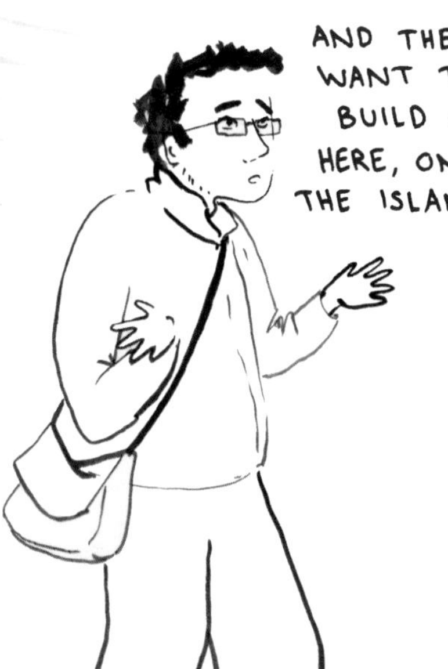

AND THEY WANT TO BUILD ONE HERE, ON THE ISLAND!

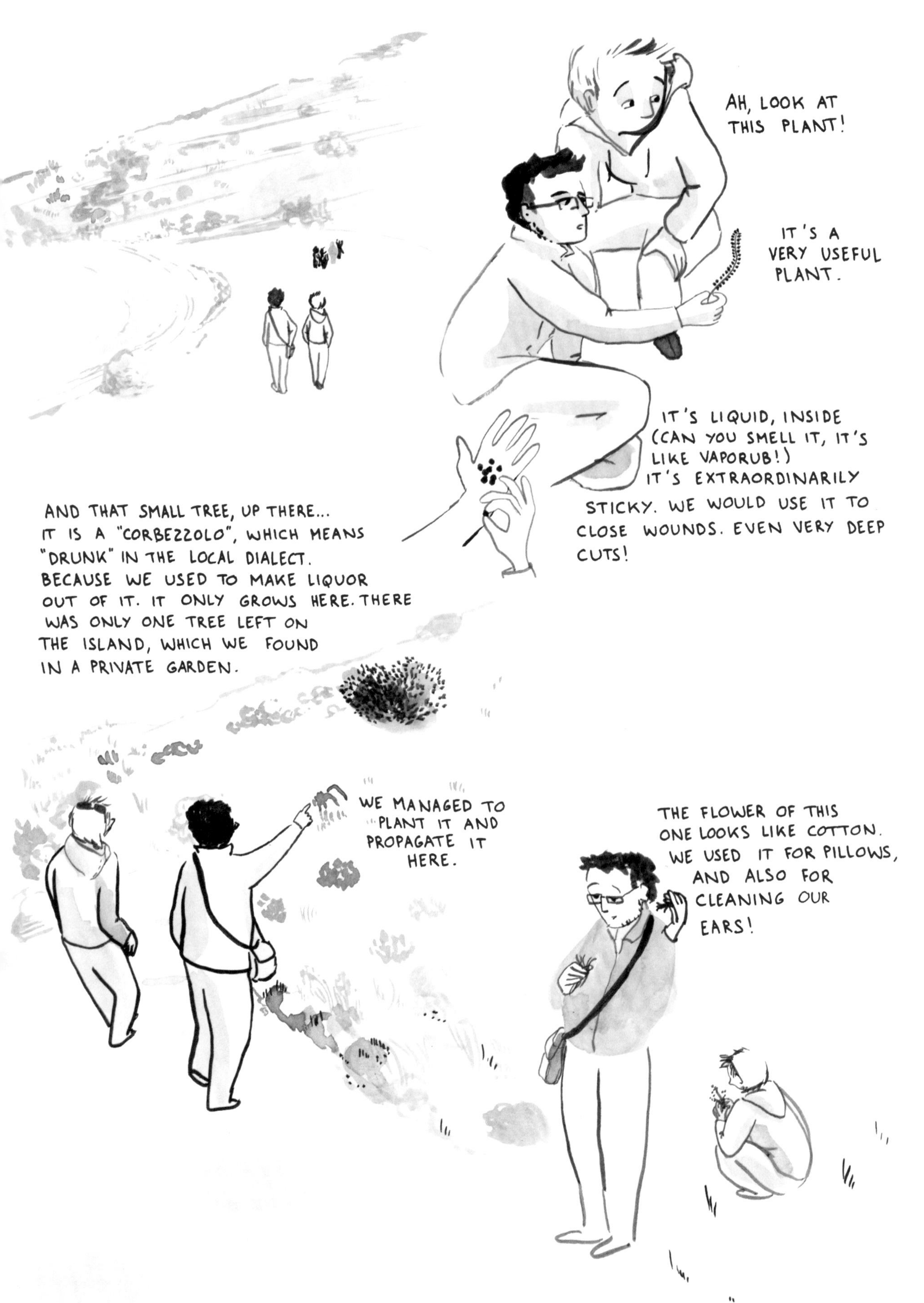

AH, LOOK AT THIS PLANT!
IT'S A VERY USEFUL PLANT.
IT'S LIQUID, INSIDE (CAN YOU SMELL IT, IT'S LIKE VAPORUB!) IT'S EXTRAORDINARILY STICKY. WE WOULD USE IT TO CLOSE WOUNDS. EVEN VERY DEEP CUTS!
AND THAT SMALL TREE, UP THERE... IT IS A "CORBEZZOLO", WHICH MEANS "DRUNK" IN THE LOCAL DIALECT. BECAUSE WE USED TO MAKE LIQUOR OUT OF IT. IT ONLY GROWS HERE. THERE WAS ONLY ONE TREE LEFT ON THE ISLAND, WHICH WE FOUND IN A PRIVATE GARDEN.
WE MANAGED TO PLANT IT AND PROPAGATE IT HERE.
THE FLOWER OF THIS ONE LOOKS LIKE COTTON. WE USED IT FOR PILLOWS, AND ALSO FOR CLEANING OUR EARS!

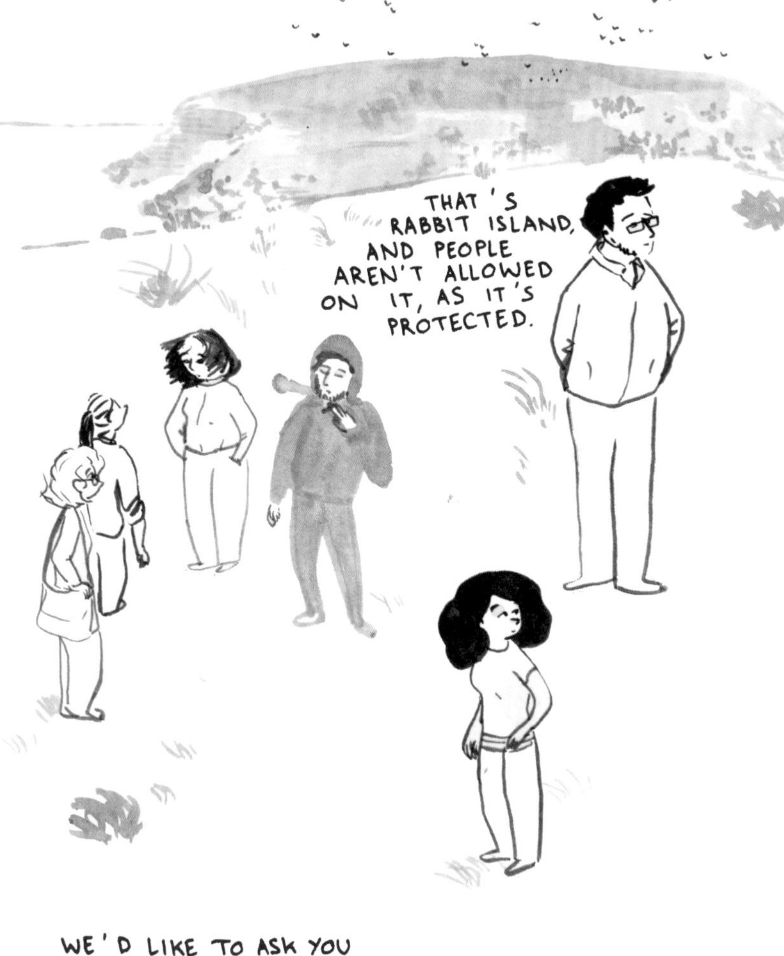

IT'S FASCINATING TO SEE AND HEAR SO MANY BIRDS!
IS IT POSSIBLE TO GO TO THE ISLAND?
THAT'S RABBIT ISLAND, AND PEOPLE AREN'T ALLOWED ON IT, AS IT'S PROTECTED.

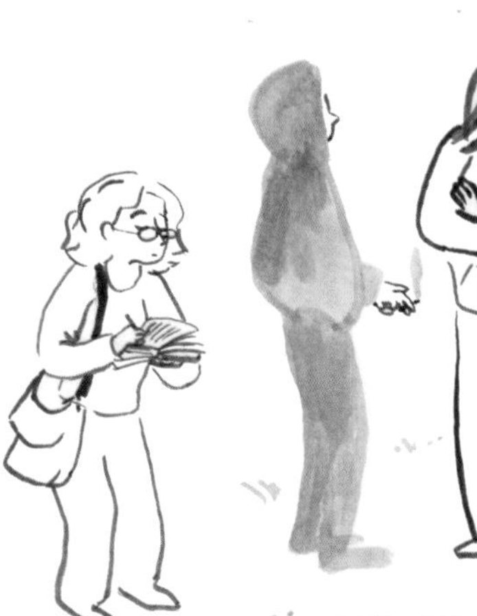

WE'D LIKE TO ASK YOU A QUESTION ABOUT THE MAYOR, GIUSI NICOLINI.

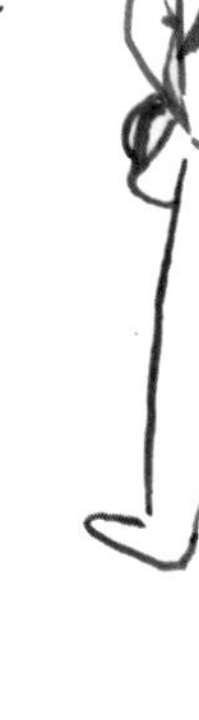

SURE! BEPPINO, PLEASE COME HERE, THEY'RE ASKING ABOUT GIUSI!
YES, BECAUSE WE'VE HEARD VERY DIFFERENT OPINIONS ABOUT HER...

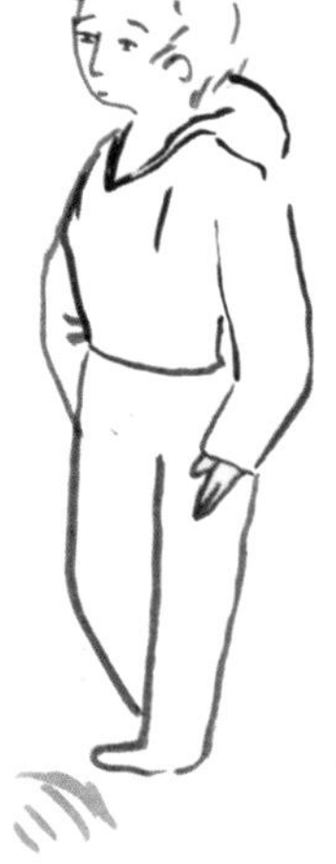

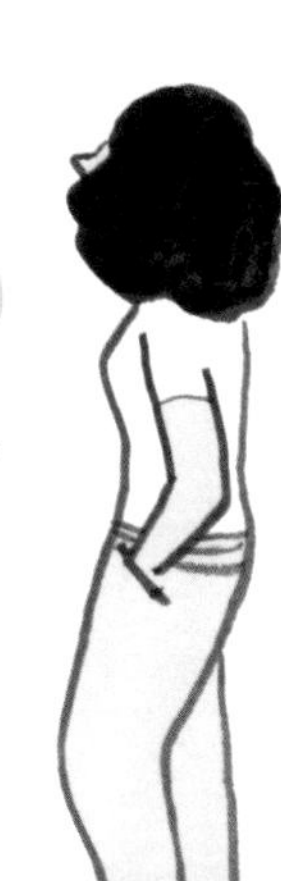

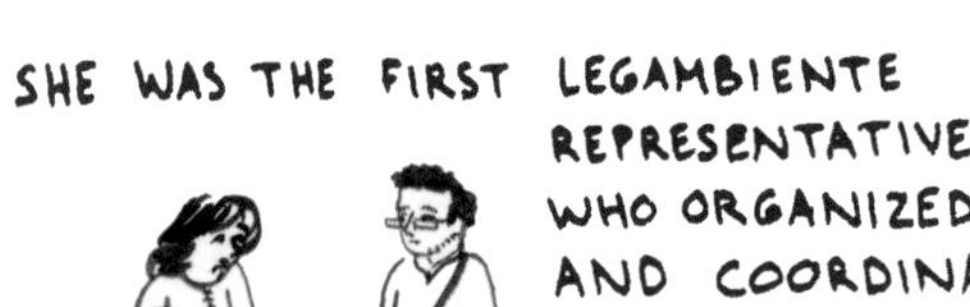

SHE WAS THE FIRST LEGAMBIENTE
REPRESENTATIVE
WHO ORGANIZED
AND COORDINATED
THE ENVIRONMENTAL
RECOVERY OPERATIONS.

SHE HAD DONE SO MUCH
FOR THIS PLACE, STUDYING AND
CONDEMNING THE TERRIBLE
CONDITIONS THAT USED TO PLAGUE
THE WHOLE AREA.

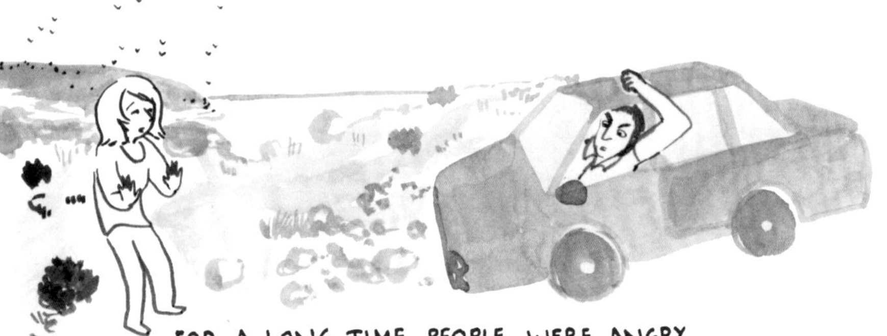

FOR A LONG TIME PEOPLE WERE ANGRY
BECAUSE THEY WERE USED TO USING THE BEACH
IN A CERTAIN WAY.

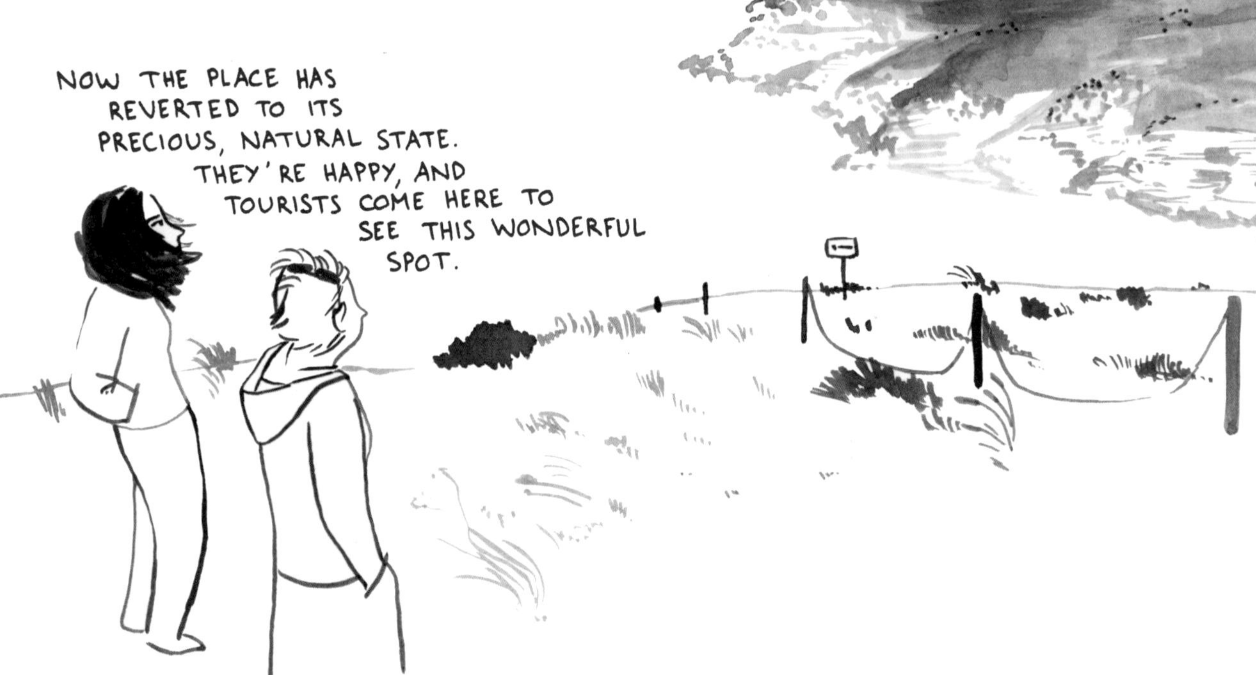

NOW THE PLACE HAS
REVERTED TO ITS
PRECIOUS, NATURAL STATE.
THEY'RE HAPPY, AND
TOURISTS COME HERE TO
SEE THIS WONDERFUL
SPOT.

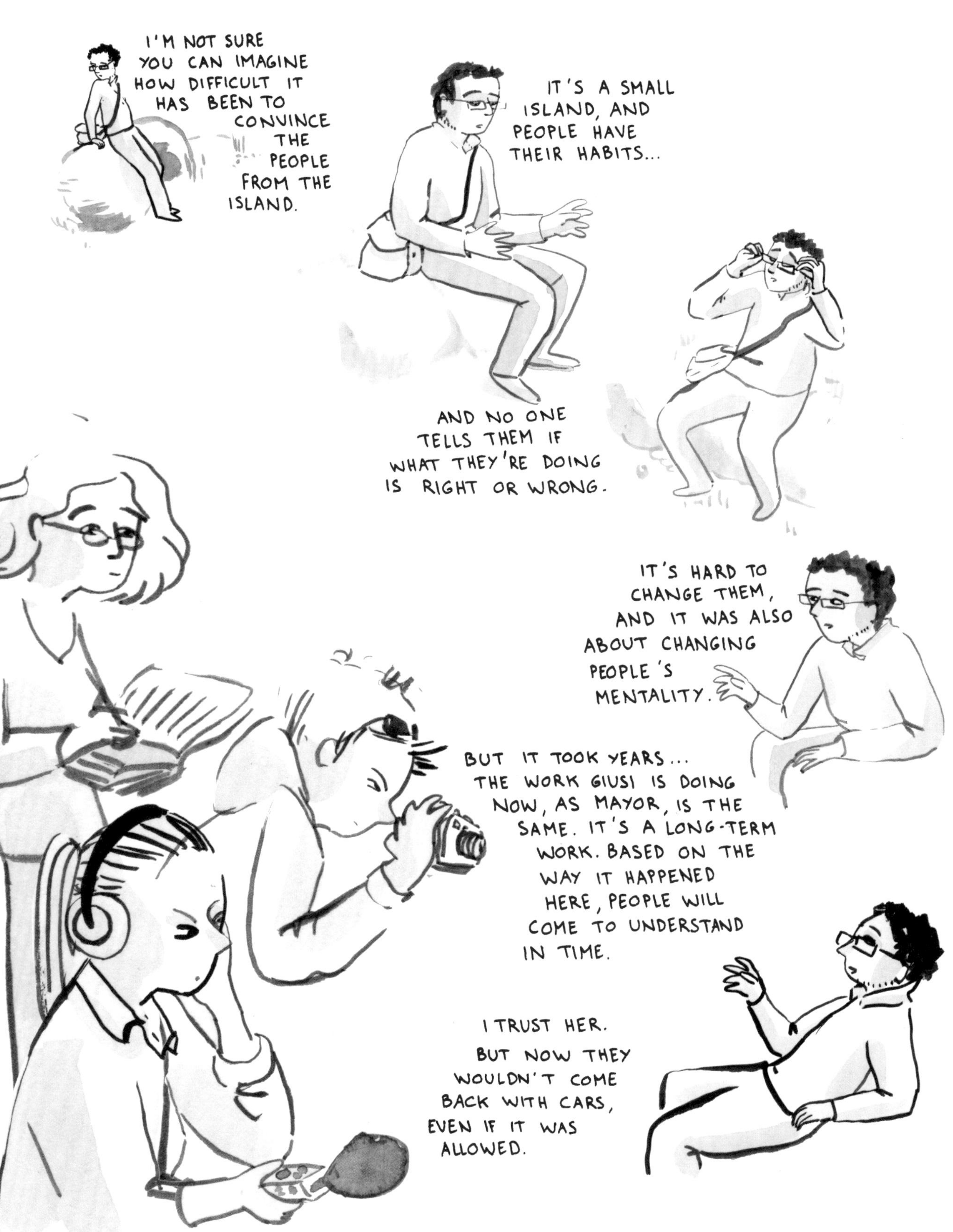
I'M NOT SURE YOU CAN IMAGINE HOW DIFFICULT IT HAS BEEN TO CONVINCE THE PEOPLE FROM THE ISLAND.
IT'S A SMALL ISLAND, AND PEOPLE HAVE THEIR HABITS...
AND NO ONE TELLS THEM IF WHAT THEY'RE DOING IS RIGHT OR WRONG.
IT'S HARD TO CHANGE THEM, AND IT WAS ALSO ABOUT CHANGING PEOPLE'S MENTALITY.
BUT IT TOOK YEARS... THE WORK GIUSI IS DOING NOW, AS MAYOR, IS THE SAME. IT'S A LONG-TERM WORK. BASED ON THE WAY IT HAPPENED HERE, PEOPLE WILL COME TO UNDERSTAND IN TIME.
I TRUST HER.
BUT NOW THEY WOULDN'T COME BACK WITH CARS, EVEN IF IT WAS ALLOWED.

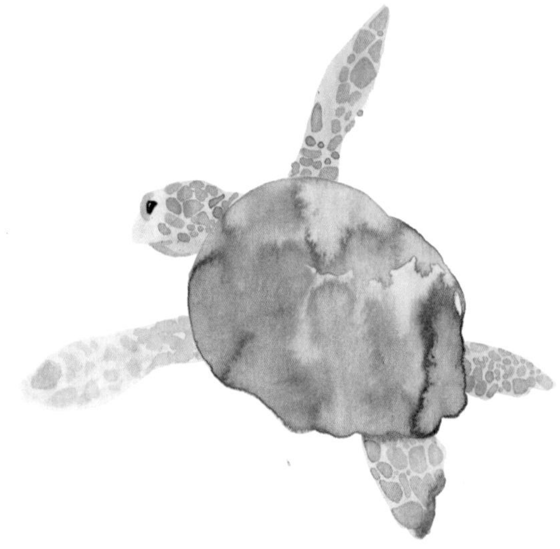

Migration, Protection, and Tourism

Elena Prazzi explains her work on Lampedusa for Legambiente

The Italian biologist Elena Prazzi works as the coordinator of Legambiente, a non-profit association whose mission is to make environmental culture the center of development. Legambiente's main activity on Lampedusa is taking care of the island's nature reserve. The reserve was established in 1996 and is managed by the municipality of Sicily. Elena Prazzi moved from North Italy to Lampedusa a couple of years ago. The Migrant Image Research Group met her there at Rabbit Beach in 2016. The interview was conducted by Elisa Calore and Anne König.

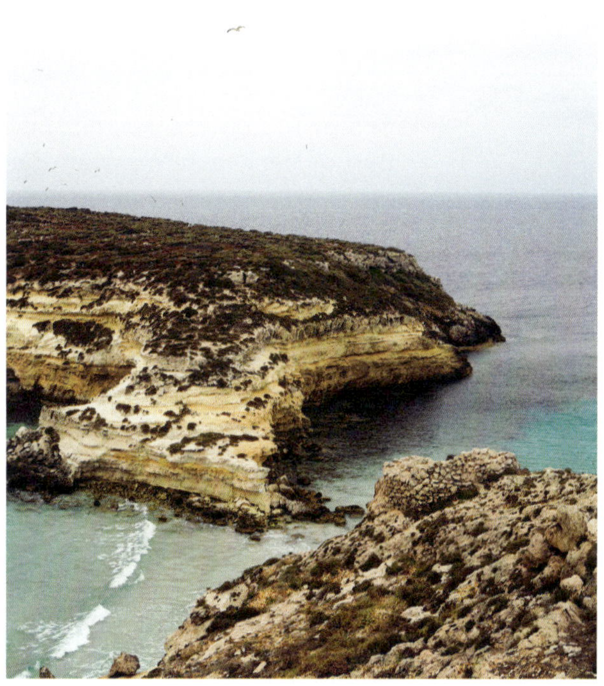

Q: *Can you tell us something about the place where we are today—Spiaggia dei Conigli?*
PRAZZI: Lampedusa has 360 hectares of coastline, but the most famous beach is Rabbit Beach, as it is popularly known here. According to the legend, the area was called "Rabbit" in

reference to the isthmus that connects the tiny Rabbit Island to the main island. *Rabit* in Arabic means "link, something that connects." This name was marked incorrectly on a map by Captain Smith and then translated from English instead of Arabic.

Q: What did Legambiente do for the reserve?

PRAZZI: Lampedusa primarily preserves endemic species—that is, species of local flora and fauna, most of them North African species. It is a rich and precious place that has to be protected.

Legambiente conducted several environmental recovery operations because before the reserve was established, the island was suffering severely degraded conditions.

Roads were opened illegally to reach the sea, paying no attention to the morphological characteristics of the place and destroying it. Previously, motor vehicles could access the beach, and, as a result, a lot of rocks, debris, and other foreign matter fell into the water, generating erosion and disturbing animals, especially turtles, whose egg deposition was affected.

After the reserve was established, motorized vehicles were forbidden. Legambiente undertook natural engineering interventions to restore the natural state of the place by organizing seed collection campaigns for native vegetation: seeds were cultivated in greenhouses and then more than ten thousand seedlings were planted on site. These operations stopped the rockfall and saved the beach.

Moreover, we started to control access to the beach: by night nobody is allowed to enter so that turtles can depose their eggs in peace. During the there is a strict tally of toys, deckchairs, and beach umbrellas and they are only allowed on a small part of the beach. We want the beach to retain its natural quality.

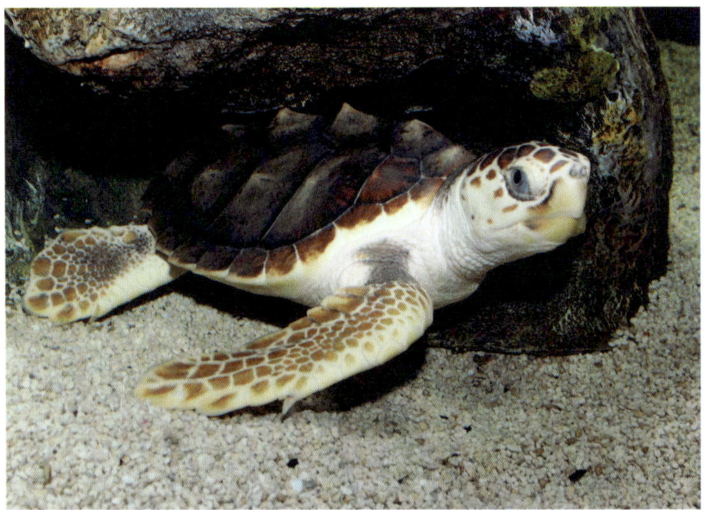

← *Q: You spoke about the turtle. Why?*

PRAZZI: In this place the loggerhead sea turtle (*Caretta caretta*) comes ashore to lay its eggs. Loggerheads are considered an endangered species and are protected by the International Union for the Conservation of Nature.

The period of deposition coincides with the tourist season, so Legambiente monitors and protects them.

Q: There seems to be a peaceful coexistence between the protected turtles and the tourists, who are still allowed to go to the beach. It

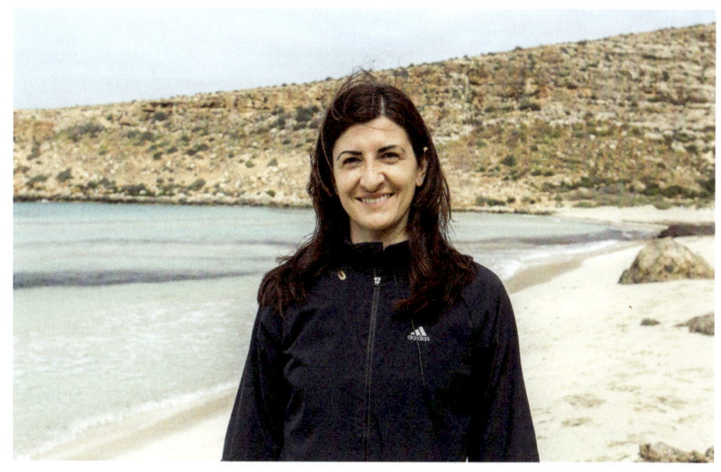

could be the other way around—in other words, when the turtles arrive on the island, Legambiente would close the beach to tourists. But you don't do that. Both are living together here.

PRAZZI: Yes, it is our intention to combine both: to protect the turtles, and at the same time to have tourism here. Female turtles arrive at the beach every four or five years. The mechanism of "natal homing" allows females to return to the beach where they were born. Each turtle lays 100–120 eggs, covers the hole, and then goes back into the Mediterranean. In the same summer they can nest up to five times. Sixty days later little turtles run as fast as possible to the sea. Knowing that mice and seagulls catch them for food, Legambiente protects the little ones till they reach the water. Then they swim continuously for forty-eight hours to get as far away as possible from danger. Female turtles are checked, and we give them a sort of name tag. We do not use GPS, but there are other research groups that use this to monitor their movements. In the Mediterranean there are feeding, mating, and nesting areas … we know that they go to North Africa to spend the winter. There are other large nesting areas in North Africa and Greece. When the turtle nests too close to the beach in a dangerous place, we dig a new hole and move all the eggs one by one to bring them to a more protected place. We have specific authorization to do this because they are a protected species.

Q: What about Legambiente's awareness campaigns that have shown the way forward for strong and combative environmental volunteerism?

PRAZZI: Legambiente operates awareness campaigns: we clarify and publicize what we're doing here, we explain the importance of this place, we talk about the turtle, and we involve local people and tourists. Moreover, we organize thousands of work camps and voluntary summer camps: teens and adults from all over Italy and from abroad come to this island to monitor and ensure "healthy" enjoyment of the site 24/7—they play an active role in our work.

Q: Do other animals migrate from Africa to the island?

PRAZZI: Due to its position, Lampedusa is an important stop-off point for migratory animals, especially for birds in spring and fall. Rare species fly from Africa to Europe, and vice versa. The little island in front of the beach is totally off limits to people. The Royal Seagull lives there and a particular North African lizard, the *Psammodromus algirus* (large psammodromus) from Algeria. Between February and March whales pass near the island and we can see them following the plankton. They move northward.

Q: *Has the arrival of migrants changed your activities?*
PRAZZI: No, it doesn't affect our activities, and in any case it's always a migratory flow, like that of animals …

Q: *And tourism?*
PRAZZI: Tourism can be negative if it isn't controlled. Legambiente promotes a wise use of natural resources, and sustainable and guaranteed tourism to allow protected species to find a safe place. In this way tourism can become a resource.

Q: *May I ask you about the involvement of Giusi Nicolini?*
PRAZZI: Giusi Nicolini, the mayor of the island, was the first Legambiente representative who worked to organize and coordinate the environmental recovery operations. She has done a lot for this place, analyzing and denouncing the previous terrible condition of the beach. People from Lampedusa at first weren't happy, because they were in the habit of using the beach in a certain way. It took a while to make them understand the importance of the operation, and now that the place has returned to its precious and natural state, they finally understand—they are happy. Tourists from all over the world come here to see this wonderful place.

Photographs as Gifts

Laura Rizzello and Fiorella Friscia from the Italian Red Cross on rescue operations in the Mediterranean

PHOTO STORY: LISA BERGMANN

Laura Rizzello and Fiorella Friscia have often acted as volunteer nurses in rescue operations in the Mediterranean. The pictures they take of their work are used internally by the Red Cross for teaching and demonstration purposes to improve the medical care provided to shipwrecked refugees. Besides their work as nurses, they also offer emotional and psychological support to the people they rescue, whom they record in private snapshots. In 2011 they gave an interview to the Migrant Image Research Group in their capacity as spokeswomen for the regional office of the Italian Red Cross in Sicily. They presented the research group with a collection of photographs they had taken during rescue operations between 2005 and 2010. Unlike with professional photographers, authorship is of no importance to the Red Cross nurses, so it is often not clear who has taken which pictures. In turn, the image itself plays a major role as it can also be used for publicity purposes to legitimize the work of the Red Cross and attract funding. The interview was conducted by Filippo Baracchi, Valeria Malito, and Laura Morcillo.

RIZZELLO: I started dealing with boat landings in June 2006. I got into it in just the same way every mission begins for a nurse: I was called and told there was a humanitarian necessity to carry out this mission helping the migrants arriving on the island of Lampedusa from North Africa, Central Africa, and the Horn of Africa.

I followed this path together with the whole group, though I had different duties, because I always worked on my own. This is how the adventure began. The only information I had was what could be gleaned from videos, newspapers, and television; I was not aware of the phenomenon until I met these people.

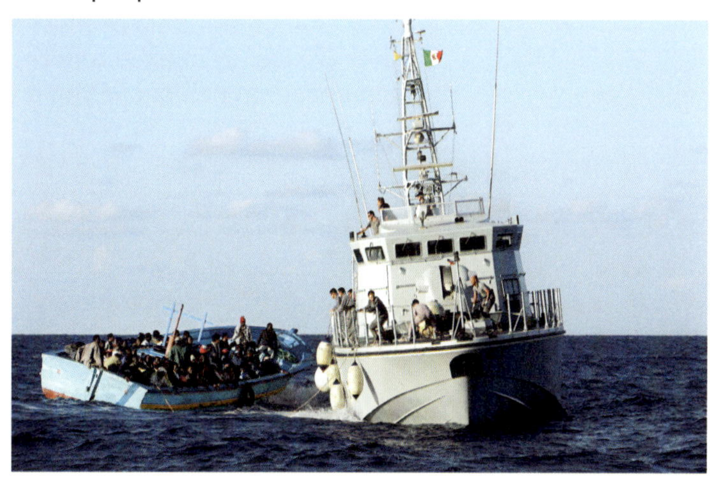

↑ During the rescue missions the emotions are very strong, as you can see in these pictures; approaching the boat is the

critical stage of the rescue, because the people all tend to move to one side of the boat, so that the vessel is at risk of capsizing right in front of the rescuers, almost like an ironic twist of fate.

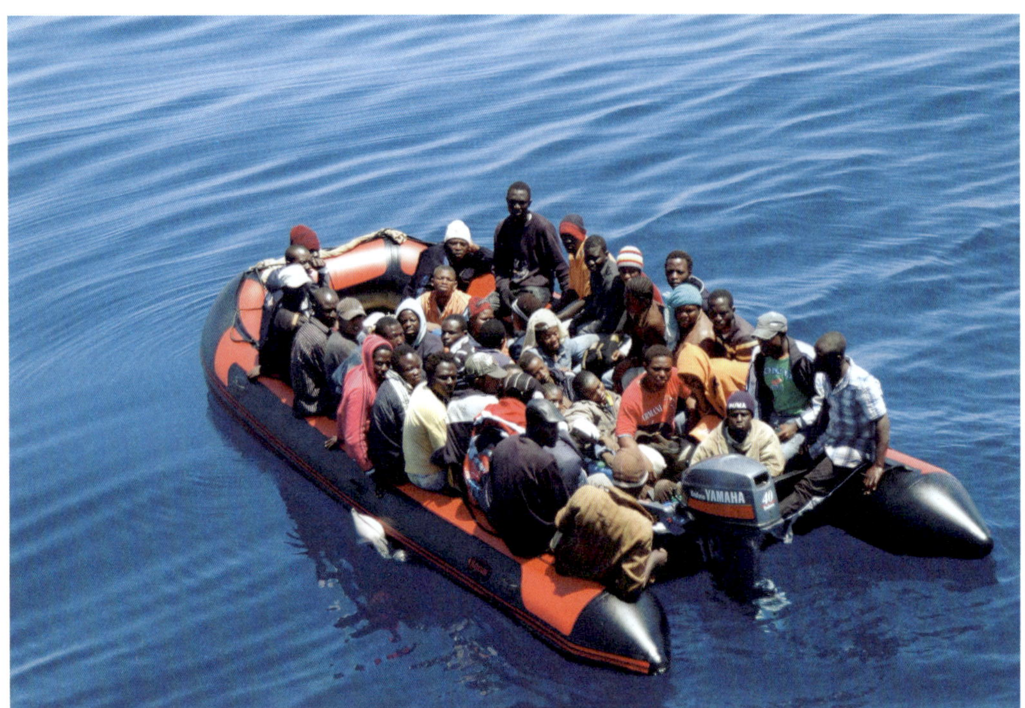

↑ On the sides of the boat there are only men. In the center there are the women and the kids. This is how they are placed. There are several reasons why they stay there. The women are there because generally they weigh less than the men. So at the sides they might be thrown overboard by the waves. They also stay there because it is the most uncomfortable position. People at the center of the boat cannot stretch their legs, they cannot stand up or move for the entire passage, because they are tightly packed together. Just one person changing their position can cause the craft to capsize.

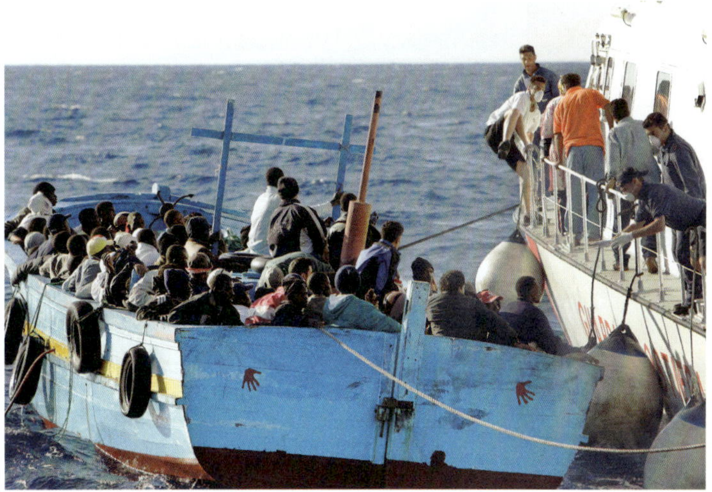

← From there the rescue staff help the people to get aboard if their boat is not able to continue its journey. This operation is called "transshipment": the people are brought on board the rescue boat to safety.

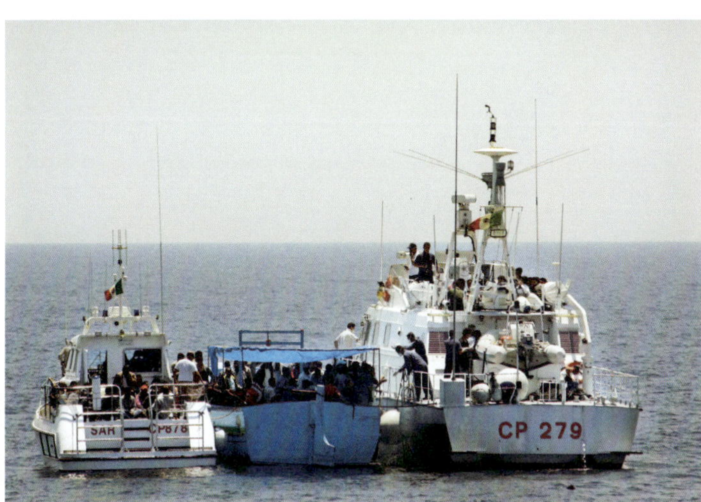

← In this video you can see that there are two boats performing this rescue: one from the port authority *Guardia Costiera* and one from the *Guardia di Finanza*; this is because on this boat, measuring 10 by 10.5 meters, there were eighty-four migrants.

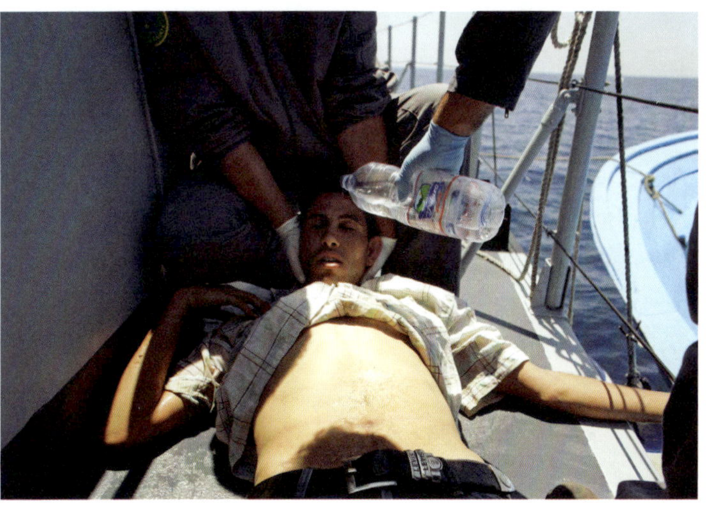

← In any case, the situation is extremely delicate. What the rescuers do at this stage is to rapidly get an idea of the general condition of the boat's passengers. Approaching and fastening the ropes, the rescuers try to get an impression of whether there are dead people on board, people with health problems, pregnant women. They are immediately transshipped, and once on board we perform a triage. Triage means assigning priority to whoever is most in need.

Other tasks include talking with the women, asking them whether they are pregnant, how far along they are, whether they have problems, if they are in pain or have contractions; in this case not only is practical support fundamental but also psychological support, in order to make them feel safe.

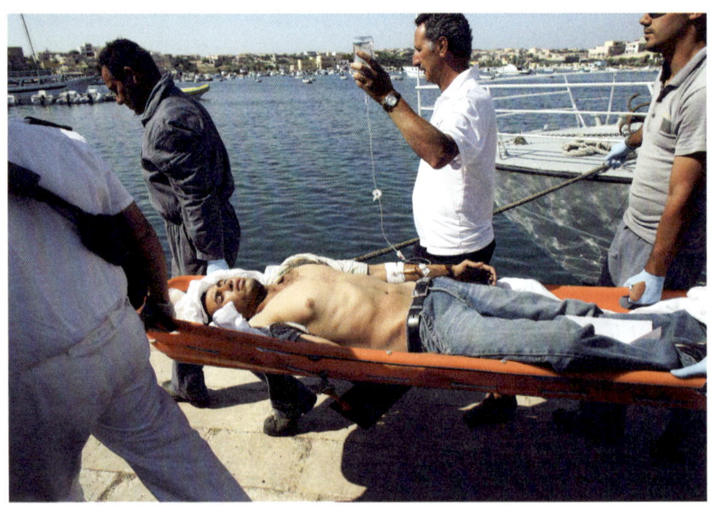

← You also have to coordinate everything with the boat's crew: if there is someone in need of urgent assistance, the commander has to alert the next rescue level, such as a navy helicopter, or at least to communicate how many hours it will take to get into port, to schedule the arrival of ambulances and paramedics if necessary.

This stage of triage and collaboration with the military's technical staff is fundamental. For example, the communication with the Knights of Malta is extraordinary. They tell us how many patients there are—they do the triage and we achieve an even higher level of synergy in our work.

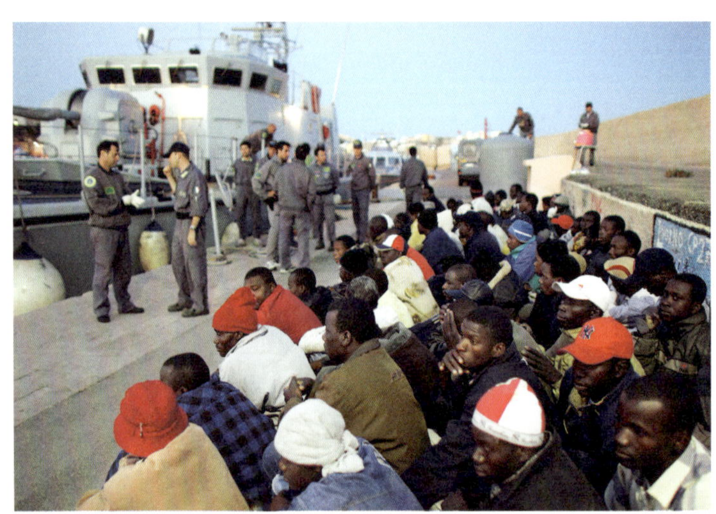

← When there are very large numbers of arrivals, it can take quite a bit of time just to sort everything. The people on the quay have to be transferred to the reception center for the next steps, to check them for scabies, for instance—not a serious ailment, but one that requires different accommodation inside the center because they have to receive treatment.

Afterwards there is the pre-identification phase, in which the migrants have to state where they come from, their personal information. Then, on the basis of this work, the police records department takes fingerprints and enters the data in an international database. Afterwards, the migrants arrive in the residential area of the reception center. They remain there for some days, depending on a range of factors, including the maritime conditions.

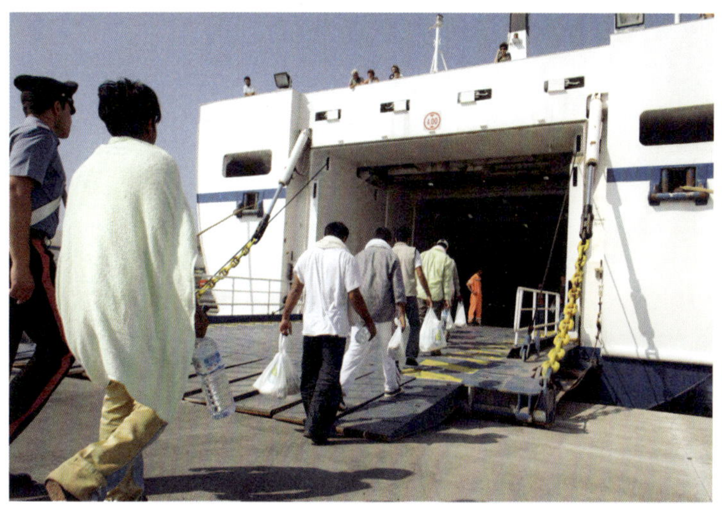

← These people may have to be moved by sea, on a ferry. But if the maritime conditions do not allow easy docking or traveling, they have to stay at the center for a few more days. This is for their security and health. Therefore it's nearly impossible to calculate the length of their stay. Normally they are there for three to four days, but there are conditions under which they have to remain longer.

The joint work with all the rescue operators can happen under difficult conditions, because often the migrants leave in good maritime weather conditions, but then on their way the conditions change. Obviously the rescuers have to intervene, even in these more complicated situations.

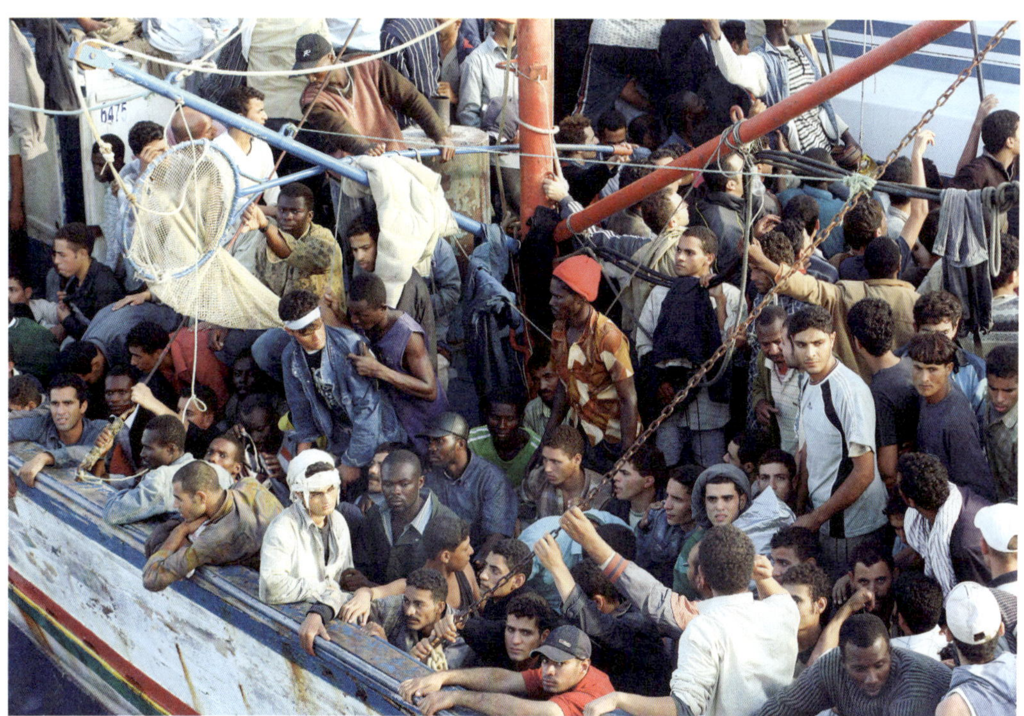

↑   These are pictures from the period in September, and as you can see, there were many people on this boat, about 380. In the hold of that boat the people made the passage lying down on their sides, head to foot, to increase the cargo capacity.

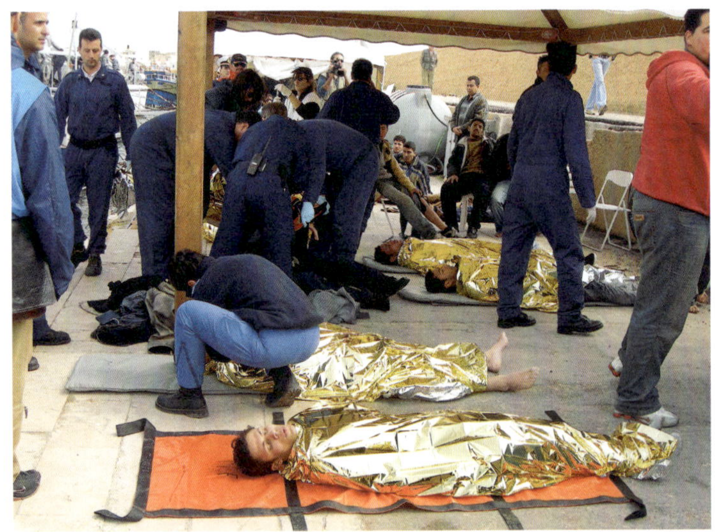

← These people arrived exhausted, because of the cold. They were suffering from hypothermia, which is one of the most frequent problems, also because of lack of air. In the hold with all these people there cannot be enough air.

These are very critical moments. These people were really suffering from hypothermia, but they were also dehydrated—two very serious conditions to deal with. In this case, everybody has been mobilized, but as you can tell from the pictures, the situation was very serious indeed.

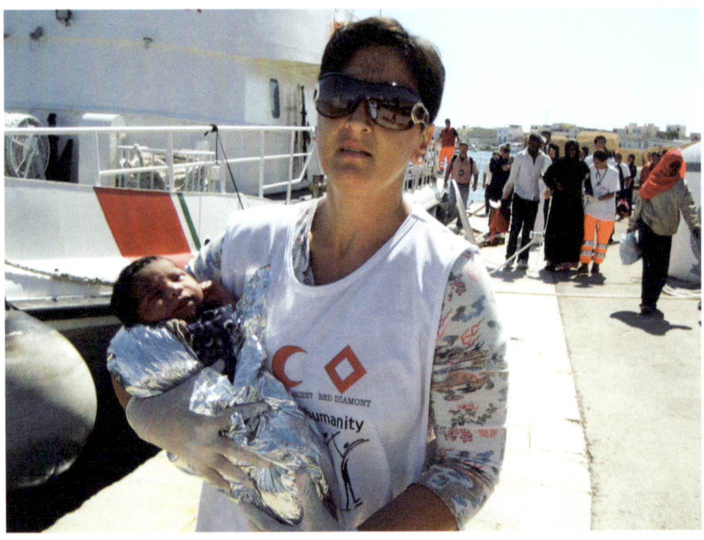

← These pictures are very private because they represent important moments for me; these are fleeting instants rather than moments.
I don't like to use the word immigrant, I prefer to say "people." Because behind every person there is a story, a family, a heart, a head, and there are often painful decisions.

The idea of traveling for a European is like this: I set off and I arrive. We have to get this idea of traveling out of our heads, because it's not only a journey, it's about hope.

To leave one's country, perhaps never to return, is definitely not an easy decision. A part of the work of the voluntary nurses consists of "active listening," because with the gathering of stories you do not only get to know people better but also the reasons why they leave. They often make un-believable journeys, and these people tell us very personal things too—about their difficulties, because they know that they can trust us. They go through 8,000 km of desert, reach Libya, perhaps experience prison there, or violence, and then they leave in these makeshift boats. They need to tell their experiences to someone.

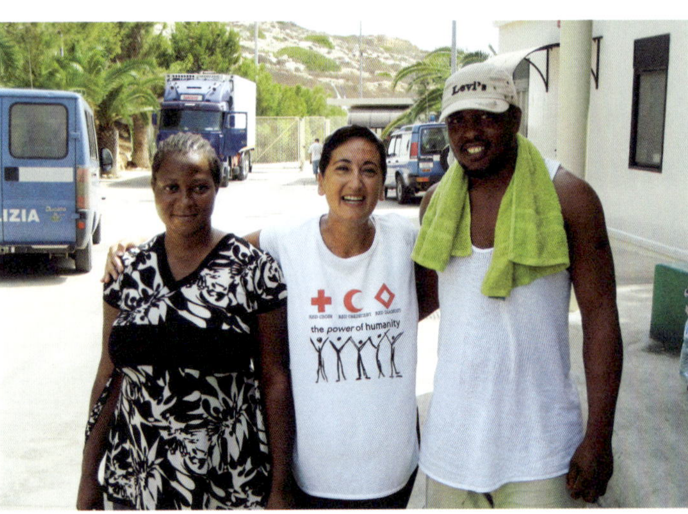

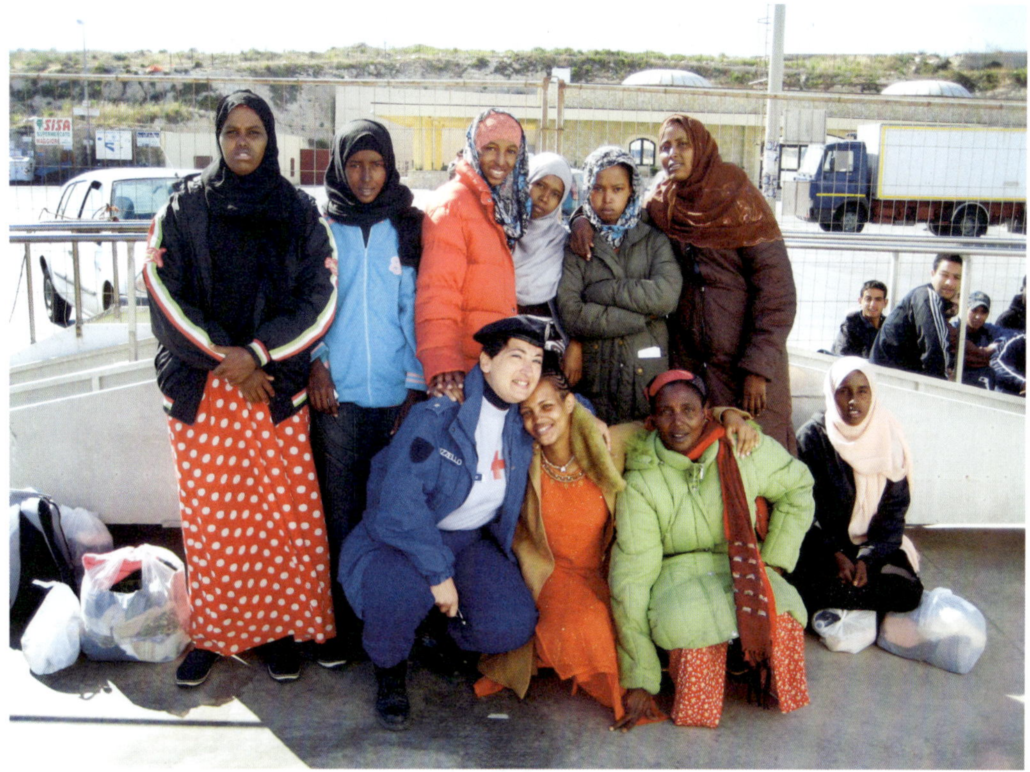

↑   These girls are posing for the camera! They asked me and the other sisters, "One picture please. I can't give you anything because I have nothing, but I can give you this." It's a beautiful, important present. If I have nothing and in that moment have the idea that creating a physical memory of me would be a way to give something to the other person, a picture of me, then I ask if it's okay to do a photo. Several times people have asked me to take a picture.

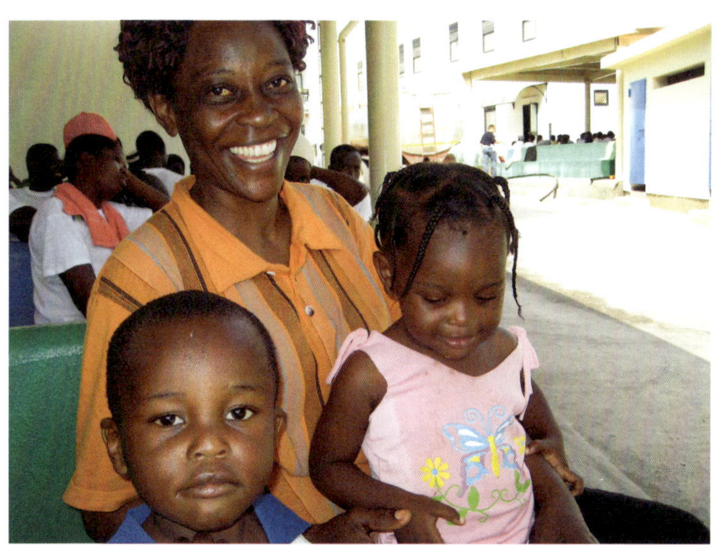

←   There is also the expectation on the part of the immigrant, who wants to occupy a space in the life of the people who have given their help—the idea, in other words, of leading a different life that is no longer only lived separately in anonymity but rather lived as part of the life of another person, a person you appreciate, because he or she helped you.

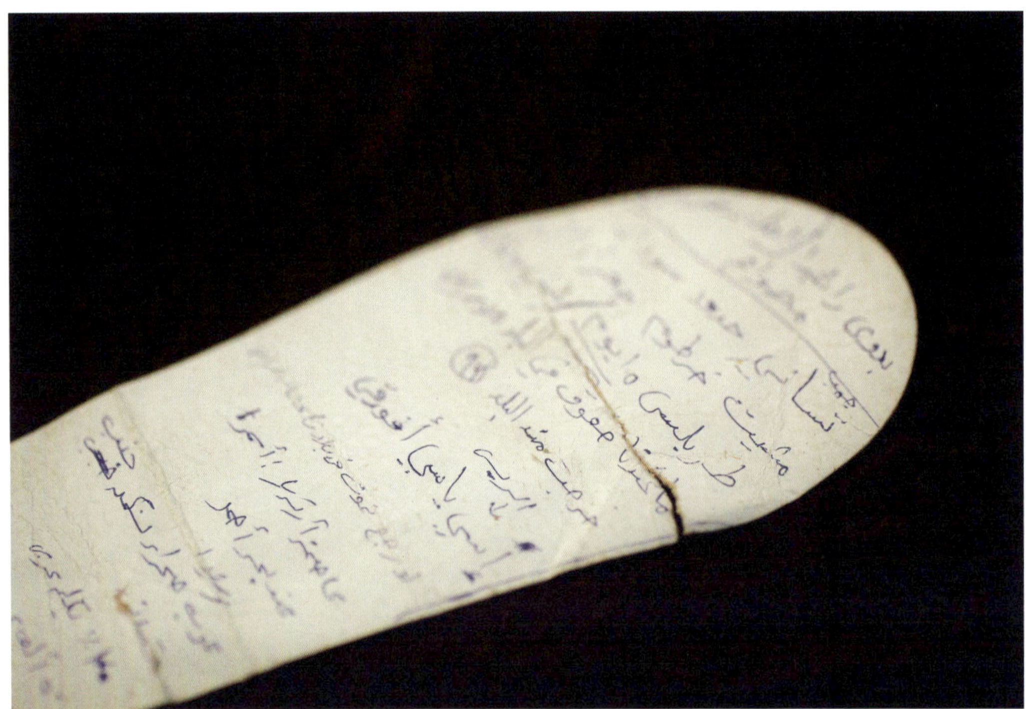

↑   This is the inside of a package from a pair of socks. Some-one wrote the story of his journey on this, of the time that passed, of what happened to him. It's poetry. For me it's one of the most beautiful presents ever. The prose finishes like this: "When I thought I wasn't going to make it anymore, I encoun-tered your smile, and I understood that life could go on." It's simply poetic. Every time I think of this young man, I can't help wondering where he is today, what he is doing …

LAST REMAINS

BY EMILIE JOSSO

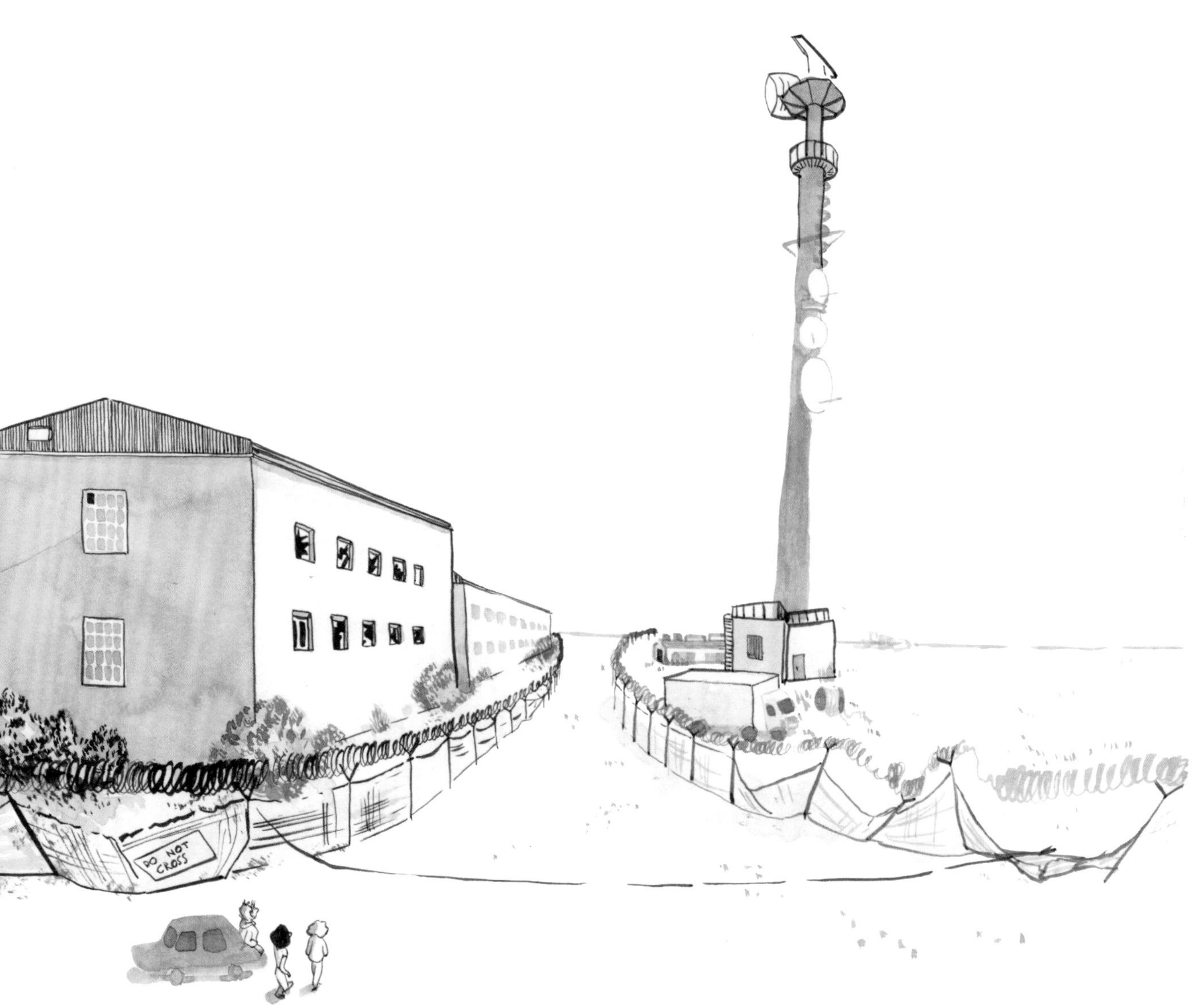

IT SHOULD BE HERE.
THE OLD
AMERICAN BASE.

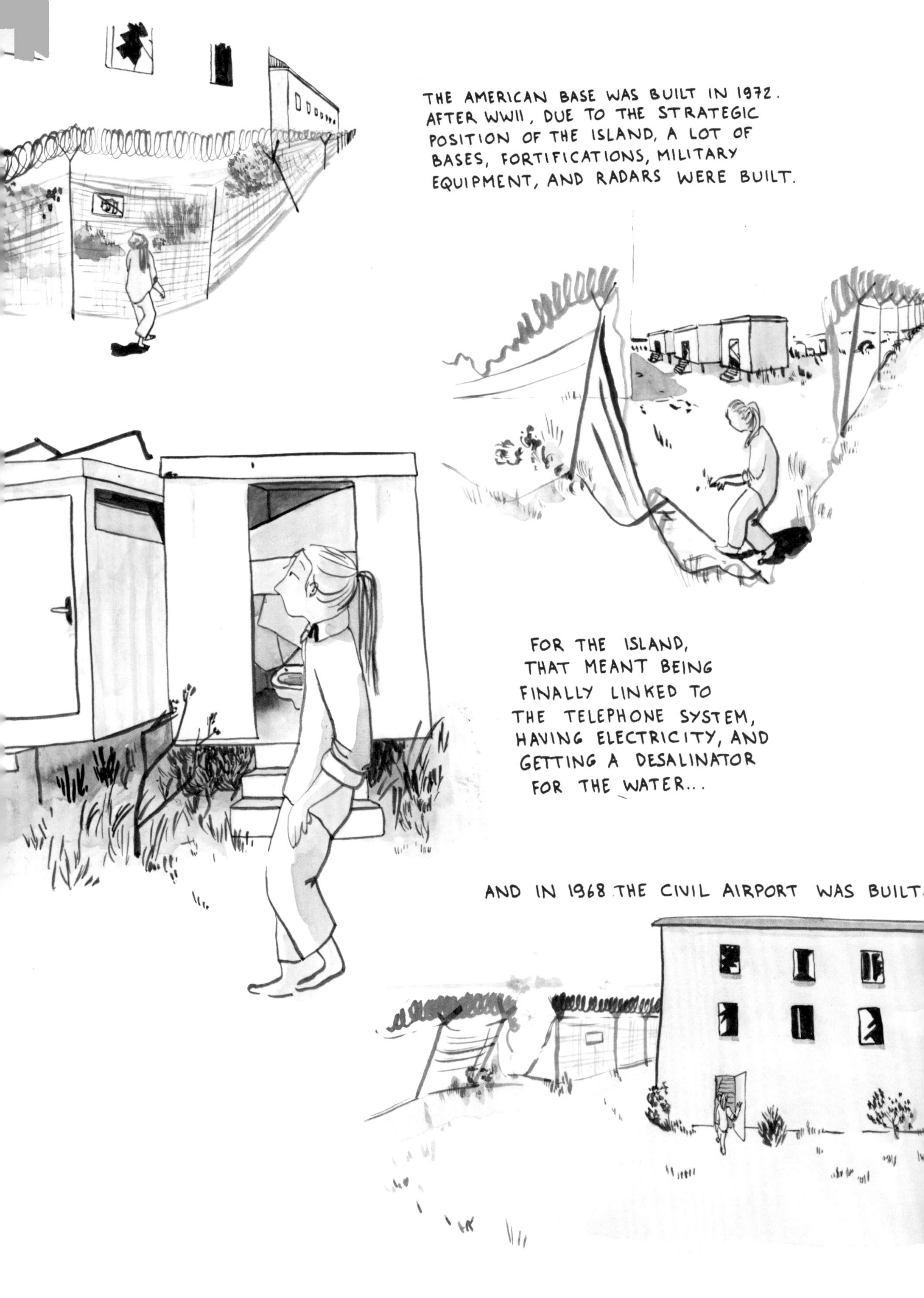

THE AMERICAN BASE WAS BUILT IN 1972.
AFTER WWII, DUE TO THE STRATEGIC
POSITION OF THE ISLAND, A LOT OF
BASES, FORTIFICATIONS, MILITARY
EQUIPMENT, AND RADARS WERE BUILT.
FOR THE ISLAND,
THAT MEANT BEING
FINALLY LINKED TO
THE TELEPHONE SYSTEM,
HAVING ELECTRICITY, AND
GETTING A DESALINATOR
FOR THE WATER...
AND IN 1968 THE CIVIL AIRPORT WAS BUILT.

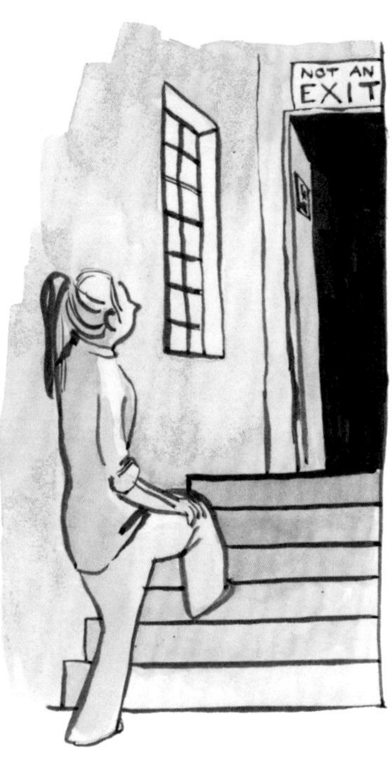

ON APRIL 15, 1986 AT 17:30, COLONEL MUAMMAR GADDAFI LAUNCHED MISSILES DIRECTED AT LAMPEDUSA, AIMED AT THE AMERICAN BASE.

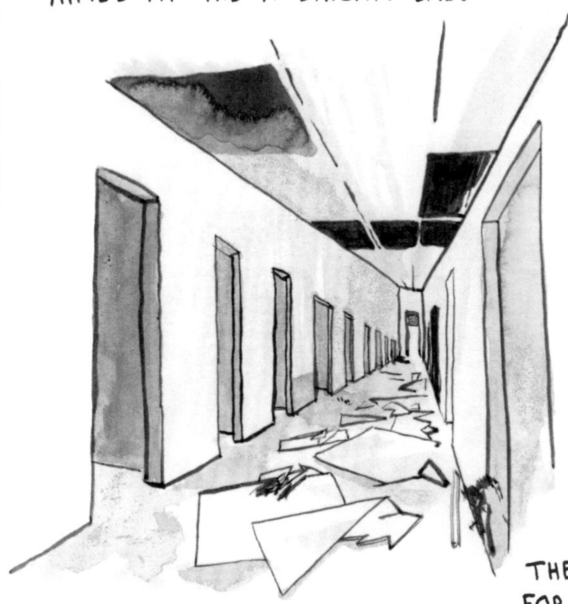

THE NEXT MORNING, FOR THE FIRST TIME, LAMPEDUSA ENDED UP ON THE FRONT PAGE OF NEWSPAPERS ALL OVER THE WORLD.

THOSE MISSILES WERE A RESPONSE TO THE AMERICAN BOMBING OF TRIPOLI (24 AIRPLANES; ONE OF GADDAFI'S DAUGHTERS WAS KILLED) THAT HAD HAPPENED THE DAY BEFORE.

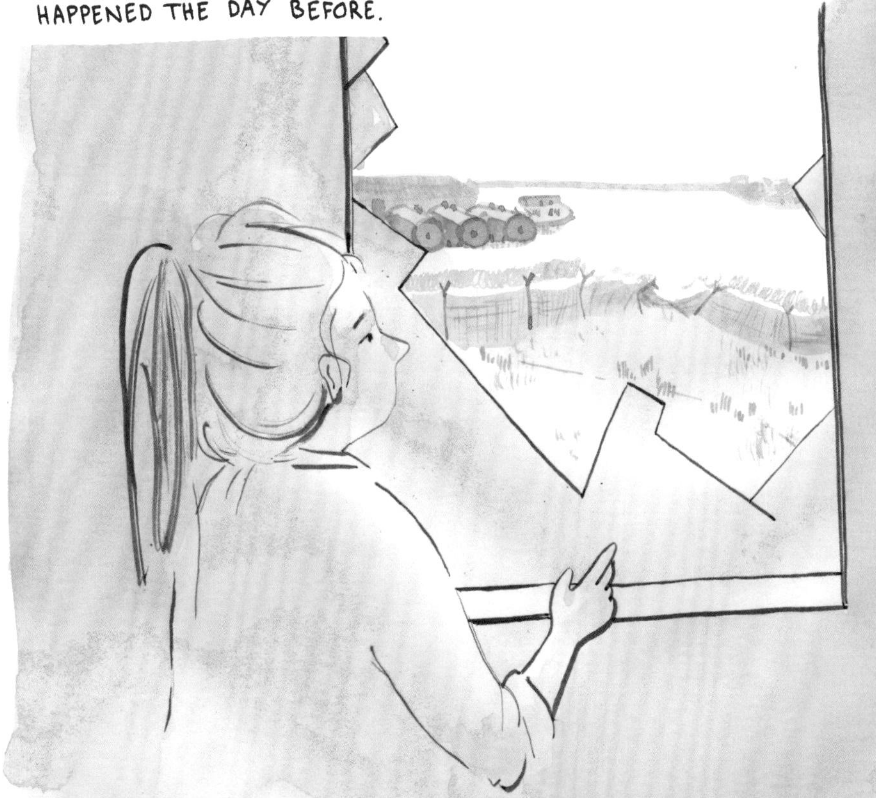

IT HAD BEEN ORDERED BY THE AMERICAN PRESIDENT, RONALD REAGAN, FOLLOWING A TERRORIST ATTACK IN A NIGHT CLUB IN BERLIN THAT WAS MAINLY FREQUENTED BY AMERICAN SOLDIERS.

LA STAMPA

REDAZIONE, AMMINISTRAZIONE, TIPOGRAFIA: 10128 TORINO, VIA MARENCO 32, Centralino 55481 - Telex 221.121

Mercoledì 16 Aprile 1986 - L. 650

La risposta di Gheddafi al bombardamento americano su Tripoli e Bengasi

Due missili libici contro Lampedusa

Gli ordigni sono caduti in mare senza fare danni - Erano diretti alla stazione radar Usa installata sull'isola - Si alzano in volo aerei italiani, ma non trovano alcuna nave: i razzi lanciati da una base in Libia - Craxi: «E' un atto di guerra» - Energica protesta della Farnesina - E' già polemica sull'efficienza delle strutture difensive nazionali, convocato per oggi il Consiglio superiore della Difesa

L'Urss annulla l'incontro tra Shultz e Shevardnadze - Uccisa una figlia di Gheddafi

Sulla linea del rischio

La crisi aperta dal raid americano su Tripoli e Bengasi ha subito coinvolto l'Italia, sia pure nell'estremo lembo del suo territorio e senza conseguenze per la popolazione dell'isola di Lampedusa. L'allarme con cui non soltanto il nostro Paese, ma l'Europa, avevano seguito i preparativi dell'azione americana, e la disapprovazione nostra e degli altri europei (con l'eccezione quasi isolata dell'Inghilterra) per l'azione compiuta, trovano così un riscontro anche troppo immediato in una «escalation» militare che i comportamenti irresponsabili del leader libico, protettore di terroristi, facevano prevedere.

Siamo così in grave allarme per il rischio di ulteriori e più diretti coinvolgimenti dell'Italia in quello che potrebbe diventare un vero e proprio conflitto, con un Paese dove diecimila nostri compatrioti potrebbero diventare altrettanti ostaggi di un leader spregiudicato e privo di scrupoli. Siamo altresì in allarme per la minaccia di una seria crisi politica tra Stati Uniti ed Europa: il dissenso tra le due metà dell'Alleanza atlantica, così vitale per la nostra sicurezza e libertà, è forte e potrebbe aggravarsi.

Anche se l'Europa, con i suoi passati silenzi e la sua inerzia, è in parte responsabile per l'isolamento dell'America, e quindi persino per le reazioni militari di Reagan, ciò non deve impedire agli alleati europei di far sentire le loro ragioni. Il presidente del Consiglio italiano lo ha fatto ieri con senso della misura, riconoscendo le gravissime provocazioni a cui l'America è stata sottoposta dalla Libia ed Gheddafi, ma confermando il nostro «dissaccordo», non possiamo non chiederci: l'America ha scelto la via giusta? O ha adottato, per combattere il terrorismo e i suoi protettori, una strategia errata, controproducente e pericolosa?

La divergenza tra gli europei e l'America non riguarda il giudizio su questo terrorismo, che tutti intendiamo isolare e combattere, ma i mezzi con cui combatterlo. Sempre dare i Dodici ha detto ieri unanimemente che, pur comprendendo le frustrazioni e le sofferenze dell'America, ritiene la rappresaglia militare, imprecisa e indiscriminata, inefficace per reprimere il terrorismo.

E poi, dove può condurre una tale strategia? Userebbe l'America la stessa forza contro la Siria, alleata dell'Urss, se le responsabilità siriane tante volte denunciate venissero in egual modo alla luce? E ancora: un'azione punitiva, che provoca in risposta altri atti di terrorismo (agli occhi libici giustificati dalle vittime civili del bombardamento americano), da quali ulteriori punizioni sarebbe seguita? Fin dove potrebbe arrivare una «escalation» di questo tipo? Infine, non offre così l'America all'Unione Sovietica (anche supponendo che per una sorta di complicità tra le superpotenze Mosca non reagisca se non a parole) gratuiti vantaggi politici nella regione, e futuri (o passati) atti d'imperio sovietici?

La strategia della rappresaglia, anche adottata da un piccolo Stato accerchiato come Israele, ha già dimostrato tutta la sua pericolosità, quando è stata portata da Begin fino alle sue estreme conseguenze con la fallimentare invasione del Libano. Ma una cosa è Israele, potenza locale e limitata, un'altra l'America, superpotenza globale. E Israele stesso ha sì usato le rappresaglie, ma ha anche cercato la via alternativa del negoziato, ma con Begin, l'uomo della pace con Sadat. Una strategia della rappresaglia avrebbe per principale risultato di stringere attorno a Gheddafi anche i governi arabi più moderati e filo-occidentali, rafforzando l'estremismo, invece d'indebolirlo.

Tutte queste sono le ragioni che hanno indotto l'Europa a pronunciarsi contro la rappresaglia reaganiana. Con il raid americano si è messo in moto un meccanismo pericolosissimo di «escalation»: si può ancora fermarlo? La sola risposta possibile è che si deve chiedere con forza che l'azione compiuta rimanga una sorta di monito e isolato, a cui segua una complessa azione politica mirante ad isolare Gheddafi e gli altri protettori del terrorismo. Non azioni militari isolate e imprecise, ma la formazione di un fronte internazionale compatto può contenere il terrorismo: non ne avevano parlato anche Reagan e Gorbaciov al vertice di Ginevra?

Giusto trent'anni fa un altro Presidente repubblicano, che si chiamava Eisenhower, fermò le due grandi potenze europee dell'epoca, Francia e Gran Bretagna, che avevano lanciato una spedizione contro Nasser, all'epoca della crisi di Suez. Ora le parti si sono capovolte, ed è giusto che l'Europa suggerisca all'America di lasciare il terrorismo e nelle armi per fare ritorno all'azione diplomatica, come suggerì allora Eisenhower agli europei. Quanto a Gheddafi, se colpirà ancora bisognerà rispondere con la necessaria durezza: questo è bene dirlo forte, sperando con forza.

Arrigo Levi

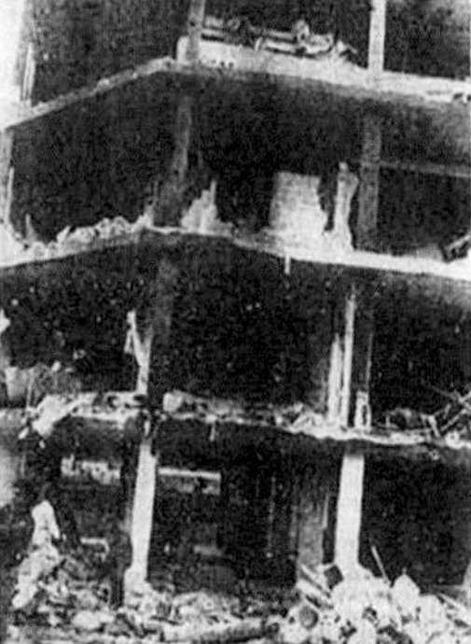

ROMA — La Libia ha cercato di colpire ieri l'isola di Lampedusa con due missili, caduti per fortuna in mare senza provocare danni. E' stata questa la prima reazione di Gheddafi al bombardamento americano di lunedì notte su Tripoli e Bengasi. In serata la Marina italiana ha reso noto che i due missili esplosi vicino alla costa di Lampedusa sarebbero stati identificati da un satellite. Usa e apparterrebbero al tipo «Scud-B» superficie-superficie, prodotto dall'Unione Sovietica. La base di lancio è libica e i due missili, di media gittata, hanno superato una distanza di 330 chilometri, al limite della loro gittata. Mezzi della Marina stanno cercando di recuperare i frammenti.

Tutto comincia intorno alle diciassette. Al Senato è in corso il dibattito sul bombardamento americano. La voce è già nelle redazioni dei giornali e i vertici dello Stato vengono travolti dalle telefonate. Quirinale, Palazzo Chigi, i ministeri della Difesa, dell'Interno, la Farnesina. E poi i centri militari, i servizi di sicurezza, i comandi Nato. Le risposte sono evasive, imbarazzate, incerte. Avanzano

le prime ipotesi e si fa osservare che comunque il grande dispositivo di sicurezza messo in piedi ieri notte dal Centro Crisi di Forte Braschi e dalla sala operativa della Difesa è stato clamorosamente bucato.

C'è un momento di panico; in attesa che Roma fornisca la sua versione, cominciano a squillare i telefoni di Lampedusa. Chiamano da tutto il mondo e la centrale va in tilt. Risponde un addetto alla radio costiera e dice che intorno alle diciassette sono state udite due forti esplosioni. Indica come possa essere possibile una base radar del la Nato, tipo Loran con 30 militari Usa di guardia. Un abitante dell'isola sostiene che i «botti» sono stati sentiti verso le cinque e un quarto.

La prima notizia rassicurante viene dal comando della Guardia di Finanza di Palermo: «Non hanno colpito alcun bersaglio». Solo in seguito il sindaco Giovanni Frapagane fornisce una versione meno approssimativa. Quarantasei anni, scapolo, preside di scuola media, comunista come tutti i venti i consiglieri comunali, riferisce di essersi recato personalmente alla base americana e di non aver trovato traccia della caduta di missili.

«Alle cinque e dieci — racconta — abbiamo sentito questi scoppi, come delle cannonate. La gente ha avuto paura, e dopo quello che è successo è avvenuto a Tripoli, la paura è più che giustificata. Ora è tornata la calma, la gente è composta e spera che la crisi possa rientrare».

Al Viminale è riunito il comitato per la sicurezza e l'ordine pubblico convocato da Scalfaro per coordinare le misure di vigilanza di tutti i possibili obiettivi del terrorismo: porti, aeroporti, ferrovie, sedi diplomatiche, compagnie aeree. Si è parlato di Lampedusa e anche stare formulare varie ipotesi. Quella di missili lanciati da un sottomarino e caduti in mare. O, ancora, quella di un peschereccio camuffato, difficile da identificare.

In attesa della versione ufficiale della Marina basata sui rilevamenti del satellite Usa, l'ipotesi del bersaglio mancato era diventata una quasi certezza e subito erano cominciate le polemiche su come era stato possibile lo sfondamento delle apparecchiature di sicurezza.

Roberto Martinelli

«Non vorremmo ripetere i bombardamenti, la scelta a Gheddafi»

La Casa Bianca avverte Craxi «Operazione finita, per ora»

DAL NOSTRO CORRISPONDENTE

WASHINGTON — Una calma minacciosa è scesa sugli Stati Uniti dopo i drammatici eventi di Tripoli e Bengasi. L'attacco libico a Lampedusa ha suscitato una reazione circospetta: «Lavoreremo gomito a gomito con l'Italia — ha dichiarato il portavoce del Dipartimento di Stato Kalb — per decidere come rispondere a questa aggressione sul suo territorio». Alla Casa Bianca, dove è stato accolto da un'ovazione, Reagan ha ignorato la rappresaglia di Gheddafi. In un breve discorso agli esponenti della Confindustria Usa, ha affermato che Washington non sottovaluta il Colonnello, ma a sua volta lo invita a non sottovalutarla».

E' il momento del bilancio, e Reagan, l'uomo della forza, oggi si mostra alla ricerca della pace. Sulla scia del massimo bombardamento compiuto dopo la guerra del Vietnam, l'America riflette sul da farsi. Voci non confermate vogliono che i sondaggi diplomatici fossero in corso la settimana scorsa, e siano ripresi ieri, per un armistizio tra Washington e Tripoli. L'amministrazione Usa e il governo libico hanno ammesso, ma il portavoce Speakes ha ammesso che approcci indiretti hanno avuto luogo — non ha voluto dire quando — tramite il Canada e il Belgio. Evidentemente i falliti, potrebbero ricominciare se la crisi non precipiterà.

Dietro questa pausa, ci ha riferito un consigliere della Casa Bianca, c'è l'attesa di cruciali sviluppi in Libia. Gli Stati Uniti sono persuasi che la posizione interna di Gheddafi si sia enormemente indebolita, ed egli rischi di essere travolto da un golpe. Nella sua trasmissione di ieri, la radio Voice of America ha praticamente invitato la popolazione libica a ribellarsi: di fronte al pericolo, il Colonnello potrebbe piegarsi a un compromesso. Sempre ieri, **Ennio Caretto**

(Continua a pagina 5 in ottava colonna)

ALLE PAGINE 2, 3, 4 e 5

- L'ora più lunga per 3 ministri mentre partono i caccia italiani *di Ezio Mauro*
- Un'azione di guerra elettronica e radar libici non «vedevano» *di Maurizio Cremasco*
- Che cosa aveva detto Gheddafi a Enzo Biagi in quell'intervista censurata
- Si prepara il piano di rientro per i diecimila italiani in Libia *di Liliana Madeo*
- I perché (e i vantaggi) della linea Gorbaciov *di Frane Barbieri*
- Schiaffo all'orgoglio della nazione araba *di Igor Man*
- Fedeltà degli americani a un duro codice morale *di Furio Colombo*
- Domani un altro consulto europeo (ma la Francia sta fuori dal gioco) *di Barbara Spinelli*
- Il no comment della Nato *di Fabio Galvano*

Mosca annuncia «Ne trarremo le conclusioni»

MOSCA — L'incontro Shultz-Shevardnadze, in programma in maggio a Washington per preparare il secondo vertice Reagan-Gorbaciov, non si farà. Questa la prima risposta concreta del Cremlino all'attacco americano contro la Libia.

Con una «dichiarazione governativa» — una forma la più solenni e gravi nella liturgia sovietica — Mosca ha ammonito «l'America a interrompere l'azione banditesca contro la Libia», altrimenti «l'Unione Sovietica dovrà trarre conclusioni» di più ampia portata. Un linguaggio forte ma pacato, che cancella d'un colpo «spirito e speranze di Ginevra».

«Molto preoccupato (come dimostrano le due esplosioni che hanno causato colonne di acqua in mare in direzione della stazione Loran. Non vi è stato alcun danno né a perso-

(A pagina 4 il servizio di Emanuele Novazio)

«Disapprovato» il bombardamento Usa sulla Libia

Il governo era pronto a una risposta armata

ROMA — Tra le 17,15 e le 18,45 di ieri il presidente del Consiglio Craxi con i ministri della Difesa Spadolini e degli Esteri Andreotti, riuniti al Senato, hanno dovuto esaminare l'eventualità di una risposta armata all'attacco libico contro l'isola di Lampedusa, ovvero contro il territorio italiano. «E' un atto di guerra contro un obiettivo italiano», ha ammesso Craxi.

Lunga è stata l'incertezza sul da farsi, soprattutto perché non si riusciva a capire che cosa fosse realmente successo. Si era parlato di un attacco di una motovedetta libica o di un sommergibile. Alle 18,45 Craxi è rientrato nell'aula del Senato, dove nel frattempo era stato sospeso il dibattito sulle dichiarazioni di governo sull'attacco aereo americano alla Libia, ed ha esposto la versione ufficiale. «Alle ore 17 sono state rilevate nell'isola due esplosioni che hanno causato colonne di acqua in mare in direzione della stazione Loran. Non vi è stato alcun danno né a per-

le nostre Forze Armate di fronte alla scelta immediata». Il Loran e una antenna alta 100 metri, che emette segnali radio per la guida della navigazione.

Craxi ha detto che gli aerei intercettori levatisi in volo subito dopo le esplosioni hanno «perlustrato per 30 minuti lo spazio di mare davanti a Lampedusa senza avvistare nessun mezzo navale. Anche il radar non hanno avvistato nulla. «A questo punto si è pensato ad un'offesa dovuta ad un mezzo missilistico portato da lunga distanza».

Poiché l'attacco è stato rivendicato da fonti libiche, il nostro governo risponderà con «una nota di energica protesta», è stata immediatamente comunicata all'ambasciatore libico a Roma. Una risposta militare avrebbe reso inevitabili l'intervento degli altri Paesi della Nato, che possono essere coinvolgere in base agli articoli 4 e 5 del Patto Atlantico.

La scelta è stata per il momento rinviata, anche perché la versione dell'accaduto fornita da Craxi non ha messo

né né a cose». Il Loran e una antenna alta 100 metri, che emette segnali radio per la guida della navigazione.

Non tutti sono rimasti convinti dalle comunicazioni di Craxi. I moltissimi hanno rilevato come il nostro apparato di difesa, decantato appena poche ore prima dal presidente del Consiglio, nella stessa sera del tutto inefficiente. L'attacco a Lampedusa ha messo in secondo piano il dibattito che si era avviato sul bombardamento americano. Alle 13 Craxi si era recato a Montecitorio per comunicare il «disaccordo» del governo italiano all'attacco Usa, definito «una decisione grave». Il primo imperativo era che ora «la situazione non degeneri», aveva detto, esprimendo un orientamento unanime del governo, concordato in una riunione del Consiglio di gabinetto.

Alberto Rapisarda

Ieri sera si è diffusa la voce (smentita) di un nuovo attacco

Tripoli parla di decine di morti

Case distrutte dalle bombe - Colpite le ambasciate francese, svizzera e iraniana

TRIPOLI — Lanci di razzi e tiri di contraerea sono stati uditi ieri sera verso le 21 a Tripoli: le esplosioni sono durate alcuni minuti e si è subito diffusa la voce di una nuova incursione aerea americana. L'agenzia sovietica Tass, senza fornire particolari, ha annunciato un nuovo raid Usa, ma il Pentagono ha immediatamente smentito. E' stata la conclusione di una giornata confusa, in cui si sono susseguite voci incontrollate mentre le radio alternavano slogan di guerra e marce militari.

Non si conosce ancora il bilancio definitivo dell'incursione aerea americana: secondo alcuni diplomatici occidentali i morti sarebbero un centinaio. I medici dell'ospedale pediatrico di Tripoli hanno annunciato che tra le vittime c'è anche una figlia

adottiva di Gheddafi, Hanna, una bimba di meno di un anno. La moglie e altri due figli del Colonnello, secondo fonti arabe raccolte a Parigi, sarebbero tra i feriti.

Case sventrate dalle bombe e devastate dagli incendi, muri e tetti crollati, linee elettriche e condutture dell'acqua danneggiate: così si presentava ieri mattina il quartiere Bin Ashur. Sette Aprile, uno dei più eleganti di Tripoli, colpito dall'incursione dei bombardieri americani. Ieri la città sembrava calma, come stordita dopo una notte di terrore e di confusione. L'ambasciatore austriaco ha raccontato che i negozi di generi alimentari erano regolarmente aperti. Soltanto davanti ai distributori di benzina c'erano lunghe file di automobili in attesa.

Un gruppo di giornalisti è

stato accompagnato dai funzionari del ministero delle Informazioni a visitare brevemente la zona colpita dalle bombe. I giornalisti sono stati seguiti da una folla eccitata che urlava slogan: «Maledetti bastardi, ecco cosa ci hanno fatto, ci hanno distrutto le case».

Le devastazioni provocate dalle bombe erano ben visibili. L'edificio accanto all'ambasciata francese è stato completamente distrutto, i tetti di altre quattro case visibilmente erano crollati. Le strade presentavano un aspetto desolato: delle gli auto danneggiate dai crolli e dalle esplosioni, alberi abbattuti. La sede diplomatica francese, che si trova al centro del distretto, è stata colpita ma non in modo grave. L'agenzia Jana ha annunciato i morti, molti di ha

nella sede diplomatica italiana, che è sorvegliata da soldati e poliziotti. Risultano colpite anche le ambasciate della Svizzera e dell'Iran.

Le devastazioni provocate dalle bombe erano ben visibili negli obiettivi stati colpiti nell'incursione. La polizia ha bloccato le strade che portano alla caserma dove vive Gheddafi. Ai giornalisti era anche stato annunciato che avrebbero visto i resti di un bombardiere colpito, ma dopo un giro in autobus sono stati riaccompagnati in albergo senza spiegazioni.

Un medico dell'ospedale di Tripoli ha detto che i medicati 60, 100 feriti e molti sono stati subito dimessi. L'agenzia Jana ha annunciato i morti, molti di

(Continua a pagina 5 in prima colonna)

NELLE PAGINE INTERNE

- **MORTO GENET** - E' scomparso ieri a Parigi l'autore di «Paraventi». Lo scrittore aveva 76 anni *(Servizio a pagina 7)*
- **MESTRE** - Brigadiere di polizia uccide un uomo in fuga, poi colto da sconforto si toglie la vita *(Servizio a pagina 10)*
- **VINO** - Il giudice ora accusa sette sofisticatori di omicidio volontario. La ventesima vittima a Monza *(Servizi a pagina 11)*
- **TOTONERO** - L'ombra della camorra sulle scommesse clandestine. Anche Allodi nella bufera del calcio *(Servizi nelle pagine di Cronaca e Sport)*

Tripoli Un condominio della capitale sventrato dall'attacco aereo

SEEING THOSE PICTURES OF THIS UNKNOWN, WONDERFUL
ISLAND IN THE NEWSPAPERS, PEOPLE BEGAN
TO THINK OF LAMPEDUSA AS A
TOURIST DESTINATION.

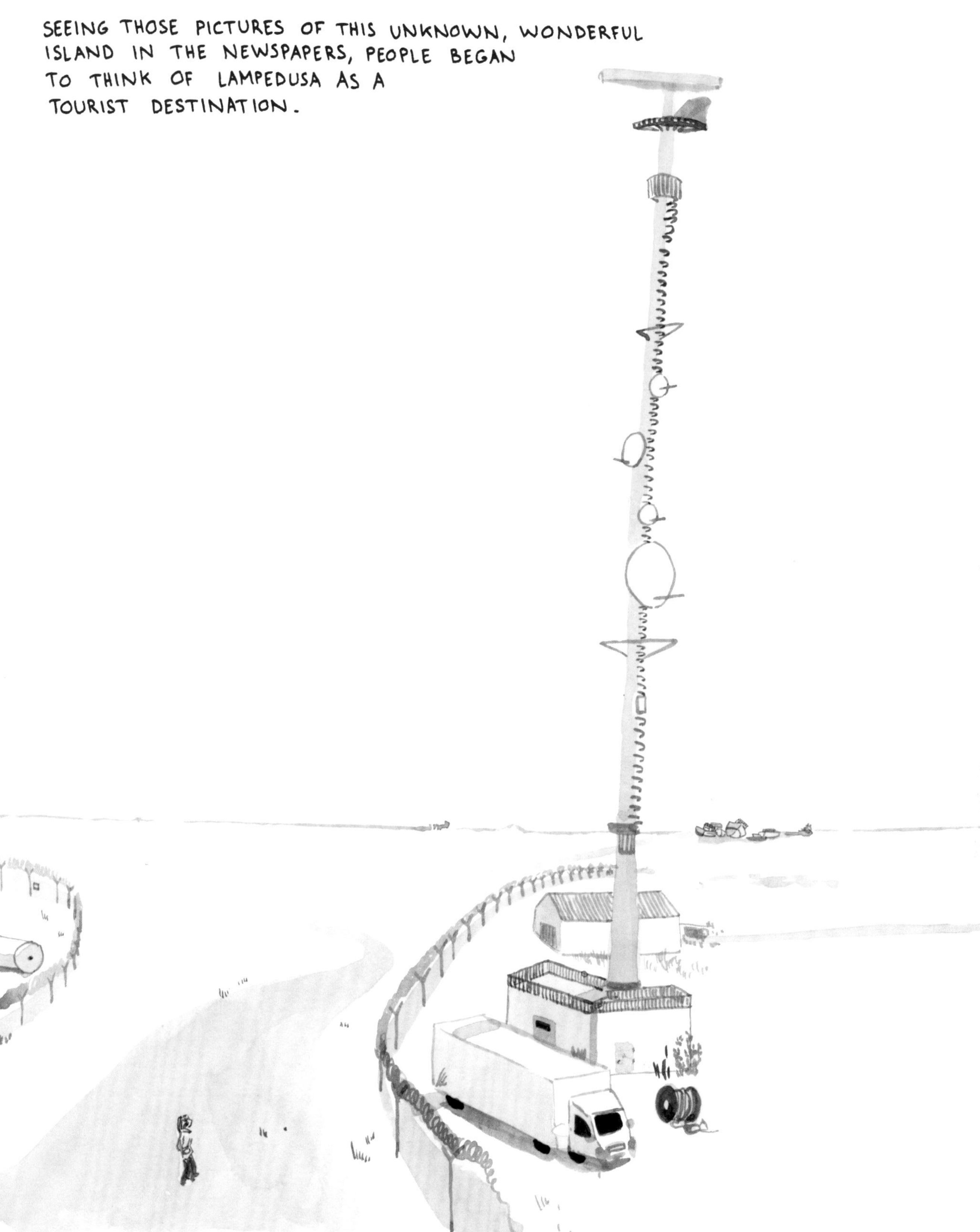

NOWADAYS, THIS PLACE IS JUST USED NOW AND AGAIN AS SOMEWHERE TO PUT THE
MIGRANTS' BOATS...

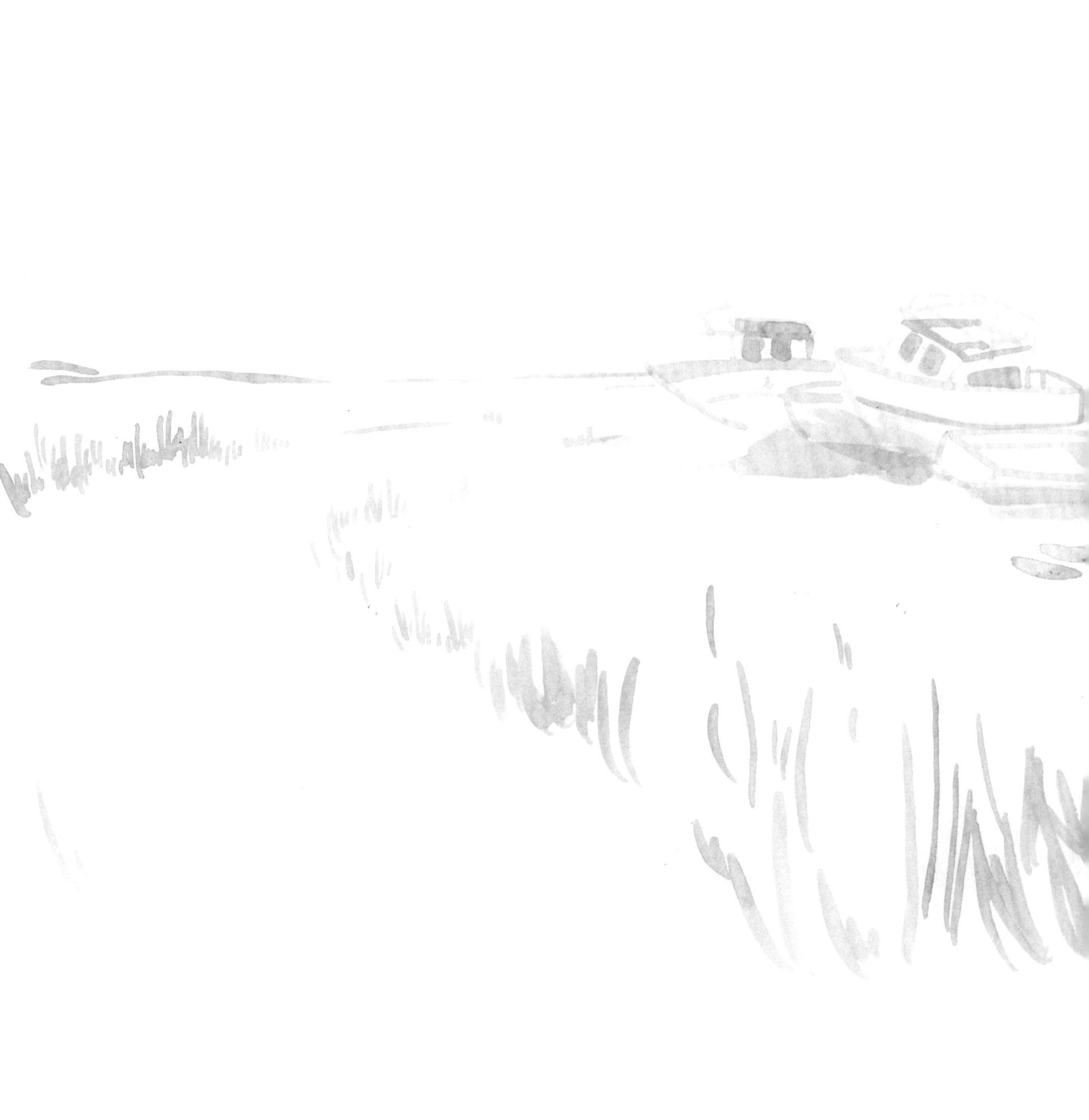

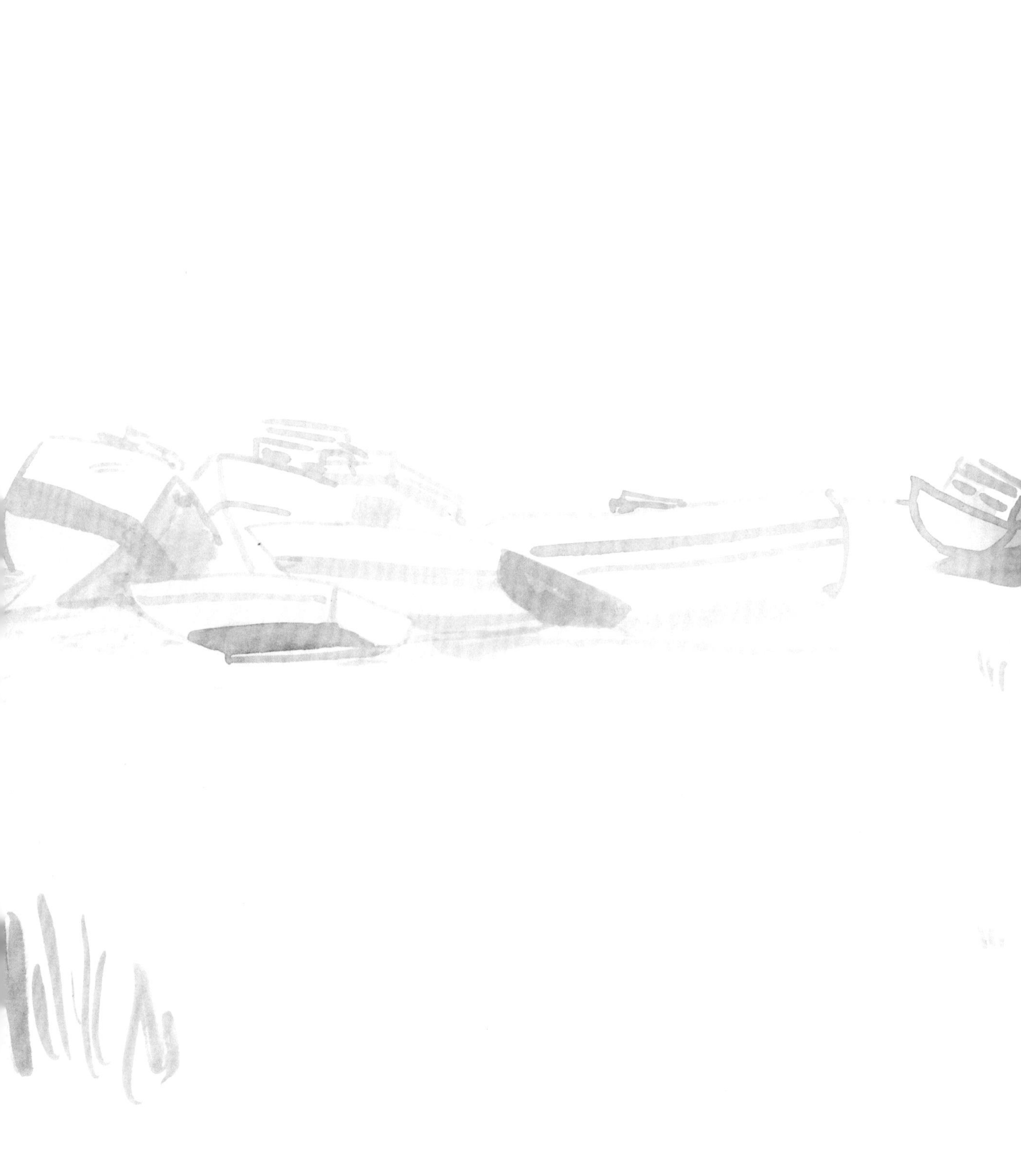

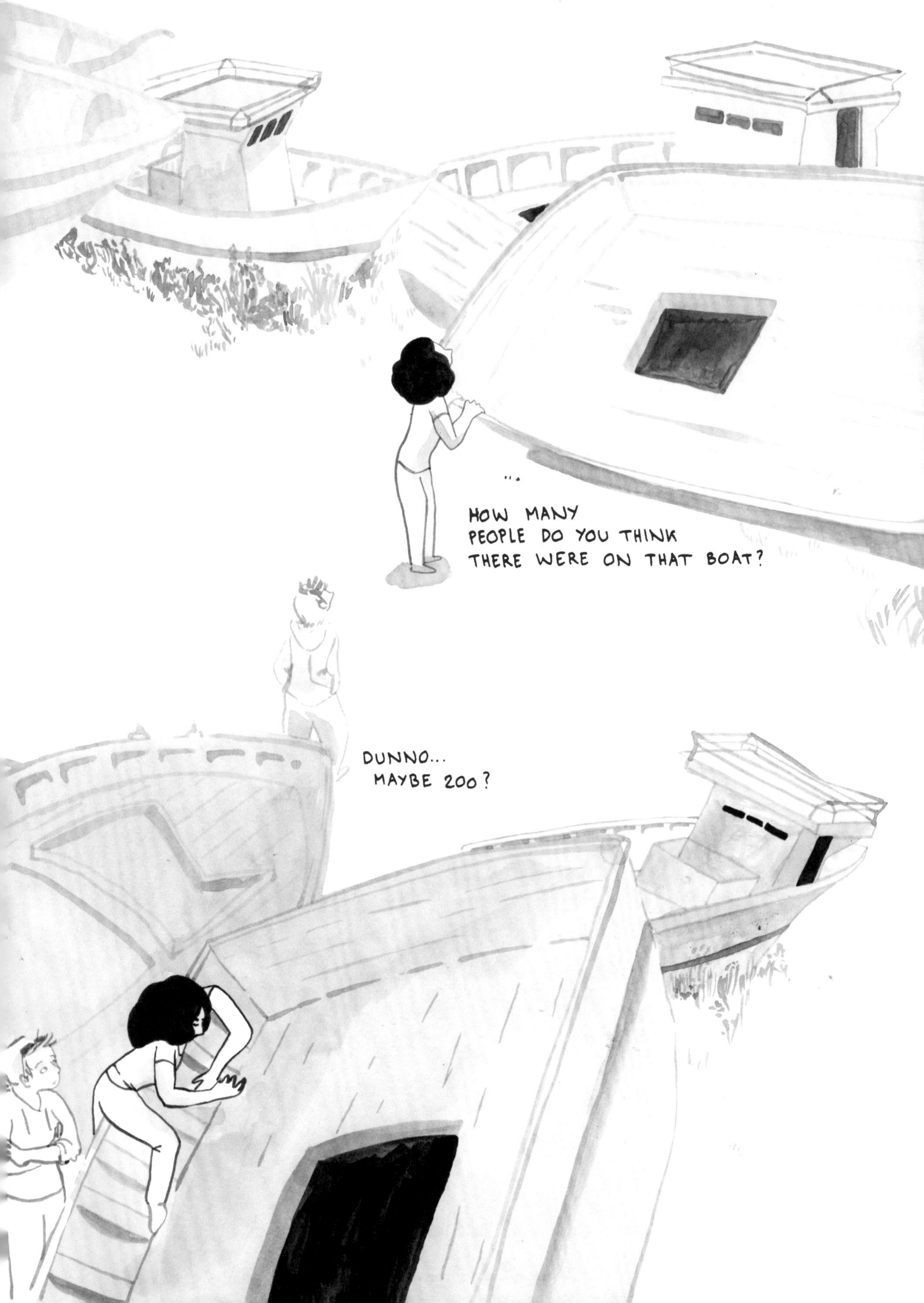

HOW MANY
PEOPLE DO YOU THINK
THERE WERE ON THAT BOAT?

DUNNO...
MAYBE 200?

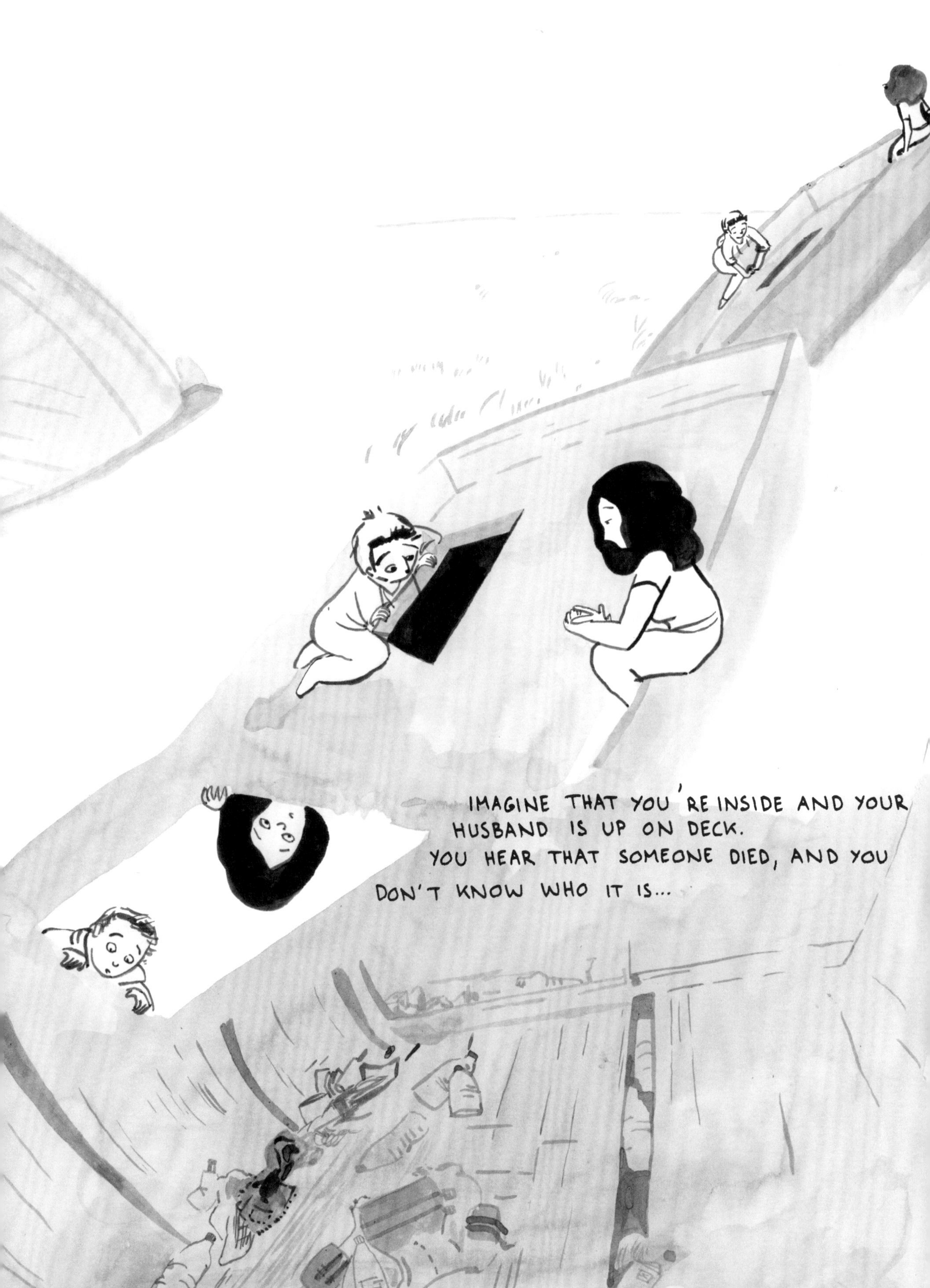

IMAGINE THAT YOU'RE INSIDE AND YOUR HUSBAND IS UP ON DECK.
YOU HEAR THAT SOMEONE DIED, AND YOU DON'T KNOW WHO IT IS...

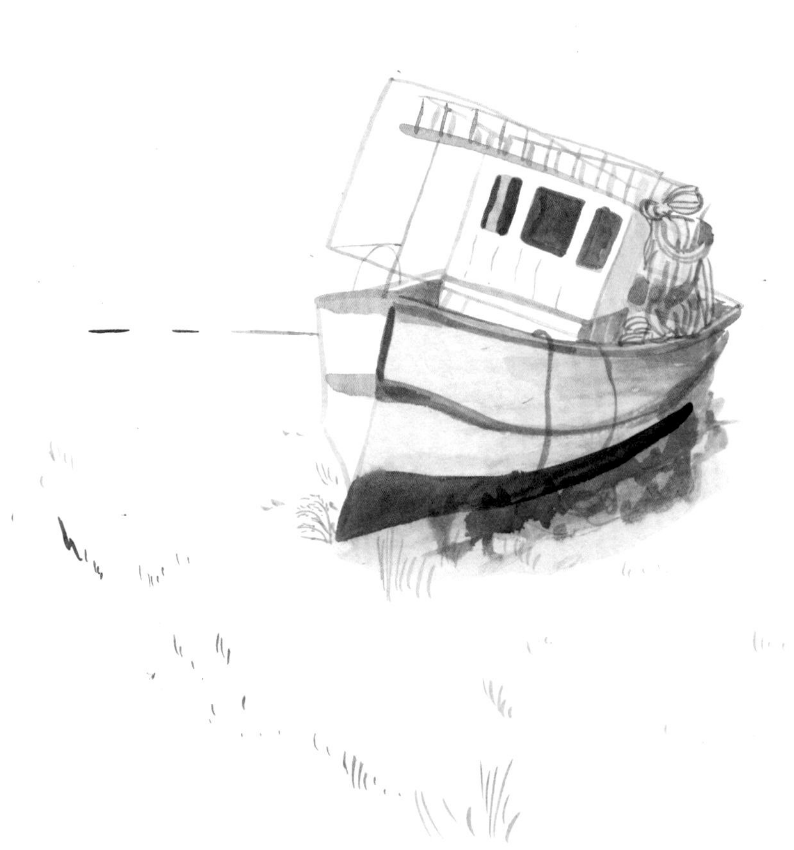

The Multicultural Graveyard

Conversation with the Syrian artist Khaled Barakeh about one Facebook post

On August 28, 2015, at 3.33 pm Khaled Barakeh posted seven photos showing six dead children on his Facebook site. All of them had met their death in the Mediterranean. Under the title "Multicultural Graveyard" Khaled's post, as he wrote it, ran: "Last night more than 80 Syrian and Syrian-Palestinian asylum seekers have drowned in the Mediterranean close to the Libyan shores trying to reach Europe." All over the world people saw these images and responded immediately. The interview between Khaled Barakeh and Anne König took place in May 2016.

Q: Where did you find these photos?
BARAKEH: Since the beginning of the revolution in Syria, as a kind of alternative way of making things happen on the ground, people have been organizing themselves in groups on Facebook to have a place to meet and plan events away from the eyes of the Syrian regime and its spies. One of these groups was created by some asylum seekers so that they could help each other find the best way to get to Europe through Turkey and Greece. One of the guys from this group, which has about 200,000 members, posted these images, and, without thinking for too long, I decided to repost them on my Facebook page.

Q: What is the Facebook group called?
BARAKEH: It's called "Immigration Garages for the Displaced." It includes a team of twenty volunteers called "Rescue and Follow-Up" who follow refugees from their starting point until the moment of their arrival in a safe haven. Members of the team are continuously present throughout the day on the group page. They communicate with the refugees via WhatsApp to make sure they are safe, and, when necessary, they contact the coast guard if the boat engine has stopped or there's been some other problem.

Q: Your post crossed between two cultural realms—the Arabic-speaking world and the English-speaking world. Was there a moment when you were thinking, should I or shouldn't I be posting these images?
BARAKEH: I saw them and my immediate reaction was to re-post them. Of course, I try to be sensitive about what I post because once I posted a harsh image from the Libyan revolution

and a friend from Denmark had a strong reaction to it, asking me why I would post something like this on Facebook! I understand that we live in different realities, if not parallel worlds, but how can we help form public opinion if we don't show reality as it is? Think about the image from Vietnam taken by Nick Ut in 1973, *The Terror of War*—the little Vietnamese girl who was running scared and naked, and how much it changed the attitude toward the American war in Vietnam. That's why I thought that these images should be seen. I also think the title of the album and its description added something to the story. It kind of opened a discourse, a call for people to wake up and to see this. In her book *Regarding the Pain of Others*, Susan Sontag says, "Remembering *is* an ethical act, has ethical value in and of itself. Memory is, achingly, the only relation we can have with the dead."

Q: You mentioned that you did a selection of images. What was shown in the other images that you didn't post?

BARAKEH: There were a few more images, but in some of them you could recognize people's faces, or the bodies were in very bad shape. There were also photos of adults, but I took the ones of the drowned children where you don't see their faces. Just to save their dignity. I tried to be responsible about what I was posting but I didn't think twice about it. I titled the album "Multicultural Graveyard" because I think that the Mediterranean is becoming the biggest graveyard in the world, as a lot of people from all over the world have drowned there, especially from the southern part of the globe. I found a description of this tragedy in Arabic that I translated into English and posted together with the photos, but later I figured out that the text had some mistakes. I discovered that the story was different from what I'd first read.

Q: How did you find out the story and what did you discover after you had posted the "Multicultural Graveyard"?

BARAKEH: When I posted the images I didn't expect them to get that much attention from all over the world. A lot of newspapers, both national and international, contacted me, wanting to know what exactly happened that night, where and to whom. But because I didn't have the facts, I didn't respond, but instead I decided to start my own investigation by searching the ocean of Facebook images to come up with some solid information. I traced the photos from one profile to another trying to get to the source. To the person who was standing on the beach that night.

Q: What was the aim of your research?

BARAKEH: I wanted to know what the real story was, as well as to find out who took the photos! Later on I discovered that the boat started its journey from the beach at Zuwara in Libya heading toward the shores of Europe! It had around 470 people on board, and more than half of them drowned. Some volunteers

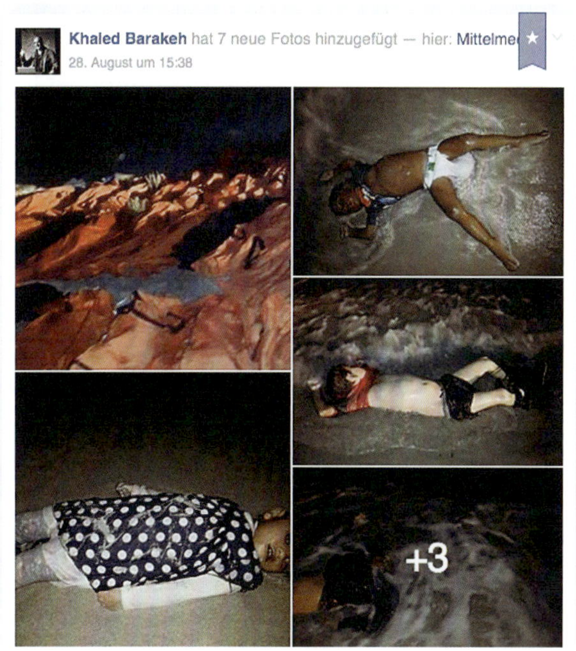

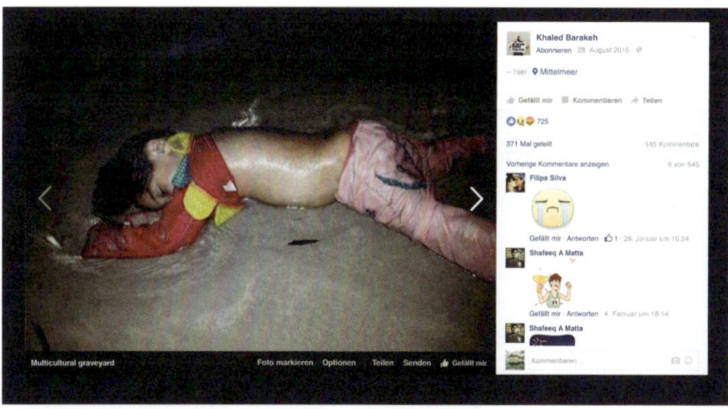

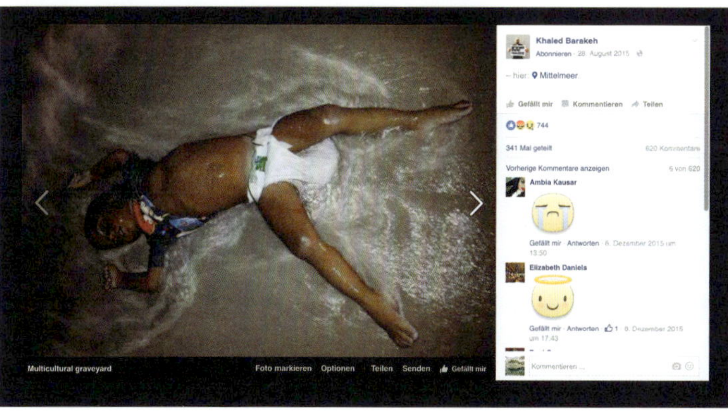

from the Libyan Red Crescent tried to save the ones who were still alive, while documenting the deaths of those who weren't so lucky. They took photos of the dead bodies and samples of their DNA for the ones they couldn't identify.

Q: *Why do you need to know who was on the boat?*
BARAKEH: Because these people have names, faces, and stories that must be heard, and I feel it is my responsibility to do this! It's like finding a baby in a basket at your front door... You can't just close the door and ignore the fact that it's there. Also since that date, if you search my name on the web, you'll find my photo side by side with the images of the drowned children.

I still don't know exactly what happened on that journey and I want to know! So I decided to go to Libya to find out more. I'm now in contact with people from organizations in Malta, Libya, and Italy, and with some locals from Zuwara in order to figure out what happened during the night of August 27.

Q: *I remember that I saw your post on the evening of August 28. Three days later, all the images you'd posted disappeared. What happened?*
BARAKEH: On August 31, after it had been shared over 140,000 times, many people who had shared the photographs noticed that the link had disappeared from their timelines, including myself, of course. I didn't receive any notification from Facebook as to why they had all been deleted, even though I wrote to them asking for an explanation! However, after many newspaper and websites commented on it, a Facebook spokesperson told mashable.com, "This content was flagged in error by our systems as spam, and we have since corrected it. We apologize for the temporary removal of this content." They stated that the album had been deleted due to an internal bug. However, by making this mistake and playing the role of censor, Facebook drew even more attention to the images after they put the album back. Writer and professor of media, culture and communication at NYU Dr. Nicholas D. Mirzoeff wrote, "With close to one billion users, Facebook is, like it or not, the public square in this fraught moment of globalization. In particular, it is being used extensively by refugees themselves and by those seeking to help them. We now need to find ways to hold them to appropriate standards for this vital resource and to agitate to make sure such censorship is not happening elsewhere."

Q: *I remember that people on Facebook responded immediately. I also felt cheated because I wanted to show the images to a friend, but then I couldn't find them any more. So I got into the public discussion of censorship on Facebook, which I followed with a great deal of interest.*
BARAKEH: In the album itself, and in each picture, there are thousands and thousands of comments and sub-comments. I also received hundreds of messages in many different

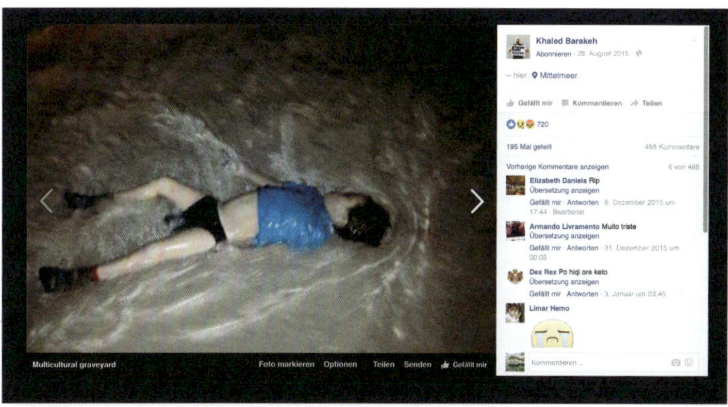

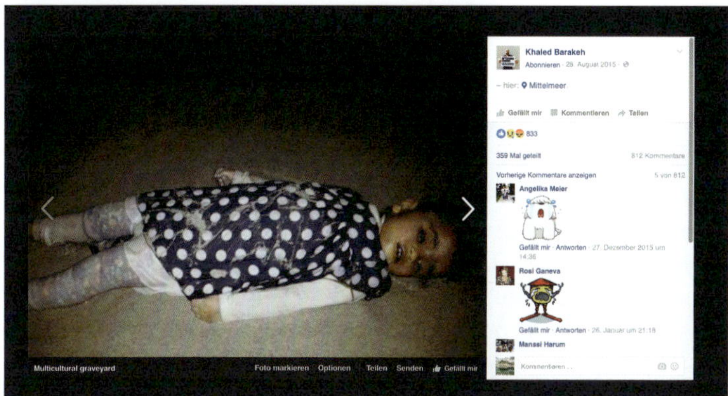

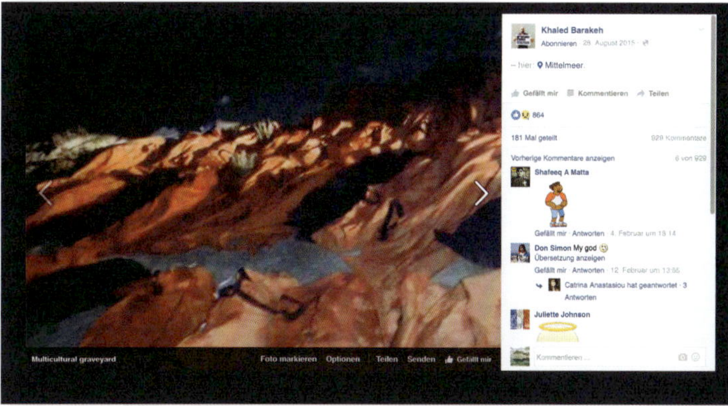

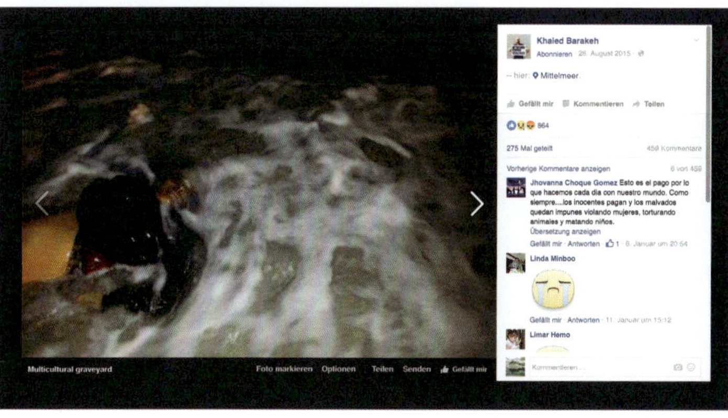

languages. Some people thanked me for posting the images because "I opened their eyes" and "everyone should know" and "I changed the world," while others blamed me for doing that and told me "to go to hell" or asked "how can I dare to post such images online?" or"what if they were my children?" etc.—all kinds of things. Some people wrote me long texts privately describing their opinions, which I found very thoughtful.

The controversy, from both sides, became a substantive debate where people raised interesting questions: Should, or shouldn't, such images be seen? What is the role of photography in our modern mass-media societies? What are the community standards in social media—and who has the right to decide these standards? Aren't our values and cultural standards different anyway? Why should the ethics of a company such as Facebook force its capitalistic values on everyone? The answers indeed were no less important than the questions, which prompted me to think about collecting them all and making a book, written collectively, about how we deal with images in our contemporary societies.

> *Q: It was September 3, 2015, when the photo of the dead Alan Kurdi, the child who drowned on the Turkish shore, was published internationally—you could find this image on the cover of all the major newspapers. There was a big discussion about whether newspapers were allowed to publish such things—should they or shouldn't they print this photo?—but then the whole conversation disappeared very quickly. The problem I have with this is that it's so focused on one single shot. But there are so many others. And I actually think it's so misleading to have only one image when there are so many other children and adults dying at sea. The single photo is always a simplification, a cutting-out of a part of the reality, and it denies the rest of what's going on around. So I found your post much more effective and closer to reality than the image of this little boy. I remember how long I was staring at each of these seven photos. One child who was already ten or eleven had a diaper on. The diaper was soaked with water and when I first saw it I couldn't make it out properly. It took me a moment to understand why this girl was wearing diapers. The reason was quite simple: they didn't know how long they would have to stay on the boat and they hadn't got a toilet there. Every image spoke to me and gave me a strong impression of what's going on, on the other side of the Mediterranean.*

BARAKEH: I don't think the images I posted were taken by professional photographers, which makes them even stronger and more real for the viewer. Personally I don't like where we are at now with photojournalism, particularly war photojournalism! The aesthetics of photos make death prettier and more acceptable. Look at any international press and photographic agencies: the editors and photographers want to make a bigger impression or be more artistic, with the result that photos lose their function of delivering reality as it is. Susan Sontag, in her book *On Photography*, says, "Although photography generates works that can be called art—it requires subjectivity, it can lie, it gives aesthetic pleasure—photography is not, to begin with, an art form at all. Like language, it is a medium in which works of art (among other things) are made."

I think we are drowning everyday in thousands of irrelevant images that leave our brain doped. So photography must be shocking to cut through this anesthetization (the image of Alan Kurdi, as an example, and all the reactions that followed). By the way, I agree with you that it is only a single shot, but I am happy nonetheless that one, at least, finally got into the international newspapers! Otherwise we would have continued our death in silence, as we have over the past five years. Also I don't think that the image of Alan monopolized the refugee crisis but rather became a symbol of it (like many other iconic images in history). What really matters is to keep the subject present in the political discourse.

Q: But a lot of newspapers did not publish the full image. Very often the Turkish policeman who picked the boy up off the ground was cut out. You could only see the little boy looking like he was sleeping on the beach.

BARAKEH: I see your point but at the same time it doesn't really matter, because the photo was circulated around the world anyway. Even right-wing newspapers weren't able to ignore it and published it the day after. And it was good, it was a call for people to wake up; and that's why it made a difference, even if it was just a single image. The whole attitude toward refugees became completely different. We really had a turning point between the time before that image appeared and after. Also look at the other side, the survivors; I'm happy for them. They reached a point where a lot of people sympathized with their cause. Germany, for example, took in one million refugees, which wouldn't have happened if those images hadn't been made public.

Q: Why this image and not another?

BARAKEH: I can't really answer that question but I will try to analyze the photo: we see a dead child alone on the beach. No past or future (no parents even), only his death is present. He is the final result of a war where it doesn't matter any more who is fighting whom. The position of his body tells his story: his head points to the sea, and what's beyond it, while his feet are pointing to the land where he came from, and his little body is stuck in the middle. In an isthmus.

He is wearing jeans and a red T-shirt like any other child. His face is down where we can't see his features. We can't tell if he is Middle Eastern, European, African, or Asian! He could be the child of any of us. Everyone can identify their children or themselves with this image.

Also there is the contrast between his death and the vitality of the beautiful beach and the blue sky. Finally there is this authority guy, the Turkish policeman standing on the beach, writing notes about his short life. Taken all together, these things make it very strong, because it's very peaceful, this image.

The conversation with Khaled Barakeh was published in the end of the world as we know it ist der Beginn einer Welt, die wir nicht kennen, *catalog of the 7th Festival for Photography f/stop by Spector Books, 2016.*

Anne König

A Misleading Caption

On October 30, 2015, an article with the title "Italian Laboratory Works to Give Names to Migrant Dead" appeared in *The New York Times International Weekly*, a supplement to the *Süddeutsche Zeitung*. The piece was accompanied by a picture from Labanof, the laboratory in Milan for forensic anthropology and odontology, showing young female students at tables, inspecting bones with their bare hands and sorting them into boxes. The caption to the picture read "Italian students examine human remains to identify migrants who died in transit to Europe, and then try to notify families."

When I saw the picture for the first time, I was immediately struck by it. Pictures showing the remains of drowned people being examined in order to assess their identity are rare in print and digital media. Headlines, always showing the same kinds of photos, usually read "29 dead on refugee boat," or "Dozens of people drowned in the Mediterranean Sea." It is not of great interest to the media what happens to the bodies. It would probably spoil the next beach holiday if the process of decomposition in salt water were described in detail.

In the article, I also read about the serious attempts made by the Italian government after the shipwrecks of October 3 and October 10, where 387 people drowned in the waters off Lampedusa, to set up a special envoy to find out the identity of the missing persons with the help of experts. Until now, Italy has been mainly working alone in this field, while the European Union has shown little interest.

Since the spring of 2014, a team around the forensic pathologist Cristina Cattaneo, director of Labanof, has been developing a database with information and pictures in order to restore the dignity and names of those people who traveled across the Mediterranean Sea without any documents. After all, issuing a death certificate can not only give some certainty to the relatives but can also help the surviving dependents to deal with legal issues.

After the shipwrecks of Lampedusa, the Italian Police prepared files for all the bodies and took pictures and DNA samples. In a cumbersome process, the relatives of the victims were contacted in Eritrea and Syria in order to verify the data. Relatives living in Europe who contacted the authorities sometimes had to take a genetic test. Occasionally, old mandibular X-rays of the dead provided by their relatives were able to contribute helpful information. Antemortem data, personal information from the lives of those who had died—sometimes even their Facebook profiles—were compared with the postmortem data to ascertain their identity. Of all the 387 victims, Labanof could only identify thirty-five people with any certainty. DNA testing was the decisive method in achieving these results.

When looking at the picture in *The New York Times International Weekly*, I didn't just notice some bones but also the bare hands of the students. If the examinations at Labanof were really to find the DNA of the victims, these young students should have worn gloves in order not to mix their own DNA with that of the dead. Something about the picture or the caption didn't make sense.

On October 2, 2015, the online edition of *The New York Times* had published an article with the title "Italian Lab Battles 'Not to Lose the Dead' from Migrant Ships." The lead picture by Fabio Bucciarelli was the same as the one in the print edition from October 30, 2015, that I had in front of me. The picture was accompanied by a slightly different caption: "Students at the University of Milan examining human remains. A lab at the university is trying to identify migrants who died trying to cross to Europe." The full stop between the two statements in the sentence indicated a slight difference between the examination of bones shown in the picture and tests conducted on bones from the bodies of refugees recovered

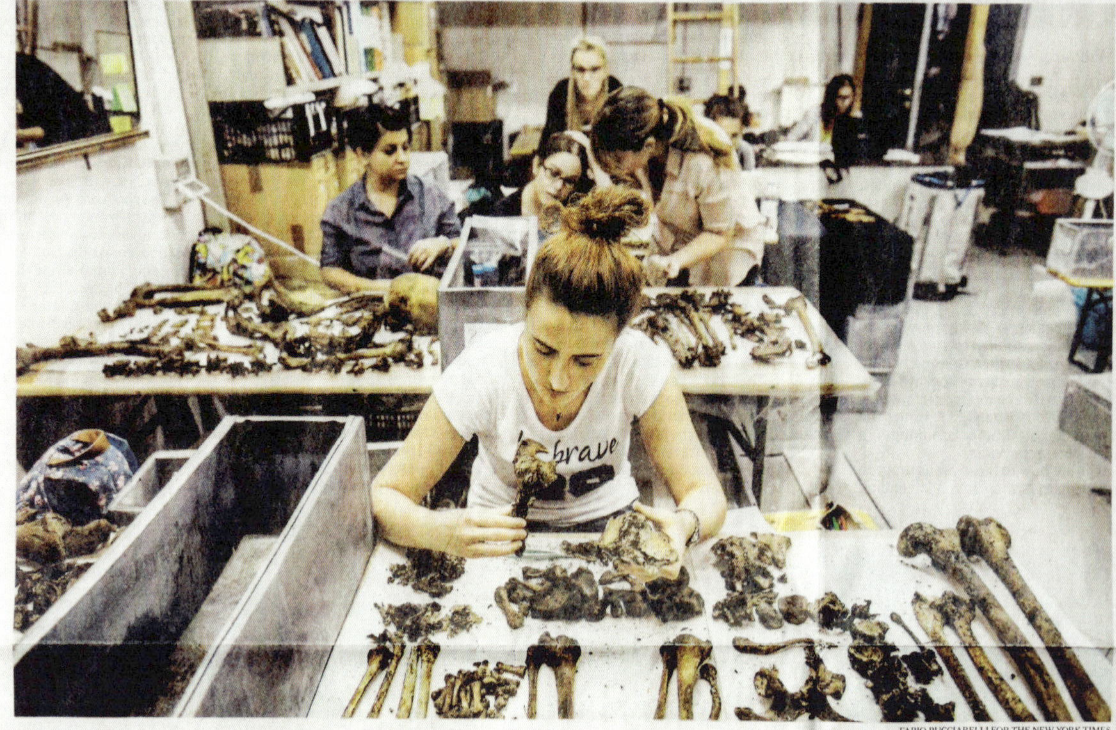

FABIO BUCCIARELLI FOR THE NEW YORK TIMES

Italian Laboratory Works to Give Names to Migrant Dead

By ELISABETTA POVOLEDO

MILAN — In one photograph, a pretty, young Eritrean woman dressed in cheerful colors smiles brightly into the camera. In another, glazed eyes stare out of a blue, bloated face, typical of drowning victims.

But it is the teeth, frozen in a grimace of death, that the scientists here were interested in. They were a match.

The finding will allow them to let the woman's family know for sure that she — their daughter, wife or sister perhaps — was among the 368 migrants who died when their boat capsized off the Italian island of Lampedusa two years ago.

So far this year, almost 2,900 migrants have drowned making the crossing to Europe from North Africa. Often, they are the nameless victims of one of this century's greatest tidal movements of people fleeing war and poverty — dying in anonymity, far from home, their loved ones left in limbo about their fates, and the authorities uncertain of exactly who they are.

Since the spring of 2014, however, this laboratory at the University of Milan has been working to give a name to those hundreds of unidentified migrants who drowned at sea in the Lampedusa wreck and others.

"Our battle is not to lose the dead," said Dr. Cristina Cattaneo, a forensic pathologist, who runs the Labanof, the laboratory that has been building a databank to help identify the victims of the migrant shipwrecks off Italy in recent years.

Even now, two years after the sinking, nearly 200 victims of the Lampedusa wreck have not been officially identified. "The more decomposed they are the more difficult it is to identify them," Dr. Cattaneo said.

Fearful of European regulations that force migrants to ask for asylum in the first country in which they land, many migrants do not carry any ID, making identification even harder.

Another challenge has been reaching the families of the victims, many of whom live in war-torn or repressive countries, or in places where medical records are difficult to retrieve.

"Our problem has been contacting relatives," said Vittorio Piscitelli, Italy's High Commissioner for Missing Persons, whose office has reached out to embassies and various humanitarian agencies — like the International Committee for the Red Cross — for assistance.

Even when relatives can be tracked down in Europe, getting them to come to Italy for the identification process can be time consuming and costly. In addition, in countries like Eritrea, where many of the Lampedusa victims came from, relatives of migrants risk repercussions from an oppressive government.

Still, over the past years, small groups of family members of presumed victims have traveled to Italy, hoping to find news of their loved ones. They bring fragments of lost lives — ID cards and photos or videos, clinical and dental records and personal effects like toothbrushes or combs — to

Using fragments of a lost life to make a match to a corpse.

help make a match.

They are interviewed by trained personnel and then pore through a database of personal effects, like bracelets or necklaces, phones or clothes, looking for identifying clues.

DNA comparisons are also made, and much of the data is culled from autopsies: tattoos, surgery scars, dental records and other biological remains.

Adal Neguse, 40, an Eritrean migrant now living in Stockholm, was the first relative to arrive in Lampedusa after the October 3, 2013, shipwreck, searching for his brother Abraham.

He spent a week looking at photographs of the victims.

"I finally had to stop because it was too disturbing," he said.

Abraham was eventually identified months later through the clothing he was wearing.

The aim of the laboratory, and of the Italian authority that oversees it, is eventually to help relatives like him identify their loved ones by setting up a broad database of all the victims of the Mediterranean crossing to Italy. In attempting to do so, Italy was "moved by humanitarian and ethical reasons, as well as a sense of pietas for the dead, and to grant relatives some peace," said Mr. Piscitelli, who coordinates the laboratory's work.

The team involves experts from four universities as well as biologists, anthropologists, forensic dentists and specialized technicians developing a single protocol that can be used in any shipwreck situation, she said.

So far, some 20 victims have been identified through the lab's work.

"It's a small number, but it means that the procedure works," Dr. Cattaneo said.

from the seabed. I asked Cristina Cattaneo why the students in the picture didn't wear gloves, and she replied that the journalist had promised to write that the students in the picture were working on the laboratory's study collection of bones. In no way were these the bones of the refugee victims in the picture, which would never be shown in this way. The person who edited the caption for *The New York Times International Weekly* certainly intended to adjust the text of the caption to the image, which did not entirely fit. If he had only mentioned the laboratory collection of bones for study purposes, the refugees would have disappeared from the picture, but that was, after all, the main topic. Or maybe the journalist herself didn't pass on the right information, in an attempt to sell the picture more effectively. This superficial way of dealing with the facts certainly doesn't cast a good light on the profession as a whole.

Later I read that the tragic shipwrecks off Lampedusa in October 2013 were those in which the largest number of drowned people could actually be identified. But what about all the others who haven't made it to the European mainland, whose bones are still lying somewhere at the bottom of the Mediterranean Sea?

— www.nytimes.com/2015/10/03/world/europe/
italian-lab-battles-not-to-lose-the-dead-from-migrant-
ships.html.
— www.sueddeutsche.de/politik/fluechtlinge-im-
mittelmeer-kreuzzug-gegen-die-gleichgueltigkeit-
1.3007141?reduced=true.
— www.swissinfo.ch/eng/business/the-mediterranean-sea-
-a-mass-grave_the-struggle-to-identify-drowned-
migrants/42238266.

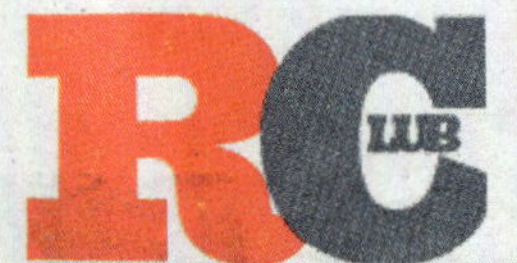

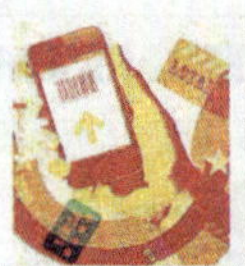

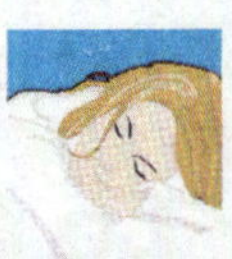

la Repubblica

Fondatore Eugenio Scalfari — Direttore Ezio Mauro

NZ — PD-1F — www.repubblica.it — Anno 38 · N. 241 — in Italia € 1,60 con "D" — (PROV. VE CON LA NUOVA DI VENEZIA E MESTRE € 1,20 CON "D" € 1,70) — sabato 12 ottobre 2013 — 9 770390 107009 31012

SEDE: 00147 ROMA, VIA CRISTOFORO COLOMBO, 90 · TEL. 06/49821, FAX 06/49822923. SPED. ABB. POST., ART. 1, LEGGE 46/04 DEL 27 FEBBRAIO 2004 · ROMA. CONCESSIONARIA DI PUBBLICITÀ: A. MANZONI & C. MILANO · VIA NERVESA, 21 · TEL. 02/574941. PREZZI DI VENDITA: AUSTRIA, BELGIO, FRANCIA, GERMANIA, GRECIA, IRLANDA, LUSSEMBURGO, MALTA, MONACO P., OLANDA, PORTOGALLO, SLOVENIA, SPAGNA € 2,00; CROAZIA KN 15; REGNO UNITO LST 1,80; REPUBBLICA CECA CZK 64; SLOVACCHIA SKK 80/€ 2,66; SVIZZERA FR 3,00; UNGHERIA FT 495; U.S.A. $ 1,50

Nuova tragedia al largo di Lampedusa: si rovescia un barcone, salvate più di 200 persone. Letta: dramma che conferma l'emergenza

Immigrati, la strage infinita

Almeno 50 morti nel Canale di Sicilia, tanti sono bambini

Grillo chiede l'impeachment di Napolitano

Berlusconi si affida ai servizi sociali: io come Timoshenko

ROMA — Ieri i legali dell'ex presidente del Consiglio Silvio Berlusconi hanno depositato al Tribunale di Milano l'istanza per l'affidamento ai servizi sociali come misura alternativa al carcere. Il Cavaliere si è sfogato con il suo entourage paragonando la propria situazione a quella della Timoshenko, l'ex premier dell'Ucraina, che si trova in prigione. Intanto Beppe Grillo, leader del Movimento 5 Stelle, ha chiesto l'impeachment per il capo dello Stato, Giorgio Napolitano.

SERVIZI DA PAGINA 9 A PAGINA 15

BEPPE, CASALEGGIO E LA MALAPOLITICA

CURZIO MALTESE

PER una volta a Beppe Grillo e Gianroberto Casaleggio possiamo dire soltanto grazie. Con il loro post, ormai giustamente famoso, sul reato di clandestinità i fondatori del movimento 5 stelle hanno infatti disvelato i meccanismi della disastrosa Seconda Repubblica e della mala politica italiana molto meglio che in centinaia di comizi. Trattandosi di persone geniali, sono bastate loro due righe.

SEGUE A PAGINA 31

dai nostri inviati
FRANCESCO VIVIANO
ALESSANDRA ZINITI

LAMPEDUSA

IL CANALE di Sicilia inghiotte un altro barcone, altri corpi senza vita galleggiano in mare.

SEGUE ALLE PAGINE 2 E 3

Il racconto

Il naufragio della civiltà

ATTILIO BOLZONI

ANCORA morti, nel mare davanti all'Italia. Ci sono ancora cadaveri da ripescare a Lampedusa e affiorano altri corpi. Altri naufraghi, fra le onde un altro cimitero. Il Mediterraneo sta diventando in queste ore una sola, grande e invisibile croce.

SEGUE A PAGINA 4

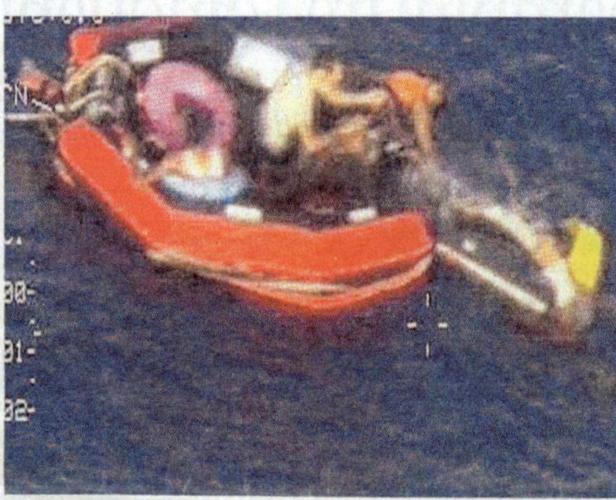

Il soccorso in mare ai naufraghi del barcone affondato ieri a 60 miglia a sud di Lampedusa

Repubblica delle idee "Mai più lutti: per i migranti noi siamo il futuro"

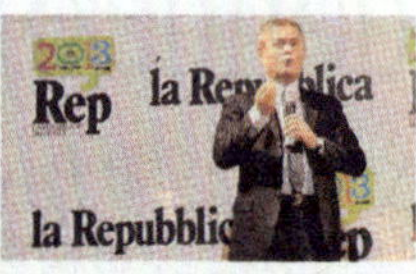

Ezio Mauro oggi intervista Enrico Letta

L'intervento

L'Europa senza qualità

BARBARA SPINELLI

ESISTE un gioco che a molti esperti pare astruso, o perché superfluo o perché poco serio e fuorviante. È il gioco della storia che *si fa con i se*: che ha dunque come oggetto non solo il mondo com'è stato fatto – come ci sta davanti – ma come avrebbe potuto essere, se invece di imboccare una strada ne avesse presa un'altra.

SEGUE A PAGINA 31

Il cda vara l'operazione da 300 milioni. Lupi: "L'ingresso delle Poste non è un aiuto di Stato"

Sì all'aumento Alitalia, ma Air France frena

Il mercato

Sulle ali dell'ultimo bluff

ALESSANDRO PENATI

DIFFICILE spiegare cosa si prova a vedere un premier e il ministro dei Trasporti in pellegrinaggio dalle aziende pubbliche solo per celare che Alitalia è fallita.

A PAGINA 26

ROMA — Il cda di Alitalia ha approvato una manovra da 300 milioni per il salvataggio della compagnia. I rappresentanti di Air France-Klm hanno tuttavia precisato che non è ancora sicura la loro partecipazione all'aumento di capitale. Sull'ingresso di Poste Italiane, il ministro Lupi: «Non è un aiuto di Stato».

CILLIS, LIVINI E MANIA ALLE PAGINE 6 E 7

Più controlli e aggravanti sulla violenza domestica

Legge sul femminicidio via libera dal Parlamento Il governo: ora le donne non sono più sole

MARIA ELENA VINCENZI A PAGINA 21

Il sondaggio

Radiografia dell'euro-entusiasta

ILVO DIAMANTI

L'ITALIA è stata, per molto tempo, lo Stato più europeista d'Europa. In particolare, negli anni della costruzione unitaria. L'Europa era un progetto in corso d'opera. D'altronde, in occasione del referendum consultivo del 1989, l'88 % dei votanti approvò la proposta di attribuire un mandato costituente al Parlamento europeo.

SEGUE A PAGINA 24

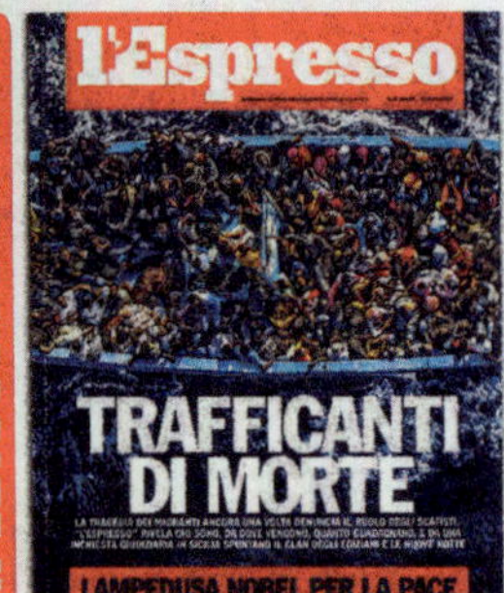

Il caso

Quel Nobel per la pace ai cacciatori di armi chimiche

VITTORIO ZUCCONI

WASHINGTON

IL NOBEL quest'anno coglie un bersaglio giusto, va ai cacciatori di gas, va ai pazzi coraggiosi che hanno fermato—per ora—la marcia della follia in Siria. Il Nobel per la Pace, spesso detonatore più di controversie che di ammirazione, è stato assegnato all'Organizzazione per la Proibizione delle Armi Chimiche.

SEGUE A PAGINA 31
SERVIZI A PAGINA 17

La storia

Priebke muore a 100 anni e lascia un testamento shock

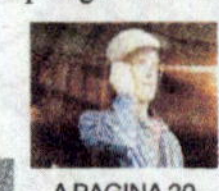

Beffati fan e polizia
'Prendete Banksy'
New York in tilt
per il graffitaro

A PAGINA 20

EMANUELA AUDISIO

È MORTO come ha vissuto. Da nazista superbo e stizzoso. Non da ex. Senza vergognarsi, né pentirsi. Scendere a patti con l'umanità non era roba per lui. Nemmeno una briciola di pietà per gli orrori suoi e della guerra. Quando lo scovarono (per caso) sulle Ande, a Bariloche, era un uomo di 81 anni libero da rimorsi.

SEGUE A PAGINA 19
ANGELI E ISMAN A PAGINA 18

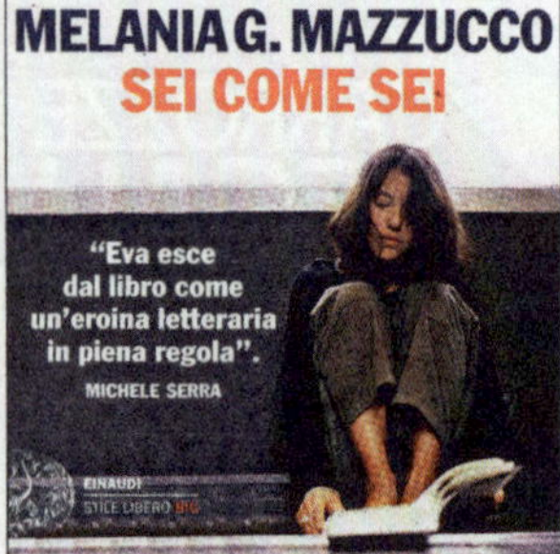

Mare Nostrum

October 18, 2013—October 31, 2014
An account of the operation in images

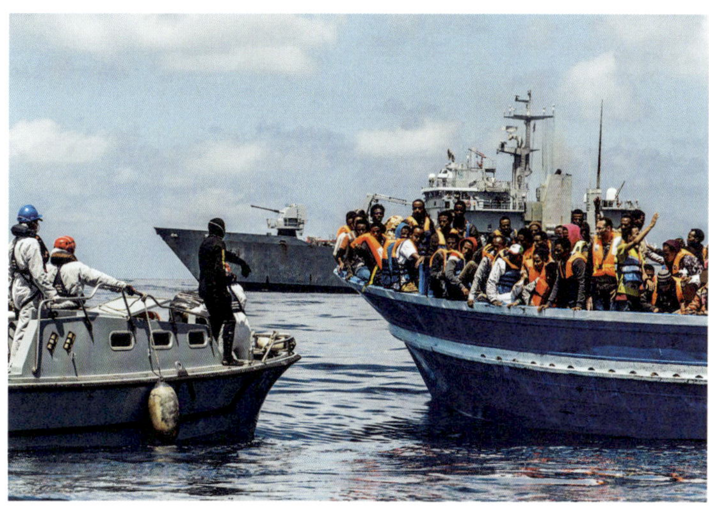

PHOTO STORY: VALERIA MALITO

Agreed on and sponsored by the Italian government on October 14, 2013, the military and humanitarian operation in the southern Mediterranean Sea known as Mare Nostrum began on October 18, 2013, in the wake of yet another shipwreck of migrants off the coast of Lampedusa. Its aim was to tackle the growing phenomenon of migration and the humanitarian emergency unfolding in the Strait of Sicily. The search and rescue operation (SAR) set out to enhance the system for controlling migratory movement that was already in place in the context of the Constant Vigilance mission. This had been carried out by the Italian Navy since 2004 and implemented together with the activities overseen by Frontex, the European agency responsible for securing and managing borders, including the Hermes operation for the control of unauthorized arrivals from Tunisia, Libya, and Algeria, and the Aeneas operation in the Ionian Sea. The Mare Nostrum operation came to an end on October 31, 2014, coinciding with the launch of the European operation known as Triton, whose main objective, however, was border control.

The mission had a dual purpose: to safeguard life on the sea and to bring to justice all those responsible for the illegal trafficking of migrants.

From an operational standpoint the program involved the personnel and naval and airborne resources of the Italian Navy,

* Mare Nostrum
— 700—1,000 military personnel
— 1 LPD-type amphibious vessel
with specific command and control
functions, equipped with advanced
medical facilities for Role 1 care,
including a shelter and biocontainment
pod. The ship can also carry landing
craft and Rigid Hull Inflatable Boats
(RHIB) and is able to receive on board
representatives of other ministries
or national/international organizations
involved in the operation
— 2 Minerva Class corvettes
— 2 Costellazioni/Comandanti Class
patrol ships, each providing 1 SH-212
helicopter: one of which is in the
fisheries surveillance role
— 1 medium-to-heavy SH90 (TRR)
helicopter carried on board the
amphibious ship, along with 2 S-100
unmanned aerial vehicles (UAV)
— 1 EH101 (MPH) helicopter deployed
ashore on Lampedusa
— 1 MM P180 aircraft and 1 PS P180
aircraft, equipped with
ForwardLookingInfraRed (FLIR)
cameras, deployed at Pratica di Mare
— 1 LRMP Breguet Atlantic deployed
at Sigonella
— 1 AW139 medium helicopter (Police)
deployed at Lampedusa
— 1 AW109 light utility helicopter
(Carabinieri) deployed at Lampedusa
— Italian Navy coastal radar
network and Automatic Identification
System (AIS)
Source: www.marina.difesa.it/EN/
operations/Pagine/MareNostrum.aspx

the Italian Air Force, the Carabinieri, the Guardia di Finanza, and the Port Authority; the personnel of the Military Corps of the Italian Red Cross, the Ministry of the Interior, and the State Police deployed on the ships of the Italian Navy, as well as all the government bodies that in different ways contribute to the control of migratory flows arriving by sea.*

The command of the mission was assigned to an admiral based on board ship, and charged with controlling and monitoring the situation. This unit also had on board personnel from the Department of Public Security's Central Directorate for Immigration and the Border Police to improve the system of checks used to identify migrants directly on board. Health controls were carried out by on-board medical staff, supported by the doctors of the ISMAF (Sea and Air Border Health Department), the personnel of the Military Corps, volunteer nurses from the Italian Red Cross, and volunteer healthcare personnel from the CISOM (Order of Malta's Italian Relief Corps) and the Francesca Rava Foundation.

During the operation's year of activity, it is estimated that 156,362 migrants were rescued in about 439 SAR missions involving 854 identified vessels.

This is the story of the rescues in their different phases, through a selection of images gathered in the area reserved for the press corps on the website of the Italian Navy. The site's server contained over one thousand files, including images and videos, divided into rescues or landings, bearing witness to the operations conducted from March to November 2014 on Italy's southern border. The material was recorded directly by the rescuers involved in the operation with video cameras installed on security devices, by members of the crew with cameras and mobile phones, and by professional photographers on board the ships who had been hired to produce reportage or provide special documentary services.

Each of the images provides important information about the operation in all its complexity and the migratory phenomenon in progress. The following pages contain captions with information about the way the files were originally archived, with specific data on their source and subject. It has also been possible in certain cases to trace the author, the device utilized, and the date of the image or video, through information embedded in the files themselves.

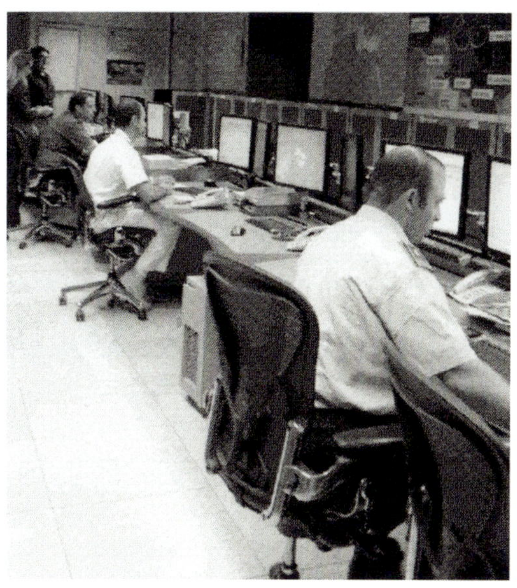

← Operations room in the Roberto Iavarone National Center of Coordination for Immigration at the Central Directorate for Immigration and Border Police (National Coordination Center – NCC) in Rome.

Besides representatives of the Italian Navy, there are also operatives of the State Police's Central Directorate for Immigration, the Port Authorities, the Guardia di Finanza, and the Carabinieri, whose job is to coordinate monitoring and sea rescue operations carried out with their own resources with those of other departments, to optimize available resources and to effectively share information. The Italian Navy also organizes the activities of its men and resources through the Operations Center of the Navy within the Central Command of the Naval Squadron at Santa Rosa, Rome. At this facility information supplied by naval and airborne craft, the coastal radar of the Italian Navy and other departments, and the naval forces of other Mediterranean countries participating in the Virtual Regional Maritime Traffic Center for the exchange of information on merchant traffic in the ports of the member countries, is gathered, compiled, and analyzed. The data are utilized to formulate a real-time image of the maritime zone where military ships are operating, and where there are possible unidentified vessels. Here too there are representatives of the agencies/commands and departments involved in the Mare Nostrum operation.

Photographer: unknown
Camera: Device unknown
Date: unknown
Source: Image from the article "Mare Nostrum, 5,700 rescued, 'Our longest day'" by Vincenzo R. Spagnolo, published in *Avvenire*, July 19, 2014, p. 10

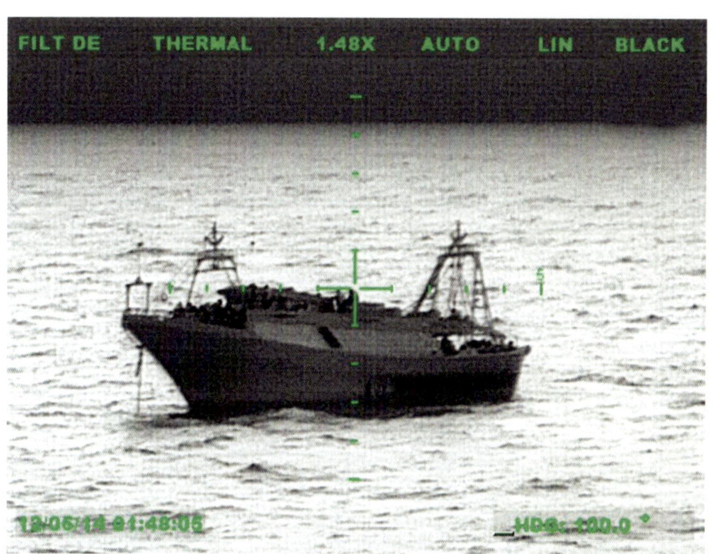

← *Infrared image of the sighting of a vessel.*
Rescue events of May 12–14
> *Nave Scirocco*
Photographer: unknown
Date: May 12, 2014
Camera: Infrared visor
Source: Italian Navy Archives

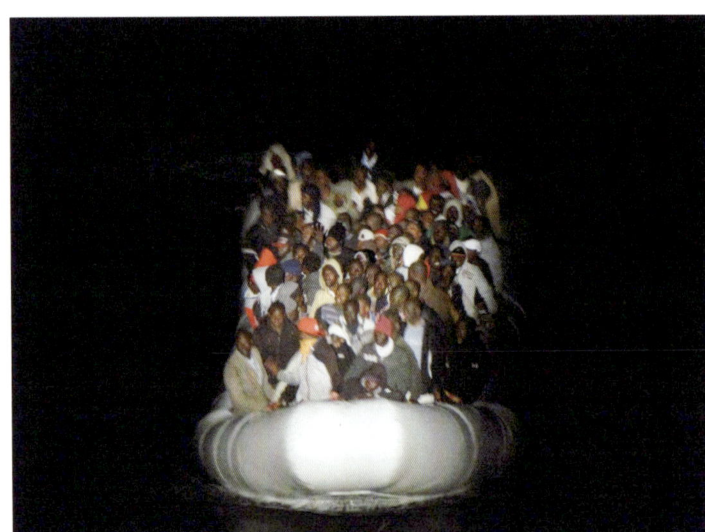

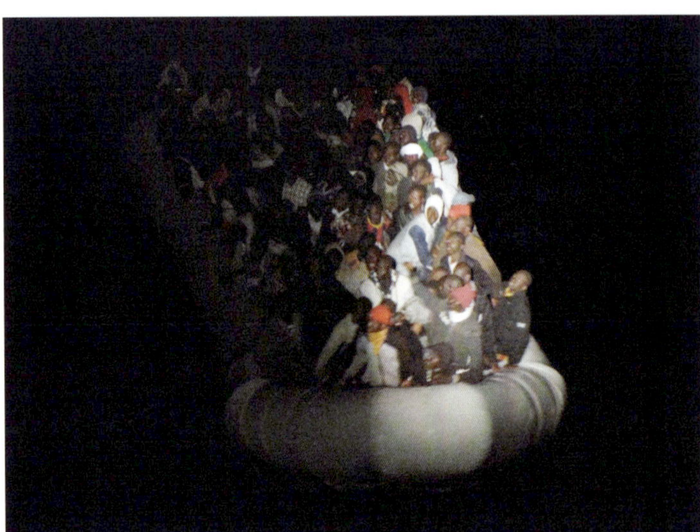

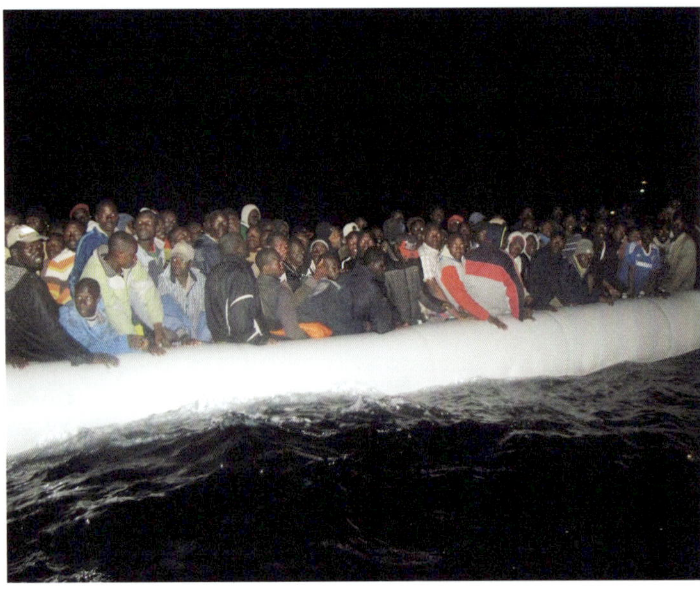

← *Sighting of inflatable raft adrift at sea and packed with migrants traveling at night without lights.* Rescue events of April 8, 9, and 10, 2014 > Rescue events of April 10 > *Nave Stromboli*
Photographer: unknown
Date: April 10, 2014
Camera: Canon PowerShot SX10 IS
Source: Italian Navy Archives

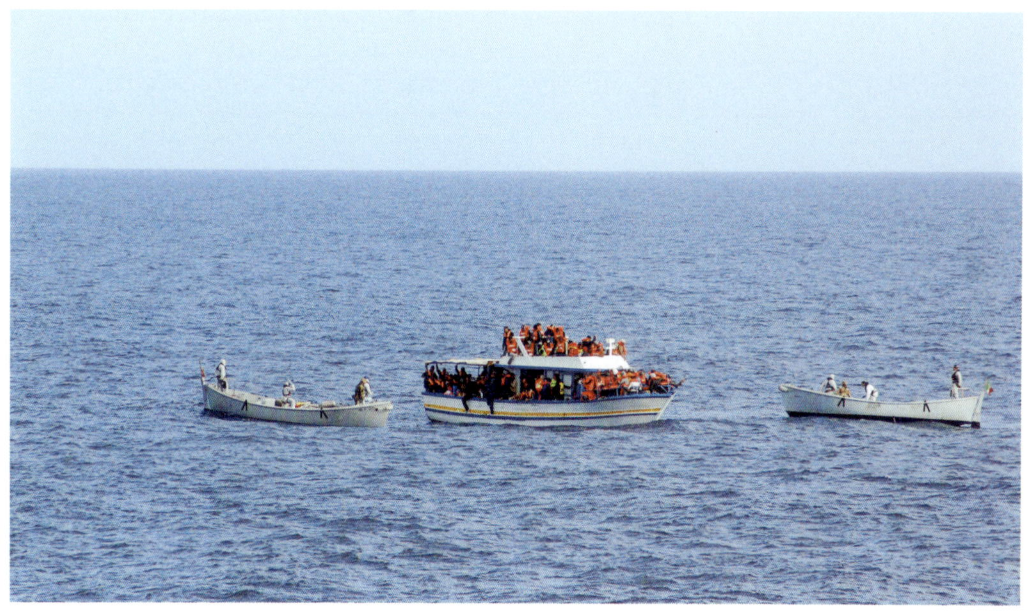

↑   *Rescue of vessel with migrants / zef*
SAR operation: two motorboats from the Nave Zeffiro *(F577)*
intercept a vessel with migrants on board. On each motorboat
the military personnel, equipped with individual single-use
safety devices (white coverall, face mask, latex gloves) are in
constant radio contact with the commander of the ship, who
coordinates the sea rescue operations from the operations deck.
Sometimes, in situations where the migrants are particularly
agitated and the vessel is in a precarious condition, members
of the San Marco Regiment are deployed on the motorboats to
support and expedite the operations.
Photographer: Primo Maresciallo Enrico Spissu
Date: January 12, 2014
Camera: Nikon D50
Source: Italian Navy Archives

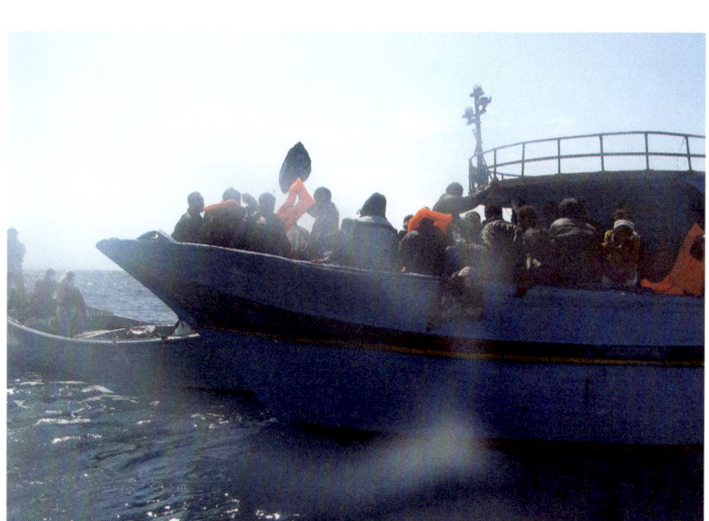

←   *Interception of vessel and distri-*
bution to the migrants of individual
life-jackets of different sizes,
contained in large black sacks thrown
onto the vessel.
Events of April 14 > Stromboli April 14
Photographer: unknown
Date: April 14, 2014
Camera: Canon PowerShot SX10 IS
Source: Italian Navy Archives

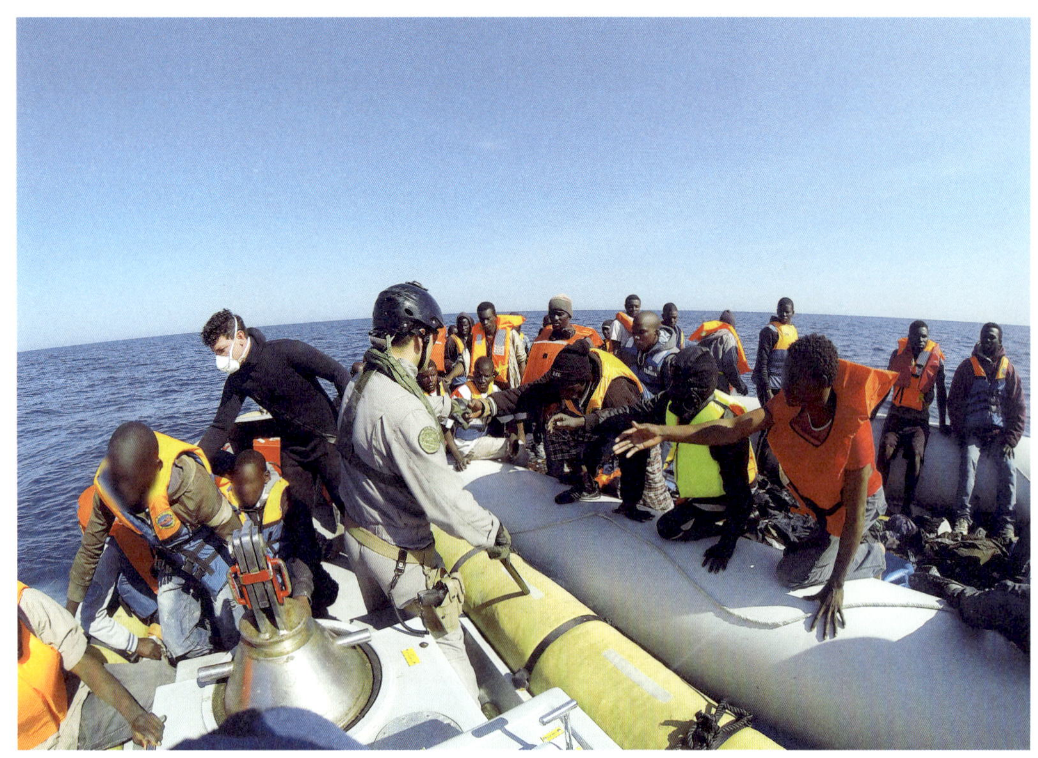

↑   *Transfer of migrants onto rigid inflatable boat belonging to the Italian Navy.*
Rescue events of April 8, 9, and 10, 2014> Rescue events of April 10 > Foscari
Photographer: unknown
Date: April 9, 2014
Camera: GoPro Hero3-Black Edition
Source: Italian Navy Archives

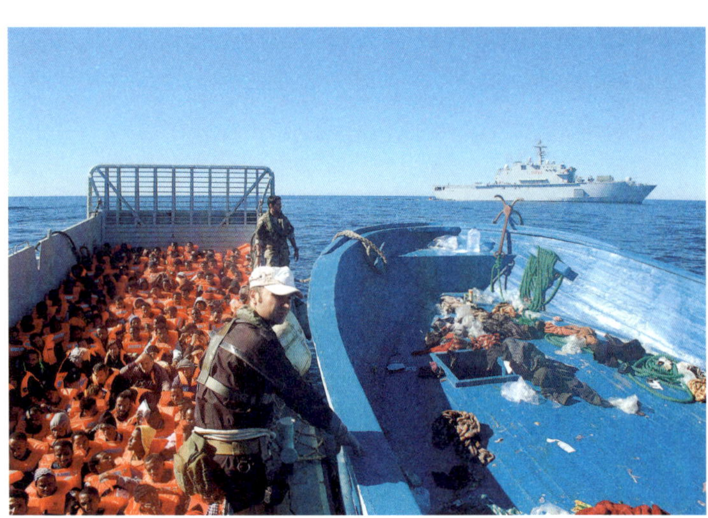

←   *Completion of transfer of migrants from the vessel to the MEN landing craft with the amphibious ship* San Giusto *in the background.*
Photographer: unknown
Date: February 16, 2014
Camera: Nikon D50
Source: Italian Navy Archives

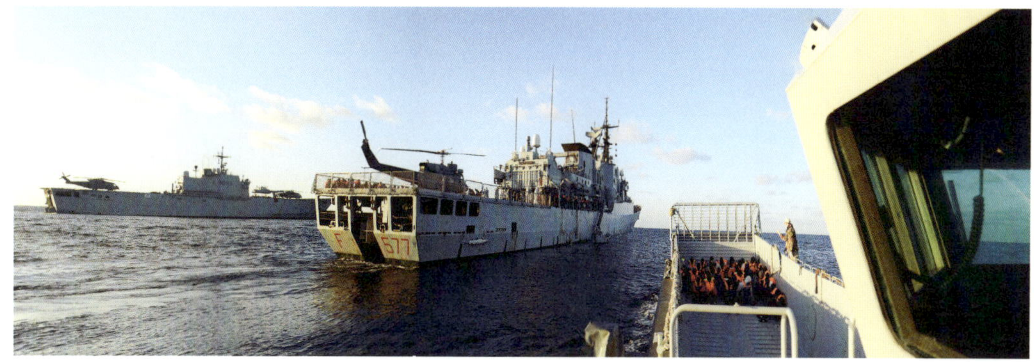

↑   *From left, the* Nave San Marco *(L9893) and* Nave Zeffiro *(F577) seen from the landing craft with migrants on board.*
Photographer: Giancarlo Silvestrin
Date: January 9, 2014
Camera: Nikon D7000
Source: Italian Navy Archives; Image from the article "Mare Nostrum: A year of struggle against the trafficking of human beings" by Carlo Disma, published in *Notiziario della Marina Militare*, Anno LXI, October 2014, pp. 8–9

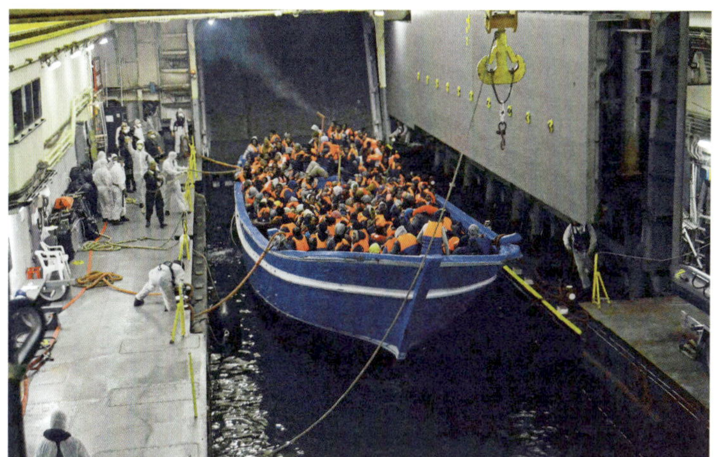

←   *Docking of a vessel carrying migrants in the floodable basin on the* Nave San Giorgio, *which is used to facilitate boarding procedures.*
Event of San Giorgio – May 20
Photographer: unknown
Date: May 20, 2014
Camera: Nikon D3100
Source: Italian Navy Archives

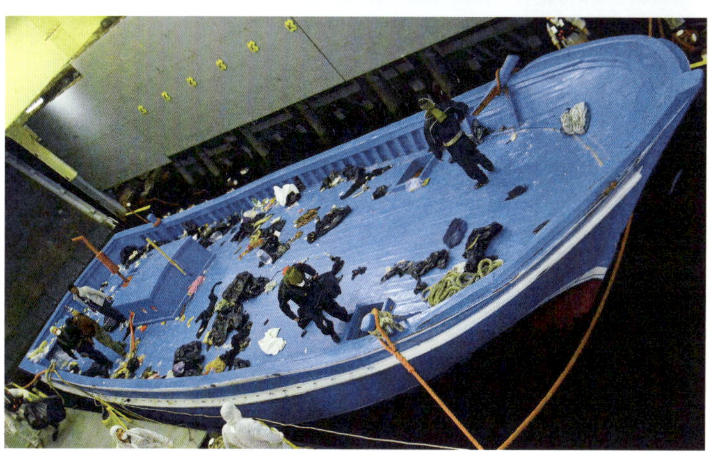

←   *After the migrants have disembarked, crew members inspect the vessel moored in the floodable basin of the* Nave San Giorgio *to check that no items of value belonging to the occupants or evidence that could enable the authorities to prosecute the traffickers have been left on board.*
Event of San Giorgio – May 20
Photographer: unknown
Date: May 20, 2014
Camera: Nikon D3100
Source: Italian Navy Archives

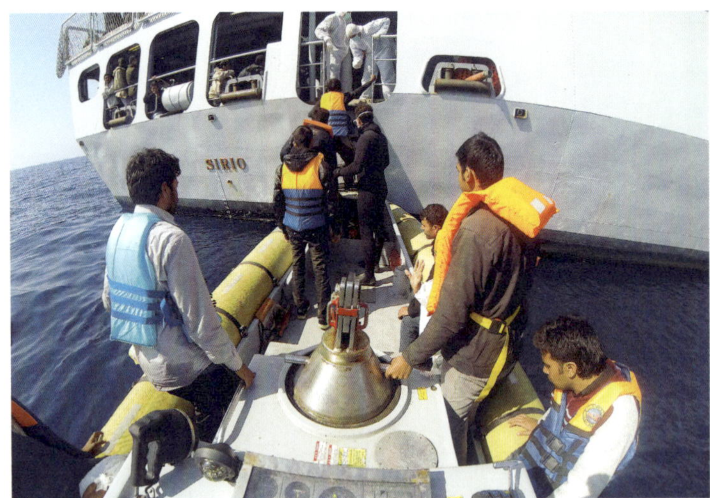

← *Members of the crew of the* Nave Sirio *assist in the transfer of the migrants from the inflatable boat.* Rescue events of April 8, 9, and 10, 2014 > *Nave Foscari* patrol vessel supporting the *Nave Sirio* – April 9
Photographer: unknown
Date: April 9, 2014
Camera: GoPro Hero3 Black Edition
Source: Italian Navy Archives

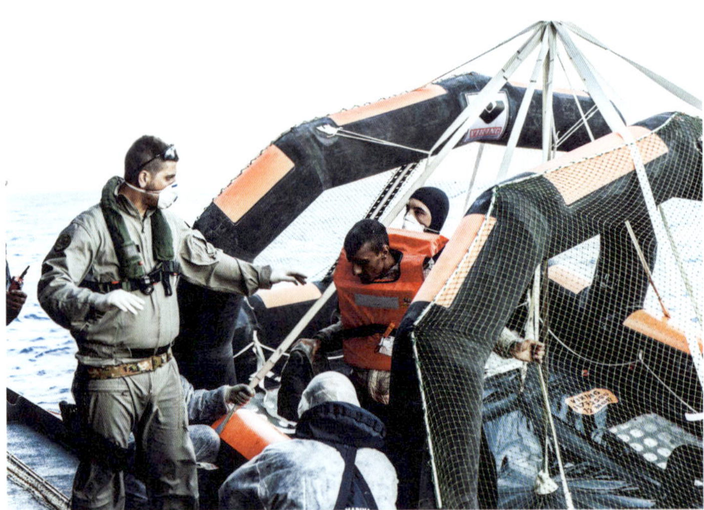

← *Crew members of the* Nave Bergamini *help to transfer the migrants from the self-inflating life raft lifted onto the deck of the naval unit.* June 5, 2014_NaveBergamini > *Nave Bergamini*
Photographer: Gabriele Lenzi
Date: June 4, 2014
Camera: Nikon D700
Source: Italian Navy Archives

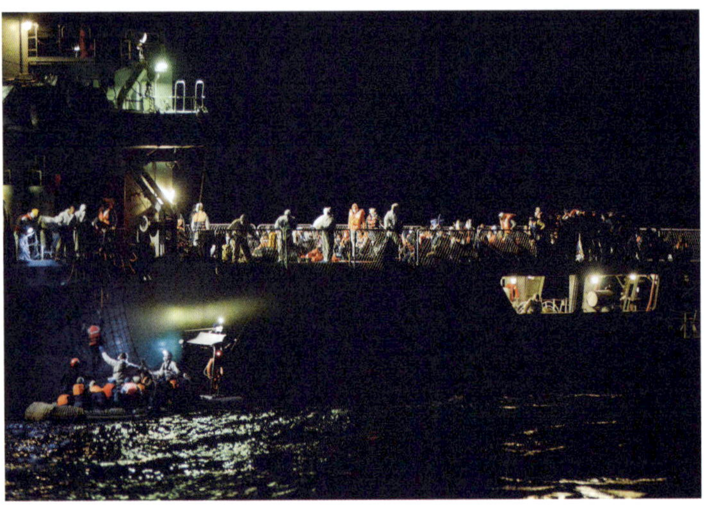

← *Transfer of rescued migrants via the "scramble net" lowered over the side of the ship, and subsequent reception and organization of the individuals on the deck of the ship.*
Photographer: Corrado Carrubba
Date: November 14, 2014
Camera: Nikon D600
Source: Italian Navy Archives

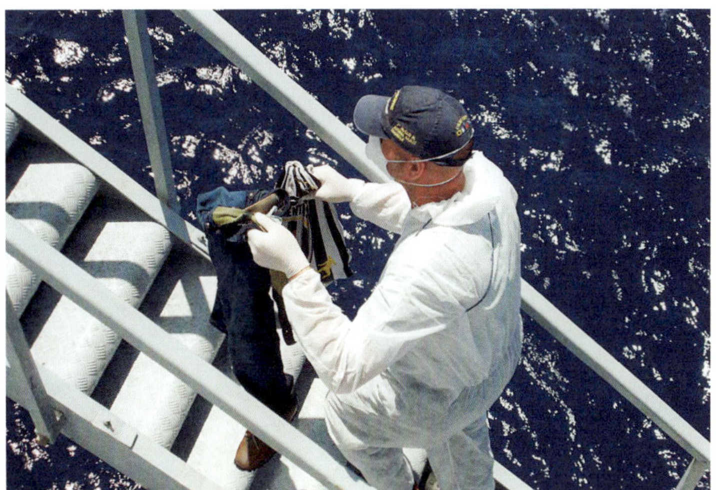

← A crew member returns personal effects and a prosthesis recovered from the intercepted vessel to a rescued migrant.
SAR events of June 12, 13, 14, 2014 >
SAR event, *Nave Orione*, June 12, 2014
Photographer: unknown
Date: June 14, 2014
Camera: Device unknown
Source: Italian Navy Archives

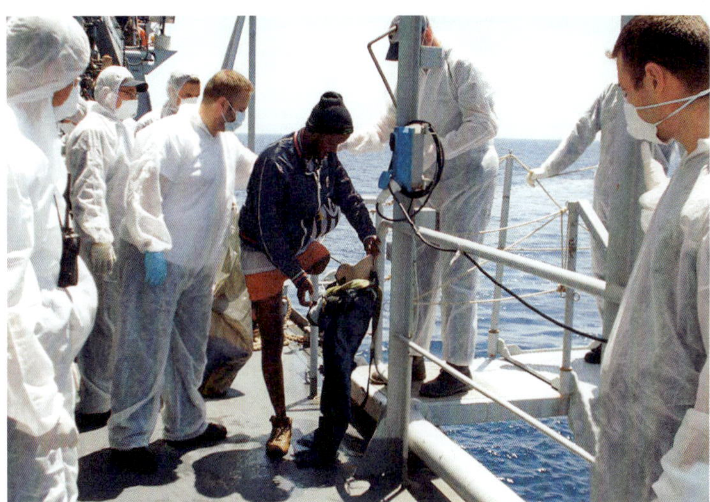

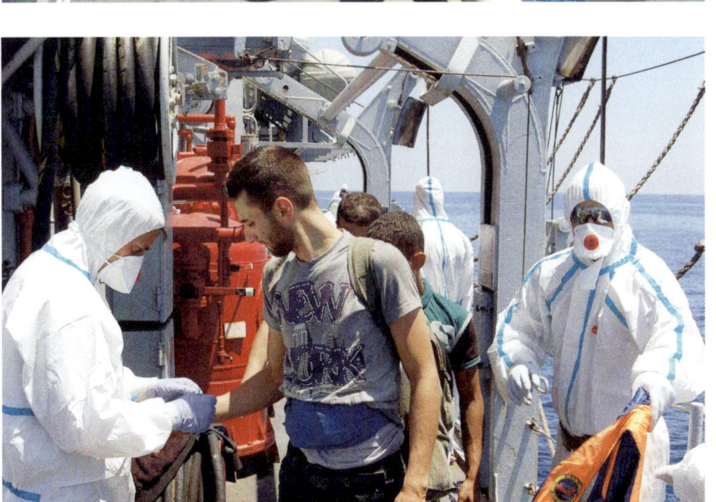

← Once on board, the migrants return the lifejackets to the crew personnel, who gather them in large black bags. The pre-identification phase begins: each individual is given a bracelet with a number.
SAR events of July 28–29 >
Nave Zeffiro
Photographer: Chief Petty Officer 2nd Class Pasquale Andrisani
Date: June 14, 2014
Camera: NIKON D50
Source: Italian Navy Archives

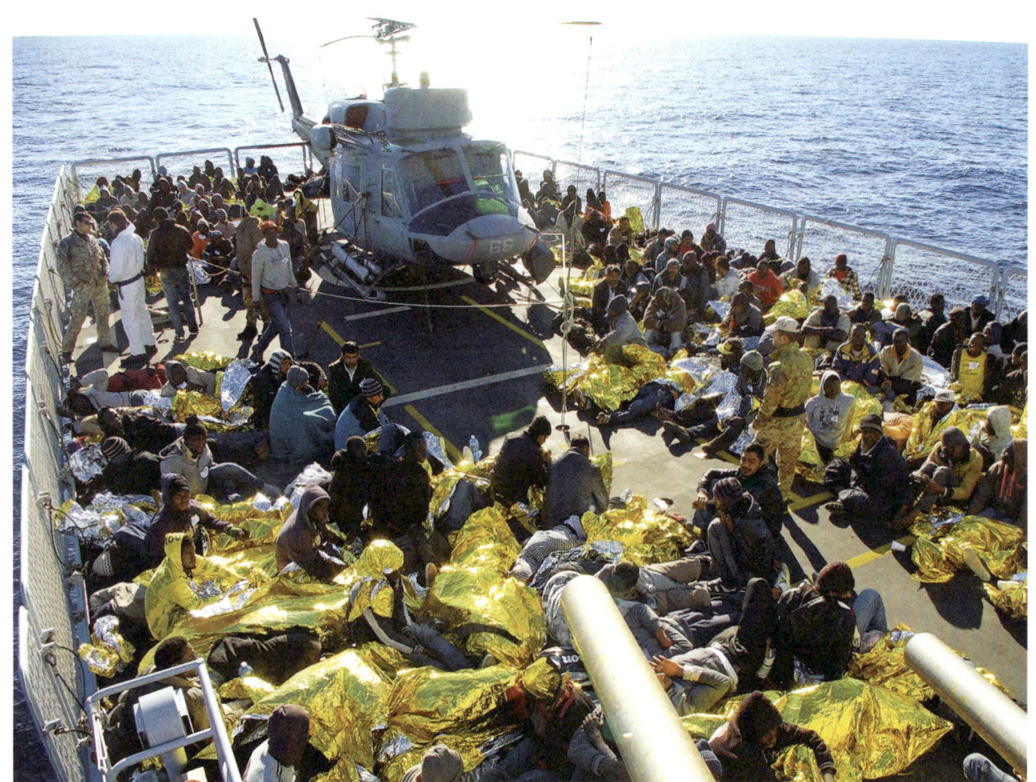

↑   *The migrants gathered on board are seated on the flight deck of the ship, wrapped in isothermal blankets, golden yellow on the outside and silver on the inside, to protect them from the cold and to stabilize their body temperature. In some cases, to protect them from the wind, physical barriers are created, or cruising speed is reduced. Depending on the number of rescued migrants, they may be placed on the flight deck, in the ship's hangar, or at the sternsheets.*

Photographer: unknown
Date: February 17, 2014
Camera: Pentax K100D Super
Source: Italian Navy Archives

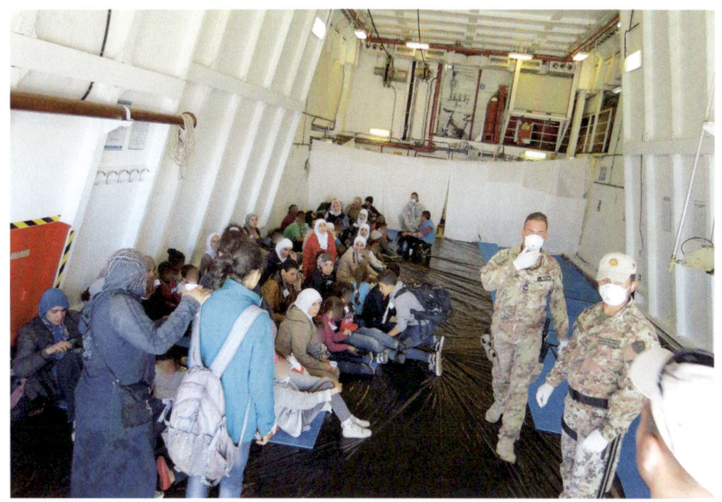

← *According to need and the options available, separate zones are created for men, women, and children, for the purposes of identification and food distribution. The biocontainment tent is set up to examine and care for the migrants rescued by the SAR operations, together with a possible field hospital.*
May 2014> *Nave Foscari* May 23
Photographer: unknown
Date: May 23, 2014
Camera: Canon PowerShot SX40 HS
Source: Italian Navy Archives

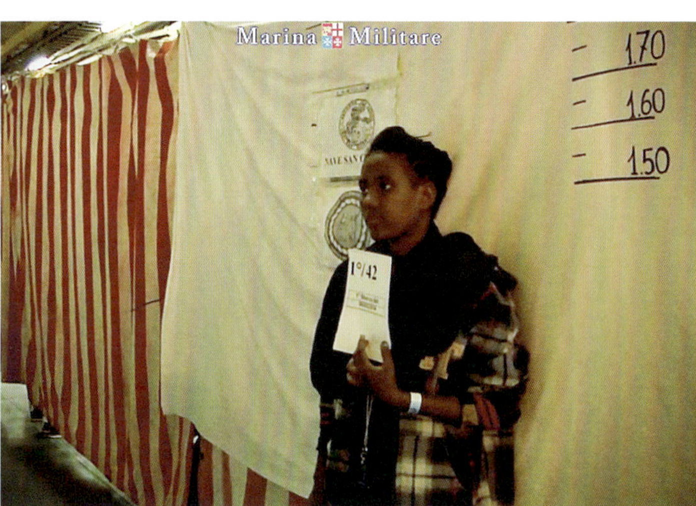

← *Pre-identification phase: Inside the ship, a zone is created for the pre-identification operations. In front of a neutral backdrop bearing the logos of the various responsible agencies and a scale to gauge the height of the individual, the migrants are photographed with the number assigned to them on their chest.*
Videomaker: Giuseppe Privitera
Date: unknown
Camera: Unknown device
Source: Italian Navy Archives, Still from the video *Mare Nostrum* screened during the day of studies entitled "Migratory flows: Impact on the public health system," at the Central Naval Squadron Command (CINCNAV), July 2, 2014

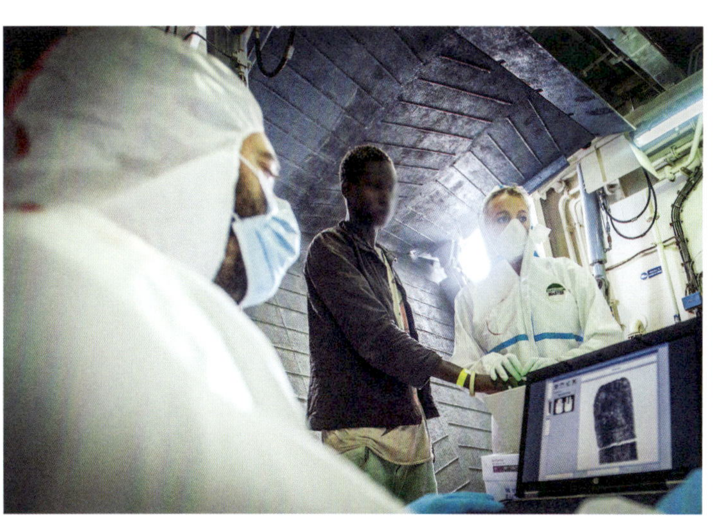

← *Pre-identification phase: Taking the fingerprints of the rescued migrants.*
Photographer: unknown
Date: November 17, 2014
Camera: Nikon D600
Source: Italian Navy Archives

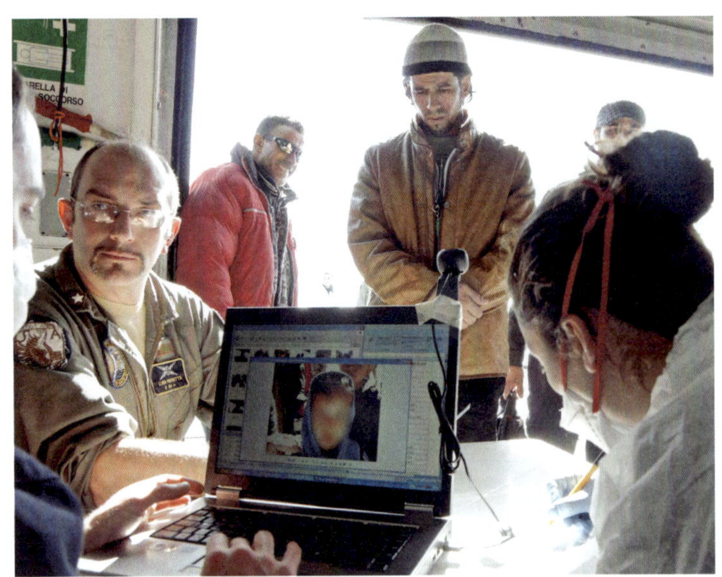

← *Pre-identification phase: Short interview conducted by personnel from the Immigration Offices of the Italian Police to gather personal information (name, age, nationality), information about the journey, and details that might help in the investigation of the traffickers. This is also the moment in which the migrants can apply for political asylum. The report from the interview and the documentation of the rescued migrants are then delivered to the local authorities at the port.*
Photographer: unknown
Date: March 18, 2014
Camera: PENTAX K-3
Source: Italian Navy Archives

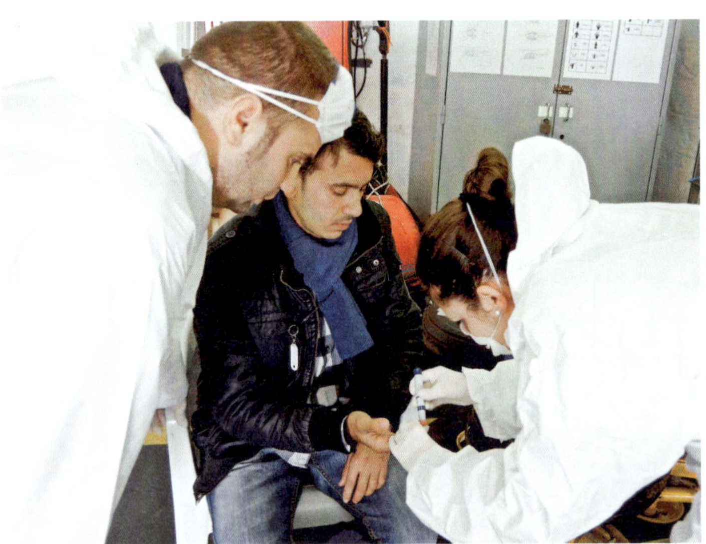

← *Two crew members provide medical assistance for a rescued migrant (blood sugar control). The doctors of the Italian Navy, together with civilian volunteers, perform an initial checkup on all the migrants (healthcare triage), and in emergencies they request the deployment of a helicopter for transfer to a ship with better facilities or a civilian hospital on land. Nearly all the rescued migrants suffered from sea-sickness, nausea, hypothermia, and ex-haustion. The most serious cases had bruises, broken bones, stab wounds, burns, or severe sunburn. There were also many pregnant women, some in an advanced stage of pregnancy.*
Photographer: unknown
Date: March 18, 2014
Camera: Pentax K-3
Source: Italian Navy Archives

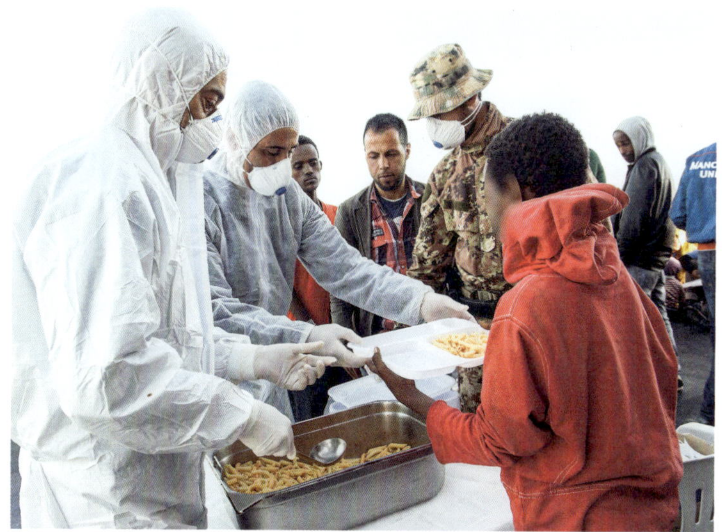

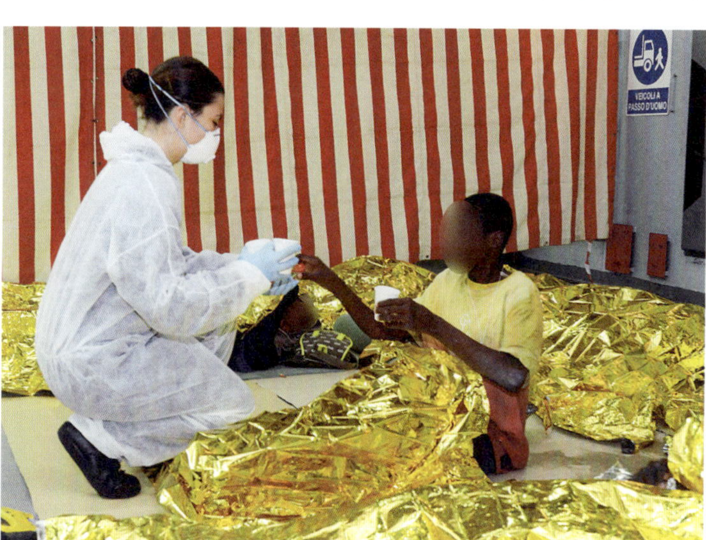

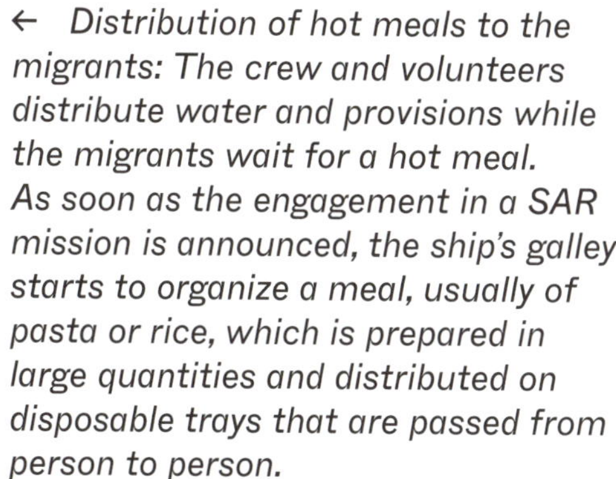

← *Distribution of hot meals to the migrants: The crew and volunteers distribute water and provisions while the migrants wait for a hot meal. As soon as the engagement in a SAR mission is announced, the ship's galley starts to organize a meal, usually of pasta or rice, which is prepared in large quantities and distributed on disposable trays that are passed from person to person.*
Photographer: unknown
Date: unknown
Camera: Nikon D800 (above) and Nikon D7000 (below)
Source: Italian Navy Archives

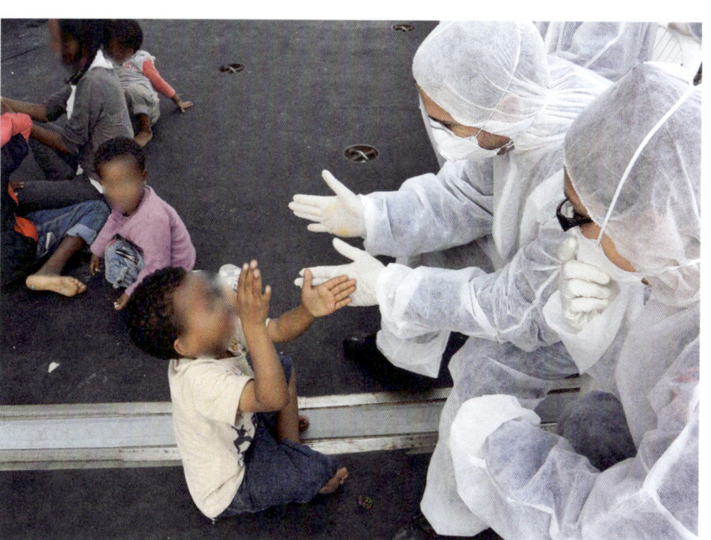

← *Crew members play with some rescued children to pass the time on the long trip to the land.*
Selection_November 2014 > Selection
Photographer: unknown
Date: May 9, 2014
Camera: Nikon 1 AW1
Source: Italian Navy Archives

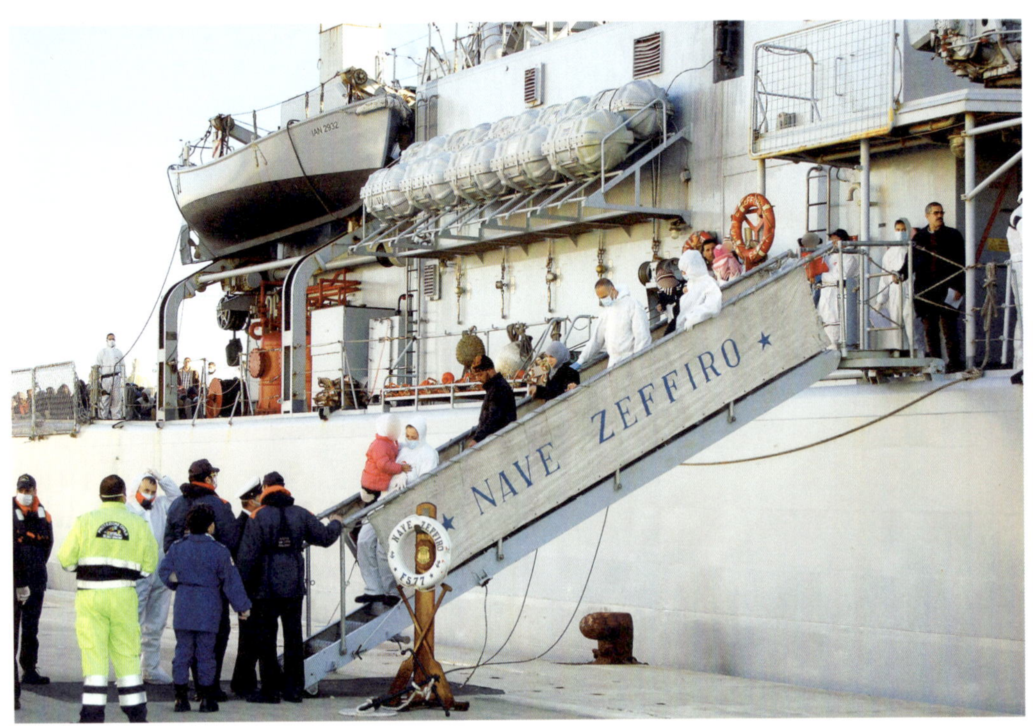

↑   *Landing of migrants from the* Nave Zeffiro *(F577) at an Italian port. The local authorities await them to carry out identification, healthcare measures, and subsequent transfer to reception centers.*
Photographer: unknown
Date: April 11, 2014
Camera: Nikon D50
Source: Italian Navy Archives

Dubious Risk Management

The Frontex border agency in Warsaw collects data and images in order to protect EU citizens

PHOTO STORY: LISA BERGMANN

Frontex was established in 2004 as the European border agency. It carries out European guidelines, while its research section promotes technological advances in the area of border security. The agency is funded by the European Member States, and its budget is decided in agreement with the European Commission and the European Parliament. The agency is not subject to any other form of control. It sees its activities as an expression of the will of the European electorate.

Information generated by the European border agency that is relevant to the security services streams into Warsaw and is distributed from there. Images and digital technology support the standardization and harmonization of national procedures and streamline processes. The goal is to create a seamless surveillance system at Europe's external frontiers that allows goods and people to move as freely as possible.

The Migrant Image Research Group has repeatedly asked Frontex to schedule a meeting. In 2014 it gained access to Frontex's headquarters in Warsaw. Lisa Bergmann, Leon Kahane, Armin Linke, and Karolina Sobel have conducted several interviews with employees of the agency.

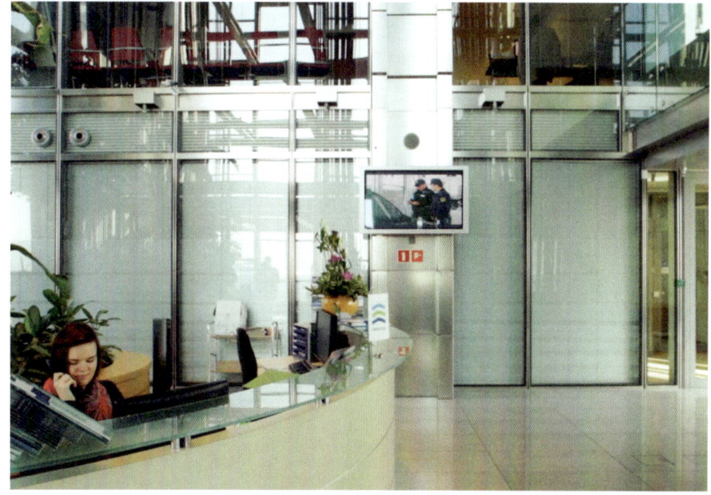

[Frontex Spokesperson Michał Parzyszek]

Q: Our main interest is in the situation on Lampedusa. Is there a mission operating now in the seas around the island?

PARZYSZEK: Hermes is an operation being conducted south of Sicily and Lampedusa.

Q: Based on the example of Hermes, can you explain the workflow of such an operation?

PARZYSZEK: The operation is always managed by the host countries, in this case Italy. We set up an international coordination center headed by the Italian officer, and then you have representatives from other countries that are taking part. They meet on a daily basis in a joint operation board and decide on what to do.

These days it has less in common with border control and surveillance because each and every action turns into search and rescue (SAR). Globally all the seas are divided into search and rescue zones. The Mediterranean is divided into approximately twenty zones with a different state responsible for mounting SAR operations. Italy, Malta, Libya, and Tunisia all have a part to play in this area. Whenever there is a boat in distress, SAR takes over. It is not that they send boats immediately, but they see which other boats are in the region. Search and rescue is an obligation for all the maritime assets in the particular vicinity.

Q: Have your regulations changed?

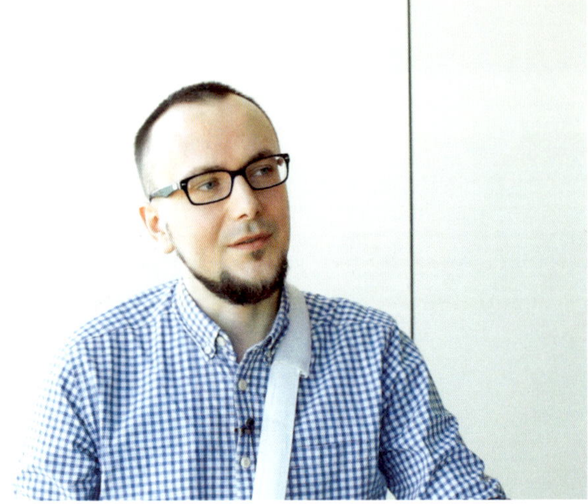

← PARZYSZEK: There have been legal changes clarifying certain rules. For some countries a little boat in the middle of the sea was already considered a case for SAR, but for other countries it was enough to give them water and fuel and to point them in the right direction. There were different interpretations and the will of the European Parliament was to establish one single interpretation for EU countries. Especially after the Hirsi judgment by the European Court of Justice, which restated that the non-refoulement principle is applicable and that people cannot be taken back to Libya because they may face prosecution there or some other threat to their lives. The possible change in how Europe approaches asylum matters is happening after the border. This is not handled by border guards or search and rescue authorities but by specialized migration authorities.

Q: Eight years ago the situation was more relaxed when fewer migrants were coming. Then there was an intensification of these movements that led up to the Italian–Libyan friendship treaty that succeeded in holding back migrants. There was another change with the Arab Spring, and now with the Syrian war Europe also feels more responsible toward people that had to flee. Did you see a change in your role and the tasks given to you by the European Union?

PARZYSZEK: Frontex is about border control and border surveillance. That hasn't changed. What has changed are the migratory flows because sometimes you have a really bad economic situation somewhere, so people start coming from that particular country to the European Union. Or there is a war and you have refugees fleeing. The Frontex mandate changed because now we have Eurosur as a pan-European surveillance system. But for border guards the situation is always the same. Only the intensity changes.

Q: One of the tasks of Frontex is integrated border management. What is meant by that?

PARZYSZEK: Integrated border management is the work of visa and consular authorities in third countries and involves cooperation with countries of origin and with neighboring countries. This cooperation continues inside the EU, where you have police forces working together. You have ID systems like the Schengen Information System, which is applicable in EU territory and also covers the return of illegal migrants to their country of origin. So control doesn't just happen at the border but before and after you cross the border.

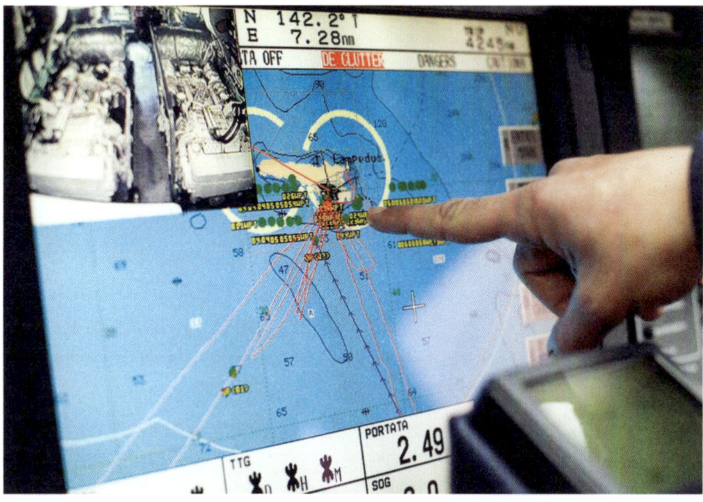

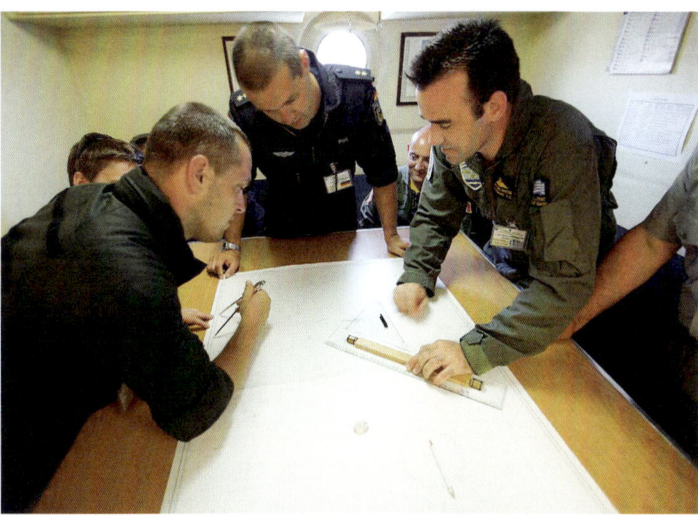

← *Q: How do you choose the pictures on your website?*

PARZYSZEK: The pictures on our website show the different types of work carried out by border guards. It is not only the person sitting in the booth at the airport. We want to illustrate this to people so they can imagine the setup of national coordination centers as in the case of Eurosur. There were some more news-oriented pictures, as the system was hotly debated. But the rest of the pictures are illustrations of what we are doing, starting with basic training. Then the moment came when we were financially able to produce videos. Not that they are very popular—we never went viral—but these are educational movies and we want to put information out there.

Q: Watching the videos, we were wondering about your need to communicate about Frontex. We had the impression that people who work here feel misunderstood.

PARZYSZEK: That's obvious, because when they read newspapers or talk to people, there is always a blurred image. People tend to refer to Frontex as the entity that is so powerful that it has an

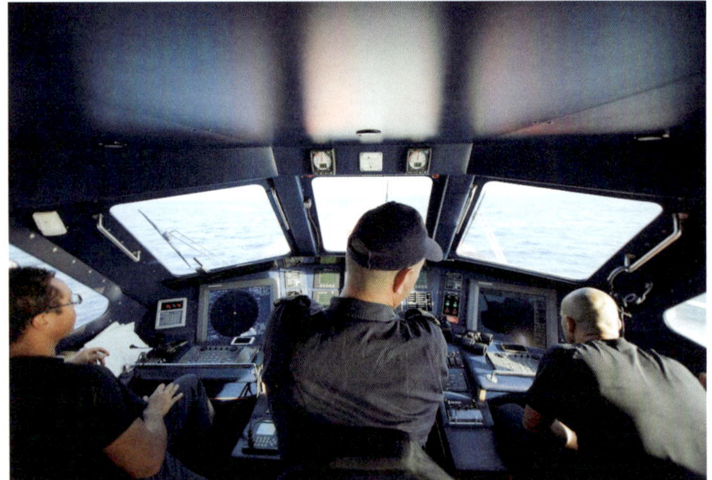

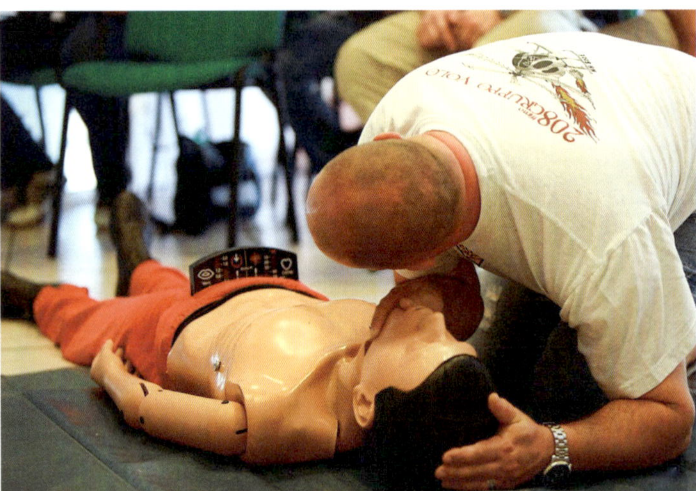

impact on everything. There are movements that are critical of Frontex, and for these people it is easier to have one entity to stand against rather than seventeen different authorities in different member states that are somehow involved in border control. These critics basically made Frontex a symbol for migration policy, asylum policy, and border management.

Q: The whole structure is very difficult to understand and it's hard to see where the discussion about Frontex is taking place in European politics.

PARZYSZEK: The policy is being made by the different member states or via their representative on the European Council. So each and every piece of legislation, if it is about migration, is done by the ministers of home affairs or of social affairs or of the interior. They go to Brussels and they decide how the legislation will be shaped. Frontex then implements the law. So it is about taking conscious decisions as a citizen regardless of whether it is at EU or national level. The frustration is usually because people are uninformed. We are always talking about the European Union as some "unidentified" entity—but this is what I was saying: the decisions are being made by national ministers and national parliamentarians who are sent to Strasbourg or Brussels. It doesn't happen in a vacuum. These are people representing a national parliament. They are not like UFOs, they have a real agenda.

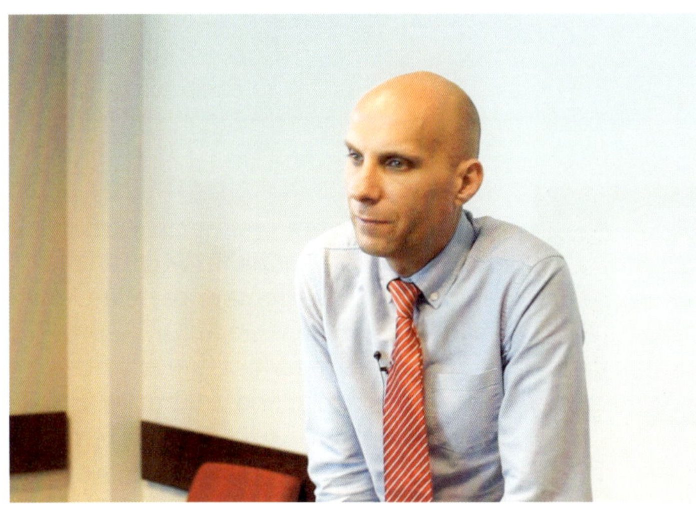

← [Situation Room—Piotr Malinowski, Service Development Team Coordinator]

Q: *Can you tell us how Frontex uses images for its operational activities?*

MALINOWSKI: Here at Frontex we have a data center to receive and store images, and we have advanced visualization capabilities with live pictures changing every couple of minutes.

We do not produce physical pictures. We are basically providing fusion capabilities. It is all about information management, data mining, and data processing. It is called Frontex fusion services and we provide technical capabilities. We do not use "images" in the standard sense—we do not handle optically fixed images. What we receive and work with are data streams. We receive data from local authorities as well as special agencies like EMSA, the European Maritime Safety Agency.

Each of our stakeholders pre-subscribes to the data stream that you see on this screen, and then they produce images themselves. We don't control the way our users produce pictures. We provide the capability to choose a different data stream and to add the data and images they select to their operational maps.

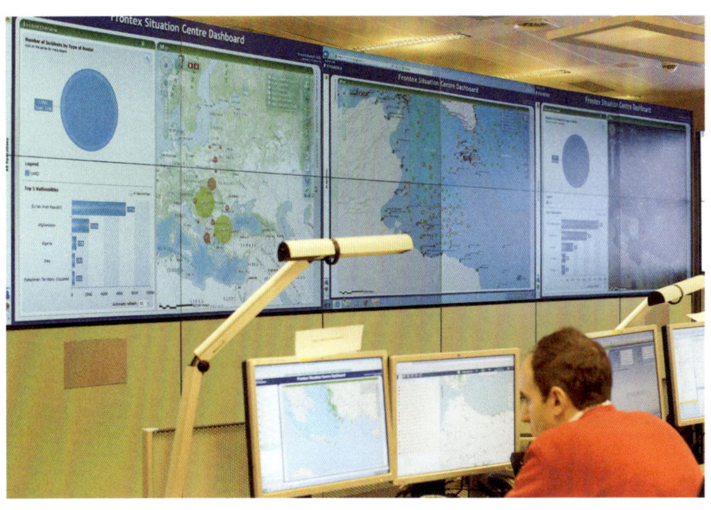

← Depending on the choice of base map, our picture will look different. This will be in the background to our operational data and we can choose between satellite images, physical maps, navigation charts, or topographic maps. That already determines how detailed our picture will be. Now officers can decide which data sets are to be implemented in our operational picture, and we have different ways of visualizing the information. Events can be clustered or presented as graphs showing the density with which they occur. There can be more layers of information, like the maritime layer, which shows the traffic of commercial ships. We include the pictures in our reports and this is what the final product looks like.

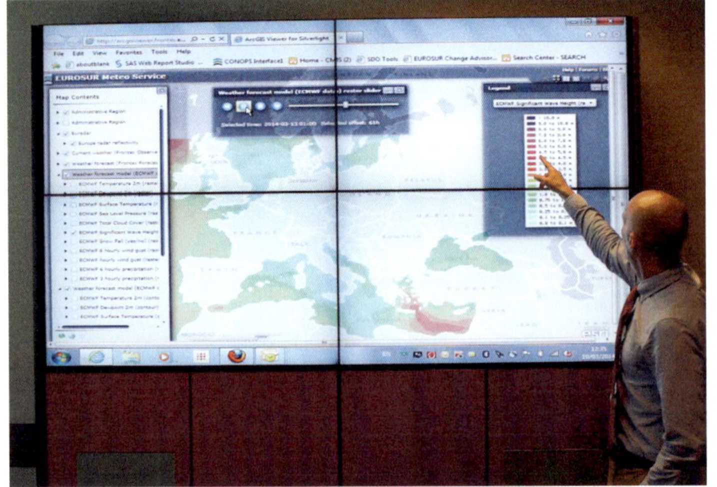

← *Q: What kinds of data and information are presented in your operational maps?*

MALINOWSKI: Weather data are received from sensors around Europe. For instance, there are buoys on the sea, several thousand, that at every moment collect data on water temperature and wave height and send it to the commercial partner organization, which sends it on to us. Weather visualizations are used to predict migratory activities. Here we know that during the next hours we will have significant waves, meaning that we cannot expect too many small boats with migrants in this area. This color means there will be a huge storm, and waves will be up to six meters high. The wind direction is also toward the coast of departure. We don't have too many instances of illegal migration now, so that is good.

Satellites provide information about ships and are used to monitor ports and track suspected vessels. This is streamed twice a day according to the satellite's orbital position, but we use several of them. If you need a picture of a specific region, you need to analyze which satellite is in that range.

In some cases, we might receive optical data from sensors that are on assets like a patrol boat, helicopter, or plane in the form of a standard photo picture. When it comes to incidents related to border patrol, these are usually pieces of information that we obtain from officers on the ground.

Q: Do you use infrared sensors as well?

MALINOWSKI: A good example of infrared sensors is the land sensors that are mounted across the Greek–Turkish border. They are detecting people trying to cross the border, but, as Frontex, we are not interested in these images. These supply tactical information that is usable right at the time when border guards receive it. When you see that image in the border station in Alexandroupoli, you immediately send a patrol. We at Frontex don't need that: it is really just operational information at a local level. We are focusing on the strategical level and the pan-European tactical level.

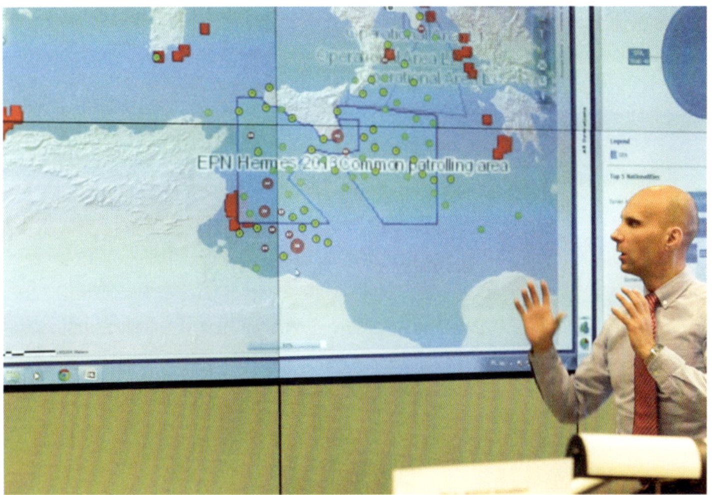

← These red dots here are uncorrelated ships, meaning they are not registered in any database. Knowing the position of these uncooperative ships, member states can easily send assets to check if these are boats with migrants, criminals, terrorists, whatever. It might just be a pleasure boat.

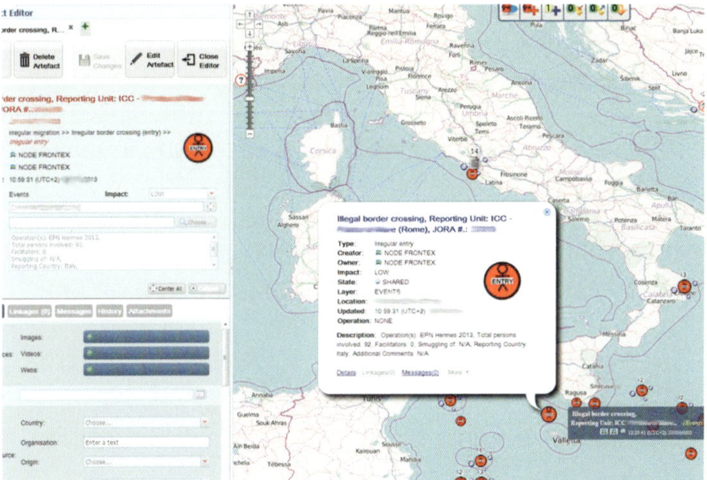

← *Q: What is Eurosur?*
MALINOWSKI: Eurosur is something new, connecting all the member states with one another. It is a big business umbrella for many different developments, and many organizations in Europe are involved in it. But for us, for now, it means a communication network and basic visualization capabilities. It is a connection between different nodes—i.e., servers in different member states—and Frontex is tasked with maintaining this system.

Q: So you provide information to the different nations, but then how this information is implemented is not your responsibility?
MALINOWSKI: We are not doing this to spend some European money but rather to satisfy three purposes: to detect, prevent, and combat illegal migration; to detect, prevent, and combat cross-border crime; and, last and most importantly, to protect and save the lives of migrants. Sometimes the general public is given the wrong message about us. After Lampedusa, thousands of people were saved—how many media reports have you seen about that?

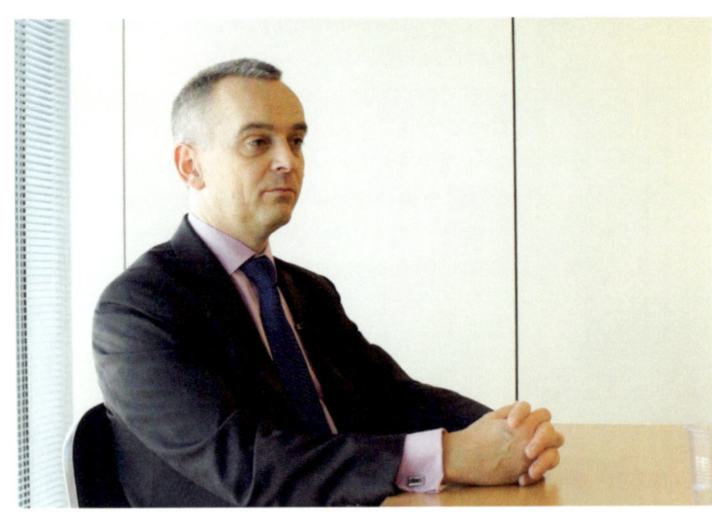

← [Research and Development—
Edgar Beugels, Head of Unit]

   *Q: What is the history of border
security?*

BEUGELS: If you leave the Schengen area, you will have to show your passport to the border guard, and if the guard is reasonably convinced that you are you, you get your documents back and travel on. This procedure goes quite a long way back, that people have to show documents in order to cross borders. It's a procedure whose development was rather limited until recently. For a long time a piece of paper was used, then photographs were added. This has been followed by the introduction of a small chip that contains your facial image. You could say that this is an additional security feature because it makes it possible not only to check if the passport photo resembles you but also if it corresponds to the image on the chip. It also means that a computer can now scan your passport and compare it with your live image, a system that is already in use at international airports like Frankfurt. And if the system is convinced that you are you, that you don't have any outstanding criminal record or fines to pay, then you can cross the border. I see this as a prelude to "new-style border control" where, as EU nationals, you will be checked less and less by real people and more and more by machines.

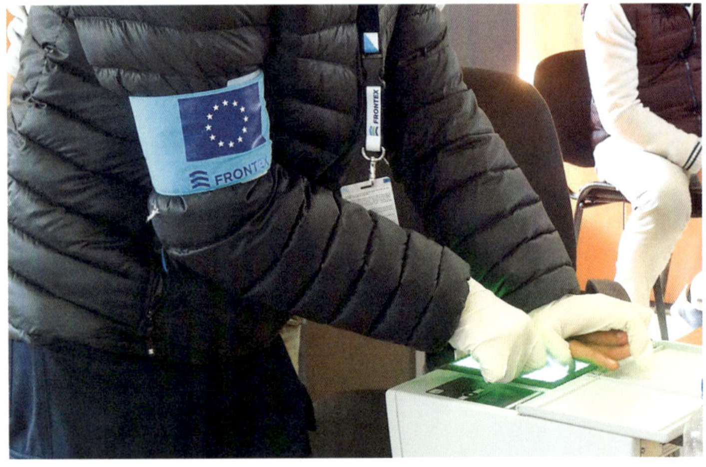

← There is already a system in place, the so-called Visa Information System for visitors from third countries, that makes use of fingerprints. Again this is about comparing images. But the procedure is somehow connected to criminality, and this is why until now it was not chosen as a biometric method for EU citizens.

   *Q: In German airports you also
have the IRIS system, right?*

BEUGELS: The IRIS system is used in Frankfurt for frequent travelers who do not want to stand in line for passport control. Your background first has to be screened in an interview. In some cases you have to pay a fee and then you can become member of a program like this. However, IRIS is not the preferred biometric system—there was a patent issue as the

American company developing this technology was not willing to give up its patent for general use.

Q: *But you are also signaling what could be an interesting development?*

BEUGELS: The number of people crossing the border is not going to decrease. On the contrary. Yet the number of border staff is not going to increase. So, on the one hand, we are seeing the introduction of automation, while, on the other, the whole process of checks is in itself a very old way of doing business.

You can check my passport and ask all kinds of questions, how much money I have on me and the purpose of my trip—and then what? Do you really know who I am? Don't you find it funny that you can check whatever you want on the Internet, but the border guard can only rely on what you tell her? As private individuals we are connected to the world, but the guard is still sitting in her isolated control booth. The person who has to determine from a professional point of view whether you are a good or bad person, he or she has almost no tools for that. The document might be a fine document, but if it was obtained in a fraudulent way, it all comes down to intentions. Everybody is potentially a bad guy. We are not able to establish if someone has good or bad intentions.

Q: *So how do you want to find out about people's real intentions? At what point do you know who someone really is?*

BEUGELS: There are some on-going developments that are looking into interview techniques measuring the reactions of people to questions. We are trying to establish different risk levels, who is more risky than other people. For that, we would need more information about travelers. People put a lot of information out there on the Internet. This information can help shape the questions a border guard might ask you about your actual activities.

Q: *Coming back to the topic of operational images, could you tell us about any possible future developments there?*

BEUGELS: We want to know earlier, we want to see what is coming toward us. We are reaching a curious situation because you can push out a border more and more—and then what? You might see things that are beyond the line of sight, that you normally don't see because of the curvature of the earth, but we should not overestimate our possibilities. There is nothing like an overview of the Mediterranean. You can't see the small boats.

Frontex: Integrated Border Management
by Lisa Bergmann

In the European Commission's "Integrated Border Management", the protection of borders is assigned in part to diplomatic and financial agreements with third countries. In 2005, after the violent trespassing of borders in the Spanish enclave of Ceuta (in Morocco), EU politicians realized that it is not possible to stop people entering Europe by building fences. From then on, the EU's strategy changed, and in addition to reinforcing physical border posts, it has moved the system of controls beyond its borders into neighboring countries.

It is for this purpose that the EU makes agreements with Egypt and Turkey, or approves of detention camps for migrants like those in Libya, where forced labor, torture, and the death penalty are common, and from where refugees are often released into the deserts of the regions that border other African states, where they are left on their own. Refugees are now being stopped en route, they no longer even arrive on the European mainland, and they lose their chance to apply for asylum. Ethnologist Bernd Kasparek has spoken of the "border regime" of the European Union.

Frontex supports the displacement of Europe's border controls by providing data, secret intelligence, and images. This border shift is taking place in the virtual space of administration, while at the same time the flight to Europe is becoming more expensive and more dangerous.

In summer 2015, the headlines and front-page news were causing panic about those people whose lives were actually in danger. In the language of EU foreign affairs officials and of Frontex, refugees are designated as a danger and a safety risk for Europe—a conscious distortion of facts that allows the EU to withdraw its responsibility for people who are risking their lives. In the logic of Frontex, thousands of victims in the Mediterranean Sea are unavoidable, in order to guarantee the safety of European citizens.

This view of migration has been described by sociologists Philipp Ratfisch and Stephan Scheel as "securitization." In the volume edited by Sabine Hess and Bernd Kasparek titled *Grenzregime—Diskurse, Praktiken, Institutionen in Europa* [Border Regime: Discourses, Practices, Institutions in Europe], they write: "The actors of security politics are are […] not reacting to objective threats, as they first construct these as such by representing certain social phenomena as a threat to the safety of a reference object established as one in need of protection."[1]

It is rarely pointed out that that Lebanon, a much poorer state, welcomes the majority of Syrian refugees, and that even though it finds itself in a very exceptional situation, it cannot afford—because of the lack of financial means—a "protection program" that would cost billions of euros.

1   Philipp Ratfisch und Stephan Scheel, Die Rolle des UNHCR bei der Externalisierung des EU-Migrationsregimes, in: Sabine Hess, Bernd Kasparek (Hg.), *Grenzregime—Diskurse, Praktiken, Institutionen in Europa*, Berlin und Hamburg 2010. Quoted in: Laura Freisberg, *Wachhund für Europa. Die europäische Grenzschutzagentur Frontex*, Manuskript Zündfunk Generator, Bayerischer Rundfunk München, 31. 7. 2011.

Things Left Behind, Found Images

Giacomo Sferlazzo on his Museum of Migration on Lampedusa

The artist, singer-songwriter, and political activist Giacomo Sferlazzo is a member of the Arci Askavusa (Barefoot) association, which studies the history of Lampedusa and its connections with global processes. A Migration Museum has developed in a lengthy process: on display, among other things, will be photographs and objects left by refugees on boats.

Together with the other members of the Askavusa collective, Sferlazzo has assembled an eloquent archive composed of ID documents, family snapshots, religious images and other items, shown in the form of an installation at PortoM on Lampedusa. In 2011 the Migrant Image Research Group visited Sferlazzo in his apartment on the island. The interview was conducted by Lisa Bergmann, Maurizio Bortolotti, Armin Linke, Valeria Malito, Laura Morcillo, and Chris Spatschek. Giacomo Sferlazzo has revised the 2011 interview and summarized his current views on the found images and the topic of migration.

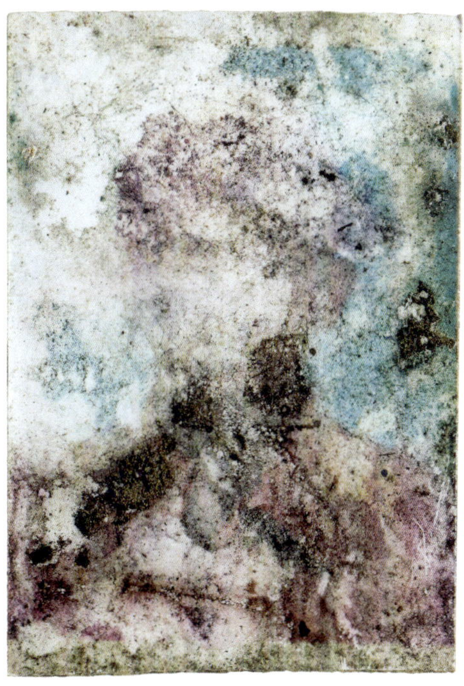

Photo ID cards: these photographs are the face of humanity. I think these are the most beautiful pictures, since there are no distinguishing features. You see there is no neck, no face, no person. It could be anyone. There is no definite image: this could be my father, my mother, my grandfather, my uncle, a friend of mine. It is true that, aesthetically speaking, maybe they are … if I say beautiful, I am referring to a whole range of things.

In 2009 large demonstrations were held here in Lampedusa against the construction of the CIE, one of the Centers of Identification and Expulsion, which Roberto Maroni, Minister of the Interior, established in Italy. In Lampedusa we forcefully opposed it, but later many of the opponents fell silent, because the government began to lodge police in the hotels and feed them in the restaurants, so the businessmen who were an important part of the protest at the start disappeared. After the Bossi-Fini legislation, all the regulations already included in the previous laws were made harsher, especially with respect to the Turco-Napolitano Act which created the CPT ("Temporary Permanence Centers") and introduced administrative detention in Italy.

The CIE are centers in which immigrants are detained until they can be identified and then repatriated. After the institution of the CIEs, the strategy shifted toward refusal of entry, pushing people back into the sea, toward Libya, applying the agreement made between Italy and Libya at the time of the Prodi administration, which had never been put into practice in terms of border rejections. Instead, the present government began to authorize this practice, which goes against many of the international treaties Italy has signed and prevents a part of the world population from moving normally, paying for a normal ticket and choosing where to go. In fact, all European regulation since the introduction of the Schengen area has moved in this direction.

Moreover, even people who could legitimately apply for political asylum are rejected, though many of them are from Africa and the Middle East and have all the qualifications they need to request political asylum in Italy. This is denied to people rejected at the border, because everyone is refused entry without their status being considered.

What we do with PortoM is very political—one cannot help taking sides. You have to take a clear position: either you are in favor of the rejections, in which case I don't understand why you would want to make a museum of migration, or you state that you are not in favor of the rejections and this policy that is being applied not only by Italy but also by Europe … because Europe too is now resorting to these solutions—this so-called total closure of the borders is also happening in Spain with Morocco, and in Greece.

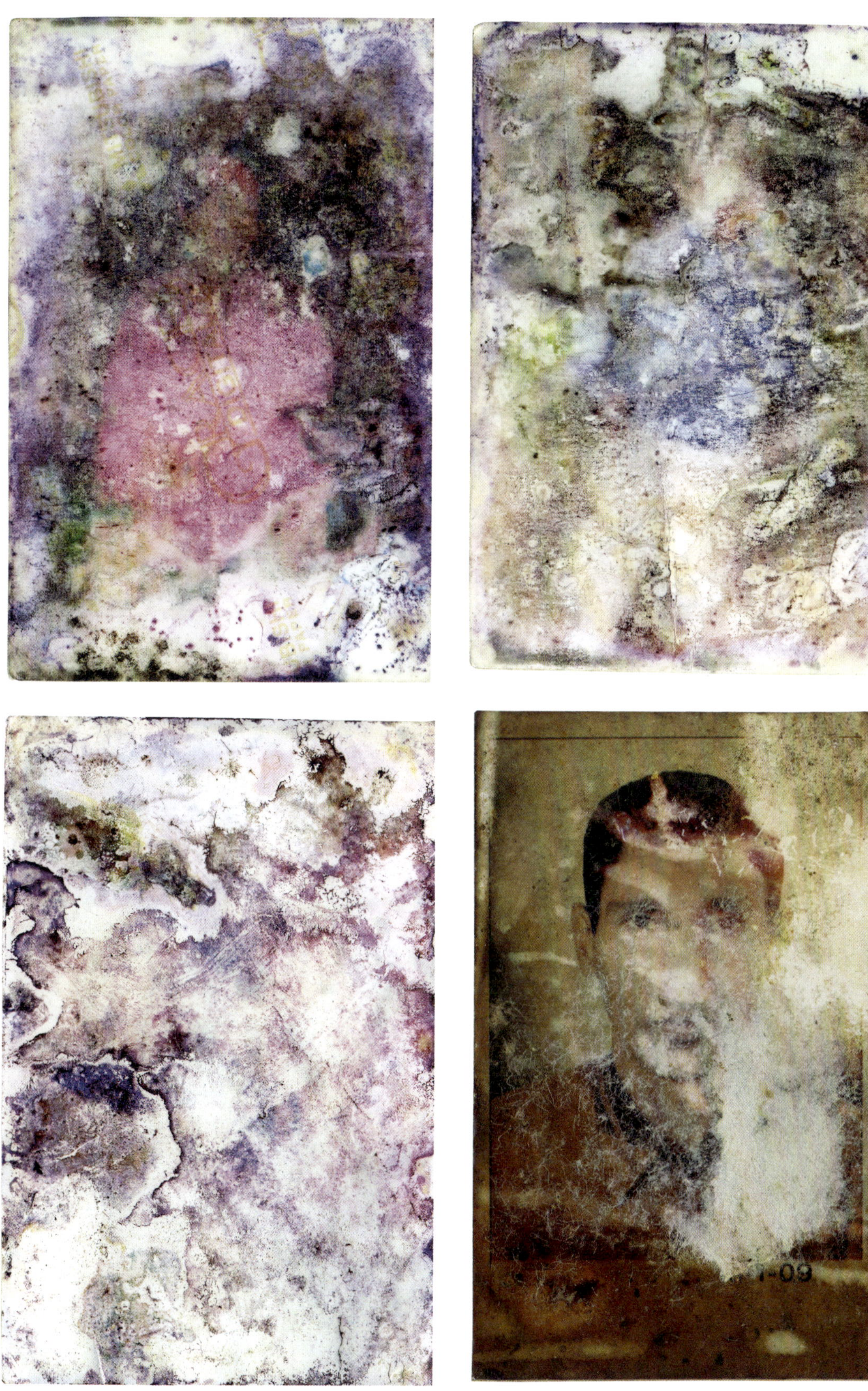

This was done by the water. It is the action of the water on the color of the photographic print that is important.

As an association, we are totally against this type of policy. We are opposed to the regulation of travel. Every person should be able to decide where to go without paying thousands of euros, without traveling for years and years, risking their lives or ending up in detention centers. But before this can happen, the EU has to put an end to its criminal tradition, which has very deep roots. In particular, it has to curb its colonial thrust, which has never ceased, and which at this moment is going through a new, aggressive phase. If many people are leaving their home countries, it is because of the policies of plunder and war of the EU, NATO, and the USA.

Italy, for example, is doing everything it can to encourage illegal aliens: a migrant in Italy who wants to legalize his status has to go through hell to do it. I mean, I don't know if you have seen what happened in Brescia: the immigrants up on a crane who were there because they had asked to become legal, to have papers—they had been working illegally in Italy for some time, and they had to spend thirty days on a crane to get anyone to pay attention to their situation. Those who want to legalize their presence in Italy have problems because Italy does not facilitate entry to the world of work, or so-called integration, which is a useless, meaningless word.

With the latest legislation, the Lega Nord even wanted to stipulate that illegal migrant women who went to a hospital to give birth were to be reported to the police: in other words, if I need medical care, the doctor has to report me. Schools also discriminate against migrant children in many areas …

But this is a consequence of the creation of the internal market and the Schengen area, which has created two types of workers: those residing in the EU, with few rights and low salaries, and those from outside it, severely exploited, without any rights and without papers. These two types of workers are pitted against each other. The goal is always the accumulation of capital in a few hands, and the destruction of the living conditions of workers.

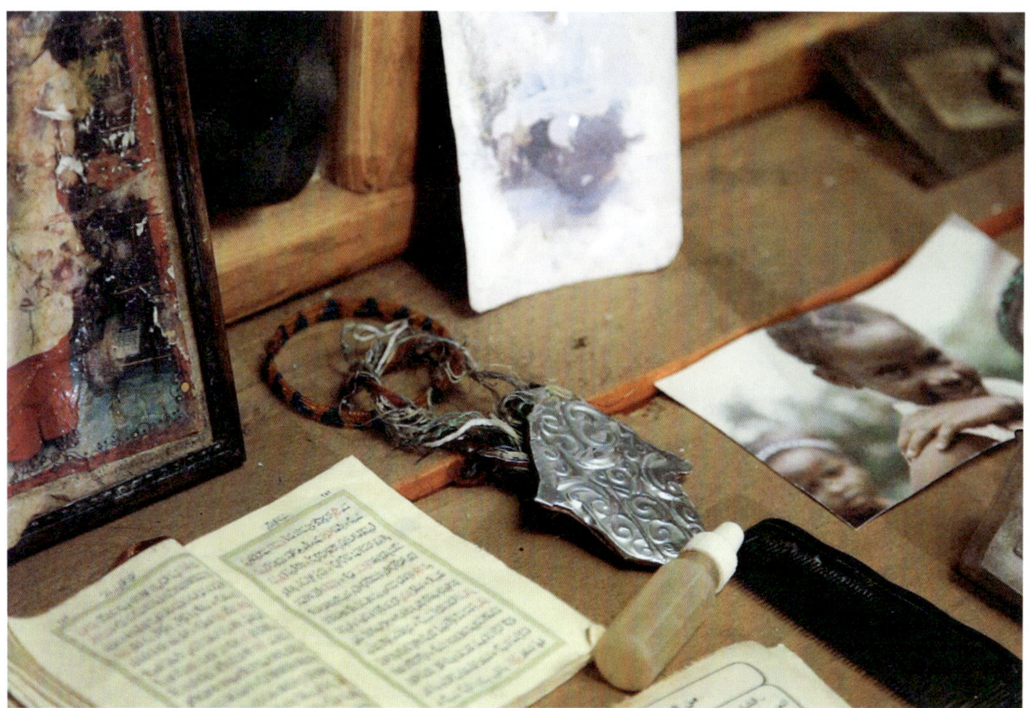

I have examined some boats even five or six years after they were confiscated.

The landings and interceptions on the sea began in the 1990s. Since 2002 boats have been picked up off the coast of Libya, and the number of migrants taken to Lampedusa has increased greatly, because since 2002 the migrant center has been run by a subcontractor, and there was an incentive to bring more migrants to Lampedusa, to make the CPT work more and to create a European militarized border. The boats the migrants came on have been destroyed by the state, involving the expenditure of hundreds of thousands of euros. The vessels were often new and could have been reutilized.

There are boats from 2002, 2004 ... The strange thing was that the objects were still there: no one had ever had been curious to look at them—never mind the civic spirit, the political sense, or even the curiosity. The Coast Guard and the police do not use the photographs for purposes of identification (though today we are not certain this is altogether the case).

The first time, I found letters, an important repository of human memories.

A person who makes a journey of that kind, defying the desert, imprisonment in Libya, then the sea, Lampedusa ... It was very moving to discover that these people bring words with them. If I had to set off on such a voyage, I don't know what I would bring with me. I might not bring a letter.

I hope that from these works you can understand my position with respect to migration.

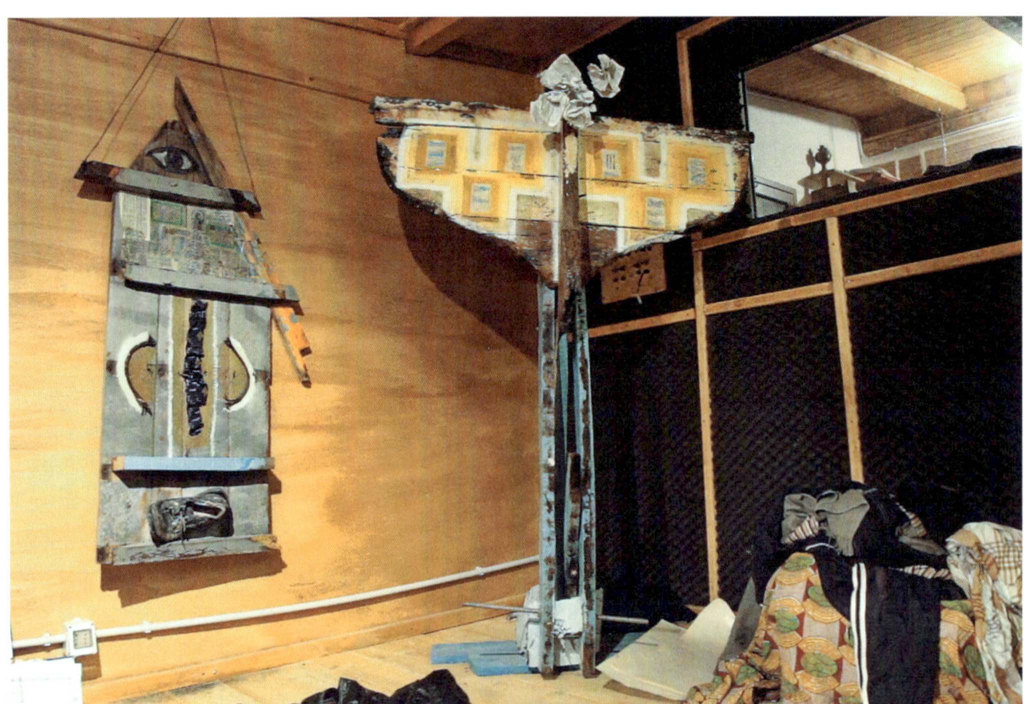

For me, immigration is the result of capitalism, of the war of capital. When I began to focus on immigration, I had a much more romantic and emotional take on the issue, I was more ingenuous and much more influenced by a certain kind of rhetoric. Today I believe the work we are doing should prompt historical and political reflection on the issue, to get beyond the humanitarian and emotional conception and to move toward a political, critical, historical approach. Emotion is an important part of human existence, but at times it can be confusing and distracting, keeping you from getting to the crux of questions.

MIGRANT PROTEST 2

BY EMILIE JOSSO

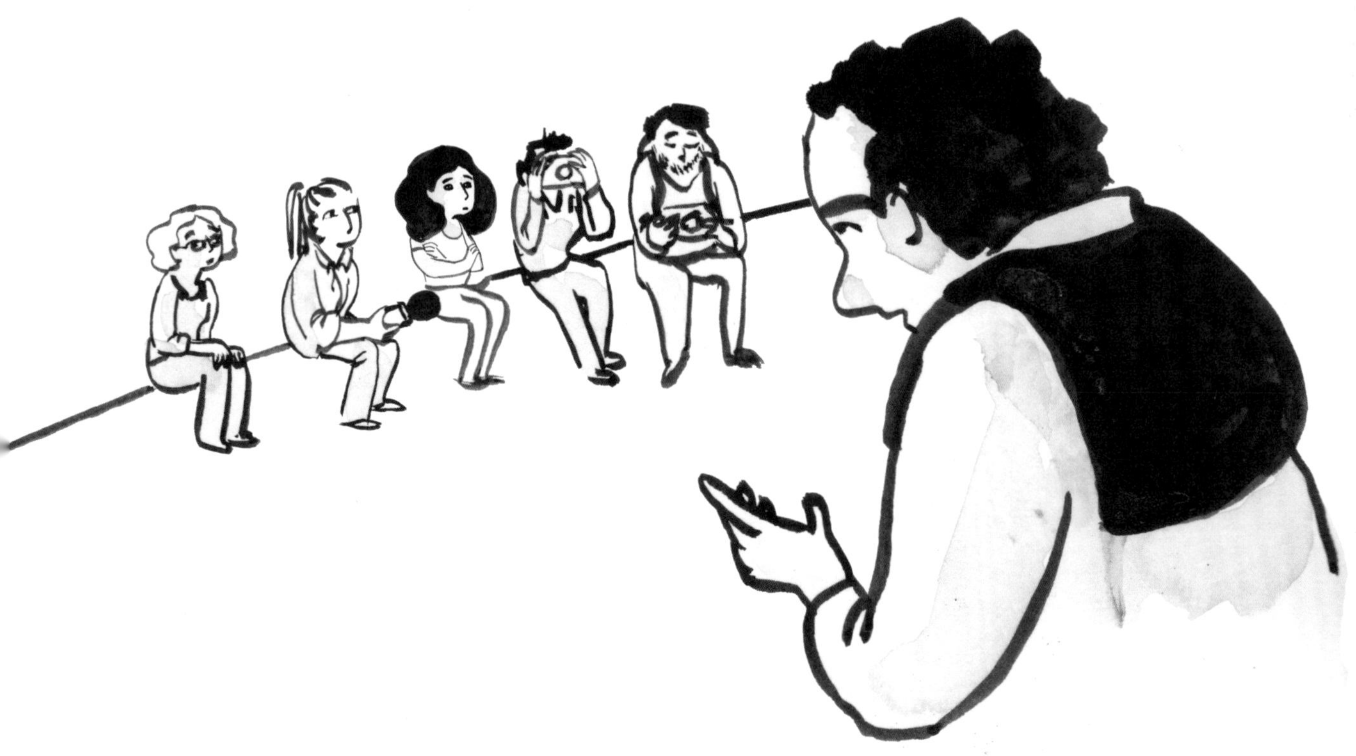

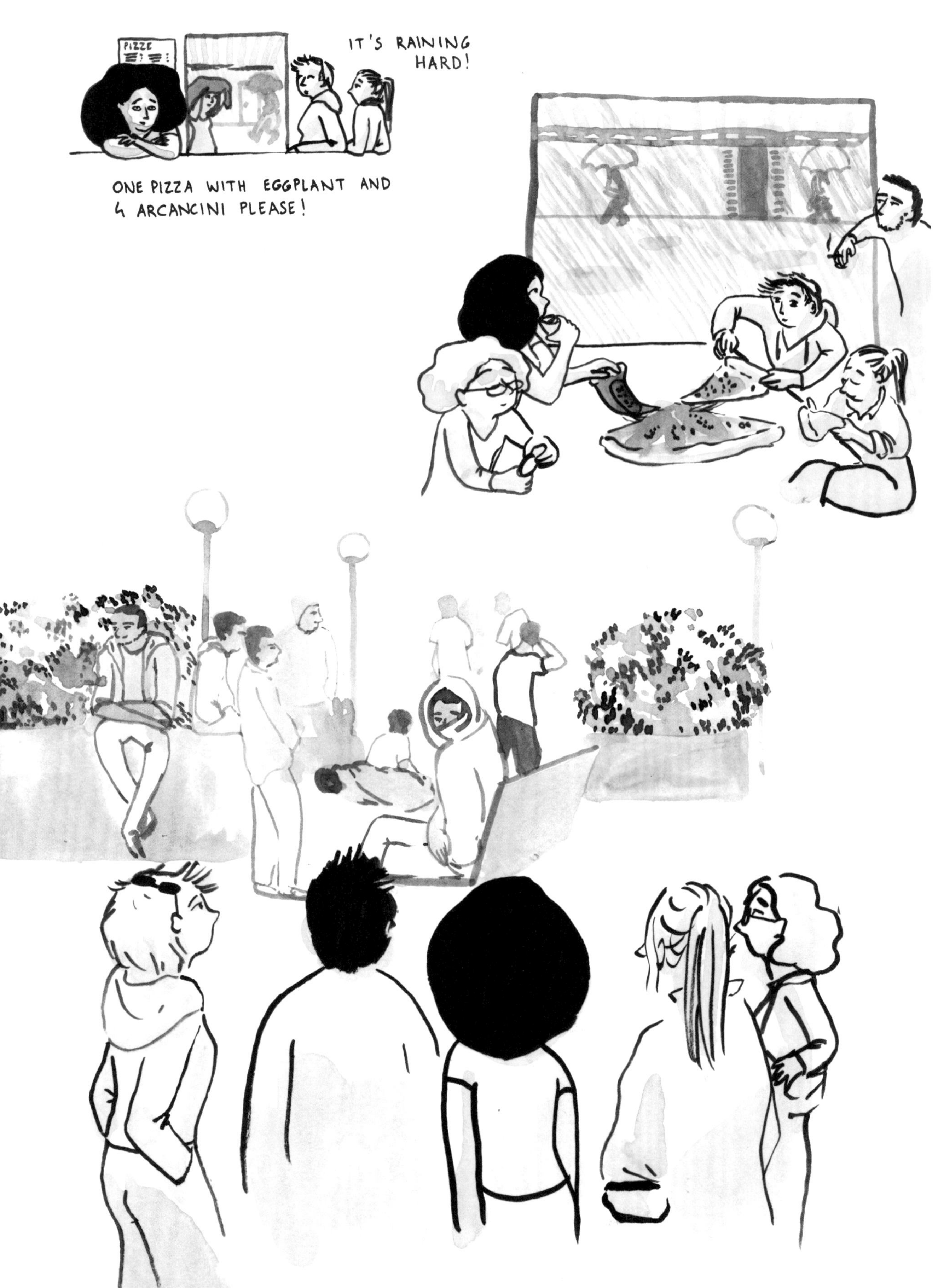

PIZZE
IT'S RAINING HARD!
ONE PIZZA WITH EGGPLANT AND
4 ARCANCINI PLEASE!

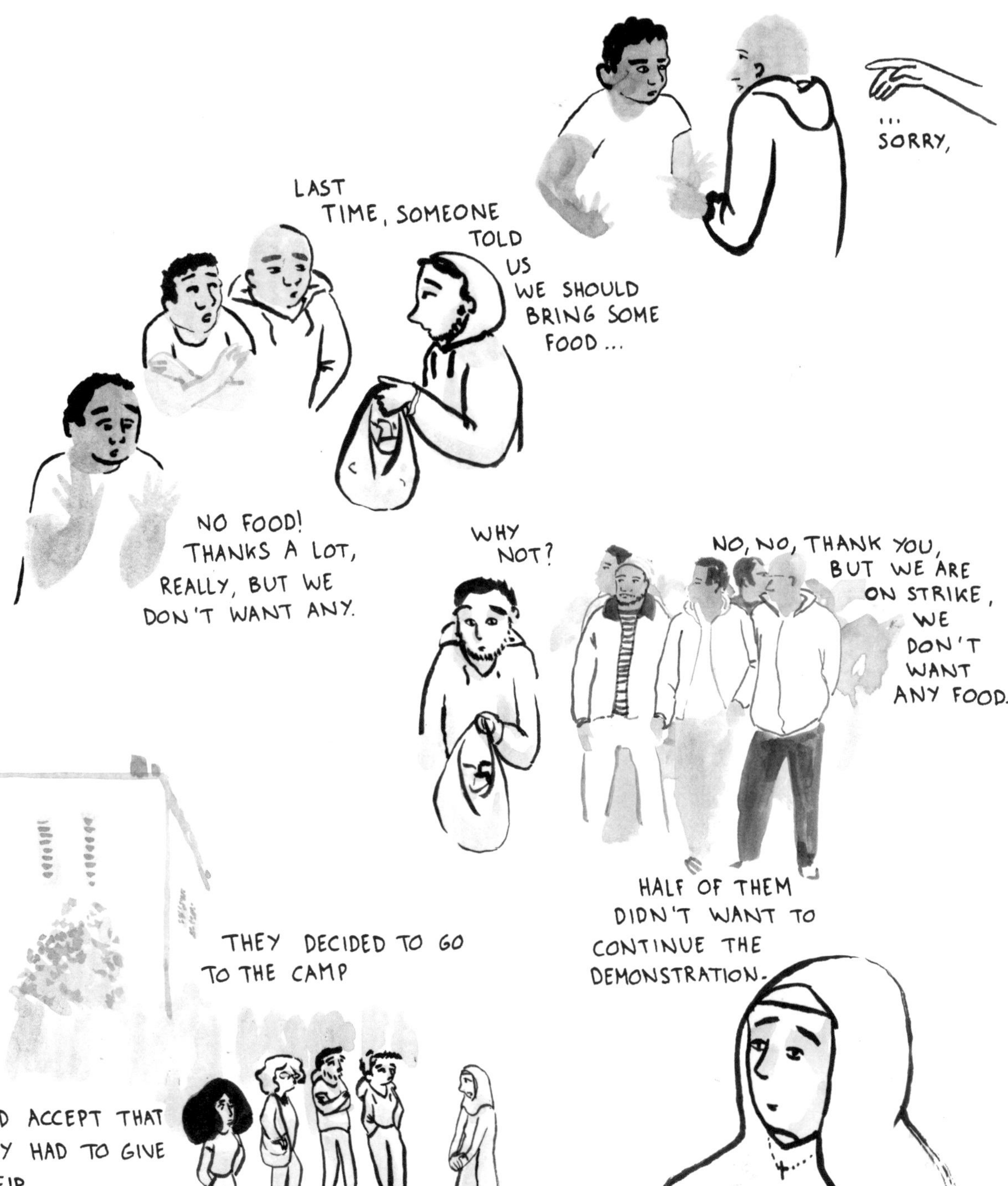
... SORRY,

LAST TIME, SOMEONE TOLD US WE SHOULD BRING SOME FOOD...

NO FOOD! THANKS A LOT, REALLY, BUT WE DON'T WANT ANY.

WHY NOT?

NO, NO, THANK YOU, BUT WE ARE ON STRIKE, WE DON'T WANT ANY FOOD.

HALF OF THEM DIDN'T WANT TO CONTINUE THE DEMONSTRATION.

THEY DECIDED TO GO TO THE CAMP

AND ACCEPT THAT THEY HAD TO GIVE THEIR FINGERPRINTS.

THE OTHER HALF FEEL BETRAYED, BY THE GROUP WHO IS LEAVING, BUT ALSO BY ALL THE PEOPLE WHO HELP THEM.

BECAUSE THEY DON'T THINK WE SUPPORTED THEM IN THEIR FIGHT.

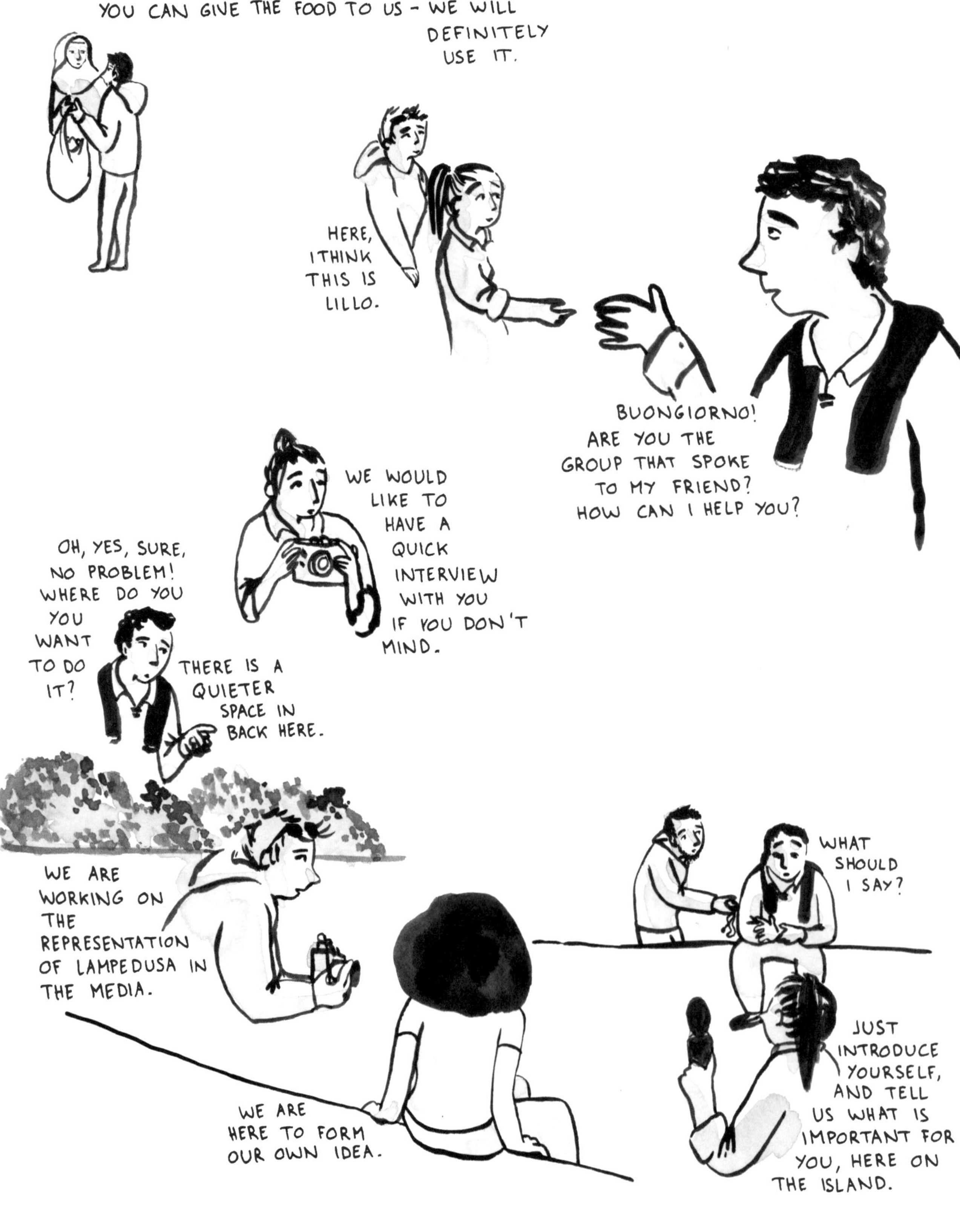

YOU CAN GIVE THE FOOD TO US - WE WILL DEFINITELY USE IT.
HERE, I THINK THIS IS LILLO.
BUONGIORNO! ARE YOU THE GROUP THAT SPOKE TO MY FRIEND? HOW CAN I HELP YOU?
WE WOULD LIKE TO HAVE A QUICK INTERVIEW WITH YOU IF YOU DON'T MIND.
OH, YES, SURE, NO PROBLEM! WHERE DO YOU YOU WANT TO DO IT?
THERE IS A QUIETER SPACE IN BACK HERE.
WE ARE WORKING ON THE REPRESENTATION OF LAMPEDUSA IN THE MEDIA.
WE ARE HERE TO FORM OUR OWN IDEA.
WHAT SHOULD I SAY?
JUST INTRODUCE YOURSELF, AND TELL US WHAT IS IMPORTANT FOR YOU, HERE ON THE ISLAND.

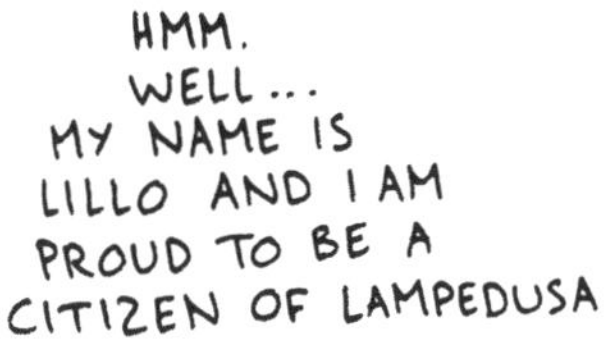
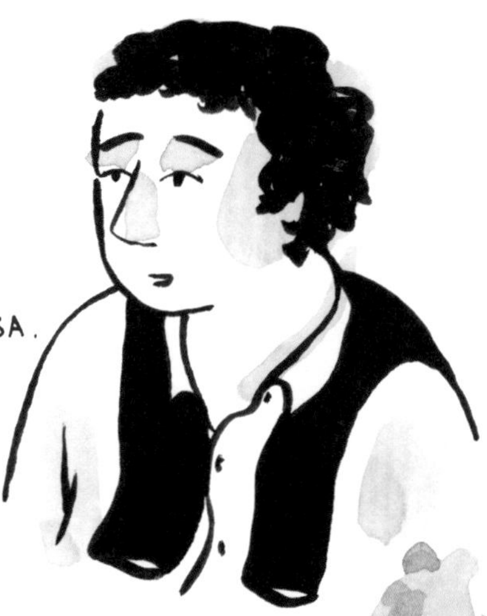

HMM.
WELL...
MY NAME IS
LILLO AND I AM
PROUD TO BE A
CITIZEN OF LAMPEDUSA.

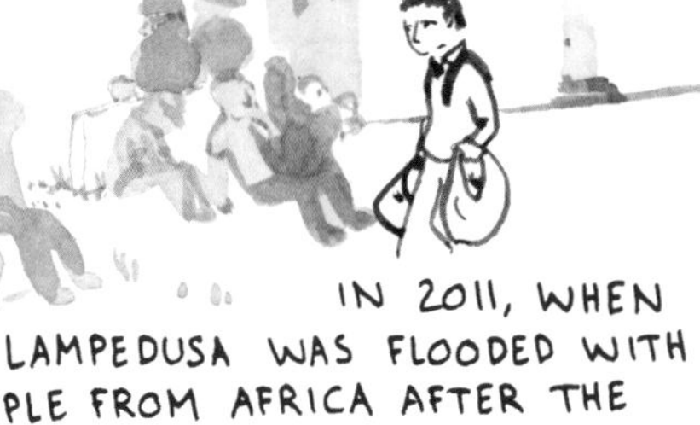

IN 2011, WHEN
LAMPEDUSA WAS FLOODED WITH
PEOPLE FROM AFRICA AFTER THE
ARAB SPRING, MY LIFE CHANGED
COMPLETELY. IN A GOOD WAY.

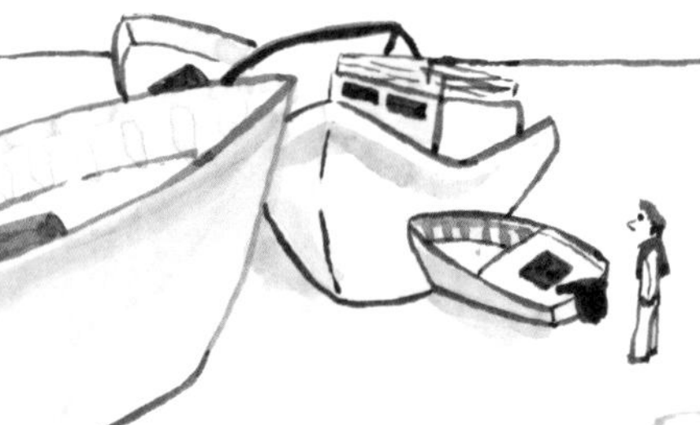

I HAD NEVER THOUGHT
THAT AT THE AGE OF FORTY-EIGHT
I COULD SEE AND TOUCH SUCH POVERTY
AND EXPERIENCE SUCH A NEED FOR
DIGNITY.

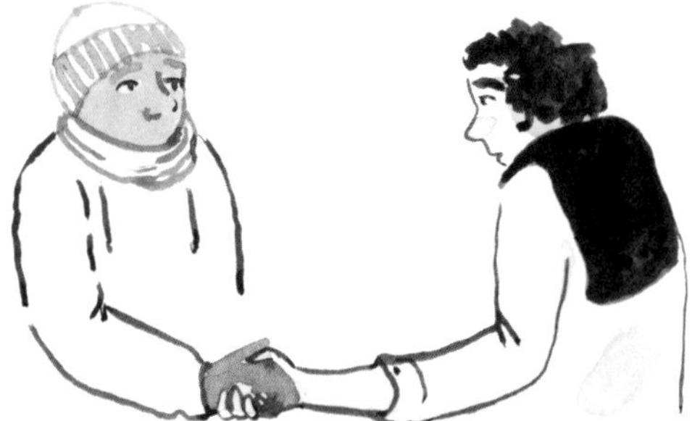

I REALIZED THAT WE HAD TO HELP.

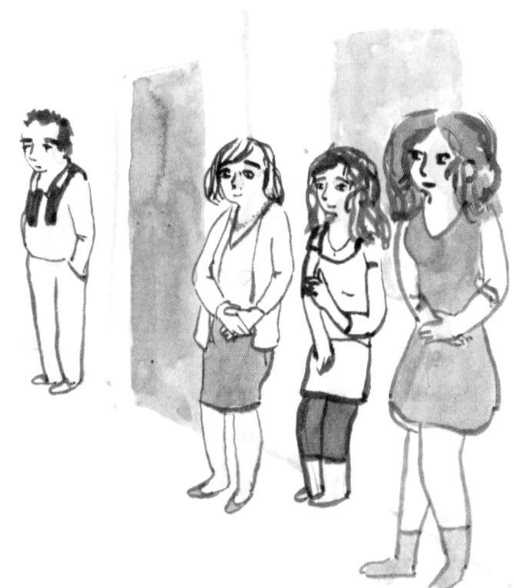

SINCE THEN,
MY WIFE, CHILDREN, AND I
HAVE DEDICATED OURSELVES TO
WELCOMING MIGRANTS ARRIVING
ON LAMPEDUSA.

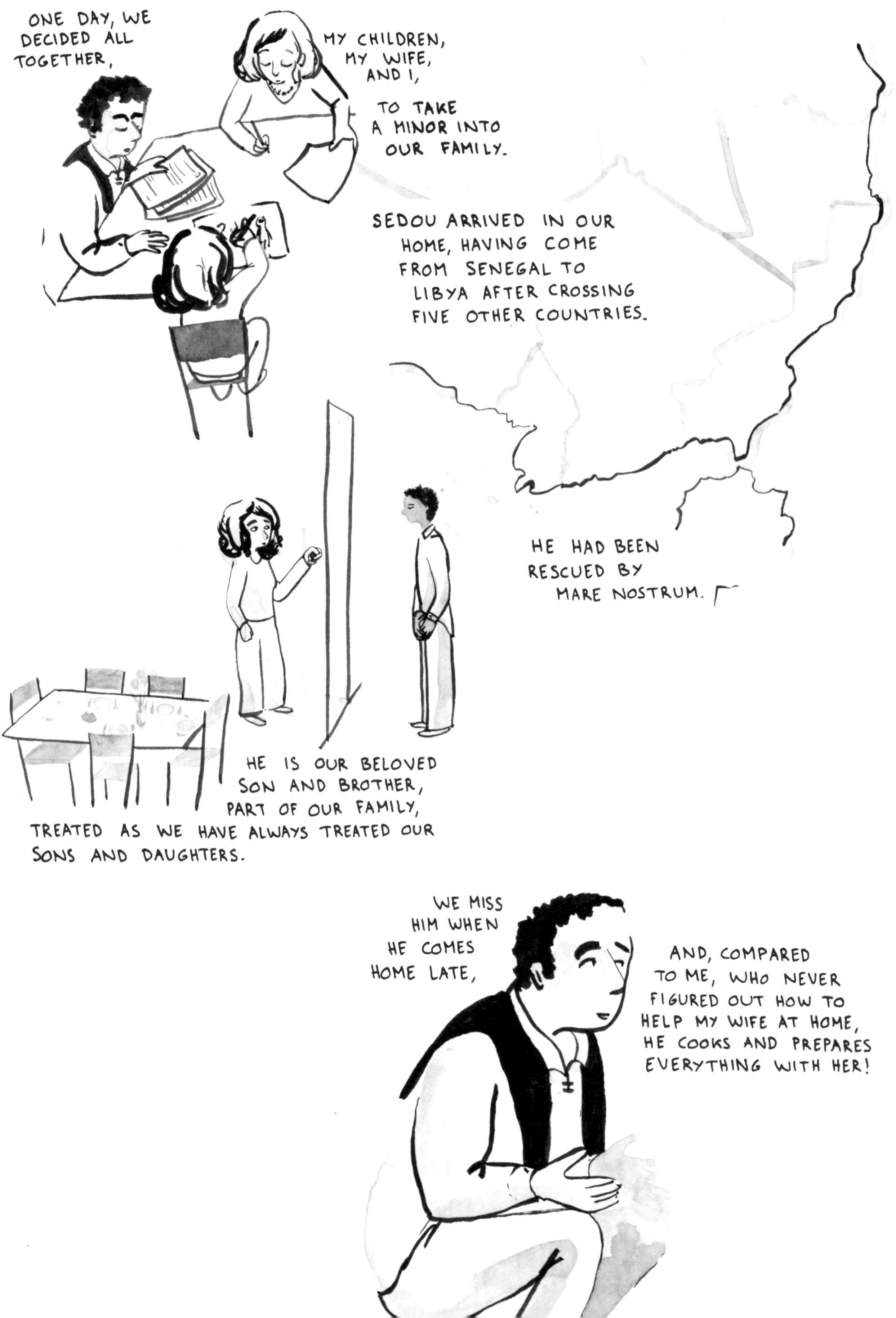

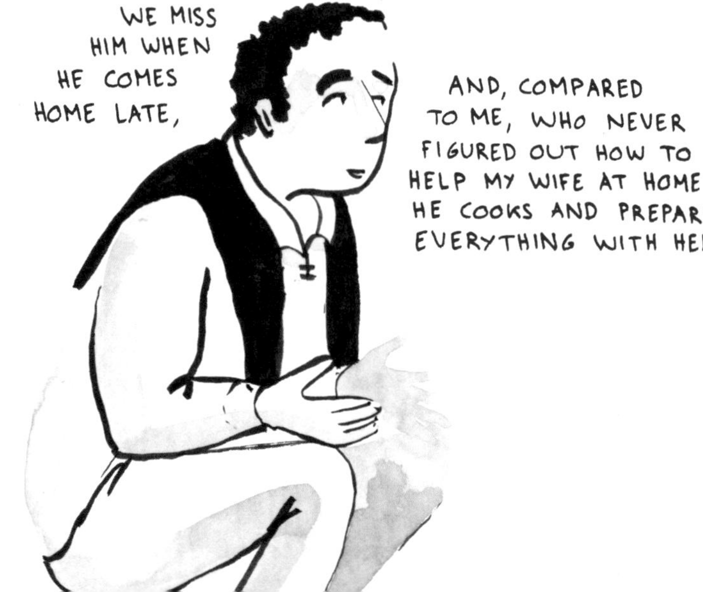

ONE DAY, WE DECIDED ALL TOGETHER,
MY CHILDREN, MY WIFE, AND I,
TO TAKE A MINOR INTO OUR FAMILY.
SEDOU ARRIVED IN OUR HOME, HAVING COME FROM SENEGAL TO LIBYA AFTER CROSSING FIVE OTHER COUNTRIES.
HE HAD BEEN RESCUED BY MARE NOSTRUM.
HE IS OUR BELOVED SON AND BROTHER, PART OF OUR FAMILY,
TREATED AS WE HAVE ALWAYS TREATED OUR SONS AND DAUGHTERS.
WE MISS HIM WHEN HE COMES HOME LATE,
AND, COMPARED TO ME, WHO NEVER FIGURED OUT HOW TO HELP MY WIFE AT HOME, HE COOKS AND PREPARES EVERYTHING WITH HER!

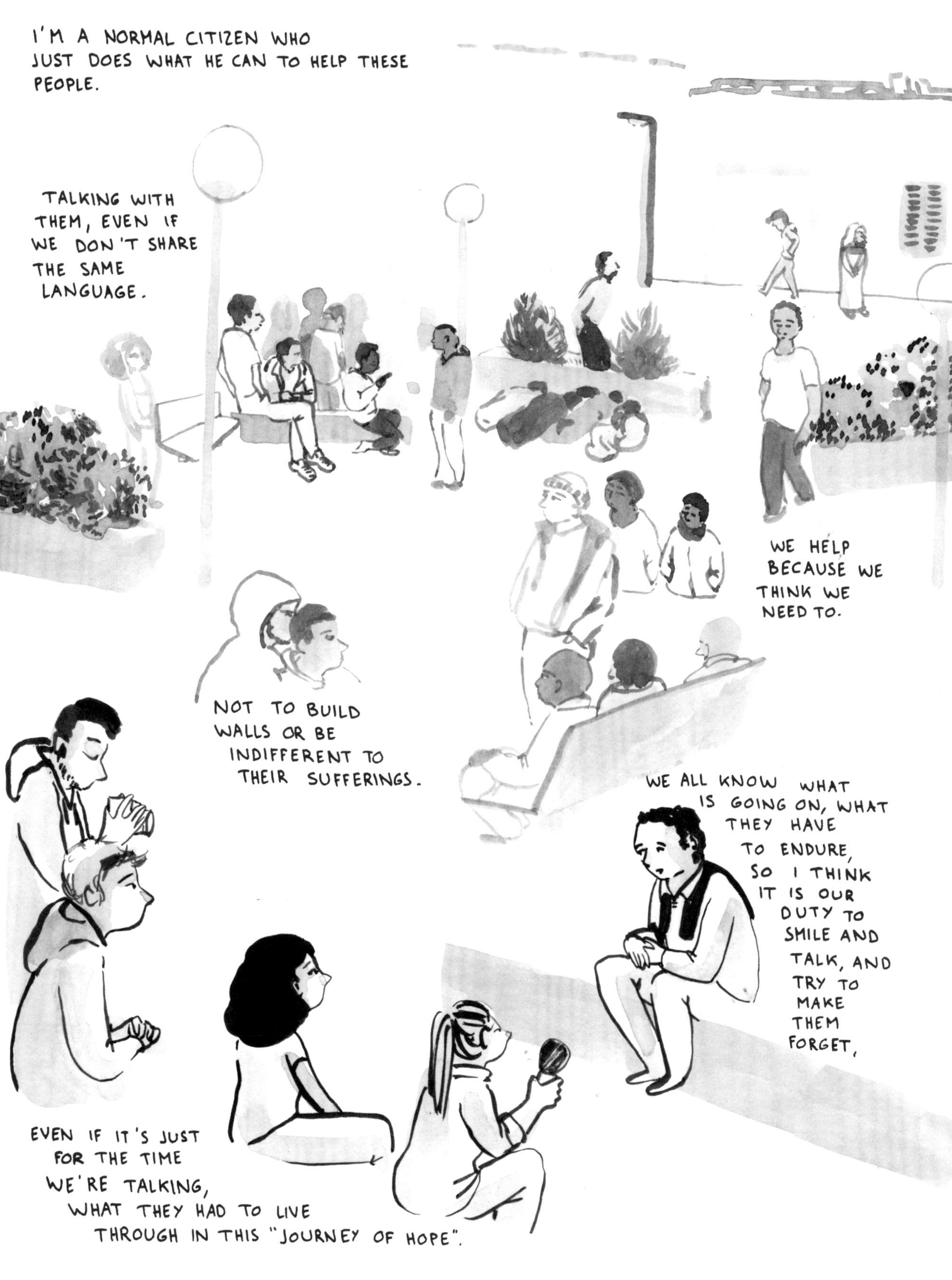
I'M A NORMAL CITIZEN WHO JUST DOES WHAT HE CAN TO HELP THESE PEOPLE.
TALKING WITH THEM, EVEN IF WE DON'T SHARE THE SAME LANGUAGE.
WE HELP BECAUSE WE THINK WE NEED TO.
NOT TO BUILD WALLS OR BE INDIFFERENT TO THEIR SUFFERINGS.
WE ALL KNOW WHAT IS GOING ON, WHAT THEY HAVE TO ENDURE, SO I THINK IT IS OUR DUTY TO SMILE AND TALK, AND TRY TO MAKE THEM FORGET,
EVEN IF IT'S JUST FOR THE TIME WE'RE TALKING, WHAT THEY HAD TO LIVE THROUGH IN THIS "JOURNEY OF HOPE".

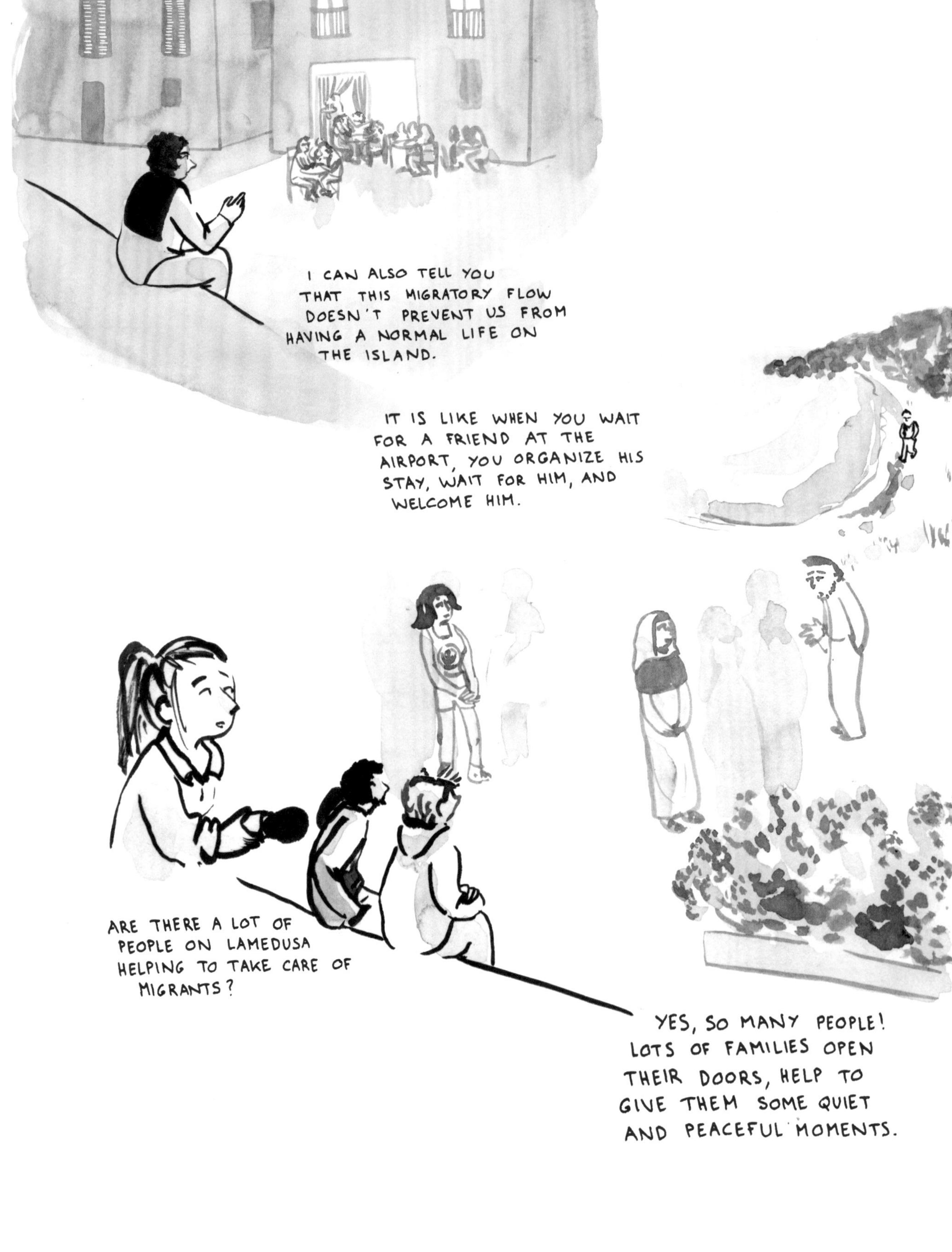

I CAN ALSO TELL YOU THAT THIS MIGRATORY FLOW DOESN'T PREVENT US FROM HAVING A NORMAL LIFE ON THE ISLAND.
IT IS LIKE WHEN YOU WAIT FOR A FRIEND AT THE AIRPORT, YOU ORGANIZE HIS STAY, WAIT FOR HIM, AND WELCOME HIM.
ARE THERE A LOT OF PEOPLE ON LAMEDUSA HELPING TO TAKE CARE OF MIGRANTS?
YES, SO MANY PEOPLE! LOTS OF FAMILIES OPEN THEIR DOORS, HELP TO GIVE THEM SOME QUIET AND PEACEFUL MOMENTS.

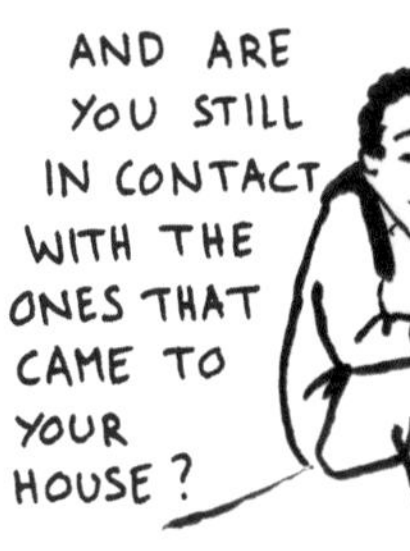

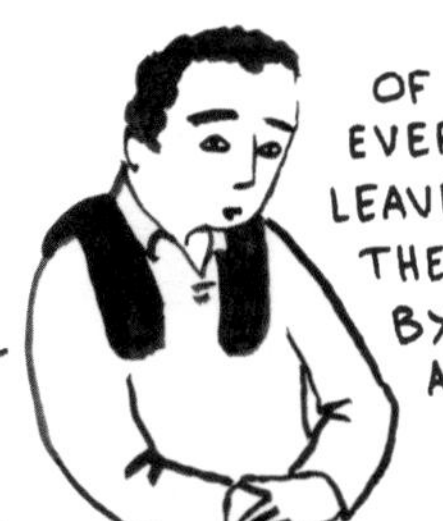

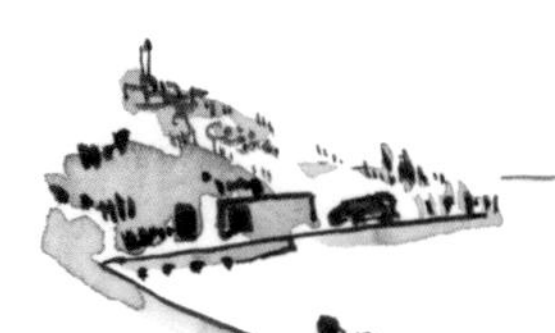

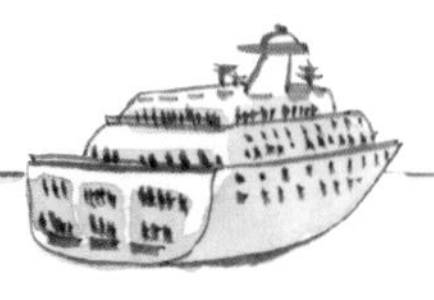

BECAUSE WE KNOW THAT ONCE THEY LEAVE LAMPEDUSA, IT IS DIFFICULT FOR THEM TO RETURN. THEY JUST PASS THROUGH HERE AND THEN GO TO COUNTRIES THAT ARE FAR AWAY.

BUT WE ALWAYS KEEP IN TOUCH. THANKS TO CELLPHONES, MAILS, FACEBOOK, AND WHATSAPP.

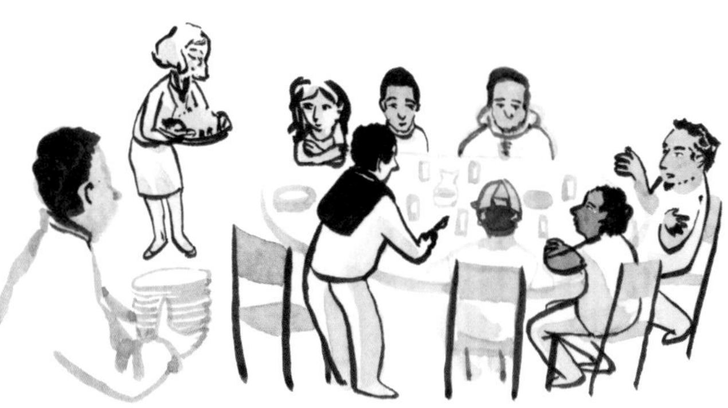

AFTER THE TRAGEDY OF OCTOBER 3, 2013, OVER A PERIOD OF A FEW MONTHS SOME OF THE ONES WHO SURVIVED OFTEN CAME TO EAT AT OUR PLACE.
WE DEVELOPED A STRONG LINK WITH TWO OF THEM: ALEX AND TAMI.

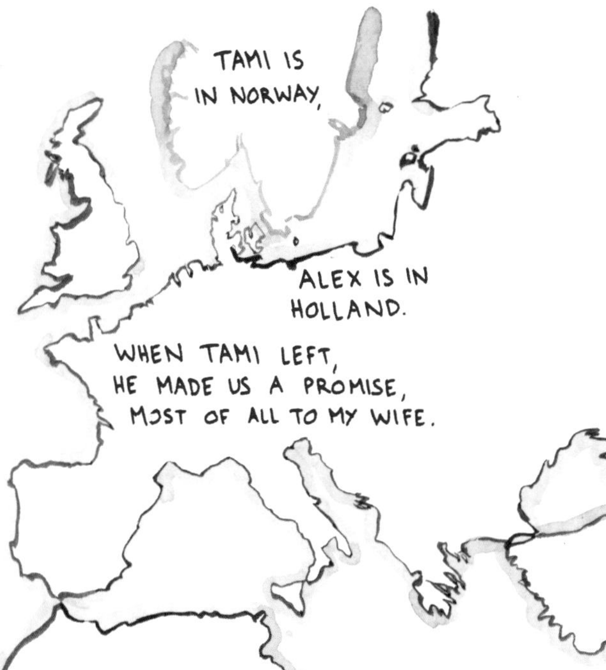

HE PROMISED THAT WHEN HE GETS MARRIED, HE WANTS TO MARRY ON LAMPEDUSA, SO MY WIFE CAN WALK DOWN THE AISLE WITH HIM.

WE TOLD HIM THAT WE WILL NOT ONLY BE HONORED TO FULFIL HIS PROMISE, BUT WE WILL ALSO OFFER HIM A WONDERFUL WEDDING.

Lampedusa
Image Stories from the Edge of Europe

Migrant Image Research Group:
Lisa Bergmann (DE), Estelle Blaschke (DE),
Paula Bulling (DE), Elisa Calore (IT),
Haitham El-Seht (EG), Mohamed El-Seht (EG),
Emilie Josso (FR), Leon Kahane (DE),
Anne König (DE), Ina Kwon (DE),
Andreas Langfeld (DE), Armin Linke (IT),
Valeria Malito (IT), Karolina Sobel (PL),
Helmut Völter (DE), Jan Wenzel (DE)

Interviews with I Girasoli, Andy Joseph Smith,
Noufou Yabré, Alessio Genovese, Maurizio
Seminara, Red Cross, and Frontex edited by
Lisa Bergmann. Interviews with Giovanna
Calvenzi, Renata Ferri, and Elena Prazzi edited
by Elisa Calore. Interview with Hani Mustafa
edited by Karolina Sobel.

The research project on the image production
in and around Lampedusa was accompanied
by many people. We would like to thank all who
supported our work:
Laura Morcillo, Christoph Spatschek, Walaa
El-Harouni, Leon Kahane, Judith Rottenburg,
Prof. Dr. Bärbel Küster, Maurizio Bortolotti
und Filippo Baracchi who participated in the
first research as well as Mariagrazia Mazzocchi,
Kathrin Schwalb, Tobias Wootton, Michel
Clegg, Elvira Heise, and Birgit Gebhard from
the University of Arts and Design Karlsruhe,
Shermin Langhoff, Aljoscha Begrich and the
Gorki Theater Berlin, Anja Casser and the
Badische Kunstverein, Florian Ebner and the
team of the Biennale für aktuelle Fotografie
Mannheim, 2017, Prof. Alexandra Kardinar und
Birgit Weyhe from the HAW University of
Applied Science Hamburg, Barbara Yelin, Jakob
Hoffmann, Philip Gaißer, Andreas Listowell
and Kwadjo Anabisa (Lampedusa in Hamburg),
Corinna Sy, Ali Maiganouhou, and Maiga
Chamseddine (Cucula, Berlin), Ali Touré,
Antonino Taranto, Lillo Maggiore, Elena Prazzi,
Beppino, Francesca Ferretti and Roberto Koch
(Contrasto, Rome), Matteo Balduzzi, Massimo
Di Nonno, Paola La Rosa, Giacomo Sferlazzo,
Giovanna Calvenzi, Renata Ferri, Andy Joseph
Smith, Noufou Yabré, Alessio Genovese,
Maurizio Seminara, Laura Rizzello and Fiorella
Friscia (Red Cross), Cettina Nicosiano and
Michele Liuzzo (I Girasoli), Hani Mustafa
(*Al-Ahram Weekly*), Frontex, Marina Militare,
Charles Heller and Lorenzo Pezzani (Forensic
Oceanography) Valeria Bonadonna, Sebastian
Baden, Giulia Bruno, Marco Bruno, Francesca
Cogni, Julia Debus, Elias Erkan, Fabrizio Fasulo,
Stefania dall'Oglio, Ralf Lenk, Francesco
Mattuzzi, Antonino Maggiore, Ornella Linke
Bossi, Mahmoud Farouk, Osama Saad Hassan,
Francis Nenik, Tobias-David Albert, Nora Höhne,
and a very special thank to Christin Krause.

RETURNING HOME

BY EMILIE JOSSO

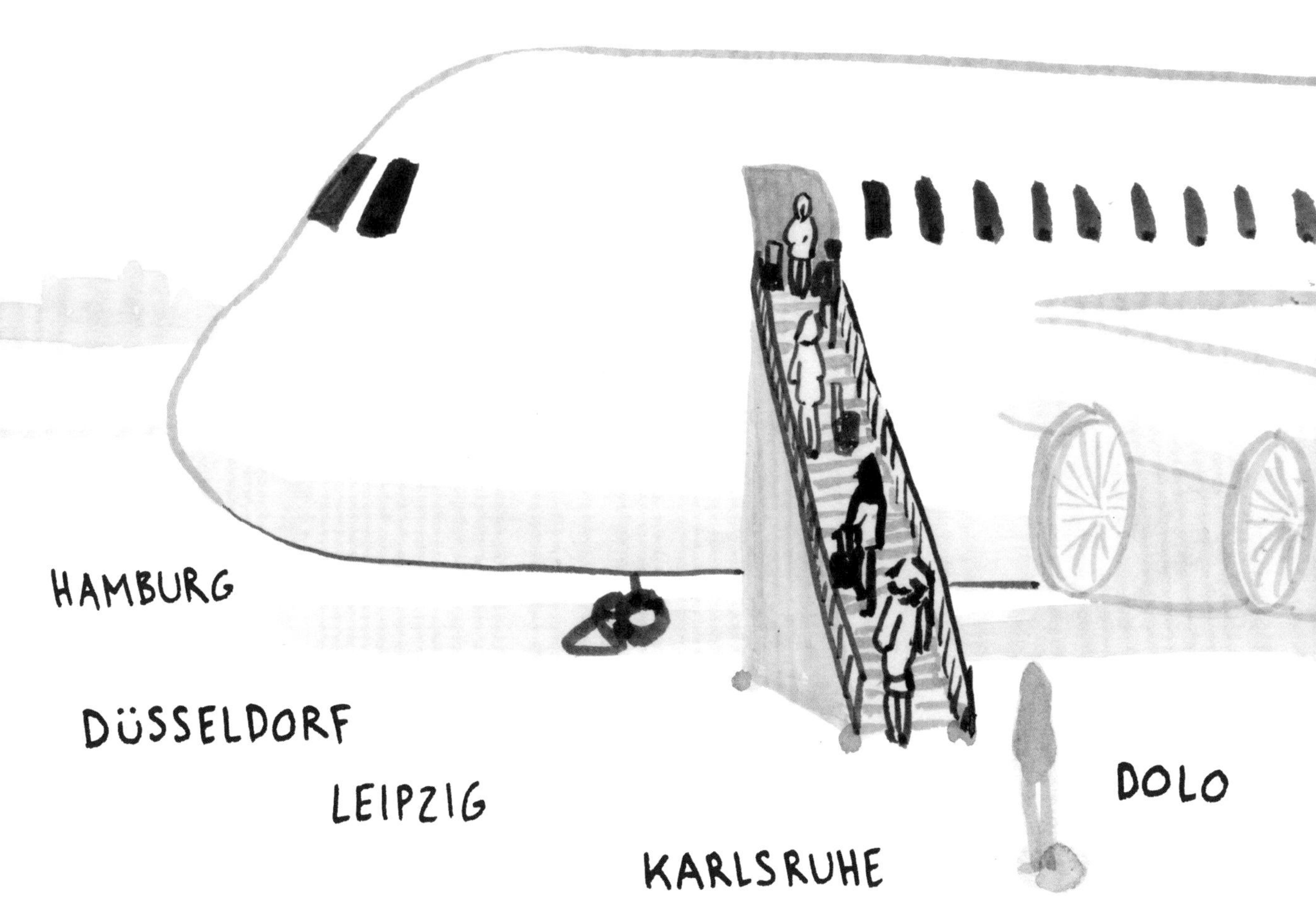

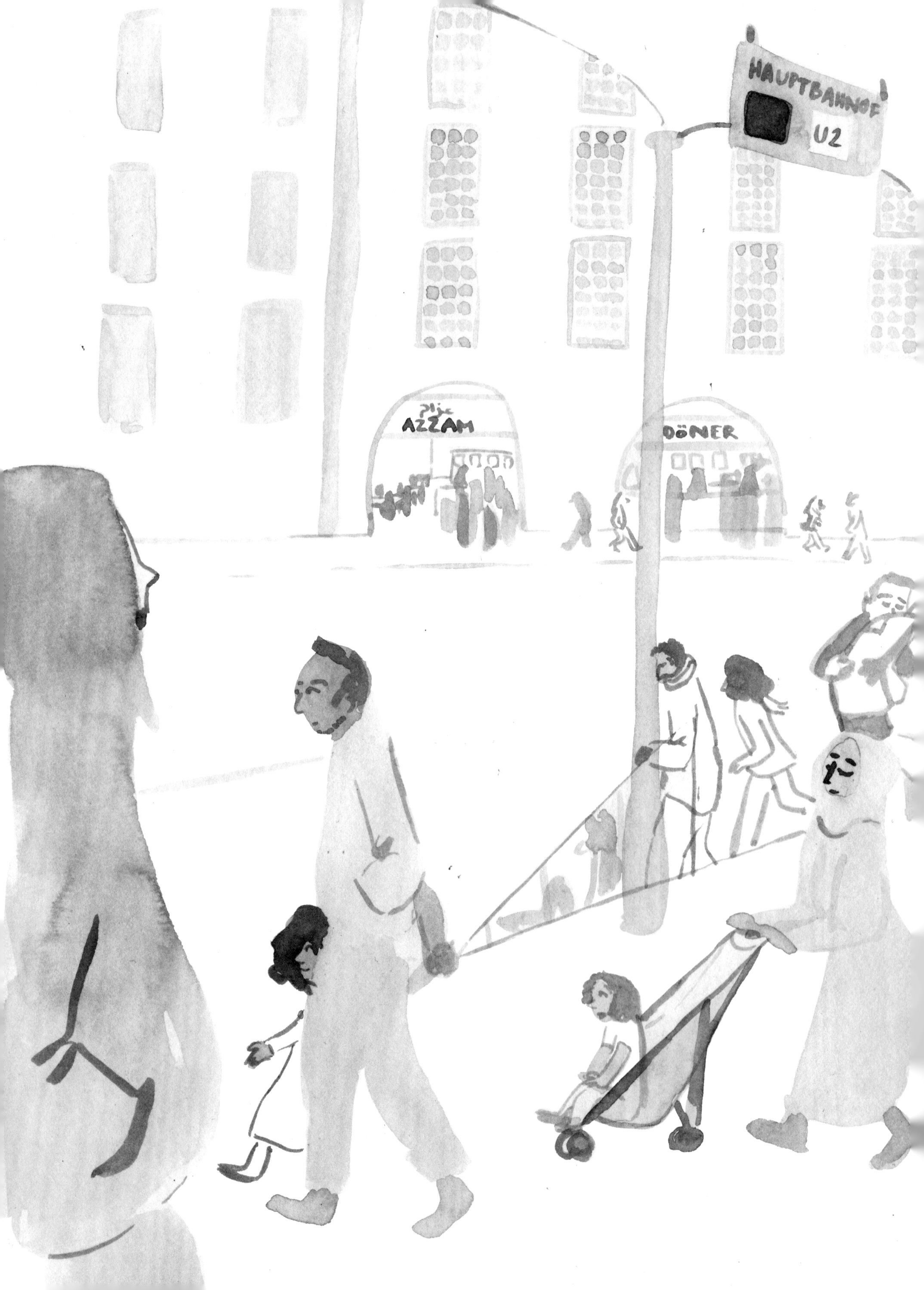

HAUPTBAHNHOF
U2
AZZAM
DÖNER

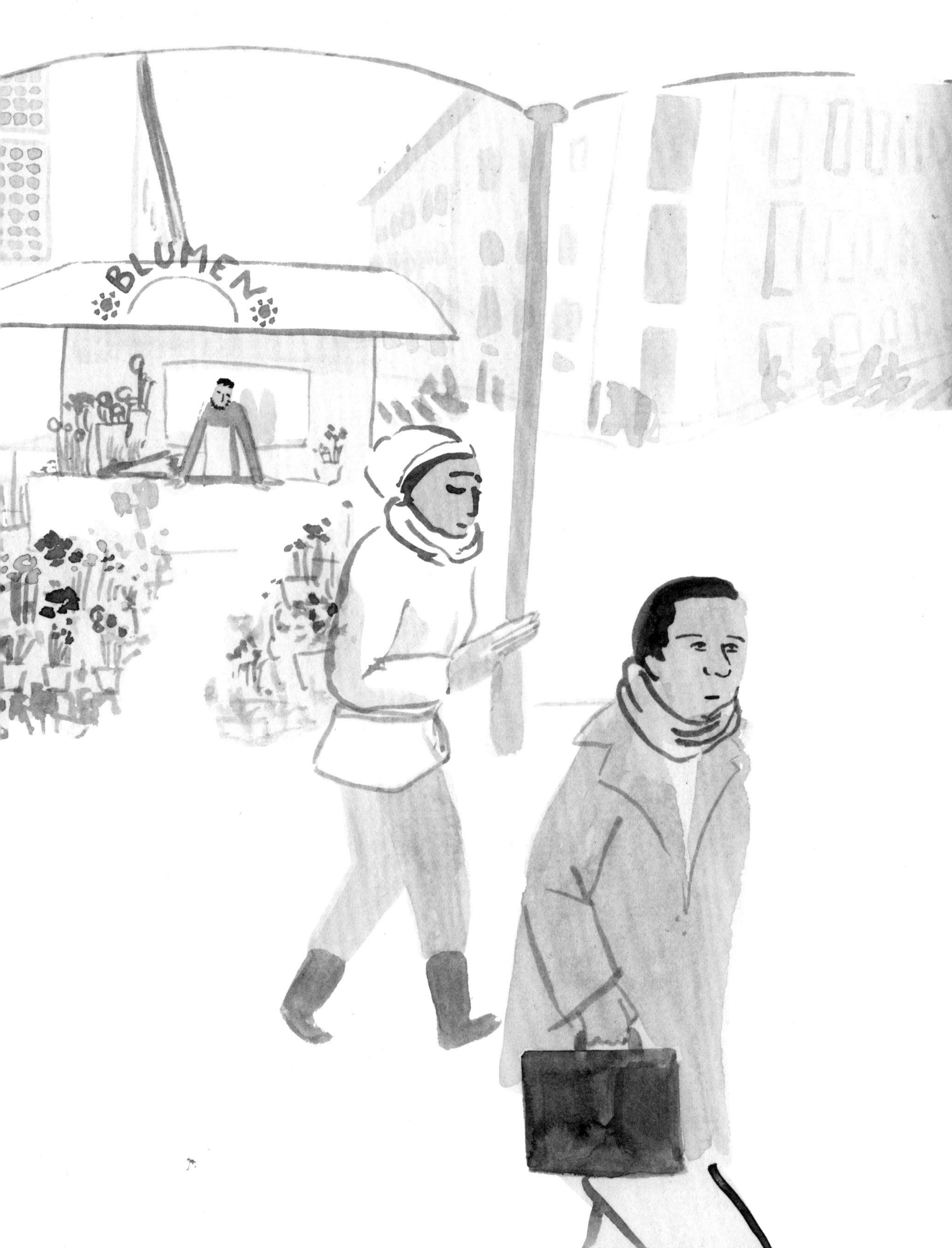

BLUMEN

Concept and editing: Anne König, Jan Wenzel
Graphic design: Ina Kwon, Helmut Völter
Lithography: ScanColor Reprostudio GmbH,
Carsten Humme (Paula Bulling)
Translation: Ger–En: Simon Cowper,
Elena Fabietti; It–En: Stephen Piccolo
Copyediting: Simon Cowper
Proofreading: Margaret May
Printing and binding: Grafisches Centrum
Cuno GmbH & Co. KG

© 2017 for the reproduced works:
Lisa Bergmann (p. 129, 216, 296, 299, 300,
301 above, 302); Verena Brüning (p. 225); Elisa
Calore (p. 91, 93, 96 above); Alessio Genovese
(p. 119–127, 176); Mohamed Abd El Ghany:
Reuters / Mohamed Abd El Ghany (p. 81 above);
Andreas Langfeld (p. 77, 203, 211, 213, 214,
247); Armin Linke (p. 295, 306); Loukas Mastis:
picture alliance / dpa / Loukas Mastis (p. 82
above); Laura Morcillo (p. 309, 310); Massimo
Di Nonno (p. 105); Antonio Parrinello: Reuters /
Antonio Parrinello (p. 96 below, 178); Giulio
Piscitelli: Contrasto (p. 87 below, 110, 231);
Stefano Rellandini: Reuters / Stefano Rellandini
(p. 97); Roberto Salomone: Roberto Salomone /
European Commission / picture alliance;
Mauro Seminara (p. 132–158, except p. 136, 137,
140 below, 141, 142, 146, 147: Mauro Seminara /
AFP, 179); Massimo Sestini: Massimo Sestini
News Pictures (p. 82 below, p. 162–164),
Karolina Sobel (p. 77, 249); Patrick Zachmann:
Patrick Zachmann / Magnum Photos / Agentur
Focus (p. 98)

Front cover: Emilie Josso (drawing),
Andreas Langfeld (photo)
Back cover: Twins Cartoon (drawing)
Flap: Paula Bulling (drawing)

The book appeares in the series:
Edition 76135 – Books from the HfG, University
of Arts and Design Karlsruhe

Published by
Spector Books
Harkortstraße 10, 04107 Leipzig
www.spectorbooks.com

Distribution
Germany, Austria: GVA, Gemeinsame
Verlagsauslieferung Göttingen GmbH&Co. KG,
www.gva-verlage.de
Switzerland: AVA Verlagsauslieferung AG,
www.ava.ch
France, Belgium: Interart Paris, www.interart.fr
UK: Central Books Ltd, www.centralbooks.com
USA, Canada, Central and South America,
Africa, Asia: Artbook / D. A. P.,
www.artbook.com
South Korea: The Book Society,
www.thebooksociety.org
Australia, New Zealand: Perimeter Distribution,
www.perimeterdistribution.com

First edition
Printed in Germany
ISBN 978–3–95905–175–0

Die deutsche Ausgabe des Buches wurde auch
von Spector Books verlegt unter
ISBN 978–3–95905–173–6

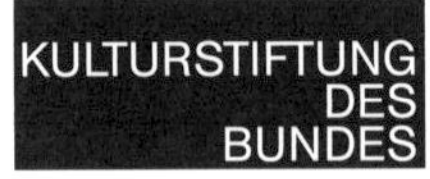

Funded by the TURN Fund of the German
Federal Cultural Foundation